D1226718

Armies of Deliverance

Armies of Deliverance

A New History of the Civil War

ELIZABETH R. VARON

OXFORD
UNIVERSITY PRESS

OXFORD
UNIVERSITY PRESS

Oxford University Press is a department of the University of Oxford. It furthers
the University's objective of excellence in research, scholarship, and education
by publishing worldwide. Oxford is a registered trade mark of Oxford University
Press in the UK and certain other countries.

Published in the United States of America by Oxford University Press
198 Madison Avenue, New York, NY 10016, United States of America.

© Oxford University Press 2019

All rights reserved. No part of this publication may be reproduced, stored in
a retrieval system, or transmitted, in any form or by any means, without the
prior permission in writing of Oxford University Press, or as expressly permitted
by law, by license, or under terms agreed with the appropriate reproduction
rights organization. Inquiries concerning reproduction outside the scope of the
above should be sent to the Rights Department, Oxford University Press, at the
address above.

You must not circulate this work in any other form
and you must impose this same condition on any acquirer.

Library of Congress Cataloging-in-Publication Data
Names: Varon, Elizabeth R., 1963– author.
Title: Armies of deliverance : a new history of the Civil War / Elizabeth R. Varon.
Other titles: New history of the Civil War
Description: New York : Oxford University Press, [2019] |
Includes bibliographical references and index.
Identifiers: LCCN 2018028897 (print) | LCCN 2018029572 (ebook) |
ISBN 9780190860615 (Updf) | ISBN 9780190860622 (Epub) |
ISBN 9780190860608 (hbk. : alk. paper)
Subjects: LCSH: United States—History—Civil War, 1861–1865. | Slavery—United States—
Public opinion. | Secession—United States—Public opinion.
Classification: LCC E468 (ebook) | LCC E468 .V37 2019 (print) | DDC 973.7—dc23
LC record available at https://lccn.loc.gov/2018028897

1 3 5 7 9 8 6 4 2

Printed by Sheridan Books, Inc., United States of America

Contents

PART THREE: *Amnesty*

Acknowledgments

OF THE MANY debts of gratitude I incurred in writing this book, none is greater than my debt to the John L. Nau III Center for Civil War History at the University of Virginia, and to the staff, colleagues, students, and interns who make up the center's uniquely supportive community. I am grateful, as always, to my colleague and Nau Center founder and director Gary W. Gallagher. He is a model of intellectual integrity and generosity, and it has been a privilege and joy to work with him. William Kurtz, the Nau Center's managing director and digital historian, has been a source of insight about nineteenth-century America and also about how our scholarship can engage with the public. I have learned so much with and from our Civil War Seminar participants—students and former students including Frank Cirillo, Mikes Caires, Tamika Nunley, Adrian Brettle, Willa Brown, Jack Furniss, Melissa Gismondi, Jesse George-Nichol, Lauren Haumesser, Shira Lurie, Asaf Almog, Clayton Butler, Stephanie Lawton, Brian Neumann, Katie Lantz, Daniel Sunshine, Joshua Morrison, Brianna Kirk, and Stefan Lund—and I cherish them, as individuals and as a team. At the heart of our work is UVA's wonderful library system and its extensive collection of Civil War books, manuscripts, and databases; I deeply appreciate the skill and helpfulness of the library staff. And I deeply value the fellowship and scholarship of UVA colleagues who work on early America and the nineteenth century, especially Alan Taylor, Max Edelson, Justene Hill Edwards, Cynthia Nicoletti, Ervin Jordan, Holly Shulman, Kirt Von Daacke, Carrie Janney, and Steve Cushman.

I am grateful to John L. Nau III for all he does to promote Civil War scholarship. His remarkable archive of Civil War documents—including thousands of unique, unpublished firsthand accounts by soldiers—is a treasure trove from which I drew much material for this book. The Nau Civil War Collection's curator, Sally Anne Schmidt, in Houston, Texas, was generous with her time and expertise in navigating the collection.

My friend Matt Gallman read the entire manuscript and offered invaluable advice for improving it. I very much appreciated the chance to workshop parts of this book at Yale's Gilder Lehrman Center for the Study of Slavery, Resistance, and Abolition, and I thank David Blight for the invitation to speak at its annual conference in the fall of 2017; I am also grateful to have received feedback at the Harvard University conference, that same fall, in honor of my treasured graduate school mentor Nancy Cott.

Oxford University Press has been wonderful throughout this process, and my thanks go to Susan Ferber and Charles Cavaliere for their editorial stewardship, and mapmaker George Chakvetadze for his expert work. The anonymous readers who vetted the manuscript for Oxford made many helpful suggestions.

I am fortunate to live in a family of writers, and I rely on all of them for inspiration: my husband, best friend, and all-time favorite historian, Will Hitchcock; our kids, Ben and Emma, whose strong voices fill us with pride and hope; my brother, Jeremy, with his fierce social conscience; my father, Bension, whose productivity leaves us all in the dust; and my late mother, Barbara, to whose standard we still aspire.

Nothing buoyed me more in the final stages of writing this book than the experience of watching my nephew Arlo, a Brooklyn sixth-grader, become a Civil War buff. Like I did at his age, he has become fascinated by the voices of the war. But he has been exposed by his teachers to a far wider range of those voices, and a more nuanced treatment of the war, than I was. His newfound passion for the study of the Civil War makes me optimistic for the future of our field, and serves as a reminder that we should never underestimate the capacity of young people to handle the complexity of history. This book is for Arlo.

E.R.V.
Charlottesville, Virginia

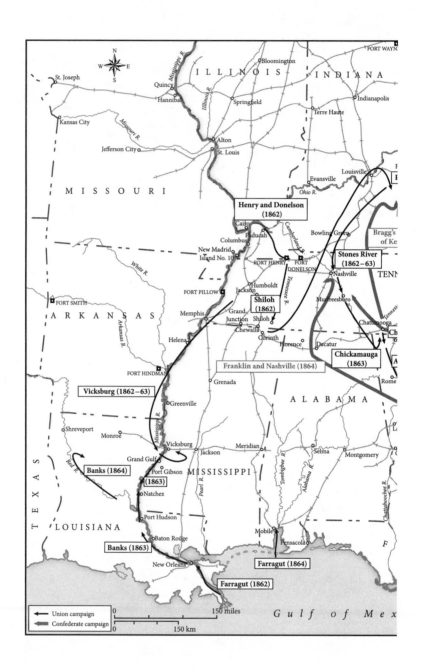

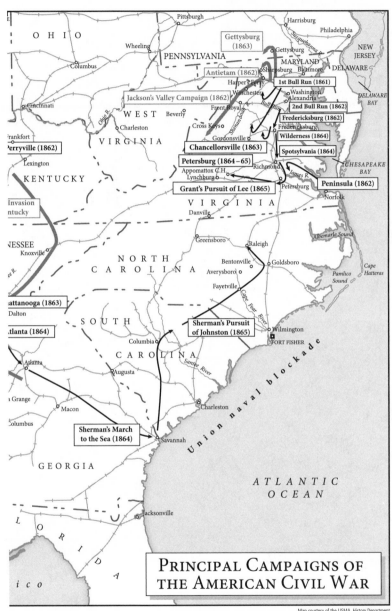

PRINCIPAL CAMPAIGNS OF THE AMERICAN CIVIL WAR

Map courtesy of the USMA, History Department

Armies of Deliverance

Introduction

"WE ARE FIGHTING FOR THEM"

IN JULY 1864, in the fourth summer of the Civil War, the popular Northern journal *Harper's Weekly* featured an article entitled "Fighting for Our Foes." The article invoked the "terrorism under which the people of the rebellious States have long suffered"—the extortion, intimidation, and violence perpetrated by elite slaveholders against the Southern masses in order to keep "their white fellow-citizens ignorant and debased." The Union army, *Harper's* pledged, would bring liberation to the South:

> Many of these wretched victims are in arms against us. But we are fighting for them. The war for the Union and the rights secured by the Constitution is a war for their social and political salvation, and our victory is their deliverance. . . . It is not against the people of those States, it is against the leaders and the system which have deprived them of their fair chances as American citizens, that this holy war is waged. God send them and us a good deliverance![1]

A modern reader might be tempted to ask: could *Harper's Weekly* have been sincere? Surely Northerners had learned, after so much blood had been shed on so many battlefields, that the Southern masses were diehard Confederates, not unwilling dupes of slaveholding aristocrats. Surely Northerners had given up waiting for Southern Unionism to come to the fore. Surely Northerners no longer cherished the naive hope of changing Southern hearts and minds.

Of all the ongoing debates over the Civil War, perhaps none has proven so difficult to resolve as the issue of Northern war aims. What was the North fighting for? Some modern scholars emphasize Northerners' bedrock commitment to saving the Union, seeing that as the central point of consensus among the majority of Republicans and Democrats. Other scholars emphasize the growing power and momentum of antislavery Republicans, and their role in establishing emancipation as the defining purpose and achievement of the war. Each of these interpretations focuses on only part of the broad Northern political spectrum. This book takes a different approach, by asking how disparate Northerners, who disagreed about the fate of slavery and the future shape of the Union, managed to form a powerful Unionist coalition and to defeat disunionism. The answer lies in the political theme of deliverance.[2]

Northerners imagined the Civil War as a war of deliverance, waged to deliver the South from the clutches of a conspiracy and to deliver to it the blessings of free society and of modern civilization. Northerners did not expect white Southerners to rise up en masse and overthrow secession. But they did fervently believe that as the Union army advanced across the South, Southerners, especially from the non-slaveholding majority, would increasingly welcome liberation from Confederate falsehood and despotism.

This belief in deliverance was not a naive hope that faded, but instead a deep commitment that grew stronger over the course of the war.[3] That is because the idea resolved the tensions within the Union over war aims. A distinct politics of deliverance—a set of appeals that fused "soft war" incentives and "hard war" punishments, and sought to reconcile the liberation of white Southerners with the emancipation of enslaved blacks—unified a pro-war coalition in the Union and sustained its morale. "As the guns of *Grant* and *Sherman* shake down their idols and clear the air," the *Harper's* essay prophesied, "these men, deluded fellow-citizens of ours, will see that in this country whatever degrades labor injures every laboring man, and that equal rights before the law is the only foundation of permanent peace and union." Grant and Sherman, symbols of hard war, also stood at the head of powerful armies of deliverance.[4]

Setting the Stage: The Secession Crisis in the North

The image of the Confederate people as the deluded dupes of scheming leaders tapped a deep vein in antebellum politics: the charge that a "Slave Power conspiracy" of ambitious planter-oligarchs and truckling Northern Democratic politicians exercised unseemly control over national politics, subverting democracy and imposing their proslavery agenda on the majority of Americans, North and South. Abolitionists warned of such a conspiracy as far back as the 1830s, as slaveholders coalesced around an aggressive campaign to expand slavery and to defend it as a "positive good" and a state's right. The fledgling Republican party took up and popularized the conspiracy theme in the mid-1850s, pointing to a series of proslavery victories, such as the 1850 Fugitive Slave Law, the 1854 Kansas-Nebraska Act, and the 1857 *Dred Scott* decision, as proof that the Slave Power was ever more aggressive in its designs and aimed at nothing less than nationalizing slavery, both spreading it westward and reintroducing it in the free states. Republican politicians appealed to the Northern mainstream by emphasizing slavery's harmful effects on whites— the economic backwardness, lack of opportunity, and absence of free speech in the South—rather than by emphasizing the themes of racial justice and equality. The party's prescription for restoring majority rule was to restrict slavery's westward expansion while at the same time spreading the free labor gospel in the South, so that white Southerners would gradually, over time, see fit to dismantle the institution. Secessionist usurpers, so Republicans charged, diverted history from its natural course, using fraud and violence to block this peaceful evolution toward freedom and sectional harmony.[5]

Abraham Lincoln led the Republican party to victory in the 1860 election, a contest in which Republicans capitalized on the recent split of the Democratic party into Northern and Southern wings. In the free states, Lincoln prevailed over his Democratic opponent and fellow Illinoisan Stephen Douglas, winning 54 percent of the popular vote to Douglas's 25 percent; two outlier candidates, Southern rights Democrat James C. Breckinridge of Kentucky and pro-compromise John Bell of Tennessee, placed a distant third and fourth. In the slave states, Breckinridge and Bell were the main attractions and Lincoln and Douglas the outliers, with Breckinridge garnering 45 percent of the popular vote to Bell's 40 percent; Douglas was third with 13 percent and Lincoln a very distant fourth with only 2 percent of the Southern vote. Republicans claimed a mandate based on the fact that Lincoln won more electoral votes (180) than all the other candidates combined. But Deep South states, which had been priming the pump for secession for the previous decade, rejected Lincoln's victory, seceded from the Union, and formed the Confederacy in the winter of 1860–61; four Upper South states followed them that spring, while the four slaveholding border states (Kentucky, Missouri, Maryland, and Delaware) remained in the Union.[6]

As Lincoln took office, he faced the challenge of uniting Northerners arrayed across a contentious political spectrum. On one end of that spectrum were abolitionists and Radical Republicans who believed the federal government should play an active role in dismantling slavery and in promoting black

citizenship. On the other end were conservative Democrats who rejected abolition and black citizenship and were content for slavery to persist indefinitely. Across the middle of the spectrum were moderates of various political
stripes who, like Lincoln himself, believed in the superiority of the free labor
system and resented the power of slaveholders but had a relatively patient attitude toward slavery's demise, wishing for its gradual extinction instead of immediate abolition. From the start, antipathy to elite slaveholding secessionists
was a strong source of Northern unity. Republicans had long scorned Slave
Power oligarchs; Northern Democrats, bitter at the fracturing of their
party, felt betrayed by the leadership class of Southern Democrats. As historian Martha Hodes notes, Northerners imagined a "simplistically divided
Confederacy" and did not carefully differentiate among the various strata of
non-elite whites. The ambiguous category of the "deceived masses" lumped
together the South's landholding yeomen farmers and landless poor whites.[7]

Very quickly, in the first months of the Civil War, the Slave Power conspiracy idea took on a new cast and increased potency. Northerners began
to argue that the Confederacy was a "military despotism" that herded white
Southerners into its ranks, seized private property for the war machine, and
suppressed dissent. This was the theme of Lincoln's first wartime message to
Congress, delivered on July 4, 1861, nearly three months after the Confederate
firing on Fort Sumter had initiated war. After "drugging the public mind of
their section for more than thirty years," the leaders of the secession movement had relied on "ingenious sophistry" (the false doctrine of state sovereignty) and on coercion (votes in which "the bayonets are all on one side
of the question") to bring "many good men to a willingness to take up arms
against the government," Lincoln insisted. A small band of conspirators had
seemingly cowed the South into submission. But how deep did support for
disunion really run? "It may well be questioned whether there is, to-day, a
majority of the legally qualified voters of any State, except perhaps South
Carolina, in favor of disunion," Lincoln speculated. "There is much reason
to believe that the Union men are the majority in many, if not in every one,
of the so-called seceded States." The Union fought to uphold the principle of
majority rule—that ballots, not bullets, should settle disputes—and did not
intend "any coercion, any conquest, or any subjugation, in any just sense of
those terms."[8]

Claims that white Southerners were "ripe for their deliverance from the
most revolting despotism on the face of the earth," as an influential newspaper,
the *New York Herald*, put it in May 1861, were standard fare in the Northern
press and among politicians in the early months of the war. Sometimes words

such as "liberation," "regeneration," "redemption," and "restoration" featured in such rhetoric. But the core message remained the same. "The people of the South are regarded as our brethren, deluded, deceived, betrayed, plundered of their freedom of inquiry, of speech and of action; forced into opposition to the Constitution and treason to the Union against their instincts, their sober judgment and free volition, by bold bad men," the *New York Times* editorialized in June 1861, in a typical formulation.[9]

In Northern rhetoric, the treatment of anti-Confederate Southerners was a form of "terrorism." While that word appears sporadically in antebellum American political discourse, it became more prominent in 1861, as Northerners accused secessionists of employing both force and intimidation to get their way. An article entitled "Southern Terrorism" in the *Milwaukee Morning Sentinel*, for example, quoted a U.S. army officer from the South who had fled Virginia and who claimed to have seen citizens there "hung for voting the Union ticket": "He says there are thousands in Virginia, and all through the South, who only wait to see Federal bayonets in order to avow their loyalty." Antislavery newspapers joined with mainstream papers in publicizing the mistreatment of Southern Unionists as evidence of the "terror which reigns in the rebel states." The war was a *rebellion to extend despotism*—despotism over white men's minds as well as over black men's bodies," the *Liberator* observed, in a May 31, 1861, article entitled "Slavery is at the Bottom of It." The border South, the *New York Tribune* opined in June, was full of men who "will be ready to act when the hour of deliverance is plainly at hand, but who dare not speak out at present."[10]

In hindsight, Lincoln and other Northern political figures and writers were clearly wrong about a Southern populace deceived and coerced into supporting the secession movement. While evidence exists of the intimidation and harassment of white Unionists, far greater evidence exists of the robust support of white Southerners for secession on the eve of war. Unconditional Unionism was in short supply among voters in the Deep South states during the secession winter of 1860–61; in the spring, the Lincoln administration's rejection of compromise proposals and willingness to use force against the insurrection moved Upper South "conditional Unionists" off the fence and into the Confederate camp.[11]

There were, nonetheless, clear military, political, diplomatic, and cultural imperatives at work in Northerners' emphasis on deliverance at the outset of the war. The free states simply did not possess the military might or the political will to conquer the Confederate South and impose a widespread and lasting military occupation. The Union had considerable advantages in manpower (a population of 18.5 million in free labor states in 1861, and another 3 million in the slaveholding border states, compared to a population of 9 million, 3.5 million of whom were enslaved, in Confederate states) and resources (90 percent of American industrial capacity lay in the North). But the vast size of Confederate territory—larger than all of Western Europe—made the prospect of winning and holding territory daunting.

As for political considerations, although Lincoln's Republican party won a resounding victory in 1860, the Democratic party represented about 40 percent of the Northern electorate, and about that same percentage of Union soldiers. Democrats intended to hold Lincoln to his promise of fighting a limited war for Union, not a revolutionary war for black citizenship and racial equality. At the start of the war only roughly one in ten Union soldiers was an abolitionist, committed to black freedom as a war aim. The other 90 percent shared an animus against the Slave Power conspiracy but not necessarily an animus against slavery itself—or any deep sympathy for the enslaved.

Proslavery Unionism was especially dominant in the slaveholding border states of Kentucky, Maryland, Missouri, and Delaware; keeping them in the fold was a major strategic priority for Lincoln. Very early on, the Union resorted to hard war measures in Maryland and Missouri, where secessionist minorities brazenly defied the will of Unionist majorities. The attack by a secessionist mob on Massachusetts regiments passing through Baltimore to Washington, D.C., on April 19, 1861, and the destruction by Confederate-sympathizing saboteurs of railroad bridges and telegraph wires in Maryland were met with stern measures on Lincoln's part, including the military arrest of rioters, saboteurs, and even several secessionist legislators, and the placing of Baltimore under martial law. In Missouri that May, Union forces captured a unit of secessionists who planned to attack the Federal arsenal in St. Louis; secessionists in that city rioted in protest, resulting in the imposition of federal martial law. Lincoln and his allies justified the suppression of dissent on the grounds that the unscrupulous secessionist elite must not be permitted to manipulate the border state masses the way it had manipulated the Confederate masses. Clashes in the border states gave rise to a "tandem strategy," as historian Christopher Phillips has put it, in which the president used political means, particularly disavowals of antislavery radicalism, to reassure border state Unionists, while selectively "allowing discretion to Federal commanders to apply the hard hand of war against civilians" whose loyalty was in question.[12]

Diplomacy was also a factor. Lincoln's administration was loath to grant the Confederacy status as a sovereign belligerent, empowered to make treaties or alliances and entitled to respect as a member of the family of nations, lest

European powers such as Britain and France openly take the Confederate side. Union officials thus characterized secession as a "domestic insurrection" within a sovereign nation and routinely referred to the seceded states as the "so-called Confederacy." The deluded-masses theory and emphasis on military despotism were essential parts of the Union's effort to cast the Confederates, for an international audience, as usurpers rather than nationalists seeking self-determination.[13]

In nineteenth-century Judeo-Christian culture, the political meanings of deliverance were inseparable from its religious meanings. The Old Testament story of Israel's exodus from Egyptian bondage was central to slave resistance and to antislavery politics; so, too, were other biblical texts with deliverance as their theme, such as the story of the year of jubilee from the Book of Leviticus, in which slaves were proclaimed free. Antebellum abolitionists such as Frederick Douglass and William Lloyd Garrison told the story of the Israelites' deliverance from Pharaoh as an "epic tale of liberation" and an "ominous tale of divine judgment," casting defenders of slavery such as John C. Calhoun as modern Pharaohs. Once the war started, Northern preachers applied biblical images to the redemption of the white South and of the nation itself—they described the white Southern majority as "crushed down and silenced by an armed minority" and yearning for liberation from such traitors, as the Reverend Horace Carter Hovey, a Massachusetts Presbyterian, declared in an April 1861 sermon. Northerners' biblical references often likened secessionists to satanic demons whose evil spell over the beguiled masses must be broken.[14]

Deliverance rhetoric filled emotional needs, too, as it reflected the conviction, pervasive among antebellum Americans, that the Union was designed by the Founders to be "affective" and consensual rather than coercive—"a political entity bound together not by force or interest, but by tender emotions such as affection and love." Americans associated the affective theory of Union with Revolutionary forefathers such as George Washington and James Madison and with antebellum heroes such as Andrew Jackson and Daniel Webster, who in times of crisis had appealed to the strong emotional bonds between American citizens. Bonds of affection were what made the Union great, and beneficial, and indeed exceptional in the world: a shining beacon of representative government, and of prosperity and progress. Secessionists argued on the eve of war that political conflicts had broken the bonds of affection between South and North and that the Union could not persist without such bonds. Unionists argued that they could reverse sectional alienation and rekindle the mutual affection and respect of Northerners and Southerners.[15]

This belief system shaped Northern war aims. While Northerners aligned themselves with the Founders' ideals, it would be a mistake to see their Unionism as nostalgic or backward-looking. Northerners upheld and defended a dynamic Union. For abolitionists and Republicans, that dynamism was best represented in the moral and material progress of America— its railroads, factories, schools, newspapers, moral reform societies, and other hallmarks of modernity. Republicans believed that they embodied the nation's free labor majority and free labor future. For Democrats the dynamism was that of "Manifest Destiny," of territorial expansion across the continent and beyond, spreading the agrarian ideal of Jefferson and Jackson. Democrats believed that their party, which had long commanded support in both North and South, was the nation's bulwark against sectional extremism. Visions of a loyal, regenerated South were at the heart of Northern nationalism during the war, and Northerners were engrossed with what Southerners thought, how they felt, what they wanted. Northern nationalism was fundamentally didactic. To achieve victory, Unionists had to do more than effect Confederate surrender: they had to teach the Southern rebels to trust them and to love the Union again. Deliverance rhetoric, by distinguishing between the guilty elite and the redeemable masses, permitted Northerners to maintain the "ideal of a consensual Union held together by heartstrings rather than military coercion."[16]

Northerners elaborated their visions of deliverance in the face of a relentless Confederate propaganda campaign aiming to show that the Union was intent on the brutal conquest of the South, not its liberation. In secessionist rhetoric, the North was in the hands of radical abolitionists who were committed to ruthless, remorseless war. "Blood, thunder, fire, smoke, rapine and entire subjugation are now the favorite terms of the Northmen, who are bent upon violence and extermination," reported the *Richmond Daily Dispatch* in early May 1861, adding, in a common trope, that Lincoln was mustering a mercenary army of "cut-throats, out laws, and vagabonds" motivated by greed and bloodlust. Such rhetoric echoed among the Confederate-sympathizing "Peace Democrats" of the North, who, drawing on antebellum campaign tactics, accused the Republicans of being abolitionist-disunionists: the Lincoln administration, they charged, never gave conciliation a chance, but instead willfully alienated and provoked the South so that Republicans could impose their radical social agenda on Southerners at bayonet point. These "Copperheads" (as Peace Democrats came to be known) sought a return to the status quo antebellum through a negotiated peace; some even accepted the legality of secession and thought Confederate independence was better than Union on the Republicans' terms. While this wing of the Democratic party was in a decided minority in the early days of the war, its message—that emancipation would endanger the economic security and racial supremacy of Northern whites as well as Southern ones—served Lincoln notice that any moves he took against slavery would meet with a fierce partisan backlash.[17]

Building a Wartime Unionist Coalition

Tracing the arc of the war from the first battle of Bull Run to Lee's surrender at Appomattox, this book will show that politics of deliverance contributed materially to the Union's military victory. Precisely because it could serve so many ends, the theme of deliverance resonated broadly for Northerners. Moderate Republicans who focused on disenthralling non-slaveholding Southern whites from the domination of slaveholding oligarchs gradually came to see the abolition of slavery as a means to that end, and they built the argument that black freedom (defined as something less than full political equality) should go hand in hand with amnesty to repentant Southern whites. For abolitionists and Radical Republicans, the emancipation of the enslaved was the key to the moral liberation of the South and the liberation of the nation from the sins of slavery and racism; in antislavery rhetoric, African Americans, in resisting slavery and then joining the ranks of the Union army, were agents of liberation, and true deliverance would bring black citizenship and racial equality. For conservative "War Democrats," the key to reunion was rekindling the allegiance of conservative white Southerners by disabusing them of the false notion that the Union was controlled by antislavery extremists, and by reasserting the power of the Northern Democratic party as a bulwark against radical change.

Northerners mobilized images of deliverance to refute the charge that they were bent on subjugating the South. Crucially, they enlisted slave-state whites in making this case. Northerners saw the slaveholding border states as Southern societies that the Union must wrest from the clutches of aspiring secessionists; their redemption was proof that the politics of deliverance could work. And so border state loyalists, such as prominent Kentucky Republicans Cassius Clay and Robert J. Breckinridge, loomed large in Northern politics, as did border state victories, such as Maryland's abolition of slavery in November 1864. Pro-war Northerners also relentlessly played up examples of white Southern Unionism in the seceded states. White loyalists willing to risk open defiance were a small minority of the population in the Confederacy. But they, too, loomed large in Northern politics, as symbols of the potential return of the Southern masses to the national fold. The most ardent and influential of these Unionists, such as Andrew Johnson and William G. "Parson" Brownlow of Tennessee, called loudly for hard war measures against the Confederates, even as they maintained that the war's primary aim was white Southern deliverance.

Deliverance politics also proved essential to establishing broad support for emancipation. Rather than conceding to Confederates or Copperheads that the advent of emancipation signaled a shift to war without mercy, Lincoln and his allies worked to harmonize the case for black freedom with the case for white Southern liberation. Each of the acts and proclamations that implemented emancipation contained inducements—grace periods, incentives, and exemptions—intended to encourage voluntary compliance by slaveholders and to reassure nervous whites that the demise of slavery was a military necessity and served the overarching aim of reunion. Over the course of the war supporters of emancipation would assiduously build the case that slavery, as the source of Southern terrorism and despotism, was the obstacle to national reunion, and that emancipation and black enlistment would benefit Northern and Southern whites alike, morally, politically, and economically. "We must disenthrall ourselves, and then we shall save our country," Lincoln asserted in his December 1862 Annual Message to Congress, connecting emancipation to the survival of democracy. "In *giving* freedom to the *slave*, we *assure* freedom to the *free*—honorable alike in what we give, and what we preserve."[18]

Black abolitionists such as Frederick Douglass and Frances Ellen Watkins Harper made their own distinct contributions to deliverance discourse. They were less inclined than whites to portray the Confederate masses as victims or to imagine that Union victory in the war would bring swift sectional reconciliation. Instead they emphasized the broad complicity of whites in the system of racial oppression, and the depths of the hatred and mistrust that system had sowed. On the eve of the war, blacks made up less than 2 percent of the population in the free states and were relegated there to a second-class citizenship. The vast majority of African Americans lived in the South and were enslaved, deprived altogether of citizenship and basic rights. In order to imagine an interracial democracy, black abolitionists had to work on two fronts: to reform the North and transform the South. They protested the persistent inequity in the North even as they acclaimed the achievements of free black communities—the infrastructure of churches, schools, businesses, and reform societies Northern blacks had built in the face of adversity. Highlighting the crucial role of slave resistance and black enlistment in undermining the Confederacy (roughly 80 percent of black Union soldiers came from slave states), black leaders argued that the only sure way to regenerate the South and reclaim it for the Union was to grant full citizenship to former slaves—the truest of the South's Unionists. Thus Frederick Douglass, hailing slavery's demise in his native Maryland in 1864, urged Marylanders to take the next step and enfranchise black men. "The more men you make free, the more freedom is strengthened, and the more men you give an interest in the welfare of the State, the greater is the security of the State," he reasoned, laying out the "true path to permanent peace and prosperity." Harper, his fellow Marylander, agreed, declaring the lesson of the war to be "Simple justice is the right of every race." African Americans expressed the cautious hope that white Southern Unionists—the diehard kind who had flatly rejected the Confederacy—could be potential allies in reshaping the region.[19]

At the heart of Lincoln's effort to reconcile black deliverance and white Southern deliverance was his program of amnesty, promulgated in December 1863. It offered forgiveness to any white Southerner who accepted abolition and pledged future allegiance to the Union, as well as readmission to states that could form an electorate of such loyalists, equal to 10 percent of the 1860 electorate. For Lincoln, emancipation and amnesty were two sides of the same coin, and his linkage of them was integral to the success of his newly christened National Union party in the presidential contest of 1864. Calling Lincoln's reelection the "great deliverance," the Reverend Cornelius Henry Edgar of the Reformed Dutch Church of Easton, Pennsylvania, marveled at how the president's conduct of the war had "magnetized—blended—harmonized—*unified*" the formerly discordant elements of Northern public opinion. Quoting Psalm 144, he prayed that God would finish the work of delivering the nation from "the hand of falsehood."[20]

The rhetoric of politicians, editors, reformers, and ministers echoed among Union soldiers, who believed that the Federal army, as it moved through the South, was bringing civilization in its wake. Union soldiers commented extensively on the Southern terrain, casting it by turns as a natural paradise from which the rebels had unjustly barred their Northern countrymen, a land of unmet potential that indolent slaveholders and ignorant poor whites had failed to cultivate and develop, or a wasteland rendered barren by slavery and the slaveholders' war. In a typical formulation, Union brigadier general Alpheus S. Williams bemoaned, while stationed in Front Royal, Virginia, in the summer of 1862, that the "beautiful valley with its productive soil" showed so "few indications of prosperity," and the houses such an "air of neglect and dilapidation." Sergeant Major Rufus Sibb Jones, a free black bricklayer from Pittsburgh serving in the 8th Regiment United States Colored Troops (USCT), wrote in a hopeful vein about the future prospects of Florida. "With a little capital and labor, on the yankee system," Florida could be "greatly improved; and in a short time, [made] . . . an enviable State," he mused while garrisoned in Jacksonville in the spring of 1864. The deliverance of the South meant reclaiming and regenerating the Southern landscape.[21]

Deliverance rhetoric also served for soldiers as a counterweight to feelings of bitterness, vengeance, and despair. Evidence abounds of soldiers venting their grief and anger in calls for the conquest and even annihilation of their Confederate foes. But retributive rhetoric never supplanted the rhetoric of redemption. Unionists yearned to establish the justness of their war by defining rules for "hard yet humane" warfare, waged with surgical precision rather than indiscriminate hatred. The justness of the Union war was measured not only by the actions soldiers took but also by the spirit in which they took them: imagining themselves as liberators of the South helped Union soldiers defend hard war tactics as righteous and free of malice. The Union army, as Corporal James Henry Gooding of the pioneering black regiment the 54th Massachusetts put it, would replace "slavery and poverty" with "liberty and prosperity." Moreover, as Copperhead Democrats grew more militant in their critique of Union war, and especially of emancipation and conscription, Northern soldiers increasingly directed their anger at this fifth column. Unlike rebel soldiers, who could be pitied on the grounds that the slaveholders' elite had kept them in ignorance, Copperheads, who lived amidst the blessings of free society, had no excuse for their treason.[22]

Women and images of femininity played a key role in Union efforts to defend hard war as humane. The armies of women who served as relief workers and hospital workers prided themselves on mitigating the pain and hatred of war and on demonstrating the moral superiority of free society, thus preparing the way for reunion. Both in the public discourse of civilian patriotic organizations such as the United States Sanitary Commission and in private letters, diaries, and memoirs, women such as reformers Mary Livermore and Harriet Jacobs contributed to a burgeoning literary genre in which tales of the exemplary suffering of loyalist soldiers and civilians and of acts of mercy to deluded rebels proved the righteousness of the Union cause. These same Union women took elite Confederate women to task for complicity in manipulating the Southern masses and perpetuating the horrors of slavery. A small vanguard of loyalist women—most notably the spies Elizabeth Van

Harriet Tubman. Tubman, who fled bondage in Maryland as a young adult, earned a reputation in the 1850s as a "Moses" figure among African Americans for leading enslaved
families to freedom in the North on the Underground Railroad. During the Civil War,
Tubman was a recruiter, spy, scout, and nurse for the Union army, and led a daring 1863 raid
to liberate slaves along the South Carolina coast. (Library of Congress LC-USZ62-7816)

Lew and Harriet Tubman—contributed directly to Union military success
and entered the circle of liberators.[23]

Deliverance politics was thus an essential tool for building a coalition
that was not only Northern but broadly Unionist: that coalition brought together Northerners in the free states (pro-war Republicans and Democrats,
and abolitionists, white and black), loyalists in the contested slaveholding
border states, and anti-Confederate Southerners (African Americans and a
small but symbolically significant number of whites) in the seceded states.
The elements of the coalition argued with each other over exactly what policies would work best to defeat the rebellion. But they found in the theme of
deliverance—with its emphasis on breaking the slaveholders' conspiracy and
bringing the benefits of free society to the South—a shared vocabulary for
battling disunionism.

Across the Union political spectrum, loyal Americans turned to metaphors to conjure how the Union war would save the South: Confederates were pupils who needed teaching, patients who needed curing, children who needed parenting, heathens who needed converting, drunkards who should sober up, madmen who needed to come to their senses, errant brethren who should return to the path of righteousness, prodigal sons who should return home. "We are actuated by love for our government and pity for our foes—a pity akin to the feelings for a misguided brother," wrote Captain Francis Adams Donaldson of Pennsylvania in the spring of 1862, as he strove to reconcile himself to the realities of hard war. Oftentimes these metaphors invoked the purifying, redemptive nature of suffering. Medical analogies, in which Southerners would be saved "by the severity of the surgeon's probe," as one Southern Unionist put it, were common and reflected the widespread Victorian-era belief that pain was a sign of the healing process. Religious images of purification, in which Southerners would be "saved as by fire," were also common, and reflected the belief that suffering could bring religious enlightenment.[24]

Such rhetoric can sound to modern ears either naively sentimental or cynical. But the commitment of loyal Americans to Southern deliverance persisted because that commitment was ideological. Unionists fit the facts to conform to their belief system—a belief system that emphasized the affective Union and humankind's capacity for moral and material progress.[25] Loyalists' hope in the possibility of changing rebel hearts and minds was renewed every time a Southerner who had fled the Confederacy testified that he left behind many fellow Unionists who yearned for liberation from Confederate despotism; every time the Federal army occupied a Southern town or city and found that its war-weary inhabitants welcomed Yankee rations and aid; every time a border state politician conceded that the institution of slavery was no longer salvageable; every time a wounded rebel prisoner expressed surprise and gratitude for medical care he received at the hands of the Yankees; every time deserters to Union lines told tales of demoralization in the rebel ranks; every time Confederate critics of the Davis administration seemed to tender the olive branch.[26] Dreams of deliverance persisted because the theory that the Southern masses awaited liberation was literally irrefutable until the work of defeating the Confederate army and destroying the Confederate government was completely done.

The longer the war ground on, the higher the toll in death and destruction, and the deeper the yearning among loyal Americans for a conversion among their enemies that would hasten the end to the carnage. A November

1864 article in the *Sacramento Daily Union*, entitled "The Dream of Peace," captured this will to believe: "The loyalists of the land will not relinquish the hope that this haughty, inexorable spirit may yield to the majestic determined power of the republic" and that "the masses who have been deluded into rebellion and trained to hate those who never hated them, will throw off a degrading yoke, sacrifice their false leaders and once more become peaceful brethren of the household."[27] Deliverance rhetoric persisted because it sustained hope in times of anguish. For loyal Americans, the dream of deliverance was a dream not only of peace but also of national greatness. Once the Slave Power was truly crushed, loyalists told themselves, America would achieve unprecedented domestic harmony as well as prestige and glory on the world stage.

The Confederate Response

This book also offers a new perspective on Confederate politics. Confederate war aims were no less complex than Union ones. Confederates sought to achieve the independence of their slaveholding republic, and independence entailed the securing of territorial integrity (meaning the exercise of political control within the new nation's borders); the cohesion of all the slave states, including those in the border South; the recognition of the Confederacy as a legitimate nation-state on the international stage; and the establishment of a new national identity and culture. Confederates pursued these aims through military and political institution-building and formal diplomacy, and also through cultural production in the realm of literature and the arts. As historian Paul Quigley has put it, "Proving that southerners were truly different from northerners—so different as to mandate political separation—formed the central problem in the Confederacy's quest for national legitimacy."[28]

Secessionists had laid the groundwork of Southern nationalism by emphasizing non-slaveholders' stake in slavery as a system of economic mobility and of racial control. On the eve of the Civil War, one in four white Southern families owned slaves, but a broad majority of whites were invested in the slave system: they hired slaves, worked for slave owners, had or would own slaves, aspired to own slaves, or were tied to the slave economy through kinship, patronage, commerce, and politics. The promise of upward mobility depended on access to land and slaves, and hence on slavery's westward expansion across the continent. Proslavery ideology rested on the fiction that any discontent on the part of slaves or political dissent by whites was attributable to abolitionist interference in the South's otherwise stable social order.

Claiming that all white men benefitted from slavery since no white man had to occupy society's bottom rung, slaveholders enlisted non-slaveholders in surveilling, exploiting, and punishing slaves and in wielding censorship and mob violence against suspected abolitionists.[29]

The long-standing anxieties of Southern whites about abolitionist infiltration crested in the late 1850s as slave resistance, especially flight through the Underground Railroad, converged with the rise of the antislavery Republican party to destabilize the electoral system. Secessionists called upon white Southerners to close ranks, conjuring dystopian images of race war, race competition, and race mixing as the fate that awaited the South should the "Black Republicans" come to power. "If the policy of the Republicans is carried out," warned a Deep South secessionist in the spring of 1861, "the slave-holder and non-slaveholder must ultimately share the same fate—all be degraded to a position of equality with free negroes, stand side by side with them at the polls, and fraternize in all the social relations of life; or else there will be an eternal war of races, desolating the land with blood, and utterly wasting and destroying all the resources of the country." Tapping their own distinct tradition of proslavery constitutionalism, Southern nationalists defended secession, by turns, as a conservative recourse to a constitutional right and as a revolutionary rejection of tyranny, echoing the colonists' defiance of the British. Modern scholars have emphasized that secessionists dreamed not only of independence but also of empire: seeing themselves as the leading champions of slavery in the Western Hemisphere, and trumpeting the profitability of "King Cotton," secessionists imagined that their new republic might eventually absorb slaveholding Cuba and expand into Latin America.[30]

Secession unfolded in the wake of Lincoln's 1860 election in two waves, with the tier of seven Lower South states (South Carolina, Mississippi, Florida, Alabama, Georgia, Louisiana, Texas) leaving first, followed in a second wave by Upper South states (Virginia, Arkansas, North Carolina, and Tennessee). Economic and demographic features distinguished the tiers. In 1860, the Lower South contained nearly 60 percent of the slaves in the United States and grew 85 percent of the South's cotton. The Upper South contained 30 percent of U.S. slaves and grew 15 percent of the nation's cotton. A third tier, the Border South (or border states), contained the remaining balance of slaves, grew almost no cotton, and resisted the siren song of secession.[31]

Given the centrality of slavery to the Confederate project, the first impulse of Confederate military strategy was to protect, through a "cordon defense" that distributed the army around the perimeter of the seceded states, as much slave territory as possible from the tramp of Union soldiers. Soon, in an effort to bolster Southern morale and depress Yankee morale, Jefferson Davis and his high command adopted a hybrid "offensive-defensive" strategy, which sought the concentration of force to drive out invading armies. This strategy produced military victories, particularly once Robert E. Lee took command of Confederate forces in Virginia in the summer of 1862. But political unity proved elusive for Confederates.

Fierce debates raged in the South over how best to achieve Confederate war aims: debates over which theater of war, east or west, to privilege; the merit of government centralization through policies such as conscription; how much faith to place in foreign intervention or Northern dissension; and which generals could get the job done. In the absence of a strong two-party system, the fault lines were factional rather than partisan, pitting a pro-administration faction against critics of Jefferson Davis and his leadership.[32]

Confederates invoked "deliverance" as a political theme in their own distinct ways. They often spoke in providential terms of the "day of their deliverance"—of divine intervention against the Yankee foe. At times, in a seeming mirror image of the North's "Slave Power conspiracy" rhetoric, Confederates described the Northern public as dupes of an antislavery conspiracy and expressed hope that they might disenthrall conservative Northern Democrats from Radical Republican influence. After initially claiming that they were fighting a defensive war against Northern aggression, Confederates soon positioned themselves as liberators, launching offensives into Kentucky, Missouri, and Maryland meant, as they saw it, to deliver pro-secession inhabitants there—"oppressed brethren," to quote Jefferson Davis—from the yoke of Yankee military despotism. Such language resonated wherever Confederates sought to take back territory that had fallen into Federal hands. But because of its "moral contradictions," John Coffey has perceptively noted, "Confederate deliverance politics lacked the force of its northern counterpart." While Confederates spoke of themselves as God's chosen people, they took care that such language would not "spill into the social sphere of slavery or overwhelm the racial barrier that separated enslaved blacks from free whites."[33]

Confederates were keenly attuned to Northern deliverance politics and determined to preempt, discredit, and silence Yankee appeals to the Southern masses. The acerbic Confederate journalist Basil Gildersleeve mocked such rhetoric as "maudlin." "They called us 'errant brethren' and 'wayward sisters,' " he wrote in a November 1863 column in the *Richmond Examiner*, and "became still more affectionate as we became less fond." Musing on the resilience of such images, he continued, "They have long spoken and written, and still speak and write, as if they believed that the Southern people are under the sway of a small slave-owning oligarchy, and that it is only necessary to get these factious noblemen out of the way in order to revive the Union feeling." But that was a miscalculation: "They count the number of slaveholders and forget to multiply by the number of the members of their families. They leave out of view all the interests which ramify from our peculiar combination of capital and labour," Gildersleeve observed, defending the idea of the solid South. In his view, talk of liberation was a smokescreen that obscured the true aim of the abolitionist leaders of the Union coalition: to extend "the area of extermination beyond the oligarchs until it embraces the whole white population of the South."[34]

The premise of the Union war was that white Southerners could be redeemed; the premise of the Confederate war was that Northerners and Southerners could never again be countrymen. Thus in their quest for unity Confederates relentlessly played up two themes: Northern barbarity and Southern victimization. Confederate rhetoric portrayed Yankees as infidels and heretics, foreign mercenaries, condescending and hypocritical Puritans, money-grubbing materialists, and socialistic radicals intent on overturning both patriarchy and white supremacy. In the 1840s and 1850s, European immigrants had flocked to the North's towns and cities, where they could find wage work, rather than to the rural South; the resulting ethnic diversity of the North and of the Union army was taken by Confederates to be a sign of degeneration, a dangerous and volatile mixing of foreign peoples and ideas. Some commentators claimed that the Yankees were themselves of a different race or ethnicity than white Southerners, Anglo-Saxon "Roundheads" to the Southern Norman-descended "Cavaliers." Confederates generally saw abolitionists as representative of Northern society and of the "Yankee character." In their own resort to medical metaphors, Confederates described Northern culture as afflicted with the chronic, incurable, and highly contagious disease of radicalism.[35]

To purge the body politic, the Confederate government designated as "alien enemies" any U.S. citizens (males over age fourteen) residing in the Confederacy who refused to embrace Confederate citizenship; such "aliens" were liable to be restrained or deported by the authorities. Homegrown Southern Unionists were treated by Confederates as pariahs, shunned and menaced until they were either cowed into submission or driven from their homes into exile. At first Confederates relied on extralegal mobs and vigilance committees to enforce loyalty, but over time they developed government mechanisms, such as the provost marshal system, for policing citizens and making an example of dissenters. As the Union's emancipation policy took shape, driven by the mass exodus of slaves to Union lines, Confederates tightened the slave system's regime of surveillance and violent coercion; they reviled the Emancipation Proclamation as the culminating proof that any reunion between the North and South was utterly impossible.[36]

The experience of Union occupation intensified the patriotic fervor of diehard Confederates. In Confederate rhetoric, the Yankee forces were, the historian Stephen V. Ash explains, "advance agents of a corrupt and corrupting civilization," bringing "violation, pollution, and degradation." Predisposed to believe that the hated Yankees would not fight fair, Confederates circulated endless stories of the invaders' "atrocities" against civilians and stressed the need for men to protect helpless women against Yankee abuses. Paradoxically, Confederate women proved far from helpless, rallying to serve the cause of Southern independence through soldiers' aid societies; by managing shops, farms, and plantations; and as clerks, factory workers, authors, nurses, and spies. Slaveholding women in particular cultivated a reputation in both North and South as especially fierce patriots. They joined with men in scorning the Yankees' pretense to be deliverers. Northern soldiers who expected a warm welcome in the South were "profoundly ignorant of the moral science of causes and effects," wrote Jane Howison Beale of Fredericksburg, Virginia. She observed, "All human experience teaches that those who suffer the tyranny of unjust warfare, learn to cling with a devotion to their principles that they would have never felt under milder influences and our Southern people will not be apt to form the first exception to this general rule."[37]

As the war escalated, Confederate leaders turned to the shared experience of wartime suffering as the "sacred adhesive of Confederate nationalism," invoking the blood sacrifice of Southern soldiers and of civilians as the essence of Southern distinctiveness and the means to victory. In early 1865, the *Richmond Daily Dispatch*, reflecting on recent reverses, imagined that "these unparalleled trials and sufferings may prove the most effectual means by which the gulf between the two combatants will be rendered forever impassable, and the heart of the country roused to that degree of energy and self-sacrifice which is necessary to its deliverance." A "dark crimson stream," which no tempting promises or seeming guarantees could ever bridge, had come to separate the Northern and Southern people.[38]

In short, a war of words—in which Unionists claimed to be "fighting for their foes" and Confederates cast Unionists as remorseless conquerors—took shape in the very opening moments of the conflict and intensified as the war grew in scope and brutality. The Union ultimately won the war of words, but its victory was incomplete. Although it helped to promote solidarity among Unionists, deliverance discourse ultimately failed to convince Confederate whites to accept peace, or black freedom, on the Union's terms. Once the shared goal of defeating the Slave Power was accomplished, the Unionist coalition lost its common purpose and its disagreements over the meanings of victory and freedom came to the fore. As former Confederates moved to discredit the Union victory and defend the righteousness of their Lost Cause, the long-lived hope that the white Southern masses would repudiate their leaders ran aground on the shoals of racism and recalcitrance.

PART I

Loyalism

March of Redemption

FIRST BULL RUN TO FORT DONELSON

"STARTLING NEWS FROM Washington—A Promising Victory Turned into a Disastrous Defeat." So the *New York Herald* reported from Manassas, Virginia, where the Federals clashed with the Confederates on July 21, 1861, along a tributary stream of the Potomac River called Bull Run. As Lincoln and his allies regrouped in the wake of this alarming start to the war, three major challenges loomed: thwarting secessionists in the slaveholding border states, resolving the status of slaves who ran from their masters to Union lines, and finding commanders who would not just win battles but also set the right tone for the war effort. Addressing these challenges was politically delicate work. Northerners struggled to discern what sorts of policies—what combination of force and incentive—would break the spell of secession and bring the Southern rebels to their senses.

Green Together

The first three months of the war saw sporadic, small-scale fighting in Virginia: at Big Bethel on the Peninsula, where the Confederates had repulsed a Union advance on June 10, and in western Virginia, where a brash young Union general, George McClellan, won the battle of Rich Mountain on July 11. The Union victory in western Virginia yielded immediate political dividends, as it gave momentum to a nascent movement among Unionists there to break from the Confederacy and establish a "restored" state of Virginia consisting of counties that had rejected secession. In June 1861, delegates to a convention in the Unionist stronghold of Wheeling elected Francis H. Pierpont governor of this new "state," and in July the Wheeling convention elected two

prominent Unionists, Waitman T. Willey and John S. Carlile, to represent
the loyalists of western Virginia in the U.S. Senate. For these Unionists, defiance of the Confederacy was an extension of a decades-old battle against the
slaveholding elite of eastern Virginia, which had denied westerners fair representation in the legislature and levied an unfair tax burden on the west. As the
Wheeling Daily Intelligencer proclaimed, westerners sought deliverance from
the "haughty yoke of Eastern Virginia" and from the "monstrous sacrilege" of
secession. Lincoln and congressional Republicans, for their part, hoped that
Unionists elsewhere in the South would be inspired to speak out by the example of the "Restored Government" of Virginia.[1]

Even as the Lincoln administration tracked developments in western
Virginia, the stage was being set for a far grander reckoning in the east, on
the outskirts of Washington, D.C. Twenty thousand Confederates were
massed a day's march southwest of the federal capital, under the hero of Fort
Sumter, Brigadier General P. G. T. Beauregard. Beauregard's position was a
defensive one: his troops were guarding a vital logistical asset, the railroad
junction at Manassas. His army nonetheless seemed to Northerners an imminent threat—Beauregard, after all, had been the aggressor at Fort Sumter.
Facing off against Beauregard was his former West Point classmate Brigadier
General Irvin McDowell, who presided over the fortification of the District
of Columbia and the securing of a buffer zone, composed of Arlington and
Alexandria, Virginia, to protect the federal capital. McDowell would have
been content to bide his time, training his troops, in keeping with General-
in-Chief Winfield Scott's proposed grand strategy for the war. According
to the "anaconda plan," the Union would move to seize control over the
Mississippi River and blockade Confederate Atlantic and Gulf ports, thereby
motivating Confederates to call off the rebellion lest they get isolated and
squeezed into submission. But Scott's plan would need time to mature, and
McDowell was under immense public pressure to move—to take the fight to
the Confederacy and initiate an offensive that would propel the Union army
"on to Richmond," one hundred miles due south. Beauregard's army was the
primary obstacle and had to be dislodged.

Northerners' sense of urgency was made more acute by the fact that
the three-month terms of service under which Union men had signed on
in April were coming to an end. Would the army be permitted to disband
without having achieved its purpose? The desire of the Northern public
for a knockout blow influenced Lincoln to embrace the idea of a summer
offensive, as did the broader strategic imperative: the Confederacy must
not be allowed, Lincoln reckoned, to consolidate itself in Virginia and

to accrue legitimacy. So when McDowell objected that his inexperienced troops were unfit to confront the enemy, the president countered that the Confederates, too, were green. "You are all green together," Lincoln noted, implying that the Federal edge must come from the quality and boldness of its leaders.[2]

McDowell yielded, and on July 16 he set his field army in motion. They reached Fairfax Court House by noon on July 17 and Centreville by nightfall on the eighteenth. A vanguard probed southward at the Confederates at Blackburn's Ford, only to be turned back in a sharp skirmish; this minor setback convinced McDowell that the best plan of action was to have a part of the Federal force demonstrate in a feint against the center of the Confederates' defensive line, which ran for six miles along Bull Run, three miles east of the railroad junction; the other part of McDowell's army would launch a flank attack across Sudley Ford, on the Confederate left.

While the plan was sound, its execution was muddled from the start. The Federal army had taken two and a half days to make a march that should have taken a single day; the delay was attributable in part to the greenness of the troops, who stopped to pick blackberries and seek water. Their foraging sometimes turned aggressive, as they importuned the locals for milk, eggs, butter, poultry, and other provisions. McDowell erred in having infantry rather than cavalry units do reconnaissance. But his most critical error was in delaying the Federal attack until the twenty-first instead of striking on the twentieth, squandering what could have been a decisive numerical advantage. As Union soldiers engaged in foraging and inefficient reconnaissance, the Confederates were rushing reinforcements to the front.[3]

McDowell's plan depended on the ability of a Union commander, Major General Robert Patterson, to pin down the Confederate force under Brigadier General Joseph E. Johnston; those two armies menaced each other, with Patterson's force numbering 18,000 and Johnston's 12,000, in the northern Shenandoah Valley, some fifty miles northwest of Manassas. Beauregard, who had gotten advance word of the Union army's movements from a resourceful Confederate spy—the popular Washington, D.C., socialite Rose O'Neal Greenhow—demanded of Davis that Johnston's army be sent east. The seventy-year-old Patterson proved himself unequal to his assigned task, letting Johnston's troops slip away from Winchester, Virginia, and board trains on the Manassas Gap Railroad that would take them directly to Beauregard's aid. By July 19, the lead elements among these reinforcements, Virginians led by Brigadier General Thomas Jackson, had arrived at Manassas Junction; the following day Johnston himself reached Beauregard's headquarters.

Ignorant of this change in tactical context, McDowell proceeded with his plan. In the predawn hours of July 21, McDowell's army moved out across Bull Run. The Federals' feint at the center failed to distract Confederates from the flank attack on the left; instead Brigadier General Nathan Evans redeployed his Confederate troops to meet the Federal flanking force. At first this counterstroke was to no avail—the Union army drove the Confederates into what promised to be a full retreat. But the tide of the battle shifted when the Confederates, following the example of Jackson, whose determined resistance in this hour won him the moniker "Stonewall," drew up a defensive line along Henry House Hill, seizing the most tactically significant piece of terrain on the battlefield. After a brief lull in the battle, McDowell sent into action two artillery brigades, only to see them overrun by Jackson's Virginia infantry. Capitalizing on the shift in momentum, Beauregard ordered a general assault, and this counterattack, which featured the debut of the caterwauling "rebel yell," sent the Union right flank reeling back across Bull Run.

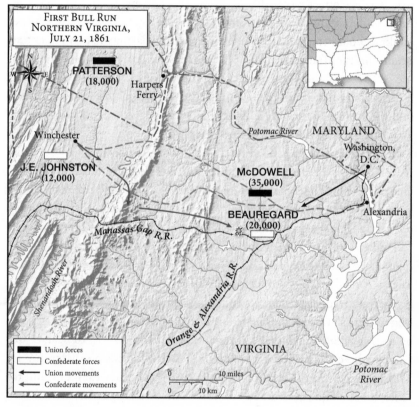

MAP 1.1

A scene of widespread panic ensued. Soon the Union columns collapsed into a desperate, headlong retreat toward Centreville and on to Washington, D.C. While some regular units maintained order, the green volunteers in particular were seized with fear. "All sense of manhood seemed to be forgotten," a correspondent for the *New York Tribune* wrote. "Even the sentiment of shame had gone. . . . Every impediment to flight was cast aside. Rifles, bayonets, pistols, haversacks, cartridge-boxes, canteens, blankets, belts and overcoats lined the road." Caught up in the chaos were civilians, including some congressmen, who had made the trip out to Virginia to witness what they had imagined would be a splendid and decisive Union victory.[4] The Confederates pursued the Federals briefly, toward Centreville, but were too devastated by the day's fighting to see the pursuit through.

The Federal casualties for the day were 2,896 killed, wounded, or missing, to 1,982 casualties on the Confederate side. Those who lived through this first great clash of the war struggled to describe the terrible and heart-rending spectacle. "To all but a scattered few it was our first battle, and its sights and wonders were things of which we had read but scarcely believed or understood until seen and experienced," wrote Charles Minor Blackford, a first lieutenant in the 30th Virginia Volunteers, in a letter home. He invoked how waves of suffering would emanate from the battlefield to the home front. Something caught Blackford's eye as he rode over the field the night after the battle:

> I noticed an old doll-baby with only one leg lying by the side of a Federal soldier just as it dropped from his pocket when he fell writhing in the agony of death. It was obviously a memento of some loved one at home which he had brought so far with him and had worn close to his heart on this day of danger and death. It was strange to see that emblem of childhood, that token of a father's love lying there amidst the dead and dying where the storm of war had so fiercely raged and where death had stalked in the might of its terrible majesty. I dismounted, picked it up and stuffed it back into the poor fellow's cold bosom that it might rest with him in the bloody grave.[5]

Most unnerving of all was the sight of the mangled men and of the makeshift hospitals in which they struggled for life. The Union artilleryman Edwin Barrett, of Concord, Massachusetts, watched ambulances bring wounded men to an old brick church turned hospital, fearing that he might discover a friend among them. He later recalled, "As these loads of wounded were brought up, blood trickled from the ambulances like water from an ice cart, and directly in front of the church door was a large puddle of blood."[6]

For all the shock experienced by novice soldiers, the image of the early war as a time of relative innocence is belied by the quickness of participants on both sides to assign blame and to demonize the enemy. William Tecumseh Sherman, colonel of the 13th U.S. Infantry, wrote his wife, Ellen, a bitter assessment of the battle, reflecting the skepticism of regular army officers about volunteer troops. He rebuked Patterson for failing to hold Johnston, but he had harsher words still for the rank and file, the "confused masses of men" whose lack of discipline had been "disgraceful." He condemned their conduct on the march to Manassas as well as their disorderly retreat: "Each private thinks for himself—If he wants to go for water, he asks leave of no one. If he thinks right he takes the oats & corn, and even burns the house of his enemy." Such rude treatment of Confederate civilians, Sherman worried, meant the Union "ought never to hope for any friends in Virginia."[7]

In the eyes of Confederates, the behavior of the Union troops toward Southern civilians was not a measure of the youthful wildness and exuberance of amateur soldiers but the fulfillment of secessionist prophecies that Northerners, at the bidding of their fanatical leaders, would wage war without mercy. On the eve of the battle of Bull Run, Beauregard issued his own proclamation to the "good people" of northern Virginia. It read:

> A reckless and unprincipled tyrant has invaded your soil. ABRAHAM LINCOLN, regardless of all moral, legal, and constitutional restraints, has thrown his abolition hosts among you, who are murdering and imprisoning your citizens, confiscating and destroying your property, and committing other acts of violence and outrage too shocking and revolting to humanity to be enumerated. All rules of civilized warfare are abandoned. . . . [I] invite and enjoin you by every consideration dear to the hearts of freemen and patriots—by the name and memory of your Revolutionary fathers . . . to rally to the standard of your state and country.[8]

Such prophecies were the lens through which Confederate civilians saw the arrival of blue-clad soldiers on their doorsteps and their demands for supplies, expressions of anger, and acts of destruction, authorized and unauthorized. Anne S. Frobel, who resided on a Fairfax County farm called Wilton Hill, described the behavior of the Union troops—their raiding of the chicken coops, burning of fence posts, commandeering of horses, and plundering of houses deserted by their owners—as the work of "horrid, vile looking savages." Their "ferocious treatment" of women and children meant that all had "a tale of horror and wrong to tell." Turning the Yankee rhetoric of deliverance on

GENERAL BEAUREGARD.—[FROM A PHOTOGRAPH FURNISHED BY E. ANTHONY.]

P. G. T. Beauregard. By the time of his Bull Run victory, Beauregard was already well known to Northerners as the commander to whom Fort Sumter had surrendered in the war's inaugural clash. The flamboyant Beauregard, who hailed from a wealthy Louisiana family, fancied himself a "Little Napoleon"—and soon earned a reputation for vanity and arrogance. (Library of Congress LC-DIG-ds-00120)

its head, she fumed, "These are the people we have been led to believe were so much in advance, and so much better, than *us poor ignorant* Southern people in morals, and manners, education, piety, sobriety, and every christian virtue I can only say deliver me from such."[9]

Confederates interpreted the battle as evidence not only of Yankee perfidy but also of divine favor for the cause of Southern independence. "I cannot regard it as mere accident," the Reverend George D. Armstrong proclaimed from his Norfolk, Virginia, pulpit in the immediate aftermath of the battle, "that our two important battlefields should bear the significant Scripture names of Bethel and Manassas." In what would be a recurring theme for Confederates, he claimed (erroneously in this case) that the Southern army had overcome terrible odds: that a Confederate force of 15,000 had bested a Union one of 35,000. But he went further still, arguing that the Confederate victory refuted the Republican argument that secession was "accomplished by an active and imperious minority." "We stand this day a thoroughly united people," he declared; this was not the rebellion of a disaffected fringe but a "great mass movement," a second American Revolution.[10]

In the aftermath of the Bull Run debacle, Lincoln summoned to Washington Major General George Brinton McClellan, fresh from his series of victories in western Virginia, and handed him command of the forces defending the capital. A distinguished graduate of West Point and veteran of the Mexican War, McClellan had left the army in 1857 and embarked on a peacetime career as a railroad engineer and executive. He returned to Federal service in May 1861, assuming command of the Department of the Ohio, comprising Illinois, Indiana, Ohio, and later western Virginia, western Pennsylvania, and Missouri. He made the most of that role by taking the fight to the Confederates, crossing the Ohio River into the mountains of western Virginia and driving Confederate troops out of that region. Lincoln hoped such boldness would be the antidote to the malaise that had settled in after Bull Run. Initially, the prospects for command harmony between McClellan and Lincoln seemed good: McClellan was committed to disenthralling the "deluded mass of rebels," as he put it, from the Slave Power. Indeed, as his army surged through western Virginia, McClellan had issued a series of proclamations propounding a policy of liberality: "We are enemies to none but armed rebels, and those who voluntarily give them aid.... [H]ouses, families, property, and all your rights . . . will be religiously respected," he promised. Such sentiments resonated in the ranks. On July 4, 1861, a newspaper run by Union soldiers who were deployed in Martinsburg, in western Virginia, offered an address "to the people of Virginia." Feeling that they had been "grossly mispresented" by secessionists, they sought to set the record straight. Their purpose was "to reestablish peace and order . . . and to reconstruct a Government which for more than three-quarters of a century proved to be all that the people of the South as well as of the North desired . . . [in order that] the many blessings handed down to us by our ancestors be permitted to descend to our posterity." Invoking the "many sacred ties" that bound North to South, they expected to find among Virginians "friends in all but those who have fallen victims to the most insane prejudices, and who will no longer hear the voice of reason."[11]

When McClellan arrived in Washington to assume his new command, he was greeted with wild enthusiasm, as the herald of victory. Dashing, dapper, and self-important, he soon earned the sobriquet "Young Napoleon." These high expectations seemed merited when he proposed to Lincoln a plan for winning the war. McClellan's August 2, 1861, memorandum to the president called for a series of amphibious operations along the Atlantic and Gulf coasts to consolidate the blockade and capture key Southern seaports, and for offensive operations in Middle Tennessee, Missouri, and the Mississippi River Valley. The centerpiece of McClellan's strategy was Virginia. The western theater was important, McClellan insisted, but not nearly so important as the east. The war would be decided in Virginia, by a great offensive against

George Brinton McClellan, the Union's "Young Napoleon." Seen as a prodigy at training and motivating men, McClellan was initially adored by the rank and file in the Army of the Potomac and trusted by Lincoln to bring decisive victories in the east. But his military caution, political ambition, and inflated ego boded poorly for his long-term success. (Library of Congress LC-USZ62-12154)

Richmond. He would need 273,000 men, so he claimed, to guarantee success. While Lincoln hoped that this offensive strategy might get under way in the summer of 1861, McClellan was loath to bring on major engagements before his troops were adequately trained and supplied. Determined not to repeat the mistakes of Bull Run, McClellan concentrated on shoring up Washington, D.C.'s defenses and on organizing and disciplining his raw recruits.[12]

Advent of the "Contraband" Policy

Among the many unsettling lessons of Bull Run were reports that slaves had provided vital labor for the Confederate army during the campaign, constructing defenses and even, according to some unfounded but nonetheless potent rumors, bearing arms and firing upon Union soldiers. This too had been warned of by abolitionists pushing for emancipation as a war aim and for black enlistment. Frederick Douglass, in a May 1861 editorial titled "How to End the War," noted that slaveholders "have no scruples against employing the Negroes to exterminate freedom, and in overturning the Government." The reports and rumors from Manassas lent credence to this argument and soon figured prominently in political debates in the federal capital. Perhaps the most lasting legacy of the battle was the impetus it gave to a nascent Union policy of confiscating slaves who fled to Union lines.[13]

That policy first took root at Union-occupied Fort Monroe, on the Virginia Peninsula, which lay between the James and York Rivers. On May 23, 1861, three slaves of a Confederate colonel named Charles Mallory, seeking to avoid further work as military laborers for their master's army (they had been building batteries at Sewall's Point), fled from the Confederate-controlled part of the Peninsula to the nearby Federal fort. The following day a Confederate major, John Cary, appeared at Fort Monroe demanding that the three men—Shepard Mallory, Frank Baker, and James Townsend—be returned to their master, as if the prewar Fugitive Slave Act of 1850 were still in effect.[14]

Cary was rebuffed by the Union commander of the fort, Major General Benjamin Butler, who insisted that "the fugitive slave act did not affect a foreign country"—and that was precisely what Virginia, which ratified its ordinance of secession that very day, claimed to be. Butler was one of the war's "political generals," promoted to leadership not because of military qualifications but for political reasons. A prominent Massachusetts Democrat, he could aid Lincoln in maintaining his fragile coalition of Republicans and War Democrats; indeed, once appointed to his generalship, Butler was generous in his public expressions of support for the Lincoln administration.

Butler was no abolitionist; in fact, he had decried abolitionism as the work of extremists. But in May 1861 he made a military calculation: keenly aware that the fugitives were representative of the countless slaves forced to construct Confederate fortifications, he reckoned that he could not return the men into the service of his enemy, but instead should put them to work for the Union cause. Butler was not emancipating the slaves; he was confiscating them, as contraband of war. In his view, the Confederates by seceding had forfeited the protections of the Constitution.[15]

Having improvised a solution to his dilemma, Butler asked the authorities in Washington to endorse his policy. He wrote Winfield Scott on May 27, reporting that still more fugitive slaves were coming into his lines, including entire families, with women and children. "As a military question it would seem to be a measure of necessity to deprive their masters of their services," he noted, adding leadingly, "How can this be done?" Within a few days, Butler got the answer he wanted: Lincoln's cabinet endorsed the confiscation policy, and thus Secretary of War Simon Cameron could instruct Butler, on May 30, to keep up the good work. Butler could both refuse to return slaves to their "alleged masters" in states under rebellion and employ able-bodied men and women to work for wages for the Union army. Cameron added one crucial condition: Union troops were not permitted to actively interfere with slavery by "enticing" slaves from their masters, but could only receive those slaves who had fled of their own accord.[16]

In July Congress took up the question of "military emancipation," with Republicans justifying confiscation as a military necessity and Democrats claiming that the Lincoln administration risked betraying its promise that it would not interfere with slavery. On July 20 Senator Lyman Trumbull of Illinois, chair of the Senate Judiciary Committee, proposed a confiscation measure declaring that masters who permitted or required their slaves to "work or to be employed in or upon any fort, navy yard, dock, armory, ship, entrenchment, or in any military or naval service whatsoever, against the Government and lawful authority of the United States," thereby forfeited the right to those slaves. Masters could not reclaim slaves who had been used for Confederate military purposes.[17]

This measure was driven by recent events—at this point approximately nine hundred slaves had fled to Fort Monroe and its vicinity—but its premise was the long-standing abolitionist theory that the enslaved had a dual status as "persons," according to the federal Constitution, and "property," according to Southern state law. Once the rebels had seceded, their state laws carried no weight; because the rebels had taken up arms against the Union, the

Slave Flight. This wood engraving, depicting the flight of refugees from slavery to Union-controlled Fort Monroe in Hampton Roads, Virginia, appeared in the June 8, 1861, edition of *Frank Leslie's Illustrated Newspaper*. Like *Harper's Weekly*, the New York–based *Frank Leslie's* reached a mass audience and represented the mainstream of Northern public opinion. Over the course of the war, these journals frequently featured images of "contrabands" fleeing to Union lines and aiding the Union war effort. (Library of Congress LC-USZ62-31165)

war powers granted the president under the Constitution kicked into effect. Democratic opponents of the measure, in Congress and in the press, asserted that any move toward federally mandated emancipation as a war aim would divide the North and anger border state slaveholders and Democratic soldiers; that it would incur Southern ire and thus prevent the restoration of peace and goodwill between the sections; and that it was inconsistent with the Republican theory that the seceded states had not left the Union and thus remained under the purview of the Constitution. Republicans countered in turn that there was no inconsistency in their position: military emancipation was not the conscious purpose of the war but an unanticipated effect of the war.[18]

In ways no one could have anticipated, the Union defeat at Manassas proved to be the Republicans' trump card. On July 21 Trumbull was among the congressmen who set out to watch the Union victory unfold at Manassas, and he was among those who witnessed and joined in the Northern forces' panicked retreat. Unsettled by this harrowing experience, he brought to the Senate debates that resumed on July 22 a new sense of urgency: the battle had furnished evidence of just how costly it was for the Union to permit Confederates to use slaves as military laborers. How could a true patriot possibly argue that such military assets should be returned to the Confederacy, rather than confiscated for use by the Union? Trumbull and other supporters of the confiscation bill thus tapped a Northern desire to see the defeat at Manassas as somehow redemptive: as a wake-up call, alerting them to the depth of Slave Power treachery and the need for renewed resolve and sterner punitive measures against the rebel leadership class. The First Confiscation Act passed the House by a vote of 60 to 48 and the Senate by a vote of 24 to 11 in early August, and was signed into law by Lincoln on August 6, 1861, justifying Charles Sumner in his assessment of the debacle at Bull Run: "The battle & defeat have done much for the slave."[19]

But how much? On August 8, in response to Butler's call for further clarification of his mandate, the War Department issued instructions. Although the Confiscation Act technically applied only to slaves of disloyal masters, Butler could receive and employ as military laborers all fugitive slaves who had come voluntarily to Union lines, regardless of their masters' loyalty or whether they had worked for the Confederate army or navy. Butler was instructed to record the names of fugitive slaves and the loyalties of their owners so that Congress could determine after the war whether loyal masters should be compensated financially for the loss of those slaves. Scholars have debated whether the 1861 Confiscation Act was an emblem of the Republicans' commitment to a war for freedom or a sign of their ambivalence about emancipation as a war aim. Historian James Oakes has argued that, taken together, the congressional act and the War Department's instructions embodied the Republican promise that runaway slaves would never again be reenslaved. Slaves seized that promise: "Within a year of its passage," Oakes observes, "tens of thousands of slaves had been freed by the First Confiscation Act." By committing themselves to military emancipation in the war's very first summer, the Republicans revealed their conviction that the war must end slavery.[20]

Other scholars see ambivalence. The policy, William W. Freehling notes, did not explicitly declare fugitives to be permanently forfeited or discharged from service, leaving open the possibility that masters could reclaim former slaves after the war. While the wording of the Confiscation Act was meant to convey that "the slave's *labor* was the property being confiscated, not the

slave himself," in holding out the prospect of financial compensation to loyal
owners of fugitive slaves the act seemed implicitly to recognize the principle
of property in man. Moreover, the measure's passage coincided with the late
July passage, with overwhelming congressional support, of the Crittenden-
Johnson resolution, which denied that abolition was a war aim: "This war
is not prosecuted upon our part in any spirit of oppression, nor for any purpose of conquest or subjugation, nor purpose of overthrowing or interfering
with the rights or established institutions of those States, but to defend and
maintain the supremacy of the Constitution and all laws made in pursuance
thereof, and to preserve the Union."[21]

Implementation would be difficult and inconsistent, as the policy tasked
army officers with the tricky work of handling the claims of slave owners
who appeared at Union lines to demand the return of runaways, but it did
not give them clear guidelines on how they should make such judgments
or ascertain the loyalty of such claimants. As a result, some Union officers
disregarded Cameron's dictates and remanded runaways or denied them
refuge. The enactment of confiscation coincided with Lincoln's appointment
of McClellan—who was committed to the limited-war principle embodied
in the Crittenden-Johnson resolution—to replace the discredited McDowell.
Meanwhile, in November 1861 General Henry Halleck, who commanded
Union forces in the western theater, between the Mississippi River and
Appalachian Mountains, issued General Order No. 3 barring fugitive slaves
from his lines and expelling them from his camps. Loath to take on the responsibility of providing for slave refugees, Halleck insisted that "it does not
belong to the military to decide upon the relation of master and man." Taken
together, these facts signal that the administration was not yet ready to declare a war for freedom.[22]

Debate over the Confiscation Act persists because there is evidence enough
to sustain both interpretations. Indeed, the confiscation bill commanded
broad support among the Northern public precisely because it was open to
divergent readings. Abolitionists and Radical Republicans pointed to the
exodus of slaves to Union lines as evidence of the "universal desire among
the slaves to be free," as the Massachusetts soldier Edward Pierce, assigned by
Butler to supervise the fugitives at Fort Monroe, put it in his published account of his "experience among the contrabands." With the Confiscation Act,
Pierce hoped, the government moved to recognize the justness of that desire
for freedom, to repudiate at last the shameful Fugitive Slave Act of 1850, and
to discredit the proslavery ideology that held white Southerners in its sway.
Union soldier Alexis J. Seymour, stationed at Camp Hamilton just outside

Fort Monroe, reported in a July 15 letter to his sister, "We have 40 or 50 of the 'contraband' in & about our camp." He added, in an arch reference to the paternalist defense of slavery (and to secessionist James Henry Hammond's famous 1858 "mudsill" speech), "Their peculiar institution is in danger & their faithful, open hearted, jolly, contented chattels ... are leaving their dear good massa's and claiming the protection of us poor mud sills." Seymour was perfectly sure that the slaves, "to a man," preferred to fight against the Confederacy than to "go back to their kind hearted & chivalrous masters."[23]

Northerners who identified themselves as moderates and conservatives could support confiscation on different, narrower grounds: as a punitive measure against disloyal masters, one grounded in military calculations rather than in social egalitarianism or moral judgments, and as an incentive, in the form of protection for or compensation to loyal masters, for slave-holding secessionists to convert to Unionism. Such Northerners hoped the measure would hasten Confederate defeat and the restoration of the Union. "Our army will use the slaves, just as they will use the other property of the Southern rebels, whenever and however they shall deem necessary. They will pay for the services of the slaves, just as the services of the cattle of loyal men, upon receiving proper evidence of that loyalty," the *New York Herald* explained in a fall 1861 editorial, "Emancipation and the War." Both the rebels and "abolition conspirators" had "deluded" the Southern masses with the lie that the Northern government was "abolitionized." In order to "attract all honest Southern men to our banners," the editorial continued, Northerners must prove that the Union would pursue a conservative course of action.[24]

Tellingly, Confederates were unreceptive to such a "conservative" message. They interpreted the confiscation policy as the culmination of a long string of Yankee depredations, fully consistent with the North's aim of sub-jugating and destroying the South. "The last step in the programme of out-rage and insolence is now initiated," fumed an August 7, 1861, *Charleston Mercury* editorial. In asserting the right to seize Southern property, it con-tinued, Northerners had declared war on Southern women and children. In the eyes of Confederates, the confiscation policy was a symbol of not only Yankee brutality but also hypocrisy: the Northern army was enticing slaves with visions of freedom, only to "take possession of them as prop-erty" and "coerce" them into service for the Union. The *Mercury* urged Southern men to derive a new sense of urgency from the advent of the contraband policy. "It is not enough that we arm and go forth to battle," it intoned. "We must do so with the conviction that we fight along the edge of a precipice."[25]

Missouri and Irregular Warfare
in the Trans-Mississippi Theater

On August 30, 1861, Major General John C. Frémont, commander of the recently created Department of the West, stretching from Illinois to the Rockies, issued a proclamation establishing martial law throughout the state of Missouri. This severe measure was justified, the proclamation explained, by the "helplessness of the civil authority, the total insecurity of life, and the devastation of property by bands of murderers and marauders, who infest nearly every county of the State, and avail themselves of the public misfortunes and the vicinity of a hostile force to gratify private and neighborhood vengeance, and who find an enemy wherever they find plunder." Frémont was decrying the emergence of a guerrilla struggle, an extension of the Kansas-Missouri border wars of the late 1850s, between Unionist and Confederate partisans in the state. Irregular warfare became so intertwined with conventional warfare there that it proved nearly impossible to disentangle them. The Confederates were led by Kentucky-born Democrat Claiborne Fox Jackson, who despite the pro-Union vote of the state's convention in March 1861 was determined to lead it into the secessionist column. He was pitted initially against Brigadier General Nathaniel Lyon, who was given command of the Union forces in the state after he and Republican congressman Francis Blair Jr. forced the surrender in St. Louis of a secessionist militia that Jackson had raised and which threatened to seize the federal arsenal there; this action had devolved into a riot that claimed the lives of some secessionist civilians. Jackson had upped the ante, appointing former Missouri governor and Mexican War veteran Sterling Price to command the State Guard and directing him to oppose the incursions of Federal forces. In abortive truce negotiations, the rebel Jackson proposed to the loyalist Lyon that Missouri maintain "neutrality" premised on the Federals' pledge not to occupy the state. Lyon responded, "This means war." Missouri was part of the Union, and Federal troops would go where they pleased.[26]

Jackson chose to form a government in exile in Missouri's "black belt," decamping from the state capital at Jefferson City and concentrating his men at Boonville. Meanwhile, on June 15, 1861, Lyon's troops entered the capital, receiving a warm welcome from its Unionist civilians. Hoping to elude the Federals, Jackson led his fugitive government and army on a long retreat to the southwest corner of Missouri. Two months of pursuit and sporadic fighting culminated in the August 10, 1861, battle of Wilson's Creek, the second major battle of the war. The stakes could not have been higher. Price had, after long pleading with Richmond, been reinforced by troops from Arkansas under Brigadier General Ben McCulloch. Their mandate was to reverse the Union tide in the state and secure another triumph as grand as Bull Run. Lyon, for his part, was keenly aware that setbacks in Missouri could have ripple effects in Kentucky and the other border states. To stop the Confederates' advance toward his headquarters at Springfield, Lyon chose a bold course: he divided his outnumbered army and attacked the Confederate encampment head-on, with his second in command, Colonel Franz Sigel, making a flanking maneuver. The Federal attack faltered, and the Union troops, despite their stern resistance at Bloody Hill, were swept back in a ferocious counterattack. Lyon was mortally wounded, shot through the heart. As at Bull Run, the Confederates were too depleted to follow up their victory by pursuing the enemy.[27]

Even as the Confederates debated how best to capitalize on this momentum, guerrilla war engulfed Missouri, with Unionist and Confederate civilians organized into partisan bands preying on each other with raids, ambushes, looting, and sometimes lethal violence. Rebel guerrillas attacked Union military resources, such as supply trains, and vulnerable soldiers, such as pickets and patrols, and then reassumed their guise as harmless civilians,

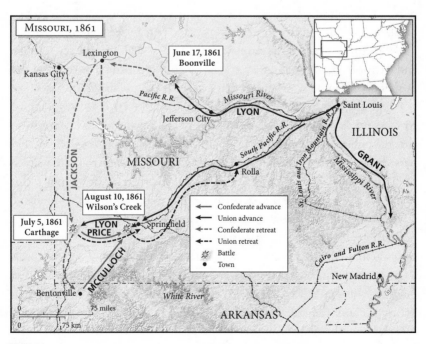

MAP 1.2

confounding the Union search expeditions sent to root them out. Unionist civilians dominated the state's "white belt" regions but were exposed to incursions from Confederate partisans based in the "black belts." Secessionists, for their part, were vulnerable to attacks from across the border by antislavery jayhawkers from Kansas and to the stern policies of Union commanders such as Brigadier General John Pope, who seized property from civilians who tried to shield guerrillas. As Frémont's declaration of martial law highlighted, not all of the irregular warfare was ideological in nature: some of it was rooted in old neighborhood rivalries, vendettas, and feuds. The violence also reflected ethnic tensions between German immigrants who were stalwarts of Missouri's Unionist Home Guards in St. Louis and elsewhere and nativists who resented the "foreigners" for picking a side in the fight.[28]

To reassert control over this deteriorating situation, Frémont in his August 1861 proclamation promised that rebel guerrillas would "suffer the extreme penalty of the law." Those taken with weapons in their hands would be tried by court-martial and, if convicted, executed at gunpoint; those aiding the rebel cause in less direct ways, by fomenting disaffection and spreading false information, would also face "severe punishment." One of Frémont's punitive measures proved especially odious to Confederates and controversial in the Union: the stipulation that any civilian "who shall be directly proven to have taken an active part with their enemies in the field" was liable to have his slaves "confiscated to the public use . . . and hereby declared freemen."[29]

With this threat against slavery, Frémont exceeded his military mandate and encroached on the political realm. Lincoln moved swiftly to bring him into line. Cautioning the general that executions would initiate a cycle of retaliation, the president implied that they must in practice be only a last resort. As for Frémont's rogue declaration of emancipation, Lincoln insisted that the policy be brought into line with the Confiscation Act Congress had passed that August. In Lincoln's view, military proclamations by commanders in the field could not settle political questions, and therefore it was not within Frémont's purview to fix the "permanent future condition" of "contraband" slaves. Only Lincoln, as commander in chief, would decide on issues where the politically fraught question of slavery was concerned, and he would do so on the grounds of military necessity. Was Lincoln's rescinding of Frémont's order a sign of the president's skepticism about black freedom? Many abolitionists feared so. "It is greatly to be regretted that the President has thought it necessary to check the ardor of the western leader, and to confine him to the mere letter of the Act of Confiscation," an editorial in the African Methodist Episcopal Church's *Christian Recorder* noted, adding, "It is a step backward,

John C. Frémont. The dashing Frémont, renowned as an explorer of the West and as the standard-bearer in the Republican party's first presidential bid, carried the weight of heavy expectations: he was out to "vindicate the judgment of the million and more citizens who desired to make him President in 1856," *Harper's Weekly* noted in July 1861. (Library of Congress LC-USZ62-127601)

and one which will dishearten the nation." In another sense, perhaps less evident to the public, Lincoln's orders to Frémont represented a step forward. The Confiscation Act had targeted disloyal states—but Lincoln was implying that it had legal sway in loyal states where there were significant numbers of rebels and thus the military necessity for punitive measures.[30]

Lincoln's exchange with Frémont revealed a political dynamic that first became visible in the border states: Federal military authorities on the ground, suspicious of professions of "neutrality" and scornful of the idea of qualified loyalty, decided to hold civilians accountable not only for actively aiding the rebellion but also for passive collusion. Conciliation would be reserved for Unionists—and slaveholding was seen as a potential marker of disloyalty.[31] Lincoln himself remained focused on the work of securing the loyalty of all of the border states. His primary objection to Frémont's proclamation was that it "will alarm our Southern Union friends, and turn them against us— perhaps ruin our rather fair prospect for Kentucky." It would not do for slave- holding Kentuckians to get the impression that Frémont "may do *anything* he pleases—confiscate the lands and free the slaves of *loyal* people, as well as of disloyal ones," Lincoln explained. When Frémont balked, Lincoln removed him from command.[32]

Democratic papers saw Lincoln's rebuke of Frémont's harsh strictures as a welcome message for the "hundreds of thousands of loyal men who cling to the flag of their country" in border states such as Missouri and Kentucky and also in Confederate states such as Virginia, Tennessee, and North Carolina, as a midwestern newspaper explained. Such views were echoed among Union soldiers who continued to believe that "kind treatment" of be- nighted Southern civilians would convert them into "good Union people." William Penn Lyon, a Wisconsin infantry officer on expedition in south- eastern Missouri, observed that the majority of people he met there were "very stupid, ignorant, dirty, and of course, poor . . . probably a fair specimen of the 'poor whites' of the South." They had been "made to believe that the Federal troops wherever they went indulged in indiscriminate rapine, vio- lence, and murder"—but when "disabused in relation to the objects of this war," such "deluded people" would embrace the Union. Lyon thus supported the removal of Frémont, and he believed that most of his fellow soldiers did, too. Frémont's replacement, Henry Halleck, took up the challenge of defining the parameters of "hard yet humane" warfare when he promulgated General Order No. 13 in December 1861. This summary of the laws of war instructed Union soldiers to be "fierce and decisive in their punishment of guerrillas" and civilians who actively aided guerrillas, but constrained in the treatment of noncombatants. Union soldiers who seized civilian property without au- thorization—or engaged in "eye-for-an-eye" vengeful reprisals for guerrilla attacks—would themselves risk the death penalty.[33]

A distinct antislavery version of the "hard yet humane" argument was also taking shape, and among its most influential proponents at this stage of the war was a maverick white Southern Unionist, Moncure Conway. An elite Virginian who had come to embrace New England Unitarianism and reform, Conway belonged during the antebellum era to an exclusive club: a tiny but determined cadre of white Southern champions of abolition. These dissenters—the Grimké sisters of South Carolina, James Birney and Cassius Clay of Kentucky, Hinton Rowan Helper and Daniel Goodloe of North Carolina, and a few others—fed the Northern hope that Southerners might one day embrace the free labor system. The war vaulted Conway to prominence. In his popular lectures in the North and in his antislavery treatises *The Rejected Stone* (1861) and *The Golden Hour* (1862), Conway defended Frémont as the "Warrior of Liberty" and denounced his removal. He implored Lincoln to enact immediate abolition under his constitutional war powers and argued that slavery, not the South, was the Union's true enemy. At the heart of Conway's rhetoric was his claim that an emancipation decree by the president would be not only "merciful to the slave" but also, as he put it emphatically, "MERCIFUL TO THE SOUTH!" Bearing witness as a Virginian, Conway conjured the "fearful proportions of ignorance" and the "licentiousness and idleness" with which the slave system had afflicted white Southerners. The answer was "smiting the South to heal her of the withering curse that is upon her." Conway reached for other metaphors— slavery was a "wild disease" that coursed through Southern veins, a poisonous "vile drug" Southerners brought to their own lips, a "tumor which now eats into our Southern brother's heart." What the crisis demanded was not a "weak love that yields and indulges" but instead merciful severity. The North must "rescue that brother," he explained, "by the painful surgical way." Emancipation, he predicted, would hasten the end of the war and the restoration of sectional amity. It would be welcomed by most non-slaveholding whites, especially in the mountain South, and end at long last the regime of the slaveholder oligarchy.[34]

Conway's message was received enthusiastically by audiences in the North, who clamored for his books and lectures; indeed, at the behest of some of his Boston supporters, thousands of copies of *The Rejected Stone* "were sent to soldiers at the front," even as it rapidly sold out in Philadelphia and New York. Conway visited Lincoln in the White House on January 17, 1862, and asked the president "whether we might not look to him as the coming Deliverer of the Nation from its one great evil." Conway left the meeting feeling the president was not yet ready to fully embrace the role. Although Lincoln believed slavery should someday end, he was preoccupied with public opinion, especially in the border states, and could not see that the golden hour was at hand.[35]

Kentucky and "Armed Neutrality" in the Western Theater of War

Lincoln was indeed preoccupied with Kentucky. Like Missouri, Kentucky had a Unionist majority, a pro-Confederate governor, and a shaky pretense to neutrality. The state's strategic importance was clear: bounded by the Ohio River to the north and the Mississippi to the west, Kentucky lay at the center of both the North's and the South's heartland. Lincoln also had an intense personal stake in Kentucky: he had been born there, had idolized the Bluegrass State's favorite son Henry Clay, and had married a Kentuckian, Mary Todd. "I think to lose Kentucky is nearly the same as to lose the whole game," Lincoln insisted, noting that with "Kentucky gone, we can not hold Missouri, nor, as I think, Maryland." In May 1861 Kentucky's governor, Beriah Magoffin, who had made no secret of his support for slavery or secession, announced a policy of armed neutrality: Kentuckians would stand at the ready to defend their state from either Union or Confederate forces. Over the course of the summer, Unionists, predominant in all but the southwestern portion of the state, secured resounding victories in legislative and congressional elections; meanwhile, Federal army recruiters positioned along the state's borders proved far more successful than Confederate recruiters did at signing Kentuckians up for military service.[36]

As Lincoln had suspected it might, Frémont's declaration of martial law in Missouri brought a backlash from Kentucky Unionists, but that proved short-lived, not only because of the president's rebuke to Frémont but also due to the Confederates' miscalculations. In a rash move Lincoln had anticipated and indeed hoped for, the Confederates were the first to violate Kentucky's neutrality. On September 4, 1861, Major General Leonidas Polk, who commanded the Confederate forces in western Tennessee, ordered Brigadier General Gideon J. Pillow to occupy Columbus, a rail junction on the Mississippi. This was a virtual invitation for Union forces, under Brigadier General U. S. Grant, to enter the state from their base at Cairo, Illinois, wearing the mantle of liberators of the state's loyal civilians. Grant captured Paducah, at the confluence of the Tennessee and Ohio Rivers, and the Federals soon exercised control over roughly two-thirds of Kentucky's territory. The Kentucky legislature instructed the governor to banish the Confederate troops from the state but to permit the Union ones to remain.

The Confederates refused to withdraw. General Albert Sidney Johnston, the renowned army veteran from Kentucky overseeing the Confederate armies in the west, ordered Polk's men to move into Bowling Green, so as to establish a defensive line from the Mississippi to the Appalachians along the Kentucky-Tennessee border. Confederates also shored up the forts they had begun constructing on the Tennessee and Cumberland Rivers. In a bloodless contest of maneuver, the two armies carved out zones of occupation, consigning Kentucky's neutrality to the ashes. On October 29, 1861, the Confederate minority in Kentucky set up a shadow government, with George W. Johnson as governor and Bowling Green as the state capital (the city was also Albert Sidney Johnston's headquarters); this rump government was admitted to the Confederacy in December 1861. Whatever the symbolic value of this show of support for the Confederacy, the fact remained that Unionists dominated the state. Twice as many Kentuckians joined the Union army as the Confederate one, and the state furnished Grant's army with manpower as well as the matériel and safe harbors in which to prepare for offensives to the south.[37]

On November 7, 1861, Grant took aim at the Confederate camp at Belmont, Missouri, which lay across the Mississippi from the rebel garrison at Columbus, Kentucky. His force of roughly 3,000 troops moved by river transports, under the cover of gunboats, and pulled off a surprise raid on the Confederate position. "The National troops acquired a confidence in themselves at Belmont that did not desert them throughout the war," Grant would write in his memoirs. Eager to capitalize on that confidence, Grant proposed a more ambitious riverine expedition, against Fort Henry on the Tennessee and then Fort Donelson on the Cumberland. His superior officer Henry Halleck, recently appointed to command of the newly created Department of the Missouri, comprising Missouri and Kentucky, shared Grant's enthusiasm for this plan; Fort Henry, as Grant explained, was a rail and river conduit to Mississippi and Alabama, and Fort Donelson was "the gate to Nashville . . . and to a rich country extending far east in Kentucky." Investing these forts was a way to breach the Kentucky section of the Confederates' cordon defense, to drive Albert Sidney Johnston out of his headquarters at Bowling Green, and to penetrate Tennessee.[38]

Grant's force of 15,000 soldiers, two gunboats, and four ironclads made short work of Fort Henry on February 6, 1862. With its disadvantageous position on the low ground, the fort was all too vulnerable to the joint operation by the Federal infantry and navy. Recognizing this, its commander, Brigadier General Lloyd Tilghman, had already sent many of his troops ahead to Fort Donelson, anticipating an attack there. Without awaiting orders on what next to do, Grant set out for this second target, some sixteen miles away, anticipating that Johnston would rapidly send additional reinforcements to Donelson. Due in part to the strong defensive position of the fort's

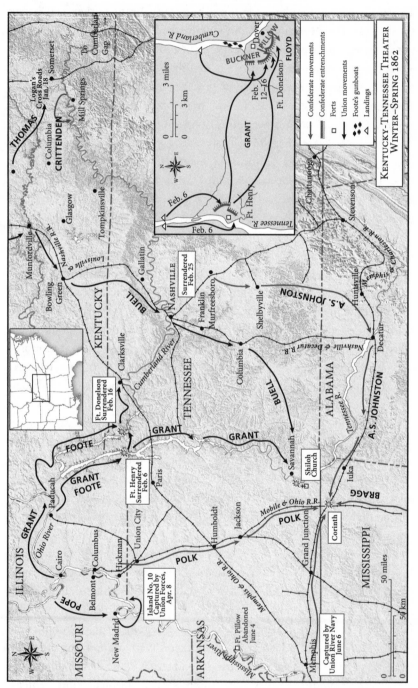

MAP 1.3

river batteries, which were located on the high ground, there would be no swift and easy Union victory this time. Grant's troops surrounded the fort by land on February 12; on the fourteenth the Federal gunboats joined the fray, coming under punishing fire from Confederate artillery. The next day, a Confederate counterattack caught the Federals off guard but then faltered. As reinforcements poured into Federal lines, the Confederate commander, Brigadier General John B. Floyd, along with his second in command, Pillow, slipped away from the fort by steamboat under cover of darkness, leaving the ranking officer left on hand, Brigadier General Simon Bolivar Buckner, the ignominious task of negotiating the fort's surrender.

When Buckner asked Grant to discuss terms, the Union general responded curtly, "No terms except unconditional and immediate surrender can be accepted." These words helped to pique the Northern public's fascination with Grant. Here was the North's first great victory in the war—a clear strategic and symbolic triumph. Grant's army captured some 12,000 Confederate prisoners, secured Middle Tennessee, and shook Confederate confidence in their western commander, Albert Sidney Johnston. The Northern press hailed the Federal army's deliverance of Missouri and Kentucky from the "plots and cabals" of secession sympathizers and from the "delusive twaddle of neutrality," and predicted that the "march of redemption" would soon spread out across Tennessee.[39]

2

Ripe for the Harvest

TO SHILOH

THE WINTER AND spring of 1862 brought the Union important diplomatic and military victories, but they came at a sobering price. Dreams of delivering the South from falsehood and terrorism continued to mobilize Northerners across a broad political spectrum, including those who saw abolitionism as an obstacle to peace and those who saw emancipation as the key to Confederate defeat. Lincoln offered border state slaveholders incentives for loyalty through the promise of compensated emancipation; medical and relief workers imagined that individual acts of mercy to Southerners would serve as models of the redemption of the region; African Americans celebrated emancipation in the District of Columbia as a long-yearned-for victory and a sign of new momentum for the cause of freedom. But the sheer carnage of the battle of Shiloh in April in Tennessee tempered Northern hopes, as the war began to spiral into a massive humanitarian crisis. How could the Union change Southern hearts and minds while exacting such a toll in flesh and blood?

Deliverance Diplomacy

In November 1861, Jefferson Davis dispatched two diplomats—his minister to England, James M. Mason, and minister to France, John Slidell—on a daring mission. The men were to run the Union blockade south to the Bahamas and then book passage to Europe, where they could make the case to the neutral British and French that the Confederacy deserved nationhood status and foreign recognition. The essence of the case was that these powers depended economically on King Cotton and that treaties of amity and commerce with the fledging Confederacy would undermine U.S. commercial power. The mission, however, soon veered off course when Captain Charles Wilkes of the U.S. Navy—having gotten wind from Cuban newspapers that the Confederate diplomats were headed east on a British mail packet, the *Trent*—resolved to stop the rebels. On November 7, 1861, Wilkes and the USS *San Jacinto* sighted the *Trent* off the Cuban coast and literally fired a shot across its bow, announcing their intention to board and search the ship. When the *Trent's* captain resisted, Wilkes decided not to confiscate the entire British vessel but only to seize Mason and Slidell and their two secretaries. In Wilkes's view, the Confederate envoys were enemy dispatches in human form and therefore contraband of war.[1]

A diplomatic firestorm ensued. Wilkes's "contrabands" were thrown into a Northern military prison. Wilkes had, the British charged, violated the neutrality of the *Trent* and the precepts of international law, which stipulated that a captured ship be brought before a prize court, expert in the rules of naval warfare, which could address the legalities of the seizure. While moving toward war footing by bolstering their forces in North America, the British government insisted on the release of the Confederate emissaries into British hands and an apology from the Lincoln administration. Would the Union meet these terms, or risk having to fight England and the Confederacy at once? Ironically, as the historian Howard Jones notes, the tense stand-off was met by a "wildfire of exultation" in both the Union and the Confederacy. Many Northerners felt that the British had already betrayed them by declaring neutrality and therefore recognizing the belligerent status of the Confederacy, rather than treating the rebels as rogue insurrectionists. Northerners depicted the treacherous Mason and Slidell as the very personification of the Slave Power. Both men had been United States senators; Mason was an architect of the proslavery Fugitive Slave Law of 1850, and Slidell had defended the extra-legal "filibustering" expeditions of slavery expansionists. "Occupying places of trust and power in the service of their country, they conspired against it, and at last the secret traitors and conspirators became open rebels," Senator Charles Sumner charged. "Treason, conspiracy and rebellion, each in succession, have acted through them." Moreover, after the disaster at Bull Run, Wilkes's daring gambit felt like a victory of sorts. For Southerners, by contrast, the *Trent* controversy seemed a dream come true: "Whether or not the British formally aligned with the Confederacy, the result would be the same: two nations fighting the Union."[2]

The controversy ended in late December when the Union, under the leadership of Secretary of State William Seward, found an honorable way to retreat: Seward issued an apology noting that Wilkes had acted on his own, had intended no insult to the British, and would have been well within his rights if only he had followed the procedure for bringing the *Trent* and her passengers to port for adjudication—that procedure would have vindicated Wilkes by disclosing that the British ship was indeed carrying actual dispatches, spelling out Confederate schemes to bring down the United States. Seward cast the release of Mason and Slidell as a defense of the very position—the rights of neutrals against belligerent maritime despotism—that the United States had upheld against Britain in the War of 1812. Finally, for the American audience, Seward emphasized that Mason and Slidell themselves were of no particular importance to the U.S. war effort.[3]

The Mason-Slidell controversy coincided with the launching of competing campaigns on the part of the Union and the Confederacy to shape popular sentiment in Europe; each side employed "unofficial agents" to lobby politicians and influence the foreign press. Southern agents played on the fears of the European elite that the Republican party was made up of "incendiary revolutionaries whose aims were to level society and overturn natural hierarchies of race and class," while Northern agents cast the Union war as a defense of republican principles against Southern oligarchs and monarchists. The Unionist press addressed itself directly to European audiences, offering the deluded-masses theory of the rebellion to counter Confederate propaganda. Rebel agents, the *New York Times* observed in February 1862, sought to "make it a matter of general European belief that there is absolute unanimity in the rebellion cause" in the South. Pointing to the warm reception the "liberating National army" had won in areas it occupied, the *Times* sought to make Europeans understand instead that the rebellion was "based on a system of organized terrorism." An article entitled "The Union Sentiment Strong in the South" in *Frank Leslie's Illustrated Newspaper* struck a similar note. "The most pertinacious attempts are made, by the rebel agents in Europe, to present the people of the South as a unit in favor of what they call 'Southern Independence,'" the piece began. "Let not Europe be deceived by false representations of the leaders of the rebellion," it continued. "With the exception of South Carolina, there is no doubt whatever of the clear existence of a clear Union majority in every Southern State." Union gunboats that had pushed up the Tennessee River after the fall of Fort Henry were met with "extravagant demonstrations of joy" from local civilians. "Whenever and wherever the pressure of rebel terrorism shall be removed, the same results will follow," the newspaper vouched. These arguments circulated in Britain among partisans of the Union; English antislavery crusader George

Thompson, for example, told an audience in Manchester that there "was no unanimity in the South, as most people thought. There were terrorism and Lynch law there." Black abolitionists practiced their own deliverance diplomacy in transatlantic reform circles, urging Britain to uphold the principles of its 1833 Slavery Abolition Act (which dismantled slavery in the British Caribbean). "Let no diplomacy of statesmen, no intimidation of slaveholders, no scarcity of cotton, no fear of slave insurrections, prevent the people of Great Britain from maintaining their position as the friend of the oppressed negro," declared abolitionist orator Sarah Parker Remond of Salem, Massachusetts, at a congress of reformers in London in 1862. Emancipation, she argued, would bring "lasting prosperity" by breaking the cotton trade's cycle of exploitation.[4]

Confederates viewed the diplomatic rapprochement between the U.S. and British administrations in the winter of 1862 as deeply disappointing, as it returned England to the posture of a neutral spectator to the American conflict. Some were skeptical that diplomacy could secure independence—they would have welcomed European support but preferred that the Confederacy focus on marshaling its own resources and achieving decisive military victories, from which recognition could follow. These skeptics, including Vice President Alexander Stephens, believed that "England and France would deliberately avoid intervention in any form in order to reap the benefits from a war that might exhaust both the North and the South." For most Confederates, this ethos of self-reliance was a position to fall back upon when diplomatic prospects seemed poor. "The military affairs of the Confederacy are not very cheering right now," a Mobile newspaper editorialized in January 1862. "Perhaps we are to pay for too joyous hopes suggested by the *Trent* affair." The lesson of the hour was that "the reliance of the South is in its own stout arms, not on the uncertain hope of a short road to independence through foreign recognition."[5]

Winter Doldrums

On February 22, 1862, one week after the fall of Fort Donelson, Jefferson Davis gave his inaugural address in Richmond, under a gloomy downpour. This speech was followed three days later by his message to the First Confederate Congress. Davis "seemed self-poised in the midst of disasters, which he acknowledged had befallen us," John B. Jones, a clerk in the Confederate War Department, observed of Davis's comportment at the inauguration. At both moments, Davis drew clear lessons from the reverses in the west: the Confederacy had too few men under arms to defend its vast territory. Reflecting back on the heady days after the fall of Fort Sumter, Davis noted, "The people, incredulous of a long War, were naturally averse to long enlistments, and the early legislation of Congress rendered it impractical to obtain Volunteers for a greater period than twelve months." The initial year-long enlistments were expiring just as the new nation faced the loss of its heartland. Now that they had been made to confront the probability that "the war will be continued through a series of years," Confederates must, Davis insisted, be willing to make long-term commitments. Davis hoped that Confederate civilians would react as John B. Jones did. The calamities in the west were a "wholesome chastening" for the South, Jones reckoned. "We shall now go to work and raise troops enough to defend the country," he resolved.[6]

In late March, Davis proposed to the Confederate Congress a conscription act that would enlist all white men between the ages of eighteen and thirty-five for a three-year tour of duty. The measure was supported by large

Jefferson Davis. With his extensive military and political experience, Davis seemed to be impeccably qualified to be Confederate president. Controversial policies such as conscription made him the lightning rod for public disaffection with his administration. (Library of Congress LC-DIG-ppmsca-23852)

majorities in both houses of the Confederate Congress and was signed into law by Davis on April 16, 1862. There were exemptions for men in civilian roles essential to the war effort—not only Confederate and state officials but also railroad workers, telegraph operators, clergymen, and miners—and a draftee could avoid duty by hiring a substitute from among those who had not yet been called up. This was the first national draft in American history, and it proved to be a source of enduring controversy in the Confederacy. Its opponents objected that it was an abrogation of states' rights; along with policies such as impressment, taxation, and regulation of the railroads, conscription exemplified a trend toward government centralization. The most vocal of these critics, Georgia's governor, Joseph Brown, barraged Davis with letters and pamphlets denouncing the draft law as unconstitutional. But Davis did not relent: he argued that the Confederate constitution had granted "broad, ample and unqualified" war powers to the Confederate Congress and that conscription was "absolutely indispensable" to a nation facing an existential threat from "armies vastly superior in numbers."[7]

As for Union morale during the war's first winter, the hopefulness and relief at Grant's successes in the west were offset by the lingering spirit of unease that prevailed in the east. In the summer of 1861, McClellan set to work recruiting, training, and organizing his army, winning plaudits for his efficiency. In the fall, despite the fact that the Federals incurred a setback at the October 21 battle of Ball's Bluff in northern Virginia, where Confederates had repulsed a Union attack, McClellan received another vote of confidence. On November 1, Lincoln appointed him general-in-chief of the Federal armies, replacing the retiring Winfield Scott, whom the ambitious McClellan had been subtly working to undermine ever since arriving in Washington. Union successes in joint army-navy operations on the Atlantic Coast seemed at first to vindicate Lincoln's choice: Union forces seized Port Royal Sound, South Carolina, on November 7, 1861, and proceeded to capture the Sea Islands, off South Carolina and Georgia; in February 1862, amphibious operations again brought victory, this time in the North Carolina Sounds, where Brigadier General Ambrose E. Burnside's command captured Roanoke Island and then, in a series of engagements extending through June, claimed additional seaport towns. These victories tightened the blockade and gave the Union forces beachheads for potential overland operations into the Confederate interior— and thus tied up Confederate troops along a defensive perimeter. They also stoked Northern hopes in Southern Unionism; Northerners imagined, based on North Carolina's tardiness in embracing secession, that that state was rife with loyalists and potential converts. Union soldiers who occupied coastal towns such as New Bern "were convinced that they witnessed loyalty to the United States," the historian Judkin Browning has observed. White refugees streamed into Union lines in two waves—first came diehard Unionists claiming the protection of the flag, and then, after the Confederate draft was instituted in April 1862, came a wave of those avoiding conscription. Lincoln tried to encourage that loyalty by appointing a native North Carolinian, Edward Stanly, as military governor of the occupied portions of the state. Stanly, who loathed secessionists and also loathed abolitionists, worked to re-kindle loyalty in coastal North Carolina by assuring whites there that Lincoln was no abolitionist and that reunion was the president's only goal.[8]

Despite these military inroads, the relationship between Lincoln and McClellan was souring, as the grand Virginia campaign McClellan had outlined in his August 2, 1861, memorandum failed to materialize. McClellan was showing a penchant for overestimating Confederate troop strength. He imagined that an army of 150,000 rebels menaced the Federal capital (the

MAP 2.1

force actually numbered 40,000) and that he could not move south until the Washington defenses, and his own newly christened Army of the Potomac, were shored up. "I owe it to my country & myself not to advance until I have reasonable chances in my favor," McClellan explained to his friend Samuel Barlow, a prominent New York Democrat, in November 1861. He added, turning to politics, "I am fighting to preserve the integrity of the Union & the power of the Govt—on no other issue. To gain that end we cannot afford to raise up the negro question—It must be incidental and subsidiary." Here was the crux of the brewing controversy over McClellan: he had a different understanding of the politics of deliverance than Lincoln did. An ardent Democrat of the Stephen Douglas school, McClellan was not a defender of slavery—he subscribed to the fantasy that voluntary, piecemeal manumission of slaves by their owners might someday bring the gradual extinction of the institution, and thought that freedom would be followed by a prolonged period of second-class status for blacks as they gradually earned the rights of citizens. But he was intensely anti-abolition—opposed to federal antislavery measures such as confiscation, contemptuous of Radical Republicans and of abolitionists, and wary at best of moderate Republicans such as Lincoln.[9]

Moreover, McClellan was scornful of politicians, believing they lacked the specialized military expertise needed to make sound strategic and tactical decisions and that they were susceptible to manipulation by radical reformers. Political meddling in military affairs, he feared, would bring battlefield defeat and would further alienate Southern and Northern civilians. Keenly aware that some Republican congressmen were complaining to Lincoln about his inaction, McClellan believed himself to be persecuted and slandered by antislavery radicals who questioned his loyalty and plotted to push the impressionable president—"an idiot" was how McClellan described Lincoln—toward emancipation by federal fiat and toward total war. In a sense, McClellan's critics were right to discern a connection between his conservative politics and his military strategy: McClellan wanted to be sure his first blow at the Confederate army in Virginia would be a knockout punch, so that he could secure the surrender swiftly, without a prolonged, grinding war that would destroy the Southern social order and obviate a harmonious reunion.[10]

Lincoln showed remarkable forbearance in the face of McClellan's truculence. His first Annual Message to Congress, on December 3, 1861, publicly sustained McClellan, urging loyal Americans to give the new general-in-chief the "confidence, and cordial support . . . without which, he cannot, with so full efficiency, serve the country." Lincoln also offered reassurances to moderates and rebuffed radicals: he defended confiscation as an "indispensable means" to achieve the war's overarching aim of preserving the Union, and he endorsed the idea that Congress should provide financial remuneration to states that undertook measures for gradual emancipation, compensating loyal slaveholders who chose to free their slaves and colonizing those freedpeople. Behind the scenes, Lincoln was increasingly disgusted by McClellan's inaction and his attitude. He wanted the general-in-chief to direct multiple offensives in the west and east—and to that end, the president on January 27, 1862 issued General War Order No. 1, ordering the Union armies to commence a coordinated advance on all fronts on Washington's Birthday, February 22, 1862. This directive further alienated McClellan—but did not prompt him to move. His grand campaign in Virginia would await the spring.[11]

The Union commanders in the west, by contrast, needed no such prompting, and the ongoing string of Federal gains there served to cast the Virginia stalemate in a harsh light. On February 25, shortly after the fall of Forts Henry and Donelson, Union forces under Brigadier General Don Carlos Buell, commander of the Department of the Ohio, captured Nashville, Tennessee; the city, the first state capital to come under Federal control, had been relinquished without a fight by Albert Sidney Johnston. Seeking to promote Southern Unionism with this victory, Lincoln sent to Nashville, to act as his military governor there, Senator Andrew Johnson. Johnson was already a man of renown. A Jacksonian Democrat of humble, yeoman origins from Tennessee, Johnson was in his first term as a United States senator when the war began, and he took a courageous stand against secession, declaring it an "odious, diabolical, nefarious, hell-born and hell-bound doctrine." He was the only Southern senator to profess such loyalty to the Union, and he paid a high price for this apostasy: his family was driven into exile, his property confiscated, and Johnson himself hung in effigy and roundly cursed by Confederates in his home state. Johnson represented not only rock-ribbed loyalty but also the plight of white refugees in the South. From the start of the war, the Northern public was keenly fascinated by the stories of exiled white Southerners; newspaper columns with titles such as "A Refugee's Statement," "Further Rebel Outrages," and "What a Southern Unionist Says" featured the testimony of individuals who had fled from Confederate oppression and lived to tell the tale. With Johnson's return to Tennessee, the tables were turned, as a March 1862 *Cleveland Herald* article entitled "The Refugee Now Governor" crowed.[12]

Johnson's Unionism was rooted in the class resentments of non-slaveholding yeomen farmers against elite planters, and in the cultural differences between the mountainous, "upcountry" regions of the South (such as Johnson's own East Tennessee) and low-country plantation districts.

Johnson would persistently press Lincoln to launch a campaign to liberate East Tennessee from the Confederates and would publicize the sufferings of East Tennesseans at the hands of the "military despotism of Jeff Davis" when such a campaign—which was logistically daunting, as the region was shielded by the Cumberland Mountains—failed to materialize. Like North Carolina's military governor, Edward Stanly, Johnson professed to abhor secessionists and abolitionists in equal measure and promised, early in his tenure, to pursue a "conservative Union policy."[13]

East Tennessee Unionism. This *Harper's Weekly* cover depicts a clandestine meeting of East Tennessee Unionists led by Colonel David Fry. They launched raids against Confederate assets such as railroad bridges, and risked execution if caught. The persecution of East Tennessee loyalists captured the imagination of the Northern public. But the Union army was slow to make inroads into East Tennessee. (Library of Congress LC-USZ62-107095)

The Federal army consolidated its momentum in the west in March 1862 with the victory of Major General Samuel R. Curtis over Major General Earl Van Dorn at Pea Ridge in northwestern Arkansas. The battle was a chapter in the struggle over Missouri. Sterling Price and Leonidas Polk were determined to regain lost ground there and to launch an offensive directed at St. Louis, bolstering the fading morale of Confederate civilians in the state. Jefferson Davis was persuaded, and he handed the task to Van Dorn, who commanded the department consisting of Arkansas, Missouri, parts of Louisiana, and Indian Territory. But the planned offensive faltered when Union forces under Curtis, heading the Army of the Southwest, struck first, driving Price's force back into Arkansas. Van Dorn's March 8 attempt to push back—he sent his divided army in two columns against Curtis, in an effort to envelop the Federals—ended in a rout. The loss at Pea Ridge, which was followed by Union Brigadier General John Pope's breach of the Confederate defenses at New Madrid, Missouri, and Island No. 10 on the Mississippi above Memphis, marked the end of Confederate hopes to assert military control over Missouri. Still another reversal played out that spring, in the Southwest. A Confederate expeditionary force raised in Texas and commanded by Brigadier General Henry Hopkins Silbey was foiled in its ill-conceived and poorly provisioned attempt to invade New Mexico. Turned back by Union regulars and Colorado volunteers at Glorieta Pass on March 28, 1862, it retreated back into Texas. The Confederates would not try their fortunes in the Southwest again.[14]

Shiloh

In late March 1862, seeking to recover momentum after the losses of Forts Henry and Donelson, General Albert Sidney Johnston effected the concentration of Confederate forces at the rail junction of Corinth, Mississippi. He united with Beauregard, to whom he had delegated command of the western wing of his army, and he welcomed reinforcements from the east, most notably Major General Braxton Bragg's army, sent from Pensacola, Florida. Keenly aware that the volunteers in his command were green and undisciplined, Johnston tasked Beauregard and Bragg with drilling the troops, supplying them with arms and ammunition, and organizing them into three corps and a reserve force. Generals Polk, William J. Hardee, and Bragg would command the corps and George B. Crittenden the reserves. Johnston intended to strike at Grant before the Union received reinforcements—but he would have liked to buy time and to delay this attack until the Confederates had received additional reinforcements from Van Dorn's Trans-Mississippi Department.

Grant, for his part, had just resumed command of his army after a clash with Halleck, who, spurred by jealousy of his successful subordinate, had spread rumors of Grant's drunkenness. Lincoln and his recently appointed secretary of war, Edwin Stanton, disregarded the rumors and stood by Grant. Under orders from Halleck to recover the Mississippi Valley, Grant's army of 40,000 moved through West Tennessee by steamboat and camped at Pittsburg Landing, a wooded plateau on the west bank of the Tennessee River, near the northern border of Mississippi and twenty-two miles from Corinth. As Grant did not expect that an attack by Johnston was imminent, the Federal soldiers were not entrenched. With Grant headquartered at the town of Savannah, downstream, his Pittsburg Landing force, under the command of Brigadier General William T. Sherman, awaited the arrival of Buell's Army of the Ohio, en route overland from Nashville. Halleck preferred that Grant not provoke a battle until the Union forces had concentrated and until he himself had come to the front to command them in a grand new offensive.[15]

When Johnston learned on April 2 from Confederate scouts that Buell would soon reach Pittsburg Landing, he knew the time had come to pounce.[16] Confederate troops began their advance toward Grant's encampment on April 3, with the intention of attacking the following day. But they soon were bogged down by poor execution of Beauregard's marching orders, which created a traffic jam on the two roads approaching Pittsburg Landing, and by torrential rain on the night of April 4. At a council of war on the evening of April 5, the Confederate generals debated whether they had squandered the element of surprise and should call off the attack. Beauregard thought so—the troops had been not just slow but needlessly noisy in their approach toward Federal lines, which had surely tipped the Yankees off. Johnston, reckoning that a retreat would demoralize the men, opted to risk an attack, over Beauregard's objections.[17]

At 6:30 a.m. on April 6, Hardee's corps fell upon Grant's position, pushing the surprised Federal soldiers out of their camps. With victory seemingly so near at hand, Confederate troops experienced a rush of elation. They tauntingly invoked their first great victory in the east, calling out "Bull Run" as they scattered the Yankees. The men's momentum was boosted by the conspicuous bravery of Johnston, who rode forward to direct the battle from the front lines rather than issuing orders from the rear; Johnston chose to abandon Beauregard's tactical scheme and revive his own preferred plan.[18] But the tide of the battle began to turn. The Confederate rush was slowed by the propensity of the men to fall out of line and to forage among the Union supplies left behind in the Federal retreat. Meanwhile, the Union troops were developing a strong point of resistance at a low ridge in an oak thicket at the right center of their line, where divisions that had fallen back converged with advance reserve divisions. Most of the Confederate brigades were working the Union flanks, leaving a vacuum in the center. The Union's stiff resistance at this sector of the battlefield—which Union veterans of the battle would later dub the "Hornet's Nest"—buoyed Federal morale and made a hero of Brigadier General Benjamin Prentiss, who held out until captured by Confederates. His stubborn defense of the Union center had bought time for Grant to form a strong new defensive line.[19]

More ominous still for Confederates was the fate of Albert Sidney Johnston. At 2:00 p.m., as the Confederate attack was losing momentum, Johnston determined to stiffen the resolve of his troops by leading a brigade directly into Union fire. At first Johnston's men believed he had survived the charge intact and successfully made his way back to the rear of the Confederate lines. But staff officers soon saw Johnston reel in the saddle and lose consciousness: he was bleeding to death after the artery behind his right knee was severed. Johnston's death left Beauregard in charge of finishing the day's work. Positioned some two miles behind the Confederate front lines, Beauregard chose instead to call off the Confederate attack. He sent a telegram to Richmond, announcing that the Confederates, after a "severe battle of ten hours," had "gained a complete victory, driving the enemy from every position."[20]

On April 7, that victory slipped away. On the night of the sixth, Federal ships ferried men and supplies to Grant while the gunboats *Tyler* and *Lexington* shelled the Confederate positions. The arrival of Grant's reinforcements permitted the Union to mount a potent counterattack, pushing the Confederates back across the ground the armies had contested the previous day and forcing Beauregard to retreat to his original position at Corinth. Beauregard's decision to call off his attack on the sixth would be a source of enduring controversy.[21] He offered up a welter of contradictory explanations: that his officers and men were exhausted, out of ammunition, and needed to regroup; that they could not fight effectively after nightfall; that he had whipped Grant's army and there was little prospect of the Union forces receiving reinforcements; that Grant had already received reinforcements on the night of the sixth and was well shielded by Federal gunboats and artillery; that the Confederates had achieved their primary purpose of executing a raid followed by an orderly retreat; and that the Confederate corps commanders were to blame for not finishing the Federals off while they had the chance.[22]

The Federals, for their part, regarded the battle as an epic victory, attributable to their own prowess and righteousness. In his General Order No. 34,

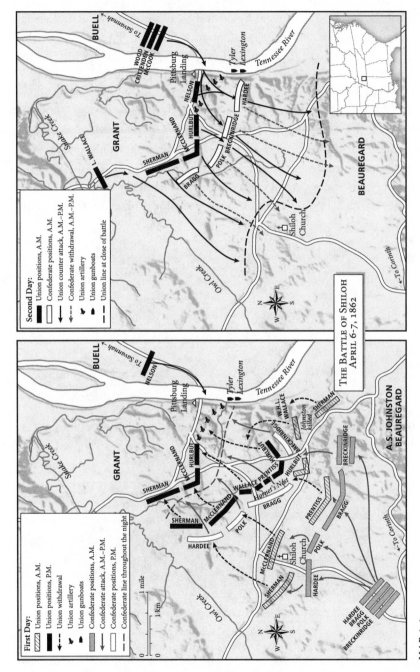

First Day:
Union positions, A.M.
Union positions, P.M.
Union withdrawal
Union artillery
Union gunboats
Confederate positions, A.M.
Confederate attack, A.M.–P.M.
Confederate positions, P.M.
Confederate line throughout the night

0   1 mile
0 1 km

GRANT
BUELL
To Savannah
Pittsburg Landing
NELSON
Tyler
Lexington
Tennessee River
Snake Creek
SHERMAN
McCLERNAND
HURLBUT
W.H.L. WALLACE
Johnston killed
SHERMAN
HURLBUT
BRECKINRIDGE
WALLACE
PRENTISS
Hornet's Nest
BRAGG
McCLERNAND
SHERMAN
POLK
HARDEE
PRENTISS
BRAGG
POLK
Shiloh Church
McCLERNAND
SHERMAN
HARDEE
BRECKINRIDGE
HARDEE
BRAGG
POLK
BRECKINRIDGE
To Corinth
Owl Creek
A.S. JOHNSTON
BEAUREGARD

N E S W

Second Day:
Union positions, A.M.
Confederate positions, A.M.
Union counter attack, A.M.–P.M.
Confederate withdrawal, A.M.–P.M.
Union artillery
Union gunboats
Union line at close of battle

BUELL
WOOD
CRITTENDEN
McCOOK
Pittsburg Landing
NELSON
Tyler
Lexington
Tennessee River
GRANT
L. WALLACE
Snake Creek
SHERMAN
McCLERNAND
HURLBUT
HARDEE
BRECKINRIDGE
POLK
BRAGG
Shiloh Church
To Corinth
Owl Creek
BEAUREGARD

N E S W

THE BATTLE OF SHILOH
APRIL 6–7, 1862

MAP 2.2

Grant congratulated his troops for having "routed a numerically superior force of the enemy, composed of the flower of the Southern army, commanded by their ablest generals, and fought by them with all the desperation of despair." He continued: "In numbers engaged, no such contest ever took place on this continent; in importance of results, but few such have taken place in the history of the world." The Union troops had fought to guarantee that future generations would "enjoy the blessings of the best government the sun ever shone upon." Moreover, open expressions of Unionist sentiment in West Tennessee seemed to surge in the battle's aftermath, as the Federal army's show of force reassured loyalists that they would have protection from Confederate retaliation. Buoyed by the results at Shiloh, Andrew Johnson predicted that once the rebel army was driven beyond the state's borders, Tennessee would "wheel back into her old place in this glorious Union by a majority of tens of thousands."[23]

Andrew Johnson. Rising from humble roots, Johnson positioned himself as a champion of the common man and critic of the slaveholding elite. During the war, Johnson became Lincoln's most important ally among War Democrats and Southern Unionists, serving as military governor of Union-occupied Tennessee and eventually as Lincoln's running mate in 1864. (Library of Congress LC-USZ62-13017)

The Union's progress could not, however, keep at bay the inevitable finger-pointing and recrimination. Perhaps the debacle of the first day of the battle—in which Grant's men were caught unawares—could have been avoided if Union commanders such as Sherman had had the prescience to entrench their forces and to camp behind defensive positions. And why hadn't Grant's army chased down the fleeing rebels and finished them off? "Just as at Bull Run," historian Russell Weigley has explained succinctly, "there was criticism on the victorious side that the winning army did not pursue vigorously enough; just as at Bull Run, the victorious army was so severely hurt by winning that it could pursue only feebly."[24]

Shiloh eclipsed Bull Run in the destruction it wrought. The Federals had sustained roughly 13,000 casualties (killed, wounded, and missing) and the Confederates 11,000; the roughly 3,400 total combat deaths on both sides were four times the total (868) at Bull Run. "I ate my dinner," one Union captain recalled of the carnage of battle, "within six paces of a rebel in four pieces. Both legs were blown off. His pelvis was the third piece, and his head and chest were the fourth. . . . Myself and other amateur anatomists, when the regiment was resting temporarily on arms, would . . . examine the internal structure of man. We would examine brains, heart, stomach, layers of muscle, structure of bones, etc., for there was every form of mutilation. At home I used to wince at the sight of a wound or of a corpse; but here, in one day, I learned to be among the scenes I am describing without emotion."[25]

War Work

Shiloh was a harbinger not only of the destructive power of the war but also of the essential role women would play in mitigating both the pain of the wounded troops and the chaos in the medical divisions of the Union and Confederacy. Robert Murray, the medical director of the Army of the Ohio, testified in his April 21, 1862, report on the battle just how ill-prepared he and his fellow Union medical officers were for the avalanche of wounded men. He lamented the "utter impossibility to obtain proper details of men to nurse them and to cook and attend generally to their wants," along with the inadequacy of the available supply of bedding, tents, dressings, ambulances, and other necessities. But he testified as well to the timely intervention of the civilians of the United States Sanitary Commission (USSC), the Washington, D.C.–based umbrella organization for the North's thousands of war relief societies, noting that USSC relief workers were "ready to receive all sick and wounded, without regard to States or even to politics, taking the wounded Confederates as willingly as our own." The head of the USSC, Unitarian minister Henry W. Bellows, was a stalwart ally of Lincoln's and a tireless purveyor of the view that the Union war was waged not against the South but "for the South," to free it from its "self-imposed sufferings." Defending the Union war as a "Holy War," Bellows intoned from his New York City pulpit, "We smite to heal, and resist to bless, and kill to make alive." Bellows and his fellow founders of the USSC, such as renowned landscape architect Frederick Law Olmsted and financier and lawyer George Templeton Strong, were part of a cadre of urban liberals who "devoted themselves to perfecting a society based on free labor." They believed that slavery had a deleterious effect on white Southern society as well as on blacks, and decried the absence of civil liberties such as freedom of speech in the South. While its primary focus was on medical and sanitary aid for Union soldiers, the USSC also extended aid to white refugees fleeing from "rebel persecution and outrage." The USSC was "self-consciously nonpartisan" in appeal and attracted widespread public support, reflecting the strong spirit of civic voluntarism in the wartime North.[26]

Although its formal officers were men, the commission had its origins in the charitable work of New York City's Woman's Central Relief Association, which was established by the nation's first female physician, Dr. Elizabeth Blackwell, and by a young prodigy of philanthropy, Louisa Lee Schuyler (the great-granddaughter of Alexander Hamilton). Powered by the labor of thousands of women, the commission represented the "feminization" of the realm of military medicine: the systematic efforts of women, at the grassroots and national levels, to apply their domestic skills to the care of soldiers. Before the war, in civilian life, sick and wounded men were often cared for by women at home, and hospitals were largely reserved for the poor and homeless. The war necessitated the rapid establishment of field hospitals, abutting the battlefront, and more comprehensive general hospitals, behind the lines—and women in the North and South lobbied for the chance to serve in both settings as hospital workers (a designation that comprises their manifold roles as orderlies, nurses, matrons, and, in rare instances, physicians). Women faced the skepticism and even outright hostility of male surgeons who felt that exposure to gravely wounded men violated the dictates of Victorian morality. They countered that they sought, as an extension of their maternal impulses, literally to provide the comforts of home—attention to nutrition, hygiene, and morale—to the suffering "boys." Male defenders of female relief work and nursing argued that women's selfless ministrations could temper the hatred unleashed by war. Major General John A. Dix of New York, a strong ally of the USSC, expressed gratitude in 1862 to the female nurses of Baltimore, noting that their willingness to attend to wounded enemy prisoners offered a "lesson of magnanimity" to the "misguided masses who are in arms against the Government."[27]

In the aftermath of Shiloh, the Sanitary Commission sprang into action, chartering boats in St. Louis, Chicago, Louisville, and Cincinnati and outfitting them with beds, nurses, and supplies to evacuate those men languishing at Pittsburg Landing. As relief organizer and nurse Mary Livermore explained, three days after the battle USSC boats arrived at the landing laden with "every species of relief": "condensed food, stimulants, clothing, bedding, medicines, chloroform, surgical instruments, and carefully selected volunteer nurses and surgeons." Among those who rushed into the void after Shiloh was Ohioan "Mother" Mary Ann Bickerdyke, a tireless caregiver who was fast establishing a reputation for setting up field hospitals and "personally superintending... the nursing of some thousands of sick and wounded men." All told, the USSC distributed "11,448 shirts; 3,686 pairs of drawers; 3,592 pairs of socks; 2,777 bedsacks; 543 pillows; 1,045 bottles of Brandy, whiskey, and wine; 799 bottles of porter; 941 lemons; 20,316 pounds of dried fruit; 7,577 cans of fruit; and 15,323 pounds of farinaceous food" to aid the soldiers after Shiloh. These supplies were gathered by Northern women in thousands of local relief societies across the country; the USSC set up regional "subdepots" in major urban centers to receive the supplies and then send them to the battlefront and to the home front hospitals to which the wounded were evacuated.[28] Meanwhile, the USSC leadership lobbied Congress and Lincoln for the passage of a medical reform act that would authorize the appointment of a properly qualified surgeon general and of a corps of medical inspectors to maintain standards among surgeons and within hospitals. The passage of the act on April 16, 1862, facilitated the creation on the Union side of a centralized general hospital system and a "nationalistic attitude toward patient care."[29]

As historian Frances M. Clarke has argued, Northern relief and hospital workers contributed, in their letters, diaries, memoirs, and other writings, to an emerging literary genre of war stories focused on "exemplary suffering." The main focus of these stories was the stoicism of Union soldiers. "Writers lavished attention on what men said and how they acted on their deathbeds or in hospital," emphasizing that Union men bore their suffering more bravely than Confederate ones, in order to hold up Northern character as the ultimate guarantor of victory. This genre also featured set pieces in which Confederate sufferers responded with gratitude to Yankee acts of kindness. For example, in Livermore's account of treating the wounded of Fort Donelson and Shiloh, she tells the story of a grievously wounded rebel prisoner from western Virginia compelled by his secessionist uncle into fighting for the Confederacy and pining on his deathbed for his Unionist mother. "I sought to buoy up his sinking spirits," Livermore remembered, "[and] talked to him as if he were my own son." In a second such story some "unlettered" poor white Southern soldiers who receive medical care from the Yankees proclaim with surprise, "You-uns is very good to we-uns." Livermore also holds up Mother Bickerdyke's willingness to extend "tender mercies" to wounded rebels as exemplary of the USSC's ethos of magnanimity. Such stories were all meant to show that the Northern war effort was "motivated by principle rather than vengeance" and that rebels had been deceived by their own leaders into viewing the Yankees as cruel avengers.[30]

The Confederates had no equivalent of the Sanitary Commission; instead army medical care was organized on the state level, and women's benevolent efforts were mostly local in nature. Confederate women nonetheless surged forward to assist the wounded, and because of the war's geography, they were far more likely than Northern ones to tend to men at or near the battle-front. Kate Cumming of Mobile, Alabama, was one of the many Confederate women who heeded the call to serve at Shiloh. Over her family's objections, she volunteered to work in the hospital division of the Army of Tennessee, and on the second day of the Shiloh battle she set out with forty other women from Mobile to Corinth, the Confederate base to which the wounded were being evacuated. Cumming's detailed wartime diary provides a window into how she acclimated to her new duties. On April 11 she wrote: "My heart beat with expectation as we neared Corinth. As I had never been where there was a large army, and had never seen a wounded man, except in the cars, as they passed, I could not help feeling a little nervous at the prospect of now seeing both. . . . Mrs. Ogden tried to prepare me for the scenes which I should witness upon entering the wards. But alas! Nothing that I had ever heard or read had given me the faintest idea of the horrors witnessed here." Cumming quickly steadied herself, noting in the next day's journal entry, "The foul air from this mass of human beings at first made me giddy and sick, but I soon got over it. We have to walk, and when we give the men any thing kneel, in blood and water; but we think nothing of it at all." Cumming also voiced her distress over the "confusion and want of order" that characterized the wards; "the amount of good done is not near what it might be, if things were better managed," she lamented, adding, "I trust that in a little time things will be better."[31]

Cumming recorded her own encounters with wounded Federal soldiers who had fallen into Confederate hands and were receiving treatment. When she brought food to a Federal officer with a broken arm, she was determined to be "polite"—but, finding the man "indifferent to the woe which they had been instrumental in bringing upon us," Cumming could "not help being indignant." "What can be in the minds of our enemies, who are now arrayed against us, who have never harmed them in any way, but simply claim our own, and nothing more!" she wrote on April 11. "May God forgive them, for surely they know not what they do."[32]

Battle Hymns

In the war's first year, Northerners and Southerners churned out songs, stories, poems, novels, and histories reflecting the escalation of the war and debates over war aims. A case in point is the story of the transmutation of the popular song "John Brown's Body." Soldiers in a Massachusetts militia battalion had penned the words in the spring of 1861, fitting them to the melody of an old folk hymn. The lyrics began by invoking the Harpers Ferry martyr's death: "John Brown's body lies a-mouldering in the grave." With its rousing refrain of "His soul is marching on" and its chorus of "Glory, glory hallelujah," the song's rhythm matched the tramping feet of marching soldiers. But it was the lyrics' very ambiguity that gave the song such broad appeal. Union soldiers and civilians who were anti-slaveholder but not antislavery could sing the words to taunt the Slave Power, knowing the image of Brown enraged Southerners, while abolitionists could sing it in a spirit of reverence for a fallen liberator.[33]

The melody itself was so compelling to Northerners that many chose to furnish their own lyrics for the song. The most enduring of these—the words to the "Battle Hymn of the Republic"—came from the pen of the Northern poet and antislavery reformer Julia Ward Howe. She was inspired by a visit in December 1861 to the outskirts of Washington, D.C., to see a grand review of the Army of the Potomac. With a husband too old to serve and children too young, and lacking the wherewithal for medical work, Howe was overwhelmed by a sense of inadequacy: "I thought of the women of my acquaintance whose sons or husbands were fighting our great battle; the women themselves serving in the hospitals, or busying themselves with the work of the Sanitary Commission. . . . Something seemed to say to me, 'You would be glad to serve, but you cannot help any one; you have nothing to give.'" The review was cut short, due to some rumors of enemy movements, and as the soldiers and spectators made their way back to Washington, they joined together in singing "John Brown's Body." One of Howe's friends suggested that she write more elevated lyrics for the song's compelling melody. That morning, as if moved by unseen hands, she did. Her "Battle Hymn" featured biblical imagery of the vindication of the righteous Union:

> Mine eyes have seen the glory of the coming of the Lord:
> He is trampling out the vintage where the grapes of wrath are stored;
> He hath loosed the fateful lightning of His terrible swift sword:
> His truth is marching on.

Howe's lyrics powerfully merged patriotism and piety: she tapped Americans' millenarian beliefs that God would redeem the United States, confirming its elect status, after an apocalyptic period of fiery trials, and that the United States would in turn serve as a millenarian agent, redeeming the world from evil and bringing it the gift of freedom. Published in the *Atlantic Monthly* in February 1862 and frequently reprinted thereafter, Howe's lyrics rivaled "John Brown's Body" in popularity. Both sets of lyrics cast Northern men as soldiers "in the army of the Lord," and both had broad appeal across the political spectrum, functioning equally well as paeans to the Union or to the cause of emancipation.[34]

Songs of War. In this autumn 1861 Winslow Homer print for *Harper's Weekly*, Union soldiers sing the "Glory Hallelujah" chorus of "John Brown's Body." The other frames feature images from popular war songs including "The Girl I Left Behind," "Hail to the Chief" (depicting McClellan), and "Dixie," depicting a "contraband." (Library of Congress LC-DIG-ppmsca-23132)

In December 1861, at virtually the same moment Howe penned the words
to "Battle Hymn," the Reverend L. C. Lockwood arranged for the publication, in Northern antislavery newspapers and as sheet music, of "The Song
of the Contrabands: 'O Let My People Go.'" Lockwood was in the vanguard
of Northern reformers, sponsored by the American Missionary Association,
who had arrived at Fort Monroe that fall to minister to the educational and
spiritual needs of former slaves who had fled to Union lines there. Like many
of the missionaries who would follow in his wake, he felt it his solemn duty to
raise the Northern public's awareness of the struggles of the fugitive slaves—
to testify to "their gratitude, their courage, their acquaintance with passing
events, their confidence that the result of the rebellion will be the liberation of
their people." In Lockwood's view, this song was the slaves' "prime deliverance
melody" and exemplified blacks' piety, suffering, and yearning for redemption
from bondage; it had been sung in the region, he noted, for many years.[35]

It began with a trope characteristic of spirituals: the likening of American
slavery to persecution of the Israelites by Pharaoh:

> *When Israel was in Egypt's land,*
> *O let my people go!*
> *Oppressed so hard they could not stand,*
> *O let my people go!*
> *O go down, Moses*
> *Away down to Egypt's land,*
> *And tell King Pharaoh,*
> *To let my people go!*

The song's final verses were not a mournful supplication but a call to action:

> *O let us all from bondage flee,*
> *O let my people go!*
> *And let us all in Christ be free,*
> *O let my people go!*
> *We need not always weep and mourn,*
> *O let my people go!*
> *And wear these Slavery chains forlorn*
> *O let my people go!*
> *. . . What a beautiful morning that will be!*
> *O let my people go!*
> *When time breaks up in eternity,*
> *O let my people go!*

For Confederates, the prime deliverance melody of the war was the wildly popular song "Maryland, My Maryland." It had its origins in a poem penned by a Louisiana secessionist in the spring of 1861, lamenting the Lincoln administration's crackdown on disloyalty and fortifying of Baltimore in the wake of the April riot against Union soldiers there. The poem, which was widely published in the Confederate press, was modified and set to music by a pair of Baltimore sisters, Hetty and Jenny Cary. The song became a favorite of General Beauregard, who distributed it among his men. "The despot's heel is on thy shore," the anthem began, and it then commanded Maryland's native sons to "avenge the patriotic gore / That flecked the streets of Baltimore." It continued, "Thou wilt not yield the Vandal toll, Maryland! / Thou wilt not crook to his control, Maryland!" The song was meant to reassure anxious Confederates that the slaveholding border states would fall into line and to assure those Maryland "exiles" who had already taken up the Confederate banner that their own sacrifices would not be in vain. As the *Charleston Mercury* explained in February 1862:

> We are glad to see this Maryland song so enthusiastically received by the Southern people. To the gallant exiles of Maryland, who are shedding their blood for our cause upon every battlefield, the fact that this song occupies the first place among "Songs of the War," will be taken as a grateful earnest of the resolution which animates the masses of the South, that, sooner or later, Maryland shall be free.

The song reflected the persistence of a myth among Maryland's slaveholding elite that without the early imposition of martial law and Federal troops, Maryland would have swung into the Confederate column. However, the historical evidence contradicts that view: in Maryland, as in Kentucky, the people "voted with their feet to join either Union or Confederate armies," and over the course of the war white Marylanders would choose the Union army "by almost a two to one margin," historian William Freehling found. Crucially, it was not at all clear to Confederate sympathizers in Maryland in the war's first year that Unionism was ascendant; that lesson would come in the fall of 1862.[36]

According to historian Alice Fahs, the contrast between "Battle Hymn," with its images of Christian sacrifice, and "My Maryland," in which Southern patriots spurn "Northern scum," reflected a "marked difference in tonality" in Northern and Southern popular culture in the early phase of the war. Southern poets were "equally as confident as their Union counterparts that God was on their side," Fahs notes, but were more inclined to demonize the enemy and emphasize the theme of vengeance, in order to "create a national identity in opposition to the North." The 1862 Confederate poem "The Guerrillas: A Southern War Song," by S. Teakle Wallis, for example, invoked the specter of Yankee assaults against helpless white Southern women and called for retribution against the "felon foe." According to the *Richmond Daily Dispatch*, the lyrics of "John Brown's Body" revealed the Yankee's true purposes. "The horse thief, murderer, and insurrectionist," the *Dispatch* intoned, referring to Brown, "was the true representative of the spirit and character of this whole invasion."[37]

Compensated Emancipation

As important as Fort Monroe, Virginia, was in the emerging narrative of wartime emancipation, no place rivaled Washington, D.C., as a beacon for fugitive slaves. Frustrated with the spotty enforcement of the Confiscation Act, Congress passed a law in March 1862 prohibiting military personnel from returning fugitive slaves to slave owners. A little more than a month later, on April 16, 1862, Lincoln signed into law Congress's bill for the abolition of slavery in the District of Columbia, freeing the city's some three thousand slaves. The bill was the culmination of a decades-long campaign by immediatists, who had long contended that slavery was a shameful blight on the capital and that Congress had clear constitutional jurisdiction to remove it. The April act also represented compromise within the Republican ranks, as abolition was coupled with compensation and colonization: loyal owners could apply to a federal commission for remuneration—roughly $300 per slave—for their lost property, and a congressional appropriation of $100,000 would cover the cost of sending away those freedpeople who wished to emigrate. Such remuneration of slaveholders had a "long lineage," as historian Eric Foner has observed: "In one form or another compensated emancipation had been implemented in the British West Indies and most of Latin America."[38]

Lincoln had mixed feelings about the D.C. abolition bill, as he preferred state-controlled, gradual emancipation. In the winter of 1861 he pitched such a program, in a test case, to the Delaware legislature (Delaware was the least enslaved border state, with slaves making up only 1 percent of the population). He proposed that the federal government would pay the slaveholders of Delaware roughly $400 for each of their slaves if the state devised a scheme whereby these slaves would be freed over a thirty-year period. Lincoln felt the logic of this plan was irresistible—and he hoped that once Delaware took the bait, the other border states would follow in short order. Here were his calculations. The cost of indemnifying border state slaveholders for their lost property was about one-third the cost of paying for a year of the war effort. If all the border states committed to gradual emancipation, Southern hopes for bringing those states into the Confederate fold would be dashed, and the Confederate war effort would crumble. As Secretary of the Treasury Salmon P. Chase put it in a December 1861 memo to the president, a scheme of compensated emancipation would expose the Confederate leadership's scheme of "extending [the] Slaveholding empire" as a fraud and "arouse, in the minds of the misled masses, irresistible desires to return to the Union, from which, in an evil hour, under coercion or delusion, they have attempted to withdraw." Slave flight was already eroding the institution in the border states, so wouldn't border state slaveholders jump at the chance to salvage some of their investment?[39]

Abraham Lincoln. Lincoln had far less military experience than his Confederate counterpart Jefferson Davis but proved far more willing to adapt his strategy and rhetoric to changing circumstances and more adept at shaping public opinion. In the early part of the war Lincoln was intent on reassuring the slaveholding border states that he was no abolitionist. (Library of Congress LC-USP6-2415-A)

To his consternation, Delaware's leadership summarily rejected Lincoln's offer, associating it with the threat of black social and political equality. Lincoln forged on undeterred and proposed a version of the plan to Congress on March 6, 1862. He reiterated his position that "gradual, and not sudden, emancipation, is better for all." He tried to sound a note of realism: "The point is not that *all* the states tolerating slavery would very soon, if at all, initiate emancipation; but that, while the offer is equally made to all, the more Northern shall, by such initiation, make it certain to the more Southern, that in no event, will the former ever join the latter, in their proposed confederacy." He stressed above all that with this plan, emancipation was "a matter of perfectly free choice" for the states.[40]

The reception of Lincoln's March message was gratifying—to a point. Congress endorsed the proposal in a resolution of its own, and the general public expressed widespread support for the president's plan. Moderate and conservative Democrats and Republicans alike saw Lincoln's state-based, gradual approach as a rebuke to the abolitionists, with their agenda of universal, immediate, federally mandated emancipation. The press praised Lincoln for reassuring whites in the slaveholding states that the federal government had no intention of imposing abolition. Although Lincoln hedged his bets on whether his message would appeal to any Confederate-state whites, Northern commentators saw compensated emancipation as a vehicle to promote Southern Unionism. The moderate Republican *New York Times* thought that Lincoln had "hit the happy mean, upon which all parties in the North and all loyalists in the South can unite," and emphasized that "loyal men at the South should look upon it as their only ark of safety in this tempest." The *Boston Daily Advertiser*, another mainstream paper favorable to the administration, thought the president's message marked "a moment when the ears of the South are fast being opened to truths to which they have long been deaf"—namely, that Lincoln would give "practical aid" for voluntary emancipation but would not force it upon "any reluctant State." Here was "tangible proof of the real attitude of our government."[41]

Many abolitionists and Radical Republicans supported Lincoln's March message on the grounds that it augured bolder measures. Horace Greeley, the brash editor of the North's most popular antislavery newspaper, the *New York Tribune*, predicted that "the 6th of March will yet be celebrated as a day which initiated the Nation's deliverance from the most stupendous wrong, curse and shame of the Nineteenth Century." The editors of the *Continental Monthly*, the Boston journal of self-styled "emancipationists" who rejected abolitionist moralism and argued for the military necessity of ending slavery, saw the president's message as "building up . . . the Union party of the South"; indeed, the journal insisted that the South's mountain counties, such as East Tennessee, were full of "loyal zeal" and ripe for "counter-revolution." For Radical Republicans, Lincoln's plan was part of an every-means-possible approach to ending slavery: as Massachusetts senator Henry Wilson put it, "I would at once abolish slavery in the District of the Columbia, repeal the black code that dishonors the National Capital, tender to the loyal slaveholding States the treasures of the Federal Government to aid them in the work of emancipation, deal justly and liberally with the loyal men of the Rebel States, but free the bondmen of rebels." The antislavery Methodist organ *Northern Independent* took a similar stance. While its editors would have preferred an "instant, peremptory decree" of emancipation by Lincoln, they were happy for him to "go for freedom in any way" and concluded, "It will be well if, with the sword and the purse both combined, we can gain deliverance from so monstrous an evil."[42]

In defiance of Northerners' optimistic predictions, border state leaders themselves remained intransigent. They saw the proposal not as a "sweetheart deal" but instead as a canny form of indirect coercion and a catalyst to antislavery extremism and even race war. Delaware senator Willard Saulsbury objected that the measure would "open the door to the agitation of abolition," while Senator Lazarus W. Powell of Kentucky called compensated emancipation "a pill of arsenic, sugar-coated." On the other end of the political spectrum, there were abolitionist holdouts, who felt, as an editorial in Garrison's *Liberator* insisted, that the president's plan was "at war with common sense": Lincoln was offering a bounty to traitors and "keeping up the old delusion of 'gradualism'" when he should instead be asserting his constitutional right to proclaim liberty. Henry McNeal Turner, a prominent Baltimore-based minister and missionary in the African Methodist Episcopal church, wrote to the church organ the *Christian Recorder* that he hoped Lincoln would be "a Moses waving a mace of independence," but instead the president's message on freedom was a dispiriting "*not yet.*"[43]

Defenders of the president's plan were undeterred by this opposition, as they had faith that his policy would eventually bear fruit. "So long as the certainty exists that compensation *may* be obtained," the *Continental Monthly* editorialized, "there will be a party who will long for it; and where there is a will there is a way." Greeley himself conceded that "years may elapse before the object boldly contemplated" in Lincoln's message would be "fully attained," but he urged his readers not to "harbor a doubt that it will ultimate in a glorious fruition."[44]

This debate over Lincoln's March message shaped the response to D.C. abolition. Moderates interpreted the congressional act as a victory for their restrained, incentive-based approach. "Looking at these principles of compensation and colonization—our abolition radicals have gained little or nothing by this bill, as an entering wedge against slavery in the States," the *New York Herald* editorialized. Lincoln, while he would have preferred border state initiative to congressional fiat, was glad that the bill remunerated slaveholders for lost property and provided for black expatriation.[45] Radical Republicans and immediatists, for their part, saw abolition in D.C. as a precedent-setting step toward the denationalization of slavery. "Kill slavery at the heart of the nation, and it will certainly die at the extremities. Down with it there, and it is the brick knocked down at the end of the row by which the whole line is prostrate," as Frederick Douglass asserted in advocating for the bill. The New York *Anglo-African*, edited by prominent free black journalist Robert Hamilton, pronounced D.C. abolition a boon to the "nation at large," for white men in the capital and in Congress could at last speak freely without "bending on their knees to Baal." The black press, historian Richard Newman has noted, "vigorously defended" each new freedom decree of the early war—Butler's contraband policy, congressional confiscation, Frémont's decree, and D.C. abolition—as a "potentially big step forward."[46]

Black communities in the North celebrated the D.C. abolition bill on their own terms, linking abolition and equality. For example, a public meeting at the AME church in Terre Haute, Indiana, "for the purpose of returning a tribute of thanks to Almighty God, for the late act of emancipation in the District of Columbia," offered up resolutions of praise for Lincoln and Congress but then closed on a defiant note. The final resolution of the meeting read:

> That we, having been born on American soil, ("The land of the free, and the home of the brave,") feel, as a natural consequence, that this is our home, and therefore we feel an attachment to this country, and will be loyal to its Government; though we have been deprived of many rights and privileges which are ours by nature.

Invoking the principles of republicanism, and of citizenship as a birthright, this resolution rejected the premises of compensation and colonization, and implicitly looked forward to a time when blacks would have chance to demonstrate their patriotism on the battlefield.[47]

The case for enlistment was made explicitly by a host of African American leaders. Hamilton's *Anglo-African*, in an article on blacks in the District,

Frederick Douglass. "To fight against slaveholders, without fighting against slavery, is but a half-hearted business": With his pen and voice, Douglass urged the Lincoln administration to embrace abolition. Douglass escaped from slavery in Maryland in 1838 and then forged a storied career as his era's preeminent champion of emancipation and civil rights. (Library of Congress LC-USZ62-15887)

asserted that "their patriotism is well informed, strong, and zealous. They understand the great question of the day—having a deep personal interest in all its practical bearings. The sacred preservation of the Union is everything to them." George Stephens, a Philadelphia cabinetmaker who signed on as the cook and personal servant of a Pennsylvania officer in the Army of the Potomac, became the most important black war correspondent of his era, sending regular reports to the *Anglo-African* from southern Maryland and eastern Virginia in 1861 and 1862. Stephens was highly critical of the Union leadership. "The Government has spurned and rejected us, and has pampered and petted its bitter foes," he lamented in March 1862. But he saw the Union army not for what it was but for what it might be: a vanguard of "progressive civilization." He emphasized that African Americans were already indispensable to the army's work. The black man was "a spy in every household of the enemy," Stephens explained. "He conveys from every point the information without which the military operations of the United States would be ineffective. When the Union soldier meets the negro in the enemy's country he knows him as a friend and asks him to strive for freedom in spite of fugitive-slave laws, proclamations and orders." Stephens offered this poignant plea: "Let the American people but say we are their brethren, and the millions of our race will flock to the national defence, and seal with blood their love for liberty, and devotion to the national cause. . . . all the scoffs, jeers and persecutions meted out to us since Crispus Attucks fell the first martyr of the revolution, shall be buried in the very deep of forgetfulness."[48]

In a Boston address, "The Black Man's Future in the Southern States," Frederick Douglass charged that the white rejection of African American volunteers was a refusal to heed the lessons of history:

Mark here our nation's degeneracy. Colored men were good enough to fight under Washington. They are not good enough to fight under McClellan. They were good enough to fight under Andrew Jackson. They are not good enough to fight under Gen. Halleck. They were good enough to help win American independence but they are not good enough to help preserve that independence against treason and rebellion.

"The field is ripe for the harvest," Douglass continued, suggesting that victory depended on the willingness of white Northerners to reap the bounty of black patriotism. Looking forward with both wariness and hope to the conflict's second year, Douglass intoned, "God forbid that when the smoke and thunder of this slaveholding war shall have rolled from the troubled face of our country it shall be said that the harvest is past, the summer is ended and we are not saved."[49]

3

Sacred Soil

VIRGINIA IN THE SUMMER OF 1862

AS MCCLELLAN'S ARMY bore down on the rebel capital in May 1862, the *Richmond Daily Dispatch* conjured images of the "pollution" of her soil by the "hireling hoards of the North." The city must be defended at all costs, it warned, for "to lose Richmond is to lose Virginia." "To die in her streets would be bliss," the paper intoned, and "would consecrate the spot anew, and wash it of every stain."[1] In Confederate eyes, McClellan's grand campaign in Virginia epitomized the dark dreams of invasion and conquest that secessionists had long imputed to the abolitionist North. But Federal soldiers who moved up the Peninsula imagined themselves to be an army of liberation: they claimed Southern soil and Southern history as American, and imagined that Union victory would both regenerate the land and perpetuate the true legacy of the Revolution and of the Virginia Founders. On the Northern home front, defenders of an expanded confiscation policy aimed to punish treason and reward loyalty in the name of military necessity, while Lincoln, whose offer of compensated emancipation was rebuffed again by the border states, laid the groundwork for emancipation by presidential fiat in the insurgent states. In the face of renewed calls for colonization, African Americans staked their own claim, based on centuries of sacrifice and labor, to American soil and citizenship.

The Peninsula Campaign

"Wherein is victory *more certain* by your plan than mine?" Lincoln wrote McClellan, with exasperation, on February 3, 1862. In the weeks that followed, against the backdrop of Union successes in the west at Forts Henry and

Donelson, tension between Lincoln and McClellan would mount. The two men were at loggerheads not only over the timing of an offensive in Virginia but also over what shape it should take. Lincoln's preference was for the Army of the Potomac to envelop Joseph Johnston's army in northern Virginia by moving overland to Centreville and by water along the Occoquan River, a tributary of the Potomac. McClellan's preference was to transport the Army of the Potomac down the Chesapeake Bay and up the Rappahannock River to the port town of Urbanna, Virginia, thereby interposing the Federal force between Johnston and the rebel capital—and forcing Johnston to come out and attack the Federals on ground of McClellan's choosing. This plan was vitiated when Johnston struck first—on March 9 he moved his army out of northern Virginia to a stronger defensive position south of the Rappahannock. Lincoln urged McClellan to take the fight to Johnston in an overland campaign, but McClellan clung to his vision of an amphibious launch for his spring campaign and identified Fort Monroe, a Federal outpost seventy miles southeast of Richmond, as the new landing point for his army; after having been transported down the bay to the fort, Federal forces would then fight their way up the Peninsula bounded by the York and James Rivers to the rebel capital. Skeptical of McClellan's strategic plan, Lincoln approved it with hesitation. He worried that too few Federal units would be left in northern Virginia to protect Washington, D.C., from a potential strike by Confederate forces.[2]

The grand spring campaign began to materialize on March 17, as Federal transports conveyed McClellan's men from the outskirts of Washington, D.C., down the Potomac and into the Chesapeake Bay to Fort Monroe. There the army massed until it reached some 100,000 soldiers. It faced a much smaller Confederate force, consisting of 17,000 men at Yorktown under the command of Major General John B. Magruder; they were arrayed along the seven miles of earthworks that stretched across the Peninsula there. McClellan, resentful of an eleventh-hour decision by Lincoln to retain McDowell's corps for the defense of Washington, began to brood about the odds. Thanks in part to the dramatic flair of Magruder, who repeatedly paraded his troops through a clearing to make the Yankees believe they faced a sizable foe, McClellan considered himself greatly outnumbered, and to the exasperation of Lincoln, he delayed launching a frontal assault against the enemy. In early April, as the drama at Shiloh was playing out in the west, McClellan opted for siege operations on the Peninsula. But his was a siege in name only, as the Confederates could leave at will. And leave they did, in a well-executed retreat on May 3–4 that caught McClellan completely off guard. McClellan declared the evacuation and the ensuing engagement at Williamsburg to be great victories.

Having squandered almost a month at Yorktown—during which time the arrival of Confederate reinforcements shrank the Union manpower advantage
from nearly six to one to two to one—McClellan's army began to move northwest along the Peninsula toward Richmond.[3]

On the Confederate side, a parallel set of tactical debates and person-
ality conflicts were playing out. Jefferson Davis and Joseph Johnston had
readily agreed to transfer Confederate forces from Manassas to the defense
of Richmond, but Davis felt Johnston had poorly executed this withdrawal.
Davis increasingly turned for counsel to Robert E. Lee. Lee had been named
with great fanfare to command the armies in Virginia in the spring of 1861.
Having been assigned to fruitless missions in western Virginia and Georgia,
he had been summoned from this purgatory by Davis in March 1862 to serve
as the president's main military advisor; in that capacity Lee helped design
the conscription law of April 1862. While Johnston was eager for Magruder's
forces to abandon Yorktown and fall back to Richmond, Lee favored pin-
ning down the Federals on the Peninsula while Richmond's fortifications
were bolstered. Davis sided with Lee and dispatched Johnston's forces to join
with Magruder's. Arriving in Yorktown in advance of his troops on April
13, Johnston confirmed that the Confederate position could not withstand
imminent bombardment by the Federal army and navy, so he ordered the
evacuation. Johnston anticipated that as he lured the Federals away from the
Peninsula (and from their supply base and naval support) toward Richmond,
he could choose a place to wheel around on McClellan's army and administer
a devastating blow that would force it, in turn, to withdraw and abandon its
offensive.[4]

To the exasperation of Davis and Lee, Johnston failed to rally his troops.
For nearly two weeks the Union invaders encountered minimal resistance,
and by May 31 they were within five miles of the rebel capital, the city's
church spires visible in the distance. But McClellan's army was nonetheless
vulnerable, because divided: three of its corps were positioned north of the
Chickahominy River, to protect the Federal supply lines, and two corps were
south of the river. The swampy Chickahominy was more imposing than usual,
due to torrential spring rains that had flooded away some of the bridges spanning the river. Under intense pressure to act, Johnston moved to capitalize
on this vulnerability, and on May 31 he ordered his right wing to lunge at the
two isolated corps on McClellan's left, near a plantation called Seven Pines
and railroad station called Fair Oaks on Richmond's eastern outskirts. Poor
communication between Johnston and his generals muddled the execution
of this plan, as did the timely arrival of Federal reinforcements from north of

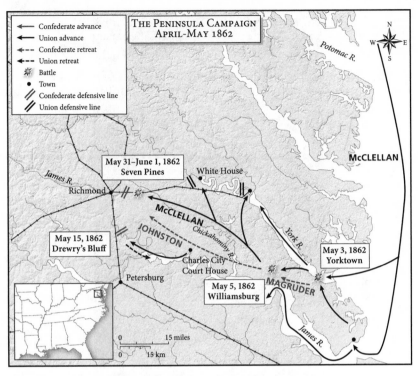

MAP 3.1

the river. A promising Confederate attack on the first day of the battle was followed by a successful Federal counterattack on the second day, resulting in a stalemate. Confederates sustained just over 6,000 casualties to the Federals' 5,000 in the battle of Fair Oaks (Seven Pines). Johnston himself was badly wounded while riding along the lines at twilight on May 31 to reconnoiter enemy positions—and would be sidelined for almost six months.[5]

Davis named Lee as Johnston's replacement on June 1; Lee christened his new command the Army of Northern Virginia. Davis granted him broader authority than Johnston had held, placing under Lee's purview armies in the Shenandoah Valley and North Carolina. McClellan for his part drew a faulty conclusion from the May 31 clash. He assumed that Johnston would not have launched an assault unless the odds of its success were favorable and thus that Johnston must possess "overwhelming numbers." McClellan, in a familiar refrain, called for and waited for more troops.[6]

Lee was determined to retake the initiative and to protect Richmond— the seat of government, symbolic heart of the Confederacy, and also an essential manufacturing and rail center—at all costs. He was acutely aware of the

Robert E. Lee. Lee's success in the Seven Days, together with Jackson's victories in the Valley, were rays of light for Confederates, ending the unrelieved slide in Confederate fortunes since February. Lee's army would become the premier symbol of Southern nationalism, and Lee was likened by Confederates to George Washington. (Library of Congress LC-B8172-0001)

North's overall superiority in manpower and resources, as well as McClellan's potentially decisive edge in engineering, artillery, and naval power. The challenge for the Confederacy was to somehow neutralize these advantages at the tactical level, by maneuver and the concentration of force against the enemy's weakest points. Certain that Richmond could not withstand a siege, Lee by mid-June devised a plan that would maneuver McClellan away from his earthworks out into the open. In Lee's view, the Federals were most vulnerable not south of the Chickahominy but north of it, where the Federal right wing, guarding McClellan's supply line to his base at White House plantation on the Pamunkey River, was exposed, lacking any protection from the terrain. Lee proposed a turning movement on the Federal right that would force McClellan to defend his communications and supply arteries.[7] Where manpower was concerned, Lee succeeded where Johnston had failed, in convincing Davis to redeploy troops from the Valley, Carolinas, and Deep South to the Richmond front; by the end of June, Lee commanded the largest army ever assembled in the Confederacy, nearly 90,000 strong. Lee moreover directed his army to improve the fieldworks around Richmond so that the city could be held with a smaller force, freeing up men to serve in Lee's flanking columns. Lee hoped additional reinforcements would soon head east from the Shenandoah Valley.[8]

The Seesaw of Deliverance in the Valley

"If this valley is lost, Virginia is lost," Stonewall Jackson wrote on the eve of his Shenandoah campaign of 1862. Rich in agricultural resources, the Valley was also a strategic prize, as it provided a route, shielded by the Blue Ridge mountains, of access to the western flanks of Washington or Richmond. Jackson's mandate was clear: with the Yankees on the Peninsula, Jackson's job was to protect the Valley while tying up the Federal armies in northern and western Virginia so that they could not reinforce McClellan. This he would do by fighting a series of battles stretching from March to June that buoyed Confederate morale and turned Jackson into the Confederacy's first folk hero. "Old 'Stonewall' is a trump and if he has half a chance he can paddle his own canoe, and whip the Yankees too," wrote Confederate private John W. Smith of the 8th South Carolina from Richmond in early June 1862. "I wish I was with him."[9]

Although the Valley campaign of 1862 would become synonymous with Confederate audacity, it did not begin promisingly. Jackson assumed command of the Valley District in November 1861 and made his headquarters in Winchester, Virginia, an important market and transportation center. In the winter of 1862, Jackson's men undertook a costly campaign to recover some of the western Virginia counties that McClellan had seized in 1861; the Confederates were so afflicted by cold, disease, and hunger that some remembered this season of war as their "Valley Forge." On March 11, with the army of Union general Nathaniel P. Banks menacing him from Harpers Ferry, Jackson evacuated Winchester, sacrificing the town to preserve his army. Under strict orders to pin down Banks and prevent him from joining forces with McClellan in the east, Jackson struck Banks at Kernstown on March 23, 1862, pitching his 3,000 men against a force three times that size. The Yankees pummeled and drove back the Confederates, but a strategic victory soon emerged from this tactical defeat: Lincoln, hoping that Federal forces could follow up and bag Jackson's army, directed Banks to stay in the Valley and McDowell to join Banks in pursuit of Jackson. McClellan was thereby deprived of reinforcements from these two Federal armies.[10]

Outnumbered, with enemy armies converging on him, Jackson moved to play his trump cards. One of them was his knowledge of the Shenandoah Valley landscape. A native of the region, Jackson was determined to use the terrain, particularly mountain passes, to his advantage. To that end he commissioned the virtuoso cartographer Jedediah Hotchkiss to prepare a detailed map of the Valley from Harpers Ferry to Lexington, "showing all the points of offence and defence in those places." The other trump cards were speed, daring, and maneuver. In the spring, with a third Yankee army, Frémont's, advancing toward the Valley from the west, Jackson went on the offensive, attacking two brigades of Frémont's force at McDowell, west of Staunton, on May 8. Using the mountains to obscure his movements, Jackson then turned on the other Federal columns, driving his army north along the Valley to attack the Federal garrison at Front Royal on May 23 and then to reclaim Winchester from Banks on May 25. Winchester yielded up the spoils of war: the fleeing Yankees left the roads lined with "knapsacks, haversacks, canteens, guns, gum clothes [and] overcoats," while abandoned wagons and captured stores disgorged massive quantities of ammunition, medicine, bacon, sugar, and salt. "Our troops are loaded with Yankee plunder," noted one Confederate artilleryman, adding that the rebels were so "rigged out in Yankee clothes" that an order had to be issued forbidding such attire, lest friends be mistaken for enemies.[11]

Jackson tracked Banks's retreating army further northward toward Harpers Ferry but abandoned the pursuit when Frémont advanced from the west and McDowell from the east in another attempt to trap Jackson; the two Federal commanders were supposed to cooperate in closing off the southern end of the Valley and the eastern mountain gaps. Jackson's troops instead raced southward, to strike Frémont's forces at Cross Keys on June 8 and a division of McDowell's army, under General James Shields, at Port Republic on June 9. With Frémont and Shields scattered and in retreat, Jackson was free to head east to join in the defense of Richmond.

The Valley Campaign soon became the stuff of legend. Jackson's nimble army of 17,000 men had bested Federal forces of nearly 60,000 men, winning five of six battles and sustaining roughly 2,750 casualties to the Federals' nearly 5,500 (more than half of whom were captured). Confederate troops had marched, relentlessly, some 650 miles up and down the Valley. Southern civilians were ecstatic at these victories. Jackson's operations "formed a series of movement and combinations," crowed the *Richmond Dispatch*, "which have not been surpassed since the days of Napoleon."[12]

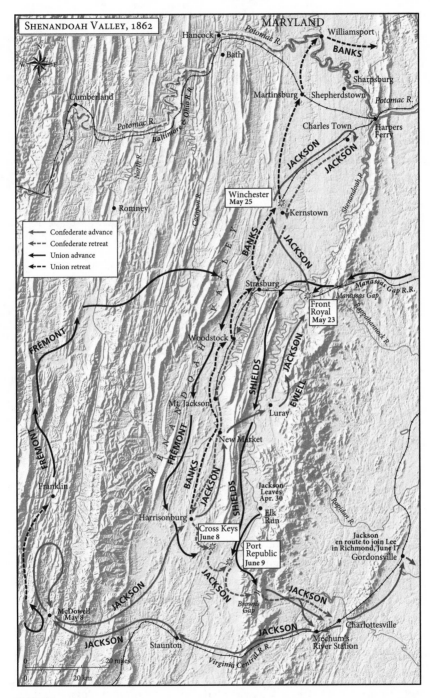

SHENANDOAH VALLEY, 1862

MARYLAND

Hancock
Bath
Cumberland
Potomac R.
North R.
Baltimore & Ohio R.R.
Romney
Cacapon R.

Confederate advance
Confederate retreat
Union advance
Union retreat

Williamsport
BANKS
Sharpsburg
Martinsburg Shepherdstown
Potomac R.
Charles Town
Harpers Ferry
JACKSON
JACKSON
Shenandoah R.

Winchester
May 25
Kernstown

BANKS
JACKSON

Strasburg
Manassas Gap R.R.
Manassas Gap
Rappahannock R.
Front Royal
May 23

FRÉMONT
Woodstock
SHIELDS
JACKSON
EWELL

Mt. Jackson
Luray
FRÉMONT
FRÉMONT
New Market
BANKS
JACKSON
SHIELDS

Franklin
Jackson Leaves Apr. 30
Harrisonburg
Cross Keys
June 8
Elk Run
Port Republic
June 9

Rapidan R.
Jackson en route to join Lee in Richmond, June 17
Gordonsville

JACKSON
Browns Gap
JACKSON

McDowell
May 8
Charlottesville
JACKSON
Staunton
JACKSON
Méchum's River Station
Virginia Central R.R.

0   20 miles
0   20 km

MAP 3.2

Thomas "Stonewall" Jackson. Jackson "was a perpetual surprise to friend and foe alike," one Confederate memoirist observed after the war, capturing Jackson's enigmatic persona. Jackson was a hypochondriac who was seemingly insensible to bodily fear during battle, a severe disciplinarian who inspired the ardent devotion of his men, and a devout Christian who favored a relentless style of warfare. (Library of Congress LC-DIG-cwpb-07475)

Winchester, which was briefly occupied by Union troops during the spring and summer (March 12–25 and June 4–September 2) only to fall back into Confederate hands, became a symbol of the seesaw of liberation. Indeed, it would change hands again and again over the course of the war, with "each successive Union occupation result[ing] in harsher measures toward civilians." Roughly 10 percent of its white inhabitants were Unionists (transplanted Northerners, and religious and political dissenters), and they paid a high price for their disloyalty: in a preemptive move, to deny the Federal army manpower, Stonewall Jackson rounded up and imprisoned scores of white male Unionists in early March, in advance of the first Federal occupation. Unionist Julia Chase's elderly father was carted off, and worries over his fate tempered her joy at the Federal troops' arrival. "Glorious News! The Union Army took possession of Winchester today and the glorious old flag is over our town, but oh, if the troops had only come a day or two sooner, then our people would have escaped the clutches of the Southern army," she wrote in her diary on March 12. The town's African Americans, enslaved and free, exulted in the Union army's arrival. "They ran back and forth calling the Union men *brothers*—they cried 'Glory!' 'Praise the Lord!' and no sleep came to their eyes that night," wrote Abigail Hopper Gibbons, a Quaker abolitionist trained by the Sanitary Commission to set up field hospitals in Virginia. Noting that the town's black residents brought food to injured soldiers at the hospitals—"Union men, and Rebels, *too*"—Gibbons commented, "They are a wide-awake people, and I think they will make their way anywhere."[13]

Some Northern soldiers imagined that their presence would have a re-demptive effect on the disloyal population. Lieutenant Colonel Wilder Dwight, a charismatic Massachusetts lawyer whose account of campaigning in the Valley decried the "reign of terror," as he put it, under which white Virginians had been living, recorded in his diary the story of a rebel soldier being treated in a Union hospital in Winchester. " 'How kind you are to us! They told us that you would kill us, and kill all the wounded,' " the Southern man marveled. "Such are some of the lies with which they keep their men up to the fighting point," Dwight archly commented. The women of the town, Dwight noted, at first only brought "delicacies for *their* wounded" to the hos-pital. But after they saw Northerners' "equal kindness," they "began to get a little humanity, and to work for all."[14]

Other Federals who occupied the town were struck instead by the intran-sigence of its Confederate residents. "We had already seen Rebel women, but in all our travels we never saw any so bitter as those of Winchester," wrote John M. Gould of Maine. "They were untiring in their efforts to show us how they hated us. If we sat upon their doorsteps a moment, they would send out their servants to wash up the spot that was supposed to be made filthy by our pres-ence." The diary of Confederate Cornelia Peake McDonald dramatizes the gap between the image Union soldiers sought to project and the impression they made. McDonald recorded a range of behavior on the part of occupying troops—she found some of the soldiers she encountered to be brusque and "vindictive" in their attitudes and others to be "courteous" and respectful. But individual instances of kind behavior did nothing to diminish McDonald's rage at the Yankees or her perception of them as ruthless conquerors. Their "great display of their finery" and the "grandeur of their equipments," the pa-triotic airs their bands pumped out as their army was "marshalled in all its pomp for parade or review," the "boastful accounts" of their newspapers—all of these compounded McDonald's sense of shame and bitter humiliation at her army's reverses. When Jackson's army reclaimed the town in late March she and her fellow Confederates united in exultation, "embracing the precious privilege of saying what they chose, singing or shouting what they chose." The Confederate press for its part attributed to the citizens of Winchester "a calm and dignified fidelity and firmness which their adversaries must have secretly respected." Winchester had resisted Yankee "pollution" and proven itself worthy of Jackson, its glorious liberator. The question remained: would Richmond face a similar test?[15]

Seven Days

With Jackson on his way to the eastern front, Lee and McClellan clashed on June 25 at Oak Grove, in the first of the contests that came to be known as the Seven Days' Battles. McClellan tried to move his siege artillery closer to Richmond's defenses but the Confederates repulsed the effort, inflicting heavy casualties on the Federals. Lee followed up this tactical victory by beginning his own offensive, mounting an attack against Federal troops at Mechanicsville, a crossroads village six miles north of Richmond. Richmond civilians anticipated a showdown, and on the morning of June 26, wrote government clerk John Jones, "hundreds of men, women, and children were attracted to the heights around the city to behold the spectacle."[16]

Richmond's small community of white Unionists experienced an altogether different sort of anticipation, imagining that their liberation from Confederate rule was imminent. The most important of those Unionists was Elizabeth Van Lew, who headed a remarkable espionage network, the "Richmond Underground," in the Confederate capital. Van Lew represented the urban Unionism that existed in pockets among former Whigs in the Upper South who favored economic modernization and sectional compromise. In the first year of the war, Van Lew rallied a circle of fellow Unionists to the assistance of Federal soldiers in Confederate prisons, helping them to survive and to escape.[17]

Confederate authorities were aware of the existence of a Unionist subculture in the rebel capital, and they targeted it with policies such as the Alien Enemies Act, which deported men who would not swear allegiance to the Confederacy; the Sequestration Act, which authorized the seizure of property belonging to Unionists; and the imposition of martial law on Richmond. In the spring of 1862, Confederates arrested a venerable Unionist politician and Van Lew family friend, John Minor Botts, and caught and hung a Union spy, Timothy Webster, who had been deployed in Richmond by the Union's primitive secret service operation. Confederates also targeted Unionism with propaganda, urging the Southern populace not to "relapse into its old associations." "There is scarcely a family in our land which has not been clothed in mourning by these Restorationists of the Union," the *Richmond Dispatch* intoned in a May 1862 editorial entitled "Unionism in the South." "Can they restore the dead that cover our plains and hillsides? Can their incantations to the Union stir those brave hearts that the grass is growing over? Can their shout of Union bring back the union of the wife with her dead husband, of the mother with her noble son, or the sister with her cherished brother?"[18]

Van Lew found all of this chilling, but she kept up her work and managed to elude the Confederate authorities. Publicly playing the Southern lady, Van Lew justified her ministrations to Union soldiers as acts of charity to the "unworthy," in keeping with the female imperative to be "benevolent." Van Lew's hopes rose and fell with the fortunes of McClellan's army. Elizabeth and her mother, Eliza, fantasized that McClellan would literally fight his

Van Lew Mansion. Elizabeth Van Lew yearned for the Union army to liberate Unionists, black and white, in her native Richmond. Her mansion was the nerve center of an underground network that aided Federal prisoners of war and conveyed military intelligence to the Union high command. (Library of Congress LC-D4-33908)

way to their doorstep. Elizabeth wrote in her wartime journal: "Mother had a charming chamber, with new matting and pretty curtains, all prepared for Genl. McClellan, and for a long time we called [it] Genl. McClellan's room." In the last weeks of June 1862, they had the room prepared "even to the water drawn for the bath."[19]

They would wait in vain. Lee, entrusting the Richmond defenses south of the Chickahominy to a smaller force under General Magruder, attempted on June 26 to bring the bulk of his army down on Brigadier General Fitz John Porter's isolated Fifth Corps, entrenched behind Beaver Dam Creek, north of the river. But this attack went awry, due to a lack of coordination by Generals A. P. Hill and Stonewall Jackson, the latter of whom had arrived, uncharacteristically, late to the scene; the Confederates sustained much higher casualties than the Union. But now McClellan's psychology became a crucial factor. Stubbornly convinced that Lee commanded 200,000 Confederates to his 100,000 Union troops, and unaware of how undermanned Magruder's position was, McClellan decided to abandon his well-laid plan of besieging Richmond and instead to move south, across the Chickahominy, bypassing the rebel capital in a strategic withdrawal. His goal was to establish a new base of operations at Harrison's Landing on the James River, some twenty miles southeast of Richmond, where his army could regain the protection of the navy's gunboats. (Union gunboats could steam as far upriver as Drewry's Bluff, seven miles from Richmond; there Confederate fortifications and sunken vessels posed insurmountable obstacles.) McClellan wrote bitterly to the War Department, "Had I twenty thousand, or even ten thousand fresh troops to use tomorrow, I could take Richmond; but I have not a man in reserve, and shall be glad to cover my retreat and save the material and personnel of the army."[20]

The prospect of transferring the Union forces—nearly 100,000 men, hundreds of field guns, and nearly 4,000 ambulances and wagons—was logistically daunting. It would be a fighting retreat. As soon as Porter established a new defensive line closer to the military bridges crossing the Chickahominy, Lee hit him again, at Gaines' Mill on June 27. Lee's savvy maneuvering had secured him numerical superiority at the tactical level: Porter had 35,000 men to the Confederates' 50,000. In the blistering summer heat, the Confederates launched a spirited series of assaults, with Brigadier General John Bell Hood's infantry finally breaking the Union lines and sending Porter reeling toward the river. The fighting was furious. "The trees were lopped and branches and leaves fell as thick as snowflakes," wrote Lieutenant Colonel Hugh S. Campbell of the 83rd Pennsylvania, "whilst the balls flew like a hail-storm, the solid shot, grape, canister, and shrapnel unintermittingly [*sic*] scattering destruction in all directions."[21]

The largest of the Seven Days' Battles, Gaines' Mill was Lee's first great strategic victory, and one for which the Confederates paid dearly, as their roughly 8,700 casualties exceeded the Union's 6,800. For the next four days Lee's swooping columns tried to pound McClellan's army as it lumbered across the Peninsula toward the James, striking its rear guard at Savage's Station on June 29 and at Glendale (White Oak Swamp) on the thirtieth. Images of the desperate combat were seared into men's memories. In 1884, future Supreme

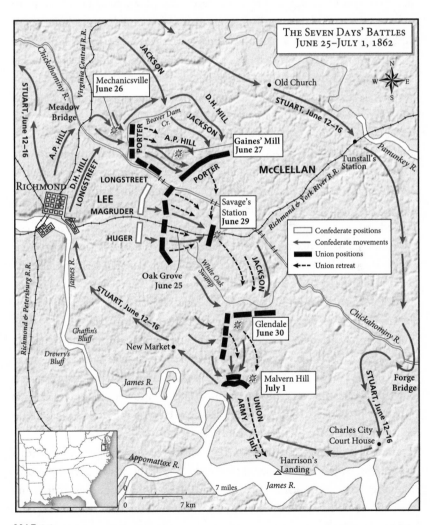

MAP 3.3

Court justice Oliver Wendell Holmes gave a Memorial Day speech in which
he recalled the last time he saw his cousin James Jackson Lowell. Both had
been idealistic young officers in 1862. "I looked down the line at Glendale.
The officers were at the head of their companies. The advance was beginning.
We caught each other's eye and saluted," Holmes remembered with pride.
"When next I looked he was gone." Lowell had been gut-shot. He lingered
for a week and then died, at the age of twenty-five.[22]

Lee's attacks further unnerved McClellan, but they failed to ensnare and
destroy the Union army, in part because Lee's army continued to be plagued
by miscommunication. The Federals were slipping away. The Seven Days'
battles concluded on July 1 with Lee's frontal assault on a strong Union position at Malvern Hill, just seven miles from the haven of Harrison's Landing;
the Federals had drawn up a new defensive line there, massing infantry and
artillery on the high ground and daring Lee to attack. Knowing this was his
last chance to cripple McClellan's army before it reached the James, Lee threw
his army at this imposing target, in wave after futile wave. By day's end, the
Confederates had suffered roughly 5,600 casualties to the Union's 2,100.
Under cover of night, McClellan's army at last reached its destination on the
James, where it would linger in defeat; in August, Lincoln would summon
it back to the North. Lee emerged a hero—the savior of Richmond. The
Richmond Daily Dispatch described his campaign as "perfect in all its parts"
and "in the highest degree ingenious." Lee's operations, the paper insisted,
showed the "unanimity" of the Southern people, as none had betrayed Lee's
movements and maneuvers to the enemy. "Where is the Union party that
were to show themselves as soon as the enemy made his appearance in force?"
the *Dispatch* asked pointedly.[23]

McClellan, although he had won tactical victories (measured in casualties inflicted) in all but one of the Seven Days' Battles and extracted his army
from a trap, was deemed a failure. McClellan's critics can point to his many
errors in the Peninsula campaign: his decision to besiege Yorktown rather
than assaulting it; his failure to attack the Richmond defenses south of the
Chickahominy when he enjoyed a two-to-one manpower advantage; and his
embarrassing absence from the front during the battle of Glendale, which he
spent safely ensconced on a navy gunboat.[24]

The week of fighting left behind a transformed landscape and frightful
carnage. Forests had been scarred by gunfire and artillery barrages; weapons,
knapsacks, and other possessions were scattered along lines of retreat; shattered human bodies and animal carcasses were strewn across battlefields.[25] The
Confederacy sustained approximately 20,600 casualties to the Union's 15,800.
Destruction of such magnitude had no precedent in American history. Sara

Pryor, a general's wife who reluctantly went to work tending the wounded in Richmond, captured the defiant yet somber mood of Confederates in her reminiscences. "Each of the battles of those seven days brought a harvest of wounded to our hospital," she wrote. "I used to veil myself closely as I walked to and from my hotel, that I might shut out the dreadful sights in the street— the squads of prisoners, and, worst of all, the open wagons in which the dead were piled. Once I did see one of those dreadful wagons! In it a stiff arm was raised, and shook as it was driven down the street, as though the dead owner appealed to Heaven for vengeance."[26]

"A Conservative Course"

McClellan's actions on the Peninsula reflected his abiding priorities, which were to minimize risk and casualties, and thereby "avoid setbacks that might inflame passions in the North"—especially the passions of abolitionists.[27] These priorities were expressed succinctly in a May 21, 1862, letter his trusted advisor Brigadier General Fitz John Porter sent from the Virginia front to Manton Marble, editor of the Democratic *New York World*. The Union would fight "in a manner which will develop Union feeling and cause Virginia to re-join us," Porter pledged. "The army goes as a disciplined body, not an armed mob, compelled to respect the private rights and to win the respect of the people." In Porter's mind a "conservative course" would "cause our enemies in the rear (the abolitionists) to be looked upon with contempt." "How they are detested here," he added, with a note of approval.[28]

This remained McClellan's official position at the end of the failed campaign. On July 8, when Lincoln visited Harrison's Landing to assess the situation, McClellan handed him a letter he had drafted in mid-June, calling on the president to commit his administration to conciliation. The war, McClellan intoned, "should be conducted upon the highest principles known to Christian Civilization." He continued,

> It should not be a War looking to the subjugation of the people of any state, in any event. It should not be, at all, a War upon population; but against armed forces and political organization. . . . In prosecuting the War, all private property and unarmed persons should be strictly protected; subject only to the necessities of military operations. All private property taken for military use should be paid or receipted for; pillage and waste should be treated as high crimes; all unnecessary trespass sternly prohibited; and offensive demeanor by the military towards citizens promptly rebuked.

McClellan's letter accepted the confiscation of "contraband" slaves provided that loyal masters were to be compensated. Such a "conservative"
policy, he predicted, would "deeply impress the rebel masses"—while
a "radical" antislavery policy would "rapidly disintegrate our present
Armies."[29]

In their letters and diaries, Union soldiers and relief workers on the
Peninsula offered their own interpretations of the dictates of civilized warfare. Some echoed the views of McClellan and Porter. Sergeant Major Elisha
Hunt Rhodes, a pious Rhode Islander, wrote from near Mechanicsville on
June 8 of how he posted a guard at the house of a frightened woman who lived
with her young children (her eldest son was in the rebel army) in a shanty
near the Federal camp. "This is a sample of what we are doing in Virginia,"
he observed earnestly. "The men are fighting against their country, and we
are guarding their families and even feeding them. But humanity demands
this much." Katharine Prescott Wormeley, one of the leaders of the Sanitary
Commission, expressed similar sentiments in letters home. She worked
as a superintendent of nurses on hospital transports that plied the James
and Pamunkey Rivers during the campaign, setting up shore hospitals and
taking aboard severely wounded men for conveyance to the North. Believing
Northern and Southern extremists shared the blame for bringing on the war,
Wormeley disapproved of slavery but also of abolitionism. She wrote home to
her mother and sister on June 20, 1862, "How deluded the body of Southern
troops and people have been by their leaders!" Based on conversations she
had with Confederate prisoners and wounded men, she reported that "*surprise* [was] their chief emotion" at "receiving kindness" from Yankees they had
been taught to regard as fanatical fiends. One prisoner said to her, "I could
change the feelings of half my country if I told them what I know now" about
the Yankees' decency.[30]

For Union soldiers, historic sites such as Williamsburg and Yorktown
made Virginia "sacred soil" and conjured images of George Washington,
Patrick Henry, and other heroes of the Revolution. At Yorktown, where
George Washington brought the British to heel in the Revolution's last
major battle, Lieutenant Colonel Charles P. Chandler of Maine marveled
"that we of this generation must attack the same place that Washington
did. . . . Heaven grant that we may gain a similar result!" Some, Chandler
included, perceived in the Virginia landscape the moral imperative to lift
the pall of slavery. As they traversed coastal Virginia, Union soldiers were
incredulous to find that the oldest settled part of the country was so underdeveloped. "This country is a wonder to all Yankees," Charles H. Brewster of

the 10th Massachusetts wrote on April 23, 1862, at Warwick Court House on the northern bank of the James. "There is no reason why this should not be as thickly settled and thriving as any country on the face of the globe. The soil is good the climate too, and everything grows here that we could wish, and it would be a magnificent region, but for the curse of slavery which has blighted it." "No one can float down the Pamunkey river, with his eyes open, and not see that this land is sleeping the sleep of torpor and moral death," wrote Lincoln's secretary John Hay near Yorktown on June 20, in his capacity as an anonymous correspondent to the *Missouri Republican*. "A pall of densest indolence and sloth rests palpably on the face of this unparalleled richness of nature." Hay diagnosed slavery as the cause of this torpor and Yankee industry as the cure that would bring the "patient . . . back to life." "The faded glories of the Old Dominion will receive fresh coloring" after the war, when "the tide of activity and honorable effort sets again to her shores, and the restored flag of the beneficent nationality again blesses her cities and protects her fields."[31]

Union soldiers and Northern civilians in the Shenandoah Valley recorded similar impressions of the Virginia landscape and its inhabitants. Commenting in April 1862 on the "beauty of the scenery and fertility of the soil" in the New Market vicinity of the Valley, James Clarke of the 5th Ohio lamented, "A farm in it would be a mine of wealth to any one who would

Patriotic Covers. Envelopes featuring patriotic messages circulated widely among soldiers and civilians. Images of the Founding Fathers, George Washington especially, were common motifs on Union envelopes such as this. (Library of Congress LC-DIG-ppmsca-34703)

give it a fair chance it seems to me that these Virginians have been trying their best to wear out the soil and cant do it. They are too ignorant to know how to use a farm and too lazy to do it if they did." The region's towns, he observed, "seem to have finished their growth about a half century or so ago . . . they now present a very dilapidated appearance, as Virginians do not think of such a matter as repairing anything." In Clarke's view the "Poor white trash" of the Valley had been "pressed into the service" by the elite, leaving behind women, children and elderly inhabitants who found that the "Yankees improve upon acquaintance." The renowned author Nathaniel Hawthorne, an iconoclastic New England Democrat who disdained abolitionism and clung to the fantasy that slavery might gradually fade away, toured Union-occupied Virginia in the spring of 1862 and published an account of his travels in *The Atlantic Monthly* that summer. Hawthorne described the landscape as squalid, decayed, and "unthrifty," spoiled both by sloth and by war. The rebel prisoners he met at Harpers Ferry, Virginia, Hawthorne regarded as "simple, bumpkin-like fellows" who lacked "the remotest comprehension of what they had been fighting for." He ventured that "the present war is so well justified by no other consideration as by the probability that it will free this class of Southern whites from the thralldom in which they scarcely begin to be responsible beings." While Hawthorne was skeptical that the Deep South could be reconciled to the Union, he deemed Virginia, along with Maryland, Kentucky, and Missouri, as "fully capable of being made free-soil" if secessionism was defeated.[32]

Perhaps no one mused so extensively on the unmet potential of Virginia as Army of the Potomac surgeon Alfred Lewis Castleman of Wisconsin. The moment he first set foot in the state with his regiment, he began a running commentary in his diary (which was published in 1863) on the condition of its "sacred soil." In his analysis, although secessionist politicians had "misled" the Southern people into believing that Yankees sought to seize and destroy their homes and property, it was those slaveholding politicians themselves who were responsible for the degradation and destruction of the once-great Old Dominion. In northern Virginia in the fall of 1861, he observed the havoc the Federal and Confederate armies had already wreaked on the landscape there, and he cast it as punishment for Virginia's "officious subservience" to South Carolina secessionism; Virginia could have "assumed the position of umpire to the belligerents" but had failed to, and now paid the price. When his regiment was deployed to the Peninsula, he deemed the region an ideal subject for the "moral as for the physical historian": it presented view after view "of the blasting influence of the institution of Slavery." "Though we are almost in sight of the historical cities of Yorktown and Jamestown, the country is not half so far advanced in improvements and culture as the new State of Wisconsin, or even the still-newer and wilder Minnesota!" he marveled in April 1862. "We may travel for miles through an almost unbroken forest." "What a commercial world this State of Virginia should be," he wrote in August as his regiment prepared to leave the Peninsula. "Alas, poor Virginia!"[33]

These feelings of pity strengthened Northern soldiers' resolve to stamp out the rebellion. "I cherish no malice or hatred for the rebels," Pennsylvania infantryman Hugh Frasier wrote his sister from Irwin McDowell's command in Falmouth, Virginia. "No doubt many of them are deceived but if they have not the caution to be sure they are on the right side they must take the consequences."[34]

Portents of Hard War

The behavior of both armies had already confounded McClellan's vision of a limited war. The Peninsula campaign furnished soldiers on both sides with ample evidence for claims of enemy ruthlessness. Northern soldiers, McClellan included, reviled as uncivilized the Confederate use of land mines (called "torpedoes") at Yorktown and on the retreat to Williamsburg. Confederates, for their part, decried the Yankee use of sharpshooters during the Yorktown siege. The main impact of both tactics was psychological. Under the ceaseless threat of Yankee marksmen, Confederate artilleryman Robert Stiles remembered, "one of our detachments broke down utterly from nervous tension." When Stiles's unit went to relieve them in the trenches, he found "some of these poor lads were sobbing in their broken sleep, like a crying child just before it sinks to rest."[35]

As they chronicled the expanding scope of the war, men on both sides noted how frequently foraging devolved into plunder. For example, on the march to Glendale, Union private Alfred Bellard of the 5th New Jersey fell out of the ranks to visit a nearby house to procure some milk. But others had beaten him to the punch:

> When I got to the place, I found that the regulars had been there before and had taken everything that was worth taking and more too. The spring house where the southerners keep their milk, cheese, hams, etc. was completely gutted, and even the woman's clothes, with the exception of what she had on her back, had been made into gun rags and appropriated by the troops, her trunks and wardrobe having been turned inside out to furnish them.

The Union commanding general on the scene got wind of this behavior and sought to remedy the situation by placing a guard at the house and banishing the foragers. But it was too late. Bellard's fellow soldiers were unrepentant, for in their view this Southern woman and her family deserved what they got: "it was generally reported that her husband was a guirella [*sic*] and had fired at our pickets the night before," Bellard noted. "Hence the destruction."[36]

Confederates, too, grappled with temptations of looting, and their principal targets were the copious supplies of ammunition, medicine, clothes, foods, and other necessities to be found in captured Union army camps and along lines of retreat and pursuit. After the battle of Seven Pines, Major General James Longstreet upbraided his men for dereliction of duty in the midst of battle, "so far forgetting themselves as to desert their ranks for plunder." But straggling and looting proved difficult to contain, as such behavior was driven not only by the impulses of greed and vengeance but also by that of survival.[37]

Firsthand accounts of the campaigning on the Peninsula reveal how nature itself challenged McClellan's vision of a limited war, as soldiers battled with hunger, exposure, and disease. The marshy terrain of the Peninsula was replete with environmental dangers: malaria-carrying mosquitoes, typhus-carrying lice, dysentery-inducing fetid water. Camp conditions offered little relief. Disease swept through camps in "crowd epidemics" of measles, mumps, and smallpox that fell hardest on "unseasoned" soldiers, particularly rural men who lacked immunities. They were followed by camp scourges such as scurvy and diarrhea. Hospitals, too, offered little relief, as they privileged the wounded over the sick, and treated diseases with medicines that were themselves toxic. During peak periods of illness on the Peninsula, 30 percent of soldiers were unfit for duty; over the course of the entire war, disease would account for two-thirds of all soldier mortality. While McClellan had imagined that his cautious strategy would save lives, the irony is that the protracted struggle on the insalubrious Peninsula took a terrible toll on both armies.[38]

Soldiers were, however, not passive in the face of these environmental threats. As historian Kathryn S. Meier has shown, they devised self-care regimens to maintain body and soul—rigging up crude tents and shelters for protection from the elements; using fire and smoke to kill predatory insects; supplementing their woeful army rations by foraging, trading for, and buying milk, fruits, and vegetables; boiling their fetid water into coffee to render it potable; stealing time for baths and for washing their uniforms. Meier notes that many of the behaviors that Union and Confederate authorities derided as straggling were efforts by soldiers—through short absences in the interest of self-care—to preserve their strength and stay in the ranks.[39]

The suffering of the armies on the Peninsula reverberated in soldier and civilian commentary over whether the time had come for the North to embrace hard war. The controversy over the Union occupation of White House, the plantation home of Lee's son, William H. F. "Rooney" Lee, is a case in point. The estate was located on the Pamunkey River near the Union's supply depot at White House Landing, and it had some historical significance, as George Washington had courted Martha Custis there. When Mary Lee, Robert E. Lee's wife, vacated the house in advance of the Federal soldiers' arrival there in the spring of 1862, she had left a note on the door decreeing that "Northern soldiers who profess to reverence Washington" should "forbear to desecrate" the house. McClellan obliged her, posting soldiers there to safeguard the home. He refused requests to use the White House as a hospital to treat the teeming mass of sick and wounded men who had been sent there from the front.[40]

In the eyes of Union men such as John Hay and Alfred Castleman, the White House was the perfect symbol of the pretenses and faded glories of Virginia; Hay commented that the property was "worn-out" and "generally, like Virginia, going to decay." When Radical Republicans heard press reports that wounded, suffering Union men were left outside, writhing on the swampy soil and exposed to the elements, rather than being admitted to the house, they were livid. Secretary of War Stanton and a host of Republican congressmen upbraided McClellan for his "cowardly policy of conciliation" toward the enemy. The way to honor Washington's memory, they insisted, was to use his ancestral home to serve Union soldiers. When Lincoln got wind of the controversy, he reversed McClellan's order. But the issue was soon moot, as McClellan decided on June 28 to abandon the White House as part of his retreat to the James. He left orders to put to the torch the public property the Union army left behind but not the private dwelling. Those orders were disregarded, and the White House was burned to the ground.[41]

For Confederates, the fate of the Lees' house was just more proof that the Yankees waged a ruthless war of subjugation. Confederate cavalry commander J. E. B. "Jeb" Stuart saw the charred remains of the White House the day after its destruction. "An opportunity was here offered for observing the deceitfulness of the enemy's pretended reverence for everything associated with the name of Washington," he remarked bitterly. The remains told a tale of "desolation and vandalism."[42]

Stuart gave voice to a central theme in Confederate political culture. Southern nationalists had long maintained that they were the true heirs and protectors of the Revolutionary legacy. They condemned abolitionism as a slander on the reputations of the slaveholding Founding Fathers and as a betrayal of the constitutional compromises that had safeguarded slavery. During the war, Confederates took inspiration from the colonists' underdog victory against the mighty British Empire, casting Lincoln in the role of the tyrannical King George III, the Yankee army as the ruthless and mercenary "Hessians," and Southern Unionists as treasonous "Tories." In the Confederate version of American history, the Northern patriots of the Revolutionary era were cowards who had never carried their weight, and the Northern founders were either false idols unworthy of emulation or fallen idols who had been betrayed by their faithless descendants. The great principle of the Revolution was not human equality or reverence for the Union but instead the idea that "humans no longer needed to blindly trust in their government," as historian Paul Quigley has explained. George Washington, whose image was featured on the Confederate national seal and on patriotic envelopes, stamps, currency, and other forms of iconography, was in Confederate culture "the Great Southerner" and belonged solely to the South. Confederates insisted that Washington had led a revolution "for the freedom of the white, and the slavery of the black race"—and that Yankees, waging a ruthless abolition war, had forfeited the right to evoke Washington's memory.[43]

Military Necessity and Black Labor

No issue loomed so large in debates over hard war on the Peninsula as that of black labor. Evidence that both sides derived military advantage from such labor was everywhere to be seen during the Peninsula campaign—and each side argued that the other, in mobilizing blacks, defied the rules of civilized warfare. Union men condemned the Confederate practice of forcing enslaved and free blacks to work for the Southern army. Black laborers cleared roads, built fortifications, and worked as teamsters and camp servants for their rebel masters. General Magruder had rounded up hundreds of black laborers to build the Confederate defenses at Yorktown, cajoling slave owners to hand over their slaves and initiating what would become the widespread practice of slave impressment; after focusing his requisitions on southeastern Virginia, Magruder reached into central Virginia and eastern North Carolina. Slave owners complained bitterly about such seizure of their property, as there was as yet no official state sanction for it (the state of Virginia did not pass a law authorizing slave impressments until October 1862), and the systems for compensating masters for the services of their slaves proved haphazard. Meanwhile, the city of Richmond commandeered enslaved and free blacks to work on the entrenchments there. Virginia governor John Letcher pithily summed up the case for impressments: "The people must yield their Negroes or submit to the Yankees."[44]

Increasingly, Union soldiers recognized how such policies translated into Confederate manpower. By using "negro servants from different plantations to work upon the fortifications," a Massachusetts private serving at Yorktown noted ruefully, the Confederates left "their soldiers fresh for other military duties." Most galling to Union soldiers was evidence that Confederates compelled some slaves to serve as pickets or sharpshooters or to man artillery batteries. One Pennsylvania soldier in the Yorktown trenches wrote his mother that he had seen a Confederate officer force a black laborer at pistol point to man a gun, and that the disturbing scene ended abruptly when a Union sharpshooter killed both the officer and the laborer. While instances of blacks in combat roles were rare, they loomed large symbolically, as proof of rebel cowardice and barbarity.[45]

Confederates, for their part, folded the issue of blacks' military labor into the case that the Yankees were not fighting fair. Slaves flocked to Union lines during the Yorktown siege, the move up the Peninsula, and the fighting around Richmond, offering their services to the Union war effort. Confederate soldiers and civilians chose to interpret these acts of slave resistance as evidence of Yankee duplicity, charging that the Union army stole and enticed slaves away—and that radical Northerners sought to incite slave rebellion. The fact that McClellan, a Democrat who professed to favor conciliation, was leading the Yankees was cold comfort to Confederates. In their eyes Radical Republicans directed the Northern war machine. Thus on June 17, 1862, as Longstreet rallied his troops to defend Richmond, he emphasized Frémont's August 1861 proclamation of emancipation in Missouri (which Lincoln had voided) as representative of Northern war aims. "Already has the hatred of one of their great leaders attempted to make the negro your equal by declaring his freedom," he warned. "Servile insurrection" was the Yankees' aim; driven by "lust" and "avarice," they would slake their thirst on "the blood of babes" and "carnage of innocent women." Longstreet concluded: "Let such thoughts nerve you to the most dreadful shock of battle."[46]

Masters tried to preempt and deter flight by moving enslaved people into the interior, or convincing them that Yankees were profit-hungry and heartless demons who would sell them into a more exacting slavery in the Caribbean. Thomas Henry Carter, an artillery captain in Johnston's army and master of more than a hundred slaves on the family's plantation, Pampatike, wrote his wife in March 1862 that the remedy for slave flight was to give slaves over to the Confederate army, as menial labor. He chastised his fellow slave owners for "procrastinate[ing] until too late" and thereby letting "negroes get off in whole families." In the same breath, Carter reassured his wife, "Ours in Pampatike are in no danger." A month later, ensconced at Yorktown, Carter realized that he himself had procrastinated too long. He wrote his wife, "I do not know what to advise in regard to the servants at Pampatike. I believe half or three fourths of them will leave when the Yankees approach in foraging & marauding parties."[47]

Confederate efforts at deterrence fell short, and fugitives kept pouring into Union lines. At each phase of the Peninsula campaign, runaway slaves represented not only labor power—bolstering Union defenses, unloading transports, piloting riverboats, keeping supply lines open—but also valuable information on the state of the rebel fortifications and movement of rebel armies. Black informants brought the Federals intelligence about the progress of the *Merrimack*, Johnston's falling back from Manassas to the Rappahannock, Magruder's evacuation of Yorktown, and dozens of other key military developments. Service to the Union army was demanding and risky—behind the lines, many Union soldiers were callous toward black refugees and some were wantonly cruel and abusive. But slaves nonetheless took the risk, understanding that the Union army brought deliverance from the certain punishments and tortures of the slavery regime. Positive interactions between slaves and Union soldiers multiplied over the course of the Peninsula campaign, as Northern men came to confront the realities of slavery and to appreciate the courage of the fugitives. Thus the flow of runaways increased over time. Ironically, although he disapproved of Congress's confiscation policy, McClellan largely complied with it and thus "oversaw the emancipation of more slaves than any other Union commander in the first year of fighting," explains historian James Oakes. New England chaplain Alonzo Quint deftly captured the "differences of opinion in the army as to the slavery question" as of July 1862. "Some want emancipation proclaimed. Some, practical and effectual emancipation without proclamations. Some, to leave slavery as it was before the war. The drifting is towards emancipation, mainly to the second position."[48]

The Second Confiscation Act

Back in Washington, D.C., Radical Republicans sought to accelerate the changes that were under way. As the Peninsula campaign unfolded, they pushed for the passage of a Second Confiscation Act and broader military use of African Americans. The new confiscation measure had been introduced by Lyman Trumbull in December 1861, but Congress did not deliberate fully on it until May and June 1862, after the April passage of the D.C. Abolition Act. It was expansive in its provisions, authorizing the immediate seizure of "all the estate and property, money, stocks, credits, and effects" of Confederate military officers and civil office-holders.[49]

The Second Confiscation Act technically opened the door to a major redistribution of wealth from the disloyal to the loyal. "Though the bill provided for limited judicial review of seizures, the Union government could have freely confiscated most southern property under this legislation," political scientist Richard Bensel has explained. But in practice, it proved difficult to enforce widespread seizures, and confiscation of rebel estates, money, and other such assets remained "haphazard and tentative." Lincoln himself threatened to veto the bill if the confiscation of rebel real estate was to last beyond the lifetime of the convicted traitors (lest innocent descendants pay too high a price for their forebears' sins), and he worked with moderate Republicans to amend the bill so that such forfeiture would not last beyond an offender's "natural life." The confiscation measures were explicitly designed to offer incentives for slaveholders to return to the Union fold: the president was authorized to warn all classes of rebels that unless they renounced the Confederacy within sixty days, they, too (along with the Confederate leadership), would be liable to have their material assets confiscated. Those who saw the light and embraced the Union could retain such property. Lincoln was also authorized by the bill to grant amnesty and pardon to repentant rebels and to make provisions for the colonization of freed slaves.[50]

Lincoln proved to be unenthusiastic about confiscating rebel real estate and material assets. The much more lasting impact of the measure was on the status of "contrabands." While the first act had applied only to slaves employed by the Confederate army or navy and had left the legal status of forfeited slaves unclear, the new act's emancipation clauses authorized the seizure of slaves from all disloyal masters and declared such persons "captives of war" and "forever free." Its provisions covered not only slaves who ran to Union lines but also those deserted by their owners and those living in zones occupied by Union forces. The act also authorized the president "to employ as many persons of African descent as he may deem necessary and proper for the suppression of this rebellion, and [to] . . . organize and use them in such manner as he may judge best for the public welfare."[51]

Moderate and Radical Republicans lined up in support of the new bill and Democrats in opposition to it. The statute's supporters reiterated arguments that they had made on behalf of the First Confiscation Act—namely, that confiscation was a wartime necessity intended to punish rebels, who had forfeited their constitutional rights and protections.[52] Republicans also advanced new arguments that reflected recent events. They cited the failure of some Union commanders (Democrats especially) to comply with the laws forbidding the return of fugitive slaves to their masters as justification for sterner measures. They cited the recently published report by the congressional Joint Committee on the Conduct of the War on the "Barbarities of the Rebels at Manassas," in which Union witnesses to the battle enumerated a train of Confederate abuses: the rebels had allegedly "murdered" helpless, wounded Union prisoners of war by subjecting them to "brutal operations" by untrained doctors, and had desecrated the bodies and graves of the dead, carrying Union bones off as trophies. "Every step of this monstrous treason has been marked by violence and crime," the report insisted—and the Union must thus embrace a vigorous prosecution of the war effort. Although laced with misrepresentation and exaggeration, the report struck a raw nerve among Northerners.[53] They cited the mounting costs of the war, noting that the confiscation of all manner of Confederate property was a way to exact compensation for the Union's financial burdens. This argument was given salience by the recent imposition of heavy taxes on Northerners to fund the war effort. As the Radical Republican *Chicago Tribune* explained, it was wrong to "tax patriotism for the benefit of treason" when the government could instead, through confiscation, establish the "principle that rebels shall pay the cost of putting down rebellion." And they noted that dire Democratic predictions about the effects of the First Confiscation Act and the D.C. Abolition Act— that these measures would radically undermine Northern support for the war effort and alienate the border states—had not come to pass.[54]

Historian James Oakes has argued that the Second Confiscation Act marked the abandonment of the Republican hope that "a submerged unionist sentiment among southern whites would assert itself." Certainly Democratic and border state critics of the Second Confiscation Act (and some conservative Republicans, too) accused Republicans of abandoning white Southern Unionists: the problem with confiscation, these critics charged, was that it would catch some loyalists and would-be loyalists in its web and "punish alike innocent as well as the guilty," thereby alienating and demoralizing Southerners who were themselves victims of the Slave Power. For example, the political pamphleteer Anna Ella Carroll of Maryland, a conservative Republican, wrote that congressional confiscation would be a "flagrant violation" of natural law, as it would punish Unionists who were already being subjugated by the hostile rebel forces. Peace could only be restored, she argued, by extending to such loyalists "the shield of the Constitution."[55]

It is important to note that moderate and Radical Republicans alike insistently rebutted that charge and pledged their commitment to sustaining and promoting white Southern Unionism. As Elijah Babbitt, a Pennsylvania congressman, put it, the confiscation bill "very properly distinguishes between the leaders in this rebellion and those whom they have deceived," targeting the property of the rebel elite only and extending all others a sixty-day grace period. Ira Harris, representing New York, announced that he agreed with Democrats that "there are many in the confederate States who have been constrained even by force to join in the rebellion" and that they should not suffer the same penalties as the "willing traitor"—and that is why confiscation fittingly applied to "the leaders only." Quoting William Brownlow's memorable aphorism that the spirit of secession was the "spirit of hell," Congressman Aaron A. Sargent of California declared, "We level not our thunders against the victims of secession rage who now fill southern prisons, or are hunted through the mountains like wild beasts by their former neighbors and friends. It is against the authors of these atrocities . . . that we aim our laws of confiscation and reprisal." Southern Unionists, along with those who seemed to favor secession but were "not secessionists at heart," he predicted, would "rejoice at any effective blow we can strike at the rebellion." Republican legislation did not strike at the "unwitting dupes of designing men," William Kellogg of Illinois observed, but instead left the masses "to be wooed back to their allegiance of the government."[56]

Republicans noted that Confederates had passed their own confiscation laws, which permitted the seizure of the property of Southern Unionists, and that such laws had rendered destitute countless loyal families and filled the Confederate treasury with millions of dollars. "Now no man can give utterance to a word of loyalty in any State yet held by the conspirators, who is not at once dispossessed of all he has and driven a wanderer and an exile from his home, while if he but profess allegiance to the rebel government his property remains untouched," lamented Congressman Edward Henry Rollins of New Hampshire. The only meaningful way to sustain Southern Unionism, Republicans argued, was to punish the tormentors of the Unionists and to make the price of rebellion higher than the price of Unionism. Senator Jacob Collamer of Vermont, who played a key role in amending the confiscation policy so that Lincoln could accept it, advocated on behalf of the bill's amnesty provision and grace period by arguing that a third of the men of the Southern states had "ridden rough-shod over the majority" in the slave states and that the white Southern masses were the people "most injured" by the "incubus" of the rebellion. Confiscation could be a useful tool to Lincoln to help suppress armed rebellion—but only if he could offer "some inducement" to Southerners "to come back to their allegiance, duty and loyalty."[57]

Moreover, Republicans invoked Southern deliverance to defend the emancipation clauses in the Second Confiscation Act, noting that slaveholders were a minority of the Southern population but overwhelmingly secessionist; policies targeting slavery would thus not in any large measure victimize Unionists and potential Unionists in the Confederacy. Indeed, insisted Charles Sumner, the liberation of the slaves was more merciful and less harsh than the confiscation of material goods, as it would break the back of the slave oligarchy and bring the Union both "complete triumph" and "assured tranquility." The "poor deluded followers" of the slave oligarchy should be shown "lenity and pardon." "Left to all the privileges of citizenship in a rejuvenated land," Sumner predicted, "they will unite in judgment of those leaders who have been to them such cruel taskmasters." Samuel S. Blair, a Pennsylvania congressman, struck a similar note of hope, insisting that the emancipation clauses were in fact magnanimous, as they would "teach the world two things better than they have ever been taught before: the unity of this nation, and the unity of the human family." With "all cause of fraternal strife banished," the nation would be "fitted for a better life" and "command the respect and the honor and love of men."[58]

During the spring and summer of 1862, the Republican press churned out a steady stream of articles reaffirming the party's determination to distinguish between the rebel chieftains and the duped masses and elaborating the case that "harsh war would in the long run be beneficial for the South." "Sincerest regard to the whole South," editorialized the *Boston Daily Evening Transcript* in a typical such formulation, "demands now the unflinching prosecution of the war." Some articles prompted readers to connect the plight of Southern white loyalists to that of slaves. For example, a *New York Tribune* piece reprinted in the *Liberator* urged Northern cities to offer asylum to "fugitives from all the multiplied forms which oppression takes in the South": to white Unionist refugees who had escaped the Confederate "reign of terror," and

Charles Sumner. Viewed by abolitionists as a heroic martyr to the cause of freedom, Sumner had been brutally caned on the floor of the Senate in 1856 by Congressman Preston Brooks of South Carolina for giving an impassioned speech against slavery extension. Sumner returned to the Senate in 1859 and led the Radical Republicans during the war. (Library of Congress LC-USZ62-128709)

"fugitives of a darker complexion," who had "endured terrorism . . . for a life-time."[59]

This line of reasoning found increasing support among soldiers. Alonzo Quint, an Army of the Potomac chaplain who professed to have no "party predilections" and to "judge measures by their need for the restoration for the Union," had come to view slavery as the "greatest obstacle to the perpetuity of our government." The rebels wielded threats and imposed punishments on Southern Unionists to suppress their loyalty; it was time, he reckoned, to make slaveholders pay more dearly, through confiscation, for their disloyalty. It would pain the white Southern elite to do without their slaves, but that was the "penalty of transgression, the price of reform," Quint observed in the summer of 1862. He added, in a medical metaphor: "When our surgeon sets a broken leg, there is pain in the operation; there is subsequent inflammation in the very process of healing; there is, for a time, helplessness; but then there comes health. . . . Society here had both legs broken; better set them."⁶⁰

Ultimately, McClellan's reverses on the Peninsula, more than any speech or editorial, vindicated the necessity of the Second Confiscation Act. The bill passed on July 17, 1862, with Lincoln's approval and widespread public support in the North. The Seven Days' Battles lent credence to the image of the Confederacy, under the sway of "military despotism," as a resilient and determined foe. Now at last the North would "strike at the vitals of the rebellion." "With Honest Abe to execute the law," the *Chicago Tribune* predicted, "the people can rest in the belief that Slavery is in process of ultimate extinction."⁶¹

Lincoln's Road to Emancipation

In the spring of 1862, Lincoln pressed on with his dogged campaign to win the trust of border state leaders. That campaign was thrown off course when General David Hunter, commander of the Department of the South, proclaimed martial law in South Carolina, Georgia, and Florida on May 9, 1862—and declared free all slaves belonging to rebels in his jurisdiction. Hunter was motivated to take this unauthorized action, as Frémont had been with his August 1861 decree, by abolitionist principles. Border state politicians and editors were apoplectic over Hunter's edict, seeing it as "an outrage" upon "humanity and the constitution . . . [and] the dictates of sense," as one Kentucky newspaper fumed. As he had with Frémont's rogue edict, Lincoln nullified Hunter's proclamation, on the grounds that the general had exceeded his mandate. Lincoln's May 19, 1862, message revoking Hunter's order beseeched the border states to undertake a "calm and enlarged consideration" of his compensated emancipation proposal, cautioning them "not to be blind to the signs of the times." Even as he disciplined Hunter, the president reserved the right to move against slavery himself if military necessity demanded that he do so. A dispatch to the *Missouri Republican*, written anonymously by Lincoln's assistant private secretary John Hay, pressed the case that the administration's border state strategy, because it rejected radicalism, was actually working: Hay averred that there were "indications each day" that slaveholders in Maryland, Missouri, and Kentucky were ready to consider Lincoln's offer "in the light of reason and common sense, not of passion and prejudice."⁶²

Lincoln would try again to persuade the doubters. On July 12, 1862, he met with representatives of Missouri, Kentucky, Maryland, Delaware, western Virginia, and eastern Tennessee. The context was now very different than it had been in the winter of 1861, when Lincoln first essayed his plan. The failure of the Peninsula campaign prompted Lincoln to call east two commanders who had seen success in the west. General John Pope, captor of the Confederate Mississippi River defenses at Fort Madrid and Island No. 10 in March and April 1862, was appointed commander of the new Army of Virginia on June 27, 1862, tasked with defending the District of Columbia and the Shenandoah Valley; his command consisted of corps that had floundered during Jackson's Valley campaign. And General Henry W. Halleck, who had directed the successful Mississippi Valley campaign that spring, was brought east and named general-in-chief of Union forces on July 11. On July 2, 1862, Lincoln had called for 300,000 volunteers to serve for three years or for the war's duration; this nearly doubled the size of the Union army. All of these moves could be seen as repudiations of McClellan's conciliatory approach to waging war: drastic actions were required to get the war effort back on course.[63]

More important still, evidence that slavery was being "extinguished by mere friction and abrasion—by the mere incidents of war," as Lincoln put it, was now ubiquitous. Slaves flocked to the Union army anywhere and everywhere it penetrated the South. The window of time in which masters might act to seize recompense for their lost property was rapidly closing. Yet again, Lincoln tried to persuade the border states that he had their interest at heart: "How much better for you, as seller, and the nation as buyer, to sell out, and buy out . . . than to sink both the thing to be sold, and the price of it, in cutting one another's throats." In a wishful bit of revisionism, Lincoln claimed that if border men had only accepted the sweetheart deal back in March, before the setbacks in Virginia, the war would have already "substantially ended." The fate of the nation was at stake—and border state slave owners had, once again, the privilege of saving it.[64]

Once again, Lincoln was rebuffed. In rejecting gradual, compensated emancipation, the border state representatives, led by Kentucky governor Charles Wickliffe, invoked their concerns about maintaining control over the black population; their skepticism that the government could and would raise sufficient funds to remunerate them for their slaves; their distaste for appeasing the abolitionists; and their conviction that emancipation measures would strengthen rather than undermine the rebels' will to fight. Invoking the deluded-masses theory, the borderites claimed Lincoln had squandered an opportunity: a "large portion" of Southerners had been opposed to secession at the outset of the war, but "now the great mass of the Southern people" were united by the belief that the Lincoln administration was "making war on their domestic institutions."[65]

Seized with "deep anxiety" at the border state response, Lincoln was ready to try a new approach—one that pursued emancipation in the rebel states under his war power as commander in chief. Having confided to Welles and Seward alone his intentions of taking "extraordinary measures," Lincoln on July 22, 1862, in a closed-door meeting with his cabinet, announced to his astonished colleagues that he would issue an Emancipation Proclamation. The draft proclamation he presented them began by invoking the Second Confiscation Act, warning rebels that its provisions for seizing their property would soon go into effect. Lincoln then reiterated his support for federally funded gradual, compensated emancipation, the purpose of which, he emphasized, was to give errant Southern states a pathway back into the Union. The last line of the draft lowered the boom: as of January 1, 1863, Lincoln declared, "as a fit and necessary military measure . . . all persons held as slaves within any state or states, wherein the constitutional authority of the United States shall not then be practically recognized, submitted to, and maintained, shall then, thenceforward, and forever, be free."[66]

Lincoln told the cabinet he had not called them together to ask their advice—his mind was made up. The brief discussion that followed yielded few surprises. Chase and Stanton were enthusiastic about the plan, while the conservative postmaster general, Montgomery Blair, opposed it. Attorney General Edward Bates, an antislavery gradualist, lent his unexpected support to the proclamation, provided it was coupled with the colonization of freed slaves. Seward offered support but with a caveat: the president, he suggested, should delay promulgating the proclamation until a meaningful military victory had restored momentum to the war effort. He wanted emancipation to appear to be an integral part of a new winning plan, not an act of desperation—"our last shriek on the retreat," as Seward vividly put it. Lincoln agreed that this was best and kept his proposal under wraps. The waiting game would stretch into the fall.[67]

Lincoln's plans for border state gradual emancipation had run aground on slaveholder intransigence, even as McClellan's military campaign on the Peninsula ran aground. What did these failures portend for Northern hopes of Southern deliverance? For some of the radicals in Lincoln's inner circle, the lessons of the summer were, as Chase observed, "that the bitterness of the conflict had now substantially united the white population of the rebel States against us," and "that the blacks were really the only loyal population worth counting." But moderates read the situation differently, concluding that the Union's failure to "conquer rebellious hearts" was not from "any lack of loyalty amongst the masses of the Southern people," as Hay put it, "but from their undying hatred of Northern fanatics." For those such as Hay who "claimed the middle ground for the administration," it remained imperative that Lincoln keep his distance from abolitionist fanaticism and reassure borderites and rebels alike that his highest hope, still and always, was the restoration of the Union.[68]

No one did more to claim the middle ground for Lincoln than the famed orator Edward Everett of Massachusetts, who gave dozens of speeches across the Northeast and Midwest in the spring and summer of 1862, including "Causes and Conduct of the Civil War" and "Duty of Crushing the Rebellion." As a statesman, diplomat, and educator, Everett had gained renown in the antebellum era as the nation's primary exponent of the meaning of the Union, the life of George Washington, and the legacy of the Founders. The vice presidential candidate of the pro-compromise Union party in the election of 1860, and a supporter of gradual, compensated emancipation and colonization, Everett moved over the course of 1862 inexorably into the Republican coalition as a strong supporter of Lincoln's.[69]

Everett embodied, for the adoring audiences that thronged his speeches, a pure patriotism and open-minded pragmatism on the slavery issue—and the staunch belief that Federal troops were enacting the will of the American people. Calling on the loyal states to furnish men and materiel to the Army of the Potomac, Everett's speeches at "war meetings" in 1862 argued that the "Union sentiment of the South has been and is crushed by a reign of terror, as despotic and wicked, I doubt not, by as small a number of arch conspirators, as that of Danton, Marat and Robespierre." In Everett's recounting of the sectional crisis, a small number of conniving South Carolinians, guided by the fell spirit of John C. Calhoun, had engineered "poor Virginia" out of the Union "against the wishes and convictions of the mass of her population," even as the spirits of Virginian Founders including Washington and Madison "pleaded from their honored graves on behalf of the menaced Union." Minor victories would accomplish little to rectify this situation—what was needed was decisive victories, which depended in turn on manpower. A commitment to Union sentiment among white Southerners revived wherever the Federal army could provide them safety from persecution and "reasonable assurance of continued protection" or, better still, "*permanent* protection," Everett noted. Responding explicitly to the Confederate argument that the Union waged a war of subjugation, Everett declared that the Union had "rescued from the fangs of secession" western Virginia, Maryland, Missouri, Kentucky, and much of Tennessee, and he expressed optimism that the rest of the South could be redeemed. He was keenly aware of the diplomatic stakes

Edward Everett. Everett was beloved by Americans as a scholarly authority on the
Founding Fathers and as a politician devoted to the Union. During the war he became a
vital ally to Lincoln, helping to sustain the North's faith in Southern Unionism. (Library
of Congress LC-DIG-ppmsca-53251)

involved. Confederates sought to persuade the European powers that the
South fought for self-determination, but in Everett's view the Confederate
treatment of Unionists such as Brownlow in Tennessee gave the lie to such
claims and revealed the Slave Power to be the true aggressor in the contest.
The Northern press lavished praise on Everett, noting that his calls for a "vigorous prosecution of the war" were met with a "volcano of enthusiasm" from
the public.[70]

Lincoln's August Gambit

In August 1862, Lincoln took two public actions that seem at odds with the
emancipation plan he had secretly shared with his cabinet. On August 14, he
met in the White House with a delegation of five free black leaders, chaired

by reformer Edward M. Thomas, to reiterate his support for colonization. "Why should they leave this country?" the president asked leadingly. And then came his answer:

> You and we are different races. We have between us a broader dif-
> ference than exists between almost any other two races. . . . I think
> your race suffer very greatly, many of them by living among us,
> while ours suffers from your presence. In a word we suffer on each
> side. If this is admitted, it affords a reason at least why we should
> be separated.

Lincoln went on, at length. He called slavery "the greatest wrong inflicted on any people," and he identified it as the root cause of the war. But he also implied that blacks should hold themselves responsible for bringing on the current crisis: "See our present condition—the country engaged in war!—our white men cutting one another's throats, none knowing how far it will extend. . . . But for your race among us there could not be war."

Lincoln then acknowledged that some free blacks rejected colonization, and he asked that they reconsider, on the grounds that they should make "sacrifices"—give up their "present comfort" for the benefit of their race. Only if they were removed from white prejudice could blacks practice "self-reliance" and progress as a people. Lincoln promoted Liberia as a destination but also promised to look into establishing a colony in Central America. He closed by asking the delegation to help him identify potential emigrants. They must act not only for the benefit of their own generation, he intoned in closing, but "for the good of mankind."[71]

A week later, Lincoln penned a public letter to Horace Greeley, the editor of the *New York Tribune*, to respond to Greeley's charge that his administration had shown too much "deference to Slavery" and too little inclination to enforce the confiscation acts. Lincoln's unwillingness to push for emancipation, Greeley insisted in his August 20 open letter entitled "The Prayer of 20 Millions," had needlessly prolonged the war and had undermined Southern Unionism; if Lincoln had moved more quickly to make the loss of slaves the price of treason, he would have offered a "powerful inducement to remain loyal." The rebels had resorted to "terrorism"—confiscation, imprisonment, murder—to suppress Southern loyalism, while the Union had "fought wolves with the devise of sheep." In his August 22 reply to this indictment, Lincoln explained his course of action:

> My paramount object in this struggle *is* to save the Union, and is *not* ei-
> ther to save or destroy slavery. If I could save the Union without freeing
> *any* slave I would do it, and if I could save it by freeing *all* the slaves
> I would do it; and if I could save it by freeing some and leaving others
> alone I would also do that.

Lincoln made a point of contrasting his "*official* duty" to safeguard the Union
with his "*personal* wish that all men every where could be free."[72]

Why would Lincoln, when he had a draft of the Emancipation
Proclamation sitting in his desk drawer, try to revive colonization and seem
to disavow abolition as a war aim? Historians have fiercely debated this question. Most modern scholars believe that Lincoln was, at this moment in the
late summer of 1862, expertly shaping public opinion. Lincoln, so this argument goes, had a deep personal affinity for the abolitionists' moral critique
of slavery; he shared their core convictions while differing with them over
timing and tactics. A pragmatic politician, he had in his decision-making to
account for multiple, competing factors, such as the prevalence of racism
in the North, the risk of alienating the border states, and the impatience of
Radical Republicans. Lincoln knew he could not appear to let his personal
loathing for slavery drive his decisions and that he could not get too far ahead
of public opinion. He had to carefully prepare the way for his Emancipation
Proclamation.[73]

Seen in this light, Lincoln's August meeting with the black delegates and
his letter to Greeley were command performances, each with its own distinct
purpose. The true purpose of the colonization meeting was to reassure the
moderate and conservative white Northerners who would read about it in
the national daily press (Lincoln had invited a reporter to take notes on the
meeting) that the president was no antislavery extremist, but instead still a
gradualist. With his eye on the upcoming fall congressional and gubernatorial elections, Lincoln used colonization as a "lullaby" to quiet the opponents
of emancipation and to stave off defections to the Democrats. The Greeley
letter, with its "brilliant layering of meanings," was explicitly designed to send
mixed messages: conservatives could read it as a rebuke to the abolitionists ("If
I could save the Union without freeing *any* slave I would do it"), and Radicals
could take it as evidence that Lincoln was finally ready to sacrifice slavery
("if I could save it by freeing *all* the slaves I would do it"). The letter reached
hundreds of thousands of readers, as it was published in the *Washington
Chronicle* and widely reprinted in the Northern newspapers. Together, the
two performances were evidence of Lincoln's political genius: he would free

the slaves by presidential edict only after having demonstrated to the public that he had in good faith tried the other options, and that colonization and gradual, voluntary emancipation had fallen short as measures for weakening the Confederacy.[74]

Dissenting voices among modern historians reject the "political genius" interpretation. They argue that Lincoln persistently lagged behind the anti-slavery vanguard of abolitionists and Radical Republicans—he was not ready to consider the prospect of black citizenship and equal rights—and that we should take him at his word when he professed to put reunion above all other considerations and to favor colonization as the destiny for freed slaves. Lincoln was not the canny strategist but a man buffeted by "the uncontrollable forces of a great war" that pushed his policies into "directions that he had not antici-pated." Seen in this light, Lincoln's colonization meeting and letter to Greeley reveal his limits: at this crucial juncture, he saw emancipation as a war measure but not as a war aim, and he clung to the hope that "soft war" rhetoric and inducements would promote the reconciliation of North and South.[75]

Each interpretation has its strengths. The first illuminates the outward effects of Lincoln's tactics. If Lincoln meant to shore up his credentials as a moderate by advocating the separation of the races, it worked. Colonization supporters got a burst of momentum, as the Lincoln administration, spurred on by Attorney General Bates, further explored the prospect of black reset-tlement in Central America and the Caribbean, particularly at Chiriqui (in modern-day Panama). The mainstream white press lent its blessing to these projects. "The experiment of black colonies in Central America and else-where is well worth trying," the *New York Times* editorialized in late August. "The negro certainly has invitations and urgings enough to leave us, and small inducements to stay. . . . Here he has but personal slavery, or social degra-dation. If he chooses to leave us, Heaven speed him!" Meanwhile, African American leaders, with Douglass at their head, lambasted Lincoln for his conduct in August, concluding that the president could not be relied upon to advance the cause of freedom. In advocating black deportation, Lincoln had betrayed his "contempt for Negroes" and his "canting hypocrisy," Douglass charged.[76]

If the Greeley letter was designed to appeal to divergent constituencies of whites, it worked in that regard, too: mainstream Northerners, including some in the border states, praised Lincoln for keeping Greeley and his ab-olitionist ilk at bay. Lincoln's letter, with its emphasis on saving the Union, had "stirred the patriotism of the People," wrote Thurlow Weed, editor of the *Albany Evening Journal* and a frequent antagonist of the Radical Republicans.

Brigadier General Orlando Willcox was another who offered praise. Recently released from a Confederate prison after being captured at Bull Run, Willcox gave a triumphant speech in his hometown, Detroit, Michigan, in August 1862, professing his support for Lincoln's handling of the slavery issue. After stating that he had always been a Democrat "opposed to interfering with the rights of the States," Willcox explained that because the war itself was "crushing out slavery," there was no need for "raising an anti-slavery flag, or making anti-slavery proclamations" that would rouse the South. "The President is right on that," Willcox concluded, with applause from the crowd, "and I stand by him in it."[77] Some abolitionists, for their part, were angered or disappointed by Lincoln's letter to Greeley. But Lincoln had not pushed too hard. Others, such as the *Tribune*'s managing editor, Sydney Gay, thought the exchange with Greeley augured well: Lincoln would soon announce, Gay expected, "that the destruction of Slavery is the price of our Salvation."[78]

The second interpretation illuminates Lincoln's inner struggle to adapt his long-held views to changing circumstances. In his eyes colonization was not just a way to make emancipation palatable to slaveholders: he thought it a genuinely benevolent solution to the problem of American race relations. Lincoln believed deeply that the Republican creed of nonextension and gradual emancipation was in keeping with the Founders' wishes. Moreover, the goal of maintaining his identity as a moderate was important to Lincoln not just politically but personally. He had long resented the efforts of his Democratic and proslavery opponents to cast all Republicans as radicals, because he felt the charge was unfair and untrue.[79]

Lincoln's prejudices were deeply rooted, too. It is instructive to compare his treatment of the border state slaveholders, to whom he pitched gradual compensated emancipation in July, and his treatment of the black delegates in August. Although the border state delegates had enervated and disappointed him, he appealed to them as countrymen who shared his love of the Union:

> You are patriots and statesmen; and, as such, I pray you, consider this proposition. . . . Our common country is in great peril, demanding the loftiest views, and boldest action to bring it speedy relief. . . . To you more than any others, the privilege is given, to assure that happiness, and swell that grandeur, and to link your own names therewith forever.

With the black delegates, by contrast, Lincoln made no allusion to patriotism. He imagined that blacks might feel some connection to America, deriving from familiarity and from their "attachment" to whites. And he asked them to make sacrifices for the good of their race. But he could not yet imagine African Americans as fellow citizens and constituents, capable of the lofty and selfless sentiment of patriotism.[80]

It was this stubborn insistence that blacks were aliens in America that so galled African American leaders. For fifty years, they had systematically made the case against colonization by asserting their Americanness, invoking their integral role in building and defending the nation. Indeed, the evangelical version of that case had cast blacks as a "redeemer race," which would save America from the sin of slavery so that the nation could fulfill its glorious destiny. Now in the midst of a new war they had once again rushed to offer their services to their country. "What sane-minded man doubts our patriotism?" asked T. H. Hubard in August 1862, as Northern free blacks rallied to repudiate colonization yet again.[81]

His voice joined a chorus. Invoking the example set by "our revolutionary fathers," the Reverend James Gloucester of Brooklyn predicted that together patriotic blacks and whites would overthrow the "bloody tyrant, slavery, and our flag become the emblem of one mighty and undivided people." Ebenezer Bassett, principal of Philadelphia's Institute for Colored Youth, called on blacks to refute "the monstrous idea that the black and white races cannot dwell together in harmony." Images of African American claims to American soil, which had been central to black protests against colonization for half a century, were central to the wartime case against Lincoln's temporizing. It was "unreasonable to think that we would voluntarily leave the land that hath 'birthed and reared us,' and go and live in the desolate wastes of Central America, or under the scorching rays of Liberia's sun," wrote a commentator with the pen name "Cerebus" to the *Christian Recorder* in August. Blacks would not be forcibly ejected, he said, "from the country for which our ancestors fought, bled and died." J. W. C. Pennington, a prominent New York minister and orator, asserted that the South in particular "belonged" to his race, as "the claims of the negro to that region were God-given, and had been earned by the blood and sweat of generations." Philadelphia abolitionist Robert Purvis proclaimed:

> The children of the black man have enriched the soil by their tears, sweat and blood. . . . I elect to stay on the soil on which I was born, and on the plot of ground I have fairly bought and honestly paid for. Don't advise me to leave, and don't add insult to injury by telling me it's for my own good; of that I am to be the judge. It is vain that you talk to me about "two races" and their "mutual antagonism." In the matter of rights there is but one race and that is the *human* race.[82]

The question of the age, the Reverend Gloucester asserted, linking emancipation and providence, was "whether God or man shall be obeyed." Lincoln was preoccupied by this very same question—but the connection between emancipation and providence was not yet clear to him. In an un- dated manuscript fragment that his secretaries dubbed "Meditation on the Divine Will" and situated in the summer or early fall of 1862, Lincoln noted that each party in the war claimed "to act in accordance with the will of God," and mused that "one must be wrong," for "God can not be for, and against the same thing at the same time." "In the present civil war it is quite possible that God's purpose is something different from the purpose of ei- ther party," he continued, as he wondered why God permitted the terrible contest to unfold. In short, Lincoln, in his humility, did not see himself as the consummate strategist. He was struggling to assimilate all of the many lessons of the war.[83]

4

The Perils of Occupation

AS MCCLELLAN WAS driven off the Peninsula in Virginia, dramas of deliverance played out in Tennessee, Louisiana, and Maryland. Andrew Johnson and Benjamin Butler, installed as occupiers in Nashville and New Orleans, learned the hard way that white Southerners would not follow their script, and that elite women in particular scorned Federal "protection." Hoping to press his advantage, Lee for his part set his sights on Maryland, determined to disenthrall it from the Yankee yoke, only to have Marylanders turn their backs on his army. A new standard for battlefield horror was set on September 17, 1862, at Antietam Creek, near Sharpsburg, Maryland, where the two armies inflicted 23,000 casualties in twelve hours of savage combat, making it the bloodiest single day in American history. For Union soldiers and the Northern public, Antietam furnished yet more proof of the power that falsehood and despotism exerted over the Confederates. For Lincoln, Antietam was an "indication of Divine will," as he told his cabinet—a sign that "it was his duty to move forward in the cause of emancipation."[1]

Carrot and Stick

After the Union victory at Shiloh in April 1862, Confederate forces under Beauregard concentrated at Corinth, Mississippi, only to evacuate the town on May 30 when it became clear they could not hold out against the much stronger Union armies at the disposal of Henry Halleck, commander of Union forces in the west. Halleck chose not to advance further into Mississippi but instead to consolidate Union control over the vast swaths of Kentucky and of West and Middle Tennessee that the string of Union victories, from Fort Donelson to Corinth, had wrested from the Confederates. By June 1862, the Union firmly controlled the Mississippi from Columbus, Kentucky, to Memphis, Tennessee. Meanwhile, in April 1862, Federal forces under

Flag Officer David Farragut, commander of the Western Gulf Blockading Squadron, and Major General Benjamin F. Butler, who commanded the Department of the Gulf (after having served earlier in the war at Virginia's Fort Monroe), set their sights on the prize of New Orleans. The city was poorly defended, manned only by 3,000 militiamen, as Louisiana troops had been deployed to the Tennessee and Virginia front. On April 24 Farragut's gunboats ran the gauntlet of New Orleans defenses, and the city capitulated the following day, opening the way for the arrival of Butler's army of occupation on May 1. Baton Rouge fell next, on May 9. Northerners expected a swift "resurrection of loyalty" among the commercial class of New Orleans that had profited so handsomely from its antebellum economic ties to the North. Such expectations conditioned what Union soldiers and sailors saw as they approached the city. "There was at least 15000 people on the Levee as we passed along," Union sailor W. H. Robert of Rhode Island wrote his wife. "Their no doubt was many Union people among them—but they dare not express their oppinion. Many women were waving secession flags & men cheering for Jeff Davis," he explained.[2]

Union occupiers in the west faced the daunting challenge of neutralizing the threat of guerrillas, dealing with recalcitrant Confederate civilians, and trying to distinguish the truly loyal Unionists from those feigning compliance. The course of occupation, historian Earl J. Hess has explained, followed a pattern. Federal authorities initially tried conciliation, encouraging the soldiers garrisoned in places such as Memphis, Nashville, and New Orleans to treat the Southern civilians there respectfully and to keep their hands off civilian property; this was the best way, it seemed, to foster loyalty to the Union. Ulysses S. Grant wrote his wife, Julia, from Union-occupied Corinth, Mississippi, in June 1862 that the citizens there seemed to be learning that the "Yankees [were] a much less bloody, revengeful and to be dreaded people, then they had been led to think." He added wishfully: "In my mind there is no question but that this war could be ended at once if the whole Southern people could express their unbiased feeling untrammeled by leaders." But as Federal occupiers encountered resistance—guerrillas who ransacked railroads, burned bridges, and fired on riverboats; the shadowy civilians who harbored and abetted them; and the large number of locals who openly scorned the men in blue—Union authorities imposed harsher measures. They demanded that white Southerners take loyalty oaths, and arrested, seized the property of, or deported those who were especially dangerous or hostile.[3]

Andrew Johnson and Benjamin Butler exemplified these policies. As military governor, based in Nashville, Johnson professed a desire to restore loyal civil, rather than military, government, and he let local officeholders willing to pledge allegiance to the Union retain their posts until new elections could be held. Rhetorically, Johnson reassured Tennesseans, "with a mixture of firmness and conciliation," that he would extend amnesty to those who renounced the Confederacy. But when most Nashvillians scorned taking the oath, Johnson cracked down: he had conspicuous critics of the Lincoln administration arrested, imposed punitive taxes on wealthy planters, and seized and closed anti-Union newspapers. Determined that only consistently loyal men, rather than opportunistic Unionists, would shape Tennessee's political future, Johnson required that anyone who sought to vote would have to not only swear allegiance to the Union but also vouchsafe that he rejoiced in the victories of the Federal army and that he abjured any peace negotiations with the Confederacy.[4]

Johnson's resort to confiscation, imprisonment, and banishment of the disloyal, and his support for emancipation as a military necessity, did not just incur the wrath of Confederates. It also won him the enmity of some conservative Unionists, who were tied by kinship and commerce to the Confederate social elite, and who sought to minimize the war's impact on the existing power structure. Johnson, by contrast, saw Union occupation as a means to level the invidious distinctions of the slave system. As they were in the east, fugitive slaves were catalysts for change in the west, flocking by the thousands to Union lines and "contraband camps" and to cities such as Nashville and Memphis, where they assumed a new place in the churches, markets, and other public spaces. Slaveholding Unionists decried the erosion of the plantation system and blamed secessionists for it. "I warned you years ago that when you began this rebellion you would destroy slavery," a Tennessee Unionist intoned, addressing himself to his rebel neighbors in a September 1862 speech in Nashville. "I own slaves. I toiled and worked for their possession for years, and your madness, and wickedness have now rendered them worthless. You rebels, and not the Unionists," he fumed with bitter irony, "are the very ones who have struck a death blow to the heart of slavery."[5]

Even as Johnson resorted to severe tactics, he maneuvered to claim the moral high ground in the escalating war of words over the treatment of civilians. Johnson represented Southern Unionists who felt that the Confederates, particularly the cavalry raiders John Hunt Morgan and Nathan Bedford Forrest, had initiated hard war, preying mercilessly on loyal civilians, forcing them into the Confederate army and out of their homes—and taking property and lives when loyalists resisted. Johnson's newspaper organ, the *Nashville Daily Union*, featured a litany of stories of guerrilla depredations against helpless women and children. "The rebels plunder without remorse or pity . . . and make sport over the groans and tears of blood which hundreds and thousands of women and children are now weeping," ran one account. Moreover, Johnson campaigned assiduously to draw public attention toward the rebel treatment of civilians in East Tennessee, where Confederate forces held sway over a Unionist majority. His main ally in this work was William Gannaway "Parson" Brownlow, a fiery East Tennessee preacher and editor whose staunch opposition to secession had led Confederates to shut down his Knoxville newspaper in the fall of 1861 and jail Brownlow that winter. After they released him and banished him to Union lines in Kentucky in 1862, Brownlow launched a personal crusade to educate the Northern public about the mistreatment of East Tennessee Unionists. His speeches drew huge crowds in the North, and his *Sketches of the Life, Progress and Decline of Secession,* published in Philadelphia in 1862, became a best-seller. Brownlow fashioned himself a martyr, with heart-rending accounts of his imprisonment and depictions of Unionists in East Tennessee as the "most abused, down-trodden, persecuted and proscribed people that ever lived on the face of the earth." Northerners were receptive to the message. "How long must these long-suffering patriots wait for their day of deliverance?" asked the *New York Times* in one of its many articles lauding Brownlow. The AME church's flagship *Christian Recorder,* based in Philadelphia and edited by Reverend Elisha Weaver, a North Carolina–born free black who had made a name for himself as a preacher in the Midwest, joined the chorus of praise for Brownlow—but with one reservation. "Mr. Brownlow is a brave and patriotic man, and, in this rebellion, has done good work, and all honor him therefore," the paper editorialized after the Tennessean had given a fiery speech in Philadelphia; the *Recorder* added disapprovingly that Brownlow's rhetoric was "grossly profane" and that such language should not become "current as the expression of intense patriotism."[6]

In New Orleans, Ben Butler tried both the carrot and the stick as strategies for occupation. He instituted policies, such as distributing food to the poor and hiring unemployed workers to clean the streets, meant to change Confederate hearts and minds and to disenthrall the masses from subservience to the elite. In an effort to identify and promote a core group of Unionists who could serve as the basis of a restored loyal government, he demanded loyalty oaths of public officials. Like Johnson, he was intent on conveying the message that protection would follow allegiance. Taking the oath brought benefits, such as access to provisions and other goods, immunity from property confiscation, the right to engage in commerce and politics, and the hope of inclusion in any general amnesty policy Lincoln might devise. Refusing the oath was costly, as

Butler vigorously appropriated the personal property of the disloyal, in accordance with the provisions of the Second Confiscation Act. Butler consciously exerted "pressure along the fault lines of class," levying assessments against rich Confederates to cover the costs of poor relief for loyalists. By August 1862, nearly twelve thousand New Orleans residents had taken the oath, making it possible for the first and second districts of Louisiana to elect representatives to the United States Congress that December.[7]

The troops in Butler's occupying force saw the wisdom in such policies. In New Orleans in May, Connecticut infantryman Charles Sherman observed of the South's common whites, "Thay do not think for themselves but let their Political Leader Lead them by the Nose whare ever thay please." Slaveholding planters had "Drilled it into them . . . that Slavery is the Normal Condition of the African Race, and that it is derogatory to the White man to Labor." Sherman looked forward to the time when this "Deluded People" would be "Brought Back to the Faith and Love of its youth." Commenting on Butler's distribution of rations to poor whites, Sherman noted approvingly that such generosity would bring misguided Southern civilians "to a Sense of their ingratude to the Best and kindest of Goverments that the Sun ever Shone

Occupied New Orleans. "Among the other outrages committed by General Butler at New Orleans," *Harper's Weekly* commented sarcastically, "is feeding the starving people whose fathers, brothers, and sons are mostly in the rebel army." Benjamin Butler spent approximately fifty thousand dollars a month to provide food to the poor white residents of Union-occupied New Orleans, to promote loyalty and drive a wedge between the elite and the masses. (Library of Congress LC-USZ62-111199)

upon." "We have to overcome a very Large amount of Prejudaic that is in the Southron mind regarding the People of the North but it will Shurely be removed," he wrote his wife in October 1862.[8]

The status of slavery in occupied Louisiana posed distinct problems. Slaves fled to Union-occupied zones in the Mississippi Valley, as they did elsewhere in the South. Among the fugitives to arrive at Camp Parapet, the Union fort a mile upriver from New Orleans, was Octave Johnson. Born in New Orleans and trained as a cooper, he was sold in 1861 to a ruthless new master. Under the threat of whipping Johnson escaped into the swamps, to eke out survival with a small maroon community of runaways there. The fugitives were hunted for months by the slave owners' bloodhounds. "One day twenty hounds came after me," Johnson remembered. The fugitive band managed to kill eight of the dogs, and then jumped into the bayou; the other dogs followed their quarry into the water and were caught and devoured by alligators, who, Johnson noted, "preferred dog flesh to personal flesh." The arrival of the Union army provided redemption from this hellscape—Johnson escaped to Camp Parapet and was employed in the commissary's office.[9]

Such stories abounded. But in Louisiana Federal officials had to deal with a substantial number of planters who professed (or pretended) to be loyal Unionists and stayed put when the Union army arrived, rather than fleeing and abandoning their lands. Butler grappled with the question of whether Union masters in this setting should be treated like loyal masters in the border states and exempted from confiscation. Lincoln, Stanton, and Butler together agreed that Butler should not return fugitive slaves to their masters but instead should employ them on plantations confiscated by the Union or provide them as wage laborers to planters willing to pay for their services. Under this scheme, loyalty afforded no immunity from the new order of things: Unionist planters who wanted to stay in business had to adopt the free labor system of yearly work contracts. They grudgingly complied, but their complaints, and the lingering ambiguities in Federal policy, were incentives for Lincoln to devise his new emancipation policy in the summer of 1862.[10]

Confederate leaders, for their part, warned the citizenry of the moral costs of pledging allegiance to the Yankees. In early 1863, the Confederate senator from New Orleans introduced in the Confederate Congress a resolution praising the "martyr-like courage" of those who had the moral strength to resist taking the oath. This prompted the Reverend Benjamin M. Palmer, who had fled occupied New Orleans for South Carolina, to publish a tract in which he strongly condemned those who had succumbed to the temptation to pledge allegiance to the Union. Palmer was aware that many such oath-takers felt "bullied or cajoled into a form of submission denied by the heart." He saw Butler as practicing a shrewd psychological warfare: dealing out "brutal and insulting threats" and "playing upon the fears" of Confederates "with imposing tests of their moral courage." Palmer had no sympathy for those who failed the test. It was an affront to God, he explained, to take an oath without meaning it. Such faithlessness was the root cause of secession: Northerners no longer respected the "covenants and treaties solemnly instituted by our forefathers." The Yankee oath was explicitly designed to make a mockery of Confederate claims of state and national sovereignty. Evoking the shame that still attached to the families whose forebears had been Tories during the American Revolution, Palmer instructed Confederates to "choose the dungeon and the scaffold a thousand times, rather than transmit the taint of this leprosy to your offspring."[11]

The "Woman Order" and Female Accountability

As Palmer pointedly noted, no policy of Butler's matched the notoriety of his controversial General Order No. 28, promulgated on May 15. Butler was disgusted by the insolent and abusive behavior of the Confederate "ladies" of New Orleans toward the Union soldiers there: women turned up their noses at soldiers, spat upon them, hurled insults, threw decayed food, and even emptied chamber pots from their windows onto Union men in the streets below. This was a brazen rejection of Butler's pretense to be a liberator for New Orleans. And so he decreed that any woman who showed such contempt for Federal soldiers would "be treated as a woman of the town, plying her avocation"—namely, she would be liable for arrest as a prostitute. The "Woman Order" caused a firestorm. Confederates interpreted it as a grant of license to Union soldiers to sexually assault Southern ladies. Innocent women, the *Richmond Dispatch* fumed, were to be made victims of Yankee soldiers' "brutal passions." "Let the memory of this threatened outrage nerve the arm of every father, husband or son in the thickest strife," the *Charleston Mercury* thundered, to "make their deliverance from such a despotism certain." Calling Butler's order "one of the most infamous proclamations ever heard or dreamed of among a civilized people," South Carolinian Emma Holmes reported in her diary on May 23 that "Beauregard had it read at the head of his army and it has everywhere roused the Southerners to a deadlier hatred." Butler would be known to Confederates thereafter as "the Beast."[12]

The Woman Order controversy is a window into a broader debate that was taking shape in both the Union and Confederacy over women's civic duty, particularly the issue of female accountability: were women to be classed as "innocents" or as political actors? The Woman Order reflected an emerging Northern discourse on the "extravagant bitterness shown toward the North by the Southern women of the higher classes," as Butler put it. In his view, elite women were fully complicit in promulgating the falsehoods of the Slave Power and manipulating the masses into war—and should be made to take responsibility for their beliefs. He offered the people of New Orleans a choice: those willing to return to their allegiance to the Union would receive forgiveness and protection, while those who persisted in their treason would feel the sting of conquest. Northerners were divided over the propriety of Butler's policies. Some felt his Woman Order was unchivalrous and an embarrassment; others felt that Confederate women had forfeited the protections of chivalry and must be punished. An article in the *New York Times* captured Union ambivalence—drawing a sharp distinction between the suffering poor of New Orleans and the guilty ladies living in "palaces of luxury," it cast elite women as having been abandoned by their old protectors (Confederate men who had surrendered the city), only to shun their new protectors in the Union army. Butler noted in his own defense that he did not actually follow through by arresting anyone—and that his rhetorical threat alone had worked to pacify the female population.[13]

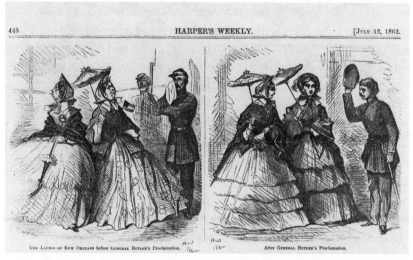

Butler's "Woman Order." While Confederates derided him as the "Beast," Butler insisted that his tough talk was working to pacify the spirit of insolent rebel ladies. The war gave rise to intense debates in the North and South over whether women should be held accountable for their political acts. (Library of Congress LC-USZ62-6533400)

But hostility simmered beneath the surface of seeming acquiescence. Sarah Morgan's account of the Union occupation of Baton Rouge illustrates how Confederate propaganda framed white Southerners' experiences of occupation and countered the Union discourse of deliverance. The privileged daughter of a wealthy family, just nineteen when she began writing her extensive diary, Morgan struggled to reconcile discordant emotions. In the first months of the occupation, she found that Union soldiers defied her expectations: "Fine, noble looking men they were, showing refinement and gentlemanly bearing in every motion; one cannot help but admire such foes." Although a committed Confederate, she was unwilling to join with her fellow elite women in proclaiming the Yankees "liars, thieves, murderers, scoundrels, the scum of the earth, etc." "I would scorn to have an inferior foe," she reasoned. "I fight only my equals." The news of Butler's "Woman Order" brought forth Morgan's condemnation, but she made a distinction between his comportment and that of the commander of Union forces in Baton Rouge, General Thomas Williams. "These people mean to kill us with kindness," she wrote on June 8, after Williams had sent a barrel of flour as a gift to the family; she continued to contrast the "quiet, gentlemanly, liberal way" of the occupying army with the "rabid, fanatical, abusive violence of our female Secession declaimers." She was tempted to bring food to sick Union soldiers convalescing in a local theater that had been converted into a hospital, but she feared that to do so would make her the "anathema of society" in the eyes of the "Ultra Secessionists." "If I could help these dying men! Yet it is as impossible as though I was a chained bear," she lamented.[14]

Before long, however, Morgan changed her tune. Butler's arrival in Baton Rouge in late June and his arrest of several prominent citizens raised her ire. From then on, Morgan's diary entries featured typical Confederate invective. "What a thrill of terror ran through the whole community!" she wrote. "God have mercy on us and deliver us from the hands of our enemies! This degradation is worse than the bitterness of death!" In August, her family fled Baton Rouge before an impending (and failed) Confederate effort to retake the city; when Morgan returned to Baton Rouge later that month to find her family's home had been ransacked by the Union army, she was filled with rage. "I say War to the death! I would give my life to be able to take up arms against the vandal[s] who are laying waste our fair land!" She was particularly incensed at the idea that her possessions might be redistributed by the Yankees to former slaves. "I would rather have all I own burned, than in the possession of negroes," she fumed. Even as she railed in her diary against her enemies, Morgan also complained that women were relegated to the role of passive victims. "Why was I not a man?" she asked in July 1862. "What is the use of all these worthless women, in war times?"[15]

Rewards as well as punishments were at stake in debates over female accountability. As they took on greater responsibilities, Union and Confederate women who filled the ranks of hospital workers pressed for recognition of their expertise, hard work, and patriotic sacrifices. But such recognition proved elusive, as male authorities remained ambivalent about the prospect of female authority. In Richmond, for example, women were pushed out of the business of managing their own private hospitals. In the first year of the war, sixteen female-run hospitals operated in the Confederate capital—and they boasted mortality rates lower than those in male-run hospitals, as female caregivers paid greater attention to patient hygiene, nutrition, and morale than male surgeons did. But in the fall of 1862, the Confederate Medical Department, seeking more centralized control, fiscal efficiency, and military discipline in medical care, ordered the private hospitals closed. They were to be supplanted by state-run, male-run general hospitals. Only one hospital manager, Sallie Tompkins, a well-connected member of Richmond's social elite, was permitted to keep her own hospital open, and she was required to adhere to regulations enforced by male inspectors. The loss of the private hospitals galled soldiers, who far preferred them to the general hospitals. Virginia soldier Alexander Hunter wrote of the Chimborazo general hospital—the largest hospital in the world and the pride of the Confederate medical system—that the three days he spent in "that Hades" were "the most terrible" of his life. Tompkins's Robertson hospital, by contrast, he described glowingly as "incomparably the best in Richmond."[16]

The move to close private hospitals did not deter female volunteers; indeed, the success of the private hospitals ensured that women would be called upon to contribute to the general hospitals not just as nurses but as "matrons"—that is, superintendents of the kitchens, laundries, and wards. Chief matrons had considerable authority, supervising workforces consisting of poor white women, convalescing soldiers, free blacks, and slaves, and acting as confidants and advocates for the patients (helping them, for example, to obtain furloughs). But such authority was always circumscribed by the supervision of male surgeons and military officers, who typically were high-handed or openly hostile to the women. For example, Phoebe Yates Pember, a Chimborazo matron, drew the wrath of her male superiors when she "made a concerted effort to protect the hospital's liquor supply, which was rationed daily to the patients, from the predations of the surgeons and other male hospital staff." Contests over female accountability and authority would multiply as the war ground on.[17]

Second Bull Run

In northern Virginia, Major General John Pope was forging his own reputation as a "beast" as he promulgated open declarations of hard war in
July 1862. His General Order No. 5 directed Union soldiers to "subsist
upon the country." General Order No. 7 targeted guerrillas by holding
local civilians responsible for repairing and remunerating Federals for any
damage caused to railroads, wagon roads, or telegraphs. Moreover, Federal
soldiers were directed to arrest and destroy the dwellings of civilians
suspected of firing upon them and to shoot down those caught in the act.
General Order No. 11 gave Pope's commanders leave to "arrest all disloyal
male citizens within their lines or within their reach" and to force them to
take an oath of allegiance as the price for their release; if they broke the
oath, they could be executed without trial. For Pope, the orders served to
announce that there would be no more McClellan-like conciliation—and
no more strategic retreats. "I have come to you from the West, where we
have always seen the backs of our enemies," Pope declared to his troops
as he took command. "Success and glory are in the advance, disaster and
shame lurk in the rear."[18]

Taken together, Confederates charged, these directives invited the
Yankees to plunder private property and to harass, abuse, and indiscrimi-
nately murder innocent civilians. Lee deemed Pope a "miscreant" and looked
forward to punishing him on the battlefield. But Lee faced a dilemma. When
Pope assumed command of the new Army of Virginia, McClellan was still
ensconced on the Peninsula; he would not begin withdrawing his troops
from Harrison's Landing to Fort Monroe until mid-August. In mid-July,
there was a stalemate of sorts on the Richmond front. In truth, neither Lee
nor McClellan had the strength to initiate a new offensive—but Lee could
not know for sure that McClellan would not move on Richmond a second
time. Meanwhile, Pope's army could potentially threaten Richmond from the
north. Lee could not afford to let Pope and McClellan combine their forces,
or to trap him in a vise.[19]

This dire situation grew more ominous when Pope, on July 12, sent an
advance guard south to Culpeper Court House, en route to Gordonsville,
an important rail junction; the east-west Virginia Central Railroad passed
through there, connecting Lee's army and Richmond's civilians with the
food supplies of the Shenandoah Valley. Lee was nervous about thinning the
defenses of Richmond, but he could not risk losing his supply line, so he sent
Jackson with 14,000 men west, to checkmate the Yankee advance. At Cedar

John Pope. Like Butler, Pope was a symbol in Confederate eyes of the Union's "hard war" policies that targeted civilians and their property. Pope failed to translate his tough talk into a victory against Robert E. Lee and was relieved of command after losing the Second Battle of Bull Run in August 1862. (Library of Congress LC-DIG-cwpb-06342)

Mountain on August 9, Jackson, who had been reinforced by Major General A. P. Hill's division, confronted Nathaniel Banks and his corps of 8,000 men and drove them back. The supply line to the Valley was safe. But Pope's army was intact—and was poised to receive reinforcements from McClellan, who was about to extricate himself from the Peninsula.[20]

Determined to hit Pope before he was reinforced, and leaving behind a small force to defend the rebel capital, Lee left Richmond for the Rapidan front, joining Jackson and Longstreet north of Gordonsville on August 15. Intimidated by the Confederate show of force, Pope pulled back to a position north of the Rappahannock River. Lee then boldly decided to divide his army, sending Jackson on a flank march around Pope's army to get between Pope and Washington, D.C., and cut off his communications and supplies along the Orange and Alexandria Railroad. Longstreet and

Lee would hold the line against Pope on the Rappahannock. Jackson's detached column marched fifty-four miles in two days and on August 27 fell upon the Federal supply depot at Manassas Junction, feasting upon some of the foodstuffs stored there. Pope withdrew from the Rappahannock to deal with this threat on his right flank. Jackson established a strong defensive line across the original Bull Run battlefield, and Pope took the bait, attacking him there on August 29; the assault was poorly coordinated and faltered.[21]

Meanwhile, Longstreet was rushing to the scene with reinforcements. Longstreet's August 30 blow against the Union left flank sent the Federals reeling, retreating back to Washington, D.C., over the very same ground they had covered in the first Bull Run fiasco. The result was "a complete victory over the boastful Pope," as Virginia infantryman John Dooley put it. Indeed, the battle was a tactical as well as strategic triumph for the Confederacy, with Federal casualties numbering roughly 16,000 and the Confederates 9,000. A disgusted Lincoln turned Pope's men over to McClellan, despite rumors that McClellan had purposely undermined Pope's campaign by withholding his own troops from it.[22]

These developments certainly took a toll on support for the Union among white Virginians. The shallow variety of loyalism, based not on political principles or grievances but on a desire to align with whatever side had the upper hand, waned in the wake of Union failures in Virginia. True-blue Unionists, "waiting and watching for that deliverance which seemed as if it would never come," the *New York Times* editorialized, "realized the bitter heartsickness which springs from hope deferred."[23]

Confederate morale surged. Jefferson Davis declared a day of Thanksgiving on September 8, saying of the Second Manassas victory, "Our enemies have renewed their attempt to subjugate us at the very place where their first effort was defeated, and the vengeance of retributive justice has overtaken the entire host in a second and complete over throw." Moreover, the Confederates seemed poised to regain lost ground in the border states. Lee followed up the victory by probing into Maryland in early September. In a September 7 letter, written at Frederick, Maryland, to his wife, Adjutant General E. F. Paxton of the 27th Virginia Infantry gave voice to the great expectations stoked by Second Manassas. The victory "will secure our recognition in Europe and be a step at least towards peace with our enemies." Lee would not hesitate to strike while the iron was hot. "I think it likely we will not stay here," Paxton wrote. "This time next week will find us either in Pennsylvania or Baltimore."[24]

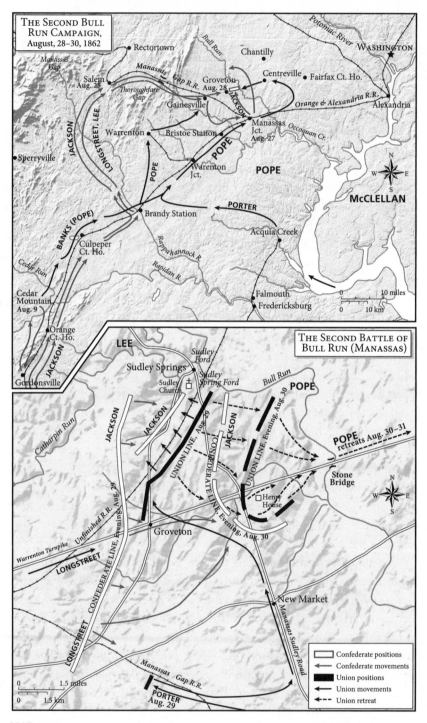

THE SECOND BULL RUN CAMPAIGN, August, 28–30, 1862

Rectortown •   Chantilly •   *Potomac River*   WASHINGTON

Manassas Gap   *Bull Run*

Salem Aug. 25   *Manassas Gap R.R.*   Groveton Aug. 28   Centreville •   Fairfax Ct. Ho. •

Thoroughfare Gap   Gainesville •   JACKSON

JACKSON   *Orange & Alexandria R.R.*   Alexandria •

LONGSTREET, LEE

• Sperryville   Warrenton •   Bristoe Station •   Manassas Jct. Aug. 27   *Occoquan Cr.*

POPE   POPE

Warrenton Jct.   **POPE**   McCLELLAN

BANKS (POPE)   PORTER

Brandy Station

Culpeper Ct. Ho.   Acquia Creek •

Cedar Run   *Rappahannock R.*

Rapidan R.

Cedar Mountain Aug. 9   Falmouth •   Fredericksburg •

Orange Ct. Ho.   JACKSON   0   10 miles   0   10 km

Gordonsville •

THE SECOND BATTLE OF BULL RUN (MANASSAS)

LEE   Sudley Ford

Sudley Springs   Sudley Spring Ford   *Bull Run*   POPE

Sudley Church   JACKSON   UNION LINE, Evening, Aug. 30

Catharpin Run   JACKSON   UNION LINE, Aug. 29   JACKSON

CONFEDERATE LINE

POPE retreats Aug. 30–31

Stone Bridge

Unfinished R.R.   CONFEDERATE LINE, Evening, Aug. 29   CONFEDERATE LINE, Evening, Aug. 30   Henry House

Warrenton Turnpike   Groveton

LONGSTREET

LONGSTREET

New Market

Manassas Sudley Road

0   1.5 miles   0   1.5 km

Manassas Gap R.R.

PORTER Aug. 29

Confederate positions
Confederate movements
Union positions
Union movements
Union retreat

MAP 4.1

The War in the West

In the aftermath of the Second Bull Run debacle, Lincoln opted to send the disgraced John Pope west, to suppress a Dakota Indian uprising in Minnesota. Pope's charge, according to Secretary of War Stanton, was to "quell the hostilities and afford peace, security, and protection to the people." Even as he reassigned Pope, Lincoln met with Cherokee leader John Ross, who led the Unionist faction in that tribe and had come to Washington to plead for military support and protection against the Confederates in Indian Territory. The warfare that unfolded in Minnesota and in Indian Territory (in present-day Oklahoma) illustrated the Union and Confederate governments' mutual disregard for the rights, sovereignty, and humanity of Native peoples.[25]

The Civil War divided Indian Territory, the lands to which the Five Civilized Tribes of Cherokee, Choctaw, Chickasaw, Creek, and Seminole had been displaced by Indian removal. Both the Union and Confederacy contended for supremacy in this borderland between Union-controlled Kansas and Confederate Arkansas and Texas. Filling a vacuum created by U.S. forces' initial abandonment of the region, the Confederacy recruited 3,000 soldiers from among the Native Americans there, only to lose ground as the Federal army reoccupied much of Indian Territory in 1862 and 1863. As historian Bradley R. Clampitt explains, Indians chose sides "for myriad reasons unique to their own experience": "existing treaties with the United States and dependence upon the federal government for a degree of financial support and reliance upon its military for physical security motivated some to remain loyal to the Union, while resentment of the United States, a genuine belief in the propriety of slavery, and a stronger cultural connection with the American South motivated others to support the Confederacy." Even after the Federal army had gained the upper hand, Indian Territory was devastated by warfare, with civilians victimized by guerrillas on both sides and plagued by shortages of food and medical supplies. Thousands became refugees; Unionist Creek families, for example, fled Confederate forces into Kansas. After the war, the federal government used the Confederate allegiance of some Indians as the pretext for punishing all, regardless of their loyalty, forcing Native Americans to forfeit large swaths of lands and curtailing what little sovereignty they exercised by consolidating congressional control over Indian Territory.[26]

In the Far West, Native Americans of the plains and prairies took advantage of the transfer of U.S. army regiments to the South and pushed back against the line of white settlement. In the summer of 1862, Dakota Sioux led

by Little Crow, angered at white disregard of treaty provisions, staged an uprising in southwestern Minnesota. It was met by Pope's campaign to clear out
the hostiles and by the hanging of thirty-eight Sioux men—the largest mass
execution in U.S. history—accused of complicity with the uprising. Lincoln
stayed the execution of scores of others, but this gesture of clemency failed to
impress critics, who noted that there were innocent men among the executed.
Lincoln was under intense pressure from westerners such as the Minnesota
newspaper editor Jane Grey Swisshelm to avenge any depredations against
whites. Swisshelm was an abolitionist but utterly unsympathetic to the
Dakota, whom she suspected of having been incited by Confederates, and
whom she regarded as "wild beasts" unfit for civilization. In the antebellum
era, abolitionists such as William Lloyd Garrison had typically positioned
themselves as opponents of Indian removal, favoring the project of cultural
assimilation over forced dispossession. Swisshelm, by contrast, called for abolition and extermination in the same breath. Her rhetorical efforts to reconcile these positions illustrate how malleable the "Slave Power conspiracy"
theory was. Swisshelm likened the Dakota to the South's slave-owning
aristocrats: both sets of enemies, in her view, shunned productive labor, were
obstacles to the "inevitable advance of civilization," and plotted treason and
murder. "A Sioux has as much right to his life as a hyena," she fumed in her
newspaper, the *St. Cloud Democrat*.[27]

Vengeance was the rallying cry for the brutal raid led by Colorado state
troops under Colonel John Chivington as they massacred and mutilated
more than 150 peaceful Arapaho and Cheyenne men, women, and children at
Sand Creek, Colorado, on November 29, 1864. This was a campaign of extermination, driven by an implacable hatred: Chivington instructed his troops
to "kill and scalp all, big and little; nits make lice." Although he faced some
criticism in the east, Chivington was regarded as a hero by western settlers.
Their continued encroachment on Indians' traditional hunting grounds set
the stage for the decades of Plains warfare after Appomattox. "For Native
people gazing east from the banks of Sand Creek," historian Ari Kelman has
written, the Civil War "looked like a war of empire, a contest to control expansion into the West, rather than a war of liberation."[28]

"My Maryland"

Back east, Lee sought to capitalize on the advantage he had seized from the
overmatched Pope. "We cannot afford to be idle, and though weaker than our

opponents in men and military equipments, must endeavor to harass, if we cannot destroy them," Lee wrote Jefferson Davis on September 3, 1862. A large-scale raid of the North, Lee reckoned, would accomplish multiple aims: it would liberate fellow Southerners from oppression, favorably impact public opinion, and relieve the logistical pressure on Virginia, as he could provision his army in U.S. territory. Lee's decision to have his army cross the Potomac into Maryland—and thus to assume the strategic offensive—reflected both long-standing assumptions and new contingencies. The idea that slaveholding Maryland was a natural part of the South and that Confederate incursions there would be acts of liberation rather than conquest was an initial premise of Confederate war aims. Lincoln had resorted to martial law and to garrisoning large numbers of Federal troops in Maryland to keep its secessionists at bay, and Marylanders, so Confederates told themselves, resented this and were eager to throw off the Federal yoke. The idea that decisive Confederate battlefield victories would swell a chorus of anti-Lincoln Northern dissenters—and perhaps bring to power Northerners willing to recognize Southern independence—was also an initial premise of the Confederate high command. It seemed more salient than ever in the fall of 1862, with Northern midterm state and congressional elections pending in mid-October.[29]

Confederate hopes for British recognition, or for European mediation of the war with Southern independence as the outcome, too seemed especially plausible in the fall of 1862. "It is difficult to exaggerate the profound impression produced in this country by the brilliant successes of our arms," wrote the London-based diplomatic agent Henry Hotze to Confederate secretary of state Judah P. Benjamin in September, referring to the Peninsula campaign and Second Bull Run. "The sympathies of the intelligent classes are now intensified into a feeling of sincere admiration" for the South, Hotze boasted. Lee's victories had indeed emboldened British advocates of intervention, most notably Foreign Secretary John Russell and Chancellor of the Exchequer William Gladstone. On September 17, Russell wrote Prime Minister Lord Palmerston that since the Federals had "made no progress in subduing the insurgent States," the time was ripe for "offering mediation to the United States Government, with a view to the recognition of the independence of the Confederates." Swirling rumors encouraged many Confederates to believe that European intervention was close at hand.[30]

Moreover, the bountiful supplies and stores of rural Maryland and Pennsylvania beckoned the poorly provisioned Confederates. Lee knew he had to keep up the initiative. Virginia had been churned up in the summer of 1862. He did not have the men and resources to besiege the Washington fortifications, nor did it make sense to hunker down in northern Virginia and give the Federals time to rebuild their armies, with the new recruits that Lincoln had summoned to fill the ranks. Better to strike while the Federals were still demoralized—and to bank again on the excessive caution of the Union high command.[31]

Meanwhile, Lincoln opted after the fiasco at Second Bull Run to reinstate McClellan to command the forces defending the capital. According to Attorney General Edward Bates, the command dilemma had pitched Lincoln into the "bitterest anguish." But Lincoln felt he had no other good choice: who would be better than McClellan at restoring morale, training green troops and integrating new regiments, and merging the disparate units of the Army of Virginia and Army of the Potomac? At first McClellan seemed to reward this act of trust, directing his army in early September to move out from the Washington defenses northwest into Maryland in pursuit of Lee; McClellan's force numbered roughly 85,000, with some 72,000 Union troops having been left behind to man the capital's fortifications. "I think we shall win for the men are now in good spirits—confident in their General," McClellan wrote his wife on September 7. "If I defeat the rebels I shall be master of the situation."[32]

THE REBEL CHIVALRY

As the Fancy of "My Maryland" painted them.   As "My Maryland" found them.

"My Maryland." This cartoon contrasts the rarified image of the Southern army in Confederate propaganda with the shabby condition of the rebel troops Lee led into Maryland. (Library of Congress LC-USZ62-96016)

Maryland's supposedly oppressed civilians neglected to follow Lee's script. The Confederate forces converged on the town of Frederick on September 7, with military bands playing the secessionist anthem "My Maryland" to announce the deliverance of this Southern territory from the Yankees. "It was plain the deliverance they meant was from the rule of law and order," wrote Frederick native Lewis H. Steiner of the scene. A Sanitary Commission doctor, Steiner spoke for the Unionist majority in the town. He and many of his fellow loyalists were appalled at the condition of the Confederate army. "A dirtier, filthier, more unsavory set of human beings never *strolled* through a town," he wrote, explaining, "Marching it could not be called without doing violence to the word." This motley crew—the "chivalry," Steiner dubbed them, with irony—soon fell upon the stores of Frederick for supplies; many of the Confederates were "shoeless and stockingless." Some Confederates made the empty gesture of paying merchants for what they took with Confederate notes—bills so worthless they "depreciated the paper on which they were printed," one citizen wryly noted. "Stauncher, stouter, stronger did Unionism in Frederick grow with each passing hour" of Lee's occupation, Steiner concluded.[33] It has seemed obvious to historians that Lee miscalculated—if he had entered the southeastern plantation districts of Maryland, he would have encountered a much warmer reception than he did in the Unionist northwest. But the idea of a rebel Maryland persisted as Confederate propaganda. A week after Steiner expressed his contempt for the "chivalry," the *Richmond Dispatch* was reporting, "Our troops were well received in Frederick, and . . . Confederate money was readily taken for every article that our worn troops desired to purchase." The conduct of the Confederates at Frederick had "greatly strengthened feeling in our favor in Maryland," the newspaper continued, and "gallant Marylanders" were flocking to the Frederick recruiting station the Confederates had opened up. This was a comforting fiction.[34]

More miscalculations were to follow, on both sides. On September 9, while in Frederick, Lee devised and issued Special Order No. 191, his plan for his northern raid. Jackson was to take two-thirds of the army to capture Harpers Ferry and its garrison and thus secure a line of communications with the Shenandoah Valley. Lee and Longstreet would proceed west through the South Mountain gaps to the vicinity of Boonsboro, Maryland, where they would await Jackson; once the armies were reunited, they could forge on into Pennsylvania and dare McClellan to attack them on terrain chosen by Lee. Lee was counting on McClellan to be slow in his pursuit. But on September 13, as McClellan's men encamped on ground near Frederick that Confederates had just passed through, a Yankee corporal, Barton W. Mitchell of the 27th

McClellan enters Frederick. When McClellan's army passed through Frederick, Maryland, in pursuit of Lee on September 12, 1862, it received a much warmer welcome from the residents than Lee's army had. This image was drawn by *Frank Leslie's* staff artist and field correspondent Edwin Forbes, one of the premier illustrators of the Civil War. (Library of Congress LC-DIG-ppmsca-20512)

Indiana Infantry, made a stunning discovery: he found lying in the grass a copy of Lee's Special Order No. 191, wrapped around three cigars and tucked into an envelope. McClellan crowed that this windfall would permit him to catch the rebels in their own trap. He told one of his corps commanders bluntly, "If I cannot whip Bobbie Lee, I will be willing to go home." This improbable story gets more bizarre. A Confederate-sympathizing Frederick civilian was on hand at Federal headquarters on the morning of September 13 at the very moment when the "lost order" was delivered to McClellan. This discerning individual gleaned from the Federals' joyous reaction to the reading of the order that they had learned of Lee's plans, and the civilian promptly rode to rebel lines to inform Lee. So by the evening of the thirteenth, Lee knew that McClellan knew that the rebel army was divided.[35]

But could McClellan act quickly enough to capitalize on Lee's vulnerability? Lee moved decisively to neutralize the Federal advantage, ordering Longstreet and Major General D. H. Hill to concentrate on blocking the passes at South Mountain to buy time and prevent the Federals from relieving Harpers Ferry. McClellan squandered some of his advantage by waiting until the morning of September 14 to send his columns forward.

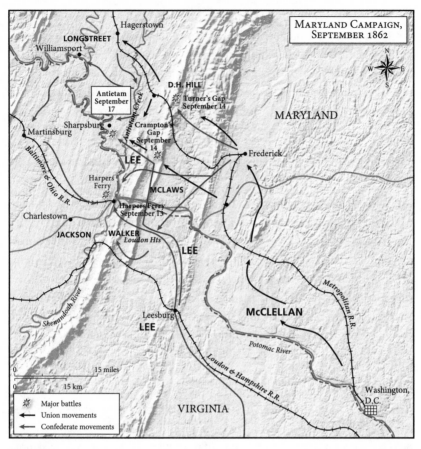

MAP 4.2

Nonetheless, the Federals performed well in the fight for South Mountain that day, forcing Longstreet and Hill to fall back to the town of Sharpsburg, near Antietam Creek. At day's end Confederate prospects seemed bleak— and Lee considered calling off the campaign and returning to Virginia. But daybreak on the fifteenth brought news that changed everything: Lee learned that Jackson had effected the surrender of the 12,000-man Federal garrison at Harpers Ferry, and so Jackson could thus join forces with Lee at Sharpsburg before McClellan could thread the rest of his imposing army through the two major passes at South Mountain. Lee perceived, moreover, that the terrain on the west side of Antietam Creek was favorable: a commanding plateau there, overlooking the creek valley, could afford the Confederates a strong defensive position, especially for artillery. So Lee decided to make a stand, aware that until Jackson could reach him, he had a mere 19,000 men to face down a Federal force of more than 80,000.[36]

McClellan, meanwhile, reverted to form and again failed to move with alacrity. He tarried on September 15, remaining "east of South Mountain . . . congratulating himself on the mighty victory he had won in the mountain gaps the day before," as historian Russell Weigley has explained. McClellan also squandered the sixteenth in unproductive reconnoitering—and this delay enabled Jackson to arrive at the Antietam front, meaning Lee was outnumbered only two to one, rather than four to one.[37]

Antietam

McClellan chose September 17 as the day for his attack and devised a tactically sound plan. Major General Joseph Hooker's First Corps would strike first, at Lee's northernmost left flank, and then Major General Ambrose Burnside would attack the Confederate's southernmost right flank, forcing Lee to weaken his center to bolster the flanks; when either or both of these movements had driven the Confederates back, the Union center would finish Lee off. The day began promisingly: Hooker's columns pushed Jackson's brigades back through the West Woods with the "crushing weight of a landslide," as Confederate brigade commander John B. Gordon put it. But a timely counterattack by Major General John B. Hood thrust the Federals back, compelling McClellan to send more men, Joseph Mansfield's Twelfth Corps, into the fray. Brutal fighting across a thirty-acre cornfield at the edge of the West Woods left Mansfield dead and Hooker wounded. "By charges and counter charges," Gordon wrote, "this portion of the field was lost and recovered, until the green corn that grew upon it looked as if it had been struck by a storm of bloody hail." The carnage in what would prove to be the war's deadliest day shocked even experienced soldiers. "The slain lay in rows precisely as they had stood in their ranks a few minutes before. It was never my fortune to witness a more bloody, dismal battlefield," Hooker would observe in his battle report.[38]

Major General Edwin V. Sumner's Second Corps now weighed in, with one division joining the action on the Confederate left, at Dunker Church, and two more attacking D. H. Hill's division at the Confederate center, along a sunken, rutted farm road that would go down in history as the "Bloody Lane." The Confederates' strong defensive position there was encircled by waves of Union attacks. Observing this portion of the battle alongside McClellan at the Federal command center on the high ground east of Antietam, Lieutenant Colonel David H. Strother, a Virginia Unionist, watched the hollow road fill up with the Confederate dead. "Among the prostrate mass I could easily distinguish the movements of those endeavoring to crawl away from the ground; hands waving as if calling for assistance, and others struggling as if in the agonies of death." For McClellan, this grim scene promised redemption. "The studied calmness of his manner scarcely concealed his excitement," Strother wrote, recording that McClellan exclaimed, "By George, this is a magnificent field, and if we win this fight it will cover all our errors and misfortunes forever!"[39]

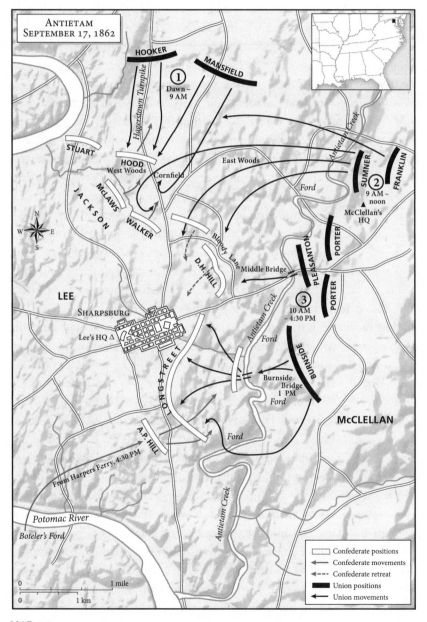

ANTIETAM
SEPTEMBER 17, 1862

MAP 4.3

But McClellan was even at this moment compounding his past errors with new ones. Rather than sending in his reserve units to follow up on the Union momentum on the left and center of Lee's line, McClellan held these reinforcements back, thus permitting the battle to shift to the south. There Burnside was trying to take the stone bridge crossing Antietam Creek; bluffs on its west bank gave the Confederates a strong vantage point for blunting the Union frontal assault, and it was not until one o'clock that the Union men finally got across the creek and rolled up the Confederate right. Again the Union dissipated its momentum, as Burnside waited two hours before resuming his advance at three o'clock. Just as Burnside's men seemed to have finally won the day, driving the Confederates back to the edge of Sharpsburg, A. P. Hill's reinforcements arrived at the scene from Harpers Ferry and counterattacked. This "single rebel division was able to transform Burnside's attack from a seemingly irresistible battle-winning—and possibly war-winning—stroke to a shattered mass of retreating soldiers," historian Ethan Rafuse has observed. Again McClellan chose not to send reserves, Porter's Fifth Corps, into battle, to Burnside's rescue. Burnside's men fell back and the battle ended in a tactical draw, with the two armies having each suffered roughly 12,000 casualties— and scarcely shifting the positions they had assumed at the battle's outset.[40]

Rather than beginning the withdrawal of his troops across the Potomac and back into Virginia under cover of darkness on the night of the seventeenth, Lee chose to stand his ground and dared McClellan to renew the contest. This was an act of bravado, a staking of the claim that the Confederates had not lost the battle. It showed Lee's "audacity as a commander, & his supreme confidence in his army," Edward Porter Alexander, Longstreet's artillery chief, would later note with pride. McClellan failed to risk a new attack, and the Confederates executed an orderly retreat, on their own terms, after dusk on the eighteenth. For Confederates, the denouement of the battle was a form of vindication. "The loss was very heavy on both sides," wrote John O. Casler of the Stonewall Brigade, "but neither army was defeated." When General Lee did fall back, "the Federal army was too much crippled to follow."[41]

McClellan's decision not to finish Lee off has been an enduring source of second-guessing. For his modern-day critics, this was the last in a train of mistakes—McClellan had once again overestimated the enemy's troop strength and failed to capitalize on the Federal manpower edge, opting for piecemeal consecutive attacks rather than bringing the full force of his army to bear at once; he failed to use his own reserves; and he failed to feel the "pulse of the battle," opting instead to watch the action unfold from a safe distance. Russell Weigley has summed up this indictment by insisting that McClellan's generalship at Antietam was "a model of how not to fight a battle." Other historians have softened this verdict, noting that McClellan was preoccupied on the eighteenth by concerns over the battered state of his army, and that his front-line commanders shared his hesitancy to risk an attack with exhausted troops. McClellan himself was sapped by anxiety and by a new bout of the recurring scourge of dysentery. They note, too, that McClellan planned to attack Lee on the nineteenth and was stymied by the Confederate retreat. But neither image—of a McClellan chastened by battle or of a general itching to strike another blow—accords with his own self-aggrandizing assessment of Antietam. In a September 20 letter to his wife, McClellan declared that his mission of turning back the rebel invasion was accomplished, irrevocably: "Our victory was complete & the disorganized rebel army has rapidly returned to Virginia—its dreams of 'invading Penna' dissipated for ever."[42]

Combat Motivation

Antietam was the first American battlefield to be photographed while still covered with unburied corpses. This forbidding work was done by Alexander Gardner, a virtuoso photographer affiliated with the New York studio of the renowned portrait photographer Mathew Brady. The two men were determined to produce a visual record of the war's great moments and personas. The task Gardner and his assistant James Gibson took on at Antietam was physically and emotionally harrowing. They had to move their cameras and darkroom wagon, as well as apparatus of tripods and tarps, glass plates and bottles of pungent chemicals, from site to site one step ahead of burial crews. The resulting images were exhibited at Brady's New York studio in October 1862, under the heading "The Dead of Antietam," and were rendered in the form of woodcuts for reproduction in periodicals such as *Harper's Weekly*. One reviewer hoped the photographs would elicit not only "terrible fascination" but also real sympathy, for the soldiers had died to teach the world a great truth: that there were "wrongs and shames more to be dreaded than death."[43]

The carnage of Antietam raises questions about soldier motivation: it is relatively easy to explain why men enlisted in the first flush of war, but what nerved them for battle once they had experienced the horrors of combat? Private David L. Thompson of Burnside's Ninth Corps published a postwar account of Antietam that sheds light on these issues. "The truth," he explained, is that "when bullets are whacking against tree-trunks and solid shot are cracking skulls like egg-shells, the consuming passion in the breast of the

The Dead of Antietam. Entitled "A contrast! Federal buried, rebel unburied, where they fell at the Battle of Antietam," this Alexander Gardner photograph shows a man contemplating a Union soldier's grave, next to which an unburied Confederate corpse is curled. (Library of Congress LC-DIG-ds-05166)

average man is to get out of the way. Between the physical fear of going forward and the moral fear of turning back, there is a predicament of exceptional awkwardness." Civil War soldiers' "moral fear of turning back" was rooted in a wide range of pressures and incentives that were shared by Northerners and Southerners: the need to prove one's manhood through bravery, the fear of dishonoring one's family or community through cowardice, the impulse to please and emulate one's superiors, the ambition to rise through the ranks, the desire to protect and defend one's brothers-in-arms. Political and ideological commitments were inseparable from these social and cultural ones. Soldiers had a moral dread of individual failure and an equally intense dread of collective, national failure.[44]

Firsthand accounts of Antietam elucidate how men coped with both physical and moral fear and steeled their nerves for "going forward." In the tense prelude to battle, soldiers articulated their sense of the profound stakes of their actions. Union General Alpheus Williams wrote his family that the night of September 16 was agonizing and surreal, as soldiers knew "that the morrow was to be great with the future fate of our country. So much responsibility, so much intense, future anxiety!" "If I lose my life, I shall be missed by but few," wrote another Union soldier in anticipation of Antietam—"but if the Union be lost, it will be missed by many." In a September 24 letter to the *Richmond Dispatch*, a Confederate artilleryman in Longstreet's corps conjured his feelings on the night of the sixteenth:

> As we lay down upon the field and look up into the great sky, we can but blush for the wickedness of man. Oh, how calmly and reproachfully do the bright stars move on their courses! It was a beautiful night, and no man who lay upon that field, and realized the deep tragedy which was to be enacted on the morrow, could be but sad and thoughtful. The past was present as well as the future, and we scanned the three together and tried to learn wisdom from the study. We thought of dear ones far away, and were glad that they knew not of the trying hour that the setting stars were bringing rapidly on.[45]

The raw excitement of combat itself could, paradoxically, provide relief from such solemn dread. Rufus Dawes of the 6th Wisconsin Volunteers remembered the fighting on the morning of the seventeenth, at the cornfield, this way:

> As we approached the edge of the corn, a long line of men in butternut and gray rose up from the ground. Simultaneously, the hostile battle lines opened a tremendous fire upon each other. Men, I can not say fell; they were knocked out of the ranks by dozens. But we jumped over the fence, and pushed on, loading, firing, and shouting as we advanced. There was, on the part of the men, great hysterical excitement, eagerness to go forward, and a reckless disregard of life, of every thing but victory. . . . "Forward" is the word. The men are loading and firing with demoniacal fury and shouting and laughing hysterically.

Dawes and his comrades were experiencing what modern historians have called "combat narcosis" or "fighting rage" or the "glaze of war": a physiological condition, brought on by the rush of adrenaline at a moment of extreme stress, causing an altered state of consciousness.[46]

Officers were expected to act as beacons in the storm, inspiring their men with conspicuous acts of bravery. Thompson remembered "seeing an officer riding diagonally across the field—a most inviting target—instinctively bending his head down over his horse's neck, as though he were riding through driving rain." Private Edgar Warfield of the 17th Virginia Infantry described his company's bravest lieutenant, Tom Perry, as "calm and serene" in battle, "as if waiting for the dinner horn to blow." In his postwar memoir, Confederate artilleryman Royall Figg recalled the stirring speech of Colonel Stephen D. Lee as he rallied his troops at Antietam. The words were "written in letters of fire on the tablet of memory." Lee had proclaimed, "You are boys, but you have this day been where only men dare to go! Some of your company have been killed; many have been wounded. But recollect that it is a soldier's fate to die!" The fearless Lee seemed to Figg "a very god of war, and his eyes flashed command, not entreaty." Wilson J. Barnett of the 53rd Pennsylvania Infantry wrote his parents an account of the stoic death of the "most gallant Officer," a Lieutenant Weaver, in his regiment. "Tell my Mother I died like a brave man" were Weaver's last words—a message intended as much for his men as his mother.[47]

Again and again, soldiers who sought to convey the lethality of this battle and the stoicism of the troops noted that corpses lay in perfect rows, where men had stood their ground. "Their battle lines can be distinctly traced by the heaps of dead . . . they did *not run*—they *melted away* in their places," Barnett wrote of the Confederates, adding, "They fought with a desperation worthy of a better cause." "We mowed the Rebbles like grass before the mashine," wrote Ephraim Brown of the 64th New York to his parents and siblings back home. "Such Death Grones was never heard." Many men who survived Antietam professed their inability to capture the experience in words. "The wildest flights of imagination can not possibly create a picture so horrible, but what it would be a parradice compared with that bloody field," New York cavalryman Charles M. Wyvell wrote a friend. "It beggars all attempt at discritpion." "I had before been near battles, at battles, in battles," wrote Alfred Lewis Castleman, surgeon of the 5th Wisconsin, in his diary on the evening of September 17. "But never till to-day was I *through* a battle. For miles around me, it has been one continuous battle field. Look where I would, and when I would, the battle was all around me." The suffering Castleman beheld left his mind reeling. "So terrible has been the day; so rapid and confused the events, that I find it impossible to separate them, so as to give, or even to form for myself any clear idea of what I have seen," he confessed, adding, "I hope it will be different when the mind has accustomed itself a little to thinking over the events and the horrors of the scene."[48]

The aftermath of battle often brought a physiological crash to earth and deep despondency, as the fears that were banished during combat came rushing back, and as soldiers confronted the scale of the slaughter. For General George Henry Gordon, a Union brigade commander, the "field of carnage" was a sight "too horrible to be real, and yet too real to forget." Nightfall on the seventeenth "filled the scene with mystic images and unreal shapes." "If phantoms from the spirit world could ever come forth to bewilder mortals," Gordon wrote, "sure never was there a time or place so seasonable." Eighteen-year-old corporal Samuel B. Mettler of the 16th Connecticut, who survived the brutal fighting of the cornfield, walked the battlefield the next day, finding its "piles of bullet-ridden corpses" too "horrid" to describe. Worse still were the hospitals, where he saw "heaps of arms and legs cut off." "Oh, such groaning—it is enough to make me cry to think of it," he wrote in a letter published in late September in the *Hartford Daily Times*. Some soldiers experienced the acute reaction to extreme stress now identified as post-traumatic stress disorder. A colonel in the 20th Massachusetts "went to pieces after Antietam," historian James McPherson relates. He rode away from camp the day after the battle, without informing his comrades, and was found later, filthy, sick, penniless, "just like a little child wandering away from home."[49]

The aftermath of battle was also a time for the rank and file to second-guess command decisions. Many Union soldiers at Antietam decried McClellan's decision not to renew his attack and to let Lee retreat. The Union officer Josiah Marshall Favill observed in his diary that "Lee's army ought not to have got away so easily, but should have been pushed to the wall, and fought without mercy every day. From experience, however, we know that General McClellan is not equal to great occasions, and therefore it is useless to expect brilliant results while he is in command." Alfred Castleman was even more harsh, writing on September 19 that "the feeling against Gen. McClellan today is no longer expressed in muttered disaffection, but in loud and angry execration. The soldiers cannot be reconciled to their disappointment." McClellan, Castleman regretfully concluded, was "nothing short of an imbecile, a coward, or a traitor."[50]

For Confederates, the key source of recrimination about the campaign was the high toll straggling had taken on Lee's army. The hard fighting of the summer and the move into enemy territory prompted thousands of Confederates to desert, and Lee's retreat left many stragglers, and many wounded men, at the mercy of the Federal army. As Lee himself explained in his report on Antietam, "The arduous service in which our troops had been engaged, their great privations of rest and food, and the long marches, without shoes, over mountain roads, had greatly reduced our ranks before the action began. These causes had compelled thousands of brave men to absent themselves, and many more had done so from unworthy motives." Some Confederates regarded the shift in strategy, from defense to offense, as simply too costly, and they vowed never to cross the Potomac again. For Lee's men, the myth of a Confederate Maryland was wearing thin.[51]

Northern soldiers on the Antietam campaign maintained their self-image as liberators of the benighted South; indeed, that self-image was renewed by their experience of moving north from the battlefields of Virginia into Maryland. "We found the villages in Maryland to be neat, and the tall church spire looks better than the jail we found in every Virginia town," recorded New Englander Elisha Hunt Rhodes in his journal. Oliver Willcox Norton, a Pennsylvania schoolteacher turned infantryman, contrasted the "swamps of the Chickahominy" with the productive villages and farms of Maryland; he considered Maryland to be a southern place, but a relatively "civilized country" compared to Virginia. "Maryland will yet be free and then she will be a noble state," he wrote his sister in a September 1862 letter on the Antietam campaign. Moreover, the condition of the Confederate army itself—"ragged and filthy, sick, hungry, and in all ways miserable," as the Union surgeon Thomas T. Ellis confided to his diary—made for a sharp contrast with the well-provisioned Union army. That army represented for him the "rich and luxurious landscape" of the North, and its "super abundant plenty."[52]

For the Northern press, Antietam offered another opportunity to indict the rebel leadership class for its manipulation of the masses. Confederate leaders had falsely led the rank and file to expect a warm reception in Maryland, despite warnings from "every sane man" in the state that it would be otherwise. Those who led the ill-fated invasion should "now hang their heads with shame at this withering rebuke from the living victims of their deception, whilst five thousand of their dupes cry from the graves they have found on Maryland soil, and ten thousand more are groaning their maledictions from beds of pain and suffering," the *Daily National Intelligencer* of Washington, D.C., reported in a September 29 article entitled "Southern Views of the Late Battle." In an article on the Army of the Potomac in the fall of 1862, the *Wheeling Intelligencer* invoked the desperate straits of Southern whites—the "starving condition of Southern women and children" and the "squads of men . . . driven at the point of the bayonet into the army." The Army of the Potomac, it predicted, would "march to the deliverance of a great and good people in the South, from the power and oppression of their greatest enemies—themselves, and their own sins."[53]

Northern soldiers offered their own indictments. "We have a desperate foe to contend with who comes at us in taters and rags . . . and fight[s] 'like Devils from Hell,'" wrote infantryman George Howard in an October 1862 letter from Maryland to his family back in Vermont. Howard told his kin about an encounter with a rebel prisoner, a poor private, who "expressed deep regret that the country was in such a state of war" and "stoutly laid the cause of the present state of affairs . . . to the 'little State of South Carolina' Seceding and dragging the other states along with it against the wishes of the people." The rebel "did not expect to be treated so kindly by the yankies," Howard observed, adding, "If the Soldiers only knew how well they would be treated here they would fast give themselves up without fighting but they are grossly decieved by their leaders." In keeping with the "exemplary suffering" trope in Union accounts of the war, Howard believed that the Confederates' mendacity and treachery literally disfigured them. The Confederate dead bore "on their faces a fearful repulsive Hideous and demoniac grin," while the Federal dead "universally wear a pleasant smile as they fall in defence of our country." Union soldiers looked for signs of redemption in the desolation of the battlefield. Lieutenant Samuel Fiske of the 14th Connecticut Infantry sent a letter to a newspaper back home, the *Springfield* (Mass.) *Republican*, in the aftermath of Antietam. He described a setting "forlorn and desolate," strewn with the mangled and putrefying corpses of men and horses. "And yet I saw over all this scene of devastation and horror, yesternight," he wrote, "one of the loveliest double rainbows that ever mortal eyes looked upon. . . . I took it as an emblem of success to our blessed Union cause, that out of the horrors of battle shall arise the blessings of a more secure freedom and stable system of liberal government."[54]

Dissenters from the deluded-masses theory, who saw in the carnage at Antietam evidence of the deep commitment of the Southern rank and file to slavery and Southern independence, lamented the sway of deliverance rhetoric over Northern public opinion. "We are not yet cured of our folly in believing what deserters and spies tell us," namely that "there are men in the rebel army who have no love for the cause," observed a correspondent for the *Christian Recorder* as he visited hospitals in and around Sharpsburg. He offered his own accounts of conversations with wounded rebel prisoners. He found them to be a "poor, miserable-looking set," but he did "not find one forced into the rebel service." "They generally spoke of the Abolitionists wanting to free the negroes as the cause of the war. Some said John Brown began the war, and they appear to be fighting him yet," the correspondent noted soberly. In his view, the rebel army was "not in the least danger of breaking up." "There is *perfect discipline*" in its ranks, he found, "and the most resolute determination" and "bitter hatred . . . real and intense."[55]

The fact that Lee's army slipped away from McClellan's grasp threatened to drain the meaning from the Union victory at Antietam. The time had come for Lincoln to act. On September 17, the very day of the battle, the *Pittsburgh Gazette* printed a prescient article entitled "The Crisis Hour," which captured the stakes of the moment. "President Lincoln holds the thunderbolt in his hand that could crush slavery forever. But he hesitates— he refuses. The Lord commands him, 'Let my people go, that they may serve me' but he turns a deaf ear; and so, war and desolation roll their awful tide over the land." The article's author, "Milonius," offered this prescription for victory: "The President has but to speak the words of 'Universal Freedom'—when those words, with Talismanic power, would immediately become the nation's battle-cry, ringing over all the hills and through the valleys of the North, and soon reaching the cotton-fields and pine glades of the South, to be hailed by the weary bondman with shouts of joy and with a mighty uprising for Deliverance." Little did Milonius know that Lincoln was about to hurl the thunderbolt.[56]

PART II

Emancipation

5

Countdown to Jubilee

LINCOLN'S HUNDRED DAYS

ANTIETAM WAS THE victory Lincoln had waited for, and on September 22, 1862, in keeping with the secret pledge he had made to his cabinet, he promulgated his preliminary Emancipation Proclamation. The document reiterated the standing offer to loyal slaveholders: if they undertook their own voluntary measures to gradually dismantle slavery, Lincoln would urge Congress to provide them with pecuniary compensation for their lost property and federal aid for colonization of the freedpeople. It reprised the major provisions of the Second Confiscation Act, underscoring that U.S. military forces would no more act as slave catchers: all slaves of rebels who came to Union lines or under Union occupation would be "deemed captives of war . . . forever free of their servitude and not again held as slaves." But Lincoln's edict also went beyond the earlier colonization proposals and Confiscation Acts. Levied under his presidential war powers, the preliminary proclamation was a warning: as of January 1, 1863, Lincoln told disloyal Southerners, "all persons held as slaves within any state, or designated part of a state, the people whereof shall then be in rebellion against the United States shall be then, thenceforward, and forever free." Implicitly acknowledging both the self-emancipation of fugitive slaves and the army's role as the beacon for flight, the proclamation promised that the federal government and military would "recognize and maintain the freedom of such persons" and "not repress . . . any efforts they may make for their actual freedom." While the two Confiscation Acts had targeted individual slave owners (persons who used slaves for military purposes, in the first act, and persons engaged in rebellion, in the second), the preliminary proclamation acknowledged the scope of the rebellion and applied broadly to the Confederacy.[1]

The hundred days between September 22, 1862, and January 1, 1863, were a period of intense uncertainty in the Union, as the Federal armies met with stalemate in the west at Vicksburg and a crushing defeat in the east at Fredericksburg, and the Republican party lost ground in the fall state elections. Although defenders of emancipation pressed the case that it would have broad benefits for the South, as the year came to an end Lincoln seemed to waver in his commitment to black freedom. Would the embattled president have the will to follow through on his promise of deliverance?

This Righteous Decree

The preliminary proclamation touched off an intense debate in the North, the contours of which Lincoln anticipated and tried to shape. On September 13, the very same day that Corporal Mitchell found Lee's lost battle plans in Maryland, Lincoln met with a delegation of Chicago ministers, who called on him at the White House to present him with a memorial pleading the cause of general emancipation. Americans could not "expect national deliverance," they warned, until the nation "heard the voice that sounded above the wail of desolated Egypt—'Let my people go.'"[2] Lincoln's response to their memorial—published by the *Chicago Tribune* on September 23, the day after he issued the proclamation—is a remarkable window into both his tactical savvy and his personal development. Lincoln began by telling the delegation that he had been pondering the question of emancipation for months and that it was his "earnest desire to know the will of Providence in this matter. *And if I can learn what it is I will do it!*" But failing a direct revelation, Lincoln continued, he had to dispassionately assess the "merits of the case." Lincoln then posed a series of questions to the Chicagoans:

> What *good* would a proclamation of emancipation from me do, especially as we are now situated? I do not want to issue a document that the whole world will see must necessarily be inoperative, like the Pope's bull against the comet! Would *my word* free the slaves, when I cannot even enforce the Constitution in the rebel States? . . . And what reason is there to think it would have any greater effect upon the slaves than the late law of Congress, which I approved, and which offers protection and freedom to the slaves of rebel masters who come within our lines?

His own answers, which he proceeded to spell out, were meant to position Lincoln as a pragmatist, not an ideologue—and thereby to neutralize his critics on both the left and the right. The issues at play, Lincoln began, were not constitutional but "practical": as commander in chief of the army, Lincoln had the right to "take any measure which may best subdue the enemy." While the Chicagoans insisted that emancipation would please God, thrill the Northern people and the "whole civilized world," and spell Confederate defeat, Lincoln offered a more measured assessment, selectively affirming the logic of certain pro-emancipation claims. Yes, Lincoln conceded, emancipation would "help us in Europe . . . and help *somewhat* at the North." Yes, it would "weaken the rebels by drawing off their laborers, which is of great importance." No, it would not alienate as many border state loyalists as it might have a "year ago, or as six months ago," as "every day increases their Union feeling." The 50,000 border state Unionists in the Federal army were "getting their pride enlisted," Lincoln noted with satisfaction," and "want to beat the rebels."[3]

Gratified that Lincoln had met them halfway, the Chicagoans responded by invoking the ground they shared with moderate Republicans: their commitment to constitutional government and their antipathy to the Slave Power, "that aristocratic and despotic element among our free institutions . . . that had nearly wrought our ruin." Lincoln assured the delegates that the subject of slavery was on his mind "day and night, more than any other," and pledged to hold the matter of general emancipation "under advisement."[4]

Lincoln's careful defense of emancipation remained a counterpoint to the ecstatic reception the preliminary proclamation found among committed abolitionists and the venomous fury it elicited from his political opponents. Abolitionist and Radical Republican newspapers tried to outdo each other in invoking the surpassing significance of Lincoln's September 22 decree. "So splendid a vision has hardly shone upon the world since the day of the Messiah," proclaimed the *Chicago Tribune* in an article reprinted in the *Liberator*. "From the date of this Proclamation begins the history of the republic as our fathers designed to have it—the home of freedom." "God bless Abraham Lincoln," declared the *New York Tribune*. "It is the beginning of the end of the rebellion; the beginning of the new life of the nation." Henry McNeal Turner, writing for the AME *Christian Recorder*, praised Lincoln's pragmatism and his courage. Lincoln had "proved himself above the fledges of partyism, by killing Gen. Fremont on the one side, and Gen. McClellan on the other" and then issuing his emancipation edict "over which the triumphant notes of heaven rolled . . . [and] reverberated in overpowering rapture." Turner had come to regard Lincoln's support for colonization as a "strategic move" to prepare the way for emancipation, not as a looming threat. Frances

Ellen Watkins Harper of Baltimore, a leading free black writer, orator, journalist, and Underground Railroad agent, agreed that Lincoln's days of "dabbling with colonization" were numbered and anticipated that blacks could persuade him that they had a "birth-right on the soil" and a key role to play in rebuilding the country and repairing the scourges of war. The proclamation, so its supporters claimed, nullified Confederate hopes for foreign intervention, as it "placed the North on the side of justice and civilization, and the rebels on the side of robbery and barbarism," to quote *Douglass' Monthly*. Moreover, abolitionists regarded the proclamation as irrevocable, claiming that Lincoln's very slowness to issue it was a kind of guarantee against its retraction. His word had "gone out over the country and the world, giving joy and gladness to the friends of freedom and progress," Frederick Douglass explained, and to retract it would only increase the rebels' pride and "sense of power." "Abraham Lincoln," Douglass vouchsafed, "will take no step backward." While abolitionists were unenthusiastic about the three-month probation period, they minimized its importance; it was exceedingly unlikely, they reckoned, that Confederates would lay down their arms before the January deadline and thereby avoid emancipation. Lincoln's decree pledged him to bring the hammer down on slavery and hasten the rebellion's doom.[5]

Many Northern soldiers agreed with such assessments. "I say *strike* the *deadly blow*," wrote a Union soldier to his sister from Maryland in October 1862. "There is one thing I think is going to help finish this war and that is the *Presidents proclamation* May God speed the right," he continued. Lieutenant John Quincy Adams Campbell of the 5th Iowa looked forward to January 1, 1863, as "the day of our nation's second birth." Alluding to Confederate vice president Alexander Stephens's well-known March 1861 speech declaring slavery the "corner-stone" of the Confederacy, Campbell added, "The President has placed the Union pry under the corner stone of the Confederacy and the structure *will* fall." Corps commander George Henry Gordon of the Army of the Potomac, in another such allusion, observed that as the South had established its government on the "corner-stone of slavery," it was time for the Union to establish itself "on the corner-stone of freedom." He thought his men would find in Lincoln's proclamation a "new inspiration" for "another advance into Virginia."[6]

Other soldiers, while supportive of Lincoln, were not sanguine about the prospects that the proclamation would hasten victory. Referring to predictions that the proclamation would break the rebels' spirit, Oliver Willcox Norton of the 83rd Pennsylvania wrote his sister on September 19, 1862, "Pleasant prospect, but I 'don't see it.' I approve of the proclamation, but I don't think it is going to scare the South into submission." The coming winter, Norton feared, would witness unprecedented bloodletting, and the war would grind on. "Seward was right—the 'irrepressible conflict' will continue till freedom or slavery rules the nation."[7]

The idea that the proclamation would prolong the war was one of many charges laid at the president's table by his Northern critics. Some moderate Democrats and conservative Republicans reacted with restraint to the proclamation, emphasizing that the right to own slaves was to be respected in the loyal states and in rebel states that returned to their allegiance by January 1, and that Lincoln was still committed to the idea of compensating loyal masters who chose to free their slaves. The *New York Herald* offered a steady stream of articles in the fall of 1862 that pushed a conservative vision of Southern deliverance. In that narrative, the rigorous pursuit of military victories would work together with Lincoln's offer of exemption for loyal slaveholders and with the Confederates' own increasing exhaustion and despair to effect the return, before the looming deadline of January 1, 1863, of the rebel states to the Union. "A sober second thought will come over the spirit of the conservative portion of the South, and bring them to their senses in time to avail themselves of the amnesty promised in Mr. Lincoln's emancipation proclamation," the *Herald* promised.[8]

With the fall elections pending, most Democrats felt the time was ripe to exact electoral revenge on Lincoln's party and its radical wire-pullers. Some ridiculed the proclamation, noting that it applied only to those areas under rebellion, where Lincoln had no power to enforce it. Most assailed it as unconstitutional and even criminal. The *Springfield Register* of Lincoln's home state claimed that the proclamation heralded "the permanent disruption of the republic, a permanent standing army, endless civil war, the Africanization of the Southern states, anarchy in the North, to end in despotism." Other newspapers added to this litany the specters of race competition, as "hundreds of thousands of negroes" would flood North to "compete with the white laboring man"; race war, as Lincoln's proclamation would spark "servile insurrection"; and mass disaffection in the Union army, where soldiers had come to see Lincoln as "Military Dictator" and to favor a "change of dynasty." Northern voters, the *Louisville Journal* urged, must "manifest their righteous detestation by returning to Congress none but the avowed and zealous adversaries of this measure."[9]

In the eyes of his Democratic critics, Lincoln's emancipation edict was inseparable from his September 24, 1862, proclamation suspending the writ of habeas corpus nationwide. The imposition of martial law had been a supercharged political issue since the first months of war. While Lincoln had revoked Frémont's August 1861 emancipation order, he upheld the use of courts-martial to try disloyal civilians, and Federal authorities in Missouri zealously used military commissions to target rebel saboteurs, such as those who burned bridges and tore up railroad tracks to impede the army's progress. Lincoln subsequently extended the suspension of the writ to certain other trouble spots in the South, but the real precedent for his sweeping September 1862 habeas proclamation was the War Department's August 8, 1862, order authorizing military arrest, imprisonment, and trial for "any person or persons who may be engaged, by act, speech, or writing, in discouraging volunteer enlistments, or in any way giving aid and comfort to the enemy." The order was intended explicitly to enforce the July 17, 1862, Militia Act, which required states to register and if necessary draft militiamen who could then be called up by the federal government to serve for up to nine months. As historian Mark Neely has explained, a wave of arrests of civilians took place pursuant to the August 8 order, targeting men who sought to evade the militia draft by leaving their states or the country. Lincoln's late September measure affirmed a system for restricting civil liberties that was already in place and that predated his emancipation edict. But his Democratic critics thought the two September measures to be twin evils, the crowning proof of Lincoln's radical disregard for the Constitution: the recent proclamations, McClellan wrote from Sharpsburg to a prominent New York Democrat on September 26, 1862, "at one stroke of the pen" changed "our free institutions into a despotism."[10]

Scholars canvassing these reactions to Lincoln's preliminary Emancipation Proclamation have noted that its actual effects were more subtle than those its champions and detractors predicted for it. There was indeed a great deal of discontented grumbling among those soldiers who felt that they had not signed up to "free the negroes," but "in the end, most soldiers kept their personal feelings subordinate to their military duty," historian Louis Masur has noted. Union soldiers who lacked sympathy for enslaved people but loathed slaveholders could accept emancipation as a punitive measure, on the pragmatic grounds of military necessity.[11]

Where foreign recognition is concerned, the proclamation was less crucial than the military victory at Antietam in shaping British policy. British advocates of mediation had gained ground in August and September by arguing that they had a humanitarian duty to staunch the carnage in America. They played up the idea that the South was the victim in the struggle, invoking Northern abuses such as Butler's "Woman Order," and claimed that the permanent separation of North and South would set slavery on a path to extinction, as the Confederacy would eventually have to yield to international pressure and abolish the institution. Finally, advocates of a British-brokered armistice pointed to the suffering the cotton embargo had brought to the English people, resulting in a rising number of textile workers who were unemployed and thrown onto poor relief.[12]

Word of the Union victory at Antietam did not reach Britain until the end of September, and word of Lincoln's proclamation did not cross the Atlantic until early October. The preliminary proclamation was controversial. On the one hand, British abolitionists were disappointed and perplexed that it did not apply to the loyal slaveholding border states; on the other, the conservative British press, led by the *London Times*, echoed American conservatives in charging that the proclamation was an inflammatory document inciting servile war. Lord John Russell and William E. Gladstone condemned it as "vindictive"; Russell redoubled his efforts to forge a pro-mediation international alliance with France and Russia. Anti-intervention forces countered by pointing to the pervasive antislavery sentiment of the British masses, who were rightly proud of Britain's role in world abolition; to the resilience of the British economy, which was offsetting the effects of "King Cotton diplomacy" through privately funded poor relief, the promotion of new trades and skills, and a turn to India, Egypt, and Brazil as alternative sources for cotton; and to the political risk of bringing on a war with the North if Britain recognized and favored the South. But more than anything, it was the failure of Lee's invasion that gave anti-intervention forces the upper hand in British politics. Lord Palmerston and many in his cabinet and Parliament felt that the Union victory at Antietam "revealed a serious weakness in the Confederate army." To the intense relief of Northerners, the mediation gambit went down to defeat in November 1862. Confederates refused to accept this defeat as final and would continue to press for great-power intervention, especially from France, which, so it was hoped, might bestow foreign recognition in exchange for Confederate acquiescence in France's imperial incursions in Mexico. As part of his "Grand Design" to restore monarchy, spread Catholicism, and promote French commercial interests in the Americas, French emperor Napoleon III deposed the Mexican president Benito Juarez and established a puppet regime under the Hapsburg archduke Maximilian. In a bid to curry favor with the French, Confederate diplomats were "instructed to repudiate the South's earlier imperialist ambitions for a tropical empire in Latin America," historian Don Doyle has explained. But ultimately, Napoleon III declined to recognize the Confederates unilaterally, without British support.[13]

On the question of how the preliminary proclamation affected the fall elections of 1862, the record is ambiguous. Republicans did suffer setbacks, as Democrats picked up more than two dozen seats in Congress, with notable gains in the key swing states of Pennsylvania, Illinois, and Indiana and victories in the gubernatorial races in New York and New Jersey. New York's newly elected governor, Horatio Seymour, saw these triumphs as proof that the Democratic party—and it alone—could deliver the white Southern masses from the twin despotisms of abolitionism and secessionism. The Democratic resurgence "teaches the loyal men at the South," he argued in an October 1862 speech, "that the conservative men at the North are able to put down fanatical agitators and meddling disturbers without the help of a single vote from a Southern State."[14]

The election results caused considerable handwringing by the Republican leadership and press. Illinois senator Orville H. Browning told Lincoln frankly that his "disastrous" emancipation and habeas corpus proclamations had "revived old party issues" and given the resurgent Democrats "a rallying cry." Some tried to explain away defeats by noting that more Republicans than Democrats had gone off to war and were therefore not able to vote; others noted that the preliminary proclamation had been an asset in certain races, as in Michigan and Massachusetts, and surmised that what the election results really meant was that voters were impatient with the old measures for winning the war and eager to try a new way. All Republicans could take some comfort from the knowledge that their party still commanded sizable majorities in Congress and controlled most state houses and legislatures.[15]

As for the Democratic charge that emancipation would bring race war and race competition, Lincoln's supporters countered such dystopian scenarios by further developing the argument that emancipation would benefit whites economically, politically, and morally. On September 24, two days after he issued the proclamation, a jubilant crowd gathered in Washington, D.C., to serenade Lincoln at the White House. After Lincoln briefly addressed them, offering praise for the soldiers in the field, the crowd processed to the home of Treasury Secretary Salmon Chase, where they heard a rousing speech from Kentucky Unionist Cassius Clay. Clay hailed the preliminary proclamation as a victory for "down-trodden humanity," predicting "it would find its way all over the South, everywhere liberating all the oppressed of both races in this country." Lincoln's secretary John Hay, in one of his anonymous dispatches to the *Missouri Republican*, took approving note of Clay's speech and of how it resonated, more than any other defense of emancipation, with the throng of well-wishers. "The emancipation of the non-slaveholding white population of the South, upon which [Clay] most specially dwelt as the result of the President's action, seemed to be received with more cordial and intelligent assent than any other proposition advanced," Hay observed. That night, Hay added in his diary, the Republican politicians and generals who gathered inside Chase's house all "breathed freer," feeling that abolitionism had earned new legitimacy. The proclamation "had freed them as well as the slaves."[16]

In the ensuing months, emancipation's defenders kept up this drumbeat. The white Southern masses had been "misled by artful demagogues" into believing that the North was waging a "fiendish war of subjugation and rapine," Horace Greeley maintained in an October 1862 *Continental Monthly* article entitled "Southern Hate of the North." To dispel such "egregious falsehoods," Northerners had to embrace emancipation: "Let Slavery disappear, and all incitement to alienation or bitterness between the North and the South will have vanished." North and South were economically the "natural complement of each other," and the demise of slavery would bring an increase in the South's population, industry, and wealth. "The South will soon realize that the death of Slavery has awakened her to a new and nobler life—that what she at first regarded as a great calamity and downfall, was in truth her beneficent renovation." The *New York Post*, edited by acclaimed poet and antislavery reformer William Cullen Bryant, made a similar plea for emancipation. "One thing alone distinguishes us; one thing alone disturbs our complete peace and harmony; one thing alone nullifies the ties of common blood, common language, common pursuits, common religious faith, and common destinies; and that thing is slavery," the editorial intoned. The South could neither be subjugated by force of arms nor be "coaxed into a superficial compromise": only Lincoln's proclamation, a "high and sovereign act of both military and civil necessity," could once again make the country "homogenous, consistent, peaceful, noble and fruitful."[17]

Ralph Waldo Emerson's defense of the proclamation, published in the *Atlantic Monthly* in November 1862, reiterated the case that freedom would remove the danger of slave rebellion and actually "relieve" whites of black "opposition": "The President by this act has pardoned all the slaves in America; they will no more fight against us; and it relieves our race once for all of its crimes and false position." An editorial in the antislavery *Pacific Appeal*, entitled "Prejudice," made a similar point. "To some Northern men Emancipation is a ghost, that continually haunts them with more terror than the ravages of the marauding rebels and the slaughter of our soldiers," the writer noted. But the truth was that "the white American would be benefitted, in the event of carrying out the principles involved in the President's Emancipation

Proclamation, by having no more competition with slave labor." William Furness, a prominent antislavery minister in Philadelphia, hailed the proclamation as a "message of hope" to Southern slaves and of moral liberation for whites:

> I think now of my own race, to whom it is an equal announcement of freedom, freedom from an oppression which did not scar our bodies, but which stamped its burning impress upon our souls, which did not forbid us to be educated, but which made it hazardous to use the liberty of thought and speech, without which education is worthless. Now we may hope that there will come an end to all the miserable confusion of thought, to all the absurd and inhuman talk which have for long years distracted and wearied us.[18]

These were familiar abolitionist arguments: slavery and not abolition was the cause of racial violence; the presence of slavery debased white morality and degraded white laborers; free labor would generate prosperity and civilization. But in the crucible of war, they took on new currency and legitimacy. Nothing illustrates this better in the weeks after Lincoln promulgated his preliminary proclamation than the pledge of support the president received on September 24, 1862, from a meeting of the North's "loyal governors" in Altoona, Pennsylvania. Eleven state executives, including the Radical Republican John Andrew of Massachusetts, centrist Andrew Curtin of Pennsylvania, and Francis Pierpont, representing the "Restored" government of Virginia, signed a statement that hailed "with heartfelt gratitude and encouraged hope the proclamation of the President, issued on the twenty-second instant, declaring emancipated from their bondage all persons held to service or labor as slaves in the rebel States, whose rebellion shall last until the first day of January now next ensuing." Invoking white Southern deliverance, the governors upheld "the duty of the government to liberate the minds of all men living therein by appropriate proclamations and assurances of protection, in order that all who are capable, intellectually and morally, of loyalty and obedience, may not be forced into treason as the unwilling tools of rebellious traitors."[19]

Familiar antislavery arguments also had tangible new effects. Lincoln's proclamation, James Oakes has observed, was quickly translated into military orders promulgated to the Union army, commanding them to comply with the Second Confiscation Act and to consider any slave who made it to Union lines to be permanently free. As a practical matter, this meant that fugitive slaves were to be paid wages. With generals such as Grant and Sherman implementing wage labor among "contrabands" in the Mississippi Valley, the preliminary proclamation was already hastening the social and economic transformation of the South.[20]

Confederates predictably condemned the proclamation as an open call to slave rebellion. "It is certainly full time that the severest retaliatory measures should be taken," Emma Holmes noted in her diary on October 1, 1862, while reporting with approbation that the Confederate Congress had just passed a resolution endorsing any such countermeasures Jefferson Davis judged necessary. The rebel Congress recommended that any Yankee officer who "shall incite slaves to rebellion, or pretend to give them freedom" by "abducting" them or "inducing them to abscond" should be, if captured, summarily executed. And it declared, "This conflict has ceased to be a war as recognized among civilized nations, but on the part of the enemy has become an invasion of an organized horde of murderers and plunderers, breathing hatred and revenge for the numerous defeats sustained on legitimate battlefields." Invoking

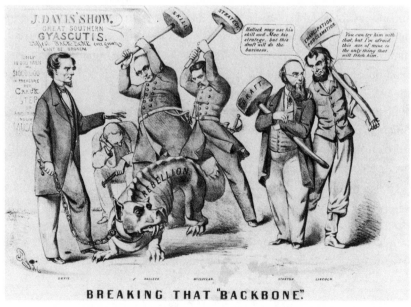

Emancipation as a Military Necessity. "You can try him with that, but I'm afraid this axe of mine is the only thing that will fetch him": In this Currier & Ives print of 1862, Lincoln tells his generals and secretary of war that only his weapon (an axe labeled "Emancipation Proclamation") can break the backbone of the rebellion (represented here by the fanged, dog-like beast on Jefferson Davis's leash). (Library of Congress LC-USZ62-42560)

the Haitian Revolution, the *Staunton Spectator* charged that Lincoln sought to "enact the bloody scene of St. Domingo through the limits of the Southern Confederacy." Lincoln had exceeded even "Beast" Butler in his villainy: "Butler is a saint compared to his master. In addition to all that Butler authorized, Lincoln adds butchery—even the butchery of babes! . . . 'Murderer' is a term of honor compared to Lincoln's crime," the *Spectator* seethed.[21]

The astute Confederate diarist John B. Jones offered a more ambivalent take on what the proclamation, together with the Democratic party's success in the Northern elections, meant for Confederate morale. He took heart from the Democrats' strident critiques of Lincoln's policies, and was at times swept up in the hope that the Yankees were losing the will to fight; Democratic rhetoric could serve to buttress the Confederate case that Lincoln was a tyrant and headed for a fall. But Jones also worried that if Southerners placed too much stock in the idea of a Democratic resurgence and negotiated peace, they would lose their own will to fight for the cause of independence. Jones was wary of moderate newspapers such as the *New York Herald* that were "*tempting* [Confederates] to return to the Union, by promises of *protecting slavery*." If Lincoln was toppled, Northern Democrats would wage a war "for the restoration of the Union . . . according to the rules of civilized nations," and a "very formidable party in favor of RECONSTRUCTION might spring up in the South," Jones fretted. The Confederates needed abolition radicalism to bind them together. "The excesses of the Republicans compel our people to be almost a unit. This is all the better for us," Jones concluded in November 1862.[22]

Confederate commanders in the field seized upon the preliminary Emancipation Proclamation to stiffen Confederate resolve. In Kentucky with Braxton Bragg's army, Confederate general Simon Bolivar Buckner issued his own proclamation, declaring that Lincoln's policy would bring race war to the Bluegrass State. "If the will of the abolition autocrat can be fulfilled, he will make his people a nation of bandits, and will light the incendiary torch around every Kentucky fireside," Buckner intoned ominously. Lincoln's extremism must inspire Southern solidarity: now was the time for border state slave owners to rally to the Confederate standard.[23]

"Liberating" Kentucky

In a drama that had been unfolding since late August in the west, Confederates launched a counteroffensive in the fall of 1862 to regain control of Middle Tennessee and open a pathway into Kentucky. This phase of fighting in the west pitted the cantankerous Braxton Bragg, a stern disciplinarian who assumed control over the Army of Mississippi from the ailing Beauregard, against Don Carlos Buell, commanding the Federal Army of the Ohio. Leaving Generals Sterling Price and Earl Van Dorn in Mississippi to keep an eye on Union forces under U. S. Grant, Bragg devised a plan whereby his own army of 31,000 men would advance north from Chattanooga and Edmund Kirby Smith's Confederate force of 10,000 would move north in a second, parallel column from Knoxville; they would converge on Buell in Kentucky and, after finishing him off, go and hunt down Grant. Each Confederate general had some initial success: Kirby Smith's force occupied the state capital, Frankfort, on September 3 (the pro-Union government had fled to Louisville), and Bragg's force captured a Union garrison at Munfordville two weeks later. Buell, meanwhile, moved out from garrisoned Nashville north to Louisville, Kentucky, beating Bragg there and securing the defenses of the city. Bragg chose not to pursue Buell to Louisville; instead the Confederates veered eastward to Bardstown, where they could reprovision. Under pressure to take the tactical offensive, Buell moved out to confront the Confederates, and the armies collided at Perryville, roughly fifty miles southeast of Louisville, on October 8. The Federals should have had a great advantage, as Bragg had not yet been able to unite with Edmund Kirby Smith's army and was greatly outnumbered. But a bizarre atmospheric phenomenon called an "acoustic shadow"—whereby layers of air dampen sound—kept two of Buell's three corps in the dark as to the battle's disposition, and out of the action. The ensuing battle—a Confederate assault and Federal counterattack—was vicious, with the "dead, dying, and wounded of both armies . . . blended in inextricable confusion," as Confederate private Samuel R. Watkins put it. The battle was poorly handled by both commanders, with the Confederates winning a tactical victory in the casualty count (roughly 3,200 to the Federals' 4,200) but experiencing a strategic loss, as their foothold in Kentucky was untenable and they were forced to fall back into Tennessee. On the Union side, Buell's failure to chase down Bragg's army as it withdrew incurred the ire of Lincoln and resulted in Buell's replacement, on October 30, by William S. Rosecrans.[24]

Bragg worked on the same premises as Lee: that the citizens of the loyal slave states yearned to throw off the yoke of their Yankee occupiers and that the border slave states were a "natural" part of the Confederacy. On September 26, in Bardstown, Kentucky, Bragg had issued a proclamation "to the People of the Northwest," staking the claim that his was an army of liberation, not conquest. The Confederate government was "waging this war

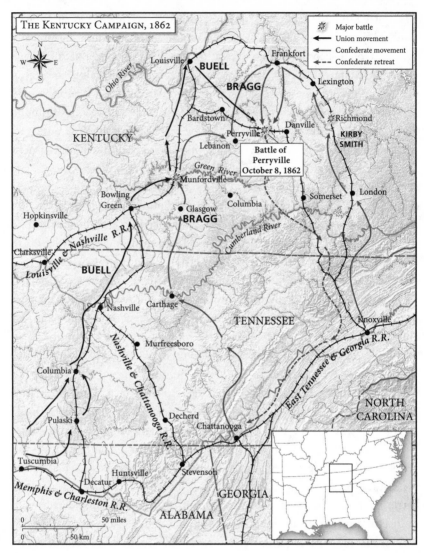

THE KENTUCKY CAMPAIGN, 1862

Major battle
Union movement
Confederate movement
Confederate retreat

Louisville BUELL Frankfort

BRAGG Lexington

Richmond

Bardstown Danville

KENTUCKY Perryville

Lebanon **Battle of**
Perryville
October 8, 1862 KIRBY
SMITH

Green River
Munfordville

Bowling Somerset London
Green Glasgow Columbia

Hopkinsville **BRAGG**

Cumberland River

Clarksville Nashville R.R.

Louisville **BUELL**

Nashville Carthage

Murfreesboro TENNESSEE Knoxville

Columbia East Tennessee & Georgia R.R.

Pulaski Decherd NORTH
CAROLINA

Chattanooga

Tuscumbia

Decatur Huntsville Stevenson

Memphis & Charleston R.R. GEORGIA

ALABAMA

0   50 miles

0   50 km

MAP 5.1

solely for self-defense," he explained, against an "enemy who pursues us with an implacable and apparently aimless hostility." Bragg had been reassured by Kentuckian John Hunt Morgan, whose cavalry had successfully raided Buell's supply lines, that thousands of Kentuckians would flock to the Confederate standard. But like Lee had been in Maryland, Bragg was to be disappointed by the response of civilians in Kentucky, who turned deaf ears to Bragg's recruitment pleas; he blamed this indifference to duty on their "love of ease and fear of pecuniary loss." Historians have pointed up Bragg's many other miscalculations and missteps in the campaign: he failed to gain accurate information about Buell's intentions; failed to coordinate with Kirby Smith and to concentrate his forces with alacrity; failed to secure reliable supply and communications lines; and failed to control refractory generals such as Lieutenant General Leonidas Polk, who on two critical occasions during the campaign disregarded Bragg's orders. Bragg's detractors also note that he took a costly detour on October 2 to attend the inauguration in Frankfort, Kentucky, of the so-called governor of the shadow Confederate government in the state. Bragg's recent biographer Earl J. Hess has tempered these criticisms by emphasizing Jefferson Davis's responsibility for the outcome of the campaign. Davis "deserves primary blame for the fact that neither Bragg nor Kirby Smith had the authority to command each other," Hess notes— and Davis was keen on the installation ceremony for the governor, hoping it would give an aura of legitimacy to the Confederacy's claim of Kentucky and help attract recruits to the army.[25]

As Lee had in the aftermath of Antietam, Bragg defended his campaign's success, arguing that it had permitted Confederates to subsist off enemy possessions, had reasserted Confederate control of Middle Tennessee, and had "only given up territory that the Confederacy had never before possessed." The Northern press mocked such claims of victory. The "deliverance from LINCOLN tyranny" that Bragg promised Kentucky, the *Philadelphia Inquirer* editorialized, was the deliverance "the wolf gives to the lamb, the spider to the fly, the cat to the mouse." Now that the Union army had driven the rebels back, Kentucky would be "more firmly devoted to the Union" than ever before.[26]

Meanwhile, the months of September and October witnessed a third Confederate offensive (along with the Maryland and Kentucky ones) in northern Mississippi, where Earl Van Dorn and Sterling Price aimed to combine forces and take on Federal armies under Rosecrans and Grant. Price clashed with Rosecrans at the railroad town of Iuka and was forced back, and then linked up with the reckless Van Dorn to attack Union-occupied Corinth on October 3. The Confederates pushed the Union troops into the city's inner defenses, but a blistering Union counterattack on the fourth, which devolved into hand-to hand combat, drove the Confederates off and into retreat. The Confederates' offensive tide, historian Russell Weigley notes, "had dissolved into anticlimax." The Federals were far from contented, as Northerners had hoped for something more than merely "standing fast" after the great victories at Forts Henry and Donelson and at Shiloh. But the Union successes nonetheless augured well. Reflecting on the results of Corinth, U. S. Grant would

Braxton Bragg. Bragg won Jefferson Davis's undying admiration when Bragg's troops rescued Davis's during the Mexican War. That support became more and more controversial
over the course of the Civil War as Bragg, whose men regarded him as a merciless autocrat,
blundered his way into a string of military defeats. (Library of Congress LC-USZ62-4888)

write that the battle was a "crushing blow to the enemy, and felt by him much
more than it was appreciated at the North." With the safety of his jurisdiction
secured, Grant was ready to pivot to the next challenge: "I suggested to the
general-in-chief a forward movement against Vicksburg."[27]

Vicksburg Is the Key

The Union had failed in its first attempt to take the rebels' Mississippi River
stronghold of Vicksburg, in the summer of 1862, and topography had a great
deal to do with the failure. Vicksburg was built on a two-hundred-foot vertical
bluff, shielded on three sides by the river and interlaced bayous and swamps,
and could be attacked from dry ground only from the east. The city of five
thousand was the second-largest in the state of Mississippi and a crucial railroad

hub, as there were railheads there on both sides of the river, connected by ferry. Lincoln declared early in the war, as he gazed over a map of the Confederate interior, "See what a lot of land these fellows hold, of which Vicksburg is the key." The city was the key to the Union's strategy of controlling the Mississippi, transecting the Confederacy, and squeezing it anaconda-like in a blockade. The citizens of Vicksburg, many of whom had thrived off the river trade with the North and had been wary of secession, clung to the hope that the war might bypass the city and that the Yankees might choose other targets. They were shaken from this delusion in late May 1862, when Yankee naval squadrons began to bombard the city as a prelude to a major assault by David Farragut and David Porter's fleet in June. The defense of the city by some 10,000 Confederate soldiers under Earl Van Dorn quickly transformed Vicksburg from a symbol of Southern ambivalence to one of Southern pride: the Union bombardment was not able to knock out the rebel batteries, and the Confederates' heavy artillery, which ran along a three-mile stretch of the river, took a heavy toll on the Federal fleet. The Confederate success at turning back Farragut and Porter in late July was virtually the only good news to come out of the western theater in the opening phase of the war. Coinciding as it did with Lee's victories over McClellan in Virginia, the failure of the Union's first Vicksburg campaign buoyed Confederate hopes; a crucial two-hundred-mile stretch of the Mississippi, between Vicksburg and Port Hudson, Louisiana, remained in Confederate hands.[28]

The Union high command had failed to realize that a joint army-navy overland and river campaign was needed in order to take the strongly garrisoned city. To resume the momentum, the Union turned to Major General Ulysses S. Grant, who in October 1862 assumed command of the Department of the Tennessee and began to devise a new strategy for taking the city. His aim was to move his 40,000-man army from Tennessee into northern Mississippi to lure the Confederate forces out of Vicksburg, even as Sherman's army of 32,000 would move on gunboats and transports down the Mississippi River and up the Yazoo River to strike at Vicksburg's presumably weakened Northern defenses. The Vicksburg campaign dramatizes the expansion of hard war measures. Slaves sought refuge with the Union army as it moved into the Delta. Confederate guerrilla hit-and-run operations harassed Union ships and cut communications and supply lines, and Union soldiers often arrested suspected guerrillas and spies and wreaked vengeance through acts of vandalism on Southern homes, including the seizure of cotton. Such actions, which needlessly embittered the locals, prompted Grant to issue Special Field Order No. 1 in the fall of 1862, condemning looting and illegal trading and promising to make an example of those actions. None other than Sherman decried the "indiscriminate and extensive plundering" by Union men as a violation of God's law and man's and as a blight on the nation's honor. These pronouncements, and punishments meted out to rule-breakers, deterred some Union men but not all: "Many harbored such hatred for Rebels that they willingly ran the risk of consequences." Confederate civilians, for their part, were embittered not only by Yankee depredations but also by the way their own army commandeered—or impressed—foodstuffs, livestock, and even slaves, and burned cotton so that it wouldn't fall into Yankee hands. Civilians took to hiding valuable property and goods when they saw either army coming.[29]

Grant faced off in this second phase of the campaign against Major General John C. Pemberton. A West Point graduate and Mexican War veteran, Pemberton had forsaken his Pennsylvania roots; having married a Virginia woman, he adopted the political orthodoxies of the Southern elite,

Ulysses S. Grant. "I can't spare this man; he fights": Lincoln counted on Grant, victor at Forts Henry and Donelson and Shiloh in 1862, to capture the Confederacy's "Gibraltar" at Vicksburg. Controlling the Mississippi River would allow the Union to split the Confederacy in two. (Library of Congress LC-DIG-ppmsca-39802)

to the deep dismay of his Northern family. Pemberton was charged with directing Confederate operations in southwestern Tennessee, Mississippi, and eastern Louisiana, and he reported to General Joseph Johnston, who commanded a vast swath of the western theater. With his headquarters in Jackson, Mississippi, Pemberton delegated ground operations to Van Dorn, who retained command of Confederate forces in Mississippi.[30]

This arrangement would prove fraught with difficulties—but in the winter of 1862 it worked well enough, as the Confederates were able to stymie Grant's invasion of northern Mississippi. Van Dorn's cavalry launched a successful raid on Grant's supply depot at Holly Springs, Mississippi, on December 20, even as Brigadier General Nathan Bedford Forrest struck at Grant's rail supply and telegraph lines in Tennessee. These coordinated raids pointed up the logistical obstacles faced by a large army trying to subsist and maneuver while isolated deep in enemy territory. Sherman, for his part, attacked the rebel position at Chickasaw Bluffs, three miles north of Vicksburg. The Union had a more than two-to-one manpower advantage, but the terrain favored the defenders: Confederate troops, under the leadership of the experienced artillery officer Brigadier General Stephen D. Lee, had positioned themselves on the high ground, overlooking a swampy bayou that afforded the Union very few routes of approach. The resulting clash proved costly for the Union: Sherman's army suffered 1,800 casualties and exacted only 200 on the Confederate side. Having learned that Grant's campaign in northern Mississippi had been turned back, Sherman withdrew his forces. Confederates at Vicksburg celebrated New Year's Day 1863 in high spirits, proud that the "Hill City" was cementing its reputation as the "Gibraltar of the Confederacy."[31]

Forlorn Hope at Fredericksburg

Back east, a fresh start for the Army of the Potomac brought fresh controversy when Lincoln in early November ordered the removal of McClellan from command and his replacement by Major General Ambrose E. Burnside. McClellan, basking in the personal glow of what he considered to be his Antietam masterpiece, had frittered away much of the fall and did not get a new Virginia campaign under way until late October, by which time Lee had once again successfully positioned himself between the Federal army and Richmond. Burnside seemed to be the answer: he had performed admirably at First Bull Run and in leading amphibious operations off the North Carolina coast. But Burnside's own frame of mind did not augur well. By this point he had already twice turned down Lincoln's offer of command of the Army of the Potomac (after the Peninsula campaign and on the eve of Antietam) and was no more eager to accept the mantle of responsibility now. Feeling himself "not fit for the position," Burnside "wept like a child" upon receiving news of his promotion, General George G. Meade reported with palpable alarm in a November 8, 1862 letter home. Many soldiers, Democrats especially, evinced bitterness at McClellan's ouster. According to Private John Haley of the 17th Maine, McClellan was the "smartest and most ill-used person on earth," and Burnside would have his hands full dealing with the soldiers' "festering and fomenting" discontent. But some soldiers were glad to see McClellan go, having lost faith in his ability to engineer lasting victories. Others, who were ambivalent at first, were brought around by Burnside's likeable demeanor. As historian George Rable has explained, although grumbling in the ranks abounded, ultimately "the men would respect Lincoln's authority as commander in chief."[32]

Lincoln clearly construed Burnside's protestations of unfitness as a refreshing display of humility. As it turned out, Burnside's want of confidence in his own abilities was justified. The Fredericksburg campaign would unfold for the Union army like a slow-moving train wreck that everyone could see coming but no one could stop. Burnside's plan was to move the Army of the Potomac, 120,000 men strong, across the Rappahannock River, seizing the city of Fredericksburg and the commanding heights behind it. This would open the way for the drive south toward Richmond. The key to success was speed: Burnside's men had to cross the river before Lee's army, which was more than a day's march to the west, at Culpeper, could arrive to defend the city. And the key to speed, in turn, was the arrival of pontoon bridges that would permit the Federals to cross the rain-swollen Rappahannock en masse (Confederates had already destroyed the bridges that had spanned the river, to deter the Federals).

On November 17, the Federals reached the north bank of the Rappahannock. At this juncture, the city, which sat on the south bank, was only very lightly garrisoned by rebels, and the river was actually fordable in some places without bridges. But Burnside did not want to risk a scenario in which the vanguard of his army crossed over only to find itself cut off if the waters rose. Unfortunately, his pontoons were nowhere in sight. Poor coordination between Burnside and Halleck, who had never fully understood nor approved of Burnside's plan, had resulted in a logistical nightmare: the necessary equipment did not arrive until November 25, by which point Lee's men had converged on Fredericksburg and had seized and begun fortifying the defensive ridge of Marye's Heights. The ominous nature of this turn of events was not lost on the Federal rank and file. "We are waiting for pontoons, which were promised to be here," observed infantryman John Haley in his journal on November 22. He added warily, "This is an upsetting state of affairs when we reflect on how much depends on our getting over there before the Rebels concentrate their forces and make it impregnable."[33]

In a remarkably prescient November 22 letter written from Falmouth, across the river from Fredericksburg, Captain William Thompson Lusk of New York wrote:

> I must say the attack on Fredericksburg is a thing I greatly dread. The field of battle with all its horrors is redeemed somewhat by the thought that the dead on both sides have fallen in a cause sacred in their own eyes at least, and this redeems them, but the wanton destruction of property and all the probable results of a successful siege develop only the most devilish propensities of humanity. . . . It may be a good thing to use severe measures to bring deluded men to a sense of their errors. Still I think, were low ignorant ruffians to visit my home while I was away fighting, burn my house, lay waste my property, insult mother and sisters, beggar the little children I might love, taunt the gray hairs I might respect, leave starvation in the place of plenty, I should feel singularly strengthened in my early delusion.

Lusk hoped that Burnside, with his "nobler nature," would prove better at imposing discipline in the Federal ranks than Pope had.[34]

A tense limbo period ensued, with Federal artillery massing on Stafford's Heights, on the river's left bank (as it flows past Fredericksburg); Lee's men digging in behind the city; most of Fredericksburg's civilians evacuating their homes and heading to Richmond or Petersburg or Charlottesville—and the weather turning bitter cold. The Federal army's odds of success worsened each day, as Lee's force, having been joined by Jackson's from the Valley, now numbered approximately 75,000 men. But Burnside was under intense pressure not to show the same penchant for excessive caution that McClellan had. Calling off the offensive and settling into winter quarters simply was not an option. So Burnside opted instead to be bold: he would send one of his three grand divisions, commanded by Major General Edwin V. Sumner, across pontoon bridges and right through the city of Fredericksburg to drive Longstreet's men off the high ground, while a second grand division, under Major General William B. Franklin, would cross the river two miles downstream, south of

Ambrose Burnside. Burnside's desire to match Robert E. Lee's aggressiveness resulted in the tragic, costly Federal defeat at Fredericksburg. One of the five commanders of the Army of the Potomac, Burnside had succeeded McDowell and McClellan and was succeeded by Joseph Hooker and then George Meade. (Library of Congress LC-DIG-ppmsca-40543)

the city, to take on Stonewall Jackson's corps. The third of Burnside's grand divisions, under Joseph Hooker, would be largely kept in reserve.[35]

Federal engineers tried to set the stage on December 11 by assembling the pontoon bridges—three for Sumner's force and three for Hooker's. But the work on the Union right, in front of the city, was accursed, as Confederate sharpshooters with Brigadier General William E. Barksdale's Mississippi Brigade kept picking off the engineers. Bristling with anger, Burnside ordered an artillery bombardment of the town, and for two hours the 150 guns on Stafford Heights blazed away at Fredericksburg, reducing many blocks of the commercial district, private homes, and even churches to rubble. Civilians sought refuge in basements and cellars, or fled in panic and despair. Images of women and children driven into the pitiless winter by the Union bombardment confirmed Confederates' contempt for the Yankees.

"I never saw a more pitiful procession than they made trudging through the deep snow," wrote artillerist Robert Stiles of the Fredericksburg refugees. "I saw little children tugging along with their doll babies . . . and women so old and feeble they could carry nothing and could barely hobble themselves. . . . Where they were going we could not tell, and I doubt if they could." Meanwhile, Barksdale's men stood firm. Edward Porter Alexander, who commanded an artillery battalion in Longstreet's First Corps, watched the bombardment from Marye's Heights. "I could not but laugh out heartily, at times," he would later recall, "to catch in the roar of the Federal guns the faint drownded pop of a musket which told that Barksdale's men were still in their rifle pits & still defiant. The contrast in the noises the two parties were making was very ludicrous."[36]

Burnside had no choice but to ferry detachments of Union troops across the river to roust the snipers. These assault parties neutralized the Confederate sharpshooters, permitting the Union engineers to finish the bridges. Flush with their success, the Union soldiers proceeded to ransack the city. "Every house and Store was being gutted! Men with all sorts of utensils & furniture— all sorts of eatables & drinkables & wearables, were carried off," Brigadier General Marsena Patrick of the Army of the Potomac wrote with disgust in his diary. He tried to restrain his own men: "I found one fellow loading up a horse with an enormous load of carpeting & bedding I ordered him to unload it, which failing to do, I gave him a cut or two with my riding whip . . . & then put him in with my prisoners." But such efforts at discipline failed to turn back the tide of pillaging. Many Union soldiers felt the Confederates had brought this woe upon themselves. Noting that Burnside had warned the rebels that the town would be destroyed if they did not vacate it, Private Haley remarked caustically, "Instead, the inhabitants of Fredericksburg chose to be very patriotic. Result: ruin!"[37]

On December 12, as Union troops squandered energy in looting, Burnside refined his battle plans. The attack the following day would begin on the Confederate right flank, toward Hamilton's Crossing; success there might force Lee to transfer troops from his own left and open the way for Sumner's men to capture Marye's Heights. But coordinated attacks never materialized. Burnside's orders to Franklin were muddled, and thus the Federal attack on the rebel right flank proceeded piecemeal, with a single division, rather than in force; here were depressing echoes of Antietam. The harassing fire of a brash young rebel artillerist, Major John Pelham, helped delay the Union advance. Even so, that one division, under General George G. Meade, almost broke through the Confederate line—and might have succeeded in doing so if properly reinforced by the rest of Franklin's troops. Instead, the Confederates launched a successful counterattack, plugging the gap in their lines.

Franklin's failure should have prompted Burnside to call off the attack on the Confederate left. But, tragically, it did not. At Marye's Heights, Sumner's men and then Hooker's attacked Longstreet's impregnable position, mounting fifteen hopeless assaults. The topography was deadly for the Union troops in every way: the Federal troops had to move out of the city into a

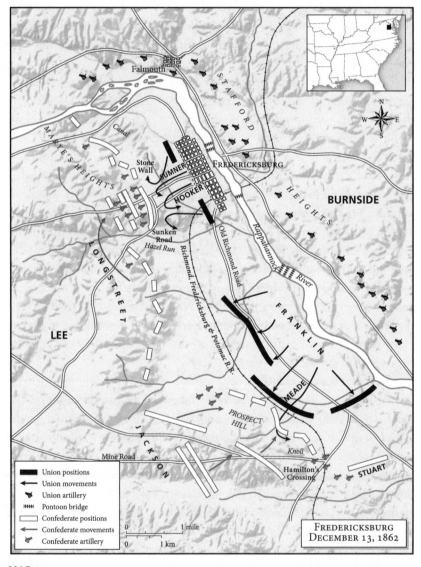

Union positions
Union movements
Union artillery
Pontoon bridge
Confederate positions
Confederate movements
Confederate artillery

0   1 mile
0   1 km

FREDERICKSBURG
DECEMBER 13, 1862

MAP 5.2

valley, across a canal ditch, and then across upward-sloping open ground toward the Confederate line, where men and artillery were entrenched in a sunken road behind a half-mile-long stone wall. While Lee energetically reinforced the stone wall, Burnside could send in only one or two brigades at a time, thanks to the way the canal ditch served as a funnel. "Practically every brigade broke up & retreated at or about the 100 yards line," Edward Porter Alexander recalled, "which was where our infantry fire began to get in its full strength. For our men would not fire at long range but would purposely let them get nearer." As the Federal army ran this gauntlet, the area in front of the stone wall soon became a "complete slaughter pen," as a Georgian hospital steward put it. The Federals sustained nearly 13,000 casualties, most of them on Marye's Heights, more than twice as many casualties as the Confederates.[38]

In another echo of Antietam, Union men could find no more fitting metaphor than to observe that troops seemed to melt away under the blistering fire. As an unidentified New York infantryman put it in a December 21, 1862, letter, "Our columns melted . . . like dew before the morning sun." For Confederates, by contrast, the battle was "truly a grand spectacle to witness," a Virginia private wrote. "Charge after charge was made and as often repulsed, and each time such a shout went up along the whole line as almost to drown out the roar of the musketry." Burnside finally relented and aborted the attack in the late afternoon. Racked with grief, Burnside accepted full responsibility for the outcome of the battle. December 14 found both armies tending to the wounded and confronting the scale of the carnage—many of the dead were "mashed into one complete jelly," as one horrified soldier put it. Other, more intact corpses were tempting targets for looters of clothing, blankets, shoes, and rifles. "Just as Federals had lost their moral compass in sacking Fredericksburg," historian George Rable has pointed out, "so Confederates now foraged among the dead with an alacrity they would have once found shocking."[39]

The news of the Fredericksburg debacle brought the inevitable public backlash against the Union's leaders. Burnside was the main lightning rod for the Northern public's disgust and frustration, but the Lincoln administration was also held to account. Contrasting the probity of the ousted McClellan with the incompetence of "Halleck, Stanton & Co.," the *New York Herald* fumed, "Never before, perhaps, in the history of war, was such ignorance, vacillation and imbecility exhibited by men at the head of a great nation." Lincoln could right the ship only if he was willing to "discard the destructive abolition malignants that surround him." Morale in the Union army plummeted to a new low, and desertions spiked. Some soldiers were keenly nostalgic for McClellan, claiming that he never would have consigned men to face such terrible odds and that only he could revive the shattered army. But others perceived that the seeds of this latest failure had been sown long before Burnside took charge. "Oh for a month of that beautiful weather that we wasted in autumn," lamented Lieutenant Samuel W. Fiske on December 15, in his postmortem of the battle. Another Union officer noted philosophically that McClellan "did not know when to order his army forward into the works of the enemy, and Burnside did not know when to call them back from inevitable disaster."[40]

Confederate morale again surged, stoked not only by the lopsided military victory but also by the ideological vindication Southerners derived from the Yankee bombardment of Fredericksburg—it was interpreted as further proof of Yankee barbarity, and the carnage of Marye's Heights as fitting retribution. While some Confederate soldiers acknowledged the courage Union men had shown in their fruitless assaults on the rebel defenses, the official line taken by Confederate propagandists was that Federal soldiers were demoralized and disaffected to the point of insubordination. For example, the *Richmond Dispatch*'s December 19 article "Feeling in the Yankee Army" gauged Northern morale from interviews with prisoners of war and concluded that the Federals had "very little hope of ever accomplishing the object for which they enlisted . . . [They] frankly admit that they have no Generals equal to those commanding the armies of the Confederacy . . . [and] are heartily sick of the task in which they are engaged." The Confederate press contrasted Yankee demoralization with Southern discipline, noting that at Fredericksburg, unlike in the Maryland campaign, very few Confederates fell out of the ranks. Lee's army "had but this single vice of straggling," the *Charleston Mercury* declared with satisfaction, "and now that has been conquered." Lee, exhilarated by the victory, had uttered while watching his men repulse the Yankee attack on December 13, "It is well this is so terrible! we should grow too fond of it!"[41]

In time this Confederate confidence would seem to be hubris. Although they were chastened, Union soldiers had not lost hope or their faith in their cause and each other. "Simple patriotism remained strong," George Rable has observed of Union morale in the aftermath of Fredericksburg, "and it was bolstered by staunch loyalty to comrades." Such patriotism was most visible to civilians in the hospital wards—there were more than fifty hospitals in Washington, D.C., alone—where the Fredericksburg wounded were treated and then convalesced.[42] Louisa May Alcott could see it: in December 1862 she came to the District of Columbia from her home in Concord, Massachusetts, to work as a nurse, and her account of that experience would be published in 1863 under the title *Hospital Sketches*. Upon first encountering the maimed veterans of Fredericksburg, she thought, "There they were! 'our brave boys,' as the papers justly call them, for cowards could hardly have been so riddled with shot and shell, so torn and shattered, nor have borne suffering for which we have no name, with an uncomplaining fortitude, which made one glad to cherish each as a brother."[43]

The poet and journalist Walt Whitman saw it: he, too, came to Washington in the aftermath of the Fredericksburg battle, in search of his brother George, who was listed as having been wounded there. Whitman found George in the camp of the 51st New York, alive and well, but he then began visiting the less fortunate in the sick wards and was transformed by the experience. "Really nothing we call trouble seems worth talking about," Whitman wrote

Louisa May Alcott. In the winter of 1862, Alcott worked twelve-hour shifts nursing wounded soldiers in the Union Hotel Hospital in Washington, D.C., only to fall ill herself with typhoid fever, necessitating her return home. Her account of her nursing experience, *Hospital Sketches*, was the first of her many acclaimed books; her best-selling *Little Women* would be published in 1868. (Library of Congress LC-DIG-ppmsca-53264)

his mother on December 29, after seeing a "heap of feet, arms, legs &c. under a tree in front of a hospital." In subsequent letters, Whitman, who threw himself wholeheartedly into nursing the wounded, would describe the soldiers as "never vulgar, ever calm, without greediness, no flummery, no frivolity—responding electric and without fail to affection, yet no whining—not the first unmanly whimper have I yet seen or heard." These stoic sufferers were "the best expression of American character" Whitman had "ever seen or conceived."[44]

Lincoln's Second Annual Message

The Fredericksburg campaign repeated what was by this point in the war a familiar pattern: as the Union army approached, slaves sought refuge behind Union lines. Joseph Lawson, a free black cooper living in Fredericksburg, recalled,

> As soon as the Yankees got hyar the slaves began to run away from their mistresses and masters. They went by hundreds. You'd see 'em gittin' out of hyar same as a rabbit chased by a dog. Some carried little bundles tied up, but they couldn't tote much. Often one of the women would walk along carrying a child wrapped up in a blanket. Fifteen miles from hyar they got to the Potomac, and the Yankee gunboats would take 'em right to Washington. Then they'd pile in wherever they could git. They never come back this way.

And yet Burnside's defeat seemed to many a potential setback for emancipation: would Lincoln, with Union fortunes and his own party's popularity ebbing low, follow through on issuing his final proclamation? Speculation that Lincoln might reverse course was already rife after the fall election setbacks for the Republicans and was lent further credence by the president's seemingly equivocal December 1, 1862, Annual Message to Congress. That speech found Lincoln quoting at length from his own First Inaugural Address and updating the case for gradual, compensated emancipation. After arguing that there was literally no way for North and South to separate that would not invite further division and harm the prospects for prosperity of all involved, Lincoln proposed constitutional amendments providing for the extinction of slavery by 1900, with masters to be compensated by the federal government for their lost property and authorizing Congress to appropriate money for colonization. Such a plan, Lincoln insisted, would "secure peace more speedily, and maintain it more permanently, than can be done by force alone." Was Lincoln reverting to the discredited formula of voluntary emancipation and abandoning his plan for military emancipation by presidential fiat? Some moderates thought so, believing the speech was intended to rein in Radical Republicans and abolitionists. "That they should be told by Abraham Lincoln to wait for thirty-seven years for the abolition of Southern slavery, and be told this upon the heels of his emancipation proclamation, is certainly very wonderful," quipped the *New York Herald*. "I like 'Old Abe's' emancipation plan as developed in his message very much. . . . Father Abraham has proposed the wisest plan I have heard of yet," wrote William Thompson Lusk in a December 3 letter home, explaining that in his view the slaves were not ready for immediate emancipation. Samuel Cormany, a devoutly evangelical cavalryman from rural Pennsylvania, likewise approved. "Read Pres Lincolns message to Congress—A great paper indeed," he observed in his diary on December 5.[45]

Careful readers of the speech could discern a different purpose and harmonize its recommendations with Lincoln's standing promise to issue his final Emancipation Proclamation on January 1, 1863. While Lincoln's proclamation "dealt only with rebel communities," the *Boston Journal* explained, his proposed amendments provided for "universal emancipation under the flag of the Union, so that the nineteenth century should close on no American slave." While his proclamation, made under his war powers, relied for its justification on military necessity, and might be in danger of repeal during peacetime, his amendments would outlast the war. While Lincoln once again, in his 1862 Annual Message, strongly advocated colonization, he also argued at length, for the first time, against its central premise. Directly disputing the "largely imaginary, if not sometimes malicious" argument that black freedom without deportation would bring social chaos and economic competition, Lincoln asked pointedly whether "colored people can displace any more white labor, by being free, than by remaining slaves." He predicted that after emancipation blacks would largely choose to remain in the South, "with people of their own blood and race," and that the demise of slavery would enhance the economic prospects of all laborers, white and black, North and South. Even without deportation, in other words, emancipation would bring material progress.[46]

Lincoln closed the December 1 annual message by reiterating forcefully that he saw emancipation as an indispensable means to the primary goal of saving the Union and a way of enhancing the freedom of whites:

We *say* we are for the Union. The world will not forget that we say this. We know how to save the Union. The world knows we do know how to save it. We—even *we here*—hold the power, and bear the responsibility. In *giving* freedom to the *slave*, we *assure* freedom to the *free*—honorable alike in what we give, and what we preserve. We shall nobly save, or meanly lose, the last best hope of earth.[47]

Two weeks later, after the nightmare at Fredericksburg, with the Union in deeper peril, emancipation seemed to many to take on the aura of a desperate act—the very situation Lincoln had hoped to avoid by issuing the preliminary proclamation in the wake of a victory, after Antietam. Border state representatives denounced the proclamation as a dangerous usurpation of power by the president and pressured Lincoln to postpone if not scrap it, and Lincoln's most reckless Northern critics even insinuated that he had willfully engineered the Fredericksburg defeat to demonstrate the "military necessity" of emancipation as a means to victory. Confederates for their part both mocked the idea of gradual compensated emancipation and repeated the time-worn charge that black freedom would bring insurrection and race war.[48]

But supporters of emancipation kept up counterpressure, urging Lincoln to stay true to his purpose and advising him on how best to ensure that the January proclamation would have broad public support. Pragmatic abolitionists such as John Murray Forbes of Boston thought that the "ground of 'military necessity' should be even more squarely taken than it was on 22d September." This was the best way, Forbes reckoned, to convey respect for the "constitutional scruples" of a "large class of Democrats, and self-styled 'Conservatives,' whose support is highly desirable." Forbes believed that "a good strong Proclamation full of vigor, of freedom, and of *democracy,* would almost compensate us for the dreadful repulse of Fredericksburg." His friend Charles Sumner hoped Lincoln's final proclamation would aim higher. "It should have something in it showing that though an act of military necessity and just self-defense, it was also an act of justice and humanity, which must have the blessings of a benevolent God," Sumner wrote Forbes on December 28, 1862.[49]

For African Americans who carefully planned myriad celebrations to mark the New Year, there was no question that emancipation was a sacred cause. "Let us prepare, in the intervening twelve days, between this and the 1st of January," urged a December 20 editorial in the free black *Pacific Appeal,* "to have a Thanksgiving to Him who rules the destinies of nations, for the deliverance, at last, on that auspicious day, of thousands, at least, if not millions

"Waiting for the Hour." This carte de visite depicts the hopefulness and anticipation of enslaved African Americans as they count down the moments, on New Year's Eve of 1862, until the Emancipation Proclamation goes into effect. A man draped in the American flag stands in the open doorway of the slaves' cabin. (Library of Congress LC-USZ62-119987)

of those who are identified with us by the kindred ties of blood and common origin, from the galling chains of Slavery." Sacred, too, was the work of saving the Union and redeeming it from the scourge of prejudice—and emancipation alone would not effect that redemption. On December 28, Frederick Douglass gave a speech at the Spring Street African Methodist Episcopal Church in Rochester, New York, in which he proclaimed, "Out of a full heart and with sacred emotion, I congratulate you my friends, and fellow citizens, on the high and hopeful condition, of the cause of human freedom and the cause of our common country, for these two causes are now one and inseparable and must stand or fall together." He continued: "This is no time for the friends of freedom to fold their hands and consider their work at an end. The price of Liberty is eternal vigilance."[50]

6

The Emancipation Proclamation

LINCOLN INSCRIBED THE Emancipation Proclamation into law at
2:00 p.m. on January 1, 1863, after the conclusion of a three-hour New Year's
Day reception at the Executive Mansion. The president's hand trembled as he
wrote his name, a sign of physical wear from glad-handing with the public.
But his sense of purpose was unshakeable. "I never in my life felt more certain
that I was doing right than I do in signing this paper," he said to Seward.[1]

What exactly did Lincoln accomplish at this pivotal moment? In
keeping with the premises of his preliminary decree of September 1862, the
Emancipation Proclamation declared free all persons held as slaves in "States
and parts of States wherein the people thereof respectively, are this day in
rebellion against the United States." To ensure that it was legally defensible,
Lincoln cast emancipation as a "fit and necessary war measure for suppressing
said rebellion," deriving its constitutional authority from his war powers
as commander in chief. The preliminary proclamation had promised that
Lincoln would, on January 1, designate exactly which states and areas of the
South were in rebellion and therefore under the purview of his decree, and
that he did: the Emancipation Proclamation applied to all of the Confederate
states, while the loyal slaveholding states, and certain Union-controlled areas
of the South (those that had sent duly elected representatives to the U.S.
Congress, and Tennessee, which was reconstructing under Andrew Johnson)
were exempted from its requirements. The exempted regions included New
Orleans and surrounding parishes, the newly formed loyal state of West
Virginia, and some Eastern Shore counties of Virginia.[2]

The fact that Lincoln's policy contained exemptions gave rise to a critique of the proclamation as misdirected or even hollow: Lincoln declared
free enslaved persons in those very areas under Confederate control where
he could not actually enforce emancipation, and it left in chains slaves in

Unionist areas, where he did have the power of enforcement. But such a critique fails to appreciate how the proclamation gave new momentum and direction to changes already under way and how its supporters drew strength from its spirit as well as from its content. Lincoln's decree worked to extend freedom on all three Southern fronts: within the Confederacy, within the exempted areas, and within Union-occupied areas that were not exempted.

New Birth of Freedom

Lincoln's January decree moved far beyond his preliminary proclamation of September 1862. In late December 1862, the president had asked his cabinet one last time for their input on his draft, and he acceded to Salmon Chase's suggestion that he add some language highlighting the moral significance of the act. The final proclamation described emancipation as an "act of justice" and invoked the "gracious favor of Almighty God." Lincoln also dropped the preliminary proclamation's references to colonization and voluntary, gradual, compensated emancipation. He had not lost hope altogether that colonization might be an outlet for the free black population, but he had concluded—after being rebuffed so many times—that the offers of compensation and colonization would not induce slaveholders to give up slavery or rebels to give up rebellion. Implicitly acknowledging white fears that emancipation would bring social strife, Lincoln asked the freedpeople to abstain from all violence. But he included the qualifying phrase "unless in necessary self-defence." Here was an unprecedented acknowledgment by an American president that African Americans possessed the fundamental right to protect themselves from white violence. Most important, Lincoln declared on January 1 that freed slaves would be "received into the armed services of the United States to garrison forts, positions, stations, and other places, and to man vessels of all sorts in said service." The congressional Militia Act and the Confiscation Act of July 1862 had opened this door by authorizing Lincoln to enlist black troops; after some hesitation, he walked through the door. Before January 1, 1863, there had been localized efforts to raise black regiments by individual commanders in Kansas, Louisiana, and South Carolina. Now there was a Federal mandate for large-scale enlistment.[3]

With regards to Confederate-controlled areas, the proclamation signaled a change in Union policy. Up until this point, even as Congress had implemented confiscation, the official practice of the Union was to passively receive fugitives but not to actively entice them away from their masters. Lincoln's proclamation set in motion a change in Union policy, reflected

Reading the Emancipation Proclamation. This 1864 engraving, in which an enslaved family gathers around to hear a Union soldier read the Emancipation Proclamation from a newspaper, emphasizes the role of Federal armies as heralds of deliverance. (Library of Congress LC-USZ62-5334)

immediately, James Oakes notes, in orders from the War Department to commanders in the field. From now on, Union soldiers were to take an active role in attracting fugitives. "They are to be encouraged to come within our lines," as Adjutant General Lorenzo Thomas, who worked to implement the proclamation in the Mississippi Valley, put it. The change had a measurable effect, with slaves more inclined than before to run off in large groups toward Union soldiers, who were literally bearing the news of freedom; many Union soldiers had had distributed to them, by the government and private companies, booklet-sized and even pocket-sized copies of the proclamation for distribution in the South. Union authorities were counting on the slaves' clandestine information networks—their "grapevine telegraph"—to reach deep into the South, even into places the Union army had not yet penetrated. And they were not disappointed: by the spring of 1863, some Union commanders were reporting that the slaves arriving at their lines had often traveled "from long distances in rebeldom," as Captain Charles B. Monroe, the "superintendent of contrabands" at Fortress Monroe, Virginia, wrote.

Fugitives had recently arrived from some two hundred miles away in North Carolina. "They knew all about the Proclamation and they started on the belief in it," Monroe explained.[4]

In other words, the proclamation was a catalyst to self-emancipation. It clarified the legal status of those slaves who came under the Union army's purview, either by virtue of flight or when the army arrived at their farms and plantations. The questions that had clouded the confiscation policy—Was a given slave's master disloyal or loyal? Was a given Union commander or picket inclined to welcome fugitives into his army camp or to turn them away? Would the army recognize the freedom of enslaved persons it found on plantations? Would masters feel entitled to one day reclaim the slaves they left behind?—were set aside. Union forces had to recognize the de jure freedom of all African Americans in the Confederacy, no questions asked.[5]

Moreover, the Emancipation Proclamation, with its language specifying that "all persons held as slaves within said designated States, and parts of States, are, and henceforward shall be free," was intended to provide legal protection against the threat of reenslavement. The proclamation drew strength from a November 1862 ruling by Attorney General Bates that free blacks born

Effects of the Emancipation Proclamation. "They said that it was known far and wide that the President has declared the slaves free": This image from the February 21, 1863, issue of *Harper's Weekly*, of freedpeople entering Union-occupied New Bern, North Carolina, illustrated the "first-fruits of the glorious emancipation proclamation." (Library of Congress LC-USZ62-112158)

in the United States were citizens, entitled to the full privileges and immunities thereof; Bates invoked the long-standing principle in Anglo-American law of birthright citizenship. Did this ruling extend to blacks who became free as a result of Lincoln's decree? Bates and many other Republicans and abolitionists believed that it did: those blacks born into American slavery became citizens once emancipated. Bates's ruling hardly settled the fraught question of black citizenship; just how to define full citizenship, and who possessed it, would continue to be bitterly disputed. But he had furnished an important precedent. If restored Southern states one day tried to reassert the precedence of state law and argue that fugitives should revert to slavery, supporters of emancipation would have their answer: citizens of the United States could never be enslaved.[6]

In the exempted areas, the proclamation hastened the demise of slavery by strengthening the hand of pro-emancipation Union authorities and Southern Unionists, and emboldening fugitives to seize the new opportunities for military service. Exempted areas were the very border and occupied regions where the friction and abrasion of war, as Lincoln put it in one of his futile appeals to loyal slaveholders, had already done the most to erode the authority of masters. Now military recruiting became a major source of friction and abrasion. By mid-1863, Union soldiers established army recruiting stations in the border states and excepted areas, a process aided by the May 1863 creation of the Bureau of Colored Troops, which coordinated the raising of regiments. At first recruiters only took into the ranks volunteers who had been slaves of disloyal masters, but with so many able-bodied fugitives imploring the army for the chance to enlist, recruiters soon turned a blind eye to the technicalities of the Emancipation Proclamation and accepted slaves of loyal, nonconsenting masters, granting them freedom with their enlistment. Tellingly, by war's end Louisiana would lead the way in the number of black Union army recruits, with 24,052, and Kentucky was a close second, with 23,073. Therein lay an irony: "It was far more common for slaves to be freed by Union troops in areas that the proclamation explicitly exempted," Oakes notes, "than in areas it technically covered."[7]

That irony was perhaps nowhere so pointed as in Tennessee. It was a Confederate state in name, but largely Union-controlled. Its military governor, Andrew Johnson, had requested of Lincoln that it be exempted from the Emancipation Proclamation, on the grounds that it might undermine Unionism there if loyalist slaveholders felt that Lincoln was levying punishment on them. Lincoln agreed—Tennessee is not even mentioned in the Emancipation Proclamation, exempted by omission. But emancipation made progress there nonetheless. As Brigadier General William Sooy Smith

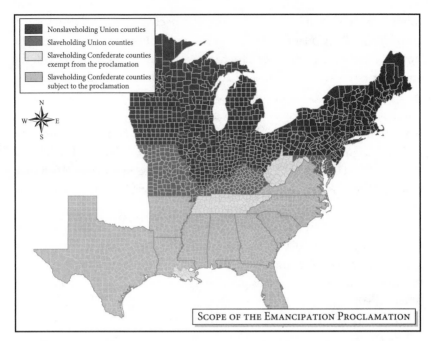

Nonslaveholding Union counties
Slaveholding Union counties
Slaveholding Confederate counties exempt from the proclamation
Slaveholding Confederate counties subject to the proclamation

SCOPE OF THE EMANCIPATION PROCLAMATION

MAP 6.1

observed in March 1863, "whole families" were "stampeding and leaving their masters" and heading to Union army camps. Johnson, driven by his animus against the slaveholding elite and by his political ambitions, rolled with the tide. In August 1863 Johnson freed his own slaves, seeking to set an example for his fellow white Tennesseans. In the year that followed he delivered a series of speeches in which he called slavery a "cancer upon the body politic," and he appealed to Tennesseans to pass a state constitutional amendment abolishing the institution. At Lincoln's urging, Johnson promoted black enlistment, with dramatic effects in places such as Memphis, which the army designated in 1863 as the primary recruiting stations for black troops in the upper Mississippi Valley. More than 20,000 African American Tennesseans would wear the Union blue.[8]

Of course, no one could know with precision in early 1863, as Lincoln's proclamation went into effect, how much it would impact the exempted areas. But it is revealing to note that African Americans in those areas celebrated the initial announcement of emancipation as though Lincoln's words applied to them. For example, thousands of blacks took to the street in Union-occupied, exempted Norfolk, Virginia, on January 1, 1863, to mark the occasion. "This has been a great day among the negroes," wrote Presbyterian minister Isaac W. K. Handy, a pro-Confederate civilian, in his diary entry on New Year's Day. "Under the impression from Lincoln's proclamation that 'the hour of Jubilee has come,' they have had a wonderful procession through the streets of Norfolk, with banners, flags, sashes and whatever things are used on such occasion. It is difficult to estimate the number in this grand turn out; but it has been variously estimated from 3,000 to 15,000, including men, women, and children. . . . The United States flag was conspicuous among the various ensigns; and at various certain stages of the wandering, three cheers, each, were given to the U.S. flag, President Lincoln and Liberty." With such rituals, African Americans insisted that the spirit of Lincoln's proclamation transcended its letter.[9]

A similar dynamic was visible in Union-occupied areas of the South that were not exempted by the proclamation. These scattered regions—along the Mississippi in Arkansas, the Atlantic coast of north Florida, eastern North Carolina, the Sea Islands of Georgia and South Carolina, and certain Shenandoah counties of Virginia—were in a kind of limbo. The Union army had a strong presence there, but the areas did not meet the requirements for exemption (representation in the U.S. Congress and the absence of Confederate resistance). The Second Confiscation Act applied there, but it still designated freedpeople as "captives of war" and did not gesture at their citizenship—and it left in slavery blacks on the peripheries of Union outposts. Lincoln's proclamation resolved these ambiguities, affirming the freedom of some fifty thousand African Americans in these borderlands.[10]

The case of the Sea Islands is illustrative. It was the site of a singular rehearsal for Reconstruction that dated back to November 1861, when a Union navy flotilla had secured Port Royal Sound, South Carolina, and its networks of coastal islands and inlets; this was a great prize, as the deep-water port could be used to support the blockade, and the region's plantations grew some of the most valuable cotton in the South. The Port Royal victory was a major step in the process of emancipation, as the Union amphibious operation sent planters fleeing to the mainland, leaving behind nearly eight thousand enslaved men and women on abandoned plantations; soon slaves in turn began fleeing the mainland to get to the Union-controlled islands. In May 1862, Union general David Hunter, in a move akin to Frémont's in Missouri, had issued a rogue emancipation edict, declaring slaves in his department (comprising coastal South Carolina, Georgia, and north Florida) to be free. Lincoln had overturned this edict as he did Frémont's. Thereafter, a trio of Massachusetts abolitionists—Edward L. Pierce, General Rufus Saxton, and Colonel Thomas Wentworth Higginson—would shape policy on the Sea Islands. Treasury Secretary Chase (who had purview over abandoned lands) delegated to Pierce the task of overseeing the transition of the "contrabands" to freedom, and Pierce implemented a system—a joint endeavor of the federal government and Northern philanthropic and missionary societies—in which blacks would work for wages, on plantations or in Union army camps, and at the same time receive education, food, clothes, and medical assistance. Their calculus was that if this free labor experiment could produce high cotton yields, it could both provide revenue for the Union war effort and prove to skeptics that freed blacks would be industrious and productive.[11]

The spring of 1862 witnessed the arrival on the Sea Islands of an eager troupe of Northern volunteers, motivated by antislavery convictions to educate, evangelize, and provide humanitarian relief to the former slaves. Negotiations, at times tense, ensued between the freedpeople, who wanted the economic autonomy to grow foodstuffs and the chance to obtain the confiscated lands on which they worked; the cotton agents and plantation superintendents, who sought high yields and profits; and the missionaries and other do-gooders, with their agenda of social uplift. Northerners at Port Royal saw themselves as an advance guard of Southern deliverance. As the occupation newspaper *New South*, published in Port Royal by Union army postmaster John Henry Sears, put it, if news of the experiment's success could somehow reach the "deluded and unfortunate people with whom we are contending," they would "perhaps see how desperate is their own condition, and submit more readily to the government which has never wished to do more than bring them back to their allegiance." Charlotte Forten, an antislavery activist from a prominent Philadelphia free black family, was one of those who helped spread the word, publishing an account of her work as a schoolteacher in which she attested to the desire and capacity of former slaves for knowledge and hailed the "Northern improvements" that Yankees brought to the underdeveloped region. For the sake of sustaining the new free labor system, freedpeople abided both cotton production and the reformers' paternalism. Port Royal was also the site of early recruitment of African American troops. In August 1862, General Saxton, Hunter's replacement, secured from Stanton permission to raise a black regiment, and Saxton would bestow command of that regiment—the 1st South Carolina Volunteers—on his fellow Massachusetts native Higginson; the regiment performed well in raids on the Georgia coast that fall.[12]

In a technical sense, the African Americans in the Sea Islands milieu were freed by the confiscation policy, which had referred specifically to slaves on abandoned plantations as well as to fugitives. Pierce and his cadre of investors, superintendents, and philanthropists routinely described Sea Island blacks in 1862 as "freedmen." But African Americans nonetheless celebrated January 1, 1863, as a day of deliverance. Indeed, the best-documented and most stirring of all the emancipation ceremonies in the occupied South took place at Camp Saxton, on Port Royal Island in South Carolina's Beaufort district. A large assemblage—white Union officers, soldiers, clergymen, government agents, reformers, reporters, and reformers, and African American soldiers (in the 1st South Carolina Regiment) and former slaves—gathered together in a live-oak grove on New Year's Day 1863 to hear prayers offered, speeches given, and emancipation proclaimed. "The multitude were chiefly colored women," observed Higginson, who presided over the festivities. Many of those women were actively aiding the Union cause. For example, Susie King Taylor, a Georgian who fled to Union lines, worked as a teacher, nurse, and laundress for the 1st South Carolina, and penned an influential memoir of her experiences as a camp follower, in which she described the Camp Saxton celebration as "glorious."[13]

Susie King Taylor. After escaping slavery, Taylor worked as a nurse and teacher for the 1st South Carolina (33rd USCT) regiment, and exemplifies the contributions of countless African American women to the Union war effort. Her postwar memoir, *Reminiscences of My Life in Camp*, was published in 1902. (Library of Congress LC-USZ61-1863)

The services began with a reading of the Emancipation Proclamation by the Reverend William Henry Brisbane—a "thing infinitely appropriate," observed Higginson, as Brisbane was a rare white South Carolinian abolitionist who decades earlier had renounced slavery, emancipated his slaves, and left his native Beaufort for the North. In the midst of the day's proceedings, right after regimental colors were presented to the black troops, there transpired an "incident so simple, so touching, so utterly unexpected and startling, that I can scarcely believe it on recalling," Higginson would later write in his memoirs.

> The very moment the speaker had ceased . . . there suddenly arose, close beside the platform, a strong male voice (but rather cracked and elderly), into two women's voices instantly blended, singing, as if by an impulse that could no more be repressed than the morning note of the song-sparrow.—
> "My Country, 'tis of thee,
> Sweet land of liberty,
> Of thee I sing!"
> . . . Firmly and irrepressibly the quavering voices sang on, verse after verse; others of the colored people joined in. . . . I never saw anything so electric.[14]

Charlotte Forten also testified that the impromptu performance of "My Country 'Tis of Thee" was "touching and beautiful," and she praised Higginson for acknowledging in his remarks that the song was "far more effecting than any speech he could make." Forten was moved, too, by the dress parade of the black troops, "in their brilliant uniforms, with bayonets gleaming in the sunlight." "What a grand, glorious day this has been," she wrote that evening in her journal.[15]

Why did the day carry such weight for those who were "nominally free already," as Higginson put it? Because they knew, he explained, that until this moment of jubilee, freedom had "yet to be established on any firm basis."[16] The Emancipation Proclamation mattered: now the president, and not only Congress, had declared for freedom; now freedom was linked to citizenship, embodied by black soldiers who would act as liberators; now those slaves beyond the Union army's reach were legally entitled to their freedom and would be actively encouraged to claim it.

The reach of the Emancipation Proclamation is hinted at in another scene from the New Year's Day celebrations of 1863. In Washington, D.C., a group

Freedom Days. The Camp Saxton celebration: "Whatever our readers' politics may be," *Frank Leslie's* editorialized in its January 24, 1863, issue, "they cannot fail to feel a stern satisfaction in the simple fact that within a few miles of that 'most errant of sisters,' Charleston, Emancipation-day, as it is called, was celebrated with great pomp." (Library of Congress LC-USZ62-88808)

of former slaves, many of them fugitives from the South, gathered at the headquarters of Danforth B. Nichols, the "superintendent of contrabands" in the District, to mark the issuing of Lincoln's decree. As the proclamation was read, an article in *Douglass' Monthly* reported, "explanations were made showing the different portions of Virginia in which Freedom was declared." "Many of the contrabands recognizing their native counties, cried out, 'That's me,' 'I'm free,' 'That means this child.' " In their eyes, these Virginia counties were no longer fortresses of slavery that cast a legal shadow over the free North but zones marked out for liberation and redemption. An "aged contraband" at the D.C. gathering summed up the promise of Lincoln's proclamation for Southern blacks when he gave a prayer asking the Lord to bless the Union army and to be the "burning lamp" lighting its way into the benighted South.[17]

Reactions to the Proclamation in the North

"To day has bin a memorable day and I thank god I have been sperd to see it the day was religiously observed all the churches were open we had quite a

Jubilee." These were the first lines, penned on January 1, 1863, in the diary of Emilie Davis, a free black seamstress in Philadelphia. In the North, while some abolitionists muttered about the limits of the Emancipation Proclamation, most chose to interpret it expansively. A central theme was the idea that emancipation was a "consummation": blacks had long ago proven their patriotism, and now it was time for "reclaiming and holding our withheld rights," as Robert Hamilton of the *Anglo-African* put it. Commentator after commentator stressed that blacks' nativity, sacrifice, and service had earned them citizenship, and that Lincoln was finally recognizing that status—not granting it conditionally. African Americans had since the time of Crispus Attucks proven themselves "ready to worship, or die, if need be, at Freedom's shrine," William Nell intoned. He gave as a recent example of black heroism the story of Robert Smalls, a South Carolina slave who in May 1862 had commandeered the Confederate military transport on which he worked as a wheelman (pilot) and sailed it through the Confederate fortifications of Charleston harbor and into open waters, to safety with the Union's blockading force. Smalls, whose daring escape won praise from antislavery Northerners, lobbied Lincoln in August 1862 to permit blacks to serve in the military. With the door opened to enlistment, Nell rejoiced, African Americans would en masse affirm their citizenship on the battlefield.[18]

Many black commentators spoke proudly of America's distinctive promise as a beacon for democracy. "I am proud in being an American citizen," Robert Purvis asserted, "proud of this mighty young nation—this awakened young lion, with power so vast, varied and exhaustless as to fill with consternation and terror the haughty despotisms of the Old World." Such expressions of national pride blended with references to the emancipation as a global process— to the course of freedom in Haiti, Liberia, England, France, the Netherlands, Russia. No longer would America lag behind. "The paper proclamation must now be made iron, lead and fire, by the prompt employment of the negro's arm in this contest," Frederick Douglass declared in a February 6, 1863, speech on how Lincoln's decree was a "mighty event for the bondman . . . but a still mightier event for the nation . . . [and] the cause of truth and justice throughout the world." These developments, black abolitionists all agreed, were providential. "While admiring the conduct of our President as an instrument," a correspondent to the *Christian Recorder* wrote, "our emotion of gratitude should be expressed to God who defeated the purposes of men" and brought "this great deliverance." The biblical proverb "Ethiopia shall soon stretch out her hands to God," long a favorite antislavery motto, was invoked at the moment of Lincoln's proclamation as a prophecy fulfilled. Indeed,

biblical images abounded in African American commentary on the proclamation. "The Year of Jubilee Has Come," the *Pacific Appeal*'s January 1, 1863, editorial proclaimed. The deep lamentations of slaves, "How long, how long, O
Lord, before our deliverance shall come to pass?," were answered. They were
no longer bound by the "soulless political theories of the impious slaveocracy,"
and America could now "loom up with grandeur."[19]

Abolitionist whites, too, emphasized the broad scope of the proclamation
and considered it a long-awaited vindication. For Wendell Phillips, speaking
in Boston, the proclamation was "sunlight, scattering the despair of centuries." For Henry Adams, in London assisting his father, Ambassador Charles
Francis Adams, the proclamation was the death knell to Confederate hopes for
British recognition. "The Emancipation Proclamation has done more for us
here than all our former victories and all our diplomacy," he wrote home to his
brother Charles, a Union officer. "It is creating an almost convulsive reaction

Harriet Beecher Stowe. Her 1852 novel *Uncle Tom's Cabin* catapulted Stowe to international fame. During the war she joined with other prominent Northerners in arguing
that emancipation would ultimately benefit Southern whites as well as the freedpeople.
(Library of Congress LC-DIG-ppmsca-49807)

in our favor all over this country." For Harriet Beecher Stowe, the proclamation promised the redemption not just of slaves but of their Southern masters, too—it would deliver "our misguided brethren from the wages of sin," she explained, and the descendants of the very Confederates who were killing Union soldiers would "grow up in liberty and justice."[20]

Yet even as they offered tributes to the proclamation, antislavery Northerners, black and white, gestured at the long road that lay ahead. "The old monster dies very hard," Henry Highland Garnet warned, referring to the destructive power slavery still possessed.[21] Obstacles and threats to freedom were everywhere to be seen. Among white Northerners, the proclamation met with a ferocious backlash and exposed a fault line within Democratic ranks between War Democrats and Peace Democrats (the latter earning the derogatory nickname "Copperheads").

While War Democrats, in the tradition of centrists such as Stephen Douglas, offered their party as an alternative to the extremism of radical abolitionists and militant secessionists alike, Peace Democrats reserved their ire for abolitionists and often expressed respect for the principles and courage of Confederates. While War Democrats accepted that some antislavery measures, such as confiscation of slaves, could be a means to the end of the restoration of the Union, Peace Democrats argued that all antislavery measures had radical intent and effects and aimed at nothing less than the overthrow of white supremacy. While War Democrats were ambivalent about Lincoln and clung to the hope that they could steer him toward moderate policies, Peace Democrats were more inclined to see Lincoln as irredeemably radical. While War Democrats wished for a return to the conciliatory policies of the early war, as exemplified by McClellan's Harrison Landing letter, Peace Democrats believed that the Lincoln administration had waged hard war from the start and had never given conciliation a chance—and that Lincoln's hard war policies had brought abject failure.[22]

War Democrats were the majority of the party faithful, but Peace Democrats were coalescing and gaining momentum with the argument that "the Union could never be restored by the war, especially now that Lincoln had turned it into an unconstitutional war against slavery." The timing of Lincoln's proclamation, in the wake of the Fredericksburg debacle, raised a hue and cry that the president cared more about the well-being of slaves than that of white soldiers. Copperheads often engaged in flagrant race-baiting, retooling secessionist arguments that antislavery Republicans were race traitors, and that emancipation would bring on race competition and race mixing. Lincoln had rendered the war into an "unconstitutional crusade for the liberation of three millions of negro barbarians and their enfranchisement as citizens," the *Chicago Times* fumed, while the *Cincinnati Enquirer* insisted that reunion was now impossible, as the South would "shrink with horror and loathing from a connection with a people who would countenance the stirring up of servile insurrections among them, the inevitable concomitants of which are arson, rapine, and the slaughter of women and children." Copperheads appropriated the word "terrorism," turning it back on the Lincoln administration with the charge that confiscation and emancipation were "devices of terrorism" used to wage a war of subjugation against the South and of political proscription in the North.[23]

In the face of these accusations that Lincoln's January 1 edict was extremist, moderate Republicans, together with some War Democrats, defended it as pragmatic: it was not a radical transformation of American society but an act of national self-defense and self-preservation. They emphasized that Lincoln had given fair warning to rebel slaveholders; that he had urged freedpeople not to resort to violence; that he would use former slaves to do menial labor for the military but not to bear arms.[24] Disavowing any interest in racial equality or full citizenship, moderates offered a narrow interpretation of the scope of the proclamation, insisting that it conferred on blacks nothing but freedom—primarily the right to be remunerated for their labor. As the *New York Times* explained, emancipation rested on the principle that the inferiority of blacks entitled them to white protection; a black man had the right to "his wages, his wife, his children, and his own body." "We do not advocate, because we do not believe in, negro equality," the paper continued. "We would not, if we could, give negroes a share in the Government." The *Waynesboro Village Record* in Pennsylvania offered an even more circumscribed interpretation of Lincoln's January 1 decree. To critics who objected to "fighting for the niggers," the *Village Record* responded that Lincoln was simply taking away the "labor that sustains the power of the South" to add to the "military power of the North." "Suppose the rebels were using a great many oxen . . . and the President found out some means by which he could detach the oxen from them and make them serviceable to him in putting down the rebellion, would you refuse to fight on the plea that you were fighting only for oxen?" Such a reading was a far cry from that of Purvis or Nell.[25]

Moreover, mainstream supporters of federal emancipation cast it as an extension, not a repudiation, of Lincoln's plans for state-based, gradual emancipation: part of a dual strategy in which the Union would rid itself of slavery "peaceably if we can, forcibly if we must," as the *North American and United States Gazette* put it on January 2, 1863. Centrist commentators noted with satisfaction that Lincoln's freedom decree came at the same moment as his signing of West Virginia's statehood bill, which provided for gradual rather than immediate emancipation in that fledgling state. The region's statehood movement dated back to the secession summer of 1861, when Unionists in Wheeling, spurning the Richmond convention's secession vote, called for the formation of a "Restored" Virginia government under lawyer and coal industrialist Francis H. Pierpont. The statehood bill Lincoln signed on December 31, 1862, stipulated, following a proposal by Senator Waitman Willey, that slaves under age twenty-one as of July 4, 1863, would become free when they attained that age. West Virginia would join the Union on June 20, 1863. Despite the efforts of Confederate-sympathizing guerrillas in its southern-most counties to uproot this new government, West Virginia persisted (and would support Lincoln in the 1864 presidential election).[26]

Equally encouraging to moderates was the surprising turn of events in Missouri, where gradual compensated emancipation, which had been summarily rejected by the state's leaders in the summer of 1862, picked up support after Lincoln issued his preliminary proclamation. Staunch Unionists gained seats in the state legislature and in Missouri's congressional delegation in the fall elections, and they embraced Lincoln's previous offer of compensated emancipation "so as to salvage something from the impending wreck of slavery." While they did not yet have enough votes to enact their plan over the opposition of proslavery legislators and of a small but growing group of immediatists, Missouri's gradualists, like West Virginia's, gave hope to Northerners who were looking for signs that slaveholders might as yet be persuaded to renounce slavery. Highlighting West Virginia's statehood bill and Congress's appropriation of funds to promote compensated emancipation in Missouri, the *North American* declared triumphantly in January 1863 that the fortunes of those regions were "no more identified with the south, but with those of the free north," and that "Kentucky must soon follow." In the *North American*'s calculus, Lincoln's offer of gradual compensated emancipation had been a "serious wound" to the principle of involuntary servitude, and his new proclamation would prove the "death blow." Such assessments of border state trends were repeated again and again by Northerners. At a public meeting in response to the proclamation in Bangor, Maine, for example, a local politician praised the president's "conservative and forbearing" treatment of slaveholding rebels ("He has warned them, but they have refused to yield"), "alluded to the gratifying change of sentiment in the State of Missouri," and

predicted that emancipation would "elevate all labor, white as well as black."
A January 2, 1863, editorial in Milwaukee's *Semi-Weekly Wisconsin* heralded
the "progress of public sentiment" not only in Missouri but also in Maryland,
which had "turned away with a shudder from the rebel army that visited her
soil."[27]

Some defenses of Lincoln's proclamation focused directly on the suffering
of Southern whites and what they stood to gain from the demise of slavery
and of the Confederacy. In the pages of the *Continental Monthly*, Frederick
Perry Stanton, a Tennessee Democrat turned Republican, cast Lincoln's
proclamation as a blessing in disguise to the white South, a seeming punishment that would in time do momentous good. Repeating the mantra that
the Federal army sought the "regeneration and redemption" of the Southern
people, not their subjugation, he argued that the triumph of the free labor
system would not only increase the "population, wealth, activity, and intelligence" of the South but also dispel "force, fraud, and self-delusion." "The
masses of the people," Stanton predicted, would soon "look on themselves as
the victims of designing men, who, for selfish purposes, have partly seduced
and party impelled them into the perils and disasters of a gigantic but fruitless
rebellion." The Union called to them with "paternal tenderness" to accept its
"magnanimous protection." Linking black liberation and white deliverance,
the February 2, 1863, offering of the *New Haven Daily Palladium* insisted,
"There is not a State in the South where men are not longing for the triumph
of the Union arms. And while the slaves of the South are flocking to our
standard, as they do by thousands wherever opportunity offers . . . white men
of the South who love our country are reaching out their hands from every
State saying, 'Come over and help us.'" The rebels "may visit the patriots of
the South with their whole catalogue of tortures" but "they cannot destroy a
patriot's love for his country," the paper proclaimed, looking forward to peace
and reunion.[28]

Home front debates were mirrored in the ranks, as the proclamation
escalated a battle to mold the opinion of the soldiery. Democrats end-
lessly repeated the charge of Republican treachery and callousness. "It is
not because we can not whip the South that this war has continued so
long, but because those dirty Abolitionists at Washington are spending all
their time thinking of the [slave], instead of looking to the poor soldier,"
a soldier writing to the *Cleveland Plain Dealer* charged. While racist ful-
minating abounded, "there was also quiet support for emancipation in the
army," as George Rable has explained. He elaborates: "Entrenched racial
prejudice among the troops was often impervious to argument, but not

to the course of the war itself. Military developments and to some degree the performance of black troops would vindicate the wisdom of emancipation and change white soldiers' attitudes as well." Most Union soldiers accepted emancipation on the grounds of military necessity. As an infantryman in the 48th Ohio, stationed in Memphis, related in a published letter, "Very few Abolitionists of the Sumner and Giddings school can be found in our army, yet a majority of us, here at least, are Abolitionists in the sense that the negro is 'contraband of war,' and, as such, should be put out of reach of their rebel owners." In a similar vein, Corporal Henry C. Baldwin of the 15th Connecticut wrote home that he did not care "how many Negroes . . . get their heads broak if it will help to end the war."[29]

Some Union soldiers explicitly connected emancipation and white Southern deliverance. Taking heart from the new policy of black enlistment, Private Charles W. Sherman of the 12th Connecticut Volunteers wrote from southern Louisiana to his family back in New England that the "vigorous mesuers that will be carred through by Uncl Abraham to fill the Union Armies" would "Convince the Traitors . . . that they have been sold and decived." He continued: "The Southron People are Suffering more then you can think but they are kept down [by] the Iron hand of Military Despotism, and thair is no help for them till the Fedral Arms brake the Chains by which thay are held Down."[30]

Other Union soldiers saw emancipation as a part of their own moral renovation. Charles W. Hill of the 5th Massachusetts, a self-described "red-whiskered, big-mouthed, awkward Yankee," was moved by the experience of seeing fugitive slaves seek refuge in Union-occupied New Bern, North Carolina. He wrote his wife, Martha, on January 6, 1863:

> The iron heel of *despotism* has been upon them and deprived them of the privilege of learning and they must seek their freedom . . . leiving behind dear friends, dear to them as ours are to us, in *slavery* of whose fate they shall never learn until a just God shall summon oppressors and oppressed before Him in judgment. How great to them must be the worth of *freedom* when sought at such a cost. Sometimes whole families join us father, mother, and children, even infants. . . . I have no doubt many are compelled to fall behind and again fall into the hands of the cruel taskmaster.

Complaining to Martha that many of the men in his regiment were mean-spirited to the freedpeople, Hill added, "I *hate* slavery as I never hated it before." A few months later Hill revealed that as much as he missed his wife and family, he felt that soldiering had developed his character. "Are we not more to *each other* now," he asked Martha, "that we have been willing to make this sacrifice for what we believe to be a great and good cause? It does one good sometimes to get out-side of *self.*" Applauding the enlistment of black troops as a hopeful sign, Hill wrote, "I think that whenever we are willing to do justice to *all* men *white* or *black*, we shall be on the road to success."[31]

George Snell of the 15th New Hampshire had his own awakening, as he explained to his brother Aaron in March from Camp Parapet near New Orleans: "I am a stronger aberletionest, since I came out here than I was in New Hampshire I have ben to the Negroes meeting and it was a good meeting the spirit of the living God was with them. . . . I tell you Aaron altho they are ignorant God has put somthing in them that they will tell all about the Relegion of his Dear Son." It was time, Snell had come to see, "to whip out Rebeldom and slavery both together."[32]

Those soldiers who accepted emancipation worked to convince the skeptics to try the experiment in good faith. Whether black freedom and black enlistment were "good or bad policy is a matter of opinion," Halleck told Grant in the spring of 1863; the real character of these measures could "only be determined by a fair trial." "It is expected that you will use your official and personal influence to remove prejudices on this subject," he continued. "The north must either destroy the slave-oligarchy, or become slaves themselves."[33]

"Contraband" Camps

The range of opinion within the Union army was dramatized by conditions in the so-called contraband camps—in zones of Union control such as Corinth, Mississippi; Helena, Arkansas; and Memphis, Tennessee—at which fugitives converged. Some of the Union officers and superintendents (often army chaplains) who administered these camps were solicitous of the well-being of the refugees and appreciative of their contributions to the war effort. One Union camp in particular, the Freedman's Village in Arlington, Virginia, was designed to be a showcase of the freedpeople's capacities. The April 1862 D.C. Abolition Act and the military campaigns in Virginia had brought a steady stream of refugees to the District; by the fall of 1862 there were some six hundred "contrabands" at Camp Barker, within the city limits, and another one thousand in nearby Alexandria. The announcement of Lincoln's proclamation turned the stream of arrivals into a flood, and with conditions in the

MAP 6.2

overcrowded urban camps rapidly worsening, Union military officials decided
to set up a new camp in the country. They chose a site rich in symbolism—
the confiscated estate of Robert E. Lee's family, just across the Potomac. The
village featured carefully laid out streets, homes, shops, parks, churches, and
schools. Able-bodied men and women worked for wages, doing farm labor or
learning trades, such as carpentry for men and sewing for women. But beneath
the veneer of a model community was another story—of hard labor, poor pay
and rations, high rents, strict military discipline, and gradual overcrowding.[34]

Elsewhere in the South, Union officials and rank-and-file soldiers were
generally ambivalent about or indifferent toward black refugees. Many
were unsure of their obligations. In the military culture of the era, soldiers
were not accustomed to regarding the care of refugees as their responsibility. The new directive that the army was to actively withdraw resources
from the Confederacy translated not only into the enticement of slaves away
from masters but also into the impressment of black laborers by the Union
army, with little concern for their consent. Those freedpeople who could not
be put to work by the army—children, the aged, and the infirm—posed a
special problem. Did the army have any moral obligation to offer housing,
rations, and other precious resources to them? The "fear of dependency ran
like a cancer throughout the rhetoric of Union officials in the Civil War
South," historian Jim Downs has noted. The association of poverty and indolence ran deep in nineteenth-century culture, as did racist stereotypes of free

blacks as unproductive. Union officials worried that offers of government assistance, especially to women and children, would lead freedpeople to refuse
to work.[35]

Still others were actively cruel. Halleck alluded to the problem of soldier
recalcitrance in his letter to Grant, disdaining those Union officers who "not
only discourage the negroes from coming under our protection, but, by ill
treatment, force them to return to their masters." As three officers at Helena,
the site of several refugee camps, complained, "The contrabands are left entirely to the mercy and rapacity of the unprincipled part of our army." Black
laborers were routinely exploited—not paid at all, or paid in counterfeit
money, or, if they had been paid in real money, robbed by Union soldiers.
Freedmen had no protection for their families, and camps were sites of sexual
danger. "The wives of some have been molested by soldiers to gratify their licentious lust, and their husbands murdered in endeavoring to defend them,"
the Helena officers noted with horror. The lack of shelter, clothing, food, and
sanitation bred diseases such as typhoid fever, measles, smallpox, pneumonia,
and dysentery, and medical care was nonexistent or woefully inadequate;
the "negro hospital" at Helena was "notorious for filth, neglect, mortality &
brutal whipping." The Helena officers asked plaintively: "For the sake of humanity, for the sake of Christianity, for the good name of our army . . . cannot
something be done to prevent this oppression?" A similar picture emerges
from the testimony of eight camp superintendents in Grant's Department of
the Tennessee, to whom a questionnaire on conditions among the ex-slaves
was circulated in February and March 1863. While the Corinth superintendent reported that his camp was well regulated and that Union soldiers
there were cooperative, his Memphis counterpart attested that "many soldiers
and some officers manifested only bitterness and contempt" in their treatment of freedpeople.[36]

Significantly, all of the superintendents emphasized the refugees' "universal desire to obtain their freedom" and profound longing to enjoy its full
benefits. None wished to return to slavery—and "many would die first." This
was a recurring theme in the commentary of Union authorities, one that
dated back to the arrival of the first "contrabands" at Fort Monroe in Virginia
in 1861. Colonel Nathan W. Daniels, who commanded one of the first black
regiments mustered in Louisiana as it garrisoned an island off the Mississippi
coast, said this of his troops: "The taste of Liberty is too sweet and death is far
preferable to them than renewed slavery—To hear these men reiterate 'that
they will die sooner than be taken,' . . . one can but *know* that they are the men
to battle and conquer, one can but feel that in their action is success."[37]

Freedman's Village. This photograph of the Freedman's Village in Arlington, Virginia, shows African Americans reading books in front of their barracks. Established on land confiscated from Robert E. Lee's family, the village was intended as a temporary refuge but became a substantial settlement with several thousand residents. (Library of Congress LC-DIG-ppmsca-34829)

This push and pull between whites who were hostile to emancipation and blacks who were determined to shape it made camps at once places of "despair and death," historian Thavolia Glymph has written, and sites "of refuge and hope and the making of freedom." Harriet Jacobs attested to this paradox. She did relief work among refugees in Alexandria, Virginia, and bore witness to their suffering, sending reports of the dire conditions there to the Northern press, to inspire the benevolent to step forward with aid. She described men, women, and children languishing in destitution—but still displaying faith in the Union and clinging to those moments in which the promise of freedom seemed to materialize. "Amidst all this sadness, we would sometimes hear a shout of joy," she wrote. "Some mother had come in, and found her long-lost child; some husband his wife. Brothers and sisters meet."[38]

For Jacobs, the human dramas that unfolded in the camps were a powerful indictment of slavery itself. What but the love of freedom, she asked, could compel slaves to seek refuge in such flawed sanctuaries? To well-minded whites who had an interest in assisting the freedpeople, Jacobs preached empathy: "Trust them." In letters she sent north after the proclamation had been issued, Jacobs compiled evidence of progress in the camps—of weddings, night classes, sewing circles, and other manifestations of the freedpeople's fitness for full citizenship. "Many have found employment, and are supporting themselves and their families," Jacobs wrote to abolitionist Lydia Maria Child in March 1863. "They are quick, intelligent and full of the spirit of freedom." Small victories sustained her: "I can but feel with my heart the last chain is to be broken, the accursed blot wiped out."[39]

Confederate Reactions to the Proclamation

For Confederates, the Emancipation Proclamation was a bitter blow. In his January 12, 1863, annual message to the Confederate Congress, Jefferson Davis set the tone for the Confederate response, attributing the proclamation to Northerners' "revenge and thirst for blood . . . mercenary and wicked passions . . . [and] lust of conquest." The only passage of the proclamation that Davis quoted directly was Lincoln's clause urging freedpeople to "abstain from violence unless in necessary self-defence." This, for Davis, was an "insidious recommendation" that slaves perpetrate "a general assassination of their masters." In one loud chorus Confederate civilians and soldiers joined Davis in charging that Lincoln's purpose was "to incite servile insurrection in the Southern States and thus consign our women and children to butchery," as a Charleston newspaper put it. While Confederates agreed about Lincoln's intent, they disagreed about his edict's likely effects. Some commentators, clinging to the fantasy of the "loyal slave," insisted that blacks did not desire liberty and would refuse to heed the proclamation's call to rebellion. Some protested defiantly that slavery had never been safer or more profitable. "Just at the very time when Lincoln declares they are to be emancipated, they command higher prices than ever before," the *Staunton Spectator* editorialized on January 6, 1863. "Could anything demonstrate more satisfactorily the futility of his infamous proclamation?" Those looking for evidence of the proclamation's futility also purported to find it in news reports from the North rehearsing the Copperheads' pointed attacks on Lincoln; perhaps, Confederates reckoned, these heralded the overthrow of the Republicans at the hands of Northern voters.[40]

On the whole, however, Confederates were far more likely to play up than to play down the proclamation's possible effects in the South—and to call for renewed solidarity and swift retaliation against the insurrectionists. Lee dubbed emancipation a "savage and brutal policy . . . which leaves us no alternative but success or degradation worse than death, if we would save the honor of our families from pollution." The "day has passed for argument," the *Natchez Daily Courier* intoned. "The hour has come for quick retribution on the heads of the invaders. . . . Drive back and destroy the invading foe, and take no officers as prisoners except to hang them by the neck until they are dead, DEAD, DEAD!" Confederates escalated their charges that Yankee soldiers were demons incarnate bent on merciless destruction, that any kind of reconciliation was an impossibility, and that black freedom would bring the enslavement or extermination of Southern whites. The South Carolina diarist Emma Holmes captured all of these themes in her February 14, 1863, entry. Invoking the "baseness and treachery of the Yankee character" and the "despotism" of the Federal government, Holmes asked, "Is it possible for any sane man to dream for an instant after such reiterated acts, of *Re-construction*"? She vowed: "Rather let every man, woman and child perish in one universal self-immolation and our blessed country become a wide-spread desert than become the slaves of such demons as they have shown themselves." She would not "submit to the descendants of the witch burning Puritans, whose God is the almighty dollar!"[41]

Whatever their rhetorical stances, slaveholders left nothing to chance in their actual treatment of bondspeople. They ratcheted up measures intended

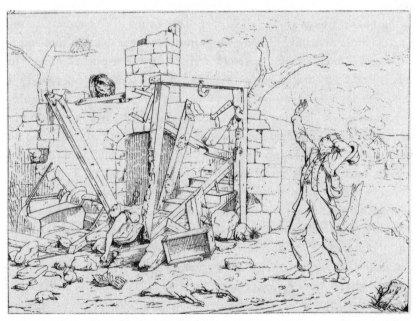

"Tracks of the Armies." Typifying Confederates' dystopian depictions of the Union war, this etching by Adalbert J. Volck shows a Confederate soldier returning home to find it burned, his belongings destroyed, his wife dead in the ruins, animals slaughtered, and perched vultures contemplating their prey. A German émigré living in Baltimore, Volck served as a smuggler and courier, as well as propagandist, for the Confederate cause. (Library of Congress) [Metropolitan Museum of Art, Harris Brisbane Dick Fund, 1938, 38.13.15]

to deter slave flight, relocating slaves to farms and plantations far away from the Federal army; strengthening slave patrols, local militias, and home guards; advertising runaways and posting rewards for their recapture; and meting out brutal punishments to fugitives who were recaptured, to make an example of them. For example, under directions from the governor, the citizens of Kenansville in eastern North Carolina, not far from Union-occupied New Bern, created a new twenty-man patrol guard in 1863 and "purchased a pack of Hounds at heavy cost to accompany them" in the work of tracking down and remanding fugitives. This "preventive" measure worked, the patrols' sponsors attested: "Since the organization of this Company . . . the whole number of negroes (save one, & he was shot and killed *near* the Yankee lines) were Captured & returned to their owners."[42]

Southern civilians looked to the Confederate army to enforce racial control, and it worked aggressively to catch and punish runaways, and to seize and reenslave blacks through raids of Union-controlled plantations and contraband camps, and ambush attacks on small Union commands or isolated regiments that traveled with vulnerable contingents of camp followers.

No mercy was shown to those who were ensnared. "Yesterday a negro was caught armed and killed two dogs in the attempt to catch him and finally shot himself inflicting a severe wound," C. R. Barteau, a Confederate officer in Okolona, Mississippi, reported to his superiors on January 8, 1863. The wounded man revealed that he had learned of the Emancipation Proclamation in Union-occupied Corinth and had been given a pistol by the Yankees and instructed to go back out into the countryside to spread the word. What was to be done with such captured men, Smith asked, if they resisted reenslavement by refusing to disclose the names of their masters? The answer from an adjutant: "When you take Negroes with arms evidently coming out from the enemie's camp . . . proceed at once to hold a drum head court martial and if found guilty hang them on the spot." Regional patterns distinguished the particular kinds of risks runaways took on. Because of the density of Confederate forces there, it was more difficult in the east than in the west for a fugitive to evade capture on the road to Federal lines. But refugees were relatively safe if they succeeded in making it to the Union strongholds on the Virginia and North Carolina coasts. A fugitive in the west, by contrast, had somewhat better odds of evading capture on his journey to Union lines but was more vulnerable to later being reenslaved, due to the frequency of Confederate raids on undermanned Union positions.[43]

Even in the absence of flight, the proclamation could change the dynamics in Southern households: those slaves unable or unwilling to take on the risk of running away worked to destabilize slavery and hasten emancipation by ratcheting up their own daily acts of resistance, such as refusing to work, feigning illness, breaking tools, and engaging in truancy (short-term flight). Some slaves changed their demeanor: "They tossed aside the use of coded speech," Thavolia Glymph has noted, "and spoke openly of freedom, calling for an end to the brutalities associated with slavery, especially violence against women." For example, Ann Wilkinson Penrose of New Orleans complained bitterly in her diary of her slaves' growing recalcitrance; her February 2, 1863, entry fumed that the enslaved woman Old Lyddy was "very insolent indeed, telling Rebecca that she was free, and signifying she would do as she please." But the proliferation of this kind of resistance brought in turn waves of reprisals from whites, most notably plantation mistresses, who vented their anger at the emancipation policy in violent acts of vengeance against the enslaved persons in their midst, rendering Southern households more volatile and fraught than ever.[44]

With Confederates launching a concerted counterattack, the progress of emancipation was neither linear nor certain. Instead, the tide of freedom surged forward and receded with the fortunes of the Union army. However strong an incentive the proclamation provided, flight toward Union lines was not a viable choice for the overwhelming majority of slaves living in the Confederate interior—the regime of slaveholder surveillance and punishment was too strict, Union lines were too far off, the conditions in contraband camps too forbidding, the prospect of leaving loved ones behind too heart-wrenching. "Slaves were more likely to be freed during the war by the arrival of the Union army than by escaping to it," James Oakes has noted, underscoring the risks of and obstacles to flight and the crucial role of direct intervention by the Federal forces. For liberation to come into view, the Union army had to penetrate vast reaches of the Confederacy that had not heard the tramp of blue soldiers—and to break the strategic stalemate that prevailed in the existing zones of combat. And in the winter of 1863, as Lincoln's decree went into effect, Federal armies were fighting to a bloody draw in Tennessee and literally bogged down along the Mississippi and on the Virginia front.[45]

7

Fire in the Rear

TO CHANCELLORSVILLE

IN MARCH 1863 the *Milwaukee Sentinel* published a revealing letter from a soldier in the 66th Illinois Volunteers (also known as the "Western Sharpshooters") who was manning a stockade near Corinth, Mississippi. "Another year of victories for us, and the C.S.A. will pass away 'and there will be a new heaven and a new earth,'" the correspondent predicted. He professed his great faith both in Lincoln's "saving ordinance" of emancipation and in white Southern Unionism. "Refugees come to our lines frequently seeking protection from the power of Davis, the Southern tyrant and dictator," he observed, noting that none other than the Honorable John W. Wood, one of only two delegates to the Mississippi secession convention to reject secession, was among the recently arrived refugees. "He is now in our camp and tells many wonderful tales of tyranny, oppression, suffering in the South. He states that even the most sanguine supporters of rebellion have no faith in their ultimate success and their only hope seems to be derived from expectations of foreign intervention of a division of the North," the letter explained. "The treasury is without credit and many poor families are starving throughout the country. The people are without power, and wholly in the hands of the Government." The correspondent added with a flourish, "These are common tales, and well known to be true." Before the year was over, John W. Wood, safely installed in Union-occupied Memphis, would publish a pamphlet there recounting the suffering of persecuted Deep South loyalists and pledging his commitment to "effecting a re-union in feeling and sentiment between the masses of the people of the United States." "When re-united and harmonious, we will be the greatest military and maritime power on the globe," Wood proclaimed. "Uncle Sam will never be caught napping again."[1]

These were bold prophecies. But in the spring of 1863, Union progress in the western theater was again offset by demoralizing reversals in the east, this time at Chancellorsville in Virginia, where Lee flatly outgeneraled his latest Federal rival, Joseph Hooker. Increasingly, setbacks for the Federal army had ripple effects in partisan politics, with Copperhead Democrats getting more strident in their censure of emancipation and their calls for a negotiated peace; the controversial Ohio politician Clement Vallandingham painted Lincoln as a despot and condemned the government's resort to martial law and conscription as an abrogation of white men's rights. Loyalists tried to close ranks in the president's defense through the new Union League movement, which cast criticism of the war effort as disloyalty and laid out the broad benefits, to whites and blacks, of abolition. Unionists continued to scan the horizon for signs of Confederate disaffection and drew hope from the bread riot that rocked the rebel capital in April. Meanwhile, the men in the ranks displayed a greater and greater animus against Copperheads, who seemed to be actively aiding and abetting the rebels.

Hell's Half Acre

After the failure of Braxton Bragg's invasion of Kentucky in the fall of 1862, he took his army to Murfreesboro, Tennessee, hoping to preempt Union advances on Chattanooga, to the south. Meanwhile, some thirty miles northwest in Nashville, Rosecrans's Army of the Cumberland concentrated forces and gathered supplies, under intense pressure to take the offensive and dislodge Bragg. The day after Christmas Federal troops got orders to strike tents, draw three days' rations, and prepare to advance; they soon set out toward Murfreesboro, in a cold rain, and arrived at its outskirts three days later on December 29, finding the Confederate army drawn up in a defensive line amidst the red cedar groves along the Stones River, two miles northwest of the city.[2]

On the morning of the thirty-first, Rosecrans sent an order through the ranks exhorting his troops to be ready for a battle that "may today decide the fate of the nation." Rosecrans's battle plan was to attack and roll up Bragg's right flank. But Bragg beat him to the punch. The Confederate plan, as it happened, was a mirror image of the Federal one, targeting the Yankee right flank, and the Confederates acted first, launching their assault while many Federals were still finishing their morning coffee. "Dropping our pots and pans, leaving our haversacks and blankets, we snatched up our cartridge-boxes and rushed for our guns," R. B. Stewart wrote. "We stood to deliver [one round of] fire and say good morning, then took to our heels and ran." Bragg's blow sent two Federal divisions reeling, forcing them into a fighting retreat. The Federals avoided total collapse thanks to the leadership of Brigadier General Philip Sheridan, who led a counterattack that dissipated the Confederate momentum, and to the stubborn resistance of Colonel William B. Hazen's brigade, at a point in the Federal line dubbed "Hell's Half Acre." The battle's first day ended with the Confederates having the clear advantage.[3]

Both sides stood down on New Year's Day, but the carnage commenced again on January 2, when Union forces took a hill east of the river and Bragg ordered John C. Breckinridge's division to retake it. In one of the legendary charges of the war, some 4,500 rebel soldiers threw themselves at a Federal position that was well defended by closely packed artillery, forty-five guns strong, on the other side of the river. "The bravery of the rebel officers amounted almost to insanity," commented Marcus Woodcock, a Unionist Tennessean fighting in the Federal 9th Kentucky Infantry. "Obstinately did the disappointed rebels fall back after once thinking that they had already gained a victory; but our boys pressed on with such fury and determination, rendered almost desperate by the terrible loss they sustained among comrades and friends." The battle of Stones River ended with a Confederate retreat, and with more than 3,000 dead; the 24,000 total casualties of the two sides combined was nearly one-third of the men engaged. Both sides claimed victory, but the Union had the more plausible case: the Confederates withdrew to Tullahoma, thirty miles to the southwest, relinquishing fertile farmlands in Middle Tennessee. "What a bloody and useless sacrifice!" wrote Lieutenant Lot D. Young of the Confederate 1st Kentucky Brigade as his epitaph for the battle. While the Federals failed to pursue the rebels and instead hunkered down at Murfreesboro, they did slowly consolidate their gains: in the battle's wake, the Army of the Cumberland, together with large numbers of ex-slaves, built a massive fort, Fortress Rosecrans, spanning two hundred acres, as a supply base for future operations against Chattanooga.[4]

The battle of Stones River was one of the bloodiest of the war, and soldiers' accounts of it provide a window into shifting constructions of death. The impulse to create idealized "good deaths" for soldiers—in which they were calm and reposed in their acceptance of God's will and tended to by sympathetic witnesses who could hear their dying declarations—remained strong and suffused condolence letters, eulogies, obituaries, and other such testimonials. But the growing scope and lethality of the war made it increasingly difficult, if not impossible, to contextualize death in this way. "Individuals found themselves in a new and different moral universe, one in which unimaginable

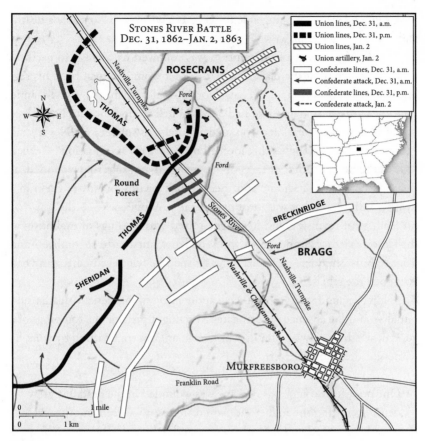

MAP 7.1

destruction had become a daily experience," historian Drew Faust has written. "Doubt threatened to overpower faith—faith in the Christian narrative of a compassionate divinity and a hope of life beyond the grave." The internal struggle of soldiers to reconcile peacetime ideals and wartime realities is evident in Marcus Woodcock's account of the aftermath of Stones River. He and his fellow able-bodied soldiers were detailed to collect the dead and wounded from the battlefield; this gruesome task was generally the responsibility of the victorious army, which held the field of battle. The first wounded man Woodcock came across was his comrade Andrew Bray, who was dying from a shot that had just missed his heart. "He insisted that I should hear him talk awhile ere I attempted to remove him," Woodcock wrote of Bray. The wounded man testified "that he was prepared to meet the great Judge before the bar of Eternal Justice and render a clear account of his stewardship while on earth. He prayed for the souls of mankind and *for the nation*." Woodcock took some solace from being able to serve as a witness to "so noble a death" and to hear Bray's dying words.[5]

That brief moment of redemption was followed by a crash to earth as Woodcock arrived at the place where the other wounded men from his regiment were being collected. "What a horrid sight here met my eyes!—amid the light of the glaring fires that had been kindled around the spot I could see 14 dead bodies and near fifty wounded and helpless soldiers. . . . Never shall I forget the awful thoughts that loomed up before my imagination . . . when I heard the heart-rending shrieks of our mangled and suffering wounded, as they lay there far from home and their dearest friends—many of them in a dying condition." What was most distressing to Woodcock was the way that his feelings of revulsion and heartache mixed with feelings of exaltation at the Union's victory. Stones River was Woodcock's first taste of combat—and it made him "shudder" to realize how satisfied he felt because his army had "whipped the rebels."[6]

Soldiers shuddered, too, at the anonymity of battlefield deaths and burials—and the absence of surrogates who might provide the trappings of a good death. Ira S. Owen, an Ohio infantryman, was traumatized by what he witnessed after Stones River:

> One poor fellow who was near me was wounded in the head. He grew delirious during the night, and would frequently call his mother. He would say: "Mother, O, Mother come and help me!" The poor fellow died before morning with no mother near, to soothe him in his dying moments. . . . Next morning rows of men were laid out side by side ready for the soldier's burial. No weeping friends stood around, no coffin and hearse to bear them away to the grave, no funeral orations delivered; but there, away from home and kindred, they were wrapped in the soldiers' blanket, a trench dug, and their bodies placed side by side, like they fought, a few shovelfuls of earth thrown upon them.[7]

The nameless dead had the power to haunt soldiers long after these encounters. Confederate Samuel Watkins wrote of Murfreesboro (as the Confederates called the battle of Stones River) in his postwar memoir, casting it as a Confederate victory. He recalled that as he passed over the battlefield, his eye was drawn to a dead Yankee colonel. "He had on the finest clothes I ever saw, a red sash and a fine sword. I particularly noticed his boots," Watkins continued. "I needed them, and had made up my mind to wear them out for him." Watkins took hold of one of the dead man's feet to try to wrestle a boot off, but then he happened to look up, and what he saw stopped him cold: "The colonel had his eyes wide open, and seemed to be looking at me." Watkins dropped the foot, recoiled, and gave up his macabre task. "It was my first and last attempt to rob a dead Yankee."[8]

Return to Vicksburg

Even as Rosecrans drove back Bragg, Union forces under Grant were determined to regain momentum along the Mississippi. The Federals had failed in their prior attempts to capture Vicksburg, in December 1862. Back to the drawing board went Grant, who in mid-January "decided to take personal field command of operations against Vicksburg." Reviving a stalled element of the first Vicksburg campaign, Grant deployed thousands of soldiers and former slaves in digging canals that might redirect the river into new channels and thereby permit the Union forces to avoid exposure to the batteries on Vicksburg's bluffs. The work was dangerous, as pneumonia, malaria, and other deadly ailments coursed through the ranks. And it was ultimately futile, as the river and bayous, whose water levels the army simply could not control, refused to cooperate. But the project served the important purpose of keeping Grant's men busy while he searched for a more practicable scheme.[9]

In February, the Union forces tried again to manipulate the tangled Delta waterways: Federal explosives blew up a levee at Yazoo Pass so that Admiral Porter's armada could enter the Yazoo River via its tributaries and attack Vicksburg from the northeast. But the Confederates lay in wait at Fort Pemberton, an unimpressive structure built of dirt, sand, and cotton bales, positioned at a narrow pass, and surrounded by swamps that the Union gunboats could not navigate. The fort held out against multiple attacks, and the Federals had no choice but to retreat. In mid-March, a second attempt by the Union navy to approach Vicksburg using the Yazoo River—this time the plan was to enter the river through the waterways of Steele's Bayou—foundered, as the boats encountered numerous topographical obstacles, including low-hanging tree limbs and felled trees, which the Confederates hoped might trap the Union fleet in the swamps. Another Union retreat ensued.[10]

On the face of it, Confederates had the upper hand as spring came to the Delta in 1863. But as historian Michael B. Ballard has noted, the Confederate commander John Pemberton was in fact stuck in a strategic rut: he was content with shoring up his defensive works and reacting to Grant's initiatives and proved averse to mounting counteroffensives or taking the initiative himself. Because of this passive mindset, Pemberton had squandered the

The Vicksburg Campaign. In the summer of 1862 and then again in the winter of 1862–63, Union forces attempted to cut a canal opposite Vicksburg so that the Federal fleet could bypass the city's artillery defenses. Both times, disease and exhaustion took a heavy toll on the former slaves and Union soldiers doing the heavy labor, and Grant eventually abandoned the idea and changed tactics. (Library of Congress LC-USZ62-138293)

opportunity to trap Porter's fleet or to pursue them in their retreat. Lulled into a "false sense of security," Pemberton failed to appreciate that while victory had eluded Grant, the Union had nonetheless made headway over the last three months: Union operations had forced the Confederates to spread their already thin manpower across a wide front.[11]

Grant, under fire in the North from critics who argued that his futile campaigns had consigned too many Union soldiers to ignominious deaths in

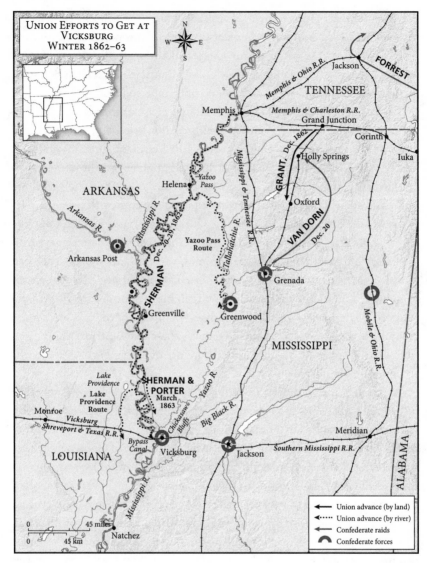

UNION EFFORTS TO GET AT VICKSBURG WINTER 1862–63

MAP 7.2

the swamps, nonetheless remained certain that Vicksburg eventually would be his. His new plan, one that had taken shape over the course of the vexing winter months, was to send Union gunboats and supply craft downriver, running the four-mile gauntlet of the Vicksburg batteries and landing some thirty-five miles south of the city, where they would be met by infantry corps that had marched along the west side of the river; the boats, in an amphibious operation of unprecedented scale, would then ferry the men to the east bank, and they would march north to beset Vicksburg, where its defenses were weakest. Meanwhile, to screen these movements from Pemberton and induce him to send his troops to the wrong places, Grant had Sherman effect a mock attack on the outskirts of Vicksburg near Chickasaw Bluffs, while Colonel Benjamin H. Grierson led an ambitious cavalry raid on Pemberton's railroad supply.

Porter's fleet successfully executed the first phase of the plan on April 16 and 17. His men shielded their craft with cotton bales, hay, sandbags, and logs, and the vessels moved slowly, hugging the Louisiana shoreline and with lights extinguished, in the hopes that they might glide past the batteries undetected. When Confederate sentries spotted the convoy and the Vicksburg artillerists opened fire, Porter shrewdly directed the convoy to cross the river to the Mississippi shoreline, so that the Confederate batteries high upon the bluffs would struggle to find effective shooting angles. As a result of the diversionary Sherman feint and Grierson raid, when Grant's men were ferried across the Mississippi to Bruinsburg, they encountered negligible resistance from the Confederates. Grant would write in his memoirs of the Bruinsburg landing, "I felt a degree of relief scarcely ever equaled since. . . . I was on dry ground on the same side of the river with the enemy. All the campaigns, labors, hardships and exposures from the month of December . . . were for the accomplishment of this one object."[12]

As Grant's forces moved inland, east toward Port Gibson, Pemberton rushed reinforcements to the new front—but the Confederate force of 8,000 massed too late and was no match for Grant's 23,000 troops. Victorious at Port Gibson, Grant's men defeated a heavily outnumbered Confederate force at Raymond on May 12 and continued to move east, toward Jackson. Grant's army was by now 44,000 strong, as Sherman's corps had been transported downriver, but the army was nonetheless vulnerable: it had moved away from its supply bases on the Mississippi River and would have to live off the land. Union foraging increased in intensity. "The country will supply all the forage required," Grant reasoned; a Union soldier added that it was "excellent 'war policy' to quarter a hungry army on the produce of the enemy and on his own land." That Confederate forces failed to exploit Grant's vulnerability is attributable both to Pemberton's weaknesses and to a crippling disharmony in the Confederate high command. Pemberton had been warned in April by the astute brigadier general John S. Bowen that the Yankee forces aimed to run the Vicksburg batteries and establish a beachhead to the south of the city. But Pemberton, still trying to direct operations in the region from his headquarters at Jackson, had failed to see, both literally and figuratively, this Federal plan as it unfolded.[13]

Pemberton finally transferred his headquarters to Vicksburg, but this move failed to bring strategic clarity, for Pemberton was distracted and confused by the rivalry between his two powerful superiors, Joe Johnston and Jefferson Davis. Johnston, who arrived in Jackson to assume personal command on May 13, urged Pemberton to leave the river city's defenses and move a force south, to contest Grant's inland campaign; it is ironic that such advice, for Pemberton to go on the offensive against Grant, issued from the defensive-minded Johnston. By contrast, Davis—who mistrusted Johnston and had ordered that Pemberton report directly to Davis himself—insisted that the Confederates must make the protection of Vicksburg itself their top priority. This accorded well with Pemberton's cautious mindset, and he focused on shoring up Vicksburg defenses. Here was another missed opportunity: if Pemberton's Vicksburg force of 30,000 and Johnston's Jackson force of 8,000 had acted in concert, they might have caught Grant's army in a vise. But instead Grant's own spirit of daring had given the Federals momentum. On May 14, Johnston relinquished the poorly defended Jackson and retreated northward; the Union destruction of military assets such as mills and warehouses left the town in ruins and with the nickname "Chimneyville." Grant then pivoted to the west to confront Pemberton, who had relocated his command to the front to direct operations in person. The rebel general was outmaneuvered and forced to retreat by Grant at two final battles on the Union army's road back to Vicksburg, at Champions' Hill on May 16 and Big Black River, ten miles outside of Vicksburg, the following day. The Confederates were left with no choice but to seek refuge within Vicksburg's defenses and to steel themselves for a last stand.[14]

At this very moment Pemberton issued an extraordinary proclamation to the Confederate soldiers and civilians who struggled to defend the town. "You have heard that I was incompetent, and a traitor; and that it was my intention to sell Vicksburg," Pemberton began defensively. But he continued defiantly, "Follow me, and you will see the cost at which I will sell Vicksburg. When the last pound of beef, bacon, and flour, the last grain of corn, the last cow and hog and horse and dog have been consumed, and the last man shall have perished in the trenches, then and only then will I sell Vicksburg." Pemberton's words were intended both to silence his critics, who had whispered that this Pennsylvanian-turned-Confederate was not a true-hearted Southerner, and to nerve the faithful to stay strong in the face of a Yankee assault they knew was imminent. Pemberton intended for his words to have a heroic ring.[15] But the proclamation signaled that the prickly Pennsylvanian, who had acquired the image of a vain martinet, was losing

John C. Pemberton. A carte de visite of the controversial defender of Vicksburg. A native Pennsylvanian who had married a Virginian, Pemberton never fully convinced the Confederate public of his loyalty to the South. (Library of Congress LC-USZ62-130838)

the faith of his army and of Vicksburg's civilians. As one surgeon put it, "Pemberton is either a traitor, or the most incompetent officer in the confederacy." His fatal flaw was "*Indecision, Indecision, Indecision*," the surgeon noted with disgust. Major Maurice Kavanaugh Simons of the 2nd Texas Infantry Regiment, connecting Pemberton's northern roots and his tactical failures, hoped that the embattled general would have the decency to resign. "He may be true to our cause," Simons confided to his diary, "but it looks very suspicious."[16] Confidence in the Union ranks, by contrast, ran high. "We have not known defeat since we left Fort Donelson, and we propose to keep our good record up," Osborn H. Oldroyd of the 20th Ohio Volunteer Infantry wrote on May 17, reflecting on the Union Army of the Tennessee's successes in the western theater and on the prospects for taking Vicksburg at last. "We have seen hard times on some hotly contested fields, but mean to have nothing but victory."[17]

Slough of Despond

Such confidence was in short supply back east within the Army of the Potomac, as the winter and spring campaigns only exposed the depths of the Union's command problems. Private John Haley's January 1, 1863, journal entry captured the state of play in the aftermath of Fredericksburg: "General Burnside, smarting under a severe castigation and the criticism of his enemies, naturally has a strong desire to retrieve his late disaster." But redemption would prove elusive. Burnside's new plan for dislodging Lee from the Fredericksburg defenses—he would flank Lee upriver, from the west—soon ran aground, as bitter winter rains rendered the clay dirt roads impassable and left man and beast alike mired. "It seem that Mud is really King," wrote Lieutenant Theodore A. Dodge of the 101st New York on January 23. "The horses sank into mud up to their bellies, and it is said down near the river you sometimes have to put sticks under the mules' necks to prevent their being engulfed in the very slough of despond. How inspired and confident the men feel in their leaders you can well imagine." Burnside had little choice but to abort this offensive and return his men to their camp near Falmouth; the notorious "Mud March" would linger in the memories of Union veterans as a low point in the war.[18]

Lincoln turned to Major General Joseph Hooker as the newest designated savior of the Army of the Potomac. Hooker had a reputation for hard drinking, gambling, and fighting—and for confidence bordering on arrogance. He quickly instituted policies to rebuild the fighting capacity of his men: he revamped the cavalry corps, placing it under the command of Brigadier General George Stoneman; appointed the capable colonel George Sharpe to head the new Bureau of Military Information, an intelligence-gathering arm; beefed up both pickets and furloughs to stanch the flow of deserters from Union ranks; and generally reequipped the troops. By April, thanks to reforms and reinforcements, the Army of the Potomac was 134,000 strong—stronger than ever before and more than twice the size of Lee's army. Tactically, Hooker's abiding principle was to avoid the kind of fruitless frontal assault on Lee's Fredericksburg entrenchments that had ended in disaster in December. He favored a campaign of maneuver—a grand turning movement that would hit Lee's army at the flank and rear.[19]

Meanwhile, the Confederates in their winter camps had abundant confidence in their own leaders and their fighting ability but were woefully lacking the practical necessities. "We are in a liquid state at present," Lee wrote in February, "up to our knees in mud & what is worse on short rations for men & beasts. This keeps me miserable. I am willing to starve myself, but cannot bear my men or horses to be pinched." The farmland around Fredericksburg had been denuded of food and forage, and Confederate transportation networks and logistical management were inadequate; the commissary general, Lucius Northrup, was an incompetent administrator who hung on to his job only because of his friendship with Jefferson Davis. Short rations together with exposure to the winter elements—including unusually low temperatures and heavy snowfalls—translated into high rates of disease, including scurvy, smallpox, and scarlet fever.[20]

Moreover, there was "ruinous competition between the army and the citizenry for the available supplies," historian Stephen W. Sears has explained. This fell hardest on working-class civilians, as dramatized by the Richmond Bread Riot of April 1863. The Richmond riot was part of a wave of female-led food riots in the Confederacy that spring, beginning with a March riot in Atlanta and followed by mob actions in locales including Salisbury, North Carolina, and Mobile, Alabama. The riots reflected a crisis of subsistence. In Richmond, basic foodstuffs were in short supply and prices were exorbitant, with flour at $40 a barrel and turkeys $15 apiece; the average family was paying ten times more for basic foodstuffs than before the war. In order to feed and equip the starving soldiers, the army "impressed" or seized the food and material of civilians; the military was legally required to pay a "fair price" for such goods but more often than not failed to properly compensate civilians for it. For working-class women, cash was hard to come by and wages could not keep pace with inflation. Women clamored for factory jobs at places such as the Tredegar Iron Works, though the wages were inadequate and the work dangerous. On March 13, 1863, an explosion at the Confederate ordnance lab on Brown's Island took the lives of at least forty-five and injured twenty-three others, including a nine-year-old girl who had been among those workers filling cartridges with gunpowder.[21]

With the threat of famine hanging like a dark cloud over the Confederate capital, a group of two hundred to three hundred women convened on April 1 at Belvidere Hill Baptist Church on Oregon Hill to share their grievances and make a plan for ameliorating conditions. The meeting was presided over by Mary Jackson, the wife of a sign painter with one son in the Confederate army. The women chose from among their ranks a committee to go to Capitol Square the following day to call on Governor Letcher and make the case that they deserved to obtain food from the government storehouses at the same low prices the government paid civilians when it impressed goods from them. On April 2, when the committee reported back that their meeting with Letcher had proven fruitless and that he had ushered them out empty-handed, the crowd of women became enraged and made its way out of Capitol Square down Main Street, shouting out a battle cry of "Bread!" James Craig, a Scots Unionist who lived on Main Street and saw the riot firsthand, fled the city shortly afterward and upon making it to Union lines offered the following account to the Federal authorities: "Armed with axes and hatchets, and the ringleader Mrs. Jackson with a pistol, they commenced an attack on the provision stores and with the help of some blacks carried off the flour, bacon &c. An attack was also made on clothing and shoe stores. . . . [T]he city guard was ordered on the ground and Mayor Mayo read the riot act. . . . Governor Letcher then made his appearance and addressed them saying that the proceedings were disgraceful to the Southern Confederacy." Only when Jefferson Davis arrived on the scene with a detachment of Confederate troops and warned the rioters that if they did not disperse in five minutes they would be fired upon did the crowd break up.[22]

The response of the Confederate elite to the riot reflected a lack of empathy for the poor, unabashed sexism, and deep anxiety about the machinations of the "secret enemies" of the South. Confederate officials quickly went into damage control mode: the War Department ordered that neither the telegraphs nor the newspapers send out any word of the riot for fear of humiliating the Confederacy and stoking further acts of protest. Josiah Gorgas, the Confederate chief of ordnance, represented the views of the elite when he observed in his journal that the rioters' "pretense was bread; but their motive really was license." President Davis, Gorgas noted, had put the rioters in their place when he announced to them that the "course they were pursuing was the one most likely to bring scarcity of food on the city." Gorgas simply refused to acknowledge that the women had any legitimate grievances. "There is scarcity, but little want," he observed of conditions in Richmond. Forty-seven individuals were arrested and processed through the Mayor's Court at city hall; at least twelve were convicted. The press described the accused in negative terms—Mary Jackson was, according to the *Richmond Examiner*, "a good specimen of a forty year old Amazon, with the eye of the Devil," and her fellow rioters "prostitutes, professional thieves, Irish and Yankee hags and gallow birds from all lands."[23]

Even as public opinion condemned the rioters, city, state, and Confederate government officials took measures to address the riot's underlying causes. As historian Stephanie McCurry has demonstrated, "prosecution of the rioters proceeded in tandem with a massive expansion of the system of public relief": the appropriation of twenty thousand dollars for the relief of poor families and the establishment of a new market with free food for the indigent in

Richmond, and similar programs in other Southern cities and states. Asserting identities as soldiers' wives, working-class women had successfully forced the problem of the starving poor onto the public agenda and positioned themselves as constituents, albeit aggrieved ones, of the state.[24]

Lee's rank and file clearly saw the connections between their own plight and that of the rioters. Private Milton Barrett of the 18th Georgia Infantry wrote his brother and sister from Fredericksburg in mid-April, describing the riot: "A bout one thousand women arm ther self with axes and clubs and firearms and march in to the city and broak open stoers grocers and comassary's took what every tha wanted in spite of military or sivel authority." The efforts at damage control left him cold: "Our newspapers have bin very cearful not to say anything a bout it But I see the Yankees have got a full history ot it ... the fack is to wel known to be disputed that we ar running short of suplyes." "We gi no beef now," he continued, speaking of the soldiers, "and not quite half rashons of bacon and sometimes it is spoilt so we cant eat it.... The cearsity of provishosn is cosing a grate deal of uneasiness a mong the soldiers." "The Yankees cant whip us," he wrote plaintively, "only by starving us out."[25]

The Yankees did indeed piece together a "full history" of the riot by using the accounts of exchanged prisoners, deserters, refugees, and intercepted mail

"Sowing and Reaping." This image from *Frank Leslie's* shows Southern women "hounding their men on to rebellion" in the early part of the war and female rioters "feeling the effects of rebellion" in the spring of 1863. The Northern press commented extensively on the Richmond Bread Riot, pointing up both elite women's complicity and poor women's victimization in the Confederacy. (Library of Congress LC-USZ62-47636)

to supplement the meager reports in the Southern newspapers. "This was a real hunger riot, and no cloak for indiscriminate robbery, as pretended at Richmond," the *New York Times* argued. According to Northern newspapers, the rioters numbered in the thousands and were driven to violence by starvation and exploitation, particularly at the hands of "rude and rapacious" government impressment gangs that robbed the goods of common people to sustain the army, government, and elite. Some accounts took satisfaction in the irony of the situation: secessionists had predicted, the *Cleveland Daily Leader* noted archly, that Northern cities would devolve into "wild riots" from a "want of cotton." But the "curses of the traitors" had "come home to roost." In Washington, D.C., the press cast the riot as "a direct attack of the people upon the Confederate government" and took it "as a good omen of the end being nigh." The *New York Times* was more cautious, noting on April 20, 1863, that while it was sound policy to take advantage of the enemy's evident weakness and exhaustion, only "military power delivering irresistible blows" could turn the tide of the war.[26]

Chancellorsville

Hooker intended to deliver such blows. His plan for a grand turning movement began to unfold on April 26, when he dispatched Stoneman's cavalry to cut off Lee's rail supply lines to Richmond and to engage the Confederate cavalry, while two Union corps would menace Lee on the Fredericksburg front. Meanwhile, the other half of the Army of the Potomac would secretly steal a march some twenty miles upriver, crossing the wishbone of the Rappahannock and Rapidan Rivers and then heading east downriver to threaten Lee's flank and rear, thus compelling him to abandon his Fredericksburg fortifications and fight on the open ground to the southwest of the city. But on April 29, Jeb Stuart discovered Hooker's plan and informed Lee. Lee then had to make a difficult choice about how to deploy his limited troops on two fronts—at Fredericksburg, where the Yankees' strong artillery position across the river at Stafford Heights precluded an offensive, and at the crossroads of Chancellorsville, where he was greatly outnumbered. Lee chose to divide his army, leaving a single division under Jubal Early to pin down the Federals at Fredericksburg and taking the bulk of his army, with Stonewall Jackson, west to meet the Yankee turning movement head-on. Hooker meanwhile arguably squandered some momentum by holding his own army back on April 30 rather than attacking Lee then; Hooker was determined, with the Fredericksburg debacle weighing on his mind, to fight on the defensive. On

May 1, Jackson boldly had his Confederates launch a surprise attack on the Federal corps advancing slowly through the Wilderness, a dense woodland tangle of brush and bramble. Hooker was utterly caught off guard—and to the dismay of his senior commanders, he ordered a retreat back through the thickets to his positions at Chancellorsville.[27]

This gave Lee and Jackson a chance to regroup and plot their next move: having learned from Jeb Stuart that Hooker's right flank was "in the air," or shielded by no obstacle, Lee would divide his small army a second time, sending Jackson and three divisions on a long and risky march around Hooker's exposed flank, while Lee and a smaller force of only 15,000 would occupy the Federals at the current Confederate position. Jackson set out on the morning of May 2, heading southwest, then north, then southeast in a giant C-shaped arc. Hooker warned General Oliver O. Howard to expect a possible flank attack, but Howard would later claim, improbably, that the message never got through. At five o'clock in the afternoon, as the oblivious

Joseph Hooker. Nicknamed "Fighting Joe," Hooker increased morale in the Army of the Potomac and devised an ambitious plan to turn the Confederate left flank, only to be outmaneuvered by Lee's much smaller force at the battle of Chancellorsville. (Library of Congress LC-DIG-ppmsca-49605)

Federals in Howard's Eleventh Corps were settling in for dinner, Jackson launched his second surprise. Union private Warren Goss recalled the scene:

> The soldiers of the Eleventh Corps, with stacked arms, were boiling their coffee, smoking their pipes, lounging in groups, and playing cards among the baggage wagons, pack-mules, and teamsters, when rabbits, deer, and other game driven by Jackson's advance came into our lines. Some of the men were chasing the rabbits with shouts of laughter, and all were unprepared, when a few shots were heard . . . and Jackson's men . . . burst upon them like a clap of thunder from a cloudless sky.

To the din of bugles and the "rebel yell," the Union men reeled back in panic. Jackson's strike had paid off. While the battle would rage on for two more days, the Confederate momentum was irreversible. Hooker himself was a casualty of the day's fighting, having suffered a concussion when the fragments of a wooden beam hit by a shell struck him in the head at Chancellor House, his command center. Nightfall on May 2 brought some temporary relief for the Federals and bad news for the Confederates, as Jackson was gravely wounded by friendly fire while doing reconnaissance on the front lines. But his aggressive spirit continued to inspire the Confederates, who, under Jeb Stuart, continued their attacks on the Federals at Chancellorsville on May 3 and then, under Lee, drove back the Federals who had advanced from Fredericksburg to attack the Confederate rear at Salem Church on May 4. On May 5 and 6, Hooker's broken army withdrew back across the Rappahannock toward Washington.[28]

Chancellorsville is widely considered Lee's tactical masterpiece, the crowning evidence of his audacity. For Union men the humiliation of a second thrashing, so close to the scene of the Fredericksburg carnage, demanded a scapegoat. "Twice now we have been led as sheep to the slaughter," wrote John Haley. "Twice have our plans miserably miscarried without proper cause, and somebody is to blame." Hooker had had Lee in a vise, he observed, and somehow let him slip away. Some Union commentators attributed Hooker's poor performance to his injury or to the self-inflicted wound of habitual drunkenness. Others found a scapegoat in Howard's Eleventh Corps, which contained thirteen regiments of German immigrants, who were dubbed the "Flying Dutchmen" after they broke ranks and fled on May 2; the impulse to disparage these men revealed that even the most assimilated immigrants had a kind of probationary status in nineteenth-century America, and that their loyalty and fitness for citizenship were always open to question by bigoted nativists. Because of the availability of these targets, the Army of the Potomac did not experience widespread demoralization after Chancellorsville, as it had

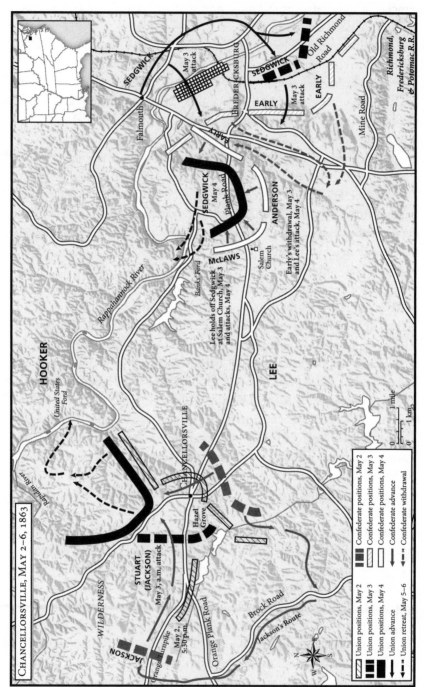

CHANCELLORSVILLE, MAY 2–6, 1863

Union positions, May 2
Union positions, May 3
Union positions, May 4
Union advance
Union retreat, May 5–6

Confederate positions, May 2
Confederate positions, May 3
Confederate positions, May 4
Confederate advance
Confederate withdrawal

MAP 7.3

after Fredericksburg. The Federals knew, moreover, that they exacted a heavy toll on their foe.[29]

Indeed, Lee's victory had chastening costs: Hooker's roughly 17,000 casualties constituted 13 percent of his total strength, while Lee's 13,000-some casualties amounted to nearly a quarter of his men. Most bleak of all for Confederates was the death of Stonewall Jackson, who after briefly rallying had succumbed to postoperative pneumonia after the amputation of his left arm. His troops were disconsolate and "wept like children when told that their idolized General was no more," as John Casler, a veteran of the Stonewall Brigade, remembered. The aftermath of Chancellorsville illustrates how providential theology was flexible enough to accommodate both defeat and terrible loss of life: each side somehow sustained the expectation of divine favor. Jackson had personified for Confederates both the pious Christian warrior and the avenging angel, and his death was a terrible blow to civilian morale—crowds of men, women, and children thronged Jackson's corpse as it was transported back to his Lexington home; mourners blanketed his coffin with flowers and wreaths. Confederates nonetheless reconciled his death to their own sense of the righteousness of their cause. Lee's general order announcing Jackson's death urged his men to "emulate his invincible determination" and assured them that Jackson's spirit lived on and would fill the whole army with "indomitable courage"—and that message resonated broadly among Confederates, who pledged that they would "not allow the soul of their hero to die, as his body had died." They consoled themselves with the thought that since Jackson had been wounded by friendly fire, the Yankees could not claim to have conquered him, and they indulged the expectation that God would bring forth another Jackson-like hero to lead the way. More than anything, Confederates insisted that their hero's death was a reminder not to make idols of mere mortal men and to trust fully and unconditionally in God to deliver victory. "God has taken him from us that we may lean more upon *Him*," wrote North Carolina diarist Catherine Edmondston, succinctly capturing the prevailing view.[30]

Union men no less than Confederates sought providential explanations for military setbacks, and those explanations reflected the range of opinions along the Northern political spectrum. Thus W. H. Cudworth wrote his brother on May 9 the following account of Chancellorsville:

> The army of the Potomac has failed again though supplied with everything to make it irresistible and apparently in splendid condition. It was God's will. I bow to it. Our national pride is not sufficiently humbled nor our great and grievous sin against the Indian and African races sufficiently atoned for, nor our greed for gain sufficiently rebuked. The

condition of our cities, the confidence and boastings of our people, the abundant supplies of our armies and the fullness of our treasury all show that we have not begun to suffer as the rebels are suffering. The multitudes of our strong men at home *reading* and *talking* about the travail of their country, which they should be in the field to relieve, show it.

To Cudworth, redemption for the Union lay in unity—the Northern people must close ranks against the "fire in the rear" from those disloyal Northerners who sought to weaken the government.[31]

General George Henry Gordon took solace, in the midst of his bitter disappointment at the Chancellorsville defeat, in evidence that the Emancipation Proclamation was hastening the demise of slavery. Responding to the active effort of his army to spread the word, fugitives poured into Union lines where Gordon was stationed in King William County, Virginia, in May and June 1863. Slave masters were reduced to the "humiliation of begging for the return of the slaves" and offered up "maudlin demonstrations" in which they claimed to be "exceedingly attached" to their slaves. Gordon had no patience for this—he relished telling them that the "attachment does not seem to be mutual" and that they should console themselves by "looking upon this change as the work of God," sweeping away an "accursed institution" and washing away its accumulated sins.[32]

Democrats, too, argued that the "nation's humiliation" at Chancellorsville was a sign of divine chastisement, but in their view the Lincoln administration was being chastised for its sins—for the "imbecility" of Stanton in particular and the ousting of McClellan. As the Franklin County, Pennsylvania, *Valley Spirit* put it archly, "Invective and abuse badly become an hour of national distress; and we have therefore only our most sincere sorrow to offer the President and his advisers for the terrible disasters they are visiting upon the nation . . . and to express the hope that in the good Providence of God they may be instrumental in bringing upon us no greater evils than we will be able to survive."[33]

Vallandingham and Civil Liberties

No one delivered the opposition critique of Lincoln with more fury than Ohio politician Clement Vallandingham. A representative of Congress from Ohio who had established himself on the national scene as a leading Copperhead by calling for an armistice and negotiated peace, Vallandingham lost a bid for reelection in October 1862 but used his lame-duck session in Congress to perfect his scorched-earth rhetorical tactics. He gave a series of speeches in the winter of 1863 that lambasted emancipation, martial law, and conscription as the tools of military despotism and social radicalism. The "freedom of the negro is to be purchased," he declared on February 23, 1863, "at the sacrifice of every right of the white men of the United States." That argument gained credence for Democrats in March 1863 when Congress passed two far-reaching pieces of legislation. The Habeas Corpus Act gave legal authority to Lincoln's practice of suspending the writ; military officers were not required to bring detainees before civil courts. The Enrollment Act (so called to avoid use of the word "conscription") required all men ages twenty to forty-five to register their names with the authorities and constitute a pool from which they could be drafted to serve until the war's end, or three years (whichever came first). This broke new ground by superseding the state-run militia system and pulling men directly into the Federal army; Congress invoked its constitutional mandate to "raise and support Armies" in defense of the measure's legality.[34]

When Vallandingham returned home to Ohio at the end of the congressional session, he was hailed as a hero by Peace Democrats and reviled by Republicans. Major General Ambrose Burnside, as commander of the Department of the Ohio, had Vallandingham in mind when he issued General Order No. 38 on April 13, 1863, specifying that "treason, expressed or implied, will not be tolerated in this department." Vallandingham gleefully took the bait, daring the Republicans to abridge his freedom of speech. He delivered an inflammatory address in Mount Vernon, Ohio, on May 1, in which he denounced the war as cruel and unnecessary and called upon his fellow citizens to defy Burnside's order. Two undercover army officers were present, and when they reported this to Burnside, he ordered Vallandingham's arrest. On May 5, a detachment of 150 Union soldiers arrived at Vallandingham's house in Dayton, taking him into custody and sending him to prison in Cincinnati. A military commission found Vallandingham guilty of disloyal sentiments and consigned him to a military prison for the war's duration. Conservatives were apoplectic. On the morning after Vallandingham's arrest, the office of Dayton's Republican newspaper, the *Dayton Journal*, was mobbed and set on fire. In the days that followed, the Democratic press lit into the Lincoln administration for its "high-handed assumption of despotic power." Democrats held protest rallies, such as a May 16 meeting in Albany, New York, chaired by Congressman Erastus Corning, a War Democrat, in which they demanded that Lincoln uphold the supremacy of civil law over martial law. Loath to watch Vallandingham play the martyr and worried about how disaffection was spreading among War Democrats and even conservative Republicans, Lincoln revised Vallandingham's sentence, setting him loose from federal prison and having him spirited under flag of truce into Confederate territory, to spend the remainder of the war there. Vallandingham found he was distinctly unwelcome in the rebel states; although Confederates welcomed his critiques of Lincoln, they rejected his goal of returning the Union to the way it was before the war. So Vallandingham tarried in the Southern states for less than a month before making his way to Bermuda, Canada, and eventually, violating the conditions of his sentence, back into the United States.[35]

But Lincoln did not stop with Vallandingham's banishment. The president also went on the offensive, justifying his actions in a public letter of June 12 addressed to Erastus Corning and offered as a response to the Albany protest resolutions. At this very same moment Democrats in Ohio, at their party's state convention, were nominating Vallandingham, in absentia, to be their gubernatorial nominee and demanding that Lincoln let him return to the Union. Lincoln's letter, which was widely disseminated in the Northern press, defended his use of military arrests, reminding readers of the provisions of the Constitution that stipulated that habeas corpus could be suspended "in cases of rebellion or invasion, when the public safety may require it"; the framers had wisely anticipated, Lincoln noted, that ordinary courts would be inadequate at such times. To the Democratic objection that such a stipulation applied only in localities where actual rebellion existed—to wit, the Southern states but not the Northern states—Lincoln countered that martial law measures were "constitutional *wherever* the public safety does require them." Vallandingham, he went on to explain, was arrested not "because he was damaging the political prospects of the Administration, or the personal interests of the Commanding General," but because he was, by discouraging enlistment and encouraging desertion, "damaging the Army, upon the existence and vigor of which the life of the nation depends." Next came Lincoln's rhetorical coup de grâce:

> Long experience has shown that armies cannot be maintained unless desertion shall be punished by the severe penalty of death. The case requires, and the law and Constitution sanction, this punishment. Must I shoot a simple-minded soldier boy who deserts, while I must not touch a hair of a wily agitator who induces him to desert? This is none the less injurious when effected by getting a father, or brother, or friend, into a public meeting, and there working upon his feelings till he is persuaded to write the soldier boy that he is fighting in a bad cause, for a wicked Administration of a contemptible government, too weak to arrest and punish him if he shall desert. I think that in such a case, to silence the agitator, and save the boy is not only constitutional, but, withal, a great mercy.[36]

"The Mower Mows On, Though the Adder May Writhe." This 1863 print contrasts the dignity of free labor—represented by the Lincolnesque farmer in the foreground and free black farmers behind him—with the grim plantation scene to the right. The image takes aim at Copperhead Democrats, represented by the snakes in the grass and wrapped around the central figure's scythe. (Library of Congress LC-USZ62-55538)

By casting Vallandingham as the "wily agitator" preying on innocent young patriots, Lincoln positioned himself as the defender of the people, in language the masses could understand. His letter drew widespread praise from Republicans, who declared it timely, wise, and unanswerable. "The letter will do great good," Horace Greeley promised, hoping that it might touch the consciences of War Democrats even as it exposed the treachery of the Copperheads.[37]

The Copperheads' argument that the war was a failure increasingly alienated the Union rank and file. Soldier anger at the Peace Democrats, historian Jennifer Weber has argued, grew steadily in the winter and spring of 1863. Copperheads "find little sympathy in the army," observed William Henry Harrison Clayton, an Iowan stationed in Missouri. Clayton bore witness to the depredations of Confederates against Southern Unionists in the region and was incredulous that any Northerners would be so naive as to talk of making peace with the ruthless rebel "scoundrels." He observed of Copperheads in March 1863, "I assure you some of them would be roughly used if they were where the soldiers could get a hold of them." "I suppose that there is some copperheads

up there tell them that they want to keep dark when the soldiers get home,"
wrote infantryman Benjamin W. Wilber, stationed in Arkansas, to his cousin
Chauncey in Wisconsin; this sort of veiled threat was becoming standard fare
in soldiers' letters. Sometimes home front correspondents matched the intensity of the soldiers' scorn. Over the course of the war, Charles W. Ingersoll,
who served as an ambulance driver in a New York regiment, exchanged frequent letters with his sister Ruth A. Whittemore. Her letters revealed her
growing contempt for the "stinking 'Secesh' Democrats" of the North. "I can
only wish that they were obliged to go South," she fumed in February 1863; in
April she added, "It is awfully disgraceful to have such miserable traitors in the
country. And yet they are upheld by the democratic party while it pretends to
be loyal." African American commentators added to this chorus of denunciation. Henry McNeal Turner called Vallandingham a "stench in the nostrils of
mankind." "His name will go down to posterity under the curse of the traitor,"
Turner predicted. "He will be known only to be hated."[38]

Union Leagues

This emerging critique of disloyalty took institutional form in a new network
of patriotic organizations, Union Leagues, which sprang up across the North.
The movement began in the fall of 1862 with the founding of Republican
secret societies in the Midwest pledged to check the growing power of
Copperhead Democrats by stigmatizing them as traitors. By the spring of
1863, there were hundreds of clubs in towns and counties across the Union,
and in May delegates from eighteen states convened in Cleveland, Ohio, to
formalize the links between these organizations. The organizations themselves varied in format. Some, in large cities such as Boston, New York, and
Philadelphia, were gentlemen's clubs for the business, professional, and literary elite—the same social milieu and often the same individuals who led
the United States Sanitary Commission. Clubs in smaller towns or rural areas
were typically mass membership organizations. Regardless of their makeup,
these organizations aimed at shaping public opinion by promoting unconditional loyalty to the national government and its policies. Union Leagues
(sometimes called Loyal Leagues) sent forth traveling agents, sponsored massive rallies, and churned out broadsides and other forms of printed propaganda through loyal publication societies.[39]

Scholars, like some contemporary critics, have tended to see the Union
Leagues as an arm of the radical faction in the Republican party. Certainly
league spokesman and publications did much to condemn Copperheadism
and defend emancipation. "As the war progressed," historian Melinda Lawson

has noted, "increasing numbers of pamphlets and broadsides argued that slavery was morally wrong and that blacks had a right to 'equal treatment.'" Such language kept most Democrats away from the Union League movement. But not all. The movement enlisted the services of a cadre of prominent War Democrats, such as New York attorney general Daniel S. Dickinson, who could embody a patriotism that put country before party. The movement also featured Southern Unionists at its rallies and in its propaganda, most notably Andrew Jackson Hamilton of Texas. Hamilton was a perfect poster boy for Southern deliverance: an anti-secession Democratic congressman, he was forced to flee Texas early in the war for his Union views; like Parson Brownlow and other celebrated exiles, he gave a series of popular speeches in the North decrying the terrorism of the Slave Power. Hamilton's frequent warnings about the vulnerability of Lone Star loyalists was dramatized in October 1862 with the roundup and mass execution by Confederates of forty Unionists and Confederate draft dodgers and deserters in Gainesville, in north Texas. In November 1862 Hamilton met with members of Lincoln's cabinet and then with Lincoln himself. The president bestowed on him the wishful title of military governor of Texas, expecting that the Federal army would soon make incursions into that state to liberate its Unionists.[40]

The Union League movement dedicated itself to harmonizing black freedom and white Southern deliverance. "The true glory of the war is not that it liberates the black but the white men of the South," a New England Loyal Publication Society broadside proclaimed, while a New York Loyal Publication Society pamphlet took aim at the concept of mastership as the root of rebellion, arguing that lasting peace depended not only on the emancipation of the slaves and uplift of poor whites but also on the "deliverance of the master population" from the "fumes of unrestrained and illicit power and dominion" that had "perverted, not their own self-consciousness only, but their whole sense of truth." Men such as Dickinson and Hamilton were particularly good messengers for these arguments. Both men described the masses of white Southerners as innocent and ignorant—as loyal at heart, but defrauded, betrayed, and coerced into secession. Both men defended the military necessity of emancipation, noting that secession and war had brought about the de facto end of slavery, and that Democrats and Southerners must accept that. Both men called for the sternest of punishments for the guilty slaveholding elite and for the malignant Copperheads who did their bidding. Most important, both men made the case that there was no moral equivalency whatsoever between the limited, targeted measures the Lincoln administration had taken to suppress treason in the North and the rank terrorism perpetrated by the Confederacy on its civilians. Like Lincoln in his Corning letter, they argued that the leading Copperheads were not merely exercising free speech but were materially endangering the Union army. Freedom of speech did not include the right to "stimulate mutiny," as Dickinson put it. The Constitution, Hamilton added, had given the government the "power to protect itself against any enemy from without or within." Increasingly, Unionist rhetoric cast Copperheads as guiltier and more treacherous than the Confederate masses. Those who would sacrifice the Union through an empty compromise were "thrice more to be distrusted than the rebel who levels his musket at your heart," Dickinson pronounced at an April 1863 Loyal Union League mass meeting in New York.[41]

In May 1863, leading female reformers in North entered the lists by forming the Women's Loyal National League (WLNL) to coordinate the activities of women's Union clubs that had formed around the North as counterparts to the male-run organizations. The WLNL "firmly embraced an antislavery agenda," historian Nina Silber has written, and in a time-honored abolitionist strategy sponsored a petition campaign to push for an antislavery amendment to the Constitution. The league also sought to foster the view of women as independent political agents, whose potential for good had gone unfulfilled because of both sexism and their own inaction. Its opening meeting featured a who's who of women's rights pioneers, including Elizabeth Cady Stanton, Susan B. Anthony, Ernestine Rose, and Angelina Grimké Weld. Grimké Weld, as she had done at abolitionist meetings for a quarter century, symbolized the hope of Southern redemption: she had been "once a South Carolinian slave-holder" but now was a "loyal woman," Stanton reminded the crowd as Grimké Weld took the stage. Both Stanton's and Grimké Weld's speeches highlighted elite Southern women's central role in secession and slavery, the ignorance and barbarism of white Southern masses, and the complicity of Copperhead women who, "breathing the pure air of our Northern hills," had no excuse for their own disloyalty. In a moment of levity, Stanton jokingly suggested that once the war was over the Union should "colonize the chivalry, with a body-guard of Northern Copperheads, to the coast of Liberia," prompting Grimké Weld to respond that it would be unfair for Liberia "to be cursed with the aristocracy of the South."[42]

Even as they decried conditions in the South and the behavior of Confederates, these women pledged themselves to the region's reformation. As Dr. Elizabeth Blackwell put it, using a medical metaphor in which the South was a wounded limb, "We have no idea of lopping off the offending member. Let us bear with it, and heal its infirmities, even if we are forced to apply the severest remedies, and to suffer cruelly ourselves from the sympathetic agony." Blackwell emphasized that only universal suffrage, in which "the Southern people, white and black, male and female, are all voters together," could be a firm foundation for reunion, while Grimké Weld emphasized that black soldiers were the heralds of victory. When white soldiers could learn to accept their black brethren, "the army of the North will thus become the angel of deliverance, rescuing the nation from the shifting sands of compromise, and refounding it upon the rock of justice."[43]

At this same juncture in the war, another female politico, Anna E. Dickinson, was attaining celebrity status as a sort of one-woman Union club. A twenty-year-old Quaker from Philadelphia, Dickinson was a staunch abolitionist and a prodigy in the art of public oratory—an art widely considered inappropriate for women, particularly if they dared to speak before "promiscuous" audiences that included men. Dickinson defied convention

Anna Dickinson. A public speaking prodigy, the Pennsylvania abolitionist achieved celebrity status in 1863 by campaigning for Republican candidates and condemning the Copperheads. Her admirers dubbed Dickinson the Civil War's "Joan of Arc" for her willingness to defy gender conventions in the name of patriotism. (Library of Congress LC-DIG-ppmsca-53271)

and was tapped in the spring of 1863 to stump for Republican candidates in New England running for state office. In a series of public appearances covered in detail by the partisan press, Dickinson excoriated Copperheads and called Union men to arms, emphasizing themes such as the benefits of emancipation for white working-class men in the North. "Give the slaves their liberty at the South and they will stay there," she told an audience in Hartford, Connecticut. "Refuse it, and they will come to the North, and slave labor will be in competition with your own." The Republican press praised Dickinson for the ways she could think on her feet—when Democrats in Middletown, Connecticut, tried to sabotage her talk there by turning off the gas and plunging the meeting hall into darkness, she quipped without losing a beat, "I read of the prince of darkness, and judging by the present display, some of his children are present! . . . I read of a creature that loves caves and dens and holes in the earth—and I suppose, from the last fact, that some of them are in this hall—copperheads I believe they are called." The Democratic press reviled Dickinson, charging her with "unsexing" herself, with advocating servile insurrection, and with generally pouring forth "odious and inhumane sentiments." Dickinson was undeterred and soon took the stage in New York City, moving "fully into the national limelight."[44]

The Lieber Code and the Laws of War

While the Vallandingham drama unfolded and the loyal movements coalesced, the Lincoln administration moved on another front to establish a sound legal basis for the escalating war effort, promulgating on April 24, 1863, General Order No. 100: "Instructions for the Government of Armies of the United States in the Field." This influential text soon came to be known as the Lieber Code, after its author, the Prussian-born jurist Francis Lieber of New York. Lieber, a soldier-turned-scholar (and New York Union League leader) who before the war taught in South Carolina, took up the challenge of defining the laws of war and the limits of just war—even as two of his sons were fighting for the Union and one for the Confederacy. Lieber had three specific issues on which he was to offer clarification: guerrilla warfare, the status of prisoners of war, and emancipation.[45]

Lieber's abiding assumption was that a vigorously prosecuted war was the most humane, because it would result in peace sooner than a halfhearted, drawn-out conflict. He sought to justify the Union's hard war measures by advancing a capacious understanding of what soldiers in conventional forces might do in the name of military necessity. But he sought also to establish that the Union was playing by clear and unimpeachable rules—legal doctrines consistent with international standards and yet suited to the turbulent realities of civil conflicts, doctrines that forbade unnecessary or revengeful destruction of life. He first had to address the persistent question of whether to define the Confederates as enemy belligerents, subject to the international laws of war, or as domestic criminals, subject to the Union's national laws and to civilian standards of conduct. The distinction was vitally important: soldiers in a state of war could legally do things that were illegal for civilians to do in a state of peace. The danger was that if the Union labeled the Confederates as "foreign" enemies, that might amount to a recognition of Confederate nationhood. In keeping with the Lincoln administration's practices, Lieber took a dualistic approach, arguing that the Union government could treat the Confederates as soldiers, subject to the laws of war and liable to punishment for breaking them (committing war crimes), without in any way conceding Confederate sovereignty.[46]

But the question remained of how to draw the line between legitimate soldiers and illegitimate guerrilla fighters. The Confederates had blurred the line by accepting into service so-called partisans, who wore uniforms but were detached from the armies and thus free to use hit-and-run raiding tactics. Such tactics were exemplified by the exploits of John Mosby, a cavalry colonel whose partisan band operated in northern Virginia, boarding in homes of civilians there and coming together for scouting and raiding duty; in March 1863 Mosby's men had humiliated the Federals by capturing a Union brigadier general, Edwin H. Stoughton, while he was asleep at his headquarters at Fairfax Court House. Lieber chose to define such partisans as belligerents, part and parcel of the army and subject to both the protections (such as prisoner-of-war status) and standards of the laws of war. Guerrillas, by contrast, were not soldiers bound by the laws of war: they were not integral to established armies, and they practiced vengeful acts such as giving no quarter to prisoners. Men such as the Missouri desperado William Quantrill, who harassed Union soldiers and robbed, looted, and terrorized civilians along the Kansas-Missouri border, were in Lieber's eyes outlaws, waging war on his own account. Union authorities could deal with such men however they saw fit—including by executing them without due process if necessary.[47]

Lieber also addressed the related issue of prisoners of war. He disapproved of the system of mass battlefield paroles, in which captured soldiers were released upon their oath that they would not again take up arms unless formally exchanged for an enemy captive. Because parolees could simply drift away from the army altogether, rather than reporting for exchange, Lieber felt that such a system favored Confederates, as it potentially attenuated the

Union's manpower advantages. He preferred a strictly monitored system of prisoner exchange—in which Union and Confederate prisoners were swapped number for number, rank for rank, wounded man for wounded man. He argued that such a system should prevail and that the Union was not required, according to the laws of war, to parole Confederates. Finally, Lieber strongly supported Lincoln's emancipation measures, insisting that the "law of nature and nations" had never recognized the legitimacy of slavery and that the institution was solely a creature of local law. Fugitive slaves who made it to Union lines were entitled to the "rights and privileges" of freemen in perpetuity, for a "person made free by the law of war is under the shield of the law of nations" and never again subject to former claims of service. Such a shield extended protection to black soldiers, too—"the law of nations knows no distinction of color." Confederates were obliged by such laws to accord African American soldiers their belligerent rights.[48]

This last injunction signaled the Lincoln administration's fear that black soldiers would become the targets of Confederate reprisals. In December 1862, Jefferson Davis had issued a proclamation denying captured black soldiers' status as prisoners of war and deeming them instead rebellious slaves, to be remanded to the Southern states and "dealt with according to the laws of said States." In May 1863, just a week after the Lieber Code was issued, the Confederate Congress endorsed Davis's proclamation with its own Retaliatory Act, specifying that the Confederate army had license to punish black soldiers and their white officers in whatever way it deemed fit—including the enslavement of black prisoners and the summary execution of such officers. The act implicitly brushed aside Lieber's doctrines while making its own appeal to the international laws of war. The Union's design "to overthrow the institution of African slavery and bring on a servile war," the Confederate Congress ruled, was "inconsistent with the spirit of those usages which in modern warfare prevail among civilized nations." Such measures as emancipation and black enlistment could therefore be "properly and lawfully repressed by retaliation."[49] Confederates imagined that African Americans might be deterred from enlisting by such policies, or that they might desert the Union army after a taste of combat and return to their masters. Many Northerners, for their part, refused to believe that the Confederates would carry through with the barbaric threats made by Davis and the rebel Congress. The coming months would confound both sets of expectations.

8

Under a Scorching Sun

THE SUMMER OF 1863

"A FEW HOT-HEADED demagogues have dragged the State of Virginia almost into beggary and turned their once beautiful country into a desert," Private John Haley lamented to his diary on June 15, 1863, as the Army of the Potomac geared up to take on Robert E. Lee again. "There was never anything so near akin to despotism in this country as is now being enacted in the so-called Southern Confederacy." A week later, Philip Hamlin of the 1st Minnesota struck a similar chord in a letter home. Deploring how the Old Dominion had been "marred by the hand of war," he added that no state "possesses more numerous or varied resources than Virginia and it would be a glorious sight to see a young and free civilization springing up here where slavery has wrought ruin." Haley, a millworker from Saco, Maine, who joined his regiment in August 1862, at age twenty-two, had fought at Fredericksburg and Chancellorsville. Hamlin, a college student hailing from the small village of Pine Island, Minnesota, enlisted in April 1861 in response to Lincoln's initial call for troops and had seen action at First Bull Run, in the Peninsula campaign, and at Antietam. Haley would survive until the end of the war to see the Union triumphant. Hamlin, who fervently believed that the nation had "a future destiny gloriously delivered from the weights and embarrassments of the past," would never see that future. He died on July 3, 1863, at Gettysburg.[1]

In the war's third summer, the Unionist coalition's commitment to the narrative of Southern deliverance would face new tests on the battlefield and the home front, as fighting at Gettysburg and at Vicksburg revealed the depths of Confederate resilience and as debates over conscription further exposed fault lines within the North. African American heroism at Port Hudson and Fort Wagner breathed new life into that narrative, as black troops took up positions as liberators.

Lee's Second Invasion

In early June, fresh off its rout of the Yankees at Chancellorsville, the Army of Northern Virginia embarked on its second invasion of the North. Considering Stonewall Jackson to be irreplaceable, Lee reconfigured his army's two corps into three: the reliable Longstreet retained command of the First Corps, Richard S. Ewell inherited command of the Second from Jackson, and A. P. Hill was assigned the new Third Corps. Lee shifted the bulk of this force, under Longstreet and Ewell, northwest from the Wilderness to Culpeper, leaving behind Hill's corps to pin down Hooker's Yankee force at Fredericksburg. Jeb Stuart's cavalry was deployed to screen the infantry's movement as it pressed on into the Shenandoah Valley, where it could veer north into Maryland shielded by the Blue Ridge Mountains. Stuart stumbled out of the gate: his grand review of his cavalry on June 5 tipped off the Federals to his presence and prompted a surprise attack by the Federal cavalry under Major General Alfred Pleasanton at Brandy Station on June 9. In what would prove the war's most storied cavalry engagement, Stuart's men regrouped and fought the Federals off, but the whole incident left a bad taste in Stuart's mouth. The Confederates under Ewell soon regained the initiative, plowing through the Valley to seize the Federal garrison at Winchester and setting their sights on the Potomac River and on Maryland.

In a sense, Lee's motivations at this juncture were similar to the aims of his fall 1862 invasion of the North: he was eager to provide respite to battle-scarred Virginia, to enable his hungry army to live off the fat of the land in enemy territory, to demoralize Northern civilians, and to press the initiative after key victories that had exposed the weaknesses in the Union high command. Indeed, Lee had received a sort of vindication of his earlier Maryland campaign when he learned from Northern newspapers, in the spring of 1863, that McClellan had found Lee's "lost order" on the eve of Antietam; perhaps the Union's strong performance in that battle was a fluke, and Lee's strategy had been sound.[2]

Yet the context for an invasion had also changed. While Lee conceded the limitations of his victories at Fredericksburg and Chancellorsville—neither victory had gained the Confederates any ground or disabled the Yankee army—his army's confidence and his aura of infallibility were at a peak. "The universal feeling in the army was one of profound contempt for an enemy whom they have beaten so constantly, and under so many disadvantages," wrote Arthur Fremantle, a British officer who had attached himself unofficially to Lee's forces and who chronicled the Gettysburg campaign in his diary. The flip side of that contempt for Northerners was Confederate reverence for Lee himself. "The boys never cheer him, but pull off their hats and worship," wrote Lieutenant Edmund DeWitt Patterson of the 9th Alabama Infantry about how Lee was regarded in the ranks. The Confederate press provided an echo, declaring Lee and his troops "the most famous Chief and army on earth at this day," as the *Richmond Enquirer* put it in May. "No leader now in the world has won so many great battles." Lee wielded this influence, rebuffing Davis's and Secretary of War James Seddon's request that troops be transferred from the eastern theater to the west, to meet the crisis at Vicksburg. A northern campaign, for which Lee required reinforcements, would relieve pressure in the west.[3]

Moreover, the agitation of the Peace Democrats in the North and the Vallandingham controversy loomed large in Lee's thinking. In two June letters to Jefferson Davis on the state of the peace movement in the North, Lee emphasized an idea he had already expressed in an April 1863 letter to his wife, Mary Custis: "If [we are] successful this year, next fall there will be a great change in public opinion in the North." Lee no longer imagined, as he had on the eve of Antietam, that border state residents would rally en masse to the Confederate banner. But he did reckon, based on his voracious reading of newspapers such as the *New York Tribune, Times,* and *Herald,* that the "friends of peace at the North" were gaining ground. In his June 10 letter on the subject, Lee expressed disappointment with Southern journalists who dismissed the Northern peace movement and the prospect of a Democratic party ouster of Lincoln. "We should neglect no honorable means of dividing and weakening our enemies," Lee argued. "It seems to me that the most effectual mode of accomplishing this object, now within our reach, is to give all the encouragement we can, consistently with truth, to the rising peace party of the North." Lee surely had in mind the recent June 3 mass meeting in New York City convened by the Copperhead former mayor Fernando Wood, which passed a series of resolutions bitterly denouncing the Lincoln administration. He had in mind, too, the discordant Confederate press coverage of the Copperhead surge. While they relished reporting on Northern dissension, many Confederate editors were loath to read too much into it, for fear of building false hope and undermining Confederate military momentum. "The Northern Democrat[s] in favor of peace, and against Lincoln and the Abolitionists," the *Richmond Dispatch* reminded its readers, "are not, as a mass, in favor of our separate nationality." Reunion, not independence, was what these Democrats had to offer;

only "great, crushing and telling victories" on the battlefield could achieve Confederate aims. In the wake of the June convention, a chorus of voices seconded this opinion: the *Charleston Mercury* opined that "Yankee *peace* talk" was "mere drivel" without victories at Vicksburg and against Hooker; the *Staunton Vindicator*, in an editorial called "Northern Toadyism," described the Northern peace meetings as "full of blather"; the *Richmond Enquirer* declared that it had no confidence in the Copperheads "unless they are aided by the continued exertions of our own Peace party, which we call the Army of Northern Virginia."[4]

Lee begged to differ. He of course sought "crushing and telling victories," but he believed that such military triumphs could be a catalyst to a major shift in public opinion in the North. It was counterproductive, Lee argued in the June 10 letter to Davis, to make "nice distinctions between those who declare for peace unconditionally and those who advocate it as a means of restoring the Union." Any spike in sentiments for peace was favorable to the Confederacy, Lee explained, because it would bring the North to the negotiating table, where Northerners would learn that Confederate independence was the non-negotiable price of peace. Lee knew that some Confederate detractors of the Northern peace movement worried that war-weary Confederates might themselves, once brought to the negotiating table, be lured into accepting reunion; Lee had faith, he insisted, that Southerners would prove "steadfast" in their insistence on their sovereignty. Lee drove this argument home in a follow-up letter to Davis on June 25: "It is plain to my understanding that everything that will tend to repress the war feeling in the Federal States will enure to our benefit." Jefferson Davis's replies to Lee's letters have not survived, but it would become clear over the subsequent year that Davis had profound doubts about the potential of Northern Democrats to aid the Southern cause and an abiding determination that Confederates rely on military and not political means to the end of independence.[5]

In Lee's eyes, the aim of effecting a change in Northern public opinion could be achieved only if his invading army took the moral high road in its treatment of Northern civilians, to offer them the contrast between Southern civility and the depredations practiced by Yankees on Southern soil. And so Lee directed his troops in General Order No. 72 not to plunder civilian property during their northern campaign but instead to "requisition" supplies, paying up with Confederate money or vouchers. The directives fell on deaf ears: the Confederate army, fired by memories of Fredericksburg and reports from Vicksburg, blazed a trail of forcible confiscation through Maryland and then Pennsylvania. "I am in Yankeedom," South Carolina infantryman Tally Simpson wrote his aunt on June 28 from Chambersburg, Pennsylvania, where Ewell's men had advanced after crossing the Maryland state line. "The country is the most beautiful I ever beheld, and the wheat and corn crops are magnificent," Simpson observed of the lush Pennsylvania countryside. He continued, commenting disapprovingly on his comrades' conduct: "The most of the soldiers seem to harbor a terrific spirit of revenge and steal and pillage in the most sinful manner. They take poultry, hogs, vegetables, fruit, honey, and any and every thing they can lay their hands on."[6]

Confederates did not stop at seizing property. They seized people, too, practicing slave catching—the rounding up of free and fugitive African Americans to send them to the South's slave markets for sale. This policy was "widely and officially tolerated" by the Confederate high command, historian Stephen W. Sears has explained, and hundreds of blacks were victimized by it. As word of this practice spread, blacks in the path of Lee's invading army took flight as refugees, many heading for Harrisburg and Philadelphia. A white inhabitant of Gettysburg recalled seeing blacks flee that town:

> They regarded the Rebels as having an especial hatred toward them, and believed that if they fell into their hands annihilation was sure. . . . I can see them yet, men and women with bundles as large as old-fashioned feather ticks slung across their backs, almost bearing them to the ground. Children, also, carrying their bundles and striving to keep up with their seniors. The greatest consternation was depicted on all their countenances as they hurried along, crowding and running against each other in their confusion, children stumbling, falling, and crying.[7]

White Pennsylvanians, too, found themselves in the grip of panic in late June, unsure of Lee's ultimate intentions. Harrisburg was a "Bedlam," the journalist Charles Coffin wrote, its railway stations and bridges serving as convergence points for white families arriving from southern Pennsylvania and Harrisburg residents departing for points still farther north. Sallie Broadhead, a Gettysburg schoolteacher, captured the prevailing mood of dread in her diary entry for June 25: "Every one is asking, Where is our army, that they let the enemy scour the country and do as they please?"[8]

Meade Takes Charge

On June 28, the same day the Confederates raided Chambersburg, General George G. Meade replaced Hooker as the head of the Army of the Potomac. Hooker had continued a downward spiral in Lincoln's estimation after Chancellorsville, by grappling with Halleck, reprising McClellan's constant nagging for reinforcements, and failing to respond to Lee's movement northward with alacrity. When Lee's invasion began to materialize, Hooker's instinct was to propose that the Federals strike at Richmond, to which Lincoln responded, with palpable exasperation, "I think *Lee's* Army, and not *Richmond*, is your true objective point." Hooker relented and moved the Federal army into Maryland, shielding Washington, D.C., but he seemed incapable of outmaneuvering Lee and regaining the initiative. Meade, a native Pennsylvanian, seemed the answer. Although not an imposing figure—tall, thin, and bespectacled, he looked like a "good sort of family doctor," one Yankee officer observed—he had an imposing record of leadership, having led a division at Antietam and Fredericksburg and the Fifth Corps at Chancellorsville.[9]

Meade acted decisively, ordering the Army of the Potomac to advance from Frederick, Maryland, into Pennsylvania. He hoped to draw the Confederates back across the border toward Pipe Creek, Maryland, where he had identified a strong defensive position for the Federals to hold. Lee, learning of the Yankee change of command and thrust into Pennsylvania, adapted his own plans. Ewell had split his force, sending Major General Jubal Early eastward to York, Pennsylvania, while taking the remainder of his command north to Carlisle; Harrisburg was their ultimate aim. On the afternoon of June 28, Early's men, seeking to cross the Susquehanna at Wrightsville, had been repulsed by local militiamen, including a company of free blacks, at the Columbia Bridge. Lee ordered his far-flung forces to concentrate, either at Cashtown or at Gettysburg to the west, so back came Ewell's men from their abortive Harrisburg campaign; the goal was to reunite with the rest of Lee's command, Longstreet's and A. P. Hill's corps, which pressed through the South Mountain gap, from Chambersburg toward Cashtown.[10]

Meade had an army of 112,700 at his disposal, to Lee's roughly 80,000. He had another crucial advantage in the realm of intelligence gathering. Lee was largely in the dark as to the disposition of the Federal forces, thanks to the ill-conceived gambit of Jeb Stuart, who had contrived a June 25 ride around Hooker's army, distracting and harassing it and stoking Northern fears for the safety of Washington, D.C. Stuart had pulled off such tactics during the Peninsula and Antietam campaigns, with much fanfare in the South—but

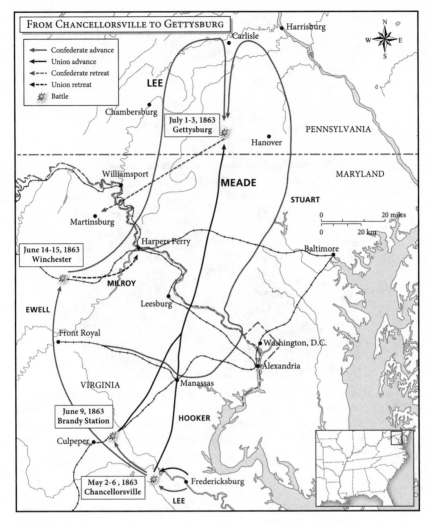

MAP 8.1

now they backfired, as his absence meant Lee was not receiving regular intelligence reports. Meade, by contrast, had at his disposal Brigadier General John Buford, "probably the best intelligence gatherer in the Potomac Army," whose cavalry force kept Meade well informed on Confederate movements. As for the morale of the Federal troops, while they could not boast of recent victories, they nonetheless had their own wellsprings of confidence and motivation. Federal troops were heartened by their reception at the hands of loyal civilians. "This is lovely country," William T. Livermore of the 20th Maine wrote of Maryland. "It seems more like a civilized land than VA does. . . . The

George Gordon Meade. Decidedly lacking in glamour, and described by one of his soldiers as a "damned old goggle-eyed snapping turtle," Meade was underestimated by both his friends and his enemies. Assuming command of the Army of the Potomac just a few days before the battle of Gettysburg, Meade succeeded brilliantly in his first major test. (Library of Congress LC-DIG-ppmsca-40717)

people are very friendly tell us all the milk eggs pies they can spare reasonable." Samuel W. Fiske of the 14th Connecticut, for his part, was gratified to get out of "abominable, barren, ravaged Old Virginia into fertile, smiling Maryland." The Union line of march took these men right through the battlefields of Manassas, still strewn with skeletons and other debris of war. But they kept focused on omens of victory—the encouraging news from the Vicksburg front and the knowledge that they had turned back the last rebel invasion, at Antietam—rather than on memories of defeat.[11]

Gettysburg Begins

The town of Gettysburg was a logical point of concentration for the armies, as it was a hub at which ten roads converged from the countryside in every direction, like spokes on a wheel. On June 30, Meade's vanguard, consisting of Buford's two cavalry brigades on reconnaissance, entered the town from the south and arrayed itself on McPherson's Ridge, on the northwestern outskirts of Gettysburg. Buford knew the main bulk of Lee's force was heading his way—and indeed, that afternoon a Confederate foraging party, looking to secure some shoes, made contact with the Federals and then withdrew after a brief skirmish. Buford, anticipating that the high ground just south of Gettysburg could offer a formidable platform for victory to whichever army seized it, called for reinforcements and awaited the Confederates' next move.

On July 1, A. P. Hill's lead division, under Major General Henry Heth, approached Gettysburg from the west (Heth was under the incorrect impression that the Yankee forces consisted only of local militia) and was met by Buford's cavalry, which was determined to keep the Confederates at bay until reinforcements could arrive, in the form of Major General John F. Reynolds's First Corps. Buford fought valiantly: he "gave way slowly, taking advantage of every accident of ground to protract the struggle," wrote Union major general Abner Doubleday. Two hours into the day's fighting, Reynolds swept in, just as Buford's stubborn defense was about to crack under the Confederate onslaught—but Reynolds was soon shot dead in the saddle and replaced by Doubleday, and then by Major General Oliver Otis Howard, whose Eleventh Corps had also arrived on the scene to reinforce Buford. Even as Howard's men tried to rally the Federals, Confederate reinforcements from Ewell's and Hill's corps streamed into action from the northeast and northwest, giving the Confederates a three-to-two manpower advantage. The Confederates turned the Union right flank and then assaulted the left, and the Federal line collapsed, with retreating Union soldiers scurrying through the town to the high ground on Cemetery Ridge to the south. "All was bustle and confusion," wrote diarist Sallie Broadhead of the atmosphere among the townspeople. "No one can imagine in what extreme fright we were when our men began to retreat. A citizen galloped up to the door in which we were sitting and called out, 'For God's sake go in the house! The Rebels are in the other end of town, and all will be killed!' " The day ended, she noted, with the town full of "filthy" Southern troops and "our soldiers having possession of the hills just beyond."[12]

Ewell's failure to follow up on the Confederate momentum, and to drive the Yankees off the heights, Cemetery Hill and Culp's Hill, south of town, has invited perennial second-guessing. Lee, who had arrived at the battlefield at around 2:00 p.m., ordered Ewell to follow up on his success of that afternoon and to take the hills "if he found it practicable." Ewell declined: the Federal position was already too strong, as the retreating Yankees had quickly drawn up a new defensive line under the leadership of the Second Corps' Winfield Scott Hancock, a major general whom Meade had dispatched to take control of the field of battle from the spent Howard. Ewell's decision set tongues wagging: he had been called upon to fill the late Stonewall Jackson's shoes, and the men who had served under Jackson could not help but speculate that their fallen idol, had he lived, would have taken the fight to the Federals on Cemetery Hill that twilight.[13]

The two armies, their bivouac fires separated by a mere mile, sought respite amid misery. Abner Doubleday's division camped on the town's cemetery. "We lay on our arms that night among the tombs," he wrote, "so suggestive of the shortness of life and the nothingness of fame; but the men were little disposed to moralize on themes like these, and were too much exhausted to think of anything but much needed rest." With the guns silent for the moment, civilians in the town crept forth from their cellar hiding places to find the streets strewn with clothes, cartridge boxes, blankets, knapsacks—and the corpses of horses and men. "As I write all is quiet," Sallie Broadhead observed. "But O! how I dread to-morrow."[14]

July 2: Day Two

The daylight found Meade's army arrayed in what would come to be known as a "fishhook" formation. The British observer Fremantle, who surveyed the scene that morning with Longstreet, described the Yankee position this way:

> The enemy occupied a series of high ridges, the tops of which were covered with trees. . . . The cemetery was on their right, and their left appeared to rest upon a high rocky hill. The enemy's forces, which were now supposed to comprise nearly the whole Potomac army, were concentrated into a space apparently not more than a couple miles in length.

The Confederates, he added, "inclosed [the Federals] in a sort of semicircle, and the extreme extent of our position must have been from five to six miles at least. Ewell was on our left; his headquarters in a church (with a high cupola) at Gettysburg; Hill in the centre; and Longstreet on the right."[15]

The Union forces, in other words, had the advantage of "interior lines." As their fishhook was more compact than the Confederate semicircle, it gave the Federals a potential edge in shifting troops between sectors of the battle. But Fremantle's setting of the scene discloses a perceived Confederate advantage, too: Meade had most but not all of his infantry corps available on the morning of the second, with the remaining troops (roughly 25 percent of his command) on their way. Lee, as he formulated battle plans on the night of the first, calculated that he must attack before those Federal troops arrived. Lee's plan called for Longstreet to lead the way with an assault on the Union left and for Ewell to then initiate an attack on Cemetery Hill and Culp's Hill on the Union right. Longstreet preferred a different plan—for the Confederates to leave behind this unfavorable terrain, slip south between the Yankees and Washington, D.C., and force the Federals to engage on terrain that the Confederates chose. Longstreet's reluctance translated into delays in his getting his troops into position for the attack, leading to speculation that he hoped against hope Lee would abandon his original plan and yield to Longstreet's thinking.[16]

James Longstreet. Lee's "War Horse," Longstreet was central to the Confederate victories at Second Bull Run and Fredericksburg. But his comportment at Gettysburg—a battle he hoped would replay Fredericksburg—would be the source of enduring controversy. (Library of Congress LC-DIG-ppmsca-38007)

Meanwhile, the Federals faced their own unexpected challenge in the form of battlefield improvisation by Major General Daniel E. Sickles, commander of the Third Corps. Without leave from Meade, Sickles (an impetuous man who was notorious for having killed his wife's lover) advanced his corps nearly a mile west of the Federal line to what he imagined was some stronger high ground, leaving his men terribly exposed, unmoored from the rest of the Federal army. When Longstreet's attack finally materialized, in the late afternoon, led by John Bell Hood's division, scenes of carnage ensued at the nest of boulders called Devil's Den, and the adjacent Peach Orchard and Wheatfield, to the north. The Federal line shook and buckled but held, thanks to heroic resistance at key points, such as the hand-to-hand combat of Maine troops, led by Bowdoin professor Joshua Lawrence Chamberlain, defending the extreme left at Little Round Top; the sacrificial counterattack of the 1st Minnesota, which plugged a gap in the Federal center, losing 215 of its 262 men; and the timely arrival of the Sixth Corps on the field of battle after an epic thirty-five-mile march to the front. Meanwhile, Ewell once again squandered the initiative, waiting until sundown to launch a series of uncoordinated attacks on the hills at the top of the fishhook. Again Federal counterattacks halted the Confederates' initial progress.

The southern quadrant of the battlefield was a vista of "harrowing pandemonium" on July 2, wrote Confederate brigadier general John Brown Gordon; of the fighting at the Wheatfield, he added poetically, "The ruthless Harvester piles his heaps of slain thicker than the grain shocks gathered by the husbandman's scythe." According to William C. Oates of the 15th Alabama, the dead and wounded on Little Round Top literally covered the ground. "The blood stood in puddles in some places on the rocks; the ground was soaked with the blood of as brave men as ever fell on the red field of battle." Federal troops looking back on the day knew they had averted disaster. "Our gain was slight," diarist John W. Haley of the 17th Maine concluded, "but we have prevented Lee's forces from carrying out their design." Confederates had no such consolation. "It was evident that we had not finished the job," lamented Lee's artillery chief, Edward Porter Alexander, "and would have to make a fresh effort in the morning."[17]

July 3: Day Three

That fresh start was premised on the arrival at the front of General George Pickett's division of Virginia soldiers and of Jeb Stuart's wayward cavalry at sundown on the second. Lee's plan for the following day was to throw

Pickett's men, along with divisions led by Brigadier General James Johnston Pettigrew and Major General Isaac Trimble, at the center of the Federal line on Cemetery Ridge, while Stuart harassed Meade from the rear, after a massive artillery bombardment had weakened the Yankee defenses. Lee reckoned that the assaults of the second day of fighting had failed because they had unfolded serially rather than simultaneously; instead he would concentrate his forces for an all-out, coordinated attack. But Meade anticipated this move and shored up the Federal center with reinforcements. At 1:00 p.m. the Confederate artillery unlimbered its two-hour barrage, setting the earth trembling; the din could be heard a hundred miles away. "Every size and form of shell known to British and to American gunnery whirled, moaned, whistled, and wrathfully fluttered over our ground," wrote war correspondent Samuel Wilkerson of the *New York Tribune*, from a position near Meade's headquarters. The Federal cannon answered—"the air seethed with old iron" in "the greatest artillery duel ever fought on this planet," as Haley put it—with the Yankee guns falling silent after an hour to fool the Confederates into thinking they had no firepower left.[18]

At about 3:00 p.m., the Confederate attack brigades, some 12,500 massed men, appeared from the woods along Seminary Ridge and began advancing, flags fluttering as if on parade, along the half-mile-long gap that separated them from the Federal line, which was anchored by Winfield Scott Hancock's corps. The Federal batteries resumed their fire, and the entrenched Yankee infantry, protected by embankments, stone walls, and boulders, poured forth lead, shattering Confederate bodies. The Confederates "continued to move on unflinchingly," as Captain Francis Adams Donaldson of the 118th Pennsylvania Infantry observed. He added: "It was a grand sight to see them, their splendid behavior calling forth bursts of admiration." Donaldson was not alone among the Yankees in acknowledging the Confederates' desperate bravery. "No troops could resist the awful attack to which they were exposed. It was a sheet of fire, backed by a wall of steel. They couldn't reach the wall and *live*," Haley noted. And yet for a few short minutes it seemed that that Yankee line might give way, as several hundred Confederates led by General Lewis Addison Armistead breached the low stone wall at what would come to be remembered as the "high-water mark" of the Confederacy. Then Yankee reinforcements poured in and overwhelmed them. What came to be known as "Pickett's Charge" played out as a Fredericksburg in reverse—indeed, men in the 20th Massachusetts, as they "bowled [the rebels] over like nine pins," shouted "Fredericksburg! Fredericksburg!" in the rush of their long-awaited retribution. For Haley, this dramatic tableau called forth the legendary St.

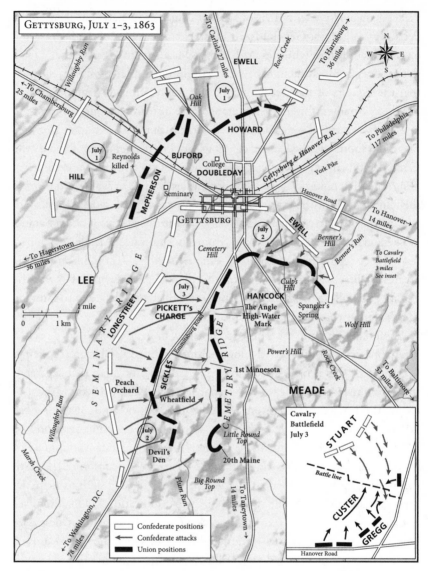

MAP 8.2

Crispin's Day battle speech from Shakespeare's *Henry IV*. On the evening of the third, he recorded these lines in his diary: "He that outlives this day, and comes safe home, / Will stand a tiptoe when this day is named."[19]

Haley's admiration did not extend to Lee himself. The rebel chief "witnessed the slaughter of his men . . . and, from the very first, it must have been plain to him that if any of his men reached the Union line, they could

George Pickett. In the ill-fated grand assault that carried his name, Pickett's men fleetingly breached the Union lines only to collapse and fall back in the face of overwhelming firepower. When urged by Lee to rally his division, Pickett purportedly responded, "General Lee, I have no division now!" (Library of Congress LC-USZ6-284)

never hold it for an instant," Haley reflected. "His feelings as he saw his troops mowed down must have been indescribable." Confederate losses in the battle were staggering: 28,000 casualties. Fifty-four percent of the men who made Pickett's Charge were killed or wounded. The command structure of the Army of Northern Virginia was ravaged. A third of Lee's fifty-two generals at Gettysburg were casualties, and in some regiments the officer corps was wiped out: for example, twenty-nine of the thirty-one officers in the 18th Virginia were killed or wounded.[20] The Union army, too, had been battered, sustaining 23,000 casualties, including frightful losses among its commanders. And so the exhausted Meade, to Lincoln's profound disappointment, decided not to renew the fight on July 4. Lee, "after holding his position long enough . . . to express his defiance," historian Russell Weigley has put it, skillfully withdrew his army, retreating back to Virginia with the Federals offering only a cautious pursuit.[21]

Lee accepted full responsibility for the defeat. Why had he asked his men to face such odds? Was he a tragic hero with a fatal flaw—arrogance, impetuousness, or bloodlust? Over the years his defenders have exonerated Lee and pointed to other culprits for the Confederate failure, with Stuart, Longstreet, and Ewell all receiving abundant blame. Historians who have sought to get beyond the blame game have emphasized that Lee had grounds for his confidence in his own army's ability to beat the odds, as well as good reason to assume that Meade, like his predecessors, would underperform. Moreover, they have placed Lee's decision-making in the context of the Confederacy's strategic dilemma. A defensive strategy was not viable, Russell Weigley has explained, for it would "multiply the advantages of the Union" by permitting the Federals to concentrate their superior numbers and resources at points of their own choosing. But an offensive strategy—one that sought tactical victories that destroyed Union armies—was also unsustainable, for it exacted too many casualties on the undermanned Confederates. Even as Lee's second northern invasion unfolded, the Vicksburg front offered evidence of the limits of defensive fighting for the Confederacy—and of the emergence of the Union general who was Lee's equal in tactical savvy.[22]

Vicksburg's Circle of Fire

As spring gave way to summer in 1863, victory continued to elude the Union on the Vicksburg front, because of the strength of the city's network of trenches, gullies, and fortifications and the stubborn resilience of its defenders. The Union army attempted a frontal assault on Vicksburg on May 19 and was repulsed by what one Federal soldier described as an "absolutely blinding" hail of lead from the Confederates.[23] Grant ordered a second such attack on May 22, and the Union troops executed it with a sober awareness of the odds against survival. Osborn Oldroyd of Ohio recounted this scene in his diary, one that calls to mind the image of World War I soldiers going "over the top" of the trenches to certain death:

> At ten o'clock we had orders to advance. The boys were expecting the order and were busy divesting themselves of watches, rings, pictures and other keepsakes, which were being placed in the custody of the cooks, who were not expected to go into action. I never saw such a scene before, nor do I ever want to see it again. The instructions left for the keepsakes were varied. For instance . . . "I am going to Vicksburg, and if I do not get back just send these little trifles home, will you?" Not

a bit of sadness or fear appears in the talk or faces of the boys, but they thought it timely and proper to dispose of what they had accordingly.[24]

Union artillery attempted to open the way for the infantry by unleashing the fearsome fire of 300 cannon; a Confederate veteran later described the roar of the cannonade as "a sublime orchestra, playing a dreadful chorus of death." But the entrenched Confederates retained the advantage and mowed down the Union attackers, leaving Grant with losses of 3,000 to Pemberton's 500. Grant would later concede that the only charge he ordered as futile as this one was the disastrous frontal assault at Cold Harbor in the summer of 1864.[25]

These May setbacks forced Grant to do what he had so hoped to avoid: to lay siege to the Confederate stronghold. For six weeks, as Federal reinforcements poured into their lines (bringing Grant's ranks to 71,000), 220 guns threw shellfire into the city and Union forces moved their trenches ever closer, and waited the Confederates out. As the infantryman Oldroyd explained in his June 19 diary entry,

> For a month we have been watching our enemy vigilantly, and a pano-
> rama, consisting of a great variety of war scenes, has, during that time,
> passed before us. We have had charging, digging rifle-pits, blowing up
> forts and firing all sizes of cannon, to say nothing of percussion shells,
> spherical case shot, times shells, parrot, grape, cannister, shrapnel,
> etc. . . . The terrible noises . . . that have rung in our ears, must echo for
> years to come. I may add our endurance of this southern sun, at times
> being short of rations, and at no time out of danger, yet all the time
> nearly uncomplaining—every one trying to make the best of it.

As Oldroyd suggested, Federal forces tried periodically to break the Confederates' defensive perimeter by digging approach trenches and attempting mining operations; on June 25, for example, the Union detonated more than two tons of gunpowder in shafts dug under the Confederate lines by coal and lead miners in the ranks. The ensuing battle over this crater did not break the Confederate line but did push it back.[26]

As the Union tried approach after approach, Southern soldiers and civilians alike languished inside the city's defenses, deprived of food and medicine. Since the spring, civilians had taken to living in caves; Dora Miller, a Southern woman who concealed her Unionist sympathies, explained, "Cave-digging has become a regular business; prices range from twenty to fifty dollars, ac- cording to [the] size of cave. . . . The hills are so honeycombed with caves that

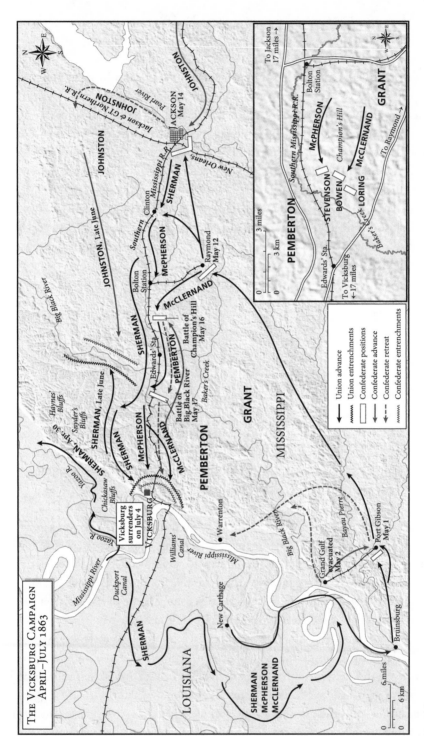

THE VICKSBURG CAMPAIGN
APRIL–JULY 1863

MAP 8.3

the streets look like avenues in a cemetery." "We are utterly cut off from the world," she wrote of the siege, "surrounded by a circle of fire. . . . People do nothing but eat what they can get, sleep when they can, and dodge the shells." The grim rhythms of the Union shellfire structured each day and filled it with terror. "There are three intervals when the shelling stops," Miller noted, "either for the guns to cool or for the gunner's meals, I suppose,—about eight in the morning, and the same in the evening, and at noon. In that time we have both to prepare and eat ours. Clothing cannot be washed or anything else done." Commenting on how the Yankee trenches encroached on the rebel ones, Sergeant William H. Tunnard of the 3rd Louisiana Infantry wrote on June 17, "The enemy's lines were so near now that scraps of paper could be thrown by the combatants into each other's ranks. Thus a Yankee threw a 'hardtack' biscuit among the men of the regiment, having written on it 'starvation.' "[27]

Port Hudson and Milliken's Bend

Meanwhile, a second Union siege on the Mississippi, at Port Hudson, Louisiana—the other remaining Confederate stronghold on the river, some 250 miles south of Vicksburg—furnished the setting for black troops to prove their mettle in combat. Union major general Nathaniel Banks, aware that Pemberton had called away some of Port Hudson's troops to come north in order to help defend Vicksburg, hoped to exploit the situation and bag the Louisiana garrison. Banks imagined that once Port Hudson was under his control, his own Union forces could veer north to assist Grant. But the Confederate defenders of Port Hudson, some 7,500 of them, had a strong defensive position on bluffs behind more than four miles of earthworks, which could neutralize the Union's manpower advantage (Banks had some 30,000 troops at his disposal). Banks was undeterred. On May 27, 1863, he ordered a general assault on Port Hudson's perimeter, throwing his divisions into a blistering barrage of Confederate firepower. On the extreme right of the Union line were two black regiments: the 1st Louisiana Native Guard, consisting mostly of free blacks from New Orleans, and the 3rd Louisiana Native Guard made up of former slaves. These Louisiana regiments offered black men unique, fleeting opportunities for leadership: while regimental commands were reserved for whites, company-level commands, at the rank of captain or lieutenant, initially included blacks (although Banks was in the process of pressuring these officers to resign, on the grounds that only whites should hold such positions). Among the line officers leading the Union assault on Port Hudson were free men of color such as Captain André Cailloux, an Afro-Creole from New Orleans's distinctive class of *gens de couleur libres*, who gave his orders to his men in French and English.[28]

The men faced a fearful scene. "Louder than the thunder of Heaven was the artillery rending the air shaking the earth itself; cannons, mortars and musketry alike opened a fiery storm upon the advancing regiments," wrote Joseph T. Wilson, who served with the 2nd Louisiana Native Guard and after the war would go on to become the premier historian of the United States Colored Troops (USCT). "'Steady men, steady,' cried bold Cailloux; his sword uplifted, his face the color of the sulphureous smoke that enveloped him and his followers, as they felt the deadly hail." This heroism proved unavailing. "Captain Cailloux was killed with the colors in his hands," Wilson wrote, and "the column seemed to melt away like snow in sunshine." Once again, a commander's choice to take the tactical offensive against a fortified defense had consigned his men to a death trap. African American soldiers sustained 600 casualties in their fruitless assault. The Union siege of Port Hudson would grind on into the summer.[29]

But as Wilson keenly realized, the action on May 27 had symbolic significance that far outweighed the tactical results. The bravery of the black troops had converted some white skeptics in the Union ranks. As Union officer Elias D. Strunke explained, he had doubted the "pluck" of black troops. But when tested, "these men did not swerve, or show cowardice." "I have been in several engagements," Strunke wrote to the chief recruiter of black troops in southern Louisiana, "and I never before beheld such coolness and daring." Banks himself testified to the brave conduct of these men, praising "the determined manner in which they encountered the enemy." While Confederate New Orleanians and some Northern Copperheads demeaned and derided Cailloux as a lackey of Lincoln, the Northern antislavery press predicted that the Port Hudson battle would "wash out the prejudices" that had so long existed against blacks, to quote Garrison's *Liberator*. The martyred Cailloux became the first African American military hero of the war, his sacrifices celebrated by Unionists in newspaper articles, poems, and a massive funeral procession in New Orleans. His decomposing corpse had lain on the Port Hudson battlefield for forty-seven days, until the Confederate fort surrendered in July 1863—only then could his remains at last be returned to his native city and he be given military honors. "Flowers were strewn in the greatest profusion, and candles were kept continuously burning" in the hall where his body lay in state, draped in an American flag; the officiating priest offered the rites of the Catholic Church and "called upon all present to offer themselves, as Cailloux had done, martyrs to the cause of justice."[30]

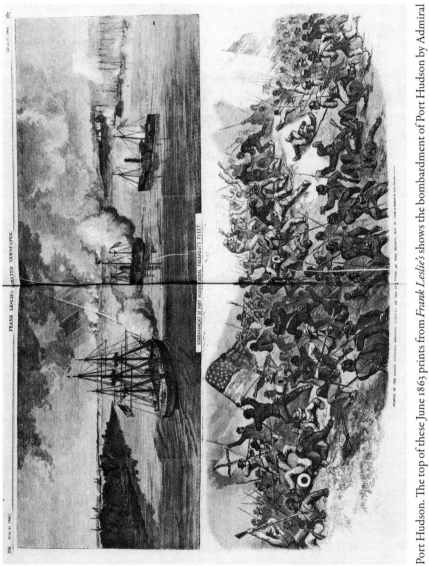

BOMBARDMENT OF PORT HUDSON BY ADMIRAL FARRAGUT'S FLEET.

ASSAULT OF THE SECOND LOUISIANA (COLORED) REGIMENT ON THE REBEL WORKS AT PORT HUDSON, MAY 27.—From a Sketch by our Special Artist.

Port Hudson. The top of these June 1863 prints from *Frank Leslie's* shows the bombardment of Port Hudson by Admiral Farragut's fleet, and the bottom shows the assault by Louisiana black regiments on the rebel works. (Library of Congress LC-USZ62-133081)

More martyrs would come forth in June 1863, at the battle of Milliken's Bend, Louisiana, about twenty-five miles upstream from Vicksburg. Determined to relieve pressure on Vicksburg and force Grant to break off his siege, the Confederates targeted Grant's supply lines on the western banks of the Mississippi and four seemingly vulnerable supply depots there. The Confederates were unaware that Grant had gotten wind of this move and had reinforced these garrisons and transferred his principal supply routes to the east of the river, where his army was operating. They learned their lesson the hard way: on June 7, 1863, in searing heat, an infantry brigade of Texas troops attacked the Federal post at Milliken's Bend and were driven back. Although outnumbered, the Union men—new, untested black regiments raised as part of Lorenzo Thomas's spring recruitment campaign in the Mississippi Valley and the white 23rd Iowa Infantry—occupied a strong defensive position behind a levee and trenches, with the Mississippi River at their backs; the approach to the levee was an obstacle course of ditches, hedges, vines, and briars. In part because the black soldiers were inexperienced and armed with poor-quality weapons, the Confederates succeeded in breaching the Federal works. The fighting along the levee devolved into brutal hand-to-hand combat, with men bayoneting each other and using their muskets as clubs. The Confederates pushed the Federal line off the levee to the riverbank, only to face the shells of the Federal gunboats. With the Federals forming a new line at the water's edge and more riverboats on the way, the Texans were forced to retreat. Their campaign in northeastern Louisiana had come to naught.[31]

Here was a victory both strategic and symbolic for the champions of black enlistment. Although undertrained and poorly equipped, the black regiments had emerged from their baptism of fire as victors. The 9th Louisiana (African Descent) especially had distinguished itself, holding its ground while other white and black units fell back, and taking 67.4 percent casualties. As in the aftermath of Port Hudson, white Union soldiers saw in this performance a rebuke to the skeptics. Captain M. M. Miller of the 9th Louisiana wrote his aunt in Galena, Illinois, that he never again wanted to hear whites opine that blacks wouldn't fight. "Come with me 100 yards from where I sit, and I can show you the wounds that cover the bodies of 16 as brave, loyal and patriotic soldiers as ever drew bead on a Rebel." While the Confederate general who led the Milliken's Bend attack, Henry McCulloch, grudgingly acknowledged the "considerable obstinacy" of the black troops, the more common reaction among white Southerners was disbelief. Kate Stone confided to her diary that it was hard to fathom that Southern soldiers had "been whipped by a mongrel crew of white and black Yankees." This contempt for an interracial army would undergird

Confederate policies on the treatment of prisoners of war. Some Union soldiers testified that the Confederates had shouted "no quarter" as they stormed the levee, and rumors circulated that the approximately two dozen black prisoners taken by the Texans had been enslaved and that two of their white officers had been jailed and executed. For black soldiers, the battle at Milliken's Bend had raised the hope of vindication but also the specter of reprisals.[32]

Vicksburg Falls at Last

For ardent Confederates, combatant and noncombatant alike, the dominant story line of the Vicksburg siege was the forlorn hope that Johnston's army, which thanks to reinforcements was now 31,000 men strong and based near Jackson, might rescue them. As the siege began, Confederate newspapers far away from the front opined, to quote the *Richmond Daily Dispatch*, that "under the skillful direction of Gen. Johnston, we have abundant reason to hope that the defense of Vicksburg will not only be successful, but triumphant." Such predictions failed to fathom the deep dysfunction in the Confederate high command. Johnston expected Pemberton to come to him: to fight his way out of Vicksburg so that the two armies, freed from the albatross of defending the beleaguered city, could join forces in a new campaign. Pemberton, upholding his mandate from Davis to hold Vicksburg, had no intention of attempting a breakout. And yet the hopes for a Johnston rescue died hard: Confederates again and again reported the rumor that help was on the way. On June 22, the Texan infantry officer Maurice Simons reported that a courier had announced the news that Johnston was "on the way here with a large force." The rumor fired Simons's spirit, if only fleetingly: "I feel confident that we will be relieved in a very few days," he wrote. "I think there will be desperate fighting yet I feel that God helping him Johnston will be equal to the task. How bright will be our prospects then. We will all feel but like birds just turned out of a cage & the cause of liberty for which we are fighting will then look bright as does a bride before the Altar all dressed in purest white." Two days later, Simons reported that a man who claimed "to be a prophet" had promised that on the following day, Johnston would attack the enemy at three o'clock.[33]

But Johnston never came. A week later, Simons faced reality and wrote a fitting epitaph for this last phase of the Vicksburg campaign:

Well the first day of July has come and almost passed away & no Signs of Johnston. The fact is we have almost despaired of his coming and the general impression seems to be that we will have to surrender. It is truly heart sickning to think of such a thing but I beleave it will be don. . . . I do not think it possible for us to fight our way out. The men have been in the trenches for so long a time on short rations & having taken no exercise all the time I do not think they could now martch five miles.[34]

On July 4, the forty-seven-day siege ended when Pemberton surrendered the city to Grant. Dora Miller wrote of the victorious Union army as it entered the city, "What a contrast to the suffering creatures we had seen so long were these stalwart, well-fed men, so splendidly set up and accoutered. Sleek horses, polished arms, bright plumes,—this was the pride and panoply of war. Civilization, discipline, and order seemed to enter with the measured tramp of those marching columns." The 30,000 surviving Confederate soldiers were paroled: they were sent back to their lines on the sworn and signed promise that they would not take up arms against the Union again unless formally exchanged. Under the elaborate prison cartel system the two sides had estab-lished, either a paroled prisoner of war went to one of his own side's parole camps to be exchanged or he went home, where he could, if he desired to get

Fall of the Rebel Gibraltar. "The Federal Army, Under General Grant, Taking Formal Possession of Vicksburg, July 4th, 1863, After the Surrender." Grant paroled the surren-dered Confederates, hoping to promote their repentance and acquiescence in Union vic-tory. (*Frank Leslie's Illustrated Magazine*)

back into the fray, await word of and then report for an impending exchange. Grant was quite forthright in the rationale for his Vicksburg terms. His leniency toward the prostrate Confederates would "make them less dangerous foes during the continuance of hostilities, and better citizens after the war was over." He hoped the parolees would melt into the countryside and into civilian life rather than report for exchange.[35]

Simons, for his part, was relieved by the lenience of Grant's terms but still defiant. "I felt proud when I thaught of the time & means that it had cost them with all their facilities to take the place & that they only got possession of it then on account of our having been starved out," he wrote on July 4. Simons was eager to get back into the fray and looked forward to "some future day when . . . things will work better for us." Union soldiers, by contrast, attributed their victory not to their overwhelming numbers and resources but to the "untiring energy, skill and forecast of our gallant leader, U. S. Grant, aided by the willing and brave hearts about him," as Oldroyd put it. He concluded: "I trust the wicked rebellion will not fail soon to near its end."[36]

A Turning Point?

It has proved irresistible for modern historians to declare the twin victories at Gettysburg and Vicksburg in July 1863 a "turning point" in the war. But such a retrospective judgment fails to fully capture the complex emotional and political realities of the moment, the distinctions each side drew between the battles, and the widening scope of the war as a humanitarian crisis. To be sure, on the Union side the twin victories produced a burst of euphoric celebration—illuminations, processions, speeches, fireworks, salutes—coinciding auspiciously with the commemoration of July 4. The status of Vicksburg as a bastion of Southern defiance made its fall all the sweeter. Lincoln, who had been skeptical of Grant's final plan to approach the river city from the south, penned an extraordinary letter to the victorious general. "I now wish to make the personal acknowledgment that you were right, and I was wrong," Lincoln conceded on July 13, in a rare moment of humility for an American president.[37]

But even in the first flush of victory, Union soldiers were made to fully confront the desperate toll of the siege on Vicksburg's civilians. "When we beheld the emaciated condition of the women and children at the entrance of their cave dwellings, along the roadside," wrote one Union soldier, "we didn't feel a bit like cheering. The boys emptied their haversacks for the little ones, and watched them devour the rations like starved animals."

The magnanimity of Grant's surrender terms and the generosity of Union soldiers to the bereft soldiers and civilians of the town were highlighted by the Northern press as it folded the story of the Vicksburg siege into the narrative of Southern deliverance. The failure of Johnston to recruit sufficient men to raise the siege, the starvation conditions into which civilians descended as the army commandeered the available resources, the deaf ear the authorities at Richmond turned to the "cries of despair" emanating from Vicksburg—these were all signs, Northern commentators noted, of the "rottenness at the root" of the Confederate cause. The misguided civilians and soldiers were "treated [by] their late enemy with great kindness," as an Ohio paper put it in a typical formulation: Union soldiers, shocked by conditions in the city, shared food, water, coffee, and alcohol with the rebels and then implemented a formal program of humanitarian relief, in which the occupying army cleaned the city of carcasses, waste, garbage, and the ghastly debris of war; distributed rations; and revived commerce and trade. "Our government will not let the innocent starve," an Illinois officer pledged, giving voice to the conviction that the Union men brought progress and civilization in their wake.[38]

Confederate civilians at first seemed grateful for the humane treatment, which stoked the hope of Federal soldiers that Southerners' minds were being "relieved from the false impressions they have received as to our real character and intentions," as Union general William W. Orme wrote to his wife on July 7, 1863. But Confederates in Vicksburg soon rejected the "occupiers' notion of progress," historian Bradley Clampitt has explained—especially as the Federals recruited black troops in the region and posted them in the city. Back on the Northern home front, moderate critics of the Lincoln administration argued that the military successes of the summer had come in spite of, not because of, its radical embrace of black freedom and enlistment. They predicted that a "few more blows" would finish the rebellion "unless the radicals should succeed in placing their abolition programme in the way of success."[39] The Copperhead press went one step further: loath to see Lincoln treat the victories as a mandate or vindication, it emphasized Confederate resilience and the staggering toll for the North of the July fighting. "The obstinacy with which Vicksburg was defended, and the terrible loss of life which it cost us," the *New York News* editorialized on July 8, "are but evidence of our incompetency to subjugate a foe that has so much vitality and force."[40]

Conditions in Gettysburg were more chastening for Northerners than those in Vicksburg. John W. Geary, a division commander in the Army of the Potomac, wrote his wife, Mary, on July 5 that he was "perfectly sick of the times": "My very clothes smell of death. The stench of the battlefields was horrible and beyond description," he lamented. "With all the consciousness and pride of victory, it is still a heart-rending sight to look upon this great burying ground," reported a Philadelphia correspondent in the aftermath of the battle. The Pennsylvania town was shattered, as if leveled by a cyclone; littered with the corpses of 8,000 men and 5,000 mules and horses; and strewn with 20,000 wounded men, a third of whom were Confederates.[41]

The battle tested and overwhelmed the Union's emerging system for the care and treatment of wounded men. That system was the brainchild of Dr. Jonathan Letterman, chief medical officer of the Army of the Potomac. Since assuming his post in the summer of 1862, Letterman had, as the battles of Antietam, Fredericksburg, and Chancellorsville unfolded, implemented a series of visionary reforms. He replaced the chaotic and inefficient methods of evacuating the wounded with a proper ambulance corps, trained crews, and well-stocked transport wagons subject to regular inspection and re-served for medical use. He established strict protocols for field hospitals, creating clear hierarchies and divisions of labor in which, for example, only

Carnage at Gettysburg. A Confederate soldier in the Wheatfield, killed by a shell at the battle of Gettysburg. Its 51,000 casualties made the three-day battle the bloodiest of the entire Civil War, and the bloodiest ever fought on American soil. (Library of Congress LC-B8184-7258)

men with technical expertise would perform surgery. He also was attentive to hygiene and sanitation, furnishing detailed guidelines for where tents were to be pitched and latrines dug, and ordering that soldiers be supplied with fresh vegetables and fruits to ward off scurvy and to aid in the healing process. Letterman's initiatives can be folded into a narrative of medical progress during the Civil War, belying the image of this era as the "end of the medical Middle Ages." Although the great breakthrough of germ theory (the role of microorganisms in disease) would not happen until the late nineteenth century, medical science did advance during the war, particularly in the use of anesthesia (the use of chloroform or ether was standard in amputations); the treatment of head wounds and gut shots; infection prevention through the use of bromide washes for wounds and hand washing in chlorinated soda; the use of qualifying exams to credential physicians; and the development of clinical research, under the auspices of the new U.S. Army Medical Museum in Washington, D.C., which provided specimens, laboratories, photographs, drawings, and lectures enabling doctors to learn from the wounded.[42]

That progress was not linear. The scope of the battle of Gettysburg confounded Letterman's best efforts. Many wounded men languished for hours or even days while the battle raged, as Letterman's doctors and ambulance drivers struggled to find evacuation routes and safe zones for establishing hospitals in the midst of the sprawling fight. Supplies of tents, bandages, and cooking equipment were all woefully inadequate, despite heroic efforts by the Sanitary Commission to supplement government stores. Wounded men were everywhere, shrieking and moaning in agony; doctors and nurses strained the limits of endurance in seemingly endless operating sessions. And then, on July 6, Letterman and most of his staff left Gettysburg, moving south with the Army of the Potomac, leaving behind 106 surgeons to attend to thousands of men, wounded, dehydrated, hungry, many too seriously injured to be evacuated to general hospitals in Philadelphia, Baltimore, and other nearby cities. On July 7, Cornelia Hancock, a New Jersey Quaker in Gettysburg to nurse the wounded, wrote her cousin, "There are no words in the English language to express the sufferings I witnessed today."[43]

Gettysburg, and particularly Pickett's Charge, has stood in popular memory as the ultimate expression of Southern men's devotion to their cause. Pickett's men were honored by the Confederate press as exemplars of valor and disciplined self-sacrifice. Northern reporters generally "endowed the enemy with superhuman qualities to enhance the reputation of the Union soldiers who had sent them reeling," historian Carol Reardon has noted. Tellingly, Northerners also folded stories of surrendered, captured, and wounded rebels at Gettysburg into the deluded-masses narrative. Some commentators made formulaic references to the theme of delusion. Michael Clover, a student at Gettysburg College, observed that after the battle the campus was thronged with hundreds of injured Confederates: "All rooms, halls, and hallways were occupied with the poor, deluded sons of the South." In his history of the 37th Massachusetts Infantry, James L. Bowen remarked that Union men at Gettysburg "never failed to succor and care for the misguided men as tenderly as though they had fallen in defense of the Stars and Stripes." Lieutenant Frank Haskell of the 6th Wisconsin, in one of the most famous and detailed accounts of the battle, lamented that the rebel dead were buried unceremoniously in trenches, remarking that he wished for better for his "brave, though deluded, countrymen."[44]

Others offered more elaborate anecdotes. In his diary entry for July 3, 1863, John Haley noted that "among the wounded is a little, flaxen-haired boy from North Carolina who is only fourteen years old, giving credence to the report that the Confeds rob the cradle and the grave. To keep the ranks full, they take old men beyond the military age and young ones who haven't reached it, and hustle them to the front." Lieutenant Samuel Wheeler of the 137th New York reported in a July 6 letter that a batch of rebels had surrendered to his regiment on July 3: "They declared themselves to be conscripts, and ... had determined to throw themselves upon our clemency rather than trust to the mercy of their own commanders, should they be compelled to fall back. This forcibly illustrates the despotism that exists in the rebel army." Reverend Edward P. Smith of the United States Christian Commission, which provided medical assistance to soldiers (along with doses of evangelism), quoted a South Carolina colonel who said, after being ministered to by a commission delegate, "I can't understand you Yankees; you fight us like devils, and then you treat us like angels. I am sorry I entered this war." Smith followed this up with the story of a wounded East Tennessean who had been forced into the Confederate army but had always kept with him the fragment of an American flag that had been torn to pieces by the rebels. Reverend William G. Browning of New York, another of the civilian volunteers who flocked to Gettysburg after the battle to assist the wounded, asked convalescing Confederates how they "came to enlist in this unnatural war" and was not surprised when they responded, "Led into it, sir!" He also reported overhearing a Yankee ask a rebel prisoner, "Were you one who thought for yourself, with reference to the cause which originated this war, or did you just believe what others told you?" The rebel answered: "Of course I believed what I was told, or I would not have been here." In her 1869 memoir, Sanitary Commission nurse Sophronia E. Bucklin cast her own ministrations to the rebel wounded as emblematic of Northern generosity, and she speculated: "Perhaps some of these men died repentant, coming back in spirit to their allegiance to the old flag." Newspaper reports echo these diary and memoir entries. A correspondent to the Republican newspaper the *Franklin Repository* was filled with pity and anger as he gazed upon rebel wounded in the aftermath of the battle. "Indignation bursts out afresh against the wicked leaders who betrayed these misguided men to such horrible sufferings," he reported. The correspondent discerned notes of repentance in the way the wounded rebels "expressed their sorrow that they had taken up arms against the Union"; he cited the example of a dying Georgian who had been "driven into the army by the bayonet."[45]

Of course, not all Northerners saw the battle as a clear moral victory. For Lincoln's foes in the North, the "butcheries at Gettysburg" were "sacrifices of our best and brightest . . . at the shrine of Abolitionism," as the *New York News* objected. Expressing bitterness at the ways the Copperheads denigrated the Union war effort, Cornelia Hancock wrote her sister on July 8 that after she read the newspaper to a tentful of amputees, the eight men quipped that they would "form a stump brigade" and go and fight the Northern traitors. Hancock ended her letter with some dark humor: "I am doing all I can, so I do not concern further. Kill the copperheads." In short, there was no consensus in the North that the July triumphs had turned the tide.[46]

Among Confederates, the Vicksburg defeat was a greater blow than Lee's failure. A "heavy sense of foreboding swept over the Confederacy as news of Vicksburg's loss gradually spread," observes historian Michael B. Ballard. It was followed in its wake by waves of name-calling among Confederates about who was to blame, with Jefferson Davis taking Pemberton's side against Johnston, and with a nascent peace movement, led by William W. Holden, editor of the *North Carolina Standard*, arguing that the Southern people should demand the end to the tragic and wasteful war. Holden believed that a negotiated peace could bring an honorable end to the grueling conflict and restore the key elements of the old order; peace would preserve the slave system, while a prolongation of the war would surely obliterate it. Most Confederates did not give in to despair, but instead took heart from the knowledge that the Army of Northern Virginia had survived to fight another day. The morale of Lee's men was buoyed by their return south. "We feel mortified at our failure, but rather pleased at the idea of once more going to Dixie," wrote George S. Bernard of the 12th Virginia on the retreat, on July 6. By the time he reached Maryland, Bernard's sense of mortification was mitigated by press reports that "the late fight at Gettysburg was not so unfavorable in its results after all. It appears that the enemy retreated at the same time, or even before we did, and it is said that their papers admit the enormous loss of 30,000." Bernard's reflections typified the efforts of Southern soldiers and civilians, and of newspapers supportive of the Davis administration, such as the *Richmond Dispatch*, to see the Gettysburg campaign as a qualified success. Confederates could take solace, such an argument ran, in their army's performance on the first day of the battle, the heavy casualties they inflicted, the stores and prisoners they captured, the elan of Pickett's Charge, and Meade's failure to drive them from the field or chase them down.[47]

Confederates drew satisfaction, too, from dramatic evidence that a Northern political revolution might come to pass even without crushing victories on Northern soil. In late July Southern newspapers brimmed with glee at news that the Northern commercial capital, New York City, had been pitched into anarchy by a massive draft riot. That such an event could transpire in the immediate aftermath of Vicksburg and Gettysburg showed, the *Charleston Courier* insisted, that "the fighting men of the Yankee nation, are tired and sick of the war." The *Richmond Enquirer* went so far as to claim that the news from New York portended "the breaking down of the whole structure of Yankee society." Would the New York convulsion shake the North to its core?[48]

The New York Draft Riot

In July 1863, the first Federal draftees were called up under the system established in the March 1863 Enrollment Act; in districts that failed to meet their quotas of volunteers, and after the enrollment of all eligible men (single men ages twenty to forty-five and married men up to age thirty-five), draftees were chosen by lottery. The provisions of the draft were inherently unfair and thus instantly controversial: in order to avoid service, draftees could hire substitutes to go in their place or pay the government a $300 commutation fee. That fee far exceeded the means of working-class men, as did the price of hiring a substitute; moreover, a shady class of bounty brokers soon emerged who took a cut of the bounties that were supposed to serve recruits as inducements for volunteering. The draft not only victimized poor men, the Democratic press charged, but also represented an abrogation of a state's jurisdiction over its own militias.

While there were small-scale, sporadic draft riots from Massachusetts to Wisconsin, New York City became the epicenter of draft resistance. For four days in the summer of 1863, July 13 to July 16, Manhattan was the scene of the most extensive mob violence in American history. The protesters, a mixture of skilled craftsmen and unskilled laborers, initially attacked the draft office at Third Avenue and 46th Street, forcing the authorities to suspend the draft. The more restrained protesters then drifted away, and the protest degenerated into an assault on the Republican party and a race riot: the rampaging white mob, led by Irish and German immigrants, and including women and children, vented its fury against any representatives and symbols of the Lincoln administration, New York's elite business class, and its vulnerable free black community. Armed with clubs, stones, and brickbats, the mob looted stores, seizing luxury goods, liquor, and weapons; sacked the homes of wealthy Republicans and torched the office of Horace Greeley's *New York Tribune*; hunted down, terrorized, lynched, drowned, tortured, and mutilated the bodies of African Americans, killing more than a dozen and burning the city's Colored Orphan Asylum to the ground; and fought pitched battles against the outmanned city police department. Describing this hellscape, the Republican *New York Times* reported that the rioters "danced with fiendish delight" around their targets, and that "the murky atmosphere and the heavy black clouds which lined the horizon, formed a strange weird spectacle, which was made the more complete by the demoniac yells of the mobs." It took regiments of Union troops returning from Gettysburg to regain control over the city, fighting for and occupying territory block by block.[49]

The *New York Times* was certain, as many Republicans were, that the riot was the work of Copperhead Democratic wire-pullers who had stoked the racism of the immigrant laboring population and put it to partisan ends. There was evidence to support that charge: Democratic newspapers such as the *New York News* had urged workingmen not to "be conscripted into the ranks of the Abolition Army" and driven "from their homes into the slaughter pen." Such rhetoric tapped a deep wellspring of economic and cultural grievances, especially on the part of the Irish Catholic poor, who had experienced nativist discrimination and were susceptible to the argument that emancipation would bring their own economic displacement by freed black workers. That fear reflected, too, the desperate squalor of immigrant slums, such as lower Manhattan's notorious Five Points, and the yawning gap between New York City's rich and poor. New York City's top 1 percent owned 61 percent of the city's wealth.[50]

Moreover, the riot is a window into the resentments of working-class white women, who, while a minority of participants, were "disproportionately important . . . in identifying targets and instigating violence," historian Judy Giesberg has established. The riots should be put in the context of an immigrant and workingwomen's culture of opposition, Giesberg explains: as these women were asked to make patriotic sacrifices, they increasingly asserted their rights to defend themselves and their families from exploitation. For example, women who filled cartridges in Northern arsenals protested dangerous and sometimes deadly working conditions there (explosions in arsenals killed scores of women). Women who could find no such paid labor and had no means of support once their husbands went to war threw themselves on the mercy of local poor relief boards and almshouses, and often felt stigmatized and ill-treated by these authorities. In the context of this economic tenuousness, the rioters believed they were "protecting their families"; "as the war drew away male wage earners, it drove working-class and immigrant women to destitution." As one rioter put it in a letter to the *New York Times*, "We love our wives and children more than the rich, because we got not much besides them, and we will not go and leave them at home to starve."[51]

Significantly, many Irish Americans, especially those serving as soldiers in the Union army, rejected this line of reasoning, and expressed their shame and regret that their fellow Irishmen and women had perpetrated atrocities in the riots. They would have preferred that the heroism and sacrifices of distinguished fighting units such as the Army of the Potomac's Irish Brigade define the image of the sons of Erin in the Union cause, and that wartime service cement the Irish claim on full citizenship and acceptance within the American polity. An estimated 25 percent of Union soldiers were immigrants, mostly German and Irish (more than 200,000 German-born and 150,000 Irish-born men wore the Union blue), and another 18 percent of the soldiery had at least one foreign-born parent, meaning that, all told, immigrants and the sons of immigrants made up approximately 43 percent of the Union's armed forces. These numbers reflected the waves of antebellum immigration by Europeans fleeing poverty and political proscription. Immigrants were 13 percent of the American population on the eve of the war, and they were clustered overwhelmingly in the urban centers of the free labor North, where jobs and communities could be found. While some served in "ethnic regiments" of fellow Irishmen and Germans, most served in nonethnic regiments. Some professed "ethnic" motivations—Irish nationalists such as Brigadier General Thomas F. Meagher, for example, saw the war as a training ground for their liberation struggle against England, and some Germans, in light of their failed revolution of 1848, saw the American Civil War as another chapter in an age-old struggle between republicanism and aristocracy. But most immigrant soldiers, historian William L. Burton has persuasively argued, "shared the motivations of [their] native-born counterparts": a sense of duty to and love for the Union. Mainstream press coverage of the riots, with its emphasis on Irish

THE MEETING OF THE FRIENDS,

Reactions to the New York Draft Riot. In this anti-Copperhead cartoon, New York's governor, Horatio Seymour, is portrayed as a ringleader of the rioters, whom he refers to, in a speech from the City Hall steps, as "My Friends." New York mayor Fernando Wood is pictured, too, with a top hat and devil's horns. The rioters terrorize and lynch African Americans and menace the offices of Horace Greeley's *New York Tribune*. (Library of Congress LC-USZ62-96391)

Catholic disloyalty, contributed to the growing disaffection of Irish Catholic immigrants from the war effort. Angered that their communities' military sacrifices went underappreciated, Irish Catholics on the home front became more susceptible to Copperhead critiques of the Lincoln administration.[52]

In a parallel trend, the New York riot sharpened the tendency of Union soldiers to see Copperheads, draft resisters, and civilian protesters as traitors. "If they would send us home to enforce the draft with our present feelings we should not be very likely to fire high for you can hardly find a soldier that would not shoot his brother almost if he resisted the draft," wrote Corporal Joseph H. Prime of the 13th New Hampshire to his wife, Hannah, on July 21, 1863. "We are protecting the rights and homes of the *damn* secessionists north and they ought to be forced to assist us if they will not do it willingly," he added. Sometimes such sentiments came with a dose of undiluted nativism. Commenting on the draft riot, artillery officer William Wheeler wrote, "I only wished they would send me with my Battery to the city for a couple of weeks to enforce the draft. I would much rather fire canister into those drunken Irish rowdies, than into the secesh brethren, who, although deluded, are worth all the paddies that ever had a brogue." James Clarke of the 5th Ohio Infantry condemned the negligence of New York's leaders for letting "the rabble have it their own way for years." "I think New York copperheadism has worked its own destruction," he wrote to a friend on July 17, 1863. "King Horatio [Seymour] and King Jeff [Davis] came down hand in hand to the domain of the first secessionist . . . where *brimstone* and *not* cotton is King."[53]

For African American victims of the mob violence, the dispiriting aftermath of the riots furnished proof of the willingness of federal, state, and municipal authorities to conciliate the disloyal Copperhead element and to disregard black patriotism. Lincoln chose not to resort to martial law in the wake of the riots and instead sought to pacify the region by making concessions to the disaffected Democrats, including putting implementation of the draft into the hands of General John Dix, a Democrat. Dix opted to use state, not federal, authorities to carry out the draft, and he decided to hold the first lottery in the rich Republican district of Greenwich Village. And county and municipal committees raised money to pay commutation fees and purchase substitutes for worthy applicants for relief. African Americans, by contrast, fled New York City in a mass exodus. Beatings and harassment of the remaining black population continued after the riot, with public spaces in the city dominated more completely than ever by whites. As they had in the wake of antebellum white rioting, African Americans struggled to keep bitterness and despair at bay. William M. Powell, a free black seaman who had hidden in a neighbor's cellar while the mob ransacked and destroyed his house, provided the following lament to the *Anglo-African*:

> As a devoted loyal Unionist, I have done all I could to perpetuate and uphold the integrity of this free government. As an evidence of this devotedness, my oldest son is now serving my country as a Surgeon in the U.S. army, and myself had just received a commission in the naval service. What more could I do? What further evidence was wanting to prove my allegiance in the exigencies of our unfortunate country?[54]

The Fighting 54th

Questions like these reverberated in debates among Northern free blacks over enlistment. The first regiment to draw primarily from northern free black

communities, the 54th Massachusetts, established in January 1863 at the behest of the Bay State's antislavery governor, John A. Andrew, was the focal
point for these debates. From the start, the model regiment drew recruits
from across the North. By March 1863, volunteers were streaming into its
training camp in Readville, outside of Boston. Nearly half of the enlistees
came from New York, Pennsylvania, and Ohio; they included Lewis and
Charles Douglass, sons of Frederick Douglass, who actively recruited for the
regiment in upstate New York. Initially, recruiting lagged in Massachusetts
itself, where some skeptics, disillusioned by the unequal terms of service (such
as the absence of black commissioned officers in the regiment and the threat
of enslavement for those captured) and embittered by having their offers
of patriotic service earlier in the war repeatedly spurned, cautioned against
embracing this new experiment. The skeptics were answered by men such as
eminent Boston activist William C. Nell and James Henry Gooding, a whaler
who enlisted in the 54th in February 1863 and chronicled the regiment's progress in dispatches published, beginning in March 1863, in the New Bedford
Mercury. (Gooding's talents as a correspondent had been honed by his excellent education, in the mid-1840s, at New York City's Colored Orphan
Asylum—the very institution the draft riot mob razed.) Nell, Gooding, and
other champions of the 54th insisted that it would work to vanquish not only
the Confederates and slavery but also Northern prejudice. They appealed to
state pride and allegiance to rouse Massachusetts men to service—the "colored
men of the Old Bay State," Gooding insisted, should not allow themselves to
be shamed by men from other states that had shown more enthusiasm. And
they reminded potential recruits that many white Northerners remained willfully blind to the achievements of black troops at Port Hudson and Milliken's
Bend. Now it was the turn of the free black men of the North, Gooding wrote
in April 1863, to refute "the base assertions reiterated by copperheads and
traitors that the black race are incapable of patriotism."[55]

By May 1863, the 54th was at full strength, and it departed Boston for
deployment in the South with a grand send-off parade, past the city's statehouse and to its expansive common, before a throng of black and white well-
wishers. "There is not a man in the regiment who does not appreciate the
difficulties, the dangers, and maybe ignoble death that awaits him if captured
by the foe, and they will die upon the field rather than be hanged like a dog,"
Gooding wrote in his last dispatch with a dateline from the North. Less than
a month later, the regiment arrived at the Union-occupied Sea Islands, the
staging ground for the Union's campaign to take Charleston. The city was
not only a vital railroad, shipping, blockade-running, and communications

hub for the Deep South but also the epicenter of secessionism and thus the premier symbol of Southern treachery. Its harbor defenses were formidable, anchored by Fort Sumter and Fort Wagner, and ringed by marshes, mines, and batteries.[56]

Initially, the 54th was consigned to a supporting role of garrison duty and menial labor, hauling logs, clearing roads, digging trenches, and other back-breaking tasks, rather than combat. Their morale was sustained in part by the reception they received from the area's "contrabands," who clearly saw the black troops as an army of liberators. "They think now the kingdom is coming sure enough," wrote Gooding in early June after his first encounters with black South Carolinians, in Beaufort. "The yarns the copperhead press have so studiously spun, that the slaves were better satisfied in their old condition than under the present order of things, is all bosh," Gooding added. "So far as I have seen, they appear to understand the *causes* of the war better than a great many Northern editors."[57]

Gooding's observation was borne out dramatically when, on June 2, 1863, Colonel James Montgomery led the 2nd South Carolina black regiment on a daring nighttime raid of the Combahee River. Snaking inland from the coast through South Carolina's most lucrative low-country rice and cotton plantations, the river was laced with Confederate batteries, trenches, and earthworks. Montgomery's gunboats succeeded in running this gauntlet thanks to intelligence provided by Harriet Tubman. Already known in antislavery circles as the "Moses" of the Underground Railroad for her liberatory raids into Maryland before the war, Tubman came to the Sea Islands in the spring of 1862 to work as a nurse and cook on behalf of the escaped slaves who were part of the Port Royal experiment. She established herself, by early 1863, as the chief scout in an espionage operation that gathered intelligence about the terrain and population of the interior. Her advance work made it possible for her to guide the Union gunboats to riverside rendezvous points where fugitive slaves awaited liberation. The June raid brought approximately 750 slaves to freedom and destroyed valuable cotton stores, commissary supplies, grist and rice mills, and plantation homes in the "Cradle of Secession." Widely covered in the Northern press, the raid brought Tubman's heroism to the attention of the Northern public, thanks to the July 17, 1863, publication in the antislavery journal *Commonwealth* of her own firsthand account (in the form of a letter she dictated to a friend). Tubman took pride in the fact that the expedition went off "without the loss of a single life on our part, though we have good reason to believe that a number of rebels bit the dust." Most important to her was that so many of those she liberated joined the ranks of liberators: "Of these seven hundred and fifty-six contrabands," she wrote, "nearly or quite all the able-bodied men have joined the colored regiments here." The Combahee expedition suggested to some skeptical whites that "negro soldiers will follow wherever a brave man dare lead," as the Washington, D.C., *Daily National Intelligencer* put it, and raised hopes that South Carolina was "about to feel the weight of the war much more than she has done hitherto." The "political effect . . . in the case of every rebel State which has been made the theatre of operations," the *North American and United States Gazette* noted wishfully, was to "bring forth a large amount of love for the Union."[58]

Fort Wagner

The stage was set for a campaign on Charleston. Due in part to active lobbying by its determined commander, Colonel Robert Gould Shaw, the scion of an elite family of Boston reformers, the 54th Massachusetts regiment finally got the chance to prove its combat mettle. On July 18, 1863, it was tapped to lead the Union assault on Fort Wagner. This was a daunting mission: the fort, consisting of sand and earthen parapets thirty feet high, was brimming with artillery, approachable only by a narrow beach pathway, and girded by a water-filled ditch filled with mines and stakes. Gooding's July 20 dispatch to the *Mercury* described the ensuing "terrible ordeal":

> You may all know Fort Wagner is the Sebastopol of the rebels; but we went at it, over the ditch and on to the parapet through a deadly fire; but we could not get into the fort. We met the foe on the parapet of Wagner with the bayonet—we were exposed to a murderous fire from the batteries of the fort. . . . The color bearer of the State colors was killed on the parapet. Col. Shaw seized the staff when the standard bearer fell, and in less than a minute after, the Colonel fell himself. When the men saw their gallant leader fall, they made a desperate effort to get him out, but they were either shot down, or reeled in the ditch below. One man succeeded in getting hold of the State color staff, but the color was completely torn to pieces.[59]

Sergeant William Carney, the man who saved the colors, would become the first African American soldier to be awarded the Medal of Honor.

The 54th sustained 42 percent casualties in men killed, wounded, and captured on July 18. Lewis Douglass wrote his future wife, "Not a man flinched, though it was a trying time. Men fell all around me. A shell would explode and clear a space of twenty feet, our men would close up again, but it was no use. . . . How I got out of that fight alive I cannot tell." Confederates, in an effort to stigmatize Shaw with their scorn and derision, buried his body in a common trench with that of his enlisted men, rather than returning it to his family. Shaw's father responded with abiding grace: "We would not have his body removed from where it lies surrounded by his brave and devoted soldiers. . . . We can imagine no holier place than that in which he lies, among his brave and devoted followers, nor wish for him better company—what a body-guard he has!"[60]

Fort Wagner would not fall into Union hands until September 1863, abandoned by the Confederates after a prolonged bombardment and siege. But the sacrifices of the 54th in the July assault were swiftly immortalized by the Northern press. The antislavery *Pacific Appeal* praised the regiment for representing the "valor of the colored freemen of the North," adding, "Braver deeds than theirs have not been recorded during the war." Mainstream papers such as the *New York Times* and *Chicago Tribune* declared that the black troops had confirmed their fitness for combat, while some white reporters who had thought blacks unfit conceded that they had been wrong.[61]

"No Holier Place." Colonel Robert Gould Shaw and the 54th Massachusetts storm Fort Wagner. For saving the flag while severely wounded, Sergeant William Carney, who had been born into slavery in Norfolk, Virginia, was awarded the Medal of Honor, the first of two dozen African American men to earn that honor in the Civil War. (Library of Congress LC-USZ62-7824)

Indeed, the champions of black enlistment elaborated a politically sophisticated defense of black soldiering that tapped the power of deliverance discourse. The image of blacks as a "redeemer race" had long been a central feature of African American abolitionism: black stoicism, resistance, and activism, so such rhetoric prophesied, would redeem the United States from the original sins of slavery and racism and fulfill the promise of the "unfulfilled Union"—namely, create a nation prepared to live up to its ideals of liberty and equality. With black enlistment a reality, redeemer race discourse focused on black heroism and patriotism as the forces of national redemption. Black soldiers were not objects or targets of liberation but agents of the state, possessed of the manly qualities—valor, discipline, and magnanimity—that would secure the Union victory and lasting peace. Tributes to the U.S. Colored Troops credited black soldiers with "fighting for all humanity and for liberty for all the races," as an article in the *Christian Recorder* put it. "You will go forward to meet a God-defying band of conspirators, arrayed against human progress, against democratic government, against the rights of the poor man, against everything that is good," proclaimed abolitionist lawyer George H. Earle at a flag raising at the USCT recruiting station Camp William Penn, just outside of Philadelphia. At a flag presentation to black troops in Baltimore, a white colonel declared black Southerners to be the truest of Unionists: "Their hearts were wedded to the Stars and Stripes. . . . Whoever else may be swayed from duty, the black remains firm. Pluck him from the very core of rebeldom and he is a true man. . . . All his aspirations are for the success of the right, the triumph of the nation."[62]

Some commentators contrasted the righteousness of black soldiers with the cowardice of Copperheads. A white soldier writing to an Illinois paper professed his admiration for black troops as "inoffensive, civil and orderly" and eager to learn, and his view of Copperheads as "the most ignorant portions of civilized society." "Morally they are so low that their highest ambition is to get drunk on bad whiskey. . . . Where then is the alleged superiority? In a hog's eye," he opined. Arming the slaves—"4,000,000 of loyal men in the very midst of 8,000,000 of rebels"—was the "only policy that has yet been adopted by the administration that has the least tendency towards the final and effectual suppression of the rebellion." Others went further and emphasized the leadership capacities of black troops. An article in the *New York Evening Post* that was widely reprinted in other newspapers, for example, noted that the 54th Regiment was "allowed to lead our veteran troops" during the Fort Wagner assault and "fronted the hottest of the battle," showing courage "sufficient to convince any unprejudiced man of the gallantry of colored troops."[63]

All of these themes came together in speeches by African American recruiters such as the venerable Philadelphia abolitionist Robert Purvis. "In this momentous struggle between freedom and slavery, between a true democracy and a tyrannical despotism," Purvis told the 6th USCT at Camp William Penn in the last days of summer in 1863, "let your rallying cry be for God, for freedom and our country. If you fall, you fall the country's patriots, heroes and martyrs." Invoking black heroism at Port Hudson, Milliken's Bend, and Fort Wagner, Purvis proclaimed that no one would ever again doubt black patriotism, unless "he belongs to that tribe of the meanest of all God's creeping things, the copperhead." The comportment of black troops was acknowledged by Lincoln himself in an influential public letter of August 26, 1863, addressed to his friend the Illinois lawyer and politician James C. Conkling. Like his June 1863 letter to New York Democrats incensed by the treatment of Vallandingham, this letter defended Lincoln's policies, emancipation especially, against detractors who felt that such radical measures were unnecessary and unconstitutional. Dispelling talk of compromise as naive, and acknowledging the prowess and prestige of the Confederate army, Lincoln emphasized that the only way to suppress the rebellion was by the success of Federal arms. No paper compromise could be "used to keep Lee's army out of Pennsylvania," he noted pointedly; only mighty armies could. Turning to the military necessity of black enlistment, he invoked testimony from generals in the field, including those who had no particular affinity for the Republican party, that emancipation and the use of black troops were the "heaviest blow yet dealt to the rebellion." Grant was the foremost of these generals, having written Lincoln just a few days before expressing his "hearty support" for the use of black soldiers.[64]

Calling to mind Port Hudson, Milliken's Bend, and Fort Wagner, Lincoln closed with a rebuke: "You say you will not fight to free negroes. Some of them seem willing to fight for you." Honor and the judgments of history were at stake. When peace comes, Lincoln observed, "there will be some black men who can remember that, with silent tongue, and clenched teeth, and steady eye, and well-poised bayonet, they have helped mankind on to this great consummation; while, I fear, there will be some white ones, unable to forget that, with malignant heart, and deceitful speech, they have strove to hinder it."[65]

These tributes, though profoundly gratifying for the black troops, did not redress the structural discrimination blacks experienced within the Union army. In the aftermath of the Fort Wagner assault, the 54th found itself again relegated to heavy labor and fatigue duty, at inferior pay. A June 1863 War Department directive had announced that blacks would be paid as "military laborers"—$10 a month, minus a $3 deduction for clothing, which came to barely more than half of what white soldiers made in a month. This contravened Governor Andrew's promise that the black troops would be paid on an equal basis with white ones. Standing on principle, the 54th (together with the 55th) refused to take the lesser sum and refused, too, the Massachusetts legislature's appropriation of funds to make up the difference. Leading Republicans such as Thaddeus Stevens, Charles Sumner, and Henry Wilson demanded that Congress pass an equal-pay bill. These lawmakers pointed up the inconsistency of "dealing out rations to white people, some of them the wives and children of rebel soldiers, by the tens of thousands" while depriving loyal black soldiers of sufficient wages to support their own families. Democrats and conservative Republicans dragged their feet. Not until June 15, 1864, did such legislation pass—and the new measure discriminated against ex-slaves, granting them back pay retroactive to January 1, 1864, even if they had enlisted earlier (free blacks' back pay, by contrast, was retroactive to their date of enlistment). The long delay and inadequate pay placed a terrible burden on black families. "Colored men generally, as a class, have nothing to depend upon but their daily labor; so, consequently, when they leave their labors and take up arms in defense of their country, their homes are left destitute," James Henry Gooding explained in one of his dispatches. In a September 28, 1863, letter intended for Lincoln, he elaborated. "Are we *Soldiers* or are we *Labourers*?" he asked. Giving shape to a tradition in which Civil War service would be a wellspring for black political leadership, Gooding then answered: "Let the rich mould around Wagner's parapets be upturned, and there will be found an Eloquent answer."[66]

PART III

Amnesty

9

Rallying Point

LINCOLN'S TEN PERCENT PLAN

"WHAT HORROR SURROUNDS me! Here I am, helpless and bleeding, my flesh lacerated, my thigh-bone broken; the dead so ghastly, the dying and the wounded all about me; my regiment falling back, the enemy advancing. What will become of me?" The terror Union private Arthur van Lisle felt on September 19, 1863, the first day of the battle of Chickamauga, is palpable, even in words he wrote thirty years after the event. Van Lisle's 1893 reminiscence continued, "My eyes are riveted to that glorious old banner.... Will it recover its lost ground and save the boys who fell where it first advanced? Will it ever reach me?"[1]

At the moment in 1863 that Lisle so vividly described, the Union was experiencing a terrible reversal of fortune, losing the impetus of the summer victories at Gettysburg and Vicksburg. The two-day battle of Chickamauga, in northern Georgia just across from the Tennessee border, was one of the Union army's worst defeats, and the bloodiest battle in the western theater. It marked the failure of General William Rosecrans, the hero of Stones River, to follow up that battle with another triumph.[2] Over the course of the fall, the Union would recover lost ground, as dramatic victories in Tennessee set the stage for the promulgation of Lincoln's December 1863 Proclamation of Amnesty and Reconstruction, also known as the "Ten Percent Plan." While it has been overshadowed in popular memory and historical scholarship by the Emancipation Proclamation, the December amnesty proclamation is just as important for understanding Union war aims and political and military fortunes. Deliverance politics came full circle, as Lincoln's administration offered forgiveness to Southerners who were willing to renounce both secession and slavery.

Chickamauga and Chattanooga

Rosecrans's assignment after Stones River was to bear down on Chattanooga, Tennessee, a rail center known as the "gateway to the Deep South." To Lincoln's frustration, Rosecrans tarried in Murfreesboro, Tennessee, for six months, from January to June 1863, before moving out; he believed the delay necessary to permit him to shepherd his supplies and strengthen his cavalry arm before the new campaign. When he finally did move, Rosecrans performed well, driving his army and forcing Braxton Bragg's Army of Tennessee, through a series of flanking maneuvers, to fall back toward Chattanooga in early July and then to abandon the city in early September; Bragg feared that the Union might seize the mountains and ridges surrounding Chattanooga and consign the Confederates to a Vicksburg-like siege. Bragg headed south toward the mountains of north Georgia, and Rosecrans sent his army, divided into three distinct columns, probing after him—unaware that Bragg was at this very juncture welcoming reinforcements from Mississippi, East Tennessee, and, most notably, elements of Longstreet's corps from Virginia.

In mid-September the two armies clashed along the Chickamauga Creek, to the south of Chattanooga, on heavily timbered terrain one Confederate correspondent described as resembling the "woods about Shiloh." After some skirmishing on September 18, the battle began in earnest on the nineteenth, with Bragg attacking the Union left, hoping to push the Union army into the mountains to the south, deeper into enemy territory and away from their supply base. Over the course of a brutal day of fighting, both commanders poured new arrivals to the front into the maw, but neither made decisive progress. "It seemed as though a terrible cyclone was sweeping over the earth, driving everything before it," wrote Colonel Benjamin F. Scribner of his brigade's ordeal. "All things appeared to be rushing by me in horizontal lines, all parallel to each other. The missiles of the enemy whistling and whirring by, seemed to draw the elements in the same lines of motion, sound, light and air uniting in the rush." On the twentieth, Bragg gained the upper hand, with Longstreet's men devastating the Union right. Were it not for the stubborn resistance of Union general George H. Thomas—the most prominent Virginia Unionist in the Federal army—the Union army would have been overwhelmed; Thomas's eleventh-hour heroics, which earned him the sobriquet "Rock of Chickamauga," bought what was left of the Federal forces time to retreat into the confines of Chattanooga. The battle, which cost the contending armies 34,600 casualties, made Thomas a hero in the North and prompted the Union high command to name him as Rosecrans's replacement. The Union press reveled in the fact that although he hailed from the "heart of the slave interest" in eastern Virginia, Thomas had "indignantly spurned all the appliances of the leaders of the rebellion to seduce him from his allegiance to the old flag." The rebel press mocked Thomas as a traitor, speculating that "his conduct can only be explained by the fact that he married a Yankee woman, old enough to be his mother, and whose money was a great influence over him."[3]

Thomas may have saved the army, but he consigned it to a siege, as Bragg surrounded Chattanooga and counted on a Vicksburg-in-reverse. The Confederate press hailed Chickamauga as a tide-turning victory; according to the *Charleston Mercury*, it was the "most important battle of the war after that of First Manassas." Not only had Southerners repelled invaders from Georgia, sending them reeling back into Tennessee, but Bragg's western theater troops had also proven their worth to Longstreet's decorated veterans from the east. The prisoners, arms, ammunition, and wagons the Confederates had seized would "go far towards equalizing our losses at Vicksburg and Port Hudson," observed the *Mercury*.[4]

It seemed the siege of Union-occupied Chattanooga would be unbreakable. The Confederates seized the heights that ringed the city to the south—the imposing, flat-topped Lookout Mountain (with a highest point of nearly 2,400 feet) and 400-foot-high Missionary Ridge—leaving the Union only a meager supply line through the mountains to the north. The Union troops would have to escape from this trap or starve. Recognizing the dire predicament, the War Department sent reinforcements to this front—Sherman from Mississippi, Hooker from northern Virginia, and, most importantly, Grant, who would command all the Union forces in the west. Grant swiftly put into action a successful plan for opening up a supply route, the "Cracker Line," to the west of the city, across the Tennessee River. Then he planned the Union breakout. Hooker was tasked with driving the rebels off Lookout Mountain, while Sherman was to roll up the northern end of Missionary Ridge in a flank attack as Thomas's Army of the Cumberland demonstrated against the trenches at the front and center of the Ridge.

Grant expected that Hooker and Sherman would be the lead players in this drama, and at first things went as scripted. On November 24, Hooker succeeded in overwhelming the heavily outnumbered Confederates at Lookout Mountain. But success eluded the Federals on Missionary Ridge, where Sherman's attack sputtered, until George Thomas's Army of the Cumberland took center stage. Grant had assumed that Thomas's men would play a supporting role in the breakout; surely their confidence and strength had been shaken by the defeat at Chickamauga and by living in siege conditions, Grant reasoned. The Army of the Cumberland defied these low expectations. On November 25,

George Thomas. A native Virginian, Thomas earned the nickname "Rock of Chickamauga" and won promotion to command of the Army of the Cumberland for his heroic stand at the September 1863 battle. He cemented his reputation with his frontal assault on Missionary Ridge that November. (Library of Congress LC-DIG-cwpbh-03123)

in one of the most dramatic and unexpected of all Civil War frontal assaults, Thomas's men charged up steep Missionary Ridge into the face of its terraces of Confederate rifle pits and entrenchments, without explicit orders from Grant or, for that matter, from Thomas. They were improvising: driven by their desire to avenge their September defeat, they chanted "Chickamauga" as they drove Confederates out of their trenches and uphill in panic. Incredulous, Grant and his staff watched this unfold. In a letter to his wife, Major James A. Connolly of the 123rd Illinois Infantry described how the Union regiments scrambled and surged across successive lines of Confederate rifle pits and breastworks, with their color guards leading the way:

> One flag bearer, on his hands and knees, is seen away in advance of the whole line; he crawls and climbs toward a rebel flag he sees waving above him, he gets within a few feet of it and hides behind a fallen log

while he waves his flag defiantly until it almost touches the rebel flag; his regiment follows him as fast as it can.... [T]he men away above us look like great ants crawling up, crouching on the outside of the rebel breastworks. One of our flags seems to be moving; look! look! look! Up! Up! Up! It goes and is planted on the rebel works. ... [O]ther flags go up and over at different points along the mountain top.... [I]n a few moments the flags of 60 Yankee regiments float along Mission Ridge from one end to the other.[5]

Only a stout defense on the Confederate right from the able general Patrick Cleburne—playing the role Thomas had played at Chickamauga—made it possible for the defeated Confederate remnants to slink to safety in northern Georgia.

The battle of Chattanooga was not unusually costly in terms of casualties (5,800 Federal and an estimated 6,000–8,000 Confederate). But it was none-theless a humiliating setback for the Confederates. "No satisfactory excuse can possibly be given for the shameful conduct of our troops . . . in allowing their line to be penetrated," the defeated Braxton Bragg lamented. "The po-sition was one which ought to have been held by a line of skirmishers against any assaulting column." Bragg speculated as to why his men might have lost their nerve, noting that they had "for two days confronted the enemy, marshalling his immense forces in plain view."[6] But even Bragg conceded that this did not explain much—those veteran troops had many times be-fore faced superior forces. Modern scholars are much more apt to emphasize Bragg's own failings: his inability to work well with his subordinates and his poor tactical decision-making, which had contributed to Confederate defeats at Shiloh and Stones River and had permitted the Federal army to slip away after Chickamauga. At Chattanooga, Bragg muddled his order to his men in the lower trenches on Missionary Ridge, leaving it unclear whether, when, and in what force they should fall back to the higher, better trenches as the Yankee attack unfolded. He had misplaced his artillery on the ridge, leaving it at ineffective angles for mowing down the enemy. At the very moment that Sherman and Hooker were reinforcing Thomas, Bragg divided his army and hastened part of it—Longstreet's divisions—away, to besiege Knoxville in East Tennessee. Most important, Bragg's constant infighting with his own generals had taken a toll on morale in his army and earned it a reputation and self-image for dysfunction. After Chattanooga, Bragg was done for: Jefferson Davis turned to Joseph E. Johnston to command the Army of Tennessee. Grant's armies, for their part, set their sights on Atlanta.[7]

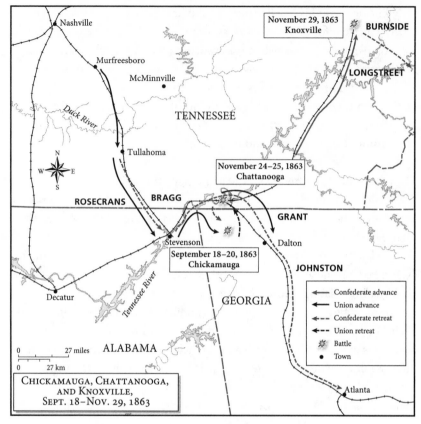

November 29, 1863
Knoxville

BURNSIDE

LONGSTREET

Nashville

Murfreesboro

McMinnville

TENNESSEE

Duck River

Tullahoma

November 24–25, 1863
Chattanooga

ROSECRANS   BRAGG

GRANT

Stevenson

September 18–20, 1863
Chickamauga

Dalton

JOHNSTON

Decatur

Tennessee River

GEORGIA

ALABAMA

0   27 miles
0   27 km

CHICKAMAUGA, CHATTANOOGA,
AND KNOXVILLE,
SEPT. 18–NOV. 29, 1863

Atlanta

Confederate advance
Union advance
Confederate retreat
Union retreat
Battle
Town

MAP 9.1

The Liberation of East Tennessee

As a set piece of Southern deliverance, no event during the war rivaled the Union army's seizure of East Tennessee and its central city, Knoxville. Thanks to the tireless publicity efforts of its Unionist champion Parson Brownlow, Knoxville was already a potent symbol, in Northern eyes, of Confederate despotism. In his popular speaking tours and pamphlets, Brownlow conveniently papered over the fact that most whites in Knoxville supported the Confederacy; he portrayed the town and region as a bastion of long-suffering loyalists groaning under the thrall of Confederate occupation. The number of Unionists in the city had actually declined over the course of the war, historian Robert Tracy McKenzie explains, and much of the remaining Unionism was in practice a kind of passive neutrality. But for Northerners, Brownlow and East Tennessee exemplified Southerners' yearning for rescue.[8]

The Union high command had previously hesitated to attempt an offensive against the mountain barriers that shielded East Tennessee. But the late summer of 1863 presented an opportunity: the Confederates withdrew their own forces from Knoxville in August to send them to the Chattanooga front, which opened the way for Ambrose Burnside's Army of the Ohio to move from Kentucky into East Tennessee in September. The Federal forces were greeted with wild enthusiasm by loyalists. "These are glorious days for the people of Knoxville," Michigan infantryman David Lane wrote on September 25. "They tell me the day of their deliverance has come at last. The story of their sufferings has been but feebly told. Even a Brownlow cannot do it justice. . . . Loyalty here is pure and unalloyed, as proven by the sacrifices they have made." When they concluded that the region and Knoxville especially were solidly anti-Confederate, Northern soldiers were in essence seeing "what they had been taught to expect," as Robert McKenzie has put it. In fact, the warm welcome was attributable in part to the fact that Confederate civilians had decamped once their army pulled out, heading toward Virginia and safer rebel communities.[9]

The Unionist press in the North and border states exulted over the news from East Tennessee. The *Cincinnati Commercial*, in an account reprinted in the *New York Times*, lingered over the details of Burnside's "triumphal march into Knoxville," proclaiming, "The day of deliverance has dawned at last, and the chains are riven from the limbs of the noblest people that ever breathed God's air." The *Wheeling Intelligencer* crowed over the "deliverance of our suffering loyal brethren of East Tennessee from the despotism of the so-called Confederacy," while the *New York Herald* praised Burnside's force as a "grand army of deliverance." *Harper's Weekly* ran a cover print in October 1863 that depicted Burnside being thronged by the grateful white Southern Unionists of Knoxville—an image that failed to acknowledge the enslaved blacks among those who greeted the Federals as deliverers.[10]

Knoxville's liberation had a second act when Longstreet's army, sent from the Chattanooga front to pin down Burnside, besieged the Yankee-occupied town and then tried in vain, in a brief campaign, to break the Yankee defenses. Longstreet's December retreat produced another round of celebrations among Knoxville's loyalists and prompted Lincoln in a December 7 executive order to declare a national day of thanksgiving:

> Reliable information being received that the insurgent force is retreating from east Tennessee under circumstances rendering it probable that the Union forces can not hereafter be dislodged from that

"The Old Flag in East Tennessee." This October 24, 1864, *Harper's Weekly* cover shows the reception of General Burnside by the Unionists of Knoxville. Their display of enthusiasm "seems to have almost overpowered our brave troops," *Harper's* noted with satisfaction. (*Harper's Weekly*)

important position, and esteeming this to be of high national consequence, I recommend that all loyal people do, on receipt of this information, assemble at their places of worship and render special homage and gratitude to Almighty God for this great advancement of the national cause.[11]

For Lincoln, with his own Border South roots in Kentucky, the disenthralling of East Tennessee was a sort of personal vindication. As John Hay explained, commenting on a meeting the president had with some exiled East Tennesseans in the White House in October 1863, "I never saw him more at ease than he is with those first rate patriots of the border. He is of them really."[12]

"Internal Reconstruction" in the Border States

Politically, the Union's fall victories in Tennessee became intertwined with Northern debates over wartime reconstruction—over when and how individual rebels and occupied rebel states might be reincorporated into the Union. Those debates reveal the resilience of the assumption that the Southern masses could be disenthralled from their Confederate allegiance. A *New York Herald* editorial on the Chattanooga victory appealed to the "long deluded, intensely suffering and dangerously situated people of the rebellious states to reflect upon the hopeless cause of Jeff. Davis, to revolt against him, and to submit at discretion to the Union, trusting to the clemency of the government, and to the fraternal forgiveness of the loyal states." By submitting now, the rebels would "avoid the ruin and confusion of absolute subjugation."[13] The *Herald* hoped Lincoln would choose clemency—policies designed to win over wavering Southerners—over subjugation.

What shape might such policies take? In the fall of 1863, Lincoln had not yet presented a comprehensive plan for reconstruction, but he was keeping a close eye on a half-dozen ongoing experiments in reconstituting the state governments. Each experiment represented a distinct blend of hard war and conciliatory policies. Three of the cases were examples of what historian Eric Foner has called "internal reconstruction"—of border states groping toward acceptance of emancipation and a consolidation of Republican rule. Maryland, Foner explains, was the first border state to experience "the disintegration of slavery from within," thanks to the presence in force of Federal troops, the energetic antislavery leadership of Radical Republican congressman Henry Winter Davis, the zealousness of fugitive slaves in seeking out and joining the Union army, and the appeal of free labor ideas and antipathy to the Eastern Shore slaveholding elite among the wage earners and capitalists of Baltimore and the small farmers in the western quadrant of the state. Lincoln and his inner circle reveled in these changes. As John Hay put it in his diary in November 1863, as Unionists came to power in the Maryland state elections, "It is the most encouraging thing in the world in consideration of the thick complications of the time to see these slave-state fellows thoroughly emancipated from the influences of a life long superstition in relation to this Mud God, Slavery." The *New York Times* agreed, seeing the vote in Maryland for "*Antislavery* Unionism" as "proof positive of the possibility of a similar change in every disloyal state." Lincoln's Emancipation Proclamation, the *Times* continued, had not alienated the border states but instead had motivated them to act against slavery. Free black editor Robert Hamilton of the New York *Anglo-African* undertook a journalistic tour of occupied areas of eastern Virginia and North Carolina in the fall and winter of 1863–64, sending dispatches back to the newspaper for publication. Hamilton had never before dared venture into slave states but was encouraged by the progress of emancipation sentiment in Maryland to undertake such a journey; he saw Maryland and Washington, D.C., as regions "cursed by the presence of slavery" but in the midst of economic and moral renovation. Marylanders themselves legislated emancipation—without compensation to slaveholders—as part of a new constitution, on November 1, 1864. A popular referendum on the constitution revealed that support for the new measures was razor thin, with Union soldiers' ballots providing the margin of victory. Lincoln's oft-repeated warning to Maryland slaveholders that the friction and abrasion of war would consign slavery to the ashes came to pass.[14]

Missouri's internal reconstruction was the most volatile, as a descent into brutal guerrilla warfare there exacerbated factionalism among the state's Republicans and contributed to the ascendance of the Radical faction. Precariously controlled by Union forces, Missouri had remained under martial law since Frémont's edict of 1861 (Lincoln had revoked its emancipation provision but let its other measures stand). Union authorities imposed a variety of tactics for rousting guerrillas and punishing those who abetted them, including banishment, random arrest, loyalty oaths, trade restrictions, and punitive taxes or levies on the disloyal. But such measures could not keep chaos at bay: in the spring of 1863, Confederate sympathizers, enraged by the Emancipation Proclamation and emboldened by the Copperheads' new assertiveness, ratcheted up their bushwhacking campaigns, taking on their mortal enemies, the jayhawkers of Kansas (who launched their own guerrilla raids against rebel Missourians), and turning southern Missouri into a wasteland of violence. This tumult triggered Francis Lieber's consideration of the rules of war, resulting in his promulgation of the Lieber Code in April 1863.[15]

Moreover, this phase of the war gave rise to a new breed of "mutant" guerrillas, as historian Daniel E. Sutherland has put it: predatory bands of "common outlaws, deserters, and other misfits" who "had no allegiance other than to themselves." The region's disorder peaked on August 21, 1863, when William C. Quantrill, a virulently anti-abolition border ruffian with an insatiable appetite for destruction, led a brutal raid on the old free soil stronghold of Lawrence, Kansas, in which his band of 450 plunderers not only looted and razed the town but also murdered in cold blood some 150 men and boys. The Union response, under General Thomas Ewing Jr., commander of Federal forces on the Missouri-Kansas border, was General Order No. 11, promulgated on August 25, 1863. The war's most drastic military act of retaliation against civilians, Ewing's order banished thousands of civilians from the counties that had supported Quantrill.[16]

The raid in turn ratcheted up the tension in Missouri between the two Republican factions there, with the Radical Republicans, led by St. Louis lawyer Charles Drake, accusing the moderates, led by Governor Hamilton Gamble and Lincoln appointee Major General John Schofield, the senior Union commander in Missouri, of being too soft on the guerrillas. In Drake's rhetoric, Missouri's Unionists were like the beleaguered loyalists of the Confederate states—victims of "outrage and defamation" at the hands of the "hell-born Rebellion." The Radical critique extended to Lincoln himself, whom Drake assailed for his excessive "tenderness towards rebels and their sympathizers." Radicals called for the more aggressive political proscription and expulsion of Confederate sympathizers; for the replacement of Schofield by someone less conciliatory, such as Benjamin Butler; and for the only measure that, in their view, would really break the back of the disloyalists in the state: immediate uncompensated emancipation.[17]

Lincoln, for his part, was utterly exasperated by the Missouri political in-fighting. He resented the fact that internal squabbles dashed his hopes for gradual compensated emancipation, which had gotten a second hearing in Missouri in the summer of 1863. Some slaveholders who had rejected Lincoln's "sweetheart deal" in 1862 reconsidered this stance after the Emancipation Proclamation was issued, hoping to salvage something of the original offer—and so, under Gamble's leadership, a special convention passed an ordinance of gradual emancipation in June 1863 (it would dismantle slavery by 1870). Unyielding slaveholders and Radical Republicans alike rejected the ordinance, and the latter, with Drake at their head, pressed their case with Lincoln.[18]

At first they encountered resistance. On October 5, 1863, Lincoln wrote Drake a rebuking response, implying that Missouri's politicians bore a share of the blame for creating an atmosphere where "universal suspicion reigns." The key to restoring order, Lincoln insisted, was not further proscription but instead unified leadership: if only Radicals and non-Radicals could unite, they "would be too strong for any foe from any quarter." But by the year's end Lincoln gave way, abandoning his hopes for gradual emancipation and embracing the Radicals' agenda of immediate abolition and their premise that Governor Gamble and General Schofield had failed in their handling of the guerrilla crisis. Lincoln was adapting to the changed political land- scape: black flight and enlistment in the Union army in Missouri discredited gradualist schemes, and the toll of guerrilla warfare increased public support for strong Federal intervention. The internal reconstruction of Missouri was gaining steam. Gamble's death in 1864 left his faction rudderless and the Radicals ascendant in state politics; they would consolidate their power by barring the disloyal from voting or office-holding. A Drake-led state conven- tion passed immediate emancipation on January 11, 1865. In a speech entitled "Missouri's Jubilee," the state's new antislavery governor, Thomas C. Fletcher (formerly a brevet brigadier general in the Union army) expressed "thankful- ness for our deliverance." "The white men of Missouri are to-day emancipated from a system which has so long lain with a crushing weight upon their ener- gies," he proclaimed. "And the black man, too, is free. The gates of a bright future are open to him as well as to us."[19]

Military Reconstruction in the Confederate States

Even as slave society gave way in the loyal border states, the Lincoln ad- ministration also promoted reconstruction in Union-occupied areas of the Confederacy, most notably in Arkansas, Tennessee, and Louisiana. Northern Arkansas, like southern Missouri, was racked by guerrilla warfare. The Confederate commander there, Major General Thomas C. Hindman, relied on irregular troops to harass Federal forces, and Union patrols responded by destroying the property of civilians suspected of harboring rebel bushwhackers. But as they had in Missouri, Confederates paid a price for their reliance on guerrilla tactics, as civilians, battered by the cycle of violence and retaliation, started to show signs of opportunism: to support whichever side in the surging struggle could restore order, even if that meant abiding by Yankee occupation. When the Union achieved a break- through victory in September 1863, with the capture of the state capital, Little Rock, Unionists came out of the woodwork, offering their services as scouts, guides, soldiers, and guerrillas. "They have been long bowed down by iron despotism," an article on Arkansas in the *Cleveland Daily Leader* reported, "and welcome the hour of deliverance with open demonstrations of joy." Private Silas W. Haven of the 27th Iowa agreed. "There is more real Union feeling here than at any other place I have been in the South," he wrote from Little Rock in September, having spent the war on duty in southwestern Tennessee. "This state will be back in the Union as soon as it can get back." Lincoln himself reckoned that the moment was ripe to cultivate a new cadre of loyalist leaders in Arkansas. To that end, the Union army embarked on an energetic propaganda campaign, organizing Union clubs and newspapers to spread the message that Federal control would bring peace and security to the war-weary region. In a typical appeal, the *National Union* urged Arkansans to embrace the "work of regeneration," assuring them that the Union army's purpose was not to "destroy property or lives" but instead to "save and protect them."[20]

A powerful national spokesman for this message broke onto the scene in October 1863. Edward W. Gantt of Arkansas was an ideal herald of deliverance: he was a Confederate general who became disillusioned with the Confederacy and converted to Unionism in the fall of 1863. In speeches and pamphlets aimed at Northern as well as Southern audiences, Gantt, describing himself as an "erring brother" who had "return[ed] from his wanderings after a mad delusion," denounced the Confederate leaders of Arkansas as merciless tyrants, urged Arkansans to recognize that slavery was "beyond the hope of resurrection," and rejoiced in the progress of loyalism in Maryland, Kentucky, Missouri, and Tennessee.[21]

In Tennessee, Burnside's September 1863 liberation of Knoxville set in motion the erosion of slavery in the eastern section of the state and fueled hopes

Union Entry into Little Rock. "Arkansas was now redeemed—nobly redeemed, by heroism and endurance which have been rarely equaled and never surpassed." In another tableau of deliverance, this postwar issue of *Harper's Weekly* depicts the Union army's September 1863 liberation of Little Rock. (Library of Congress LC-USZ62-138112)

that Unionism could be cultivated in its central and western quadrants. In late October, Union army chaplain Alonzo Quint opined, while stationed near Tullahoma, that there was "much loyalty" in Tennessee, where disgust with the "hateful ulcer" of slavery was "steadily growing." He believed the rebellion was "one based simply on the determination of a few to continue the authority of a caste—the rule of a few educated men over a mass of whites and blacks, purposely kept ignorant and poor," and that the slaveholder oligarchy could not keep at bay the "progress of free thought." Artillerist William Wheeler of New York, a self-described "extreme Emancipationist," developed similar themes in his correspondence with his family. The more of the Confederacy he saw, he wrote in November 1863 while posted near Chattanooga, the more he "felt the deepest pity for the miserable condition of the poor whites of the South," who were kept ignorant by the "so-called chivalry . . . for their polit-ical and, now, for their military purposes." The "dread of being shot or hung" was the "cohesive power of the Southern army"—but the masses were finally becoming "alive . . . to the game that has been played with them," he observed, based on reports from the numerous deserters who entered Union lines.[22]

Major General Carl Schurz of Wisconsin, a prominent spokesman for the German immigrant community, wrote his daughter Agathe an extended meditation on how emancipation would lift up Southern poor whites. While stationed outside of Chattanooga in Lookout Valley in November 1863, he observed, "You have no conception of the poverty which prevails here. The people live in log houses in which the chinks between the logs are entirely open so that light and air pass through. . . . Women and men are dressed in the most poverty-stricken way and live almost exclusively on corn bread and pork. Nearly all females smoke and chew tobacco. And then they are so igno-rant that the knowledge of reading and writing is a great rarity among them." The cause of this misery was slavery. Rich slave owners "did not want to rule merely their negroes but also, particularly, the poor white people. . . . In order to rule them better the rich people sought to keep the poor ignorant." But a better day would come with Union victory and with the infusion of Northern values. "For these people and their children the present war is a gen-uine blessing," Schurz believed, "for it shakes them out of their sleepiness and brings them in touch with keener and more active people." Looking forward to a new era of industriousness and wealth in the South, Schurz instructed Agathe, "So you see how good can come out of evil."[23]

Meanwhile, provisional governor Andrew Johnson, based in Nashville, showed new zeal in supporting emancipation. He delivered a series of speeches in which he called slavery a "cancer upon the body politic" and appealed to

Tennesseans to pass a state constitutional amendment abolishing the institution, assuring them that blacks would be productive under the "stimulus of wages and kind treatment." Johnson developed in this period a heroic self-image. In the fall of 1864, he told a crowd of African Americans in Nashville, part of a torchlight procession in his honor, "I will indeed be your Moses, and lead you through the Red Sea of war and bondage, to a fairer future of liberty and peace." That future was one, in Johnson's view, in which black freedom was synonymous with wage work, not with political rights or social equality. Instead Johnson imagined that diehard white Unionists would form the core of Tennessee's new body politic once the Confederate menace was neutralized at last.[24]

The showpiece for wartime reconstruction was Louisiana. From the start, the unusually large number of white Unionists in the occupied zones— merchants, professionals, and immigrants in New Orleans and sugar planters in the southeastern parishes—had boded well for the restoration of the state under loyal leadership. In keeping with the spirit of the amnesty provisions of the Second Confiscation Act, which had authorized the president to grant political pardon and amnesty to whomever he chose, Benjamin Butler, with Lincoln's tacit approval though not under his direction, administered loyalty oaths to the willing, constituting them a new body politic for the state. These voters, representing Louisiana's First and Second Districts, elected two Unionist representatives to Congress in the fall of 1862. As in Missouri, loyalists were politically divided. Slave-owning planters resisted emancipation, then held out for compensation, working all the while to salvage their political dominance, while businessmen and wage workers calling themselves the Free State Association pushed for thoroughgoing reform. The fact that New Orleans was home to a well-to-do and well-organized free black community, led by a creole elite of French extraction, meant that the progressive faction itself was divided, over whether full citizenship rights, including suffrage, should be granted to African Americans. In August 1863, Lincoln privately declared his sympathy for the free state movement, without acknowledging the issue of black suffrage. He instructed his commander of the Department of the Gulf, General Nathaniel Banks (who had replaced Butler in December 1862), to steer Louisiana toward a constitutional convention that would abolish slavery statewide, including in the loyal regions that had been exempted in the Emancipation Proclamation.[25]

Lincoln also entrusted Banks with the extension of the contract labor system that Butler had instituted in 1862, in which blacks signed yearly contracts to work for wages on plantations for loyal masters or lessees or government agents, with the military providing supervision. The Union victory at Vicksburg made it possible for this system to spread north from New Orleans through the Mississippi Valley. Under Banks's direction, it took on a grim overlay of regulations—such as the requirement that workers must have passes from their employers in order to leave the plantations—reminiscent of the old slave codes. This was, as Eric Foner has put it, a "compulsory system of free labor": signing an annual labor contract was mandatory; wages were poor, and often docked or withheld; the specter of impressment by the Union army for manual labor was ever present. These conditions brought forth labor disputes and protests from progressive Unionists, white and black, and made Lincoln vulnerable to the charge that he was coddling slaveholder interests.[26]

Precisely because it remained so prevalent in wartime politics, the deluded-masses theory grated on the ears of some Union soldiers, especially those in areas of the South where loyal white Southerners seemed to be nonexistent. For example, Corporal James Henry Gooding of the 54th Massachusetts USCT, stationed in coastal South Carolina, dismissed talk of "misguided brethren," "strong Union sentiment," and "persecuted loyalists" in the South as "apocryphal." The only way to demoralize the Confederates was to give "them a good sound drubbing, or else capture and put them in the penitentiary," Gooding wrote to the New Bedford *Mercury* in September 1863.[27]

Taken together, the diverse experiments in reconstruction in the border states and occupied South fueled a debate among politicians over what sort of comprehensive reconstruction strategy the Union should pursue. The two principal positions in the debate were articulated by Charles Sumner and Montgomery Blair, respectively. Sumner's September 1863 treatise "Our Domestic Relations; or, How to Treat the Rebel States" spelled out the Radical Republican position that Congress (not the president) should control wartime reconstruction, on the grounds that by leaving the Union, Confederate states had committed "state suicide" and thus reverted to the status of territories under Congress's jurisdiction. Decrying Lincoln's appointment of military governors in places such as Tennessee and Louisiana, Sumner argued that the only way to kill off the dread doctrine of states' rights and to guarantee each state a "republican form of government," in accordance with the Constitution, was to let Congress start from scratch. Land could be redistributed among "patriot soldiers, poor-whites, and freedmen": the truly loyal "who, throughout the darkness of the Rebellion, have kept their faith." In Sumner's reckoning, the experiments in internal and military reconstruction were tenuous at best: armed with states' rights sophistries, slaveholders would try to revive slavery once their states resumed their places in the Union. This terrible fate loomed, Sumner noted, even in "regenerated West Virginia."[28]

Sumner was answered by Postmaster General Montgomery Blair, whose October 3, 1863, speech in Rockville, Maryland, "On the Revolutionary Schemes of the Ultra Abolitionists, and in Defence of the Policy of the President," argued that Lincoln's approach—to "dishabilitate the rebels" and "rehabilitate the loyal men" of each state—was working wonders. Blair sustained and updated the Slave Power conspiracy theory that the Southern masses were dupes of designing leaders. It was not only the political machinations of conniving politicians that kept those masses in thrall but also "rebel military duress"—the heavy hand of a militarized Confederate autocracy. "The moment rebel military duress is removed," Blair insisted, loyalty could reassert itself. Witness West Virginia: once the Union army had delivered it from "armed brigands," loyalists came to the fore. That was why, Blair noted, Lincoln was inviting Tennessee and Louisiana to follow its example. Only the arch-traitors, the leaders of the rebellion, had committed political suicide: anyone the Union could redeem as loyal should be welcomed back into the fold. The white Southern masses should not be made to trade subjugation to "Calhounite" conspirators for subjugation to abolitionists and their radical agenda of racial equality and "amalgamation."[29]

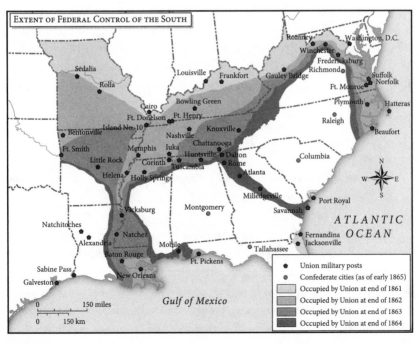

MAP 9.2

Blair's speech found much favor among moderate Republicans and War Democrats in the political mainstream. Based on Blair's exposition of the administration's philosophy, the *New York Herald* felt reassured that "Mr. Lincoln is still prosecuting the war for the Union, and not as an abolition crusade; that African slavery is still with him only an incidental and secondary issue, . . . [and] that the coast is clear for the work of peace and restoration." "We shall not be surprised," the *Herald* predicted in October 1863, if "President Lincoln, in his annual message, shall rise before the American people the recognized master of the situation, and as our great pacificator and the saviour of the Union." The *Herald* reckoned that Lincoln was waiting for a "signal military success" before going public with his reconstruction plan. Lincoln's own calculations were complex: he was holding out not just for a key battlefield victory but also for an opportune political moment. When General Rosecrans wrote the president on October 3 from besieged Chattanooga advising that a "general amnesty to all officers and soldiers in the Rebellion . . . would give us moral strength and weaken them very much," Lincoln wrote back that he planned to offer such an amnesty "whenever the case shall appear ripe enough to have it accepted in the true understanding, rather than as a confession of weakness and fear."[30]

Lincoln would, as part of his annual message in December, promulgate a proclamation of amnesty and reconstruction that fused elements of Sumner's view and of Blair's, and found widespread favor among Northerners. But first he would deliver a powerful tribute to freedom at the consecration of the Soldiers' National Cemetery at Gettysburg—and thereby help to ripen the case for amnesty.[31]

The Gettysburg Address

Lincoln's November 19, 1863, speech at Gettysburg has a well-deserved reputation as an oratorical masterpiece. Its 272 words read:

> Four score and seven years ago our fathers brought forth on this continent, a new nation, conceived in Liberty, and dedicated to the proposition that all men are created equal.
>
> Now we are engaged in a great civil war, testing whether that nation, or any nation so conceived and dedicated, can long endure. We are met on a great battle-field of that war. We have come to dedicate a portion of that field, as a final resting place for those who here gave

their lives that that nation might live. It is altogether fitting and proper that we should do this.

But, in a larger sense, we can not dedicate—we can not consecrate—we can not hallow—this ground. The brave men, living and dead, who struggled here, have consecrated it, far above our poor power to add or detract. The world will little note, nor long remember what we say here, but it can never forget what they did here. It is for us the living, rather, to be dedicated here to the unfinished work which they who fought here have thus far so nobly advanced. It is rather for us to be here dedicated to the great task remaining before us—that from these honored dead we take increased devotion to that cause for which they gave the last full measure of devotion—that we here highly resolve that these dead shall not have died in vain—that this nation, under God, shall have a new birth of freedom—and that government of the people, by the people, for the people, shall not perish from the earth.

Scholars regard the speech a crucial moment of revelation, marking the convergence of the private Lincoln, who had always loathed slavery, and the public Lincoln, who had pragmatically laid the groundwork for emancipation by stressing its military necessity and the overarching goal of saving the Union. Gone was the legalistic language of the Emancipation Proclamation with its lawyerly exemptions; here instead is Lincoln the poet, capturing, in words that soar above the carnage of war, the true meaning of the struggle. The speech's first line, invoking the sacred year of 1776 and the Declaration of Independence, and the last line, with its reference to "a new birth of freedom," signaled that Lincoln saw emancipation as a fulfillment of America's promise and as the grand purpose of the war, and equality as an essential pillar of democracy.[32]

But the address was framed by partisan politics as well. Not only did it come at the very moment Lincoln was preparing his reconstruction proclamation, but this was the moment that "semiofficially" opened the presidential contest of 1864. The state elections of 1863 had recently ended, with Democrats losing ground to Republicans and to Union party tickets that brought Republicans together with pro-war Democrats. Such fusion tickets won victories in key gubernatorial races in Pennsylvania, where Andrew Curtin was reelected over Democratic challenger George Woodward, and Ohio, where John Brough trounced Vallandingham (who had mounted his campaign while in exile in Canada). Among the newly elected Republicans in Congress were representatives from West Virginia. Lincoln played a crucial, active role in the 1863 races, arranging fundraising efforts for Republican candidates and using public letters (such as his Corning letter justifying the Vallandingham arrest) to critique Copperheads and defend emancipation. This was crucial context for Lincoln's decision to accept the invitation to speak at the Gettysburg cemetery dedication: it was a chance to meet with political allies in Pennsylvania who could help Lincoln build a Union party coalition for the presidential contest the following fall, and a chance to "bind the administration even more closely to the ideals and sacrifices that the battle, the cemetery, and the ceremony represented."[33]

The job of chronicling the battle fell to the ceremony's main speaker, the legendary orator and statesman Edward Everett. Everett's two-hour speech was masterful, providing a detailed and stirring account of the battle of Gettysburg, emphasizing that the "courage and skill" and "exalted patriotism" of the Union soldiers derived from the "consciousness that they were fighting in a righteous cause." Everett had his own distinct political agenda, one very

The Gettysburg Address. "We here highly resolve that these dead shall not have died in vain": This detail from a larger photograph shows Abraham Lincoln (hatless, facing the crowd) delivering the Gettysburg Address at the dedication of the Soldiers' National Cemetery on November 19, 1863. (Library of Congress LC-B8184-10454)

much in harmony with Lincoln's: to make the case that the rebel masses were redeemable. As had Blair's October speech at Rockville, Everett's Gettysburg speech attributed secession to the sophistries of ambitious Slave Power aristocrats, who had initiated a "reign of terror" in the Confederacy to cow the majority into submission. Everett went so far as to say, "I do not believe there has been a day since the election of President Lincoln, when, if an ordinance of secession could have been fairly submitted, after a free discussion, to the mass of the people in any single Southern State, a majority of ballots would have been given in its favor." Like Sumner, Everett denounced as unconstitutional the doctrine of state sovereignty and counted Southern blacks, "thousands of whom are perilling their lives in the ranks of our armies," as those to whom the Union owed rewards for their loyalty. Rejecting the antiwar Democrats' charge that emancipation and other hard war measures had sown a bitterness so deep among Southerners that reconciliation was impossible, Everett emphasized the Union's forbearance: despite the depredations of scoundrels such as Quantrill, he noted, the Union army had refrained from vindictiveness. The "tone of the Rebel leaders and Rebel press was just as bitter in the first months of war, nay, before a gun was fired, as it is now," Everett observed. But there was "no bitterness on the part of the masses." The hour was coming when the "power of the leaders of the Rebellion to delude and inflame must cease."[34]

Everett and Lincoln, linked by mutual respect, were drawn closer together by the Gettysburg event; Lincoln was gratified by Everett's approbation for his speech and Everett more committed than ever to throwing his prestige behind Lincoln's reelection bid. The Northern press lavished more attention on Everett's speech than Lincoln's; in keeping with the partisan context, Republican newspapers praised Everett's and Lincoln's oratory, and Democratic ones, particularly those of the Copperhead variety, found their speeches wanting. The most revealing coverage came from Confederate papers, which scorned Everett's theory that reunion could come swiftly if only the Southern masses were disenthralled. The *Richmond Enquirer* fumed,

> No matter what the original merits of the quarrel, the Yankee mode of conducting this war has made the union of fire and water a more practicable achievement than the reunion of the Southern and Northern States. . . . There is no nation on the earth which is so heartily detested and execrated in the Confederacy as the butcher nation of the North. Voluntary reunion with them! A union of hyenas, vampyres, and thugs is about as probable and practicable.

It was folly for Everett to question Southern resolve at Gettysburg, of all places, "with the stiff corpses of one thousand two hundred and eighty eight men lying in a semi-circle around him, killed dead on the field for the express purpose of giving the lie to all such statements." Everett and his ilk, the *Enquirer* countered, should worry about the divisions and discontent of the " 'weary masses' of the North," particularly about class strife and Democratic dissent. Such protestations of Confederate resolve would reach a fever pitch when Lincoln at last unveiled his plan for reconstituting the Union.[35]

Lincoln's Ten Percent Plan

The centerpiece of Lincoln's December 8, 1863, third Annual Message to Congress was his announcement of amnesty for Confederates who declared their future loyalty to the Union. Reflecting on the past year, Lincoln noted that the "policy of emancipation and employing black soldiers" had brought forth "hope and fear and doubt"—but that events had vindicated the people's hopes. The victory at Vicksburg meant that "the rebellion is divided into distinct parts, with no practical communication between them." As the rebel borders were "pressed still further back," public opinion was changing. "Tennessee and Arkansas have been substantially cleared of insurgent control, and influential citizens in each," Lincoln noted, in a selective reading of the trends in those states, "now declare openly for emancipation." Burying his own bitter frustration with border state slaveholders beneath a narrative of progress, he added, "Maryland and Missouri, neither of which three years ago would tolerate any restraint upon the extension of slavery into new territories, only dispute now as to the best mode of removing it within their own limits."[36]

With the "resumption of national authority" in a crucial number of rebel states finally within reach, it was time for a "new reckoning." All the "elements for resumption" lacked was a "rallying point." So Lincoln would provide one, in his Proclamation of Amnesty and Reconstruction. Its provisions were straightforward: to obtain amnesty, all a rebel needed to do was to take an oath of future loyalty (past loyalty was no issue) to the Constitution and Union—an oath, administered by the Union military, that included the obligation to "faithfully support" all acts of Congress and proclamations of the president. Such an act of good faith would bring full political pardon and "restoration of all rights of property, except as to slaves"; this property rights clause in effect voided the Confiscation Acts' stipulations for the seizure of land and other non-slave assets. In each rebel state (Virginia was exempted, as it already had a shadow loyal government in Alexandria), white Southerners who received pardons could set up new loyal state governments as soon as they numbered one-tenth of the number of votes in the 1860 election. Congress, Lincoln stipulated, in keeping with its constitutional duty to guarantee to each state a republican form of government, would judge whether to admit and seat the representatives sent to it by the reconstructed states.[37]

Here, in the so-called Ten Percent Plan, was another "sweetheart deal." Emancipation and black enlistment had been vindicated as war measures, and so they would stand: compliance with Lincoln's freedom decree was a core requirement of amnesty (so long, Lincoln noted, as the Emancipation Proclamation was not voided by Congress or the Supreme Court). But much autonomy was reserved to the states. They could keep their prewar names, boundaries, constitutions, and general codes of law. Rather than committing to full freedom and equality, states could enact laws for the freedpeople, by creating contract labor or apprenticeship systems that were "consistent, as a temporary arrangement, with their present condition as a laboring, landless, and homeless class." In keeping with the deluded-masses theory of Confederate culpability, Lincoln's proclamation drew a sharp line between the guilty elite and the errant populace. Certain classes of high-ranking Confederate military officers and government officials, such as those above the rank of colonel in the army, or those who resigned commissions in the U.S. army to join the rebels—were exempted from the offer of amnesty and would have to throw themselves on the mercy of Union authorities to receive pardons. The mass of rebels, should they renew their allegiance, would carry no stigma of responsibility for the war. As historian James M. McPherson has put it, Lincoln's Ten Percent Plan was a sort of emancipation proclamation for Southern white men, meant "to 'emancipate' them from their Confederate allegiance."[38]

Like the Emancipation Proclamation, the amnesty offer was to be promulgated and implemented by the Union army. It resonated with soldiers as a means to drive a wedge between the rebel masses and leaders. The Southern people might succumb if they were "assured that they would receive lenient treatment at the hands of the U.S. Govt.," Lieutenant S. Millett Thompson wrote home to New Hampshire in December; the Southern elite, by contrast, could in no way be trusted. "The people are one class—the leaders in the game quite another." These were precisely Lincoln's assumptions. At the president's direction, the proclamation was "printed in large type" and circulated in the South in handbill form. Generals such as Grant and Banks proclaimed it in their military jurisdictions, sometimes with considerable fanfare. For example, Major General Napoleon Dana, a corps commander in Texas, declared loftily of Lincoln's pardon offer that "such parental care of a people has not been exhibited to the world since the patriarchal days of old, nor since the Saviour of men cried to the multitude, 'Come unto me all ye that are heavy laden and I will give you rest!'" Wherever the Union army penetrated in the South, scouts carried the proclamation to enemy lines, cavalry expeditions were sent out supplied with it, and copies were left behind in Southern dwellings.[39]

Union authorities hoped that these announcements of the new Union policy would find their way not only to wavering civilians but also to war-weary Confederate soldiers and induce desertion. Indeed, Lincoln's amnesty was an extension of a War Department policy that gave field commanders the broad authority to release deserters from Federal custody if they swore allegiance to the Union. When handbills announcing Lincoln's proclamation appeared in Longstreet's ranks in East Tennessee in January 1864, the Confederate general wrote a letter of complaint to his Union counterpart in the region, General John G. Foster, commanding the Department of Ohio, stationed in Knoxville: Foster should have, as a courtesy, communicated the Union's new policy to Longstreet, rather than appealing underhandedly to Longstreet's men. Foster responded archly, sending Longstreet an additional twenty copies of the amnesty proclamation for him to personally distribute in his army. Meanwhile, Lincoln solicited details of the implementation of the policy. In February 1864 he sent Major General Daniel Sickles on a tour of key junctions in the Union-occupied South, such as Memphis, Helena, Vicksburg, and New Orleans, instructing him to "ascertain at each place . . . how the Amnesty proclamation works, if at all—what practical hitches, if any, there are about it—whether deserters come in from the enemy . . . and whether the ratio of their arrival is any greater since than before the Amnesty . . . and to what extent, the Amnesty is known within the rebel lines." Under pressure to clarify the status of prisoners of war who sought release in exchange for allegiance, Lincoln issued an explanatory proclamation in March 1864. It explained that his December proclamation did not apply to those who had been captured or arrested and might take the oath under duress or to escape punishment; such persons fell under the exempted classes and would have to apply for pardon. Amnesty was intended instead for those who "shall voluntarily come forward and take the said oath with the purpose of restoring peace and establishing the national authority."[40]

On the Union home front, the response to Lincoln's December 8 proclamation was overwhelmingly positive. "I have never seen such an effect produced by a public document," wrote John Hay, noting the high degree of bipartisan support for amnesty. "Men acted as if the millennium had come." The approbation among Northerners showed just how fervently they upheld the doctrine that the rebel masses could be disenthralled. Insisting that Lincoln had "never ceased to regard [southerners] as deceived and misled," Horace Greeley's *New York Tribune* asked, "What possible motive will a non-slaveholder have for persisting in rebellion after receiving due notice of the issuing of this proclamation? Merciless bands may still scour the region cursed by the revolt, and drag every man and youth into the Rebel camps—often by the help of bloodhounds: but to what end shall the non-slaveholding conscripts remain and fight?" Certain that Tennessee, Louisiana, and Arkansas would soon be "reorganized and restored to the Union" and that the "residue will gradually follow," Greeley promised, "Depend on it, this Proclamation, if seconded and sustained in the loyal States, will go far to break the back of the Rebellion." The "master-spirits of the revolt" would of course howl and curse the proclamation's insistence on emancipation—but that would serve to prove that slavery was the only substantial obstacle to peace and reunion. The antislavery *Chicago Tribune*, too, praised the amnesty policy, noting that Arkansas, Louisiana, and Tennessee were "already virtually freed from the yoke of secession" and that whites elsewhere in the Confederacy were "waiting patiently for the delivery from tyranny and bondage which our advancing arms will bring them." *Harper's Weekly* contrasted Lincoln's proclamation with Jefferson Davis's December 7 annual message, in which Davis had accused the Federal army of "the most revolting inhumanity." Davis's message was "an imposition upon a mass of ignorant and deluded followers" and a "fierce cry of rage and despair," while Lincoln's displayed his characteristic "manly faith in human rights and the people."[41]

Representing moderate and conservative Republicans, the *Franklin Repository* lauded Lincoln's proclamation for fixing blame on "those high in power in the so-called Confederate Government, upon whose shoulders rest the responsibility of this war" and opined that "many of the South are sincerely loyal and long for the blessing they once enjoyed under the United States Government." The combination of emancipation and amnesty would drive the rebel leaders into exile and open the way for the light of "Free Soil, Free Institutions and Free Government" to penetrate the South. Lincoln's offer, the *Constitution* of Middletown, Connecticut, editorialized, would do "away with the bugbear which the leaders at the South have made good use of during the war—that of subjugation.... [E]very right which they formerly possessed is restored, and they can assume their former position with honor."[42]

The leading spokesmen of white Southern Unionism stepped forward to champion Lincoln's policy. Andrew Jackson Hamilton, nominally the military governor of Texas, returned briefly to his native state when Union forces under Nathaniel P. Banks temporarily occupied Brownsville. In a January 1864 pamphlet addressed to his fellow Texans, Hamilton proclaimed, "The Government will receive with joy to its embraces all whose sins are pardonable, if, like the Prodigal Son, they repent and ask to be forgiven. . . . [He] has offered a free pardon to all except the leaders—the real responsible agents of the rebellion." The institution of slavery, he continued, had "merited and invited its own destruction"; Lincoln's requirement that Southerners accept this plain fact, Hamilton felt, was surely not too much to ask. Indeed, abolition would bring white freedom. "When you shall have been—as you will soon be—delivered from your present bondage," Hamilton told his "fellow citizens," "say to those who would question you upon the subject, that you *are* an 'Abolitionist,' not only in respect to slavery, but abolitionists as well, in respect to treason and traitors, in respect to every power, interest, institution or thing which opposes human progress, liberty and happiness." Once restored to the Union, Texas would, Hamilton promised, "set forth upon a new career of prosperity, predicated upon truth, industry and intelligence."[43]

In the winter of 1863–64, the Northern press featured many reports that Southerners were availing themselves of amnesty. Writing anonymously for the influential Baptist weekly the *New York Examiner*, Lincoln's clerk William O. Stoddard asserted in January 1864 that the amnesty proclamation was eating into rebel strength "like a potent poison": "The leaders of the conspiracy cling to their evil purposes . . . but among their subordinates a different feeling is growing up." The Longstreet-Foster exchange was widely reprinted in the Northern press and was invoked by supporters of the amnesty policy as "indubitable assurance" that it was having "its designed effect upon the rebel soldiers" by "causing desertion and disaffection," as *Harper's Weekly* commented on February 6. The *New York Herald* reported that rebel civilians and soldiers alike were entering Union lines in East Tennessee daily "for the purpose of taking advantage of the amnesty proclamation." The *Chicago Tribune* added that some rebels who came to Union lines at Knoxville waving white handkerchiefs asked to be furnished with copies of the proclamation "to circulate among their friends." The Northern media noted "a strong Union feeling" developing in Arkansas, where seven thousand people had already taken the oath of allegiance; in Louisiana and Missouri, where Union sentiment was manifesting with "great vehemence"; and in West Virginia, where disaffected rebels from the surrounding areas were negotiating to come within Union lines under the president's proclamation. "Wherever that

Amnesty has been read in the South," the *Chicago Tribune* concluded, "it has given satisfaction to all but the incorrigible rebels."[44]

The *Tribune* also condemned the "fierce hostility of the Copperheads" to the new policy. Such hostility was treasonous, for it encouraged the rebels "to hold out to the last extremity." Indeed, the Copperhead press blasted the amnesty proclamation as a radical abomination. Insisting that men take oaths to uphold emancipation as a condition of their citizenship was tyrannical, charged John Mullaly's *Metropolitan Record* of New York. The stipulation that a vanguard of one-tenth of the electorate could reconstitute the state governments embodied the "minority principle" of the Radical Republicans, themselves a "factious minority." Lincoln, Democrats charged, was "using the military to promote his own re-election" by propping up loyalist contingents who would feel beholden to him. "What right has the President to dictate who shall be a qualified elector in a State?" asked Kentucky senator Lazarus W. Powell, a frequent denunciator of the president. Moreover, the very premise of Lincoln's policy was flawed. Southerners needed no pardon, as they had done nothing wrong: they were fighting for a "just cause . . . against usurpation, and confiscation." In a similar vein, Benjamin Wood's *New York Daily News* lambasted Lincoln for demanding that Southerners consent in the destruction of slavery—Southerners who came back to the Union on such terms would find themselves enthralled, as the Northern masses were, to Lincoln's absolutism.[45]

Meanwhile, some voices on the opposite end of the Northern political spectrum took Lincoln to task for excessive lenience toward the rebels and callous indifference toward blacks' aspirations for true equality. These critics, too, rejected Lincoln's premise—in this case the idea that a simple oath of future loyalty was a meaningful marker of trustworthiness or of repentance. Certain that the all-white "ten percent" electorates would uphold the racial caste system and shut blacks out of citizenship, and that opportunistic Confederates would find it all too easy to pose as loyal Unionists in order to regain power, men such as Wendell Phillips and Frederick Douglass accused Lincoln of hewing to the cowardly principle "Make as little change as possible!" as Phillips characterized it.[46] "Tell me not of amnesties and oaths of allegiance," Douglass intoned in a January 13, 1864, speech in New York City. "They are valueless in the presence of twenty hundred millions invested in human flesh. Let but the little finger of Slavery get back into this Union, and in one year you shall see its whole body again on our backs." In Union-occupied New Orleans, African American leaders such as Jean Baptiste and Louis Charles Roudanez, through the *New Orleans Tribune*, accused Lincoln of not being radical enough: they pushed for black suffrage, highlighting the heroism of black military service, and they made the case that Congress and not the president was authorized to determine the course of Reconstruction.[47]

While most of the African American public discourse on amnesty sounded notes of caution or critique, some black commentators, even as they fully subscribed to black citizenship and suffrage, were hopeful that the Ten Percent Plan would foster Unionism and erode support for slavery. Chicago activist Sattie A. Douglass wrote to the *Christian Recorder* in February 1864 that she believed the amnesty proclamation would "greatly disaffect the entire rebel army" and promote their "bowing the penitential knee and returning to their allegiance." Philip A. Bell's *Pacific Appeal* offered an early endorsement for Lincoln's reelection in its January 9, 1864, issue, calling the Proclamation of Amnesty, with its stipulation that Southerners must draft "free State Constitutions" to reenter the Union, an act "in defiance of the slave-power." Lincoln was the "right man in the right place in the present crisis."[48]

The debate over the Ten Percent Plan hinged on the status of Southern public opinion. How strong was Southern Unionism? What toll had dissent and demoralization taken on the Confederate will to fight? Lincoln's Reconstruction plan was informed not only by his reading of trends in the border states and occupied South but also by his sense that tremors of discontent were shaking the Confederate interior. In an August 9, 1863, conversation recorded by John Hay, Lincoln expressed his view that the rebel cause was "at last beginning to disintegrate" and that it would "break to pieces" if only the Union would stand firm. Lincoln was referring to the widening gulf between two factions within the Davis administration: an anti-administration faction that hoped that foreign intervention or Northern demoralization would save the Confederacy, and Davis's own faction, which "trusts to nothing but the army." Invoking the idea that the Confederate army had become the arm of Slave Power despotism, and the need to harness military victories to political inducements, Lincoln opined that Jefferson Davis was right: the "army [was] his only hope, not only against us, but against his own people. If that were crushed the people would be ready to swing back to their old bearings."[49]

Confederate Dissent and Southern Unionism

Images of white Southern victims of and dissenters from Confederate rule proliferated in the North over the course of the war, with a focus on the waves of refugees and deserters to Union lines, and on poor white Southern civilians who availed themselves of Federal largesse. Popular press outlets such as *Harper's Weekly* and *Frank Leslie's* featured numerous depictions of white Southerners who had seemingly turned their backs on the Confederacy: Unionist scouts and guides lending their services to the Federal army, white Southerners taking oaths of allegiance or accepting food from Union commissary stores, teeming crowds welcoming Union armies of occupation, prostrate civilians preyed upon by Confederate guerrillas, refugee families reliant on the mercy of strangers. A September 1863 account in *Harper's Weekly* of "Southern refugees flying northward" lamented that countless families in Tennessee, Kentucky, and Missouri had been "thrown upon the world, without food, money, clothing or shelter." "We hear daily of tales of suffering among these Southern exiles which harrow the soul."[50]

Beyond the realm of image and anecdote, the extent of Southern disaffection with the war has proven difficult for scholars to measure. Some specificity is possible in tallying Southerners in the Federal ranks. Scholars have established that 300,000 white men from slave states fought for the Union side—200,000 from the loyal border states and 100,000 from Confederate states. These are striking numbers. As historian William W. Freehling has noted, if we add in the number of African American men from slave

VIRGINIA FARMERS' FAMILIES ON THEIR WAY TO THE FEDERAL COMMISSARY FOR PROVISIONS.
FROM A SKETCH BY EDWIN FORBES.

Encouraging Loyalty. "Virginia's farmers' families on their way to the Federal commissary for provisions": Images such as this one, from *Frank Leslie's* November 28, 1863 issue, reflected Northerners' abiding interest in the sufferings of Southern civilians and in promoting what one historian has called "loyalty of the stomach." (Library of Congress LC-USZ6-1416)

The Plight of Refugees. Sculptor John Rogers of New York created this statuette entitled "Union Refugees" in 1863, to celebrate the stoicism of Southern Unionists fleeing
to the North. The work, which was displayed at the National Academy of Design and
also available for purchase as a bronze or plaster reproduction, was one of a series of
Rogers's sculptures that sold thousands of copies on the Northern home front. (Library of
Congress LC-DIG-stereo-1s05331)

states (150,000) who wore the Union blue, the resulting total of 450,000 is
"half as many as the 900,000 Southerners who wore Confederate gray," and
enough to replace "every one of the Federals' 350,000 slain men" and then
some. The vast majority of white Southerners who wore Union blue were, like
General George Thomas, unconditional Unionists, who had never supported
the Confederate cause; only a small percentage were "galvanized Yankees"
who switched from wearing gray to blue.[51]

No such specificity is possible when gauging Unionism among white
Southern civilians. At issue is the sometimes tenuous distinction between
anti-administration Southerners, who registered protests of one kind or another against the way the Confederate government conducted the war, and
true Unionists, who worked for and welcomed Northern victory. The state of

North Carolina illustrates just how complex the political divides within the South were. Just as Missouri bedeviled Lincoln, North Carolina bedeviled Davis. As of 1862, there were two major factions among Confederates there: Davis supporters who defended polices such as conscription, impressment, and the suspension of habeas corpus as military necessities, and so-called Conservatives, led by Governor Zebulon Vance, who were wary of government overreach and criticized specific aspects of those policies, such as the War Department's refusal to let draftees choose their own regiments. But in 1863, the Conservative faction itself began to splinter, with its more libertarian elements ratcheting up their critique of the Davis administration. After the Confederacy's summer defeats at Vicksburg and Gettysburg, with desertions from North Carolina regiments mounting, a full-blown peace movement emerged in the Tar Heel State, led by William W. Holden, editor of the Raleigh *North Carolina Standard*. Appealing to the war weariness of North Carolinians, taking cues from Northern Copperhead Democrats who seemed ready to call off the war, and tapping resentment against policies such as the draft, Holden began to argue that North Carolina should seek a separate, negotiated peace with the Union to bring an honorable end to the grueling conflict. Such a peace, in which Southerners forfeited independence but regained their old constitutional rights, could preserve elements of the prewar order, including the slave system, while a prolongation of the war would surely obliterate what remained of it. In the fall of 1863, more than a hundred peace meetings sprang up in North Carolina. Half of the ten congressmen elected from the Tar Heel State in 1863 were associated with the peace movement.[52]

Beyond the bounds of such respectable political debate there were North Carolinians who actively and sometimes violently rejected the demands of Confederate nationalism. These dissidents were a volatile mix of disaffected Confederates, such as deserters and draft dodgers seeking self-preservation, and unconditional Unionists, who had never accepted secession and who sought Union victory. Among Confederate dissidents, opposition to the draft was often stoked by class resentments against the elite. In the fall of 1862, the Confederate Congress passed a measure, in response to concerns that Lincoln's preliminary Emancipation Proclamation would stoke slave rebellion, exempting from the draft one white man for every twenty slaves on a plantation (planters with large slave holdings could secure multiple exemptions). This was intended to bolster racial control on the home front. But the measure rankled small farmers and raised a hue and cry about a "rich man's war and poor man's fight"—burdens unequally borne. Desertion spiked

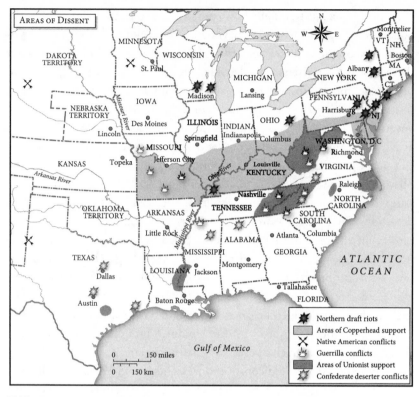

MAP 9.3

after North Carolinian troops sustained terrible causalities—the worst of any Confederate state—in the battles of Chancellorsville and Gettysburg in 1863. All told, somewhere between 15 and 20 percent of North Carolina's Confederates would desert during the war. A small but significant percentage of these deserters made common cause with outright Unionists.[53]

As for the true-blue Unionists, in North Carolina, as elsewhere in the South, African American resistance to the Confederacy was the beating heart of Unionism; slaves fled farms and plantations by the hundreds of thousands to seek refuge with the Union army and contributed to the Union victory not only as soldiers but also as nurses, spies, scouts, teachers, and day laborers. In North Carolina, like elsewhere in the South, the motivations of white unconditional Unionists were so varied as to defy generalization. Some had Northern roots or family ties to the North, but most did not; many advocated the economic development of the South, along the lines proposed by the Whig party, but some were Jacksonian Democrats; many were anti-slaveholder rather than antislavery and resented the political power of the secessionist elite, but some actively supported abolition. Strong pockets of Unionism were to be found in the mountainous, "upcountry" regions, where plantation slavery had not taken firm root, and in dissenting religious communities, such as among North Carolina's Quakers.[54]

As historian Barton Myers has shown, the Confederate military authorities aggressively fostered a culture of fear to stamp out dissent: suspected Unionists were subjected to arbitrary arrest and imprisonment; the confiscation of their property; restrictions on their freedom of speech, religion, and voting; and the depredations of guerrilla bands who committed random acts of violence, property destruction, and kidnappings. Conscription itself was used as a weapon to roust out and punish Unionists. Confederate authorities often lumped Unionists together with anti-government dissenters, regarding "Tories" and deserters as twin threats; "Confederate soldiers and home guardsmen recounted wholesale roundups of deserters, conscript evaders, and Unionists." Unionists fought back, doing battle with conscription agents, forming their own guerrilla bands to conduct hit-and-run raids on Confederate forces, slipping the Confederate dragnet to join the Union army in occupied areas like East Tennessee and coastal North Carolina—and turning out at peace meetings such as those sponsored by Holden.[55]

Myers estimates that at least 5 percent of North Carolina's population were active Unionists, and that together with anti-government dissenters, they furnished enough localized, county-level resistance to undermine Confederate control of roughly one-third of North Carolina's counties. While the Unionists never seriously endangered the Confederate governments at Raleigh or Richmond, they did force the Confederates to deploy resources, including vital manpower, to try to stabilize the contested counties.[56]

Confederate authorities worked to neutralize dissent not only through military repression but also by ratcheting up a propaganda war intended to stigmatize all dissent as treason and to preempt Lincoln's Ten Percent Plan. Davis's own views were hardening. He had at times, particularly in moments of victory and optimism, encouraged Confederates to conciliate the Unionists in their midst. For example, in an October 28, 1863, speech to the soldiers at Missionary Ridge in Tennessee, in the days when Confederates seemed to have the Yankees trapped in Chattanooga, Davis had declared his empathy for Unionists—"the misguided people of East Tennessee"—and urged that the right policy was "not to deride and abuse them, but to employ reason and conciliation to disabuse them of their error"; after all, he noted, their reverence of the Union was once a common feeling among Southerners, himself included. But in the winter of 1863–64, with Lincoln trying to coax wavering Southerners back into the U.S. fold, Davis took a different tack. He wrote North Carolina's governor, Zebulon Vance, on January 8, 1864, that the incipient peace movement in his state had to be suppressed "at any cost"—Vance could no longer abide the posturing of former allies such as Holden. Vance must, David insisted, discredit the very idea that Lincoln would negotiate. Referring to the Ten Percent Plan, Davis asked, "Have we not just been apprised by that despot that we can only expect his gracious pardon by emancipating all our slaves, swearing allegiance and obedience to him and his proclamations, and becoming, in point of fact, the slaves of our own negroes? Can there be one citizen in North Carolina so fallen beneath the dignity of his ancestors to accept or enter into conference on the basis of these terms?" A negotiated peace with Lincoln was an empty fantasy—the Confederates must focus on military victories and independence. If Vance used his "influence and position," Davis urged, the peace movement could be undermined without physical force. But Vance was to use force if necessary. Vance, tarnishing his opponent as a traitor, would go on to trounce Holden in the gubernatorial election of 1864.[57]

The rebel Congress's January 1864 address to the people of the Confederacy sent the same stern message: Lincoln's conditions for peace were tantamount to subjugation. Under Lincoln's offer of amnesty, one-tenth of the population would control the will of the remaining nine-tenths, through military force. "Can there be a man so vile, so debased, so unworthy of liberty as to accept peace on such humiliating terms?" the address asked, echoing Davis. The experiments in internal Reconstruction in the slaveholding border states had been a disaster, the Confederate Congress declared. Missouri, one a "magnificent empire of agricultural and mineral wealth," had been reduced to "a smoking ruin and the theater of the most revolting cruelties and barbarities," while Maryland groaned "under the oppressions of a merciless tyranny." New Orleans, Vicksburg, Knoxville, and other occupied cities showed the "ignominy and poverty of Yankee domination." "Retreat is more dangerous than advance," the Confederate Congress intoned—there was no going back to the Union now.[58]

Eager to put the nation on the best possible footing for the spring campaigns of 1864, the Confederate Congress complied with Davis's call for revisions to the Conscription Act, passing a measure on February 17, 1864, that dropped the lower age limit for draftees from eighteen to seventeen and raised the upper age limit from forty-five to fifty. Congress also raised taxes, established a government monopoly on blockade running, and renewed the suspension of habeas corpus (which had expired), extending the military's power to detain traitors. "However much chastened" by defeat and dissent, Davis's "administration remained in control of Confederate destiny" in the winter of 1863–64, as historian Emory Thomas has observed.[59]

The Confederate press joined with the Davis administration and the rebel Congress in countering Union promises of reunion with images of subjugation. The "Yankee nation" could under no circumstance be trusted: "No matter what might be the guaranties, treaties, amnesties, capitulations under which we should have laid down our arms, pretexts would be instantly found for evading them all," the *Charleston Mercury* insisted in a January 1864 article entitled "What Subjugation Means." In Arkansas, Confederate propagandists, based in the town of Washington, which was still in rebel hands, undertook a concerted campaign to discredit amnesty and the Unionist movement. "Shall we return [to the Union] as a dog to his vomit?" asked editor John R. Eakin of the Confederate newspaper the *Telegraph*. He derided Unionists as "the baser sort, drunkards, swindlers and ignoramuses," and predicted that after Arkansans had been "lulled into submission a Ben Butler would take over and crush the populace." Tellingly, even Davis's bitterest critics—those who blamed him for poor strategic and tactical decisions, particularly for entrusting major campaigns to incompetents such as Bragg—could rally together with Davis in opposition to Lincoln's amnesty proposals. The *Richmond Examiner* and *Charleston Mercury*, for example, which routinely bashed Davis for mishandling military matters, joined with him and his supporters in painting dystopian pictures of what would come to pass if Southerners succumbed to the siren song of amnesty. A "negro soldier will be billeted in every house, and negro Provost Marshals in every village," the *Mercury* predicted. Once-proud whites would "join the sad procession of oppressed races," the *Examiner* added. The "horrors of Peace" would prove much more horrible than the horrors of war. Confederates saw the Ten Percent Plan as cynical rather than as naive—Lincoln's aim, John B. Jones wrote, was not to end the war but to prolong it, by securing himself reelection at the head of a "radical Abolition" party.[60]

Confederate literary culture, through novels and stories, poems and lyrics, essays and articles, took on the challenge of nation-building and of sustaining morale. Because Southern periodicals lacked the personnel and resources to produce and feature large numbers of illustrations, historian Alice Fahs explains, "in the South the literary war remained primarily a war of words, not pictures; of poetic images and oratorical flourishes, rather than painted or engraved representations." Journals such as the *Southern Illustrated News* and *Magnolia Weekly* featured contributions from established literary figures such as the poet William Gilmore Simms and proslavery ideologue George Fitzhugh and also provided platforms for new talents, such as Constance Cary Harrison, who wrote patriotic poems, stories, and columns under the pen name "Refugitta." Indeed, women achieved a new level of visibility and public influence in the wartime literary realm, stoking the public's will to make the necessary sacrifices. Writers such as the novelists Augusta Jane Evans and Maria McIntosh, poet Margaret Junkin Preston, and spy-turned-memoirist Rose O'Neal Greenhow produced heralded works of Confederate propaganda and reveled in the notion that they could serve the "Cause" with their pens as men did with their swords. Negative images of Yankees as "depraved, unscrupulous, and Godless," to quote Evans, abound in women's writings. But even as they painted lurid pictures of what Confederates were fighting against, these authors also sought to remind their readers of what Confederates professed to be fighting for: their independent slaveholding republic and its distinctly tradition-bound and unitary culture. As historian Sarah E. Gardner has put it, female authors "warned southerners against being seduced into self-doubt and self-loathing by outside accounts of their culture." Evans privately lamented in January 1864 that Southerners were too fixated on "hatred of Lincoln, not love of our liberties, principles and institutions." Her 1864 *Macaria; or Altars of Sacrifice*—the Confederacy's best-selling wartime novel—features a heroine, Irene Huntingdon, who forgoes marriage and instead finds fulfillment through nursing wounded Confederate soldiers. "The pure ore of our country will be found in the ranks of our armies," Irene explains, attesting to her undying faith in the project of independence.[61]

Evans's focus on the army as the essence of Southern nationalism was typical for Confederates. As historian Gary W. Gallagher has argued, over the course of the war Confederate citizens "increasingly relied on their armies rather than on their central government to boost morale." Robert E. Lee and his Army of Northern Virginia were the focal point of Confederate hopes: "Lee's military successes in 1862 and 1863 created a belief that independence was possible as long as the Army of Northern Virginia and its celebrated chief remained in the field." Soldiers boosted the morale of civilians on the home front by projecting confidence and diehard determination. Invoking the mass reenlistment of Confederate units in early 1864, Lieutenant Ted Barclay of the 4th Virginia urged his sister back home to look to the "noble army," none of whom "shirk from their duty," as her wellspring of patriotism. Morale was strong in the western theater as well as in the east. Soldiers in the Army of Tennessee approved of their Congress's recent measures and of

Davis's decision to replace Bragg with Johnston; Johnston took steps such as increasing rations and offering furloughs, which improved men's spirits and spurred reenlistment.[62]

In short, Lincoln's December 1863 proclamation served as a rallying point for diehard Confederates. Some looked forward to the campaigns of 1864 with genuine optimism. "Nothing is shurer than our ultimate success," wrote Reuben A. Pierson of Lee's army back home to Louisiana in March 1864. Others pledged defiantly to fight on even with no end in sight. Tennessee infantryman Flavel C. Barber captured the determined mood in his army when he wrote, "Submission has been made impossible by the conduct of our insolent foe; and the only tolerable alternative left us is resistance to the bitter end. We must fight, we can do nothing else, if necessary forever."[63]

Is This Hell?

FORT PILLOW TO ATLANTA

IN FEBRUARY 1864 Brigadier General Judson Kilpatrick, a brash Union cavalry commander known for his bravery and recklessness, proposed to Stanton and then to Lincoln a plan for a raid directly on Richmond. Kilpatrick imagined that the raid would disrupt Confederate communications and supply lines, strike fear in the hearts of the city's inhabitants, and free inmates languishing in Confederate prisons; Stanton directed that Kilpatrick's raiders should also distribute hundreds of copies of the December 8 amnesty proclamation among civilians. The plan called for a carefully orchestrated joint action by Kilpatrick and his compatriot Colonel Ulric Dahlgren: Kilpatrick would attack Richmond with a force of 3,000 troops from the northwest, while Dahlgren and a smaller force assailed it from the south. The raid started promisingly enough. Setting out on February 28 and meeting little Confederate resistance, Kilpatrick's troopers reached Richmond's outer fortifications by March 1, 1864. But then the mission went off the rails. Under artillery fire from the Confederates, Kilpatrick lost his nerve and retreated, leaving Dahlgren's men isolated and forcing them to retreat as well. Groping their way through hostile terrain, under rebel pursuit in the darkness of night, Dahlgren and some ninety of his men got separated from the rest of his command and then ambushed on March 2 by rebel cavalry. The young colonel was killed and all but twenty-one of his soldiers captured.[1]

The raid soon became the focus of an intense propaganda campaign, as Confederates alleged that papers were found on Dahlgren's body instructing him and his force to sack Richmond and assassinate Jefferson Davis and his cabinet. Union authorities indignantly denied the charge and instead emphasized reports, which they gleaned from the Southern press, that

Dahlgren's corpse had been desecrated and given a "dog's burial" by the Confederates. In a typical Unionist account, the *Hartford Courant* fumed,

> The miscreants who lurked in ambush to shoot the gallant Dahlgren, showed every possible indignity to his body. His fingers were cut off to secure the diamond rings, his person was stripped and thrown in a field to save it from being devoured by hogs. It was afterwards secretly buried without coffin, winding sheet, or service. The rebels boast that none but the grim party who carried the corpse to its resting place will ever know the spot. Yet this transaction, so inhuman and fiendish, is loudly applauded by the rebel press. This shows how treason brutifies the soul.

The *National Republican* upped the ante, charging that the controversial orders supposedly found on Dahlgren's body were Confederate forgeries intended "to justify the rebels in their atrocious treatment of our prisoners." The controversy served notice that in the bloody spring and summer of 1864, Confederate treatment of surrendering, captured, and wounded Yankee soldiers would challenge Unionists' faith in the deluded-masses theory of the rebellion, even as Lincoln found himself under political siege by Northerners who regarded the war effort as a failure.[2]

Fort Pillow

On April 12, 1864, General Nathan Bedford Forrest launched an attack on Fort Pillow, an undermanned Union garrison and contraband camp on a Mississippi River bluff in western Tennessee. Forrest's aims were to seize the garrison's horses and supplies and additionally to draw Union resources and attention away from the major movement Sherman would soon launch against Atlanta. Forrest expected, with his superior numbers, to make short work of the fort. But the battle Forrest initiated, a rout that devolved into a massacre, would become synonymous with Civil War atrocity. The Union troops—poorly armed and trained units of recently recruited USCT soldiers and white Unionist refugees—were quickly surrounded by Forrest's raiders, who set the contraband camp to the torch and assailed the fort's inner defenses. Determined to stand their ground, the Federals refused, during a brief truce, to accept Forrest's demand for surrender; when the fighting resumed, the garrison was swiftly overwhelmed. As the Union lines gave way, Confederates cut down surrendering, fleeing, and wounded Federals and "contraband" women and children in a brutal bloodbath. Some 300 Union soldiers were killed or mortally wounded. Confederate cavalryman Achilles V. Clark described the scene in an April 14 letter to his sisters:

> The slaughter was awful. The poor deluded negroes would run up to our men fall upon their knees and with uplifted hands scream for mercy but they were ordered to their feet and then shot down. The white men fared little better. . . . I with several others tried to stop the butchery and at one time had partially succeeded. But General Forrest ordered them shot down like dogs. And the carnage continued.[3]

By April 15, 1864, accounts of the tragic event hit Northern newspapers, prompting Congress to investigate the incident and Lincoln to promise, in an April 18 speech at a Sanitary Commission fair in Baltimore, that if the investigation turned up evidence of a massacre, "retribution shall as surely come." Republican and abolitionist newspapers attributed the massacre to the "barbarism engendered and taught by slavery." "Is this war—or murder?" the *North American and United States Gazette* asked rhetorically, in an editorial entitled "Confederate Civilization." Noting that the "very bodies of the dead were torn with a jackal's ferocity," the editorial mocked the deluded-masses theory and scorned Southern-sympathizing Democrats. "All of this was done by 'our misguided southern brethren!'—by those with whom so many northerners are willing to fraternize." But even as the massacre provoked broad indictments of Southern society, it also illustrated the adaptability of the idea that the rebel leadership class bore the lion's share of culpability for the Confederacy's notorious deeds. A *Boston Transcript* article reprinted in the *Liberator* emphasized that "the rank and file of the rebel force simply carried out the declared purpose of their commander," while other such coverage suggested that responsibility for the massacre rested with the "chivalry of the South."[4]

In the African American press, there was a call and response on the subject of retribution for the massacre. Some argued that they must "give no quarter" to the rebels—the victims at Fort Pillow had been innocents, and the rebels were guilty and therefore deserved punishment. But others answered that the Union must not stoop to the level of barbarity and that rebel atrocities were committed in a "frenzy of failure." The *Christian Recorder* reprinted an article from the *Philadelphia Press* insisting that "no outrage is sufficient to subdue the magnanimity of the Northern people." The article cited the United States Sanitary Commission's merciful treatment of wounded rebels as "evidence

Atrocities at Fort Pillow. "The war in Tennessee—rebel massacre of the Union troops after the surrender at Fort Pillow, April 12": Coverage of the Fort Pillow slaughter brought home to Northerners the tragic consequences of the Confederacy's "no quarter" policy toward African American troops. (Library of Congress LC-DIG-ds-07662)

of national humanity." Henry McNeal Turner offered the same message in a letter to the *Recorder*, arguing against the killing of rebel prisoners. He conjured the high stakes of this debate: keenly aware that the Confederates cast black soldiers as vengeful insurrectionists, Turner urged blacks to refute that charge. "Inasmuch as it was presumed that we would carry out a brutal warfare, let us disappoint our malicious anticipators, by showing the world that higher sentiments not only prevail, but actually predominate."[5]

The Confederate administration and press took the position that reports of a massacre were trumped up, another form of Yankee propaganda. But the murder of surrendered black troops at Fort Pillow was part of a demonstrable pattern of Confederate behavior. In February, Confederates had killed in vengeance approximately twenty-five to fifty USCT troops after the battle of Olustee, in Florida, where the 54th Massachusetts had turned in another stoic performance under daunting conditions. On April 18, a similar scene unfolded at Poison Spring, Arkansas, with Confederates giving no quarter to surrendered black troops. In early May, the U.S. Congress released its report on Fort Pillow, confirming the allegations of a massacre and furnishing chilling details from witnesses and survivors, who testified that black Union soldiers had been buried and burned alive. Congress concluded that the incident was not "a spontaneous breakdown of discipline" but instead "the result of Confederate policy."[6]

Prisoners of War

The Fort Pillow massacre escalated a long-standing war of words over which side was more barbarous to its captives. The first round in that war was a controversy over Lincoln's handling of the capture of Confederate privateersmen in the summer of 1861: loath to acknowledge Confederate sovereignty, the Lincoln administration opted to treat rebel seamen as civilian criminals, charging them with the capital offense of piracy. When Davis threatened to put to death one Union prisoner for every Confederate prisoner executed, Lincoln relented, revoking the death sentences of the Confederates. With both sides amassing unwieldy numbers of POWs, the two governments reached an uneasy truce in July 1862, establishing the Dix-Hill cartel system, modeled on the agreement between the United States and Britain during the War of 1812. Each side agreed to parole and exchange captive soldiers after a given battle or campaign, man for man, within ten days (ideally), and thereby to avoid having to confine and provide for massive numbers of prisoners. Paroled prisoners pledged not to fight again until exchanged. A complex scale was devised to assess the relative worth of the various ranks (e.g., one colonel was worth fifteen privates). Excess prisoners (the balance left over after an equal exchange) would be sent to their own lines to parole camps, awaiting exchange and clearance to return to military service. Individual commanders could, with permission, make special arrangements to bypass the exchange system in certain local settings if necessary. Though the exchange system functioned to reduce—albeit temporarily—the prison populations in places such as Richmond, it was characterized from the start by a spirit of distrust and suspicion that prevailed on each side. For the duration of the cartel, Northern newspapers such as the *New York Times* featured a steady stream of reports from parolees and escapees alike on the "outrages against civilization" perpetrated by the Confederate prison system, stoking enmity and prompting public calls for Union reprisals against Confederate prisoners.[7]

In 1863, controversy over the Emancipation Proclamation crippled the already shaky exchange cartel. Davis and the Confederate Congress issued their threat that captured and surrendered black soldiers and their white officers would be punished as insurrectionists rather than exchanged as prisoners of war, prompting Lincoln to issue General Order No. 252 on July 30, 1863, suspending the cartel and ordering "that for every soldier of the United States killed in violation of the law, a Rebel soldier shall be executed, and for every one enslaved by the enemy or sold into slavery, a Rebel soldier shall be placed at hard labor on the public works, and continued at such labor until the other shall be released and receive the treatment due to a prisoner of war." Lincoln, wary of perpetuating a cycle of vengeance, backed away from the eye-for-an-eye policy, and the threat of retaliation by execution was rarely enforced. But as Confederates refused to renounce their own policy and to treat black prisoners equally with white ones, large-scale exchanges of prisoners ground to a halt by August 1863. Prisons in the North and South were soon groaning with POWs. Belle Isle in Richmond, a prison camp established on a tract of land in the James River, was designed to hold 3,000 captives; by early 1864, it held some 8,000. Rations were paltry, and boxes of food and clothing that were sent to Richmond by Northern civilians, the United States Sanitary Commission, and the federal government were withheld. "Hell is hardly a name for here a man suffers cold hunger & thirst all the time," inmate William Tippett, a sergeant in a regiment of Virginia Unionists, wrote of Belle Isle; prisoners there were reduced to catching and consuming dogs. Northerners and Southern Unionists decried Confederate treatment of Union POWs, likening it to the domination white Southerners exercised over slaves. As Richmond Unionist Elizabeth Van Lew put it, Southerners were a "people practiced in prisons . . . aye, slave prisons and jails of the most loathsome and degraded character! Prison houses, in which no eye of justice but God's ever looks, always full of innocent victims, sold for convenience, for arrogance, for lust."[8]

The Fort Pillow massacre renewed calls for direct retribution—killing a Confederate prisoner for every black soldier killed. Lincoln considered, and his cabinet debated, in May 1864, such retaliation in kind, but they again recoiled from it as inhumane: no individual Confederate was directly held to account and punished specifically for the Fort Pillow massacre. Instead, the Lincoln administration responded to the no-quarter policy by upholding the suspension of the cartel, even in the face of intense public pressure, from families of prisoners and critics of Lincoln's hard war measures, to resume exchanges. Grant's spring 1864 Overland Campaign funneled massive numbers of additional captives into the already overloaded Confederate system. By June 1864, the notorious Andersonville prison in Georgia—a sixteen-acre stockade built to receive the overflow from Richmond prisons and meant to hold 10,000 prisoners—teemed with over 18,000 captives, in conditions that were utterly unspeakable; by August the number had grown to over 30,000. As inmate Prescott Tracy of the 82nd New York would later testify of the only source of water at the camp:

> The stream, or more properly sewer, passes through the camp of the guards, receiving from this source and others farther up, a large amount of the vilest material. . . . The cook-house was situated on the stream just outside the stockade and its refuse of decaying offal was thrown into the water, a greasy coating covering much of the surface. To these was added the daily large amount of base matter from the camp itself. . . . Under the summer sun this place early became corruption too vile for description, the men breeding disgusting life, so that the surface of the water moved as with a gentle breeze.

> The new-comers, on reaching this, would exclaim: "Is this hell?"

Diseases such as chronic diarrhea and scurvy spread through ranks of starving, skeletal prisoners; some 13,000 Andersonville inmates would die, making it the war's most lethal prison. Union prisons such as Fort Delaware and Elmira were horrific in their own right, overcrowded and disease-ridden. All told, 30,000 Union soldiers died in Confederate prisons and 26,000 Confederates died in Union prisons.[9]

The captives themselves, and the Unionist public generally, puzzled over who bore the primary responsibility for this shameful record. Some condemned the Union and Confederate governments for suspending the cartel; others directed their anger at prison commandants such as Henry Wirz of Andersonville or at the ruthless guards who did their bidding; some white Unionists resented the idea that Lincoln would halt the exchanges in order to protect the rights of black soldiers. Even as they debated the issue of culpability, Northerners churned out unabashed propaganda making the case that their treatment of the rebels was more humane than Confederate treatment of Yankees. The USSC, for example, issued an extensive report on the prison system in the fall of 1864 that represented deliverance politics at its most self-serving: the report chronicled the horrors of rebel prisons and also selectively quoted Confederate prisoners who claimed they had been "kindly treated" by their Yankee captors. The U.S. government, the USSC claimed, had pursued, with "no sentiment of anger or resentment," a "Christian and magnanimous course" in its handling of POWs. The Confederate prison system, by contrast, reflected the spirit of caste in Southern society: "a too positive denial of humanity to another race, and a too positive contempt for a poorer class of their own race" had fostered the "disregard of the sacredness of human life."[10]

The idea that the Southern leadership class bore more blame than the common soldiers persisted among Union soldiers, even those who had experienced the horrors of imprisonment. Captain John James Geer of the 48th Ohio was captured at Shiloh and published an account of his captivity after

Prisoners of War. Here *Frank Leslie's* juxtaposes horrific images of emaciated Union prisoners released from rebel prisons with an article on the progress of the Union war effort, saying of the Confederate leadership, "These treacherous guides of a deluded people are now beginning to realize their folly. . . . Their hitherto unfailing devices of audacious falsehoods and brazen deceptions have failed." (Library of Congress LC-USZ62-130792)

being exchanged in 1863. He related that while incarcerated in Mississippi he had the opportunity to "study the countenances of all classes of our rebellious enemies." Such a study convinced him that the rebel army was made up of "a passive minded, illiterate citizenship" of "poor white trash" who were lorded over by the slave-owning aristocrats. He felt that the "mass of the Southern armies have been forced by the most stringent and often cruel measures to take up arms against the United States Government" and that many of his prison guards "would be loyal to the old Stars and Stripes if they dared." Geer also encountered, as many POWs did, Southern political prisoners, jailed for their Union sentiments, and found them languishing in a "most loath-some situation," on the brink of starvation. Such scenes tested Geer's faith, but prayer brought him "trust in a Higher Power—an Infinite Deliverer." "I thought of the poor Southern conscript, and the despised and fettered slave of the cotton-field, and my soul was stirred with mingled hope and compas-sion," he wrote. Captain Darius J. Safford of the 11th Vermont was captured outside Petersburg and incarcerated briefly at Libby Prison in Richmond in the summer of 1864 but managed to escape into the Virginia mountains while en route through Lynchburg and Danville to the officers' prison at Macon, Georgia. He wrote home after he had returned safely to Federal lines that he was assisted in his escape by black and white loyalists. "There are a great many Union men in the mountains of Virginia even yet," he noted, adding, "The mass of common people" would be willing to return to the "rule of the United States . . . but the aristocracy say no and they are the ones who rule in the Confederacy."[11]

Charles Mattocks of the 17th Maine, a veteran of Chancellorsville and Gettysburg who was captured in Virginia in the summer of 1864, also had his belief in the narrative of deliverance tested by his experience as a POW. Imprisoned in Macon with other officers, he compared his plight with that of the enlisted men and noncommissioned officers consigned to Andersonville:

> We hear that our men at Andersonville amuse themselves by cut-ting their names, rank and Regiment on head boards for their future graves. . . . We suffer but little compared to what our poor privates endure. As prisoners of war in what claims to be a civilized country, we suffer enough to disgrace all the military glory the Southern Confederacy can acquire in 50 years. Our long confinement and our treatment will not have a tendency to make us love our deluded Southern brothers. "When this cruel war is over" even I think we shall remember some of them. Such fellows as wantonly shoot a prisoner of

war without pretext will I think not be easily forgotten. I once heard a preacher say "Love your enemies, but not their bad actions." That is exactly our own case just at present.[12]

As evidence of cruelty to prisoners mounted, Northerners implored Lincoln to restore the cartel, but the president held fast, supported by Grant. As Grant saw it, at issue was not only was the treatment of black troops but also the marshaling of Union resources. Disappointed that some of the Confederates he had paroled at Vicksburg returned to Confederate duty (they reappeared in the ranks of Chattanooga captives) without having been formally exchanged, Grant reckoned that the cartel, by permitting captured Confederates to fight another day, attenuated the North's manpower advantage and would thus prolong the war. And Grant was determined, as he set his sights on Virginia, that the Union's superior numbers would at last prove decisive.[13]

The Overland Campaign

On May 5–6, 1864, Union and Confederate forces held each other in a death grip in the Wilderness, a dense scrub forest north of Richmond in Spotsylvania County, near where the battle of Chancellorsville had taken place the previous spring. Lee attacked Grant, although outnumbered two to one, in order to halt the progress Grant had made since crossing the Rapidan River on May 4: the heavy underbrush of the woodland, Lee calculated, would neutralize Grant's artillery and cavalry advantage. Grant, for his part, was hoping to move quickly through the Wilderness onto open ground and to flank Lee's right, getting between the rebels and Richmond. Neither general achieved his aim. The Confederates' May 5 assault met with a strong counterattack, at a ghastly cost to both sides. The men fought amidst brush fires, which erupted as the dry woods were ignited by muskets and the explosion of shells and then raged into the night, burning wounded men alive. "Every moment some souls were leaving that atmosphere of hell, their bodies to be consumed by the devouring elements," wrote Union officer Wesley Brainerd. "Hundreds of wounded on both sides, unable to crawl away from the swiftly approaching flames, could only lay and moan and roast and die." The following day, attacks by Longstreet and Gordon turned both Federal flanks, but the Union troops regrouped and halted Lee's progress. In two days of savage fighting, the Union army, which started the campaign with 119,000 men, incurred a staggering 18,000 casualties, and the Confederate army, which numbered 66,000, incurred 11,000. In an eerie echo of Stonewall Jackson's wounding at Chancellorsville a year earlier, Longstreet was hit by friendly fire; unlike Jackson, he would survive, but his recuperation would take six months.[14]

The clash in the Wilderness initiated a long-awaited, epic showdown between Lee and Grant. Grant, who on March 10, 1864, was named general-in-chief of all Union armies, conceived a strategy for breaking the stalemate in the eastern theater of war and bringing the Confederacy to its knees. Mobilizing the Union's superior manpower and material, Grant would strike multiple, simultaneous blows at the rebels: Meade's Army of the Potomac would take on Lee, while Ben Butler's army moved up the James River to threaten Richmond from the south; Franz Sigel would occupy Confederate forces in the Shenandoah Valley to keep them from reinforcing Lee. Meanwhile, in the Deep South, Sherman was to challenge Johnston's army in Georgia, while Nathaniel Banks was to take the vital port of Mobile, Alabama, and then move north to join forces with Sherman. In both the Virginia and Deep South theaters, in other words, coordinated assaults by Union forces were to trap Confederates in a vise. Offering Meade a guiding hand and protection from interference from Washington, D.C., Grant chose to make his headquarters with the Army of the Potomac.

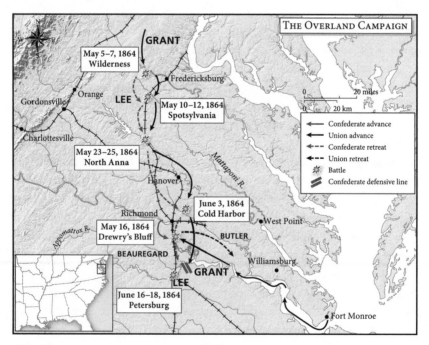

MAP 10.1

Lee got the better of his rival in the first round in their showdown, but Grant did not relent. On May 7 his Union force headed southward toward the crossroads village of Spotsylvania Court House, intending again to move around Lee's right flank. Grant's decision—for the Army of the Potomac to advance rather than retreat after a setback—was richly symbolic of his singular confidence and clear-eyed realism: Grant did not count on delivering a dramatic knockout blow to Lee, but instead envisioned a prolonged, grinding campaign. Lee, for his part, anticipated Grant's move south and was ready for him. Having won the race to Spotsylvania, Confederates drew up a strong defensive line of field fortifications—earthworks, consisting of log barriers and trenches, and abatis, or barriers of felled and sharpened trees bristling at the enemy. Because the center section of that line was a U-shaped projection, it took on the nickname of the "Mule Shoe." Union forces assaulted the line on May 10 and temporarily broke it, only to have Confederate reinforcements plug the gap. Lee, miscalculating that the chastened Federals would withdraw toward Fredericksburg, opted to remove some of his artillery from the Mule Shoe, even as Grant readied his army for a massive assault on May 12. That assault, the battle of Spotsylvania Court House, devolved into a chaotic melee, a "savage hand-to-hand fight across the breastworks," wrote Grant's aide-de-camp Horace Porter, that "was probably the most desperate engagement in the history of modern warfare." In a relentless struggle that lasted more than twenty-two hours, men trampled, bludgeoned, bayoneted, and shot each other to pieces, rendering bodies into "piles of jelly," as one soldier put it. A torrential downpour mixed water with blood, and wounded men "fell in the ghastly muck and died, some of them by drowning while helpless." With the Union sustaining 6,000 casualties and the Confederates 8,000 on May 12–13, the apex of the Mule Shoe, the sector that saw the fiercest fighting, was renamed the "Bloody Angle."[15]

The fighting briefly abated when Confederates withdrew on May 13 to a new defensive line. But Grant kept up the pressure, and the two armies continued sparring and skirmishing in Spotsylvania until May 20, when Grant pulled the Union troops from their lines and initiated a new series of flanking movements along the Confederate right, to the southeast. Even as the battle at Spotsylvania raged, Union major general Philip H. Sheridan's cavalry headed south, slashing its way to the outskirts of Richmond before turning east and then south again toward Ben Butler's army. A fierce clash at Yellow Tavern left Confederate cavalry legend J. E. B. Stuart dead in its wake. Meanwhile, Butler's Army of the James was advancing toward Richmond, facing off repeatedly with the Confederates at Drewry's Bluff, a James River fort a mere

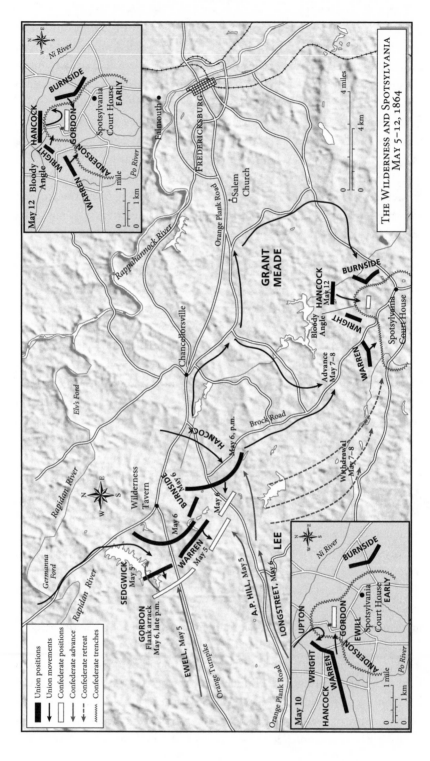

THE WILDERNESS AND SPOTSYLVANIA
MAY 5–12, 1864

Union positions
Union movements
Confederate positions
Confederate advance
Confederate retreat
Confederate trenches

MAP 10.2

seven miles from the Confederate capital. Butler's offensive ground to a halt on May 16, when P. G. T. Beauregard launched a Confederate counterattack, bottling Butler's army up in a narrow tract of land between the James and Appomattox Rivers. With Butler neutralized, and Franz Sigel disgraced for botching his mission in the Shenandoah Valley, Grant and the Army of the Potomac were on their own in the quest to vanquish the resilient Lee.[16]

Again and again Grant tried to move his left flank around Lee's right flank, to get between the rebels and Richmond, only to find Lee waiting for him, entrenched behind hastily constructed earthworks. The battle that ensued on June 3 when Grant tried to break Lee's line of defense at Cold Harbor, a crossroads just ten miles northeast of Richmond, was volcanic in its heat and destructiveness. With the Confederate defenders dug in, the surging Union troops were cut to pieces, thousands falling dead or wounded in the first few minutes of the attack. Many Union men had known that their attack would be hopeless and had pinned their names and unit numbers on their uniforms so that their corpses could later be identified. The battle cost the Union 12,700 casualties and inflicted 5,200 casualties on the Confederates. Grant would later write, "I regret this assault more than any one I have ever ordered."[17]

In the wake of the Cold Harbor disaster, Grant decided that the best course of action was to join forces with Butler's army and take the vital rail junction of Petersburg, twenty-three miles south of Richmond, thereby cutting off the rebel capital from its lines of supply. To that end, Grant dislodged his vast army from Cold Harbor and moved it south, across the James River. This daring gambit entailed finding the optimal crossing point, stealthily breaking off contact with Lee's army along a seven-mile trench line, withdrawing through the bayou-like Chickahominy swamps, and moving more than 100,000 soldiers across the imposing James on ferries, steamers, and a rapidly assembled 2,200-foot pontoon bridge. A tactical and logistical breakthrough, the crossing went as planned and set the stage for the Petersburg campaign.[18]

For four days, June 15 to 18, Federal forces probed at Petersburg's defenses, but despite the great advantage the Union had in manpower, the Yankee army was outmaneuvered and held in check by rebel forces under General Beauregard and then by Lee's army. Battered by 65,000 casualties since the Overland Campaign had begun, Grant's army faced the prospect of a protracted siege. The Union army's losses in the May 5–June 18 combat between the Rapidan and James Rivers amounted to roughly 40 percent of Grant's force (his initial 119,000 troops and 48,000 reinforcements). Lee's 32,900 casualties amounted to nearly 36 percent of his total force (66,000 troops

Crossing the James. The floating bridge, the longest of its kind yet built, over which the Union army crossed the James River in mid-June 1864. In an engineering feat, Union men built the bridge in only seven hours—a project that typically would have taken months. (Library of Congress LC-USZ62-92629)

at the outset and 30,000 reinforcements). Although the long stretch of continuous fighting had subjected the men in both armies to "relentless physical and emotional stress," Union and Confederate troops alike "showed marked resilience," notes historian Carol Reardon. In a sense, each side could claim victory. The scale of loss experienced by the Army of Northern Virginia had ample precedent in previous campaigns; Confederates saw heavy losses as "the price of Lee's successful leadership." Assessing the Overland Campaign, Confederates took pride in preventing Grant from seizing Richmond—and in Lee's skill at adjusting to defensive fighting. They regarded Grant's recklessness, particularly at Cold Harbor, as a form of desperation, and as a sign that the Yankee will to fight would soon give way. The Confederate press, for its part, closed ranks behind Lee: it reveled in his beating the two-to-one odds and inflated the Union casualties. Grant has "thrown away seventy thousand men, as though they were of no more value than so much trash, and has gained nothing whatever by the operation," editorialized the *Richmond Dispatch*. It added: "The confidence in Lee and his army is not confined to the ranks of that army and to our fellow citizens. It is as extensive as the Confederacy itself. It pervades every neighborhood and every family circle."[19]

On the Union side, some frustrated and weary soldiers "expressed freely their scorn of Grant's alleged generalship, which consists of launching men against breastworks," according to infantryman John Haley. But most Federal soldiers defended Grant's strategy, emphasizing that he had forced the Army of Northern Virginia to fight on the defensive and drained it of men it could not replace. "General Grant means to hold on, and I know he will win in the end," wrote Elisha Hunt Rhodes in his diary on June 3, after the Cold Harbor debacle. Lieutenant Colonel Stephen Minot Weld wrote his father in late June that it was "discouraging to see one's men and officers cut down and butchered time and again." But he added, "I don't wish you to think from all this that I am croaking. I feel that we shall take Richmond in time." African American troops, who participated in the initial assaults on Petersburg, as they would in the ensuing siege, stressed the symbolic significance of fighting in Virginia. Charles Brown of the 1st U.S. Colored Troops, a regiment raised in Washington, D.C., and posted outside Petersburg, wrote proudly to the *Christian Recorder* in late June 1864: "We have been instrumental in liberating some of our brethren and sisters from the accursed yoke of human bondage. They manifest their love for liberty, by every possible emotion.... What a glorious prospect it is, to behold this grand army of black men, as they march with martial step at the head of their column, over the sacred soil of Virginia."[20]

On the Northern home front, assessments of the fighting in Virginia were filtered through the lens of partisanship. Republican and moderate Democratic newspapers and journals such as the *New York Tribune* and *New York Herald* accentuated the positive aspects of the Overland Campaign, downplaying the casualties and playing up Grant's fighting spirit and the need for soldiers and civilians alike to emulate his tenacity. "Grant has more faith in square face to face fighting than in strategy," the *Chicago Tribune* observed. "It is Grant's lion heart that wins." But Copperhead newspapers such as the New York City *Old Guard* dubbed Grant a "butcher"—the antithesis of the martyred McClellan and the tool of ambitious politicians who prosecuted a remorseless war to advance their radical agenda. Grant, Copperheads charged, was heedlessly slaughtering thousands of innocent young men, with victory nowhere in sight.[21]

Grant's fortunes, on the field of battle and in the court of public opinion, were closely tied to those of his right-hand man and successor as commander of the western forces, William Tecumseh Sherman. The Northern press and civilians saw Sherman's campaign in Georgia as second in importance only to Grant's in Virginia and understood that the "success of either one depends on the other," as the *New York Herald* put it on June 6, 1864. At that same moment in early June, Andrew Evans, a staunch War Democrat, wrote his son Samuel, a Union officer stationed in Tennessee, from the family homestead in Ohio. Evans scorned the local Copperhead press and its reports that "Grant has been retreating before Lee all the time and has been whipped in every fight." "If [Lee] backs into Richmond, it will do us as well any way, I still believe that he will go in, and that Sherman will take Atlanta, and that the Rebellion must fall," Evans professed confidently, adding, "But whether the thing 'can be slid,' this season, is the great problem, the solution of which we are all, directly, or indirectly, seaking. May the God of Battles grant us a favorable solution, hastily."[22]

Atlanta Campaign, Phase One

The god of battles did not oblige, although Sherman began his Atlanta campaign with considerable advantages. His three western armies, assembled at Chattanooga and poised to enter Georgia, were 110,000 men strong, while the Confederate army, hunkered down at Dalton, Georgia, after having fallen back from Missionary Ridge, had only 54,000 men. Morale was high in the Federal ranks. Sherman felt his objective was clear: he would deprive Lee of reinforcements by compelling Joseph Johnston, head of the Army of Tennessee, to engage in a costly defense of Atlanta. The wary and cautious Johnston, for his part, was loath to take the fight to Sherman, preferring instead a defensive strategy, which would preserve his outnumbered army. Johnston would relinquish terrain while buying time, in the hopes that Sherman might make some tactical mistake that he could exploit, and that Confederate persistence might fuel opposition to Lincoln's administration in the North. The campaign opened on May 7, with Sherman eschewing a frontal assault and trying to flank Johnston out of his strong defenses at Dalton; Johnston retreated southward to Resaca and established another defensive position. A pattern was thus established whereby Sherman, while clinging to his railroad artery that ran north to south, would "pin the Confederates in their works and move part of his army group to flank each position . . . [compelling] enemy forces to retreat or risk losing their line of communications," as historian Earl J. Hess has explained. The armies fought this war of maneuver into June, with Johnston falling back toward Atlanta and "hundreds of little mounds . . . rising by the wayside day by day, as if to mark the footprints of the God of War as he stalks along through this beautiful country," as Major James A. Connolly of Sherman's army wrote to his wife back home in Illinois.[23]

The costliest fighting in the campaign's first phase took place at Kennesaw Mountain, twenty miles northwest of Atlanta, on June 27, 1864. Johnston had a strong line of entrenchments there, in an eight-mile-long defensive arc, commanding the high ground. Believing Johnston's line was overextended but unfavorable for a flanking movement, and channeling some of his men's impatience for a knockout punch after so much sparring, Sherman ordered a frontal assault. The Federals fought well but were driven back, resulting in a sobering tactical defeat that resulted in 3,000 Union casualties to the Confederates' 1,000. Sherman resumed his flanking tactics, forcing Johnston to withdraw from Kennesaw Mountain toward Marietta and then across the Chattahoochee River to the northern outskirts of Atlanta. Like Grant, who was poised outside Petersburg, Sherman hoped to avoid a siege: the Confederate ring of earthworks around Atlanta was too formidable and Sherman's army too small for siege operations. He intended to cut Atlanta's railroads while crippling the army that defended it. On July 17, that army got a new leader. Disappointed with Johnston's passivity, Jefferson Davis initiated the second phase of the Atlanta campaign by replacing Johnston with General John B. Hood, an aggressive fighter who had lost a leg at Chickamauga. Confederate troops, who were jubilant after their victory at Kennesaw Mountain, were shocked and dismayed at the news of Johnston's removal. Like McClellan had among Union troops, Johnston earned a reputation for being unusually solicitous of his men's physical well-being and morale; when he replaced Bragg, Johnston had taken measures—such as increasing rations, procuring supplies such as shoes, and issuing furloughs—that endeared him to his men. His defensive tactics had the same effect: they meant, private Samuel R. Watkins noted, that the Confederates endured "not a single rout" at the hands of the enemy while "whipping them day by day." Whether the impetuous Hood could command such loyalty was unclear.[24]

Sherman offered a trenchant summation of the May and June fighting in Georgia when he wrote grimly to his wife, Ellen, right after the loss at Kennesaw Mountain, that "the worst of the war is not yet begun, the civil strife at the North has yet to come." Even as Grant's and Sherman's spring campaigns unfolded, the presidential election contest took shape, with Lincoln facing flank attacks on his left and right.[25]

Challenges to Lincoln

Lincoln, as he sought his party's nomination, faced a sharp challenge from his left. Radical Republicans who initially professed their support for his amnesty proclamation began as early as February to show signs of souring on it. They were disappointed with how things were proceeding in Louisiana, which was pursuing readmission under the Ten Percent Plan. Lincoln's right-hand man, General Nathaniel Banks, was taking the wrong side in a factional struggle with the Free State coalition in that state. Both groups—a moderate faction led by immigrant planter Michael Hahn, Banks's hand-picked choice for governor, and a radical one led by New Orleans attorney Thomas Durant and New Hampshire–born teacher Benjamin Flanders—were committed to ending slavery and to extending citizenship to blacks, but they differed "over the pace of progress." Hahn's group hoped that a deliberate pace of change and conciliatory language would allow them to win over conservative whites; Flanders and Durant thought conservatives to be irredeemable and spoke in uncompromising terms about the need to extend education, suffrage, and economic opportunity and autonomy to blacks. Lincoln publicly favored Hahn, who soundly beat Flanders in the gubernatorial election. But the president also privately encouraged Hahn, in a remarkable March 13, 1864, letter, to push for limited black suffrage—for "the very intelligent, and especially those who have fought gallantly in our ranks"—at Louisiana's upcoming constitutional convention in May. Lincoln was likely influenced by a meeting he had had the previous day with a delegation of free blacks from New Orleans who had presented him with a suffrage petition.[26]

Hahn quietly lobbied for black suffrage during the May constitutional convention only to find that there was not sufficient support, even among liberals, to pass the measure. Louisiana's new constitution abolished slavery, without compensation, and opened up schools, militias, and courtrooms to blacks. But the fact that blacks remained disfranchised, and subject to Banks's contract labor system, rankled Radical Republicans and contributed to the rise of an "anti-Lincoln riptide," to quote historian Philip Shaw Paludan. Arkansas, too, sought readmission with a constitution that rejected slavery and secession but did not provide for black civil rights, and Tennessee seemed poised to seek readmission on similar terms.[27]

As these state struggles played out, Radicals challenged Lincoln on the national scene, registering their discontent with his moderate approach to re-union. Congress refused to seat the representatives elected in Arkansas and Louisiana. And Radicals cast about for an alternative candidate to support in the upcoming presidential election. For a time the ambitious secretary of the treasury, Salmon P. Chase, seemed to be the answer. The most liberal member of the cabinet, Chase was trusted by the Radicals and the head of a massive federal bureaucracy replete with patronage opportunities. But Chase, who had long dreamed of the presidency, played his hand poorly. In February 1864, his surrogates mistakenly leaked to the press an internal campaign document, the "Pomeroy Circular" (named after Chase's campaign manager, Kansas senator Samuel Pomeroy), that arraigned Lincoln for his "manifest tendency towards compromise and temporary expedients of policy" and offered Chase, a "statesman of rare ability," as Lincoln's replacement. The incident was embarrassing: here was the specter of a cabinet official brazenly jockeying for political advantage over his own boss during a time of national crisis. Chase denied having any advance knowledge of the letter and offered Lincoln his resignation. Lincoln took Chase at his word and refused the resignation, even as a public backlash against Chase's electioneering made the treasury secretary damaged goods. In March, Chase withdrew his name from consideration for the presidency.[28]

Disaffected Radicals, together with some key abolitionists such as Wendell Phillips, then turned to John C. Frémont as a possible standard-bearer. On May 31, 1864, a group of delegates dubbing themselves the Radical Democracy held a convention in Cleveland and nominated Frémont for the presidency. The convention platform called for federal protection of black civil rights and confiscation of rebel property (in direct contravention of Lincoln's offer that amnesty would include restoration of property). But it also reached out to Democrats by condemning Lincoln's abridgment of free speech and habeas corpus, and by nominating a former Democrat, John Cochrane of New York, as Frémont's running mate. This equivocating effort failed to really get off the ground. Frémont distanced himself from the convention's call for confiscation, seeing it as too extreme, while Democrats refused to be drawn in by Cochrane's presence on the ticket.[29]

Most important, Lincoln received ringing affirmation from mainstream Republicans when the National Union party convention met in Baltimore in June, one week after the Frémont convention. Republicans adopted the name National Union party in a show of solidarity with War Democrats, moderate border state voters, and Southern Unionists in states reconstructing under the Ten Percent Plan. The convention was a virtual showcase for Southern Unionism and Lincoln's Reconstruction program. It was chaired by Kentuckian Robert J. Breckinridge, uncle of the Confederate vice president, James C. Breckinridge. Robert was a perfect example of a redeemed white Southerner: a slaveholder and supporter of colonization before the war, his staunch Unionism compelled him to embrace immediate emancipation as a war measure. His stirring opening speech at the convention declared slavery "incompatible with the natural rights of man." To the roar of the crowd he proclaimed: "I join myself with those who say, away with it forever." Tennessee Unionists Horace Maynard and William G. "Parson" Brownlow

also took the stage to make the case for Lincoln's new running mate, Andrew
Johnson of Tennessee (who was replacing Hannibal Hamlin of Maine on the
ticket). Lincoln hoped the choice of Johnson, a War Democrat, would si-
phon off some voters from that party and also give legitimacy to the wartime
Reconstruction experiments that were under way. Maynard and Brownlow
gave stirring speeches that professed their own devout commitment to defeat
the Confederates "at all hazards, and all cost of money and lives" and that
praised Johnson for having stood loyal while "in the very furnace of the rebellion." Southern Unionists were formally vindicated when the convention
agreed to accept delegates from Louisiana, Arkansas, and Tennessee as voting
members, entitled to help choose the party's nominee.[30]

The party platform, which lauded Lincoln's handling of the war effort and demanded the unconditional surrender of the Confederacy as the
only acceptable peace terms, also supported a constitutional amendment to
end slavery, as a guarantee that Lincoln's emancipation policy would never
be repealed. The amendment had widespread support in the Republican-
dominated Senate and had passed there resoundingly in a vote on April 8,
1864, only to founder in the House on the shoals of Democratic opposition.
Its success was contingent upon Republican gains in the upcoming election.
The platform passed easily. Once Lincoln was safely renominated, he finally
accepted Salmon Chase's resignation.

The Wade-Davis Bill

While Lincoln deftly checkmated his rivals for the nomination, he could not
so easily defuse congressional opposition to his amnesty program. On May
4, 1864, the eve of Grant's and Sherman's spring campaigns, the House of
Representatives passed the Wade-Davis bill, Congress's alternative to Lincoln's
Ten Percent Plan. The plan's Republican authors, led by Maryland Radical
Henry Winter Davis, had begun their work in February, taking Lincoln up
on his promise that his amnesty proclamation represented a template that
Congress could revise and refine. That work took on a new edge as Lincoln
sided with the more moderate of Louisiana's Free State factions. The Wade-
Davis bill retained certain premises of Lincoln's plan—that states should remain intact (rather than reverting to territorial status); that the vote should be
restored to those whites who took oaths of future loyalty (with rebel leaders
requiring special pardons); and that black voting should not be a requirement
for a state's readmission to the Union. But the bill also directly challenged
Lincoln's plan by insisting that Reconstruction could not begin until military

resistance in the rebel states had been completely snuffed out and by declaring all slaves in the Confederacy forever free, thereby guarding against the possibility that Lincoln's Emancipation Proclamation, a war measure, might be rolled back once the war was over. Congress sketched out the process for readmission. The president, with the Senate's approval, was to appoint provisional governors for each of the states in revolt to oversee and administer readmission. Once military hostilities had ceased, the governor would arrange for the enrollment and oath-taking of the white male citizens in the state. Raising the bar on loyalty, the Wade-Davis bill insisted that 50 percent of a state's white men, not 10 percent, must swear an oath of future loyalty before the readmission process could continue. Those who could swear a stricter "ironclad" oath of both past and future loyalty, avowing they had never supported the Confederacy, would then vote for delegates to a state constitutional convention; only those who could take the ironclad oath could serve as delegates. The ensuing conventions were required to prohibit slavery and guarantee freedom (in essence ratifying Congress's own decree) and to bar high-ranking Confederate military and political leaders from voting and holding office in the future.[31]

The Wade-Davis bill was plainly intended to reassert congressional control over Reconstruction and to abort Lincoln's experiments in Louisiana and Arkansas, where a 50 percent loyalty yield among white men was out of reach. Supporters of the bill, such as Massachusetts Radical George S. Boutwell, defended it as a necessary first step toward the enfranchisement of blacks. "The colored people are loyal, and in many states they are almost the only people who are trustworthy supporters of the Union. Will you reject them?" he asked his colleagues. After months of debate and tinkering, the bill finally passed the Senate on July 2, 1864, by a vote of 18 to 14, just two days before Congress was to adjourn. In a shocking move, Lincoln opted for a pocket veto—to let the measure die by neglecting to sign it. In a July 8 proclamation, Lincoln laid out his reasoning. He refused to accept that the experiments in Louisiana and Arkansas should "be set aside and held for nought, thereby repelling and discouraging the loyal citizens" there. And he questioned the constitutionality of having Congress impose abolition by statute on individual states—he preferred that slavery be abolished by constitutional amendment, as endorsed in the Republican platform. Lincoln offered, in a rather wry gesture, to approve the Wade-Davis program for "any State choosing to adopt it," but he also reiterated the need for flexibility and his hesitation to be "committed to any single plan of restoration."[32]

Radicals were appalled by the pocket veto. Wade and Davis, in a seething "manifesto" they released to the press on August 5, 1864, accused Lincoln of executive tyranny and derided the Louisiana and Arkansas governments as "mere oligarchies" set up for one purpose: to ensure Lincoln's reelection. "The President, by preventing this bill from becoming a law, holds the electoral votes of the Rebel States at the dictation of his personal ambition," they charged. The pocket veto was a "great blow at emancipation," as Lincoln's plan, with its generous amnesty, left the door open for the slaveholding elite to insinuate themselves back into power. Only the Wade-Davis plan, with its ironclad provisions, would "free the masses from the old domination of the Rebel leaders."[33]

It was an irony lost on no one that this critique of Lincoln was the mirror image of the Copperhead Democrat critique—while Radical Republicans sought Reconstruction policies that were more stringent and Peace Democrats sought ones that were conciliatory, both sets of rivals charged that Lincoln's policies were motivated by his lust for power. Coinciding as it did with the opening of the presidential campaign season, the Wade-Davis challenge fueled the Peace Democrats' "Lincoln as Dictator" rhetoric. For example, in May 1864 Ohio Democratic congressman Samuel Cox argued that the Wade-Davis plan and Lincoln's Ten Percent Plan shared the same essential defect: the insistence that Southerners swear to uphold emancipation. Cox observed:

> Five months have gone, but we see no signs of thousands of southern citizens rushing to embrace this amnesty. . . . [T]here is no general taking of the oath, no genuine movement toward the restoration of the seceded States, but a fiercer spirit of resistance. . . . The President's plan has been widely published in the papers South, as the *Richmond Sentinel* says, to "animate their popular patriotism." The forgiveness offered by the President is deemed a mockery and its terms an insult.

Lincoln was clinging to this failed policy for one reason: "to secure his nomination" by hiding his own radicalism under a cloak of moderation. Democrats must, Cox urged, reject both of the Republican plans for Reconstruction and dispense with the requirement that Southerners take an "abolition oath," offering instead the only terms which could "transmute the rebel into the patriot": "the enchantment of friendship."[34]

Whether or not Lincoln's National Union party and his Reconstruction plan could command mainstream support would depend on which way the

Democrats tacked in their upcoming national convention in late August 1864. But Lincoln's fate depended even more on the Union army's progress in Virginia and Georgia—and in July and August, both campaigns were mired in tragedy.

The Crater

After his failed attempt to overrun Petersburg on June 15–18, Grant focused on cutting off its transportation lines to the south and west. As Petersburg was a supply center serving Richmond, to isolate Petersburg was to deprive the rebel capital of food, munitions, medicine, and other key logistical needs. In June and July, a pattern emerged in which both armies' methodical construction of field fortifications and trenches was punctuated by Grant's flanking offensives at either end of the lengthening siege line and by Lee's stubborn counteroffensives. The first of these actions took place on June 22–24, with Union forces damaging but failing to seize rail lines south of Petersburg. Meanwhile, the Union forces began to shell the city, forcing residents to flee or to take shelter in crudely constructed caves and bombproofs. Even as some refugees migrated out of the city, others migrated in, escaping the destruction of the Overland Campaign and the Yankee occupation of counties adjacent to the siege.[35]

Seeking to break a creeping stalemate, officers in Burnside's Ninth Corps proposed to Meade and Grant a daring gambit: to dig a long mine shaft reaching from Union lines to a Confederate salient that jutted out from the trenches a mile southeast of Petersburg, and to pack the far end of the tunnel with explosives and blow a breach into the Confederate defenses. With the high command's skeptical approval, soldiers who were peacetime anthracite miners from Pennsylvania began in late June to dig the shaft, showing great ingenuity in engineering its ventilation and drainage systems. In late July, they were ready to go: they packed the shaft with eight thousand pounds of black powder, even as Grant and Meade finally bought in, devising a plan in which Federals would follow up the detonation with an artillery barrage and charge to the high ground commanding the city. At the eleventh hour, Meade overrode Burnside's proposed order of battle. Impressed with their morale, Burnside intended to place his 4th Division, led by Edward Ferraro and made up of recently enlisted and therefore fresh African American troops, in the vanguard of the attack—and he had them trained to execute their assault by moving around the imagined blast site. But Meade insisted that white troops lead the way, on the grounds that they were more experienced—and that it would look politically suspect if black troops seemed to be sacrificial lambs in executing an especially dangerous maneuver. The commanders of Burnside's other three divisions drew straws to determine who would take the vanguard, and the lot fell to the particularly inept Brigadier General James Ledlie, known for his penchant for the bottle.[36]

In the early morning hours of July 30, after one false start due to a faulty fuse, Union soldiers detonated the massive cache of explosives, creating a blast observers likened to the eruption of a volcano and instantly killing 278 Confederates. The blast created a crater 170 some feet long, 60 feet wide, and 30 feet deep. The ensuing Union attack was a travesty. Ledlie's men ran into the crater or got ensnared in the entrenchments surrounding it, where they were easy prey. Ferraro's men, sent to the rescue, drove the Confederates, only to be forced back into the crater and into retreat by a countercharge from Confederate general William Mahone. Clueless as to these events, Ledlie and Ferraro shared a bottle of rum behind Union lines while this debacle unfolded. While some of the African American troops had shouted "Remember Fort Pillow" as they charged into action, seeking retribution for the atrocities there, the ensuing Confederate slaughter of retreating and surrendering black troops at the crater proved to be an inhuman repetition of the Fort Pillow massacre.[37] "It seems cruel to murder them in cold blood," wrote Confederate lieutenant colonel William Pegram to his sister about the treatment of black troops, adding callously, "But I think the men who did it had very good cause for doing so." General Edward Porter Alexander conceded that "some of the Negro prisoners, who were originally allowed to surrender by some soldiers, were afterward shot by others, & there was, without a doubt, a great deal of unnecessary killing of them." The battle ended with the Confederates having regained their lost ground and with Union casualties numbering 3,800 to the Confederates' 1,500—and with Grant reverting to his focus on cutting supply lines. Grant regarded this fight, which came to be known as the battle of the Crater, as the "saddest affair" he witnessed in the war.[38]

Confederate morale, in Lee's army and among civilians, rose as a result of the battle. In Confederate eyes, the use of black troops, like the shelling of cities, was a sign of Yankee barbarism and desperation. Some 1,500 Union prisoners who had somehow managed to survive the battle, 500 of them black soldiers, were paraded through Petersburg, to the delight of jeering crowds who hurled epithets at them; the white prisoners were sent off to prison camps and the black ones sold into bondage. July 30 was a "brilliant day to us," the Confederate Pegram noted, for it showed that the Yankees "cannot blow us out of our works."[39]

The Crater. This sketch, made at about 8:00 a.m. on the morning of July 30, 1864, by *Harper's Weekly* correspondent and artist Alfred R. Waud, shows Union troops advancing toward the mounds of earth thrown up by the explosion of the underground mine. (Library of Congress LC-USZ62-7056)

Northerners, soldier and civilian, reeled at the news of the Crater. It capped off a cruel month in which reversals in the Shenandoah Valley had materialized into threats against Washington, D.C. After turning back Union major general David Hunter's move on Lynchburg in June, Confederate major general Jubal Early proceeded northward through the Shenandoah Valley into Maryland, crossing the Potomac on July 5–6, winning the battle of Monocacy on the ninth, and making his way to the outskirts of Washington, only to withdraw in the face of imposing Federal fortifications and reinforcements. Early menaced Pennsylvania later in July, launching a cavalry raid on Chambersburg and burning much of the town to the ground. Although these were not major engagements, they were chilling reminders of the North's vulnerability to attack. Against this backdrop, the battle of the Crater fed multiple negative narratives: the Copperhead critique of Lincoln as tyrant, Grant as butcher, and black enlistment as harmful; the Radical charge that Lincoln was not doing enough to protect black soldiers or to reward them for their sacrifices; and the general sense that the rebels were still masters in the Virginia theater. Copperhead Chauncey Burr wrote of Grant, "Never more can he go into a town or village in the whole North where his name will not excite horror in the breasts of numberless widows and orphans." Some Union soldiers praised the courage of African American units at the battle, but others charged that black soldiers had panicked and retreated, obscuring the fact that, as historian Kevin Levin explains, "the Confederate attack also sent just as many (if not more) white troops into a full stampede."[40]

The timing could not have been worse, with the presidential election just three months away. Could Sherman bring Lincoln the decisive victories that were eluding Grant?

Siege and Stalemate

"Sherman's host still surrounds us, no, not exactly surround, but still besiege us on the North and North West trying to come in. Our general is trying to out-general and *Hood*-wink them, but it appears doubtful which will gain the point," wrote the merchant Sam Richards on August 1, 1864, in his detailed diary of life in Atlanta. "It is to be hoped the contest will not be prolonged indefinitely for there is nothing much to be had to eat in Atlanta though if we keep the RR we shall not starve, I trust." Richards succinctly summed up the tactical state of play, as Sherman expressly targeted the railroads that ran into Atlanta. To dominate those railroad lines and depots was not only to starve Atlanta's civilians and Hood's army but also to strike a symbolic blow, undermining, as historian William G. Thomas has put it, the Confederacy's claim to "modernity, wealth, and power." Indeed, Sherman's Atlanta campaign marks the apogee of what Thomas has called "railroad generalship": the Union's determination to use railroads to master the Southern landscape and control "if and how goods and people moved from one city to another."[41]

In late July Sherman divided his force, sending the Army of the Ohio and the Army of the Tennessee to cut the Georgia Railroad, east of Atlanta, while the Army of the Cumberland advanced on the city from the north. Hood's Confederates struck back on July 20, hitting the isolated Federal column north of Atlanta at Peachtree Creek; the Confederates were turned back and lost 2,500 troops to the Yankees' 1,800. Hood hit Sherman again, attacking Major General James B. McPherson's Army of the Tennessee along the eastern approaches to the city, in the battle of Atlanta on July 22. Again Hood's rashness failed to pay off and the Confederates were repulsed, absorbing staggering losses of 5,500 men. With Sherman moving his army west of the city to cut the rail tracks that ran into Atlanta from the south, the two armies clashed on July 28 at Ezra Church, where the Confederates launched an ill-timed frontal assault that resulted in a tactical disaster: approximately 3,000 Confederates were lost, with Yankee casualties numbering a small fraction of that at roughly

General William Tecumseh Sherman. Commander of Union forces in the western theater, Sherman was Grant's right-hand man in the last year of the war. Sherman was determined, in his Georgia campaign, to show the South that "war is hell." (Library of Congress LC-USZ62-72803)

650. Hood's army pulled back into the confines of the city. These costly tactical defeats dampened their morale, with some rebels now likening Hood, in his willingness to send men to the slaughter in ill-considered offensives, to the hated Grant.[42]

Meanwhile, Sherman unleashed a massive five-week bombardment of the encircled city, sending many of its residents into flight and others—municipal employees, those who sought to protect their property, and those who had no means or safe destinations for escape—underground into cellars, basements, and dugouts. "It is like living in the midst of a pestilence," wrote Sam Richards of the bombing. "No one can tell but he may be the next victim." With only one functioning rail line (to Macon, to the south) still bringing supplies into the city, and stores no longer selling wares, looting broke out, and poor families turned to the army to procure rations to eke out their subsistence. The dry, hot weather added to the tinderbox effect of the cannonading, and fires broke

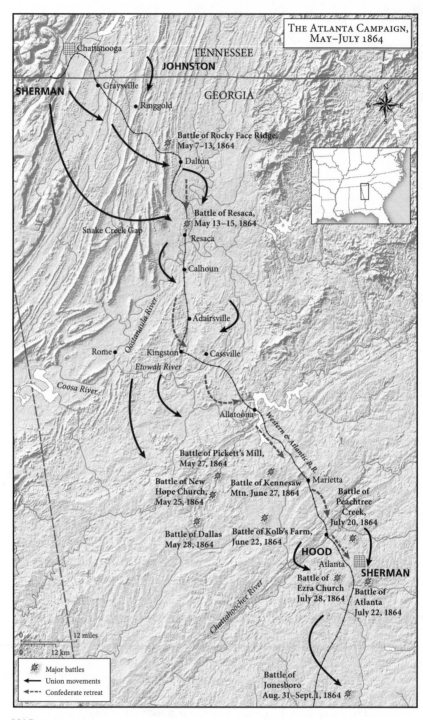

THE ATLANTA CAMPAIGN,
MAY–JULY 1864

Chattanooga

TENNESSEE

JOHNSTON

Graysville

SHERMAN

GEORGIA

Ringgold

Battle of Rocky Face Ridge,
May 7–13, 1864

Dalton

Snake Creek Gap

Battle of Resaca,
May 13–15, 1864

Resaca

Calhoun

Oostanaula River

Adairsville

Rome

Kingston

Cassville

Etowah River

Coosa River

Allatoona

Western & Atlantic R.R.

Battle of Pickett's Mill,
May 27, 1864

Battle of New
Hope Church,
May 25, 1864

Battle of Kennesaw
Mtn. June 27, 1864

Marietta

Battle of
Peachtree
Creek,
July 20, 1864

Battle of Dallas
May 28, 1864

Battle of Kolb's Farm,
June 22, 1864

HOOD

Atlanta

SHERMAN

Battle of
Ezra Church
July 28, 1864

Battle of
Atlanta
July 22, 1864

Chattahoochee River

0 ——— 12 miles
0 ——— 12 km

✳ Major battles
→ Union movements
⟵-- Confederate retreat

Battle of
Jonesboro
Aug. 31–Sept. 1, 1864

MAP 10.3

out across the city, burning down dwellings not yet leveled by the artillery barrage. The pummeling reached a peak on August 9, when some 5,000 shells poured down on the city. While only an approximated twenty civilians were killed by Sherman's bombardment, countless others were wounded and traumatized. One surgeon testified that many civilians, even children, underwent amputations during the shelling.[43]

Although Sherman inflicted severe damage on Atlanta, the bombardment did not dislodge Hood and his army. Indeed, Lincoln and the Republican party faced the possibility that Sherman, like Grant before Petersburg, was stalemated, with no breakthrough on the horizon. While Grant and Sherman were confident that they were wearing away the Confederates, the Northern public could not clearly discern this progress. The Copperheads exploited the seeming military impasse to maneuver for control of the Democratic party. They recapitulated their familiar case against the Lincoln administration, with a special emphasis on certain key themes. One of them was the connection between military and moral failure. With Burr's *Old Guard* leading the way, the Copperhead press argued that the summer's military campaigns, in which the Union had suffered 100,000 casualties since May, were not just tragic but disgraceful. Grant and Sherman, like Burnside, Butler, Pope, and Hooker before them, goaded on by Republican politicians, practiced war without mercy, in which "every species of marauding . . . seems to have been not only tolerated but encouraged," fumed Burr. "All just people," he opined, looked on "with amazement and horror at our atrocities and barbarism."[44]

Peace Democrats claimed that black troops were particularly barbarous, invoking the specters of murder, rape, and pillage in the South and of social equality and sexual "amalgamation" in the North. Copperheads produced and distributed a pamphlet, which they fraudulently attributed to abolitionists, entitled *Miscegenation: The Theory of the Blending of the Races, Applied to the American White Man and Negro.* The document was meant to "prove" to racist whites that the Republican party was committed to a policy of race mixing. As historian Jennifer Weber explains, "Reactionary papers started regularly printing accounts of African American men and white women engaging in sexual relations—something [the papers] had done on occasion before *Miscegenation* appeared but that became far more common after the pamphlet's publication."[45]

Along with the themes of military failure and social radicalism, the other major Copperhead theme was peace by compromise. During the spring and summer of 1864, peace factions in the North and South tried to capitalize on each other's seeming momentum. In the Confederacy, none other than

Vice President Alexander Stephens emerged as the most vehement anti-Davis administration voice. His faction, which some historians refer to as the "Confederate Copperheads," called for a negotiated peace on the grounds that the Davis administration had lapsed into tyranny and lost sight of the core principle of state sovereignty; that the peace elements in the Democratic party were on the ascent politically and might be primed to call for an armistice or even to recognize Confederate independence; and that neither side, North or South, had the will to keep battering each other indefinitely. This camp drew encouragement in the spring of 1864 from some intemperate congressional speeches by Northern Peace Democrats such as Alexander Long of Ohio and Benjamin Harris of Maryland, who, in arraigning Lincoln for tyranny and calling for an end to the war, seemingly acquiesced in the doctrine of secession. Southerners could find another barometer of Northern public opinion, the Stephens camp argued, in the machinations of secret peace

Alexander Stephens. Over the course of the war, the Confederate vice president became increasingly disillusioned with his own government. He critiqued Jefferson Davis for excessive government centralization, diplomatic failures, and Davis's unwillingness to negotiate for peace. (Library of Congress LC-DIG-cwpb-04947)

societies, such as the Knights of the Golden Circle, which promoted desertion in the northwest.[46]

Stephens and his allies urged that the Confederate administration
should make an overt policy of building up and strengthening the Northern
Copperheads, and that they should do so by making frequent peace
proposals to the North, especially after Southern military successes when the
Confederacy had maximum leverage. Such proposals would expose to the
war-weary Northern public Lincoln's unwillingness to treat with the South
and thus strengthen the hand of the Democrats. As a corollary, they argued,
the Confederacy should adopt a defensive military posture during the campaign season and refrain from offensive fighting, lest the renewed fear of
Confederate invasion prompt Northerners to close ranks around Lincoln.
Stephens fantasized that a Democratic victory and armistice would bring
peace and vindication: either recognition of the Confederacy or, as a fall-
back position, reunion on the South's terms (reaffirming state sovereignty,
renouncing coercion, and disavowing emancipation as a war aim).[47]

Northern Peace Democrats in turn fed on Southern peace mutterings
and pressed the case that the only real obstacle to negotiated settlement
was Lincoln's stubborn embrace of emancipation as a condition for peace.
Ominously for Lincoln, in the summer of 1864 some War Democrats and
even Republicans took up this refrain. For example, New Jersey governor Joel
Parker, an anti-emancipation War Democrat, proclaimed in speeches in his
home state that "influential men" in the South had expressed a "willingness
to talk over our difficulties, without prescribing independence," and that the
majority of people in the North "desired compromise, but the Republican
leaders would not consent to fair terms." Horace Greeley, antislavery editor of the *New York Tribune*, approached Lincoln in July with reports that
Confederate agents in Canada were eager to discuss a settlement, and he urged
Lincoln to hear them out, noting anxiously that the "widespread conviction
that the Government and its prominent supporters are not anxious for Peace"
was doing "great harm" to the Union cause and would "do far greater harm
in the approaching Elections." Yielding to the public pressure, Lincoln sent
Hay to meet the rebel envoys, but it came to light that the agents in question
were not, after all, authorized to negotiate a peace. That same month, Lincoln
granted the request of two private citizens—the minister James F. Jaquess
and author James R. Gilmore—to meet unofficially with Jefferson Davis in
Richmond, to sound Davis out on the issue of possible terms of settlement.
Lincoln knew perfectly well that the meeting would fizzle and that the envoys
would return home, as they did, bearing the message that Davis would accept

no terms other than Confederate independence. Indeed, Davis, according to Gilmore, scorned Lincoln's amnesty proclamation with the words, "Amnesty, Sir, applies to criminals. We have committed no crime.... We will govern ourselves. We *will* do it, if we have to see every Southern plantation sacked, and every Southern city in flames."[48]

On August 22, staunch Lincoln supporter Henry Raymond, editor of the *New York Times* and chairman of the National Union party executive committee, wrote the president a desponding assessment of the electoral situation, lamenting that Lincoln would lose the key states of Illinois, Pennsylvania, and New York, and therefore the election, because the voters were alienated by "the want of military success" and the "fear and suspicion . . . that we are not to have peace *in any event* under this Administration until Slavery is abandoned." Raymond suggested that Lincoln reveal Davis to be the true villain by offering Davis reunion without emancipation, "on the sole condition of acknowledging the supremacy of the constitution." Davis would summarily dismiss the idea of reunion and thus dispel the Copperhead illusion that black freedom was the obstacle to peace. Lincoln considered Raymond's plan but then rejected it, telling him that sending such a commission to Richmond with the false message that the Union might abandon emancipation "would be worse than losing the Presidential contest—it would be ignominiously surrendering it in advance."[49]

Even as he kept these peace movements at bay, Lincoln privately despaired of his reelection prospects. On August 23, 1864, he presented to his cabinet a carefully folded "blind memorandum" for them to sign, and in effect notarize, without having seen what Lincoln had written. His plan was to show the cabinet its contents after the election. The memorandum read:

> This morning, as for some days past, it seems exceedingly probable that this Administration will not be re-elected. Then it will be my duty to so co-operate with the president elect, as to save the Union between the election and the inauguration; as he will have secured his election on such ground that he cannot possibly save it afterward.

The president-elect, Lincoln anticipated, would be his old nemesis George McClellan, presumptive nominee of the Democratic party. The memorandum in effect pledged the cabinet both to accept the election results and to use the brief window between McClellan's victory and his inauguration to win the war.[50]

On August 29, nearly a week after Lincoln wrote his bleak resolution, the Democratic party finally held its national convention, in Chicago, and made its choice of McClellan official. The party had originally planned to meet on July 4 but had delayed the convention at the urging of Peace Democrats, who opposed McClellan, regarding him as too moderate; Copperheads hoped that continued military setbacks for Grant and Sherman would prime the convention to accept an out-and-out peace man as the party's standard-bearer. While they lost that bid, Copperheads did exert control over the choice of vice president—one of their own, Congressman George H. Pendleton of Ohio. And they put their stamp on the party platform, which was drafted by Clement Vallandingham, recently returned from his Canadian exile. The platform declared that "after four years of failure to restore the Union by the experiment of war . . . justice, humanity, liberty and the public welfare demand that immediate efforts be made for a cessation of hostilities, with a view to an ultimate convention of the States, or other peaceable means, to the end that at the earliest practicable moment peace may be restored on the basis of the Federal Union of the States." While moderate Democrats felt that the platform seemed too willing to concede Confederate independence, they trusted McClellan to make it clear that reunion was the basis for peace. The platform passed almost unanimously, and Democrats left their convention confident that Lincoln's days in office were numbered.[51]

II

Campaign Season

THE ELECTION OF 1864

"ATLANTA IS OURS, and fairly won," read William Sherman's September 3, 1864, dispatch to Washington, D.C., announcing his capture of the rebel stronghold. "Since the 5th of May, we have been in one constant battle or skirmish." Over four months, the Union had sustained 37,000 casualties and inflicted 32,000 on the Confederate army. This news, coming across the telegraph wires just two days after the Chicago convention declared the war effort a failure, could not have come at a more propitious time for Lincoln. In Auburn, New York, at a public celebration of Sherman's victory, William Seward offered a de facto campaign speech for Lincoln, calling the National Union party the true peace party. Propositions of peace with a restoration of the Union, he explained, would come "not from the Confederates in authority, nor through them, but from citizens and states under and behind them . . . just so fast as those citizens and states shall have been delivered by the Federal arms from the usurpation by which they are oppressed." The Union would greet liberated Southerners as "brethren who have come back from their wanderings, to seek a shelter in the common ark of our national security and happiness." And redeemed white Southerners would do the right thing by dismantling slavery, the "mainspring of the rebellion." "The Union men in all the slave states that we have delivered are even more anxious than we are to abolish slavery. Witness West Virginia, Maryland, Missouri, Louisiana, Tennessee, and Arkansas," Seward declared. The election campaign of 1864 saw Lincoln's coalition—an electoral core of Republicans and abolitionists along with some War Democrats, border state loyalists, and Southern Unionists—close ranks around the proposition that the war of deliverance was succeeding and that the disunionist Copperheads must not be allowed to imperil that success.[1]

The Fall of Atlanta

Sherman looked to be a genius. He had secured his Atlanta victory by abruptly calling off his bombardment of the city on August 25 and moving his infantry south of Atlanta to cut the city's last artery, the Macon and Western rail line. Hood's effort to repulse the Federals at Jonesboro failed, forcing him on September 1 to order Atlanta's evacuation and the blowing up of ammunition trains lest they fall into the hands of the enemy. "This was a day of terror and a night of dread," wrote Confederate merchant Sam Richards in his diary, noting that blasts from the ammunition trains shook the ground and shattered the windows as Hood's army beat its retreat.[2]

Sherman's army entered Atlanta in triumph the following day, to the jubilation of the African Americans there, who rushed into the streets to hail the liberators. Union officer James A. Connolly wrote his wife of this series of events that the Union victory at Jonesboro was so sweet that he could have "laid down on that blood stained grass, amid the dying and the dead and wept with excess of joy." Connolly saw the fall of Atlanta as a rebuke to the Copperheads. He wanted "honorable peace, won in the full light of day, at the cannon's mouth and the bayonet's point, with our grand old flag flying over us we negotiate it, instead of cowardly peace purchased at the price of national dishonor."[3]

On September 7, Sherman ordered the expulsion of the remaining civilians from the city and issued orders for the destruction of the city's depots, warehouses, and machine shops. This order brought howls of protest from the city's mayor and other residents. It has been debated ever since: while it meant suffering for poor refugees, the expulsion was carried out with some considerable consideration for Confederates of means, whom Sherman provided with boxcars to transport large quantities of goods to their new homes. Sherman defended his expulsion order in a testy exchange of letters with Hood, who accused Sherman of barbarity toward helpless innocents. Southerners had brought the scourge of war upon themselves, Sherman explained in a September 12 letter to the Atlanta mayor, and they could cause that scourge to pass:

> Once admit the Union, once more acknowledge the Authority of the National Government. . . . [I]nstead of devoting your houses, and Streets and Roads to the dread uses of War [and] I & this army become at once your protectors & supporters, shielding you from danger let it come from what quarter it may. . . . [T]he only way the People of Atlanta can hope once more to live in peace & quiet at home is to Stop the war, which can alone be done by admitting that it began in Error

and is perpetuated in pride. We don't want your negros or your horses, or your houses or your Lands, or any thing you have, but we do want and will have a just obedience to the Laws of the United States.[4]

This letter was one of many in which Sherman theorized about Southern public opinion and how to mold it; he believed himself to possess, by virtue of his prewar stint as a military college superintendent in Louisiana, a superior understanding of "the temper of the South." Sherman rejected Lincoln's Reconstruction plan as "unwise": it looked "like weakness" on the North's part to "court peace" before the South was fully conquered, he wrote his brother, Republican senator John Sherman, in late December 1863. But he embraced the deluded-masses theory of Southern public opinion, giving it his own spin. In a January 31, 1864, letter to Major Roswell M. Sawyer, an assistant adjutant general stationed with the Union army at Vicksburg, Sherman asked rhetorically, "Should we treat as absolute enemies all in the South who differ from us in opinion or prejudice, kill or banish them, or should we give them time to think and gradually change their conduct, so as to conform to the new order of things which is slowly & gradually creeping into their country?" He then answered his own question:

> For my part I believe that this War is the result of false Political Doctrine. . . . Slave owners . . . conceived their property to be in danger and foolishly appealed to War, and . . . by skilled political handling they involved with themselves the whole South on this Result of error & prejudice. I believe that some of the Rich & slave holding are prejudiced to an extent that nothing but death & ruin will ever extinguish, but I hope that as the poorer & industrial classes of the South realize their relative weakness, and their dependence upon the fruits of the earth & good will of their fellow men, they will not only discover the error of their ways & repent of their hasty action, but bless those who have maintained a Constitutional government strong enough to sustain itself, protect its citizens, and promise peaceful homes to millions yet unborn.[5]

In Sherman's eyes, there was no contradiction whatsoever between these views and his use of hard war tactics, such as the bombardment and then expulsion of Atlanta's civilians. The only strategic issue at stake was "which party can whip," he wrote to Kentucky Unionist James Guthrie in August 1864. "It is as simple as a schoolboy's fight, and when one party gives in, we will be the better friends." Sherman's own prescription for victory was a massive show of force by a unified North, fully mobilized by conscription—only such a demonstration of might, and not coaxing or cajoling, would illustrate the vulnerability of the South and thereby break the spell the secessionists had cast. Northern manpower would be more "convincing as to our national perpetuity, than an humble pardon to Jeff. Davis and all his misled host." Sherman cursed Copperheads and antislavery radicals alike for undermining Northern unity. An unabashedly racist man who thought "the negro [was] in a transition state and not the equal of the white man," Sherman accepted emancipation as a military necessity but rejected black military service—not only did he consider blacks unequal to the task of combat, but he also reckoned that the use of black troops absolved too many white men, who should be in the ranks, from pitching in. "I would use Negroes as Surplus, but not spare a single white man, not one," he wrote Stanton in October 1864. In Sherman's view, the war was a war for Union, synonymous with representative government and law and order, against the forces of "sedition and anarchy."[6]

As a result of Sherman's expulsion order, roughly sixteen hundred Atlantans were evacuated to points south. But nearly as many chose to go north—including the merchant Sam Richards, whose family made its way to New York City and there lay low, clinging to their hopes that Hood might somehow turn things around back in Georgia. For refugees who went south, Macon, Georgia, was a gathering point, and Jefferson Davis appeared in that city on September 23, ostensibly to lift their spirits. It was not Davis's finest hour. His speech decried the absenteeism in Hood's army and called upon the patriotic women of the South to use their social influence by favoring the man with the "empty sleeve" over "the man who had remained home and grown rich" and by exposing cowardly skulkers. If women "should know of any young men keeping away from the service who cannot be made to go any other way," he advised, "let them write to the Executive." Davis defended himself against the charge that he had, by not providing reinforcements from Virginia, "abandoned Georgia to her fate." Davis had chosen to deploy forces in the Shenandoah Valley, he explained, and that decision had paid off, with Jubal Early not only driving the Federals away from Lynchburg but "well nigh capturing Washington itself." Davis knew that the Valley had been a source of pride and victory in the Confederacy. But that narrative was about to change.[7]

The Burning

The fall of Atlanta was linked with two other breakthroughs in the Union's grand campaign: the fall of Mobile Bay, the Confederates' sole remaining port on the Gulf of Mexico, to Admiral David Farragut's fleet on August 5, 1864, and General Philip Sheridan's victories in the Shenandoah Valley of Virginia in September and October. The Valley campaign was not only a logistical blow to the Confederacy but also rife with symbolic meaning. "So boasted of old by Virginians, so deservingly praised by all who have visited it, whether from motives of pleasure or carnage," the Valley was "the scene of our greatest defeats in the early part of the war," as an article in the *Soldiers' Journal*, a popular Union newspaper based in occupied Alexandria, Virginia, explained in October 1864. Renewed campaigning by the Union in the spring and summer of 1864 had brought yet more defeats, with Early besting the Union generals Sigel and Hunter. In August, U. S. Grant applied the remedy by putting command of the Union's Valley forces, soon christened the "Army of the Shenandoah," into the hands of thirty-three-year-old cavalry prodigy Phil Sheridan, who had proven himself indispensable in the Overland Campaign. Sheridan's assignment was clear: to neutralize Early and seize or destroy Confederate resources and infrastructure—primarily crops, barns, mills,

Philip Sheridan. An ambitious Ohioan of Irish extraction, "Little Phil" Sheridan foiled Jubal Early's plan to use the Shenandoah Valley as a base for offensive operations in the North, and stripped the Valley, the "granary of the Confederacy," of valuable resources. (Library of Congress LC-DIG-cwpbh-01010)

livestock, and railroads—so that the Valley would no longer provision Lee's army and offer a route for invasion and a base for guerrillas. If necessary, Sheridan was to reduce the Valley to a "barren waste" by laying Confederate resources to the torch, Grant instructed him.[8]

Sheridan, commanding an army of roughly 43,000 men, bided his time for six weeks, familiarizing himself with the Valley's terrain. Acting on intelligence obtained from a local Quaker Unionist named Rebecca Wright, Sheridan finally pounced on September 19, in the third battle of Winchester, launching an attack on the Confederates that demonstrated both the ascendancy of the Federal cavalry and the shortcomings of Early as a tactician: Early "badly underestimated" Sheridan, Gary Gallagher has explained, and divided his own outnumbered and poorly armed infantry "in a manner that invited disaster." The Northern public rejoiced at this retribution. "The retreats and defeats in the Shenandoah valley, which the Union forces have so often met with, have at last been redeemed by a decisive victory," the *Christian Recorder* editorialized, adding that success in the Valley would "aid materially Grant's operations against Petersburg and Richmond." Sheridan was also striking a blow at slavery: hundreds of Valley slaves found refuge with the Union army, and many of them joined its ranks.[9]

Sheridan chased down Early and hit him again on September 22 at Fisher's Hill, near Strasburg, Virginia, flanking and stampeding the reeling Confederates, whose casualties more than doubled those of the Federals. More humiliation was in store for Early's increasingly demoralized army at Tom's Brook on October 9, where Federal cavalry again routed the Confederates, setting the stage for the campaign's coup de grâce: a Union victory at Cedar Creek on October 19 that was a personal triumph for Sheridan, who rallied the Federals for a counterattack after a surprise attack by Early had broken them. Sheridan's conspicuous bravery pulled victory from the jaws of defeat and earned him promotion to major general. Early and the Confederates, by contrast, fell into fits of recrimination, with charges circulating that Early's men had squandered their momentum by falling out of their ranks to plunder the captured Federal camps. "Our army is little better than a band of thieves and marauders," lamented infantryman Richard Waldrop of the 21st Virginia in a postmortem on the battle.[10]

In September, as he brought Early's army to heel, Sheridan also implemented the scorched-earth tactics known as "the Burning": along a forty-mile swath of the Valley of Virginia, stretching from Harrisonburg to Woodstock, Union troops, with the cavalry in the lead role, torched thousands of hay and wheat stacks, barns, and mills; captured thousands of horses; and

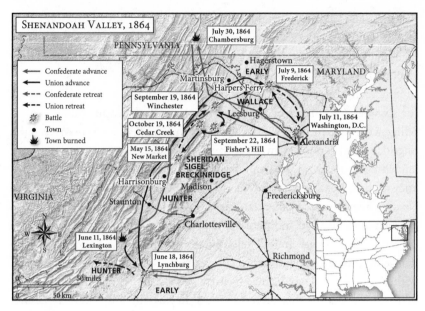

MAP 11.1

drove off or slaughtered livestock by the thousands. Historians have argued that the Burning represented not indiscriminate destruction but targeted severity: Union soldiers targeted public and quasi-public property more than private property, plantations more than farms, and the disloyal rather than loyal Unionists. These policies, although imperfectly enforced, were a buffer against wholesale devastation. In Rockingham County, for example, one of those hardest hit by the Burning, a "conservative estimate" of agricultural resources destroyed represents "less than a quarter of production levels in 1860." As historian William G. Thomas has put it, Sheridan "neither destroyed the entire Valley nor subjugated its population." But the Union's hard war tactics, as Thomas notes, nonetheless landed a blow on Confederate morale, as civilians, having found that Early's army could not protect them, "wondered whether they were forsaken."[11]

The National Union Party

On September 8, a week after the fall of Atlanta, George McClellan accepted the Democratic nomination in a letter in which he explicitly rejected the idea that there might be peace without reunion: "The Union must be preserved at all hazards. . . . I could not look in the face of my gallant comrades of the army and navy, who have survived so many bloody battles, and tell them that their labors and the sacrifice of so many of our slain and wounded brethren had been in vain; that we had abandoned that Union for which we had so often periled our lives. . . . [N]o peace can be permanent without union." This was a risky bid on the candidate's part to distance himself from the Copperhead wing of the party and the peace plank in the party platform. McClellan's letter came as a relief to moderate Democrats, who tried, in their campaign rhetoric, to thread the needle: to argue that the party fully stood behind the military leadership of Sherman and Sheridan and gloried in their victories while at the same time rejecting the Lincoln administration's stewardship of the war effort. Only a Democrat could capitalize on the army's recent success, declared McClellan spokesperson Robert C. Winthrop of Massachusetts, by promulgating "a wise, conciliatory, healing policy" to replace Lincoln's revolutionary insistence on emancipation. Lincoln's policies had "been calculated to extinguish every spark of Union sentiment in the Southern states"; McClellan would rekindle that allegiance.[12] Some prominent pro-war border state Unionists supported

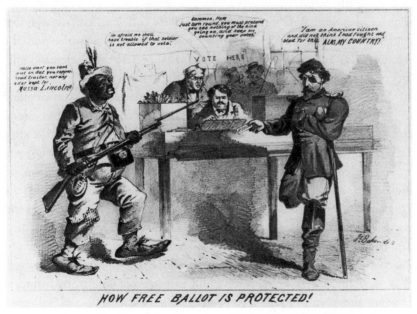

HOW FREE BALLOT IS PROTECTED!

Campaigning for McClellan. This Democratic cartoon, in which a black soldier tries to prevent a maimed white Union veteran from voting for McClellan, taps Northern racism, associating the Republicans with social radicalism and electoral fraud. The black soldier calls the white one a "copperhead traitor," and the white soldier responds, "I am an American citizen and did not think I had fought and bled for this. Alas my country!" (Library of Congress LC-USZ62-89606)

McClellan in his effort to distance himself from the Copperheads. These men, such as Kentucky's governor, William E. Bramlette, and Maryland senator Reverdy Johnson, censured Lincoln for his abridgement of civil liberties and for his "refusal to listen to terms of peace upon the simple basis of the Union and the Constitution"; they loathed Lincoln but also rejected the war failure language and cease-fire provisions in the Democratic platform.[13]

However much War Democrats tried to claim McClellan as one of their own, they could not dispel the cloud of Copperheadism. A "grand demonstration of the Democratic party" in Philadelphia in mid-September 1864, featuring a long procession of marchers bearing banners and slogans, offered tableaux of Peace Democrat campaign themes. "Abolition philosophy— handcuffs for white men and shoulder-straps for negroes," read one slogan. Another banner, the *Philadelphia Press* reported, featured the image of a "black man with a whip in his hand; before him a white man in a suppliant position." A giant transparency with the motto "Grave of the Union" depicted Grant and the Union's other leading generals "as having the bodies or forms of jackasses" and pulling a hearse with two coffins labeled "Union" and "Constitution." The featured speakers at the event amplified on these slogans. Lincoln's party, Hiram Ketchum of New York intoned, "insist[s] that the black man, the descendant of Africa, shall be raised to an equality with the white man, and they are not to be satisfied till they have the black man in the jury box, on the bench, in Congress, and in the State Legislature."[14]

The National Union movement, for its part, closed ranks in assailing the war failure and armistice planks of the Democratic party, and in associating McClellan with both. McClellan was a puppet of the Copperheads, a "mere receptacle of the thoughts and purposes of other men . . . [who] will be blindly led by the counsels of [Fernando] Wood and Vallandingham," as one pro-Lincoln paper put it. Such men had a treasonous contempt for the Union army. "They are sad when our soldiers are victorious. . . . Politicians and party leaders whose hopes of success rise upon rumors of defeat of the Union armies and fall upon intelligence of Union victories are unworthy of confidence and trust," a Philadelphia "Grand Union Demonstration" resolved. A Democratic victory would result in the demotion of Grant, Sherman, and Farragut and a return to the incompetent military leadership and "kid glove system" exemplified by McClellan, which had resulted in so many defeats. An armistice of the kind Democrats called for would leave the wily and uncompromising Jefferson Davis in power, to dictate terms to the pliable Little Mac. Campaign rhetoric often invoked the "terrible sufferings of the Union men of the South" and warned that a McClellan victory would abandon them to "wholesale slaughter," as a *Harper's Weekly* article entitled "Rebel Terrorism" put it. Robert J. Breckinridge, stumping for Lincoln in the Midwest, raised the specter of Democrats bartering away states such as Kentucky and West Virginia in peace negotiations. He urged Northerners not to desert slave state loyalists and "leave [them] to be crushed out."[15]

Lincoln's backers in the North also delighted in contrasting Tennessean Andrew Johnson's rock-ribbed loyalty to the Union with the altogether less admirable record of McClellan's running mate, George H. Pendleton. Pendleton was the very personification of the treacherous Copperhead Democrat, and the Lincoln campaign trotted out his voting record in Congress—all the many instances in which he had voted against resolutions to support and provision the troops and to raise revenue for the war effort— as proof that he was openly disloyal.[16]

Campaign appeals directly targeted the Union rank and file. Soldiers should not forget, enjoined the Philadelphia *Campaign Dial*, that the Democratic party had for three years "stigmatized them as . . . vagabonds [and] thieving marauders." "No letter that McClellan can write can possibly change the ground he has stood on," the *Dial* continued, "as the candidate of a party that proposes to the men who have been fighting the rebels for three years, and whipping them for three years, to stack their arms and stand by and see Copperhead politicians make a peace that shall acknowledge the rebel government, or practically surrender every advantage we have so bloodily won during the war." In a September letter to the *Christian Recorder,* Henry McNeal Turner, serving as a chaplain with the 1st USCT at Harrison's Landing on the Virginia Peninsula, praised Farragut and Sherman for their recent triumphs, offered a scathing denunciation of the Democrats' Chicago platform (an "infernal instrument" of "incarnate devils"), and noted with relish that the site of "McClellan's inglorious retreat in '62" was now a staging ground for black troops to assail the rebel capital. Lincoln supporters also reminded soldiers that Republicans pushed for new laws that would grant the troops the right to vote in the field, away from their own districts, or by absentee ballot, while Democrats, most notably in Illinois and Indiana, opposed such laws.[17]

While they shared an animus for McClellan, the mainstream and abolitionist wings of the National Union movement differed over the role of Lincoln's amnesty policy in securing victory and reunion. Moderate and conservative Republicans, and the contingent of War Democrats who joined their ranks, argued that emancipation and amnesty went hand in hand. The Washington, D.C., *National Republican* featured on its masthead during the campaign Lincoln's "Golden Sentences," from his December

The Spirit of Andrew Jackson. This pro-Lincoln cartoon contrasts the spineless McClellan, who bows down before Jefferson Davis, with the manly, upright Andrew Jackson, who defended the Union in 1832 against the nullification movement of John C. Calhoun (shown begging for Jackson's pardon). Jackson remained a potent symbol of Southern Unionism. (Library of Congress LC-USZ62-13212)

1863 annual address: "I shall not return to slavery any person who is free by the terms of the proclamation, or by any act of Congress," and "I proclaim full pardon to all who solemnly swear to henceforth faithfully support, protect, and defend the Constitution of the United States and the Union of the States thereof." Together, these two Lincoln policies contributed to military victory by robbing the rebellion of black labor power and white soldiers. "It is much better to win over a man who has been mistaken than to kill him," the *Chicago Tribune* declared of the amnesty policy. "It is better to get Tom, Dick and Harry to take the oath, and become good loyal men, then even to cripple them in battle. All we want of them is that they be *cured*. That once done, we are no longer at war, as far as they are concerned. . . . The Proclamation . . . not only weakens the rebel army but it gives strength to our side." At a Lincoln Campaign Club meeting in New York City in March 1864, General James H. Lane made the same point: amnesty was "calculated to weaken their armies by causing desertion. . . . May its clarion tones sound loud and clear through all the South, calling off the guilty and deluded masses from their hopeless struggle." The president still aimed "at the great end," as the *Franklin Repository* of Pennsylvania put it: "the disenthralment of a great people."[18]

"The difference between the policy of the President and the policy of the Copperheads," editorialized the *Sacramento Daily Union* on November 1, 1864, was that while Lincoln favored "conciliation for the brave, misguided democracy of the South, who do not own a pound of human flesh," the Democrats "wish to purchase peace by conciliating the minority of traitors whose guilty ambition brought all the horrors of civil war upon our land." "Once the Confederacy is broken down," the *New York Times* predicted, in the same spirit, "the Southern people will realize the utter folly of further opposition ... and, turning their backs upon the past ... adapt themselves to the new order of things."[19]

This message rang out from Northern pulpits and podiums during the presidential campaign of 1864. The Presbyterian minister Samuel Spear declared in a Brooklyn sermon that the Union must first sweep the Confederacy "from the earth as an organized military power; and then we shall be in a position to speak directly to the people of the several states, and propose to them, and not to Jefferson Davis, suitable measures for an honorable and Constitutional re-union." Spear would "meet the *masses* with a general amnesty for offenses past" while holding the guilty elite accountable.

The National Union Party Ticket. Union, law and order, emancipation, and amnesty: The Lincoln ticket appealed to moderate and conservative Northerners by justifying emancipation as a nation-saving measure. (Library of Congress, The Alfred Whital Stern Collection of Lincolniana, Portfolio 8, no. 11)

The progress of the Ten Percent Plan and of internal reconstruction in the border states was a frequent theme among Lincoln's moderate and conservative supporters. "The people of the South themselves have determined to rid themselves of the cause of their present suffering," opined the Unionist *New Orleans Era*, trumpeting restoration in Louisiana, Arkansas, and Tennessee. The *Soldiers' Journal*, published in Alexandria, Virginia, heralded the passage in the spring of 1864 of an emancipation measure by the "restored" loyal government of Virginia—the rump Unionist government that prevailed in the eastern slivers of the state liberated by the Union army—as a bellwether of how emancipationist sentiment would spread among Southern loyalists after the "*re-inauguration* of President Lincoln." The *Constitution* of Middletown, Connecticut, saw Maryland's 1864 emancipation amendment as proof that "aristocratic southerners' . . . boasted strength and power" would soon "dwindle away, and vanish like mist before the rising sun."[20]

While the campaign rhetoric of mainstream Republicans and their War Democrat allies emphasized the theme of white Southern redemption under Lincoln's policies, Radical Republicans and abolitionists foregrounded black freedom and citizenship. Garrison and his *Liberator* represented those abolitionists who supported Lincoln enthusiastically. Even if the "whole of justice has not yet been done to the negro," Garrison noted, Lincoln had still "struck the chains from the limbs of more than three millions of slaves." The *Liberator* enumerated the antislavery milestones of the previous three years, including the establishment of free labor on plantations in the liberated South and the efforts of loyalists in the reconstructing states to seek "a return to the Union on the basis of freedom," as proof that the nation was "on its way to the full recognition of the quality and manhood of the negro before the law." Other abolitionists expressed more ambivalence and conceptualized the election as a choice between "a half-friend of freedom" in Lincoln and a "thorough partisan of slavery" in McClellan. Douglass, on behalf of the Colored National Convention meeting in Syracuse in October 1864, railed against the Republican party's failure to exact sterner retribution for the atrocities against black troops and the fact that in neither the Ten Percent Plan nor the Wade-Davis bill were "colored men, not even those who had fought for the country, recognized as having any political existence or rights whatever." But still he endorsed Lincoln, for the Democratic party represented something far worse: it would "restore slavery to all its ancient power . . . and make this government just what it was before the rebellion,—simply an instrument of the slave-power." Lincoln had "depended too largely on the policy of conciliation," Gerrit Smith noted, but "uncompromising opponents of the rebellion"

Union and Liberty. This anti-McClellan broadside contrasts two visions of the future: one in which Lincoln promotes equality, free labor, and education, and another in which McClellan capitulates to Davis and perpetuates the slave system. (Library of Congress LC-USZ62-945)

must still vote for him, to defeat the "sham peace candidate." Abolitionists supported Lincoln because the choice was between "moving forward and jumping backward."[21]

Some abolitionists held out. Anna Dickinson, the Philadelphia Quaker who gained renown in 1863 as an unlikely stump speaker on behalf of Republican politicians, lambasted Lincoln's Reconstruction plan during the 1864 campaign, invoking the "fearful massacre" at Fort Pillow and asking, "Is this a time to offer amnesty and pardon? Let us leave off State making and go to work and crush out the rebellion." Dickinson spoke of her own vision of a redeemed South, in which Northerners would plant schools, churches, and mills. But she insisted, "We must elevate the blacks, or the whites will sink" into their old turpitude. Wendell Phillips lamented in an October 20 speech in Boston that the Ten Percent Plan was finding favor in the South, to evil ends. "Mr. Lincoln's offer of amnesty has been accepted by men with wealth in their hands and treason in their hearts all over West Virginia, Missouri, Tennessee and Louisiana. This is the class which has always hated the democratic tendency of the union, and still hates it. This is the class which rebelled to break the union, and their purpose is unchanged. Military defeat has not converted these men; the soreness of defeat is only added to the bitterness of their old hate."[22]

Once again Northerners were enmeshed in debates over Southern public opinion. What were Confederate perceptions of the Northern election?

Confederate Reactions to the 1864 Campaign

Confederate Copperheads who sought to expedite peace commanded substantial public support on the Southern home front in the spring and summer
of 1864, and had a brief moment of vindication when the Chicago convention called for an immediate cessation of hostilities. But the fall of Atlanta and
McClellan's acceptance letter strengthened the hard-liners led by Jefferson
Davis, who maintained that peace without independence was failure and the
offering of peace proposals was a sign of weakness that would stoke Northern
aggression. The hard-liners agreed that the Confederacy should work to
weaken the North from within by encouraging the peace elements there,
but only clandestinely, through the machinations of an unofficial diplomatic
mission, based in Canada, which could provide secret societies in the North
with "money, propaganda and organizational counsel." Confederate agents
hatched such plots as buying and hoarding gold specie in New York to spark
a financial panic and raiding prisoner-of-war camps in the northwest and
arming the inmates. It is easy to dismiss such plots, which came to naught, as
"harebrained" schemes based on "delusional" thinking, as historian William
C. Davis has succinctly put it. But they reflected the hope that the campaign
season might be "attended with violence," to quote War Bureau chief Robert
Garlick Kean Hill—that social chaos might break out or even, perhaps, an
armed mutiny on the scale of the New York draft riots.[23]

Hard-liners rejected the idea that Confederates should openly endorse
the Northern Peace Democrats on the grounds that such an endorsement
might backfire by discrediting the Democrats in the eyes of Northern voters.
Republicans would be able to say that "Jefferson Davis wants McClellan to
win!" This calculation was sound: the Republican press had a field day with
Alexander Stephens's "ray of light" endorsement of the Democratic platform. But hard-liners also invoked a deeply rooted tenet of secessionist ideology: that the Democratic party could not be relied upon to protect Southern
interests. The lesson of secession, the *Charleston Mercury* reminded its readers
in the spring of 1864, was that the South could "depend upon no party at
the North for the protection of their liberties and institutions." Noting how
many Union generals were "old Democrats"—and for Confederates Ben
Butler was the most notorious example—the editorial concluded that all
parties, Republican and Democrat, were "united in the wicked and bloody
policy" of subjugating the South.[24]

While the Confederate Copperheads put stock in the Chicago platform
as an expression of the true will of the Democrats, the hard-liners believed

the Democrats' choice of McClellan as their standard-bearer was far more revealing. McClellan, hard-liners argued, was a War Democrat who rejected Southern independence and was not to be trusted. For hard-liners, the meaning of McClellan's acceptance letter was clear. A September 19 *Richmond Dispatch* editorial commenting on the letter asked rhetorically, "Shall we be slaves to the Yankees?" and answered, "General McClellan says we shall." McClellan's stance would lose him the election, the editorial predicted, for there was no longer a meaningful difference between McClellan and Lincoln. Hard-liners had little faith that a Democratic president would do the South's bidding. Instead they wished for Lincoln's defeat because it would signal the erosion of Northern morale and would thus herald the Confederacy's military triumph. The core principle of the hard-liners was that only battlefield victories, and not political machinations, could win Southern independence—their primary aim was not to encourage Northern dissent but to revive Southern enlistment, discourage desertion, and stoke the will to fight. Jefferson Davis, during the 1864 campaign, played down the importance of the Northern election and focused instead—relentlessly—on two perennial themes: Yankee atrocities and Confederate manpower. In speeches he delivered in Georgia and South Carolina in the fall of 1864, Davis invoked the Union army's alleged outrages in Atlanta, asking, "Would you see the fair daughters of the land given over to the brutality of the Yankees?" The Yankees were dogs, he declared, and the only way to make them civil was to "whip them." "And you can whip them," he told Confederate men in October 1864, "if all the men capable of bearing arms will do their duty."[25] The fate of the Confederacy, Davis insisted, lay in the hands of the Confederates themselves.

With the Peace Democrats losing ground in the wake of Northern battlefield victories, Alexander Stephens publicly accused Davis of failing to do the right thing—that is, failing to promote the Northern peace party—and he speculated in a controversial letter, penned on November 5, 1864, and widely reprinted in the Confederate press, that Davis actually preferred Lincoln's election to McClellan's. Davis considered this a scurrilous charge and publicly accused Stephens of having fabricated it. The Confederate president and vice president were at war. Many of their Confederate countrymen did not align themselves with one camp or the other, but instead careened back and forth between them in "somersaults of reasoning," to quote the apt metaphor of Jason Phillips. Such mental acrobatics became ubiquitous after the fall of Atlanta and the Valley setbacks, as Confederates increasingly went into damage control mode and argued that there was no functional difference between Lincoln and McClellan or that Lincoln's election might indeed be preferable. After all, this last argument ran, Lincoln was the devil Southerners knew. "We prefer an ignorant, brutal fool as commander in chief of the enemy to any other man," the *Richmond Enquirer* opined. McClellan's election, by contrast, might "breathe new life into the northern war effort" and splinter the South, if credulous Southerners accepted peace on Northern terms.[26] As the Reverend Stephen Elliot, rector of Christ Church in Savannah, explained in October 1864, "The election of Lincoln is necessary for our deliverance; any other result should be disastrous to us. We need his folly and his fanaticism for another term; his mad pursuit of his peculiar ideas. . . . Lincoln's re-election will make us realize . . . [that we] must make the choice between a perpetual resistance, if necessary, and a condition of serfdom."[27]

The Result

On November 8, 1864, Abraham Lincoln was resoundingly reelected, winning 212 electoral college votes—including those of Missouri, Maryland, and West Virginia—to McClellan's 21, and capturing 55 percent of the popular vote. Little Mac prevailed only in Delaware, Kentucky, and New Jersey. McClellan had "paid the price of amateurism in politics," historian Mark E. Neely Jr. has noted: although he considered himself an opponent of extremism, he allowed himself to be "tarred with extremist views." Congressional election results further vindicated Lincoln, with Republican gains in both the House and the Senate affording them the supermajority needed to propose constitutional amendments. In a Thanksgiving discourse, the Reverend Horatio Stebbins, a San Francisco Unitarian, rejoiced in Lincoln's election, the heroic comportment of black troops, and the success of the Union in wresting away from the Confederacy the states of Maryland, West Virginia, Kentucky, Missouri, Tennessee, Arkansas, and Louisiana. "The war is near its end," he prophesied. "The military and political power of the governing class in the rebellion will be broken, and the people will find themselves under the protection of the Flag; and they will weep at their delusion, and thank God they have been saved as by fire from the power of their misguided passions and wicked leaders." Black abolitionist Frances Ellen Watkins Harper struck a similar chord in a November 15 speech, reprinted in the *Christian Recorder*. "The age is speaking grand and glorious things. Maryland is free; the curse is rolled back from Tennessee!" rejoiced Harper, lauding "glorious Andy" Johnson for his role in vanquishing the "enemies of freedom." In early December, Lincoln's fourth Annual Message to Congress emphasized the progress of loyalism and freedom in Arkansas, Louisiana, Missouri, Tennessee, Kentucky,

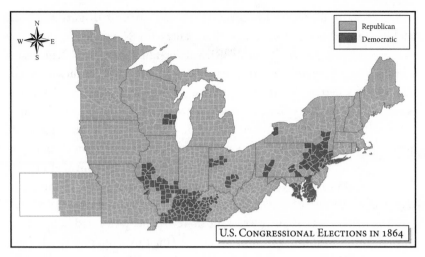

MAP 11.2

and especially Maryland (with its November 1864 antislavery constitution), and the incentives the Southern masses had to "reaccept the Union"; the door to amnesty and pardon was still open, he explained, but it would perhaps not be open indefinitely.[28]

Lincoln had successfully forged a coalition that included Republicans, War Democrats, border state and Southern Unionists, and abolitionists. In the end, even the critics Anna Dickinson, Wendell Phillips, and Ben Wade and Henry Davis, of the Wade-Davis manifesto, had come around and supported the president. But the key to the president's margin, scholars have long contended, was the soldiers' vote: Lincoln claimed nearly 80 percent of their ballots. Or did he? Historian Jonathan D. White has noted that roughly 20 percent of soldiers eligible to vote chose not to, and that this abstention reflected disillusionment with both candidates. White has also brought to light evidence of Republican intimidation and coercion of Democratic soldiers—tactics such as withholding furloughs or campaign literature and ballots, dismissing Democratic officers from service, or court-martialing men for disloyal speech were used to suppress Democratic turnout. Such tactics, usually implemented by officers, reflect how deeply they had internalized the Republican message that Copperheads posed a material threat to the Union army. In the final analysis, roughly 50 to 60 percent of the eligible soldiers voted for Lincoln—a majority but not an overwhelming one.[29]

Many soldiers, White observes, voted for the national Republican ticket out of "disgust" with the Copperheads' war failure message rather than "out of support and admiration for Republican war aims." Firsthand accounts by soldiers furnish considerable evidence of disgust for both McClellan and Pendleton. In his diary entry for November 1, 1864, for example, Wisconsin artilleryman Richtmyer Hubbell cast a Democratic victory as a nightmare scenario: "An Election will come off in which will be decided whether the nation shall live or die, for I believe if McClellan is elected our nation will be ruined." But such sources also furnish ample evidence of the positive appeal of Lincoln and Johnson. Hubbell himself avowed that "the army is almost to a unit for Old Father Abraham & the Union." John C. Myers of the 192nd Pennsylvania, a regiment that also favored Lincoln overwhelmingly, was gratified to see the Republican party take root in Charleston, West Virginia, where he was stationed in the fall of 1864. "There is a sprightly Republican newspaper published here," he reported. "Before the war a newspaper advocating Emancipation would have been pitched into the river, and the editor along with it. Now, as one of the most important results of the rebellion, free press, free speech, and freedom generally, not heretofore enjoyed in this part of the world, are no longer under the heel of the slaveholders." Among the most poignant accounts by a Lincoln supporter came from Andersonville prisoner Alexander McLean of the 117th New York, who recalled in an 1866 reminiscence that after he was transferred to Camp Lawton in Georgia (also known as Millen Prison) in the fall of 1864, the rebel officers in charge of the camp held a mock election in which the prisoners could vote for McClellan or Lincoln; if they chose McClellan, they were told, they would be paroled. The rebel officers urged the prisoners, "Dont go for a d——d negro (naming Lincoln)," but the prisoners did not oblige and gave Lincoln the majority. "The result, did not please the rebs much; no account was ever seen of it in their papers; while, if it had gone the other way, there would have been a great hue and cry raised," McLean observed. "They supposed they had starved us down and misrepresented things to us so that we would do or say anything against the government; but such was not the case; they found that the 'yanks' had some grit of loyalty left, even if nearly starved to death," he remembered proudly.[30]

The correspondence between Sam Evans of the 70th Ohio, a lifelong Democrat who voted for the National Union ticket, and his Copperhead cousin Jane provides another revealing window into how each party defined the stakes of the contest. Sam, who was stationed in Memphis, Tennessee, wrote a series of letters home to southern Ohio in the summer and fall of 1864 explaining his evolving political views. In June, he wrote his father lambasting the Peace Democrat press for disloyalty.

We would have had better Success subduing this Rebellion if 49/50 of the papers had been suppressed in the beginning [and] the army "correspondents" had been required to take a musket instead [of] the pen. This kind of warfare look[s] like tyranny, but justice to the Soldiers who are fighting the battles demands something of that nature. It is the soldier, the private soldier, who has suffered most inconveniences from these Scoundrels and are now losing their lives, because they have prolonged the war.

Evans explained that he fully endorsed the nomination of Lincoln and Johnson. "I think them both honest and competent," he offered, adding that "both have earnestly labored to conquer the Rebellion without a view to self aggrandizement or elevation."[31]

Sam's cousin Jane wrote him on September 11, upbraiding him for forsaking the Democrats. "Cousin Sam, never did I think you would vote for old Abe," she charged, reminding him that in 1860 he had scorned Lincoln and called a townsman a "Negroamus" for voting Republican. "You may call me a Rebel secesh or butternut or copperhead or any thing you please, I am for peace," Jane proclaimed. "I am getting [tired] of this war. I want to see the end of it as soon as possible and that will never be as long as old Abe Lincoln is president." Jane associated Lincoln with radicalism. "If you was fighting for the old Union as it was I would be in for it. But such a union as some of you are trying to make it!" Jane was glad, she told Sam, that her brother Laban was too young to join the army. "I would a great deal rather see him die at home than go out and fight to free the negro and no telling but what he would be buried by the side of a Negro." She concluded the letter with a pledge: "I will never change my politics as long as I live. This thing turning from one side to the other, I don't believe in it."[32]

Sam was appalled by Jane's letter and vented to his father. "It is very insulting to me or any other Union soldier to have 'would be friends' to write such sentiments to them while they are striving to protect their homes, periling their lives, and enduring a great many hardships." Perhaps it would be a good thing for Jane "if she were sent South for a month or two with the more honorable of her proclivities." Three weeks later, in mid-October, Sam wrote a scathing rebuttal to Jane. "Your letter is very unladylike," he began. "I could scarcely have believed you guilty of so treasonable language." To Jane's "Union as it was" reference Sam responded, "Was when? . . . [When] large armies were raised in the South and march[ed] North to wrest the National Capitol from us?" To her invocation of party loyalty, he responded that good

Democrats such as Grant, Sherman, and Butler had always put the Union first and that Jeff Davis, Vallandingham, and their ilk had betrayed the party. To her scorning of black soldiers, Sam responded,

> It would be more honorable to be buried by the side of "a brave Negro" who fell fighting for the glorious old banner than to be buried by the side of some cowardly Cur [dog] (in human form) who died for fear he would be drafted and who had proved himself recreant to the Boon of Liberty consecrated by the Blood of our forefathers.[33]

When the election results came in, Sam and his father, Andrew, rejoiced. "'Abe & Andy!' Glory enough for one day," wrote Andrew. "There has been many a pretty dog killed for being caught in bad company, that's Mack's fix— he is worse beaten than the Rebs beat him in his attempt to take Richmond and he has made a worse retreat."[34]

In the Confederacy, Lincoln's victory was a sort of vindication for Davis and his hard-liners: it would make the scales fall from the eyes of Southerners who had naively held out hopes that the Yankees would treat with their foes. In a November 17, 1864, letter addressed to Georgia senators who sought to know the prospects of a negotiated peace, Davis described what he took to be the Yankees' peace terms: "We should submit to their yoke, acknowledge that we are criminals, and appeal to their mercy for pardon." The Confederate diarist Emma Holmes put it this way, with her acid pen: "The Presidential election took place several days ago, & there seems no doubt from the returns already received that the vulgar, uncouth animal is again chosen to desecrate the office once filled by Washington. . . . War there must be, until we 'conquer peace.'"[35]

Sherman's March

Even as Lincoln's election sank in, a new drama unfolded in Georgia, when Sherman's men began their famous March to the Sea on November 15, 1864. Sherman tasked the dependable George H. Thomas and an army of 50,000 men with following Hood's army into Tennessee to finish it off, while Sherman would lead an elite force, some 62,000 strong, east across the Georgia countryside, in four columns across a forty- to sixty-mile-wide front, foraging off the land and destroying or confiscating the rebel property they could not use. Thomas's army, coordinating with Major General John Schofield's Army of the Ohio, succeeded in thwarting Hood's putative invasion of Middle Tennessee. Hood launched failed attacks at Spring Hill and Franklin at the end of November. Franklin was a "toe-to-toe, suicidal slugfest," as historian Benjamin Franklin Cooling has put it, in which the Confederates sustained nearly 7,000 casualties and lost six generals. Schofield's army slipped away to join with Thomas's force in Union-occupied Nashville. Hood succumbed to devastating Federal assaults at Nashville in mid-December, his Army of Tennessee disintegrating in a swirl of confusion and demoralization.[36]

On Sherman's front, Union soldiers encountered very little opposition from Confederate forces during their march, reaching the state capital, Milledgeville, on November 23 and Savannah, on the sea, a month later. Savannah was evacuated by Confederate troops and surrendered into Union hands so that it would escape the fate of siege and bombardment that had befallen Atlanta. After a month-long break, Sherman's columns then veered left and northward into South Carolina, where they ratcheted up their level of destruction, as retribution against the heartland of secessionism. When they reached North Carolina in early March, Sherman urged his men to tone down the damage, in recognition of the stronger presence of Unionism there.[37]

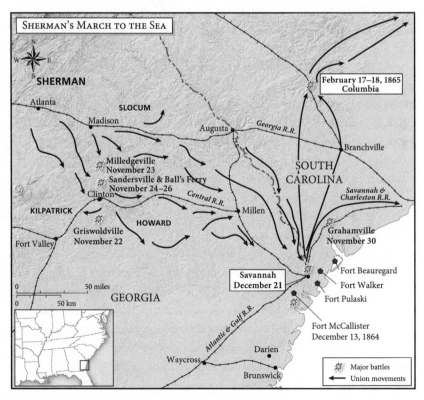

MAP 11.3

Over the course of the March to the Sea and the Carolinas campaign, military and economic resources were the Federals' principal targets—industrial and military property, foodstuffs, cotton and other crops, mills, and railroad tracks and depots, for example—but private property and domestic spaces were targeted, too, by design. Sherman instructed his soldiers that they should, as they meted out destruction, "discriminate between the rich, who are usually hostile, and the poor and industrious, usually neutral or friendly." Technically, only authorized details of foragers were supposed to seize resources for the army's use from civilians. These rules were observed in the breach, with bands of "Bummers" wreaking havoc in Southern households, carrying away not just provisions to supply the army but valuables and souvenirs for their own use. Historian Lisa Tendrich Frank has shown that such tactics were a premeditated form of gendered psychological warfare on Sherman's part, intended to "break the will of elite female Confederates" by invading their private domestic spaces—parlors, kitchens, bedrooms—and laying hands on articles such as clothes, quilts, and jewelry in symbolic acts of violation. Elite women openly defied the Yankee invaders in verbal and sometimes even physical altercations, knowing full well that such recalcitrance would likely stoke the Yankees' desire for vengeance. Sherman's tactics, Tendrich concludes, had the effect of reinvigorating elite women's Confederate patriotism. In Camden, South Carolina, for example, Emma Holmes confronted two of Sherman's men with her "bottled wrath" and a warning: "We would never be subdued, for if every man, woman & child were murdered, our blood would rise up and drive them away." "I taunted them with warring on women & children," Holmes wrote in her diary, and "laughed at their pretence of 'fighting for the old flag.'"[38]

Sherman's March is a tale of devastation and defiance, but also of the promises of deliverance. Sherman's strategy was based on his belief that he could "arouse the latent enmity" of Georgia to Jeff Davis—an enmity that Alexander Stephens, "a Union man at heart," represented better than anyone, as Sherman opined in a letter to Lincoln. This view was echoed in the Northern press. Even before Northerners had discerned Sherman's exact plan of operations, they felt they knew his purpose. A December 3, 1864, article in the *Chicago Tribune*, entitled "Sherman's March," asserted that "it is well known that Alex. H. Stephens . . . is Union at heart" and speculated that there were many other such men, especially businessmen in the major cities and towns, to whom Union victory would be "right welcome." "When Sherman shall have subdued the Secession element in Georgia we shall see these men come forward with songs of thanksgiving for their deliverance," the paper predicted. The wildly popular Union anthem "Marching Through Georgia," penned by the influential songwriter Henry Clay Work and published in February 1865, featured lyrics sung in the voice of Sherman's soldiers, who rejoice in bringing the jubilee to enslaved blacks and to Southern whites: "Yes, and there were Union men who wept with joyful tears, when they saw the honored flag they had not seen for years," runs the song's fourth verse.[39]

Savannah proved to be a test case for this theory. The city's mayor and leading citizens not only submitted without resistance to the Union but also publicly pledged that, "laying aside all difference and burying by-gones in the grave of the past, we will use our best endeavors to bring back the prosperity and commerce we once enjoyed." Sherman in turn supported a relief program to feed the poverty-stricken residents of the city, many of them refugees; he made available to the city council confiscated rice, which it could trade with Northern cities such as Boston and New York for foodstuffs and other provisions. "I will take infinitely more delight in curing the wounds made by war, than in inflicting them," Sherman wrote from Savannah to the Southern Unionist Caroline Petigru Carson in New York. These developments gave rise to breathless reports in the Northern press that a "strong Union sentiment" was "winning its way among the citizens," who were "availing themselves of the President's Amnesty Proclamation" and attesting their "fealty to the old flag," as the *New York Times* put it. "The 'undying Southern hate' for Yankees, which rebel papers love to prate about, is a ferocious delusion." New Yorkers and Bostonians were so moved at the thought of helping the suffering poor women and children of Savannah that they determined to do so as a matter of charity, not commerce, sending donations without taking rice in return. Northern charity represented Southern "deliverance from the irresponsible power of the Rebel Government."[40]

But when Union ships eventually steamed into Savannah harbor bearing the promised provisions, elite residents of Savannah, including those who stood in the relief line to receive rations, gave voice to bitter resentment against the Yankees for doling out condescension and hypocrisy along with supplies. "They think they are so liberal, giving us food," wrote one woman, adding that "they stole more from one plantation" than all of New York now offered as charity. The Confederate press excoriated Savannah's mayor, Richard D. Arnold, for submitting to the Yankees, and wrote off his "traitorous and weak kneed" allies as Northern transplants and foreigners who did not represent the "real sentiments of the Southern people." As for Sherman, he was "playing a new game," the *Richmond Daily Dispatch* insisted, "to blind the people" with seeming mildness and conciliation. Southerners would soon find, the paper predicted, that his "savage instincts" had not changed.[41]

Sherman in Savannah. "I beg to present you, as a Christmas gift, the city of Savannah," Sherman wrote Lincoln on December 22, 1864. Here Sherman reviews his army in Savannah before starting on his Carolinas campaign. (Library of Congress LC-USZ62-161)

The Confederate press felt vindicated in such an assessment when Sherman's troops hit South Carolina, cutting through the heart of the state toward its capital city, Columbia, and leaving much of it in ashes. While modern scholarship has established that Confederates, torching cotton warehouses as they evacuated Columbia, were the ones who started the series of fires that destroyed roughly a third of the city's structures, Confederates at the time attributed the disaster to the "terrible diabolism" of the Yankee invaders. "The horrors that attended the destruction of Atlanta were ten times repeated at Columbia," an Augusta, Georgia, paper charged, acknowledging the Yankees' special animus against the Palmetto State. Although Sherman had cautioned his men to treat North Carolinians with fairness, Confederate civilians who lay in his path felt as though a storm had swept over them, as a letter in a Raleigh newspaper explained. "After destroying everything we had, and taking from us every morsel of food," the female correspondent wrote, "one of these barbarians had to add insult to injury, by asking me 'what you (I) would live upon now.'" The woman replied, "Upon patriotism . . . you and your blood-handed countrymen may make the whole of this beautiful land one vast graveyard, but its people will never be subjugated."[42]

Special Field Order No. 15

When it came to the liberation of slaves, Sherman was at best a grudging deliverer. Slaves in Georgia flocked to his lines during the Atlanta campaign and March to the Sea; as many as 20,000 black refugees trailed his army. They provided vital aid as sources of military intelligence, guides to the terrain, foragers, and menial laborers. In keeping with his view that blacks were not fit as combat troops, Sherman "stubbornly resisted attempts by Halleck, Grant, and even Lincoln to permit black recruitment along his line of march through Georgia," historian Bruce Levine has observed. Evidence abounds that anti-black Union soldiers in Sherman's ranks were capable of terrible cruelty to these refugees. Some soldiers destroyed or looted what little slaves had by way of material possessions. While Sherman's hard war tactics did not sanction the rape of white women, black women were frequently targets of sexual assault by Federal soldiers. The most galling incident of Federal callousness took place at Ebenezer Creek in early December 1864, when a Union brigadier general's decision to remove a pontoon bridge his troops had just used to cross the icy river left thousands of refugees (mostly old men, women, and children) still on its other side, trapped and at the mercy of the Confederate cavalry raiders that had been pursuing the army; some of the refugees drowned trying to escape, while others were shot by the Confederates or captured and reenslaved. Some of the Union soldiers who watched this tragedy unfold were horrified, and their outraged reports inspired Secretary of War Stanton to travel to Savannah to look into Sherman's treatment of the freedpeople.[43]

Stanton asked Sherman to meet with local African American leaders to hear their views on the transition to freedom. On January 12, 1865, at Sherman's Savannah headquarters, a remarkable three-hour "interview" took place between Sherman, Stanton, and twenty black ministers and church officers, ranging in age from twenty-six to seventy-two and led by Garrison Frazier, a Baptist minister. They were asked about the war's causes and object, and Frazier, as their spokesman, offered this cogent overview of the Union's evolving war aims:

> The object of the war was not at first to give the slaves their freedom, but the sole object of the war was at first to bring the rebellious States back into the Union and their loyalty to the laws of the United States. Afterward, knowing the value set on the slaves by the rebels, the President thought that his proclamation would stimulate them to lay

down their arms, reduce them to obedience, and help to bring back the
Rebel States; and their not doing so has now made the freedom of the
slaves a part of the war.

Asked about "the feeling of the colored people in regard to Gen. Sherman,"
Frazier answered diplomatically, "We looked upon Gen. Sherman prior to his
arrival as a man in the Providence of God specially set apart to accomplish
this work. . . . We have confidence in Gen. Sherman, and think that what
concerns us could not be under better hands." Asked to "state in what manner
you think you can take care of yourselves," Frazier answered, "The way we can
best take care of ourselves is to have land, and turn it and till it by our own
labor. . . . We want to be placed on land until we are able to buy it and make
it our own."[44]

In response to this meeting, Sherman issued, on January 16, 1865,
Special Field Order No. 15, which "set apart for the settlement of the
negroes now made free by the acts of war and the proclamation of the
President" abandoned rice and cotton land in coastal South Carolina and
Georgia (reaching thirty miles inland); the settlements would be divided
by Union officers into forty-acre plots, and "sole and exclusive management of affairs" in this designated region was to be "left to the freed people
themselves, subject only to the United States military authority and the
acts of Congress." Field Order No. 15 made it possible, by the war's end,
for roughly 20,000 freedpeople to settle and possess 100,000 acres of this
land.[45]

How is it that Sherman, an unabashed racist, released the most radically
egalitarian field order of the war? Some scholars see the order as Stanton's
work, while others note that Sherman "aimed primarily to relieve his army
of the burden of caring for thousands of black refugees, not to frame a social revolution," as Eric Foner has argued. Crucially, the order did not guarantee that the grants of "Sherman land" would be permanent, and President
Andrew Johnson would revoke the freedpeople's titles to that land in the
summer of 1867. But it is important to remember that in the winter of
1864–65, both Sherman's meeting with the Savannah delegation and his
subsequent policy seemed to have great import. Accounts of the meeting
were printed in the *New York Tribune* and then in other newspapers. The
African American press took pride in the "clear, calm, succinct, statesman-
like manner" in which the delegates had made their case to Sherman and
Stanton, while James Lynch, one of the delegates, wrote to the *Christian
Recorder*, "We all went away from Gen. Sherman's headquarters that night,

blessing the Government, Mr. Secretary Stanton, and General Sherman. Our hearts were buoyant with hope and thankfulness."[46]

Nearly five hundred miles away in Virginia, on the Richmond siege front, Thomas B. Webster and his U.S. Colored Troops regiment rejoiced in the winter of 1865 in the progress of Sherman's March. "What are the enemy fighting for?" he asked in a letter to the *Christian Recorder*. "The rebels see that their cause is hopeless; but their wicked hearts will not let them acknowledge their defeat." "They have been offered peace or war; but they preferred war, and now they have it," Webster intoned, sounding very much like Sherman himself. Webster was confident that deliverance was at hand: "They will have to succumb shortly, or, like Pharaoh, be overthrown."[47]

12

Malice Toward None

THE UNION TRIUMPHANT

"IT WILL BE impossible for me to send sufficient troops from this army to oppose Sherman's and at the same time resist Grant," Robert E. Lee wrote Confederate congressman William Porcher Miles of South Carolina on January 19, 1865, in response to requests that Lee's men rally to the defense of Charleston. "If the people in South Carolina & Georgia would turn out in all their strength," Lee advised, "the advance of Sherman ought to be checked." A month later, Charleston fell at last to Federal forces, in the culmination of siege operations on its harbor defense that dated back to July 1863. Calling the city's surrender the "knell to the Southern ear," the *New York Times* editorialized:

> On the Southern masses, easily affected by auguries and events, the capture of the secession cradle will fall with a tremendous moral power. The front banner, ever flaunting in the van of their desperate warfare, has gone down. . . . Every ignorant, "poor white," will understand this. The lying press will no longer deceive them with stories of victories over the "cowardly Yankees." All that large class who desire to save what they can from the general wreck, will leave the falling cause.

The *Times* speculated that the fall of Charleston would embolden loyal North Carolinians to welcome Sherman's army and to set up a new loyal government in that state. Its rival paper, the *New York Herald,* took a similar tack, noting with satisfaction that the Union Provost Marshal Office established in Charleston was "besieged by citizens desirous of taking the oath of allegiance to the national government."[1]

Such reports were utterly at odds with accounts in the Confederate press. The *Richmond Dispatch*, for example, saw the fall of Charleston as a hollow victory. Confederates had evacuated the city, taking with them their precious cotton, the paper reported, and leaving it a hollow shell; the only whites left there to welcome the Union army were men of "Northern birth." Indeed, the *Dispatch* urged that the evacuation of Charleston should "rather inspire cheerfulness than gloom," as it freed up troops to join Joseph Johnston in defending North Carolina against Sherman's advancing force. In a February 22, 1865, article entitled "Spirit of Our Soldiers," the *Dispatch* depicted Lee's army as unbroken and indeed defiant in spirit. The article reprinted resolutions passed in the Petersburg trenches by the 32nd Virginia Infantry. They read, "Whereas, the enemy is still invading our soil with the original purpose of our subjugation or annihilation; therefore . . . [We] accept the issue, and are determined to resist until our independence shall have been acknowledged or extermination reached." "We are determined to follow wherever Jeff. Davis directs or General Lee leads," they pledged.[2]

At no time was the propaganda war over the disposition of the Southern masses more intense than in the final months of fighting. Confederate defeat offered the ultimate test of the deluded-masses theory of the rebellion, as well as which vision of deliverance would prevail.

The Richmond-Petersburg Front

Lee's decision not to send men to reinforce Charleston's defenses reflected his view that his undermanned and poorly provisioned army could not long keep Grant's Virginia siege force at bay. In the summer of 1864, trench warfare, in which "Lee's Miserables" endured constant sharpshooting and shelling, blistering heat and drought, and short rations, had taken its toll on his army, with desertions spiking in August amidst complaints about poor pay and scanty supplies. In three months of fighting after the July 30 bloodbath at the Crater, Grant launched a series of offensives aimed at capturing the railroads that supplied Petersburg from the south and at hooking the southernmost part of his own line around Lee's rightmost flank; at the same time, Grant extended his lines to the north and probed at Richmond, above the James River, largely to draw Lee's attention and his troops away from the defense of Petersburg's railroads—and also to prevent him from sending troops to aid Early against Sheridan in the Valley. In late August, on the south end of the siege line, Grant succeeded in seizing the Weldon Railroad, leaving Confederates to rely on the South Side Railroad, which entered Petersburg along the Appomattox River, to the west. Meanwhile, the Federal attacks at Deep Bottom above the James, while they failed to break the Confederate defenses of Richmond, inflicted casualties Lee could not afford.[3]

Confederates seemed briefly to regain the momentum with their victory at Reams Station on August 25, where they drove off Federals who were busy destroying the Weldon Railroad, twelve miles south of Petersburg, and with Confederate general Wade Hampton's mid-September "Beefsteak Raid" of a Union supply corral in northern Virginia, which brought desperately needed rations to Lee's men. But Grant resumed the offensive in late September, as Ben Butler's army attacked the Confederate works at New Market Heights (with U.S. Colored Troops units playing a pivotal role) and then captured Fort Harrison, above the James. "In the attack on Fort Harrison," historian Joe Glatthaar has noted, "there were so few Confederate defenders that they stood ten feet apart." Meanwhile, Federals breached the Confederate outer defenses at Poplar Spring Church, south of Petersburg. In late October, Grant again launched coordinated assaults on Confederate lines both north and south of the James, with the Confederates successfully fighting on the defensive and clinging to their last tenuous transportation links, but further depleting their ranks. As the two armies went into winter quarters, Lee feared his army would be starved into submission. He put the situation tersely to Confederate secretary of war James Seddon in January: "There is nothing within reach of this army to be impressed. The country is swept clear. Our only reliance is upon the railroads."[4]

Meanwhile, the Union was flexing its logistical muscles: since June 1864, City Point, Virginia, Grant's headquarters and primary supply base for military operations against Petersburg (which lay eight miles away), had been transformed from a modest hamlet into one of the world's busiest ports. The once sleepy village was quickly studded with wharves and warehouses, hospitals and barracks, railroad lines, engine houses and locomotives, water tanks and repair shops. On an average day 1,000 barges, 75 sail vessels, and 40 steamboats plied the waters of the James, bringing supplies from the North to the port; mail service and passenger service to Washington, D.C., was available daily. The Union's railroad construction corps built up and extended the rail line so that supplies could be whisked to the army in the trenches: 25 locomotives and 275 railroad cars were shipped in by barge. The army stored 9 million meals at City Point on an average day; the camp bakery daily produced 100,000 rations of bread. City Point had 110 hospital buildings; the sprawling Depot Field Hospital, covering some 200 acres, treated as many as 10,000 wounded soldiers a day.[5]

City Point not only supported the troops at the front but also symbolized the Union army's logistical, technological, and industrial might and its ability to transform the Southern countryside. A construction corps of 2,000 to 3,000 men worked alongside more than 1,000 carpenters, blacksmiths, teamsters, wheelwrights, clerks, and laborers to build, maintain, and extend its vast facilities. Hundreds of hospital workers staffed the seven hospitals at City Point and earned the Depot Field Hospital a reputation as the finest such facility in the land; consisting of twelve hundred tents and ninety log barracks, the Depot was described by Lieutenant Colonel Theodore Lyman of Meade's staff as a "huge canvas town." The workers toiling there included the indefatigable New Jersey Quaker Cornelia Hancock. On June 29, 1864, she wrote her mother that she had 180 patients to look after. "I work all day long and at night fall right down and sleep," she confessed, adding, "The cannonading is perfectly deafening even at this distance" from the Petersburg front. It is "sickening when you know what a scene it must bring to us," she wrote of the artillery barrage.[6]

Hundreds of African American refugees acted as laborers, cooks, laundresses, nurses, and scouts for the Federal forces. City Point was also a magnet for Northern civilians, including U.S. Sanitary Commission agents bringing supplies to the troops and teachers who offered instruction to the freedpeople and to the USCT soldiers in the camp. U.S. Christian Commission agents saw City Point as a field for missionary work; they erected prayer tents and kept the camp abuzz with religious revivals.[7] City Point was a transit point for a great throng of Confederates as well as Unionists. Hundreds of prisoners of war were brought there in flags-of-truce boats for exchange; scores of civilian refugees arrived from Richmond and Petersburg; and hundreds of deserters slipped free of the rebel army, "fast leaving the sinking ship," as a *New York Times* article put it in March 1865. Deserters were often driven by hunger: they could not but contrast the dire conditions in besieged Petersburg with the abundant resources flowing into Union lines. The price for provisions was loyalty: only those deserters who took an oath of allegiance to the Union were issued rations and granted passage on government steamers to points north.[8]

Confederate desertions were folded into the Union narrative of deliverance. "We have the pleasure of greeting many of the prodigal sons of Father Abraham, who, having repented, are returning honorably to worship at the shrine of their former devotion," Thomas Morris Chester, the free black newspaper correspondent embedded with the Army of the James, wrote of rebel deserters in the fall of 1864. The deserters told Chester that more Confederates would flee but for their fear that they would be treated harshly once behind Union lines. "The light, it is to be hoped, will soon dawn upon their darkened minds," Chester noted, so that they could "accept the proffered mercy of General Grant before it is too late." As the siege ground on, Chester's dispatches from the Virginia siege lines to the *Philadelphia Press* repeatedly held up deserters as windows into Southern morale, emphasizing the "demoralization of the enemy on account of his scarcity of provisions" and the growing "peace feeling" manifested by the starving civilians of Richmond. By March 1865 Chester had come to believe, based on the "large number who daily come into our lines," that the Southern rank and file were "disgusted with the rebel authorities for continuing a struggle in which no one has the slightest prospect of success." Chester concluded from deserter reports that the war was "continued merely to save those most guilty from the impending penalties" and that the officer class was plotting its escape into Texas and then Mexico and would "leave their deluded followers to their fate."[9]

John W. Haley's extensive journal entries on the Petersburg siege reveal how his belief in the deluded-masses theory wavered at times of vulnerability only to snap back into place when the Union had the upper hand. In mid-October 1864, an incident in which a rebel picket shot a Union soldier going to the rear for water brought forth a torrent of condemnation from Haley. "I have many times tried to cover these acts with the mantle of charity in the belief that the privates in the Rebel army are not as venomous as the higher grade of Rebel, and that in many cases they are simply the tools of those in authority. But it won't go down. No one *compels* them to attempt to scatter our brains around." Five weeks later, on November 23, thankful for Lincoln's reelection and attuned to signs that the coming winter would take a hard toll on the Confederates, Haley observed that thirteen deserters had come to Union lines seeking food and shelter from the cold. "Under ordinary circumstances I would despise men who desert their cause . . . but when men know, as these do, that their cause is hopeless and that all their sacrifices are thrown away, it then becomes both right and sensible to desert." Haley added contemptuously, "Not one in ten of the Rebel army can tell what all this mess is about." He was as convinced as ever that "Southern leaders [had] dragged the low-bred whites into the war."[10]

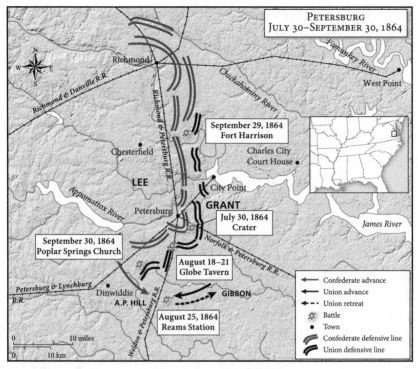

MAP 12.1

The Richmond Underground

In addition to its logistical advantages, the Union capitalized in the war's last year on its superior military intelligence operations. Beginning in the winter of 1863, spymaster Elizabeth Van Lew and her fellow Richmond Unionists were formally enlisted into the Federal secret service by Union general Benjamin F. Butler. During Grant's siege of Richmond and Petersburg, Van Lew's intrepid couriers kept up regular communications with City Point via five stations positioned along the treacherous stretch from the rebel capital to the Union headquarters. Theirs was a resourceful if primitive tradecraft: posing as ordinary civilians selling farm produce, they hid letters, maps, and plans, written in invisible ink and a crude cipher, in the hollowed-out soles of their shoes and in dummy eggshells hidden among real eggs. Intelligence reports provided by this network had immediate tactical applications. As Grant struck blows at Lee's trench line, the Richmond underground furnished Grant with key insights about the movement of men and matériel in the vicinity of Richmond, about the strength of the picket

posts and fortified lines that girded the rebel capital, and about the movement of Confederate reinforcements back and forth between Lee's army in
the east and Early's army in the west.[11]

Van Lew and her fellow Unionists knew that Grant relied on them not only
for military intelligence but also for assessments of the political atmosphere
and of living conditions in the besieged capital. Taken together, Unionists'
reports from the last year of the war provide a picture of increasing desolation in the rebel capital—business suspended, rampant inflation, old men
and boys being herded into the army, public bitterness at the fall of Atlanta
to Sherman and at Lincoln's reelection, and constant rumors that Richmond
was to be evacuated. The most cogent summary of Van Lew's significance to
the Union war effort comes from the pen of George Sharpe, Union chief of
military intelligence for the Army of the Potomac. He wrote in a postwar
letter that "for a long, long time, she represented all that was left of the power
of the U.S. government in the city of Richmond."[12]

Van Lew escaped detection for her spy work in part because Confederate
authorities simply could not imagine that a woman was so skilled a spymaster. She had one very close call: in September 1864, acting on a tip, the
Confederate authorities launched a formal investigation of Van Lew, gathering incriminating testimony about her Unionism from her estranged
sister-in-law. But they concluded that Van Lew was nothing but a harmless woman: though she was "very unfriendly in her sentiments towards the
Govt." and "like most of her sex . . . [had] talked freely," Van Lew had not
actually "done anything" disloyal. No action was taken against her. The doctrine of female accountability had gained ground during the war but had
not fully displaced older ideas of female political impotence. The sexism of
the men whose job it was to root out disloyalty disinclined them to believe
that a frail spinster "lady" could be capable of politically significant acts of
disloyalty.[13]

Confederate Emancipation

As Grant's siege took its toll, a controversial proposal for solving the
Confederacy's manpower problem took center stage in Confederate politics: the idea of enlisting slaves in the Southern army and offering them
freedom as a reward. The idea was first pushed forcefully in the winter of
1863–64 by General Patrick R. Cleburne after the reverses at Chattanooga.
Confederates faced a stark dilemma and must make a bold choice, he
explained: "Between the loss of independence and the loss of slavery, we

assume that every patriot will freely give up the latter—give up the negro slave rather than be a slave himself." As historian Bruce Levine notes, it was not until the fall of 1864 that the idea gained traction. Reeling from Sherman's and Sheridan's victories and Lincoln's reelection, Jefferson Davis, who had scorned the idea of black enlistment, now "abruptly reversed course" and endorsed bringing slaves into the army. By this point Confederates had only a quarter as many soldiers available to them as the Union had; how else could the South close this gap?[14]

A heated and prolonged public debate ensued, with opponents of black enlistment arguing that it would offend and alienate the Confederate rank and file, undermine agricultural production, encroach on property rights, raise the specter of race war if armed blacks turned against their former masters, and, most importantly, undermine slavery, the very institution Confederates fought to defend. Defenders of black enlistment, Robert E. Lee prominent among them, argued that it would preserve what was left of plantation slavery. "Their plan would not emancipate and arm *all* of the South's slaves but only a relatively small proportion of them," Levine observes. "These black soldiers would then, by salvaging the Confederate military effort, secure Confederate independence—and, in the bargain, secure the continuing enslavement of all the rest." Crucially, advocates of such measures noted that the freedom granted to recruits would be something less than full freedom—only white men would have political rights, and they could continue to "make laws to control the free negro," as Dr. John Henry Stringfellow put it; blacks would be relegated to a perpetual serfdom, as a subordinate laboring class, akin to slaves. Such rhetoric carefully steered clear of any references to the deliverance or liberation of slaves, choosing instead much more circumscribed language. Lee, for example, in his own recommendations, spoke of "employing" the slaves, tapping their "long habits of obedience and subordination" in an effort to "secure their fidelity" and "faithful service."[15]

In the end, those favoring black enlistment won a hollow victory in the form of a tepid congressional bill, passed in March 1865, that invited slave owners to volunteer their slaves for service (while retaining legal title to them) and slaves to volunteer on the shaky promise of a conditional, limited freedom. Davis "remained unwilling to impose manumission on a single master." Not surprisingly, masters and slaves alike were uninterested in heeding this call, and the measure produced negligible results. It succeeded only in signaling that the Confederate government was spiraling into desperation.[16]

The Thirteenth Amendment

Meanwhile, the Republican Party's proposed Thirteenth Amendment to the U.S. Constitution, abolishing slavery, entered its final phase of debate in the wake of Lincoln's reelection and finally passed in the House of Representatives on January 31, 1865, by a vote of 119 to 56. The principal champion of the amendment, the Radical Republican Ohio congressman James M. Ashley, had begun pushing for it in December 1863, and the measure passed the Republican-dominated Senate by a vote of 38 to 6 in April 1864. Its success hinged in part on the fact that its wording avoided the difficult issue of whether freed blacks would gain full legal equality. It sounded the death knell of slavery without heralding civil rights: "Neither slavery nor involuntary servitude, except as a punishment for crime whereof the party shall have been duly convicted, shall exist within the United States." Lincoln, focused on promoting state-based antislavery amendments in the border states, finally lent his public support to the federal amendment in June 1864, only to see the measure founder in the House of Representatives that month, in a vote along party lines, with Republicans voting in favor of the amendment and Democrats against it; the Republicans fell 13 votes short of the requisite two-thirds majority. The Republican party included support for the amendment as a platform plank in the 1864 election, but the amendment garnered little attention in Lincoln's campaign. As Michael Vorenberg has explained, "Much more than a popular decision for emancipation, the vote of 1864 was a call for the return of stability under the Union."[17]

And yet Republicans chose, in the wake of the election, to treat Lincoln's victory as a referendum on the constitutional amendment—and Lincoln took the same tack, asking the lame-duck Thirty-eighth Congress, which had already rejected the measure, to defer to the electoral verdict and pass it, before the incoming Thirty-ninth Congress (which boasted a strong antislavery majority) had the chance to steal their thunder. In Lincoln's view, if he could win over key votes among border state and Democratic representatives, he could consolidate support for the Union party that had carried the election and chart for it a bright future. He could also neutralize the Democratic argument that his own emancipation policy was an obstacle to peace by claiming that the amendment's fate lay in the hands of the states during the ratification stage. Moreover, the fact that three-fourths of the states had to ratify the amendment for it to become law meant that at least two formerly Confederate states had to offer their support—thus the states reconstructed according to Lincoln's Ten Percent Plan would be key, and Congress would have an incentive to recognize their legitimacy.[18]

While Ashley, Lincoln, Secretary of State Seward, and a group of lobbyists including the wily Tennessee lawyer William N. Bilbo (a Confederate turned Unionist) worked to "entice a key bloc of the amendment's former opponents—border state Unionists and Democrats—either to switch their stance or to absent themselves from the key vote," the House of Representatives plunged into debates over the bill. Democrats opposed to the amendment marshaled familiar anti-abolition arguments—that the measure was an unconstitutional infringement on states' rights and an emblem of the Republicans' desire to subjugate the South; that the Republicans' insistence on abolition was the root cause of the war and the only real obstacle to peaceable reunion; that slavery was a suitable and even benign condition for blacks (Ohio Democrat George Bliss opined that emancipation had victimized the slaves, many of whom were "now sighing for the happy homes from which they have been seduced"). Some Democrats also argued that the progress of emancipation in the border states—Maryland had already abolished slavery and Missouri would do so during these debates—precluded the need for a federal constitutional amendment.[19]

But the amendment's supporters brought to bear an arsenal of powerful counterarguments. Ashley led the way, defending the constitutionality of the measure (stressing the sovereignty of the national government), the "great advantage of free over slave labor," and the "wishes and judgment" of soldiers in the field, who had voted overwhelmingly for Lincoln and his agenda. If Congress should pass the amendment, he claimed, "a shout will go up from our brave men in front of Richmond, at Savannah, and all along the Union lines and throughout the entire country, such as never before arose from the heats and lips of the men on the passage of any act by the American Congress."[20]

Images of Southern deliverance were central to the case for the amendment. Republican Glenni W. Scofield of Pennsylvania responded with indignation to the Democratic charge that Republicans aimed at Southern subjugation: "Subjugate the South! No, sir; it is the purpose as it is the duty of the Government to liberate the South, to drive out the usurpers, and to restore to the deluded and betrayed masses the blessings of a free Republic." The government, he reiterated, was "not vindictive" but instead would "constantly tender to the deluded masses pardon and protection." Congressman Thomas T. Davis of New York struck a similar note, blaming the "demands of the slave power" for the war and pledging that he had "no feeling of bitterness toward the misguided and deluded people of the South," but sought only to end an institution that had "shed too much of innocent blood."[21]

Democrats who supported the amendment offered a different set of rationales, noting, as Representative Alexander H. Coffroth of Pennsylvania

"Freedom for All, Both Black and White!" This broadside, issued in 1865, illustrates the argument that emancipation would uplift the South's poor whites as well as liberating blacks from the horrors of slavery. On one side, representing the future, a public school welcomes Southerners under the banner "Education to All Classes," while on the other, representing the past, an overseer brutally whips a female slave. (Library of Congress, The Alfred Whital Stern Collection of Lincolniana)

did, that the issue of slavery had "breathed into existence" abolition fanaticism and that the death of slavery would mark the death of abolitionism and the revival of Democratic dominance. In his view, the fact that the people of Maryland and Missouri rejected slavery of their own accord was a sign that emancipation could no longer be objected to on the grounds that it would alienate key allies and potential converts to the Union cause. Border state men made their own case. Like moderate Republicans and War Democrats, they disavowed any belief in racial equality or affinity for the radical abolitionism and instead cast the amendment as "the real conservative measure," to quote Kentucky's George Helm Yeaman. Emancipation, Yeaman claimed, echoing Coffroth, would rob both the secessionists and the abolitionists of their power by neutralizing the issue they had exploited. The war had killed slavery, and what remained was to "remove the rubbish" of the institution. The fact that even the Confederates were now considering emancipation, Yeaman noted, was proof that it was "high time for conservative men here to cease halting and doubting upon the subject."[22]

In the end, Democratic and border state votes proved crucial to the amendment's success, with eleven representatives who had opposed it in June flipping their votes, including Coffroth and Yeaman. Upon the announcement of the final tally in the House, the *New York Tribune* reported, "the tumult of joy that broke out was vast, thundering, and uncontrollable. Representatives and Auditors on the floor, soldiers and spectators in the gallery, Senators and Supreme Court Judges, women and pages, gave way to the excitement of the most august and important event in American Legislation and American History since the Declaration of Independence."[23]

The ratification process would take nearly a year and bring the Republicans some disappointment on the way toward their final triumph. Delaware, Kentucky, and New Jersey would reject the amendment. But the border states of Maryland and Missouri and the reconstructed governments of Louisiana, Tennessee, and Arkansas (along with the Pierpont government in Virginia) would accept it, vindicating Lincoln in his belief that amnesty and emancipation could march hand in hand. Indeed, the Thirteenth Amendment's passage vindicated Lincoln's state-based work on behalf of emancipation. "Discussions in states such as Maryland and Missouri about amending their constitutions to end slavery," historian Christian G. Samito observes, "helped make more favorable the climate for proposing a national amendment to make the United States fully free."[24]

SCENE IN THE HOUSE ON THE PASSAGE OF THE PROPOSITION TO AMEND THE CONSTITUTION, JANUARY 31, 1865.

The Thirteenth Amendment. The scene in the House of Representatives on the passage of the Thirteenth Amendment. *Harper's Weekly* observed, "Slavery in a Union like ours has been, and always must be, the root of civil war. Congress, therefore, recommends the constitutional abolition of Slavery, and the country cries Amen!" (Library of Congress LC-USZ62-127599)

Lincoln's Second Inaugural

Given his twin victories at the ballot box and in Congress, Lincoln was entitled to strike a triumphal pose during his second inauguration. But he refrained from doing so. Modern scholars regard Lincoln's March 4, 1865, Second Inaugural Address as a window into his political and spiritual growth. He invoked providence, in stronger terms than he had ever done before, in order to place the war effort on a moral plane that transcended electoral politics. He cast disunion as the chastisement and purification not just of the South but of the whole sin-soaked and guilt-ridden nation. In this formulation, Allen Guelzo reminds us, providence was mysterious, something human beings could scarcely comprehend. Seeking a way to explain that the war "might have a purpose beyond the restoration of a perpetual Union," Lincoln intoned that "the Almighty has His own purposes":

> If we shall suppose that American Slavery is one of those offences which, in the providence of God, must needs come, but which, having continued through His appointed time, He now wills to remove, and that He gives to both North and South, this terrible war, as the woe due to those by whom the offence came, shall we discern therein any departure from those divine attributes which the believers in a Living God always ascribe to him? Fondly do we hope—fervently do we pray—that this mighty scourge of war may speedily pass away. Yet, if God wills that it continue until all the wealth piled by the bondsman's two hundred and fifty years of unrequited toil shall be sunk, and until every drop of blood drawn with the lash, shall be paid by another drawn with the sword, as was said three thousand years ago, so still it must be said "the judgments of the Lord are true and righteous altogether."[25]

It has been observed that this rhetoric is so much like that of the pioneering abolitionists of the antebellum era—David Walker, William Lloyd Garrison, Frederick Douglass, and even John Brown—that the Second Inaugural marks a moment when Lincoln's inner abolitionist comes out. But the speech can also be read as evidence of continuity: of Lincoln's persistent determination to refute the charge that Republicans desired war as the instrument of their own political triumph. In that light, Lincoln offered on March 4, 1865, a rebuke to critics who had accused him of radical abolitionism. His speech makes no mention of and gives no credit whatsoever to the antislavery movement, nor does it acknowledge the agency of the slaves themselves. As Douglas Wilson puts it, "For a speech addressed to an audience comprised of one of the warring parties, this is astonishingly even handed, and of course intentionally so.... [T]he duration of the war had proved that great suffering on both sides was part of God's plan." In rejecting triumphalism and moral certainty to emphasize the inscrutability of providence, Guelzo notes, Lincoln offered "an appeal against the Radicals, and anyone else so full of themselves as to think both the questions and answers obvious."[26]

Malice Toward None. A jubilant crowd gathered on March 4, 1865, to hear Lincoln de-liver his Second Inaugural Address, on the eastern portico of the Capitol. The crowd in-cluded USCT soldiers who marched in Lincoln's Inaugural Parade. The day was foggy and wet, but witnesses attest that the sun broke through the clouds the moment Lincoln began to speak. (Library of Congress LC-USA7-16837)

Although it is now widely seen as one of the finest examples ever of pres-idential oratory, Lincoln's speech received mixed reviews in its own day. Northern moderates lauded its commitment to reconciliation. "The words with which the address closes should be engraven on every heart," declared the *Cleveland Daily Leader*, quoting Lincoln's final pledge:

> With malice toward none, with charity for all, with firmness in the right as God gives us to see the right, let us strive on to finish the work we are in, to bind up the nation's wounds, to care for him who shall have borne the battle and for his widow and his orphan, to do all which may achieve and cherish a just and lasting peace among ourselves and with all nations.

Hailing these sentiments, and the "simple and earnest manner" in which the speech was delivered, an Iowa newspaper hoped "that the sunlight of truth is about to shine upon the people of this nation, and cause them to see eye to eye, while the star of Peace shall arise to guide them in the way of reconciliation." There was not the "slightest trace or egotism or of boasting" in the address, the *Pittsburgh Gazette* marveled, noting that Lincoln stood ready "with open arms to welcome back to duty and allegiance all who come."[27]

The abolitionist press praised the speech's "noble simplicity and directness" but also chided Lincoln for not going far enough in acknowledging "the nation's debt to the freedmen, and the duty of prompt discharge of it," as the *Liberator* put it; the freedmen were owed "every kind of help, national and individual." But at the other end of the political spectrum, Democrats hostile to Lincoln found nothing whatsoever to like in the speech. A Milwaukee paper declared it a "profane and incoherent homily," and a Detroit one found it "more worthy of a puritanical hypocrite, than of an American Executive"; not to be outdone, the *Cincinnati Enquirer* dubbed the Second Inaugural "the most blasphemous document that has ever emanated from a public man in America." Lincoln's Democratic critics rejected both his antislavery reading of American history—"God permitted slavery," the *Brooklyn Eagle* insisted, "that through it the negro might be rescued from barbarism"—and rejected, too, Lincoln's profession of "malice toward none." "The political friends of Mr. Lincoln profess to see the evidence of some progress during the last four years in the work of restoring the Union," the *Daily Milwaukee News* noted, reflecting on the course of war since Lincoln's First Inaugural. "In confirmation of their view they point us to conquered cities and to a quantity of desolate and almost depopulated southern territory. Is this Union?" Democrats kept up the pressure on Republicans, in other words, to disavow subjugation and an agenda of radical change.[28]

The Fall of Richmond

On March 25, 1865, Lee made one last attempt to break Grant's siege line, with a predawn attack on Fort Stedman, near Petersburg. The assault was a bloody and heartbreaking failure for the Confederates. With death and desertion eating away at the tattered remnants of Lee's army, public anxiety in Richmond crested and measures were taken to prepare for the evacuation of its inhabitants. The hammer soon fell: in the wake of the Fort Stedman fiasco, Grant counterpunched with a forceful blow at Lee's right flank. Grant intended this action to cut the last functioning railroad out of Petersburg and to prevent Lee's army from escaping to the west. On April 1, Federal soldiers smashed the Confederate-entrenched position at Five Forks, which

Lee had ordered General Pickett to hold "at all hazards." Despite spirited Confederate resistance, the line gave way, and by nightfall Five Forks was in Union hands. This final major clash of the long siege was the beginning of the end of the Confederacy. On the night of April 1–2, Grant unleashed an artillery bombardment, hammering Lee's position from the Appomattox River to Five Forks with the heaviest barrage of the entire war, shaking the very ground beneath the rebel capital. The morning of Sunday, April 2 brought a massive Federal attack that encircled Petersburg and forced Lee to recommend to the War Department that both Petersburg and Richmond be abandoned. Jefferson Davis was attending services at St. Paul's Episcopal Church in Richmond when he received the grim news of the collapse of Lee's army. The Confederate president left his fellow parishioners to their prayers and promptly assembled his cabinet for its last session. He directed government officials to prepare to depart Richmond for Danville, to the southwest, via the last working rail line; Davis himself would leave the beleaguered capital a little before midnight. With Confederate statesmen on the run, control over the city devolved to the municipal authorities. Federal forces entered Petersburg in the pre-dawn hours of April 3, raising an American flag above the courthouse there and preparing the way for Abraham Lincoln's triumphant visit to the newly occupied city later that day.[29]

The fall of Richmond, the subject of so many stirring eyewitness reports, is one of the most dramatic scenes in all of American history. For Confederates, the long-dreaded event was nothing less than an apocalypse, one shot through with searing irony, as it was the conduct of Confederate officials rather than of the occupying Union army that brought about the city's destruction. Following through on a plan that had been in place since the fall of Savannah that winter, the Confederate army set fire to a wide range of resources to prevent their capture by the Federals: tobacco warehouses and flour mills, arsenals and ironclads, bridges and depots, all came under the torch, giving rise, as the winds kicked up at night, to an uncontrolled and rapidly spreading conflagration. To make matters worse, the Richmond city council put into effect its own ill-considered decision to destroy all the liquor in the city, hoping to prevent the intoxication of either the armies or civilians. Unfortunately, the plan utterly backfired; alcohol released from storehouses ran through the gutters of the burning city, becoming a conduit for the streaming flames, to the dismay of desperate soldiers and civilians who sought to lap up the liquor and save it for their own use.[30]

By the morning of April 3, the *Richmond Whig* reported, the city "presented a spectacle that we hope never to witness again . . . The air was lurid with the smoke and flame of hundreds of houses sweltering in a sea of fire." Law and order had ceased to exist. As one Confederate captain tells it, a "mob of men, women, and children, to the number of several thousands," descended upon the now unguarded government commissary depots and threw open the doors, unleashing a "demonical struggle for the countless barrels of hams, bacon, whisky, flour, sugar, coffee, etc. etc." For Sallie Brock, who had been such a careful chronicler of the Confederate spirit, the destruction of Richmond spoke of millennial judgment: "All the horrors of the final conflagration, when the earth shall be wrapt in flames and melt with fervent heat, were, it seemed to us, prefigured in our capital." Union troops under the command of General Godfrey Weitzel began to enter the city at around 8:00 a.m.; when they reached Capitol Square, they raised the American flag to the strains of "The Star-Spangled Banner." "It was a requiem for buried hopes," Brock wrote of hearing that song for the first time in four long years.[31]

The Federal soldiers who entered Richmond on April 3 watched the spectacle with a mixture of jubilation and pity. For Edward H. Ripley, commander of one of the occupying brigades, the fall of Richmond was not an apocalypse but a near "holocaust," as he put it, brought on by the ruthless barbarity of the Confederate authorities to the Southern people. "The Confederacy," he reflected, died like a "wounded wolf . . . gnawing at its own body in insensate passion and fury." To that barbarism he contrasted the behavior of Union troops who threw themselves into the work of saving Richmond from the flames. For Southern Unionists such as Elizabeth Van Lew, the fall of Richmond was a long-awaited liberation and vindication. Of the Union troops' arrival in the city Van Lew wrote:

> There were wild bursts of welcome from the negroes and many whites as they poured in. In an incredibly short space of time, as by magic, every part of the city was under the most kind and respectful of guards.
>
> The Federal soldiers, immediately on entrance, went to work to arrest the progress of the flames. Had it not been for them, the whole city would have been a map of smouldering ruins. The loss of public and private property was immense. Our beautiful flour mills, the largest in the world and the pride of our city, were destroyed. Square after square of stores, dwelling houses and factories, warehouses, banks, hotels, bridges, all wrapped in fire, filled the sky with clouds of smoke as incense from the land for its deliverance.[32]

Richmond Redeemed. On April 4, 1865, Lincoln visited the rebel capital and the "late residence of Jefferson Davis," as this *Frank Leslie's* cover put it. Elizabeth Van Lew spoke for the city's Unionists when she wrote: "Oh, army of my country, how glorious was your welcome!" (Library of Congress LC-USZ62-6932)

Northern reactions to the fall of Richmond cast the event as a parable of deliverance. Hearing rumors that the Federals had the rebel capital in their grasp, crowds began to gather in Washington, D.C., as early as the morning of April 3. Secretary of War Stanton in a impromptu address to a rejoicing throng at the War Department declared, "In this great hour of triumph, my heart, as well as yours, is penetrated with gratitude to Almighty God for his deliverance of the nation. . . . He will teach us how to be humble in the midst of victory, how to be just in the hour of victory . . . to secure the foundations of this Republic, soaked as they have been in blood, so that it shall love forever and ever." The next evening at the Patent Office another such crowd heard a local dignitary proclaim, "You will have to excuse me with the simple exclamations of congratulations for this great deliverance of our great nation. We have passed the Red Sea of its blood, and now the promised land is in view. . . . We have learned the strength that is in us, the strength inherent in us, though we did not know it." Press coverage of Richmond's fall highlighted the presence of loyalists there—a Unionist newspaper in Wilmington, North Carolina (a city in Federal hands), the *Herald*, commented that as the blue legions entered Richmond, "Many Union flags were displayed, and great rejoicing manifested at the deliverance so long and so anxiously looked for." *Harper's Weekly*, in its own gloss on these events, credited the Union army with liberating "thousands of their fellow-citizens from the most relentless despotism." Echoing Lincoln's promise of "malice toward none," the article continued, "With no hatred of our fellow-citizens with whom we have fought, and whom we know were deluded by leaders who can never be forgiven, without scorn or vituperation but with devout gratitude to Almighty God for this crowning mercy, let us all . . . resolve that the peace they have secured for us shall be as broad as liberty and as eternal as justice." In the days after Richmond's fall, as Lincoln himself toured the still-smoldering ruins of the city, Northern generosity and industry were already making a difference, the *New York Herald* reported—Union forces were repairing railroads and other infrastructure and dispensing medicine and food to the poor. "The gaunt figures, sharp features and general attenuated appearance of the applicants, showed plainly enough how truly they must have suffered," the *Herald* observed, imagining their relief that "deliverance [had] come at last."[33]

The Surrender at Appomattox

After abandoning the trenches of the fallen cities of Richmond and Petersburg, Lee's army began its flight west. Grant's goal was not merely to pursue Lee's army but to intercept it and prevent him from veering South to join the Confederate army of Joseph Johnston in North Carolina. Sheridan, in the vanguard, was determined to shape the course of the retreat by using his fast-moving cavalry to repeatedly strike Lee's columns, particularly his wagon trains. Lee planned for his columns to concentrate at Amelia Court House, where they would meet awaiting supply trains and pick up the tracks of the Richmond & Danville railroad, leading south. But the provisions never arrived and the Confederates wasted a day in fruitless foraging. Desertion literally wore Lee's army away, with thousands of Confederates drifting away from the retreat, driven by deprivation, despair, and thoughts of home. Lee's men endured a harrowing night march westward on April 5, but the Federals caught up with the Confederates in the muddy bottomlands of Big and Little Sailor's Creek, a tributary of the Appomattox swollen from recent heavy rains. There the three interlocking battles of Sailor's Creek would be fought on April 6 under gray skies and spring showers, with Sheridan leading the Union to a resounding victory. Lee divided his army after the Sailor's Creek debacle, with he and Longstreet moving south of the river to Farmville, and

John Brown Gordon and William Mahone crossing the High Bridge to get north of the river. But High Bridge turned out to be the scene of another set-back. Confederate cavalry fought off a Union raiding party there on April 6, opening the way for the infantry corps to cross the bridge; the plan was for Confederates to then set the structure to the torch to frustrate the Union pursuit. But Major General Andrew A. Humphreys's Second Corps arrived on the scene in time to douse the flames on the lower wagon bridge, and they used it to cross the river and continue their harassment of the retreating Confederates.[34]

Meanwhile, on the morning of April 7 in Farmville, Longstreet's famished men were falling upon the rations issued them—their first in four and a half days. But soon they were ordered to move out, hungry still, as one of Sheridan's cavalry divisions and Major General Edward Ord's Army of the James swarmed in. Lee chose to direct his retreating columns back north across the Appomattox using the railroad and wagon bridges there and, after burning those bridges, to use the river as a protective cordon as the Army of Northern Virginia moved toward Appomattox Station, where rations were sent from Lynchburg. Unfortunately for Lee, Humphrey's Second Corps had successfully crossed the High Bridge, so he, too, was north of the river. He attacked Lee's flank at Cumberland Church, five miles away from the High Bridge crossing. Confederate forces under Mahone and Longstreet beat back a series of Federal attacks, but this was another hollow victory. Meade and Grant recognized the need to reinforce Humphreys north of the river, and by day's end, help was on the way, in the form of Major General Horatio Wright's Sixth Corps, which improvised a footbridge and commandeered a pontoon bridge to cross the Appomattox River at Farmville.[35]

Grant arrived in Farmville on April 7 and set up headquarters at Randolph House, where he conferred with Ord. Late that afternoon, Grant penned a two-sentence note to Lee:

> GENERAL: The result of the last week must convince you of the hope-lessness of further resistance on the part of the Army of Northern Virginia in this struggle. I feel that it is so, and regard it as my duty to shift from myself the responsibility of any further effusion of blood by asking of you the surrender of that portion of the C.S. army known as the Army of Northern Virginia.

This note inaugurated a correspondence with Lee leading to the April 9 meeting at Appomattox. As those letters passed back and forth between the two men, Grant was carefully laying a trap, with Federal armies converging on Appomattox north and south of the river, while Lee was maneuvering to somehow slip that trap. On April 8, the final battles of the campaign were joined, with the Federal cavalry seizing the Confederate supply trains at Appomattox Station, occupying the high ground west of Appomattox Court House, and blocking the Lynchburg Stage Road. This set the stage for Lee's last breakout attempt, on the morning of the ninth—the failure of which forced Lee to agree at last to Grant's proposal that he capitulate.[36]

Grant's instructions from Lincoln were to offer lenient terms of surrender to Lee—on the condition that the rebels accept emancipation and the reestablishment of national authority. This policy was spelled out in Lincoln's February 3, 1865, meeting with Confederate peace commissioners, led by Confederate vice president Alexander Stephens, aboard the *River Queen* at Union-occupied Hampton Roads, Virginia. Lincoln brusquely disabused the Confederates of the idea that peace could come without reunion and emancipation. On March 28, 1865, Lincoln clarified his position again in a meeting on the *River Queen* with his right-hand men, Grant, Sherman, and Porter. There could be no mistaking Grant's brief: his terms were to encompass the surrender of a hostile army and not seek to resolve the political questions of the defeated Confederates' civil rights and criminal liabilities, or of their pardon and amnesty; those questions would be taken up by the civil authorities, within the liberal framework Lincoln had constructed.[37]

Lee and Davis, by contrast, were not in agreement. Davis, who had fled from Richmond to Danville, Virginia, the putative new seat of the Confederate government, resoundingly rejected the conditions for peace that Lincoln invoked at Hampton Roads as "degrading" and "humiliating." He rejected, too, the idea of an honorable capitulation; Davis would have the Confederates fight to the last ditch. Lee, for his part, held out hopes for a negotiated peace, one in which the Confederacy, even if forced to capitulate, could still impose conditions on or extract concessions from the Yankees to secure "a restored Union, an independent Confederacy, or perhaps something in between," as historian Steven E. Woodworth has explained. Even in the wake of the Sailor's Creek debacle Lee believed power to influence any future negotiations could still be gained by further resistance. Only when Lee's depleted army failed to break the Federal trap at Appomattox Court House did Lee finally concede the cause was lost.[38]

In their storied meeting at the McLean House at Appomattox Court House on April 9, Grant offered to Lee surrender by parole. In exchange for their pledge that they would never again take up arms against the United

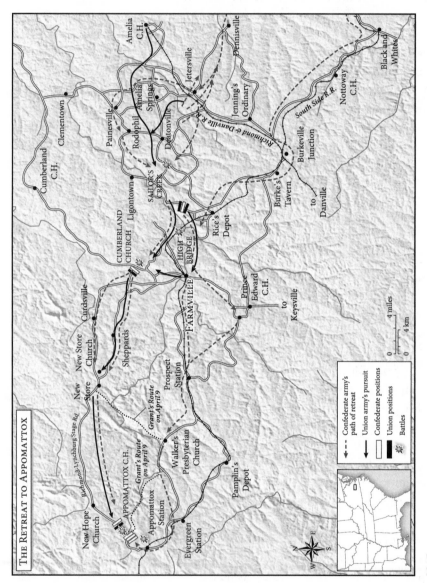

THE RETREAT TO APPOMATTOX

Confederate army's path of retreat

Union army's pursuit

Confederate positions

Union positions

Battles

New Hope Church

Richmond-Lynchburg Stage Rd.

New Store

New Store Church

Curdsville

Sheppards

APPOMATTOX C.H.

Grant's Route on April 9

Grant's Route on April 9

Appomattox Station

Walker's Presbyterian Church

Prospect Station

Pamplin's Depot

Evergreen Station

CUMBERLAND CHURCH

Ligontown

SAILOR'S CREEK

FARMVILLE

HIGH BRIDGE

Rice's Depot

Prince Edward C.H.

to Keysville

Cumberland C.H.

Clementown

Painesville

Rodophil

Amelia Springs

Deatonville

Jetersville

Amelia C.H.

Dennisville

Jenning's Ordinary

Burke's Tavern

Burkeville Junction

to Danville

Nottoway C.H.

Black and White

Richmond & Danville R.R.

South Side R.R.

0   4 miles
0   4 km

N
E
S
W

MAP 12.2

Surrender at Appomattox. The McLean House at Appomattox Court House in central Virginia, site of Lee's April 9, 1865, surrender to U. S. Grant. (Library of Congress LC-B8171-7292)

States, Confederates would effectively be set free: "Each officer and man will be allowed to return to their homes, not to be disturbed by United States authority so long as they observe their paroles and the laws in force where they may reside," the terms stipulated. Grant allowed Confederate officers to keep their sidearms, horses, and baggage, and then acceded to Lee's request that every Confederate who owned a horse or mule be permitted to take the animal home. Grant, again at Lee's request, provided food for the starving Confederate troops; twenty-five thousand Union rations would be directed from Sheridan's commissary to Lee's. When news of the surrender reached the Union lines, the jubilant soldiers commenced firing a salute of a hundred guns in honor of their victory. But Grant "sent word . . . to have it stopped." "The Confederates were now our prisoners," he explained, and there was no need to "exult over their downfall." "We were ordered to treat them as 'erring brothers,'" John Haley wrote at Appomattox on April 10. "They must be spared all those humiliating scenes which a foreign foe would have been compelled to undergo."[39]

Some soldiers felt that Grant's terms were too magnanimous. "Our authorities are paroling *Gen'l Lee's Army* and letting them go home," William

Chase of the 45th New York wrote home from Farmville on April 14. "I cant hardly approve of that," he added. "Now the Rebel Officers are going to ride around the town here with their swords and side arms on. . . . I am afraid they are dealing to lightly with traitors." But most of the Union rank and file saw the surrender as Grant did: they believed that Union victory unburdened the South both of the haughty planter aristocracy and of the retrograde institution of slavery, and that Southerners would respond well to mercy. "Our government stands vindicated," Corporal Richtmyer Hubbell wrote in his diary on April 10. "And not only the North, but the South too, must rejoice to be reli[e]ved from the Reign of Terror that has overpowered them for the last four years. . . . May the time not be far distant when a free, united, and flourishing people may extend from the Atlantic to the Pacific and from the Gulf to the Northern Climes." The Union victory, Pennsylvania army chaplain Hallock Armstrong wrote his wife, would "knock off the shackles from millions of poor whites" and give the North "a field of benevolence opened before it as wide as the whole South . . . [in] the great work of regenerating the misguided millions." He closed, "I say, Amen and Amen. Let the work be completed."[40]

The Advent of Peace

Even as Grant chased down Lee during the week-long Appomattox campaign, Northern civilians began to reflect on just what the impending peace might mean. At no time were images of deliverance more resonant than in the last days and hours of the war in Virginia. "Never had a nation better cause of rejoicing than ours has now," the *Pittsburgh Gazette* editorialized on April 8, as Lee's army disintegrated. "It is not only the day of triumph but the day of deliverance; and in all the fervent rejoicings that have burst spontaneously from the masses, the sense of deliverance is plainly predominant. The people feel as if a great weight had been lifted off them." There was "nothing in it of the sensation of anticipated vengeance," the paper noted, only "rejoicing that the blessing of Peace would once more return to the country." That same day, the Washington, D.C., *National Republican* painted a wishful picture of such blessings:

> The rebellionists . . . have nearly got the *lesson by heart* that their pretensions of superiority, so long and so vauntingly persisted in, were ill-founded; and this discovery is fast preparing them to return to the Union fold wiser men and better citizens. The Union

re-established with all roots of bitterness plucked up and buried in oblivion, the North and South, East and West joining hands frater-nally—a more homogenous people than ever before. . . . Under such benign auspices, intellectual advancement will be as certain as rapid; literature and the arts and sciences will receive the amplest encour-agement, and the accomplishments and refinements of society their highest polish.[41]

The news of Lee's capitulation on April 9—Palm Sunday—brought forth an outpouring of providential rhetoric from Northerners. The *New York Times* highlighted Northern piety in an April 11 editorial entitled "The New Epoch—the Advent of Peace":

> We had a hidden strength which the world did not understand. It was Faith . . . the moral elements of the national cause made it irresist-ible. . . . The religious faith is fitly followed now by a religious grati-tude. It is wonderful to mark the solemn character of the joy that now spreads the land. . . . Never since the hosannas of that Palm Sunday in Jerusalem has such irrepressible praise roiled up from a city street to the pure vault of heaven. . . . With this gratitude for deliverance is mingled a fresh assurance that Heaven has reserved for our republic a destiny more glorious than can yet be conceived. Americans now feel that it is less than ever a presumption in them to believe themselves a chosen people.[42]

A sermon on victory by the Reverend J. A. Thome of Cleveland, Ohio, cap-tured perfectly the mood: "Our captivity has been turned; our captivities, I may say, for the war has been a captivity, slavery has been a captivity, to the nation as well as to the negro, and the dread of a just and avenging God has been a captivity." The Confederacy's demise marred the nation's "liberation from all these bondages."[43]

Yet however powerful this shared sense of liberation, it could not fore-stall debates over precisely what shape peace should take. While there was widespread enthusiasm in the North for Grant's lenient terms at Appomattox, Northerners differed over precisely what political ends mag-nanimity should serve. On one end of the Northern political spectrum, abolitionists and Radical Republicans claimed that Northern leniency would secure the South's assent to emancipation and pave the way for black citizenship. No one made this case more fulsomely, or with more fanfare,

than the Reverend Henry Ward Beecher. On April 14, 1865, he delivered
the keynote address at a symbolic raising of the Union flag at Fort Sumter,
South Carolina, on the four-year anniversary of the opening scene of the
war; Beecher had been deputized by Lincoln himself to play the starring
role in this ceremony. Beecher had a reputation as an uncompromising foe
of slavery. But in his April 14 address, he sought to harmonize amnesty and
forgiveness with racial equality and justice. Standing at the epicenter of secessionism, Beecher intoned, "I charge the whole guilt of this war upon
the ambitious, educated, plotting political leaders of the South." These aristocratic conspirators "suborned their own common people with lies, with
sophistries, with cruel deceits and slanders, to fight for secret objects which
they abhorred, and against interests as dear to them as their own lives." They
"renewed the plagues of Egypt, not that the oppressed might go free, but
that the free might be oppressed." For such men, Beecher had no mercy—
they should be punished for their crimes and would face divine judgment.
"But for the people misled, for the multitudes drafted and driven into this
civil war," Beecher continued, in a familiar mantra, "let not a trace of ani-
mosity remain. The moment the willing hand drops the musket, and they
return to their allegiance, then stretch out your own honest right hands to
greet them.... Our hearts wait for their redemption."[44]

Beecher then enumerated at great length the benefits the "common
laboring people of the South" would derive from Union victory and emancipation. No longer would the "subtle poison of secession . . . rankle in the
blood." No longer would Southerners cast aspersions on Northern manhood,
for the war had bred mutual respect. With slavery gone, the region would
no longer lag behind in industry, piety, and education: "Schools will multiply. Books and papers will spread. Churches will bless every hamlet." No
longer could white Southerners deny the "capacity, moral and military, of the
black race," for blacks had proved themselves to "be not second to their white
brethren in arms." Black education and citizenship, Beecher insisted, would
bring the South prosperity. Addressing himself directly to white Southerners,
he pledged, "We do not want your cities or your fields. . . . All we ask is un-
swerving loyalty and universal liberty." The South's own historians would
someday write, he predicted, that "from the day the sword cut off the cancer
[of slavery] she began to find her health."[45]

The Northern free black press also linked magnanimity to black citizenship, but with an emphasis on the black military heroism and particularly the
crucial role of USCT regiments in the Appomattox campaign. "We the colored soldiers have fairly won our rights by loyalty and bravery," wrote William

McCoslin of the 29th Regiment USCT to the *Christian Recorder*, summing up the case that the surrender was a vindication of the cause of black citizenship. The fact that black soldiers had defeated Lee lent additional symbolic meaning to the surrender, for Lee and his Army of Northern Virginia typified in the eyes of the black Union soldiers the haughty slaveholding elite and its pretense of racial superiority. African Americans reveled in the fact that USCT regiments had been among the first to enter Petersburg and Richmond, and to proclaim in those cities "freedom to all mankind," as Garland H. White, chaplain of the 28th USCT, put it. The fact that black regiments had blocked Lee's last escape route at Appomattox on the morning of April 9 was also an enduring source of pride. In the "last hour of the Slave-holders' Rebellion," USCT veteran and pioneering historian George Washington Williams would later write, the "brilliant fighting" of black troops had ensured the triumph of the Union.[46]

In the middle of the political spectrum, moderate Republicans and War Democrats claimed Grant's terms for the supremacy of the Union and for a cautious approach to Reconstruction. Henry J. Raymond, editor of the moderate Republican *New York Times*, rejected the equation of Appomattox with the prospect of black citizenship and instead defended Grant's magnanimity as the means to promote "order and fraternity." Dispelling the "bug bear of perpetual war and a vast standing army," the Republican *Pittsburgh Daily Commercial* editorialized, "We apprehend no serious difficulty in the way of reestablishing order and government throughout the South." The "great body of the Southern people" would "hail the restoration of a benign government, as a deliverance, after four years of such miserable despotism as they have been groaning under."[47]

On the other end of the spectrum, Copperhead Democrats claimed Grant's Appomattox terms as a rebuke to abolitionist reformers and Radical Republican politicians. Eager to deny Lincoln's Republican Party a victory or a mandate, the Copperhead press focused on the costs of the war, lamenting that it had steeped the country in misery and in the Republican party's "antislavery dogmas." Copperheads charged that antislavery extremists sought vengeance and would undermine Grant's "humane and magnanimous settlement." The *Lancaster Intelligencer*, for example, charged that Radical Republicans were "full of venom towards the white people of the South" and desired "to make the African the ruling race in the Southern States." The Radicals intended to "reduce the white inhabitants of that portion of our country to the lowest state of poverty—to make them, if possible, hewers of wood and drawers of water for 'freedmen.'"[48]

Confederate Interpretations of Lee's Surrender

Copperheads essentially parroted the dominant Confederate interpretation of Lee's surrender: the view that the North's victory was one of might over right, attributable to overwhelming resources and brutal force, not to skill and righteousness. Lee himself staked out that case on April 10 in his "Farewell Address" (drafted under Lee's guidance by his aide Charles Marshall). It began, "After four years of arduous service, marked by unsurpassed courage and fortitude, the Army of Northern Virginia has been compelled to yield to overwhelming numbers and resources." Confederate troops had "remained steadfast to the last," Lee continued, and could draw satisfaction, even in this bitter hour, "from the consciousness of duty faithfully performed." In the context of Confederate ideology, the reference to overwhelming numbers was a kind of code, conjuring up images of the heartless efficiency of Northern society. In the wake of the surrender, Lee's officers developed this theme, churning out speeches, articles, and memoirs designed to disseminate the idea that Lee had faced insurmountable odds of five to one or worse in the final campaign. Lee's "eight thousand starving men" at Appomattox, Colonel Walter H. Taylor put it, had surrendered to an unworthy foe that "had long despaired to conquer it by skill or daring, and who had worn it away by weight of numbers and brutal exchange of many lives for one." This doctrine referred not only to the size but also to the social composition of the Union army. Lee's lieutenants lamented that they had been compelled to surrender to a mercenary army of their social and racial inferiors—"German, Irish, negro, and Yankee wretches," as Brigadier General William N. Pendleton put it bitterly in a June 1865 letter to his daughter. Scholars have since established that Lee faced odds of two to one at Appomattox, no worse than odds he had beaten before. But in its day, the numbers game had a distinct political purpose. By denying the legitimacy of the North's military victory, former Confederates hoped to deny the North the right to impose its political will on the South.[49]

At Appomattox, Lee moved to cast the surrender terms in the best possible light. Hoping their paroles could confer on his men a measure of immunity from reprisals at the hands of the victorious Federals, he requested of Grant at their April 10, 1865, meeting on horseback that each individual Confederate be issued a printed certificate, signed by a Union officer, as proof that such a soldier came under the settlement of April 9. Grant readily assented to Lee's request. In keeping with the language of the surrender terms, a parole certificate vouched that if a soldier observed the laws in force where he resided, he was to "remain undisturbed." This seemingly simple phrase would prove deeply problematic. In Confederate eyes, the paroles represented the promise that honorable men would not be treated dishonorably.[50]

The vast majority of Southern whites supported Lee's interpretation of the surrender—that the Union had overwhelmed and not outfought the Confederacy, and that Confederate soldiers were both heroic and blameless to the last. Soldiers acknowledged the depleted state of Lee's army and yet were utterly shocked at the news of its capitulation. As Dr. Hodijah Baylies Meade explained, he had seen "innumerable & unmistakable signs" of the Confederate demise but had retained his "implicit confidence" in Lee: "I believed[d] he would deliver us in a way we knew not of," Meade later confessed. Like Lee's lieutenants, the Southern army's junior officers and rank and file were loath to concede to the enemy any courage and skill. Instead, they portrayed the Yankees as a fundamentally unworthy foe. The April 9 diary entry of Captain Henry A. Chambers of the 49th North Carolina fumed: "These worthless fellows whom we have so often whipped, whose cowardly backs we have so often seen, have at last by sheer force of numbers, numbers swelled by contributions from almost every race and color on the face of the globe, have compelled us to come to this." In their reckoning, the Yankee army had grown baser even as it grew larger over the course of the war, its hosts filled by "foreigners of every nationality" and "regiments of our former slaves," as artilleryman Edward A. Moore contemptuously put it. Major Edward M. Boykin of the 7th South Carolina Cavalry estimated that the Federal army numbered 150,000 at the end and "varied in its nationality"; its "recruiting stations were all over the world," beacons for immigrants lured by the "almighty American dollar."[51]

Confederate newspapers churned out estimates of the fearful odds Lee had faced in the last battles, and fanciful reports of the surrender meeting. According to one newspaper account, widely circulated in the Confederate press, Lee offered Grant his sword at Appomattox but Grant refused to take it, saying: "Gen. Lee, keep that sword. You have won it by your gallantry. You have not been whipped but overpowered, and I cannot receive it as a token of surrender from so brave a man." In reality, Grant never said any such thing—but the report seemed credible to Confederates because it affirmed their "might over right" interpretation of their defeat. In this interpretation, Grant's leniency was a form of homage to Southern valor.[52]

Confederate civilians were unwilling, at the bitter end, to acknowledge the flaws or divisions in their society, and pessimistic about the prospect of reconciliation with the hated Yankees. Many regarded the conciliatory surrender terms that Grant offered Lee as a transparent bid to lure Southerners into accepting renewed subjugation. Emma LeConte wrote in her diary in late April, "I used to dream about peace, to pray for it, but this is worse than war. What is such peace to us? . . . It is too horrible. What I most fear is a conciliatory policy from the North, that they will offer to let us come back as before. Oh no, no! . . . Let them oppress and tyrannize, but let us take no favors of them." Diarist Sarah Morgan was equally unrepentant. She learned of Lee's surrender on April 13. To those around her who seemed to welcome the return of "blessed Peace," she had this to say: "Never! Let a great earthquake swallow us up first! Let us leave our land and emigrate to any desert spot of the earth, rather than return to the Union, even as it Was!"[53] Such protestations bespeak these women's deep investment in the Confederate cause, and their profound bitterness at the loss of slavery.

White Southern Unionists, for their part, were more crucial than ever. Could they bring their benighted Southern masses around to appreciate the blessings of the Union? Would they be inclined toward mercy or vengeance against the hated secessionist elite? How much social change would they abide? These questions would soon dominate the politics of reunion, as a Southern Unionist took the nation's helm.

The Assassination

Loyal Americans saw Appomattox as the effective end of the war: with Lee's army neutralized, Confederate independence was a dead letter. It seemed to be only a matter of time before Joseph Johnston's army in North Carolina would yield to the relentless Sherman. Davis and his government were in flight but could not long elude the grasp of the Federals; the same was true of the remaining Confederate forces scattered in Alabama, Mississippi, and the Trans-Mississippi theater.

Even the most battle-hardened veterans of Sherman's army clung to the hope that surrender would bring on the part of the white Southern masses a swift return to allegiance. "We are going to pursue Johnston's Rebel Army until we can overtake it," General John White Geary—a hero of Gettysburg and veteran of Sherman's March—wrote his wife, Mary, on April 14, 1865, from Raleigh, North Carolina. He anticipated a climactic "collision" between Sherman and Johnson that would test the Yankees' "temper & steel." But he also believed North Carolina to be ripe for redemption. "The inhabitants of the state," he predicted, "will vote *two to one* to return to the Union, as soon as the rebel army is driven away." Once Johnston was defeated, the war would truly be over, Geary reassured Mary, and he would be free at long last to "go home (sweet home)."[54]

Tragedy disrupted such reveries of peace when John Wilkes Booth assassinated Abraham Lincoln on the evening of April 14, 1865. In a cabinet meeting that morning, Lincoln had reiterated his desire that the country transcend "feelings of hate and vindictiveness." He would countenance "no persecution, no bloody work, after the war was over." As for the leaders of the rebellion, Lincoln expressed his hope that their fate would be exile—that they could be frightened out of the country and left to languish in isolation, without the honor of martyrdom. After the cabinet meeting, the president and his wife, Mary Todd Lincoln, had gone on a cheerful carriage ride, eaten dinner at home, and then proceeded on to Ford's Theatre for a welcome evening of entertainment. Lincoln, attended by only one bodyguard despite his having received numerous death threats over the course of the war, was set upon by Booth in the president's box. Booth delivered a point-blank shot from his derringer to the back of Lincoln's head, and then leapt to the stage, hissing out the state motto of Virginia—*Sic simper tyrannis*—and disappearing into

John Wilkes Booth, Assassin. Northerners saw the assassination as a base bid to rob the Union of the victory that its commander in chief, with Grant's army as his instrument, had just won at Appomattox, and to plunge the country once again into hatred, bloodshed, and chaos. (Library of Congress LC-DIG-ppmsca-19233)

the night. News of Booth's attack on Lincoln reached the Northern public around 10:30 p.m. Booth's co-conspirator Lewis Paine had attempted to assassinate Secretary of State William Seward, attacking him in his home, but had failed. On Saturday the fifteenth, Northerners learned that Lincoln, who never regained consciousness, had passed away, Booth's bullet lodged in his brain.[55]

Booth was enraged that Lincoln had, in his last speech, on April 11, endorsed limited black suffrage. Lincoln delivered that address in the euphoria of victory, before the concourse of serenaders who thronged the White House grounds, in a city aglow with bonfires and illuminations. Reading from his carefully crafted text, Lincoln grappled with the challenges of Reconstruction. He defended his amnesty policy and the good it had done in Louisiana in particular: the new constitution of the state duly upheld emancipation, which was the groundwork for future progress. Signaling that he had moved toward the Radical Republican position on the issue of black citizenship, Lincoln, for the first time, publicly endorsed black suffrage, saying he would prefer that the vote be conferred "on the very intelligent, and on those who serve our cause as soldiers." The nation must, Lincoln insisted, send a strong message of support to those Unionists in Louisiana, white and black, on whom the future depended—to nerve them to "fight" for the principles of Union and of "perpetual freedom." Lincoln closed by promising to make "some new announcement to the people of the South" about how the work of Reconstruction would proceed. Booth, who was in the audience when Lincoln gave this speech, vowed at that very moment, "Now, by God, I'll put him through. That is the last speech he will ever make." Booth's ardent secessionism and commitment to white supremacy had mixed, in a lethal blend, with his delusions of grandeur and his persecution complex. He took aim on April 14 at the prospect of black suffrage.[56]

Among Northern civilians, the assassination brought forth a tidal wave of grief. Countless Northerners gathered to hear sermons preached to their martyred president; an estimated seven million (one in every four Americans) watched his funeral train over the course of its thirteen-day trip to Springfield, Illinois; and more than one million paid respect to his remains as he lay in state in the cities the train passed through. Among those who paid such respects was the free black diarist Emilie Davis of Philadelphia. "The President Was assasinated by Som Confederate villain," she wrote tersely on April 14; "the city is in the Deepest sorrow." On April 22 Lincoln's body was conveyed with military escort to Independence Hall in Philadelphia. Davis called the procession "the gravest funeral I ever saw." Communities across the

North held meetings to mourn and honor Lincoln. For example, on April 16, the "colored citizens" of Bloomington, Indiana, met in the AME church and passed a resolution: "[We] do hereby express our grief, and mingle our tears with the great *loyal and liberty-loving* masses of the American people . . . we, as colored American citizens have lost a *tried friend*—A GREAT DELIVERER—A REAL BENEFACTOR."[57]

In their pain and anger, some Northerners cried out for stern retribution against the South and for policies more stringent than Lincoln's own merciful approach to reunion. "The government has been too lenient—these arch traitors, and fiends, must be put out of the way, or there will be a scene [of] murder and midnight assassination, unparall[el]d in the history of the world," Ann Eliza Smith observed to her husband, Governor J. Gregory Smith of Vermont. Of Lincoln she wrote, "Kind, merciful man, he will I am sure find mercy with God." John C. Rutherford, a surgeon in the 17th Vermont, took rhetorical aim at rebels and Copperheads alike, decrying "the gross folly of being too lenient to these hell born traitors not only at the South but in the midst of our N.E. homes. We are all coming home soon: and our first work will be to clean out every traitor and tory." Leading Copperheads worried that calls for vengeance would drown out the rhetoric of magnanimity. "This is the beginning of evils," an Ohio Copperhead journal predicted. "The hearts and hopes of all men—even of those who had opposed his policy earliest and strongest—had begun to turn toward Abraham Lincoln for deliverance at last . . . for his course for the last three months has been most liberal and conciliatory." His death was the "worst public calamity" imaginable, for Radicals would come to substitute vindictiveness for conciliation.[58]

In fact, Northerners' deep investment in the deluded-masses theory structured their responses to Lincoln's assassination, serving to check the impulse toward retaliation. In her study of responses to Lincoln's assassination, historian Martha Hodes finds that Lincoln's white mourners blamed the Confederate leadership for the assassination and exempted the masses; such a posture "let slide the fact that the vast majority of white southerners in 1865 remained loyal to white supremacy." Clergymen led the way in blaming Booth's act on leaders and elites. In his sermon at Lincoln's burial ceremony in Springfield, Illinois, the Methodist bishop Matthew Simpson promised that the Union would both hold the leading rebels to account and uphold the president's spirit of clemency toward the Southern people. "To the deluded masses we will extend the arms of forgiveness. We will take them to our hearts, and walk with them side by side, as we go forward to work out a glorious destiny." Ohio Methodist minister Maxwell Pierson Gaddis gave an April 16 sermon in which he praised Lincoln's amnesty policy and condemned Booth as a "despiser of mercy." Imploring his congregants to follow Lincoln's example, Pierson painted a picture of a rejuvenated, restored South, "made more lovely and productive than ever, because planted and tilled by the hands of free labor," with poor whites finally "raised by education and social influence to their true position in society."⁵⁹

Such sentiments were echoed by politicians and military leaders. Radical Republican senator Zachariah Chandler of Michigan urged the new president, Andrew Johnson, to be merciful to the masses, advising, "You have only to hang a few of these traitors and all will be peace and quiet in the South. A few men have done the mischief, and the masses of the people were misled by them." Massachusetts Radical Republican George S. Boutwell, a champion of black citizenship and suffrage, delivered an April 19 eulogy to Lincoln at Lowell, Massachusetts, in which he drew a distinction—as many eulogists did—between retribution and justice. He cautioned, "Let not the thirst for vengeance take possession of our souls," even as he called for stern punishment of the leading rebel conspirators. Boutwell was hopeful that the Southern masses could be made to see themselves as "recipients of the boon of freedom." "The white people of the South will yet rejoice in the knowledge of their own deliverance," he imagined, explaining that Lincoln's Emancipation Proclamation was designed not only to release blacks from bondage but also to save the nation. On the same day as Boutwell's eulogy, General George Henry Gordon, commanding occupying forces in the Eastern District of Virginia (covering Fort Monroe, Norfolk, Yorktown/Williamsburg, and the Eastern Shore), addressed the surrendered Confederate troops who were flocking into the district. "To those erring and misguided persons who have been allowed to return to their homes . . . this order is promulgated," Gordon began. "You have experienced the might of your Government; you are now permitted to enjoy its clemency. . . . Let there be thanks to God that the heart of the Nation has been turned to pardon, rather than to punishment; but take heed that offence not cometh again!" he warned.⁶⁰

African Americans, Martha Hodes notes, although they "joined the chorus that blamed the Confederate leadership for secession, war, and the assassination," also "raised the problem of racism among the so-called white masses of the South," understanding the broad complicity of whites in the slave system. On May 10, 1865, Frederick Douglass gave a speech entitled "The Need for Continuing Anti-Slavery Work" at the thirty-second annual meeting of the American Anti-Slavery Society. He was responding to calls by William Lloyd Garrison and others to disband the anti-slavery movement now that the work of emancipation was done. Douglass rejected such a position and reiterated the theme that African American commentators had emphasized all along: the demise of slavery would not spell the end of prejudice unless blacks were granted the full freedom of citizens. "Slavery is not abolished until the black man has the ballot," Douglass insisted. Alluding to the powerful impulse among Northern whites to see Southerners as repentant, Douglas asked pointedly, "Think you, that because they are for the moment in the talons and beak of our glorious eagle, instead of the slave being there, as formerly, that they are converted? I hear of the loyalty at Wilmington, the loyalty at South Carolina—what is it worth? . . . They are loyal when they see 200,000 sable soldiers, with glistening bayonets, walking in their midst. But let the civil power of the States be restored, and the old prejudices and hostility to the Negro will revive."[61]

The Final Surrenders

In the immediate aftermath of the assassination, Andrew Johnson upheld the distinction between the guilty few and deluded many. In a series of addresses to visiting dignitaries and delegations in April and May, the new president repeatedly promised clemency to "the unconscious, deceived, conscripted—in short, to the great mass of the misled" and stern penalties to the "conscious, intelligent, leading traitors." White Northerners trusted that, with his "intimate knowledge of the Southern masses," Johnson could "best tell what to do," devising policies "as severe and inflexible as it is necessary to be, and as lenient and merciful as he can be," as a Kansas newspaper put it in early May.[62]

The challenges of balancing mercy and justice were dramatized by Joseph Johnston's surrender to William T. Sherman at Durham Station, North Carolina, on April 26, 1865. Sherman and Johnston had negotiated an agreement on April 18 that seemed to recognize the Southern state governments, extend amnesty to all Confederates, and even restore the property and political rights of the rebels. Sherman had been manipulated by Johnston, who, acting at the behest of Jefferson Davis and his cabinet, was trying to impose a series of favorable conditions on his inevitable surrender. This accord was promptly rejected by President Johnson, Secretary of War Stanton and the rest of the cabinet, and Ulysses S. Grant himself as contravening Lincoln's explicit orders that military commanders not negotiate political settlements, and as contrary to the letter and spirit of both Lincoln's December 1863 amnesty measure and Grant's terms to Lee. Grant was dispatched to North Carolina to carry word of the administration's displeasure directly to Sherman and to enjoin the wayward general to secure a new peace in line with Grant's April 9 terms. When Jefferson Davis learned that the Union cabinet had nullified the Johnston-Sherman pact, he ordered Johnston to resume fighting. Johnston, knowing full well he was cornered, wisely refused. On April 26, Sherman and Johnston signed a new surrender accord, in keeping with the Appomattox model, and Davis and his cabinet continued their flight to the southwest.[63]

Sherman's initial terms sparked a heated debate in the press. In the eyes of some critics, Sherman had in effect promised the rebels that "they were still to be permitted to *hold their slaves* in spite of the Emancipation Proclamation," as one of the many negative press accounts of "Sherman's fiasco" put it. The Republican press attributed Sherman's behavior to his long-standing "disinclination towards the Anti-Slavery policy of the government." Sherman defended himself by noting that tensions were at a fever pitch on April 18, as news of Lincoln's assassination was fresh in the minds of Northern and Southern troops alike. His terms, he asserted, were calculated to keep passions in check and to prevent Johnston's army from dispersing and doing "infinite mischief." He believed he had co-opted Johnston into urging the surrender of the last rogue rebel forces. Sherman also protested that his initial terms were consistent with Grant's terms and with Lincoln's wishes for a restoration of the Union. Democratic papers in the North rushed to Sherman's defense, lambasting radicals for impeaching Sherman's loyalty.[64]

The Johnson administration's decisive efforts to bring Sherman into line confirmed some in their belief that the new president would hold the rebels to account. The fact that Grant was called upon to secure the final settlement of April 26 only reinforced his image in the North as "The Capturer of Armies," to quote a *New York Times* article of May 5, 1865. "The whole South is now at his feet," it concluded, "its great armies 'melted into thin air.'" With the surrender of General Richard Taylor's army to Union major general E. R. S. Canby in Citronelle, Alabama, on May 4; the capture of Jefferson Davis by Union forces in Irwin County, Georgia, on May 10; and General Edmund Kirby Smith's capitulation to Canby at Galveston Harbor, Texas, on May 26, the Confederate military effort collapsed. On June 19, 1865, General Gordon Granger, newly appointed commander of the Department of Texas, promulgated General Order No. 3, informing Texas slaves of the passage of the Emancipation Proclamation, and thus belatedly granting Texas's quarter of a million slaves freedom.[65]

In a May 29, 1865, article entitled "Peace Completed," the venerable *North American and United States Gazette* of Philadelphia declared, "At length the great problem is finally solved. The last remnant of civil war disappears with the surrender of the rebel forces in the trans-Mississippi department." Edmund Kirby Smith had failed to rally Confederates to defend their last frontier, the *Gazette* editorialized, because the populations under his command (in Texas, Arkansas, Louisiana, and Missouri) had lost their taste for war and "yearned for the return of prosperous repose" under Lincoln's amnesty policy. In a striking illustration of the potency of deliverance discourse, the *Gazette* predicted, "In coming back to her duty under the old flag, Texas will do so with less reluctance than any of the rebel States, because she knows from experience what benefits the Union brought her, and how poorly she could afford to try independence again." Such visions, which had been sources of hope in the dark days of war, would serve the Unionist coalition poorly in its struggle to forge a lasting peace.[66]

Conclusion

"DELIVER US FROM SUCH A MOSES": ANDREW
JOHNSON AND THE LEGACY OF THE CIVIL WAR

ON SEPTEMBER 30, 1865, Kentucky Unionist Robert J. Breckinridge gave an address at Union College in upstate New York entitled "The Great Deliverance and the New Career." The address reprised themes Breckinridge had developed in countless speeches over the course of the war: the argument that the Southern masses had been deluded and misled into treason by scheming conspirators; that the Confederacy had been a "relentless military despotism"; that emancipation was a military necessity for defeating the rebellion; that Lincoln had shown Americans the path of righteousness; and that America, delivered from the scourge of war, was poised to fulfill her destiny of greatness. In Breckinridge's view, the mutual duties of the vanquished and the victors were clear. Confederates must "accept the overthrow of their insurrection as an everlasting finality." The victors must be careful not "to wound, to exasperate, to afflict, nor even to punish" the Southern masses but instead must "accept their restoration as fully and completely as we require them to renounce their hostility." Breckinridge counseled Northerners to reject Radical Republican proposals for black enfranchisement and citizenship, as such measures were sure to offend white Southerners; in his view, blacks were deserving of a nominal freedom and a "comfortable existence" but were "wholly unfit" for political participation and incapable of ever achieving equality with whites.[1]

A few months later, in December 1865, the Reverend Charles R. Bliss, pastor of the Congregational church in South Reading, Massachusetts, offered to his flock a sermon entitled "Deliverance from the Furnace." In many respects it echoed Breckinridge's oration. Bliss invoked the suffering and sacrifice of loyal Americans in the "iron furnace of war," the "generous favor of God" in delivering the nation from war and from slavery, and the heroic example set by the martyred Lincoln. As Breckinridge had, Bliss stressed that Northerners should accord "gentle treatment" to their "late enemies." "No wanton deeds or words, no useless boasting, no uncharitableness or feelings of revenge, should be allowed to exasperate anew the feelings of those who are willing to become loyal men again," he cautioned. Unlike Breckinridge, however, Bliss declared that Americans must vanquish racial discrimination as they had vanquished slavery. "Though the shackles be struck from his limbs by the national authority," the black man would "yet be a slave, if denied the position of an equal." With access to education, the freedpeople were "rapidly proving [their] capacity." Invoking the "doctrine of the Declaration of independence," Bliss urged Northerners to mobilize the resources to promote black uplift. "The statement that dark color indicates inferior manhood, so persistently made by multitudes," he contended, must "take its place with that uncounted number of declarations which the war has falsified." Only then would the nation rest upon a firm foundation and "enter upon a career of unexampled prosperity."[2]

In the first months of the peace, the politics of Reconstruction severely tested the wartime alliance that men such as Breckinridge and Bliss had forged. Northerners discovered that there were not nearly as many anti-Confederate whites in the South as they had imagined, that these Unionists were divided among themselves, and that many of them were susceptible to appeals, grounded in racial solidarity, by their former Confederate enemies. Persistent "rebelism" on the part of Confederates—an unwillingness to acknowledge moral defeat—raised thorny questions about what sorts of incentives and proscriptions were necessary to secure Southern acquiescence in reunion. Andrew Johnson's amnesty program dramatized these hard lessons. Johnson's Reconstruction policies selectively appropriated aspects of the deliverance narrative and harnessed them to a goal of restoration. Johnson used the presidency to push a reactionary argument: that the Southern masses who had been the victims of the slaveholding oligarchy during the war were, during postwar Reconstruction, rendered the victims of Radical Republicans and their egalitarian agenda of black suffrage and civil rights. Johnson adapted the zero-sum-game argument of race relations—that black gains would bring white losses—by defining black freedom narrowly and associating the enfranchisement of blacks with the prospect of "negro rule." He determined that the Southern masses should ally with the old slaveholding class in defense of white supremacy.[3]

Johnson's Amnesty Plan

When he first took office after Lincoln's assassination, Johnson seemed determined to deal sternly with traitors: he approved the death penalty for four of those convicted of Lincoln's assassination, and he clapped the former Confederate president, Jefferson Davis, into prison to await an uncertain fate. But Johnson seemed to change course when, on May 29, 1865, he formally proclaimed his Reconstruction policy. His Amnesty Proclamation stipulated that Confederates who took an oath of allegiance to the United States government would have their political and property rights swiftly and fully restored. There were exceptions: high-ranking Confederate officials and members of the antebellum elite would have to apply directly to the president for pardons. Johnson believed that his Amnesty Proclamation was an extension of Lincoln's own December 1863 proclamation. But in practice, he soon charted his own distinct course. He granted pardons gladly and extravagantly, issuing at least fifteen thousand to individual rebels over the course of his time in office. At the same moment he announced his amnesty policy, Johnson also laid out the procedure by which the errant rebel states would be readmitted to the Union. He would personally appoint provisional governors for each of the seceded states and give each governor the authority to fill appointive offices and to hold elections for a state convention. Such a convention would take the remaining steps for readmission to the Union by repudiating secession and endorsing the Thirteenth Amendment, which ended slavery. Under Johnson's plan, the electorate in each state would consist of those who both had taken an oath of allegiance to the Union and had been eligible to vote in 1861. Johnson's plan was thus a rejection of the proposal advanced by Radical Republicans in Congress that the federal government should insist on black suffrage as a precondition for readmitting the Southern states to the Union.[4]

It was coming to light that Johnson and Radical Republicans represented two different understandings of Lincoln's legacy. Johnson believed, as Lincoln had, that the Southern states had never legally left the Union and that they should swiftly be restored to it, in a spirit of forgiveness. Indeed, Johnson preferred the word "restoration" to the word "reconstruction." Radicals such as Charles Sumner and Thaddeus Stevens, by contrast, believed Lincoln's legacy was a "new birth of freedom" and that the Confederate states should be reconstructed from the ground up, according to the principles of social justice and equality. Radicals did not reject the deluded-masses theory of the rebellion but instead used it as a framework for dispensing punishment. Stevens, for example, proposed that the government confiscate the estates of very wealthy rebels (those with property worth more than ten thousand dollars or exceeding two hundred acres) and use it to provide plots of land to freedmen, to pay off the war debt, and to pay damages to loyal Unionists. "The poor, the ignorant, and the coerced should be forgiven. They followed the example of their wealthy and intelligent neighbors," he stipulated. The ignorant masses constituted "a large majority of the people, though possessing but a small portion of the wealth," he continued, speculating that nine-tenths of Southern whites would be exempt from confiscation and would instead stand to benefit from it.[5]

While Johnson believed that the power to set the terms of reunion lay with the executive branch, Radicals believed that power lay in Congress. Congressional Republicans pressed the case that the United States must continue to operate on a war footing, sustaining an occupation of the South in which martial law superseded local, civil authorities. Congress's own war powers consisted of its ability to regulate the military, and it extended to the army a set of tools—the authority to make and void labor contracts, to adjudicate freedmen's complaints, to try civilians in courts-martial or military commissions, to monitor newspapers, to ban the sale of liquor or require permits for gun ownership, to arrest and punish outlaws, to override oppressive state laws, and to displace recalcitrant local officials. President Johnson at first saw the necessity for the extension of martial law, and for a time, a hybrid system of governance prevailed, in which Johnson's provisional governors shared power with the military commanders the army had assigned each state. But by the winter of 1865, Johnson and Congress were at odds, with the president eager to shift the balance of power away from the military and toward the civil governments he had sponsored. Moderate Republicans, who dominated Congress, were caught in between: they were wary of black suffrage, but they agreed with Radicals that Congress had the constitutional authority to direct Reconstruction.[6]

Johnson's May 1865 proclamations initiated a period of "self-reconstruction" in the South, during which his provisional governors appointed thousands of former rebels to political office and the new Southern state governments pushed the freedpeople into a state of subordination as close as possible to slavery. Retooling the old antebellum "slave codes," the new Black Codes, which took shape by the end of 1865, were designed to enforce white supremacy. The codes pressured blacks to sign annual labor contracts with white employers, typically their former masters; made it a crime to act "insolent" to whites; permitted white judges to seize and apprentice out any black children whose families did not meet with white approval;

levied regressive and punitive taxes on black property; and increased the penalties for crimes such as larceny and trespassing. This regime was enforced by an all-white police and judicial system. Carl Schurz, a Union general and Radical Republican who undertook a fact-finding mission to the South in the summer and fall of 1865, sent Johnson a series of despairing reports on the resurgence of ex-Confederates. "The colored people as well as the small number of faithful Union-men are perfectly helpless in the hands of those who but recently were the open enemies of the Union," he lamented, condemning both the continued sway of the old Southern leadership class and the "vindictive spirit and bad passions of the masses." The true Union men felt like a "conquered people" and the former rebels "act like conquerors."[7]

The Republican press echoed this assessment. Articles with titles such as "Rebel Obstinacy," "Spirit of the South," and "What to Do with Them" observed that the government had "dealt with the deluded people with gloved hands," only to find its "generosity and paternal tenderness" met with defiance and contempt. Johnson's leniency to the Southern elite, in the form of his pardons and his choice of provisional governors, had sent the wrong message to the masses, encouraging them to see the rebellion's "extreme leaders" as "worthy of respect." Justice to the masses required that some leaders be held to account—deprived, at the very least, of the opportunity to resume "positions of trust and honor." Northern free blacks added to this chorus of criticism. Having surveyed conditions in the South while on a mission to establish Masonic lodges among freedmen in Virginia and the Carolinas, eminent Boston reformer Lewis Hayden told his fellow black Masons in Massachusetts "that in each of the places I visited, there is evidently a deep and unalterable purpose in the hearts of the old oppressors to blast, or at least crush out, the rising hopes and dawning prospects of their late bondmen." Hayden blamed Johnson, who had "given new license to traitors to perpetrate outrages and crimes." Invoking the October 1864 Nashville speech in which Johnson had posed as a liberator of slaves, Hayden declared, "Deliver us from such a Moses," and commented, "I fear he will prove to be the Pharaoh of our day."[8]

Southern Unionists appealed to Johnson on their own behalf. African American leaders in the former Confederate states petitioned Johnson for suffrage, emphasizing their role as liberators of the South. "We cannot understand the justice of denying the elective franchise to men who have been fighting for the country, while it is freely given to men who have just returned from four years fighting against it," stated a North Carolina petition. A smattering of white Southern Unionists supported black suffrage; without black votes to bolster the loyal electorate, warned a white Tennessee Unionist in May 1865, "rebels will re-elect rebels."[9]

That is exactly what came to pass. Under Johnson's Reconstruction plan, state governments were handed over to former Confederates. Scores of former Confederate officials were elected to serve in the Thirty-ninth U.S. Congress, which would convene in December 1865. Congress refused to seat these representatives or to recognize the restored governments, and it formed a Joint Committee on Reconstruction to assess the impact of Johnson's policies in the South. Congress's refusal to seat representatives from the rebel states was a delaying tactic designed to preserve the period of legal limbo in which the U.S. government could exercise war powers in the South, and to buy time in which constitutional protections for the freedpeople could be devised and instituted.[10]

Historians have attributed Johnson's appeasement of former rebels to his deep-seated racism, his pleasure in having the planter class come before him on bended knee to receive their pardons, his commitment to states' rights, and his desire to build a new electoral constituency, composed of conservative Democrats and Republicans, for a presidential bid in 1868. All of these factors were on display when a delegation of "respectable citizens" (former Confederates) of nine Southern states called on Johnson in September 1865 to tender their support for his policies. Pledging their "sincere respect and regard" for the president, these men, led by Virginian William H. McFarland (a Richmond financier and former member of the Confederate Congress), praised Johnson for his commitment to "maintain[ing] Southern rights in the union." Johnson's response reveals a great deal about his politics and mentality. He told the delegation he felt deeply honored by their "manifestations of regard" and their willingness to abide by the results of the war. He explained that he had always had the interests of the South at heart and that the men who had opposed him during the war were the very "gentlemen" he had hoped to "befriend and guide" and to save from their own errors. And he promised that just as he had stood fast against the disintegration of the Union, he would stand fast against "consolidation"—namely, the Radical Republicans' efforts to give Congress overweening power over the states. In Johnson's view, his unique suffering and martyrdom as the leading wartime champion of Southern Unionism entitled him to political deference; he expected repentance from elite rebels, but he saw their willingness to defer to him as proof of a properly penitent frame of mind.[11]

Former rebels, as they implored Johnson to lift the occupation, exulted him as the defender of a "white man's Government" against the "Radical

Destructionists," as a Nashville lawyer, R. Weakley Brown, wrote to Johnson in late September 1865. The "Southern people are rallying to you as in days of yore," Brown noted, invoking the broad support Johnson had commanded as a leading Democrat before the war; the president could, Brown imagined, build a new coalition of conservative Republicans, Northern Democrats, and the "United South." Pro-Johnson press organs developed a case that the president was the "great barrier" against the "destructive disunionists in Congress and of the press, who invoke vengeance in coming ages upon the crushed masses of the South." During the war Johnson had sought to deliver the South from Confederate military despotism; now, his allies argued, he could deliver the South from Radical Republican military despotism.[12]

For Johnson and his supporters, the Freedmen's Bureau became the primary symbol of Radical Republican "despotism." Congress had created the Bureau of Refugees, Freedmen and Abandoned Lands in March 1865 to operate for one year after the war's end. A pioneering federal social welfare agency, the bureau's brief was to manage abandoned lands; aid the transition to peacetime for loyal white Southern refugees and freedpeople; provide Southerners in war-torn regions with humanitarian relief such as food, clothing, fuel, shelter, and medical aid; and assist in negotiating labor contracts and setting up schools. White Southerners, including those who had supported the Confederacy, benefitted materially from the bureau's work— white Georgians, for example, received 170,000 rations from the bureau from June 1865 to September 1866, and whites received much more bureau relief than blacks did in Alabama, Arkansas, Missouri, and Tennessee. Former Confederates nonetheless condemned the federal agency as a symbol of their humiliating defeat and of Congress's radical agenda of racial equality. Johnson himself took direct aim at the Freedmen's Bureau, dispatching the conservative Union general Joseph S. Fullerton to the South to compile complaints against it; Fullerton obligingly reported that the bureau extended aid only to blacks and withheld aid from poor whites (this was false). White Southerners reached out directly to Johnson with protests that bureau agents were acting as imperious "overseers," lording it over whites and doing the bidding of blacks. When Congress passed bills in February and July 1866 to extend the life of the bureau, Johnson vetoed both. Northern Democrats joined with former Confederates in supporting Johnson. An Ohio Democratic newspaper, for example, responded to Johnson's first veto message by proclaiming, "Great Victory for the White Man. Rejoice, White Man, Rejoice! The Hour of Your Deliverance Has Come."[13]

The reports that Congress received from the South—harrowing accounts of anti-black violence and proscription—prompted moderate Republican senator Lyman Trumbull, chairman of the Senate Judiciary Committee, to propose in early 1866 a Civil Rights bill that would invalidate the Black Codes. Although it did not broach the subject of black suffrage, the Civil Rights Act guaranteed the right of national citizens, defined as those born in the United States, to make contracts, bring lawsuits, hold property, and claim the "full and equal benefit" of the laws protecting persons and property. Emboldened by the sense that he was successfully building a constituency among Northern Democrats as well as among former rebels, Johnson vetoed the bill on March 27, 1866. His veto message claimed that the bill didn't simply level the playing field but instead discriminated against whites: "The distinction of race and color is by the bill made to operate in favor of the colored against the white race."[14]

Republicans overrode Johnson's vetoes and declared him to be a traitor to the party and to the Union—they called him a Copperhead, and they accused him, too, of being prone to "alcoholic rowdyism." As a safeguard against the possible repeal or judicial review of the Civil Rights Act, Congress formulated the Fourteenth Amendment to the Constitution in April 1866—guaranteeing the freedpeople the equal protection of the law and due process—and required Southern states to accept it as a condition of their return to the Union; that amendment passed Congress in June 1866 and awaited ratification by the states. Meanwhile, tragic events in Memphis, Tennessee, dramatized the need to offer additional protections for black citizenship. On May 1, 1866, a white mob, led by city policemen, began a wave of attacks against African Americans in South Memphis. The violence would stretch out over three terror-filled days. The context for the mob violence was white fear and resentment at the prospect of "social equality" between the races—a prospect, so Southern whites charged, heralded in the passage of the civil rights bill. Radical Republicans shot back that Johnson and his policies, by emboldening ex-Confederates, were responsible for the Memphis affair and for an equally tragic race riot in New Orleans.[15]

Johnson fought back against such charges, embarking in August 1866 on his "Swing Round the Circle"—the ill-fated tour of Northern cities that he undertook in order to drum up support for his agenda of restoration. This was an open bid to influence the looming 1866 congressional elections, and it went terribly awry. Provoked by hecklers, Johnson repeatedly lashed out at the crowds that gathered to hear him, hissing that he was as prepared to "fight traitors at the North" as he had been to fight Southern traitors. Republicans countered by sending out Southern loyalists such as Parson Brownlow of Tennessee and Andrew J. Hamilton of Texas to make the case to Northern audiences that "rebels had taken charge across the ex-Confederacy" and that the Fourteenth Amendment was a necessary safeguard of the Union's victory. Johnson's intemperate speechifying during the "swing" cost his allies votes, as he alienated many moderate Republicans and Democrats alike; in the fall of 1866, anti-Johnson Republicans increased their congressional majority.[16]

The Republican perspective was given a striking visual representation by Thomas Nast, the brilliantly acerbic illustrator for *Harper's Weekly*. In the October 27, 1866, issue, Nast offered up his depiction of "Andy's Trip." At the center was Johnson as martyr, with the caption "Who Has Suffered More for You and for This Union than Andrew Johnson?" But the surrounding panels dramatized the Republican critique of Johnson as a traitor to the Republican Party and to the Union. Johnson was flanked by images of the suffering of Union soldiers and loyalist civilians during the war, with captions reading "Andy forgot our soldiers & sailors" and "Andy forgot our wives and children." At each bottom corner were extracts from Johnson's wartime speeches, in which he had promised to mete out stern punishments to the leading rebels. And ringing the center were depictions of Johnson's many sins: handing out pardons, booting loyal Republicans from office, and acting in public like a common brawler. The message was clear: Johnson had betrayed the Northern public, and betrayed the promises of deliverance.[17]

"Andy Forgot Our Soldiers & Sailors." This cartoon by Thomas Nast contrasts Johnson's self-image as a martyr to the Union with his postwar policies of appeasing the former rebels. (Library of Congress LC-DIG-ds-09704)

Congressional Reconstruction and Beyond

In 1867–68, Congress implemented its own Reconstruction plan and impeached the president, very nearly driving him out of office. Congress's March 1867 Reconstruction Acts inaugurated an unprecedented experiment in interracial democracy in the former Confederate states, as the newly enfranchised freedmen formed a governing coalition with white Southern Unionists and Northern Republican transplants to the South. The congressional program enfranchised approximately one million African Americans and gave them a voice, for the first time, in Southern politics. African Americans held public office at the municipal, county, state, and federal levels. The Republican coalition, with the support of Johnson's successor as president, U. S. Grant, implemented measures to modernize the South, providing public education and social services for black and white citizens alike. These were remarkable and even revolutionary changes. Yet some things did not change. Whites continued to dominate Southern politics: the numerically dominant element in the Republican coalition was white Southerners, some of whom were former Unionists but many of whom had supported the rebellion. Ex-Confederates largely retained the right to vote; indeed, black politicians typically argued against the disfranchisement of Confederates, in an effort to uphold as sacrosanct the principle of universal manhood suffrage. Even at the height of Congressional Reconstruction, African Americans were underrepresented in Southern politics: they held roughly 15 to 20 percent of elective offices in the South. The former plantation elite retained and recovered their economic power, measured in land for producing staple crops and capital for investments in new ventures such as railroads and textile mills.[18]

Congressional Reconstruction was assailed by propaganda and violence from the very moment it started. During the presidency of Johnson's successor, Ulysses S. Grant, former Confederates ratcheted up their campaign to preempt and turn back social change. That campaign disparaged Union soldiers as "mongrels" and "mercenaries," cast black participation in politics as the imposition of corrupt and vindictive "Negro Rule" on the prostrate South, perpetrated widespread electoral fraud and intimidation, and conjured the violence of the Ku Klux Klan and other white supremacist terrorists to drive the Unionist coalition out of Southern politics. The resurgence of the Southern Democrats went hand in hand with the spread of Lost Cause ideology, which idealized the slave system and the Old South; depicted Confederates as united, blameless, and righteous martyrs who were overwhelmed by the ruthless Yankee war machine; and sought to justify vigilante violence as a legitimate means to "redeem" the suffering South from Radical Republican misrule. This myth explicitly repudiated the deluded-masses theory of the rebellion. There were no dupes or dissenters in Lost Cause histories, only diehard Confederates and faithful white women and slaves. Citing the fact that the University of Virginia had sent nearly all of its student body into the Confederate ranks in 1861, UVA alumnus and Confederate veteran Randolph McKim, in his postwar memoir, asserted "the falsity of the theory . . . that the uprising of the Southern people was the result of a conspiracy of a few ambitious leaders. . . . [T]he resistance offered to coercion in 1861 was in no sense artificial, but free and spontaneous . . . the act of the people, not of the politicians." Lost Cause histories swept under the rug the wartime experiences of Southerners, black and white, in the Union coalition.[19]

Union veterans contested the Lost Cause narrative in memory traditions of their own. White veterans, celebrating the "Won Cause" as the triumph of democracy over aristocracy, featured the deluded-masses theory in their postwar regimental histories and memoirs, condemning the slaveholding elite for bringing on the war and for the South's moral and economic backwardness. But those memories did not translate into active support for black civil rights; for most white Union veterans, as Barbara Gannon has explained, "the triumph of free labor over slavery did not require social and political equality for black Americans." Such an attitude underlay what historians have called the Northern "retreat from reconstruction" in the 1870s: a loss of commitment to federal intervention in the turbulent South and a growing inclination, at a time when the North was grappling with political corruption, labor unrest, and an economic crisis, to see Congressional Reconstruction as a political liability. As historian Mark Wahlgren Summers has noted, white Northerners reckoned that "if Reconstruction had been to secure freedom and make the reunification of the nation permanent, it had succeeded." The specters of slavery, secession, and civil war had been banished. "The crisis of the Union had passed and with it the need to put none but loyal men on guard down south."[20]

African Americans and the small number of whites committed to full racial equality dreamed of something more: of a nation "where no color line ran its barriers through law, politics, or institutions." Black veterans, writing in an "emancipationist" tradition, shared white soldiers' pride in bringing Slave Power aristocrats to heel, but drew on that victory as a wellspring for activism in the ongoing civil rights struggle. "History proves beyond a doubt," U.S. Colored Troops veteran Joseph T. Wilson wrote in his 1882 book *Emancipation*, "that the advancing spirit of freedom has always been met by a relentless war waged by the oppressors of mankind." Wilson and his fellow activists saw the quest for freedpeople's citizenship in the South as inseparable from free blacks' long-standing campaign for full equality in the Northern states, where they remained, even after the Fifteenth Amendment provided for black male suffrage, second-class citizens, proscribed by custom and law. Like other black leaders of his generation, Wilson exposed the injustices in Northern society while also emphatically rejecting any false equivalency between the Confederate cause and the Union cause. As he argued in his pathbreaking 1887 history of African American military service, *The Black Phalanx*, barbarity toward blacks was Confederate policy, promulgated from on high by Jefferson Davis, who sought to bring about a "war of extermination against the negro soldiers." USCT troops had worked to save a flawed Union so that its ideals of equality could be realized and its destiny as a beacon of freedom could be fulfilled.[21]

No one offered a more powerful exposition of the promises of deliverance than Frederick Douglass in his 1878 Memorial Day speech, "There Was a Right Side in the Late War." Douglass began the speech by paying homage to the "heroic deeds and virtues of the brave men who volunteered, fought, and fell in the cause of the Union and freedom." For Douglass, Union and freedom were properly understood as one cause, not as two causes. He invoked the high stakes and drama of the war years, a time of trial when "each day of the week saw thousands of brave men in the full fresh bloom of youth and manly vigor, the very flower and hope of the hearts and homes of the loyal and peaceful North . . . periling all that was most precious to them for the sake of their country." "May your memory never perish!" Douglass intoned.[22]

But then, as he turned from the past to the present, Douglass's speech became a lamentation. The "great work" the Union army had sought to accomplish was still incomplete. A "lawless and revolutionary spirit" was rampant in the South, where unreconstructed rebels were "endeavoring to paralyze the arm and shrivel the body of the National Government so that it cannot protect the humblest citizen in his rights." Douglass acknowledged the pervasiveness of the deliverance trope when he observed, "I do not affirm that friendly feeling cannot be established between the people of the North and South . . . but I do say that some steps by way of conciliation should come from the other side. The prodigal son should at least turn his back upon the field of swine, and his face toward home, before we make haste to fall upon his neck, and for him kill the fatted calf. He must not glory in his shame, and boast his non-repentance. He must not reenact at home the excesses he allowed himself to commit in the barren and desolate fields of rebellion." He continued, "We have always been ready to meet rebels more than half way and to hail them as fellow-citizens, countrymen, clansmen, and brothers beloved." But the premise of this magnanimity, he insisted, was the conviction that the cause of Union and freedom was righteous. Claiming the Declaration of Independence for the forces of freedom, Douglass described the Civil War as a "war of ideas": "a war between the old and new, slavery and freedom, barbarism and civilization; between a government based on the broadest and grandest declaration of human rights the world ever heard or read, and another pretended government, based upon an open, bold, and shocking denial of all rights, except the right of the strongest." Alluding to the way that Southerners claimed to suffer persecution at the hands of the North, Douglass set the record straight. The South had "suffered to be sure, but she has been the author of her own suffering." Invoking Lincoln's words and legacy, Douglass refused to yield the moral high ground: "There was a right side and a wrong side in the late war, which no sentiment ought to cause us to forget, and while to-day we should have malice toward none, and charity toward all, it is no part of our duty to confound right with wrong, or loyalty with treason." Douglass kept faith that the "heart of the nation" was "sound and strong," and that "in the future, patriotic millions, with able captains to lead them, will stand as a wall of fire around the Republic, and in the end see Liberty, Equality, and Justice triumphant."[23]

The story of Civil War–era deliverance politics is both bounded by a specific time and place and boundless, with modern echoes. Nineteenth-century Americans had their own distinct political lexicon, consisting of words, such as "Union," "disunion," and "benevolence," that would fade from use, or change in meaning, during the modern era. In a sense, "deliverance" is such a word: as American politics became less steeped in providential references, the word became less prevalent as a political signifier. But it retained its power as a signifier in the freedom struggle. As historian John Coffey has observed, "The collapse of Reconstruction in the South ensured that the biblical story [of Exodus] retained its resonance. Living under Jim Crow and segregation, black Protestants found they had neither reached the Promised Land nor got clear of Egypt." Over the course of the long civil rights crusade, generations of African American activists, together with some white allies, have again and again drawn on the symbolic power of the Exodus story and of deliverance narratives. And whites opposed to change, in a grammar of recalcitrance with its own long history, have revived the rhetoric of Southern victimhood whenever the system of racial privilege is challenged.[24]

Notes

INTRODUCTION

1. "Fighting for Our Foes," *Harper's Weekly*, Jul. 30, 1864, 482–83. *Harper's Weekly* and *Frank Leslie's Illustrated Newspaper* were the two leading illustrated newspapers of the Civil War era. Based in New York City and run by the Harper & Brothers publishing company, *Harper's* had a circulation of roughly two hundred thousand and an effective readership of half a million people. It had endorsed the Democratic candidate Stephen Douglas in the 1860 election but supported Lincoln once the war began.

2. For an emphasis on saving the Union as the overarching Northern war aim, see Gary W. Gallagher, *The Union War* (Cambridge, MA: Harvard University Press, 2011), William C. Harris, *With Charity for All: Lincoln and the Restoration of the Union* (Lexington: University Press of Kentucky, 1997), and Adam I. P. Smith, *The Stormy Present: Conservatism and the Problem of Slavery in Northern Politics, 1846–1865* (Chapel Hill: University of North Carolina Press, 2017); for an emphasis on the centrality of emancipation to Union war aims, see James Oakes, *Freedom National: The Destruction of Slavery in the United States, 1861–1865* (New York: W. W. Norton, 2013), Chandra Manning, *What This Cruel War Was Over: Soldiers, Slavery and the Civil War* (New York: Knopf, 2007), and Graham A. Peck, *Making an Antislavery Nation: Lincoln, Douglas, and the Battle over Freedom* (Urbana: University of Illinois Press, 2017); for studies that emphasize change over time from Union to emancipation as the primary war aim, see Mark Grimsley, *The Hard Hand of War: Union Military Policy Toward Southern Civilians, 1861–1865* (Cambridge: Cambridge University Press, 1996) and William W. Freehling, *The South vs. the South: How Anti-Confederate Southerners Shaped the Course of the Civil War* (New York: Oxford University Press, 2001).

3. Scholars acknowledge the prevalence of the deluded-masses theory in the early days of the war but have failed to recognize its persistence; the strong consensus is that Northerners' belief in latent Southern Unionism evaporated as the Federal strategy

shifted from conciliation to hard war. See, for example, James M. McPherson, *Battle Cry of Freedom: The Civil War Era* (New York: Oxford University Press, 1988); Charles Royster, *The Destructive War: William Tecumseh Sherman, Stonewall Jackson, and the Americans* (New York: Knopf, 1991); Grimsley, *The Hard Hand of War*; Earl J. Hess, *Liberty, Virtue and Progress: Northerners and Their War for the Union* (New York: Fordham University Press, 1997); Freehling, *The South vs. the South*; Harry S. Stout, *Upon the Altar of the Nation: A Moral History of the Civil War* (New York: Viking, 2006); Oakes, *Freedom National;* Timothy S. Huebner, *Liberty and Union: The Civil War Era and American Constitutionalism* (Lawrence: University Press of Kansas, 2016). For an excellent historiographical survey and critique of the narrative of soft war to hard war, see Wayne Wei-Siang Hsieh, "Total War and the American Civil War Reconsidered: The End of an Outdated 'Master Narrative,'" *Journal of the Civil War Era*, Sep. 2011, 394–408. For two rare works that recognize the persistence of the deluded-masses theory throughout the war, see Nancy Isenberg, *White Trash: The 400-Year Untold History of Class in America* (New York: Penguin, 2016), 158–61, and Martha Hodes, *Mourning Lincoln* (New Haven, CT: Yale University Press, 2015), 131–36.

4. "Fighting for Our Foes," 482–83. I am indebted to two works that elaborate the concept of "deliverance politics": Mona Harrington's *The Dream of Deliverance in American Politics* (New York: Knopf, 1986) and John Coffey's *Exodus and Liberation: Deliverance Politics from John Calvin to Martin Luther King Jr.* (New York: Oxford University Press, 2014). Harrington argues in her account of twentieth-century U.S. statecraft that American politics has been shaped by a myth, traceable back to the Founding, that deliverance from wrongful power is always possible if society can devise and adhere to an equitable rule-making system. Coffey argues that biblical traditions of liberation have suffused American politics from the colonial era to the present day.

5. On antebellum politics and the Slave Power idea, see, for example, Leonard L. Richards, *The Slave Power: The Free North and Southern Domination, 1780–1860* (Baton Rouge: Louisiana State University Press, 2000); Eric Foner, *Free Soil, Free Labor, Free Men: The Ideology of the Republican Party Before the Civil War* (New York: Oxford University Press, 1995); Elizabeth R. Varon, *Disunion! The Coming of the American Civil War* (Chapel Hill: University of North Carolina Press, 2008); Andre Fleche, *Revolution of 1861: The American Civil War in the Age of Nationalist Conflict* (Chapel Hill: University of North Carolina Press, 2012).

6. Michael F. Holt, *The Election of 1860: "A Campaign Fraught with Consequences"* (Lawrence: University Press of Kansas, 2017), 194–95.

7. Hodes, *Mourning Lincoln*, 132–33.

8. Abraham Lincoln, "Message to Congress in Special Session," July 4, 1861, in *Lincoln's Selected Writings*, ed. David S. Reynolds (New York: W. W. Norton, 2015), 245–47.

9. *New York Herald*, May 25, Aug. 28, 1861; Jun. 19, 1862; *New York Times*, June 5, 1861; *Boston Daily Advertiser*, Sept. 5, 1861.

10. *Liberator*, May 31, Oct. 4, 1861; *New York Tribune*, Jun. 28, 1861. While not a comprehensive index, newspaper databases are suggestive of patterns in word use: a July 26, 2018, keyword search of U.S. newspapers in the digital database Newspapers .com showed 118 hits for the word "terrorism" in 1859, 145 hits in 1860, and 778 in 1861; a search in Readex's America's Historical Newspapers database yielded 15 hits for "terrorism" in 1859, 27 in 1860, and 124 in 1861.

11. See, for example, Daniel W. Crofts, *Reluctant Confederates: Upper South Unionists in the Secession Crisis* (Chapel Hill: University of North Carolina Press, 1993) and William Link, *The Roots of Secession: Slavery and Politics in Antebellum Virginia* (Chapel Hill: University of North Carolina Press, 2003).

12. Franklin, PA, *Semi-Weekly Dispatch*, May 10, 1861; Christopher Phillips, "Lincoln's Grasp of War: Hard War and the Politics of Neutrality and Slavery in the Western Border States, 1861–1862," *Journal of the Civil War Era*, Jun. 2013, 184–210.

13. Don H. Doyle, *The Cause of All Nations: An International History of the American Civil War* (New York: Basic Books, 2015), 6–7.

14. Horace Carter Hovey, *Freedom's Banner: A Sermon Preached to the Coldwater Light Artillery, and the Coldwater Zouave Cadets, April 28th, 1861* (Coldwater, MI: Republican Print, 1861), 9. Coffey has argued that abolitionism tapped an Anglo-American tradition of "Protestant deliverance politics," rooted in an understanding of the Reformation as a "movement of liberation from popish servitude." Coffey, *Exodus and Liberation*, 6–8, 19–21, 124–25, 134–38. See also George C. Rable, *God's Almost Chosen People: A Religious History of the American Civil War* (Chapel Hill: University of North Carolina Press, 2010); Timothy L. Wesley, *The Politics of Faith During the Civil War* (Baton Rouge: Louisiana State University Press, 2013); and Edward J. Blum, "'The First Secessionist Was Satan': Secession and the Religious Politics of Evil in Civil War America," *Civil War History,* Sept. 2014, 234–69.

15. Michael E. Woods, *Emotional and Sectional Conflict in the Antebellum United States* (Cambridge: Cambridge University Press, 2014), 16, 20–30, 234–35; Matthew Mason, *Apostle of Union: A Political Biography of Edward Everett* (Chapel Hill: University of North Carolina Press, 2016), 315–21.

16. Mason, *Apostle of Union*, 316 (quotation). Much of the modern scholarship on Northern nationalism paints it as sectional and oppositional, overlooking Northerners' preoccupation with winning over white Southerners. See, for example, Melinda Lawson, *Patriot Fires: Forging a New American Nationalism in the Civil War North* (Lawrence: University Press of Kansas, 2002); Susan-Mary Grant, *North over South: Northern Nationalism and American Identity in the Antebellum Era* (Lawrence: University Press of Kansas, 2000); and Phillip Shaw Paludan, *"A People's Contest": The Union and the Civil War, 1861–1865* (New York: Harper & Row, 1988). For insights into the didactic nature of Northern culture, see Daniel Walker Howe, *The Political Culture of the American Whigs* (Chicago: University of Chicago Press, 1984) and Leslie Butler, "Lincoln as the Great Educator: Opinion

and Educative Liberalism in the Civil War Era," in Jörg Nagler, Don H. Doyle, and Marcus Graser, eds., *The Transnational Significance of the American Civil War* (Basel, Switzerland: Springer International Publishing, 2016), 49–57. Butler argues that Lincoln embodied a strand of nineteenth-century liberalism she calls "educative liberalism," in which "political leaders—along with ministers, teachers, lecturers, and writers—had a moral responsibility to work toward the 'education and redirection' of popular opinion."

17. *Richmond Daily Dispatch*, Apr. 18, May 9, 1861; *Charleston Mercury*, May 7, 1861; Jennifer L. Weber, *Copperheads: The Rise and Fall of Lincoln's Opponents in the North* (New York: Oxford University Press, 2006), 16–23.

18. Lincoln, Annual Message to Congress, Dec. 1, 1862, in *Lincoln's Selected Writings*, 296.

19. Frederick Douglass, "A Friendly Word to Maryland: An Address Delivered in Baltimore, Maryland on 17 November 1864," in *The Frederick Douglass Papers*, series one, *Speeches, Debates, and Interviews*, vol. 4, *1864–1880*, ed. John W. Blassingame and John R. McKivigan (New Haven, CT: Yale University Press, 1991), 38–49; *Christian Recorder*, Dec. 31, 1864; *The Liberator* (Boston), Dec. 9, 1864. On black politics and activism in the North, see, for example, Erica Armstrong Dunbar, *Fragile Freedom: African American Women and Emancipation in the Antebellum City* (New Haven: Yale University Press, 2008); Stephen Kantrowitz, *More than Freedom: Fighting for Black Citizenship in a White Republic, 1829–1889* (New York: Penguin, 2012); Andrew K. Diemer, *The Politics of Black Citizenship: Free African Americans in the Mid-Atlantic Borderland, 1817–1863* (Athens: University of Georgia Press, 2016); and Manisha Sinha, *The Slave's Cause: A History of Abolition* (New Haven: Yale University Press, 2016). At least 144,000 of the 179,000 blacks who served in the Union army came from slave states. Joseph T. Glatthaar, *Forged in Battle: The Civil War Alliance of Black Soldiers and White Officers* (Baton Rouge: Louisiana State University Press, 1990), 146–47 and https://www.archives.gov/education/lessons/blacks-civil-war .

20. Cornelius Henry Edgar, *God's Help: The Ground of Hope for Our Country: A Sermon Preached on the Day of National Thanksgiving, Nov. 24, 1864* (New York: Baker & Godwin, 1864), 8, 13–14, 16–17.

21. Alpheus S. Williams, *From the Canon's Mouth: The Civil War Letters of General Alpheus S. Williams* (Lincoln: University of Nebraska Press, 1995), 99; *Christian Recorder*, May 7, 1864; Gallagher, *Union War*, 68; Kanisorn Wongsrichanalai, *Northern Character: College-Educated New Englanders, Honor, Nationalism, and Leadership in the Civil War Era* (New York: Fordham University Press, 2016), 16–17, 114–17, 122–23; Adam Wesley Dean, *An Agrarian Republic: Farming, Antislavery Politics, and Nature Parks in the Civil War Era* (Chapel Hill: University of North Carolina Press, 2015), 100–101.

22. D. H. Dilbeck, *A More Civil War: How the Union Waged a Just War* (Chapel Hill: University of North Carolina Press, 2016), 3–8; James Henry Gooding, *On*

the Altar of Freedom: A Black Soldier's Civil War Letters from the Front, ed. Virginia Matzke Adams (Amherst: University of Massachusetts Press, 1991), 19.

23. On the exemplary-suffering trope, see Frances M. Clarke, *War Stories: Suffering and Sacrifice in the Civil War North* (Chicago: University of Chicago Press, 2011); for an excellent introduction to debates over women's war work and politicization, see Nina Silber, *Gender and the Sectional Conflict* (Chapel Hill: University of North Carolina Press, 2009).

24. J. Gregory Acken, ed., *Inside the Army of the Potomac: The Civil War Experience of Captain Francis Adams Donaldson* (Mechanicsburg, PA: Stackpole Books, 1998), 71; Moncure D. Conway, *Addresses and Reprints, 1850–1907* (Boston: Houghton Mifflin, 1909), 125; Horatio Stebbins, *The President, the People, and the War: A Thanksgiving Discourse* (San Francisco: Charles F. Robbins, 1864), 19, 21. On nineteenth-century understandings of pain, see Martin S. Pernick, *A Calculus of Suffering: Pain, Professionalism, and Anesthesia in Nineteenth-Century America* (New York: Columbia University Press, 1985).

25. Hess, *Liberty, Virtue and Progress*, x–xi, 10.

26. Wongsrichanalai, *Northern Character*, 123.

27. *Sacramento Daily Union*, Nov. 19, 1864.

28. Joseph L. Harsh, *Confederate Tide Rising: Robert E. Lee and the Making of Southern Strategy, 1861–1862* (Kent, OH: Kent State University Press, 1998), 7; Paul Quigley, *Shifting Grounds: Nationalism and the American South, 1848–1865* (New York: Oxford University Press, 2012), 129–31, 136, 139 (quote).

29. On antebellum Southern social dynamics, see, for example, Varon, *Disunion!*; Link, *Roots of Secession*; David Grimsted, *American Mobbing, 1828–1861: Toward Civil War* (New York: Oxford University Press, 1998); Peter Kolchin, *American Slavery: 1619–1877* (New York: Hill and Wang, 1993). On the broad spectrum of slave resistance and its inherently political nature, see, for example, Stephanie Camp, *Closer to Freedom: Enslaved Woman and Everyday Resistance in the Plantation South* (Chapel Hill: University of North Carolina Press, 2004) and Anthony E. Kaye, *Joining Places: Slave Neighborhoods in the Old South* (Chapel Hill: University of North Carolina Press, 2007).

30. Modern scholars agree that slaves' "most effective protest against the system was to run away." Link, *Roots of Secession*, 98. On the Underground Railroad, see, for example, Eric Foner, *Gateway to Freedom: The Hidden History of the Underground Railroad* (New York: W. W. Norton, 2015) and R. J. M. Blackett, *The Captive's Quest for Freedom: Fugitive Slaves, the 1850 Fugitive Slave Law, and the Politics of Slavery* (New York: Cambridge University Press, 2018). On secessionist rhetoric, see Charles Dew, *Apostles of Disunion: Southern Secession Commissioners and the Causes of the Civil War* (Charlottesville: University of Virginia Press, 2001), 98. On Confederate expansionism see Robert E. May, "The Irony of Confederate Diplomacy: Visions of Empire, the Monroe Doctrine, and the Quest for Nationhood," *Journal of Southern History* 83 (Feb. 2017): 70–73; Walter Johnson, *River of Dark Dreams: Slavery and*

Empire in the Cotton Kingdom (Cambridge, MA: Harvard University Press, 2013); Matthew Karp, *This Vast Southern Empire: Slaveholders at the Helm of American Foreign Policy* (Cambridge, MA: Harvard University Press, 2016).

31. Freehling, *The South vs. the South*, 18–19.

32. James M. McPherson, *This Mighty Scourge: Perspectives on the Civil War* (New York: Oxford University Press, 2007), 53–61.

33. *Richmond Daily Dispatch*, Mar. 19, 1862; Coffey, *Exodus and Liberation*, 135–36.

34. Ward W. Briggs Jr., *Soldier and Scholar: Basil Lanneau Gildersleeve and the Civil War* (Charlottesville: University Press of Virginia, 1998), 128–39, 178.

35. George Rable, *Damn Yankees! Demonization and Defiance in the Confederate South* (Baton Rouge: Louisiana State University Press, 2015), 6–7, 52–57; Stephen V. Ash, *When the Yankees Came: Conflict and Chaos in the Occupied South, 1861–1865* (Chapel Hill: University of North Carolina Press, 1995), 11; Michael T. Bernath, *Confederate Minds: The Struggle for Intellectual Independence in the Civil War South* (Chapel Hill: University of North Carolina Press, 2010), 48–57.

36. Mark E. Neely Jr., *Southern Rights: Political Prisoners and the Myth of Confederate Constitutionalism* (Charlottesville: University Press of Virginia, 1999), 146–47; Jarret Ruminski, *The Limits of Loyalty: Ordinary People in Civil War Mississippi* (Jackson: University Press of Mississippi, 2017), 36, 56.

37. Ash, *When the Yankees Came*, 40; Beale as quoted in Gary W. Gallagher, *The Confederate War* (Cambridge: Harvard University Press, 1997), 79. See also George C. Rable, *Civil Wars: Women and the Crisis of Southern Nationalism* (Urbana: University of Illinois Press, 1989), and Silber, *Gender and the Sectional Conflict*.

38. Quigley, *Shifting Grounds*, 181–87, 200–204 (quote on 200); *Richmond Daily Dispatch*, Jan. 2, Mar. 21, 1865.

CHAPTER 1

1. Harris, *With Charity for All*, 23; *Wheeling* (VA) *Daily Intelligencer*, Apr. 29, Aug. 6, 1861.

2. Edward Longacre, "Irvin McDowell," Encyclopedia Virginia, http://www.encyclopediavirginia.org/mcdowell_irvin_1818-1885.

3. Russell F. Weigley, *A Great Civil War: A Military and Political History, 1861–1865* (Bloomington: Indiana University Press, 2000), 58–62.

4. Richard Wheeler, ed., *Voices of the Civil War* (New York: Penguin, 1976), 46.

5. Charles Minor Blackford, "From *Letters from Lee's Army*," in Brooks D. Simpson, Stephen W. Sears and Aaron Sheehan-Dean, eds., *The Civil War: The First Year Told by Those Who Lived It* (New York: Library of America, 2011), 460–61.

6. Edwin Barrett, *What I Saw at Bull Run* (Boston: Beacon Press, 1886), 26.

7. William T. Sherman to Ellen Ewing Sherman, Jul. 28, 1861, in Simpson et al., eds., *Civil War: First Year*, 529–30.

8. P. G. T. Beauregard, *A Proclamation to the Good People of the Counties of Alexandria, Loudon, Fairfax, & Prince William* (1861), broadside, University of Virginia Special Collections.

9. Anne S. Frobel, *The Civil War Diary of Anne S. Frobel* (McLean, VA: EPM Publications, 1992), 25, 34–40.

10. George D. Armstrong, *The Good Hand of Our God upon Us* (Norfolk, VA: J. D. Ghiselin Jr., 1861), University of Virginia Special Collections.

11. Ethan S. Rafuse, *McClellan's War: The Failure of Moderation in the Struggle for the Union* (Bloomington: Indiana University Press, 2005), 100, 108–17 (quotations on 111 and 115); *American Union* (Martinsburg, VA), Jul. 4, 1861.

12. Donald Stoker, *The Grand Design: Strategy and the U.S. Civil War* (New York: Oxford University Press, 2010), 55–65; Brooks D. Simpson, *The Civil War in the East: Struggle, Stalemate, and Victory* (Lincoln: University of Nebraska Press, 2013), 17; Richard Slotkin, *The Long Road to Antietam: How the Civil War Became a Revolution* (New York: Liveright, 2012), xxii–xxiv.

13. Frederick Douglass, "How to End the War," May 1861, in Simpson et al., eds., *Civil War: First Year*, 334.

14. Glenn David Brasher, *The Peninsula Campaign and the Necessity of Emancipation: African Americans and the Fight for Freedom* (Chapel Hill: University of North Carolina Press, 2012), 32–36; Oakes, *Freedom National*, 95–96.

15. Oakes, *Freedom National*, 96.

16. Benjamin Butler to Winfield Scott, May 27, 1861, in Ira Berlin et al., eds., *Free at Last: A Documentary History of Slavery, Freedom and the Civil War* (New York: New Press, 1993), 9–10; Oakes, *Freedom National*, 99–100.

17. Matthew Pinsker, "Congressional Confiscation Acts," House Divided Project website, http://housedivided.dickinson.edu/sites/emancipation/2012/07/14/congressional-confiscation-acts.

18. Oakes, *Freedom National,* 120–22.

19. Andrew Coopersmith, *Fighting Words: An Illustrated History of Newspaper Accounts of the Civil War* (New York: New Press, 2004), 76; Brasher, *Peninsula Campaign*, 21–23; Sumner, as quoted in Louis P. Masur, *Lincoln's Hundred Days: The Emancipation Proclamation and the War for the Union* (Cambridge, MA: Harvard University Press, 2012), 22.

20. Oakes, *Freedom National*, 143.

21. Brasher, *Peninsula Campaign*, 54–60; Freehling, *The South vs. the South*, 95; Silvana R. Siddali, *From Property to Person: Slavery and the Confiscation Acts, 1861–1862* (Baton Rouge: Louisiana State University Press, 2005), 82.

22. Pinsker, "Congressional Confiscation Acts"; Freehling, The *South vs. the South*, 88–96 (Halleck quote on 96); Siddali, *From Property to Person*, 81.

23. *Christian Recorder* (Philadelphia), Nov. 23, 1861; Alexis J. Seymour to "Dear Sister," Jul. 15, 1861, University of Virginia Special Collections.

24. *New York Herald*, May 28, 30, Oct. 31, 1861.

25. *Charleston Mercury*, Jul. 26, Aug. 7, 1861.

26. Jeffrey L. Patrick, *Campaign for Wilson's Creek: The Fight for Missouri Begins* (Buffalo Gap, TX: State House Press, 2011), 116–18.

27. Daniel E. Sutherland, *A Savage Conflict: The Decisive Role of Guerrillas in the American Civil War* (Chapel Hill: University of North Carolina Press, 2009), 12–16; Patrick, *Campaign for Wilson's Creek*, 127; Rafuse, *McClellan's War*, 116–17.

28. Sutherland, *Savage Conflict*, 14–25; Phillips, "Lincoln's Grasp of War," 198–99.

29. John C. Frémont, "Proclamation," Aug. 30, 1861, in Simpson et al., eds., *Civil War: First Year*, 561–62.

30. *Christian Recorder*, Sep. 28, 1861; James Oakes, "Reluctant to Emancipate? Another Look at the First Confiscation Act," *Journal of the Civil War Era*, Dec. 2013, 462; Abraham Lincoln to Orville H. Browning, Sep. 22, 1861, in Simpson et al., eds., *Civil War: First Year*, 568–69.

31. Phillips, "Lincoln's Grasp of War," 198–99, and Christopher Phillips, *The Rivers Ran Backward: The Civil War and the Remaking of the American Middle Border* (New York: Oxford University Press, 2016), 11, 143–52.

32. Phillips, "Lincoln's Grasp of War," 196, 199; Abraham Lincoln to John C. Frémont, Sep. 2, 1861, and Abraham Lincoln to Orville H. Browning Sept. 22, 1861, in Simpson et al., eds., *Civil War: First Year*, 563, 568–69.

33. *Indiana State Sentinel* (Indianapolis), Oct. 2, 1861; letter from William Penn Lyon, Nov. 21, 1861, in *Reminiscences of the Civil War* (San Jose, CA: Muirson & Wright, 1907), 274; Dilbeck, *A More Civil War*, 26–27.

34. John D'Entremont, *Southern Emancipator: Moncure Conway: The American Years, 1832–1865* (New York: Oxford University Press, 1987), 153–61; Moncure Conway, *The Rejected Stone: Or Insurrection vs. Resurrection in America* (Boston: Walker, Wise, 1861), 100–101; *Moncure D. Conway: Addresses and Reprints, 1850–1907* (Boston: Houghton Mifflin, 1909), 106, 114, 167, 180; Moncure Conway, *The Golden Hour* (Boston: Ticknor and Fields, 1862), 5–6; Frank Cirillo, " 'The Day of Sainthood Has Passed': Abolitionists and the Golden Moment of the Civil War, 1861–1865," PhD dissertation, University of Virginia, 2017.

35. D'Entremont, *Southern Emancipator*, 160–62; Moncure Conway, *Autobiography, Memoirs and Experiences of Moncure Daniel Conway* (Boston: Houghton Mifflin, 1904), 345–47.

36. Freehling, *The South vs. the South*, 52–54; Stephen Berry, *House of Abraham: Lincoln and the Todds, a Family Divided by War* (Boston: Houghton Mifflin, 2007), 68–69.

37. Earl J. Hess, *The Civil War in the West: Victory and Defeat from the Appalachians to the Mississippi* (Chapel Hill: University of North Carolina Press, 2012), 11–17; Freehling, *The South vs. the South*, 72.

38. Ulysses S. Grant, *Personal Memoirs* (1885; reprint, New York: Penguin, 1999), 149–51.

39. Hess, *The Civil War in the West*, 34–39; Weigley, *A Great Civil War*, 108–11; *Ebensburg* (PA) *Alleghenian*, Feb. 27, 1862; *Pittsburgh Gazette*, Sep. 9, 1861; *New York Herald*, Feb. 15, 1862.

CHAPTER 2

1. Howard Jones, *Blue and Gray Diplomacy: A History of Union and Confederate Foreign Relations* (Chapel Hill: University of North Carolina Press, 2010), 83–99.

2. Jones, *Blue and Gray Diplomacy,* 93; *New York Times,* Jan. 10, 1862.

3. *New York Herald*, Dec. 29, 30, 1861; Jones, *Blue and Gray Diplomacy*, 106.

4. Doyle, *The Cause of All Nations*, 71, 100–105; *New York Times*, Feb. 14, 1862; *Frank Leslie's Illustrated Newspaper* (New York), Mar. 1, 1862; *Burlington* (VT) *Free Press*, Jan. 18, 1862 (Thompson quote); Sarah Parker Remond, "The Negroes in the United States of America," *Journal of Negro History*, Apr. 1942, 216–18.

5. Jones, *Blue and Gray Diplomacy*, 111; Henry Blumenthal, "Confederate Diplomacy: Popular Notions and International Realities," *Journal of Southern History* 32 (May 1966): 159; *Mobile Register and Advertiser* as quoted in *Christian Recorder*, Jan. 18, 1862.

6. John B. Jones Diary, Feb. 8–28, 1862, and Jefferson Davis, "Message to the Confederate Congress," in Stephen W. Sears, ed., *The Civil War: The Second Year Told by Those Who Lived It* (New York: Library of America, 2012), 82–83, 86; William J. Cooper Jr., *Jefferson Davis, American* (New York: Knopf, 2000), 413–14.

7. Quigley, *Shifting Grounds*, 187–88; James M. McPherson, *Embattled Rebel: Jefferson Davis as Commander in Chief* (New York: Penguin Press, 2014), 71–73; Jefferson Davis to Governor Joseph E. Brown, May 29, 1862, 241, in *Jefferson Davis: The Essential Writings*, ed. William J. Cooper Jr. (New York: Modern Library, 2003), 241–46.

8. Judkin Browning, *Shifting Loyalties: The Union Occupation of Eastern North Carolina* (Chapel Hill: University of North Carolina Press, 2011), 63, 77; David Silkenat, *Driven from Home: North Carolina's Civil War Refugee Crisis* (Athens: University of Georgia Press, 2016), 32–33; Harris, *With Charity for All*, 63.

9. Richard J. Sommers, "Union Strategy in the Eastern Theater, 1861–1862," in James I. Robertson, Jr., ed., *Military Strategy in the American Civil War* (Richmond: Virginia Sesquicentennial Commission, 2012), 35; Rafuse, *McClellan's War*, 73, 84–85.

10. George B. McClellan to Mary Ellen McClellan, Jul. 27, 1861, and George B. McClellan to Samuel L. M. Barlow, Nov. 8, 1861, in Simpson et al., eds., *Civil War: First Year*, 540–42, 587–88; Rafuse, *McClellan's War*, 169; Slotkin, *Long Road to Antietam*, 28. Rafuse argues that "there is no evidence that an ambition for political office drove [McClellan's] actions as a soldier" (124), while Slotkin argues that

"McClellan tried to use his position as army commander to make himself the leader of his own powerful conservative faction" (27).

11. Weigley, *A Great Civil War*, 119; Abraham Lincoln, Annual Message to Congress, Dec. 3, 1861, in Simpson et al., eds., *Civil War: First Year*, 666–69.

12. For articles on refugees, see *Christian Recorder*, Jul. 20, 1861; *Philadelphia Inquirer*, Oct. 21, 1861; *Liberator*, Feb. 14, 1862; *Daily Cleveland Herald*, Mar. 11, 1862.

13. *Life, Speeches and Service of Andrew Johnson, Seventeenth President of the United States* (Philadelphia: T. B. Peterson & Brothers, 1865), 33, 38; *New York Herald*, Apr. 1, 1862; Harris, *With Charity for All*, 53.

14. Joseph P. Harsh, *Confederate Tide Rising: Robert E. Lee and the Making of Southern Strategy, 1861–1862* (Kent, OH: Kent State University Press, 1998), 33–34.

15. Steven E. Woodworth, *This Great Struggle: America's Civil War* (Lanham, MD: Rowman and Littlefield, 2011), 93–95.

16. John R. Lundberg, "'I Must Save This Army': Albert Sidney Johnston and the Shiloh Campaign," in Steven E. Woodworth, ed., *The Shiloh Campaign* (Carbondale: Southern Illinois University Press, 2009), 19–23.

17. Lundberg, "'I Must Save This Army,'" 19–23.

18. Sam R. Watkins, *Co. Aytch: A Side Show of the Big Show* (New York: Touchstone, 1990), 42–43; Hess, *The War in the West*, 46.

19. Timothy B. Smith, "Anatomy of an Icon: Shiloh's Hornet's Nest in Civil War Memory," in Woodworth, ed., *Shiloh Campaign*, 55–74.

20. Grady McWhiney, "General Beauregard's 'Complete Victory' at Shiloh: An Interpretation," in Woodworth, ed., *Shiloh Campaign*, 110–11.

21. Beauregard to Grant, Apr. 8, 1862, *The War of the Rebellion: A Compilation of the Official Records of the Union and Confederate Armies* (Washington, DC: Government Printing Office, 1880–1901), ser. I, vol. 10, pt. 1, 111 (henceforth *OR*); *New York Times*, Apr. 16, 1862.

22. McWhiney, "General Beauregard's 'Complete Victory,'" 110–36.

23. Reports of Maj. Gen. U.S. Grant, Apr. 4–5 and Apr. 10–15, 1862, *OR*, ser. I, vol. 10, pt. 1, 110–11; Harris, *With Charity for All*, 46–47, 55 (Johnson quote).

24. Weigley, *A Great Civil War*, 115.

25. Wheeler, ed., *Voices of the Civil War*, 102.

26. Jeanie Attie, *Patriotic Toil: Northern Women and the American Civil War* (Ithaca, NY: Cornell University Press, 1998), 61–65; Report of Surgeon Robert Murray, U.S. Army, Medical Director, Apr. 21, 1862, *OR*, ser. I, vol. 10, pt. 1, 297–99; Henry W. Bellows, *The State and the Nation—Sacred to Christian Citizens* (New York: James Miller, 1861), 7, 11, 15; Bellows, *How We Are to Fulfill Our Lord's Commandment, "Love Your Enemies," in a Time of War* (New York: Baker & Godwin, 1861), 7; *The Papers of Frederick Law Olmsted: Defending the Union, 1861–1863*, ed. Jane Turner Center (Baltimore: Johns Hopkins University Press, 1986), 42, 136; J. G. Forman, *The Western Sanitary Commission: A Sketch of Its Origins, History, Labors for the Sick and Wounded of the Western Armies, and Aid Given to Freedmen and Union Refugees* (St.

Louis, MO: R. P. Studley, 1864), 128; Mark E. Neely Jr., *Lincoln and the Democrats*, 40–42; J. Matthew Gallman, *Mastering Wartime: A Social History of Philadelphia During the Civil War* (Cambridge: Cambridge University Press, 1990), 155–63.

27. Margaret Humphreys, *Marrow of Tragedy: The Health Crisis of the American Civil War* (Baltimore: Johns Hopkins University Press, 2013), 4, 34, 118, 192; *Memoirs of John A. Dix*, comp. Morgan Dix (New York: Harper & Brothers, 1883), 48.

28. Mary A. Livermore, *My Story of the War: A Woman's Narrative of Four Years Personal Experience as Nurse in the Union Army and in Relief Work at Home* (1881; reprint, New York: Da Capo Press, 1995), 133, 489, 494; Nina Silber, *Daughters of the Union: Northern Women Fight the Civil War* (Cambridge, MA: Harvard University Press, 2005), 176.

29. Humphreys, *Marrow of Tragedy*, 4, 34, 118, 192.

30. Clarke, *War Stories,* 59–63; Livermore, *My Story of the War*, 205, 221, 494. While Clarke argues that stories featuring Confederates who respond well to Yankee mercy are rare and "occasional," I have found them to be numerous and typical of the genre.

31. Kate Cumming, *Kate: The Journal of a Confederate Nurse*, ed. Richard Barksdale Harwell (Baton Rouge: Louisiana State University Press, 1998), 14–19; Humphreys, *Marrow of Tragedy*, 65–66; Libra Hilde, *Worth a Dozen Men: Women and Nursing in the Civil War South* (Charlottesville: University of Virginia Press, 2012).

32. Cumming, *Kate*, 14–15.

33. Alice Fahs, *The Imagined Civil War: Popular Literature of the North and South, 1861–1865* (Chapel Hill: University of North Carolina Press), 77–79; Christian McWhirter, *Battle Hymns: The Power and Popularity of Music in the Civil War* (Chapel Hill: University of North Carolina Press, 2012), 45–50.

34. John Stauffer and Benjamin Soskis, *The Battle Hymn of the Republic: A Biography of the Song That Marches On* (New York: Oxford University Press, 2013), 9–13.

35. McWhirter, *Battle Hymns*, 155; "Let My People Go," in Simpson et al., eds., *Civil War: First Year*, 674–77; Lewis C. Lockwood, *Mary S. Peake, the Colored Teacher at Fortress Monroe, 1862* (Boston: American Tract Society, 1862).

36. McWhirter, *Battle Hymns*, 78–82; *Charleston Mercury*, Feb. 28, 1862; Freehling, *The South vs. the South*, 51.

37. Fahs, *Imagined Civil War*, 79–83; *Richmond Dispatch*, Dec. 18, 1862.

38. Eric Foner, *The Fiery Trial: Abraham Lincoln and American Slavery* (New York: W. W. Norton, 2010), 182.

39. William C. Harris, *Lincoln and the Border States: Preserving the Union* (Lawrence: University of Kansas Press, 2001), 160–65; *Inside Lincoln's Cabinet: The Civil War Diaries of Salmon P. Chase*, ed. David Donald (New York: Longmans, Green, 1954), 69.

40. Lincoln, "Message to Congress," Mar. 6, 1862, in *Lincoln's Selected Writings*, 260.

41. *Daily National Intelligencer* (Washington, DC), Mar. 10, 1862; *Cleveland Daily Herald*, Mar. 10, 1862 (*New York Times* quote); *Boston Daily Advertiser*, Mar. 8, 13, 14, 1862.

42. *Cleveland Daily Herald*, Mar. 10, 1862 (*New York Tribune* and Wilson quotes); *Northern Independent* (Auburn, NY), Mar. 13, 1862; "Southern Aids to the North," *Continental Monthly*, Mar. 1862, 242–45.

43. Harris, *Lincoln and the Border States*, 164–69; *New York Herald*, Mar. 7, Apr. 4, Jul. 29, 1862; Freehling, *The South vs. the South*, 105; Phillips, *Rivers Ran Backward*, 215 (Powell quote); *Liberator*, Mar. 14, 1862; *Cleveland Daily Herald*, Mar. 10, 1862; *Christian Recorder*, Mar. 22, 1862.

44. "Southern Aids to the North, II," *Continental Monthly*, Apr. 1862, 449.

45. Winkle, *Lincoln's Citadel*, xv; Oakes, *Freedom National*, 269–77; Carwardine, *Lincoln*, 202.

46. *New York Herald*, Apr. 18, 1862; Douglass, "The War and How to End It," *Douglass' Monthly*, Apr. 1862; *Anglo-African* (New York), Apr. 19, 1862; Richard S. Newman, "The Age of Emancipating Proclamations: Early Civil War Abolitionism and Its Discontents," *Pennsylvania Magazine of History and Biography* (Jan. 2013), 34, 36.

47. *Christian Recorder*, May 17, 1862.

48. *Anglo-African*, Apr. 19, 1862; *A Voice of Thunder: The Civil War Letters of George E. Stephens*, ed. Donald Yacovone (Urbana: University of Illinois Press, 1997), 150, 152, 188, 193, 203–4.

49. Frederick Douglass, "The Black Man's Future in the Southern States," Feb. 5, 1862, in Louis P. Masur, ed., *The Real War Will Never Get in the Books: Selections from Writers During the Civil War* (New York: Oxford University Press, 1993), 109–11.

CHAPTER 3

1. *Richmond Daily Dispatch*, May 16, 1862.

2. Lincoln to George B. McClellan, Feb. 3, 1862, in *Lincoln's Selected Writings*, 259; Rafuse, *McClellan's War*, 178, 195–96; Simpson, *Civil War in the East*, 28; Peter Cozzens, *Shenandoah 1862: Stonewall Jackson's Valley Campaign* (Chapel Hill: University of North Carolina Press, 2008), 6. Dramatic events in early March at Hampton Roads, a key Chesapeake Bay shipping channel, were a further cause for concern. Confederates in Norfolk had salvaged an abandoned Federal steam frigate, the USS *Merrimack*, covered its hull with three-inch-thick armor plates, and relaunched it as the ironclad CSS *Virginia*. On March 8, the *Virginia* attacked a Federal squadron at Hampton Roads, consigning one wooden-hulled vessel to a watery grave and crippling a second vessel—and thereby securing Confederate control of the harbor. At the Federal navy's dark hour, relief came just in time, in the form of the Union navy's own ironclad experiment, the armored raft christened USS *Monitor*. It steamed into Hampton Roads on the night of March 8 and faced off with the *Virginia* the following day. The two vessels pummeled each other for four hours, and the battle ended in a draw. The *Monitor* had succeeded in defending its wooden fleet. But the question remained whether the Federal ironclad could continue to keep its Confederate counterpart at bay.

3. John T. Hubbell, "The Seven Days of George Brinton McClellan," in Gary W. Gallagher, ed., *The Richmond Campaign of 1862* (Chapel Hill: University of North Carolina Press, 2000), 29–31; John S. Salmon, "Land Operations in Virginia in 1862," in William C. Davis and James I. Robertson Jr., eds., *Virginia at War 1862* (Lexington: University Press of Kentucky, 2007), 6.

4. Simpson, *Civil War in the East*, 28–33; Harsh, *Confederate Tide Rising*, 49; Gary W. Gallagher, *Becoming Confederates: Pathways to a New National Loyalty* (Athens: University of Georgia Press, 2013).

5. Herman Hattaway, *Shades of Blue and Gray: An Introductory Military History of the Civil War* (Columbia: University of Missouri Press, 1997), 86–87; Harsh, *Confederate Tide Rising*, 45–46.

6. Craig L. Symonds, *A Battlefield Atlas of the Civil War* (Charleston, SC: Nautical and Aviation Publishing, 1983), 31; Wheeler, ed., *Voices of the Civil War*, 131.

7. Harsh, *Confederate Tide Rising*, 74–81.

8. Brian K. Burton, *Extraordinary Circumstances: The Seven Days Battles* (Bloomington: Indiana University Press, 2001), 401–3; Harsh, *Confederate Tide Rising*, 84.

9. Cozzens, *Shenandoah 1862*, 121 (Jackson quote); Royster, *Destructive War*, 41–45; John W. Smith to S. E. Smith, Jun. 8, 1862, Nau Civil War Collection, Houston, TX (hereafter NCWC).

10. Salmon, "Land Operations in Virginia in 1862," 6.

11. Jedediah Hotchkiss, *Make Me a Map of the Valley: The Civil War Journal of Stonewall Jackson's Cartographer*, ed. Archie P. McDonald (Dallas: Southern Methodist University Press, 1973), 10; Dear [N.A.] to Aunt, Jun. 11, 1862, letter from unidentified soldier in Papers of Elizabeth Ann Willson, University of Virginia; Cozzens, *Shenandoah 1862*, 371.

12. Salmon, "Land Operations," 8–9; *Richmond Dispatch,* May 28, 1862.

13. Jonathan A. Noyalas, *Stonewall Jackson's 1862 Valley Campaign: War Comes to the Homefront* (Mt. Pleasant, SC: History Press, 2010); Jonathan M. Berkey, "Winchester During the Civil War," Encyclopedia Virginia, www.encyclopediavirginia.org/Winchester_During_the_Civil_War; Virginia R. Bensen, "The Women of Winchester," Emerging Civil War, November 30, 2011, https://emergingcivilwar.com/2011/11/30/the-women-of-winchester-virginia (Chase quotes); *Life of Abby Hopper Gibbons: Told Chiefly Through Her Correspondence*, ed. Sarah Hopper Emerson (New York: G. P. Putnam's Sons, 1897), 1:433.

14. Elizabeth Amelia Dwight and Wilder Dwight, *Life and Letters of Wilder Dwight: Lieut.-Col. Second Mass. Inf. Vols* (Boston: Ticknor, 1891), 53–54, 219.

15. Gould as quoted in Cozzens, *Shenandoah 1862*, 143; Cornelia Peake McDonald, *A Woman's Civil War: A Diary, with Reminiscences of the War, from March 1862*, ed. Minrose C. Gwin (Madison: University of Wisconsin Press, 1992), 24, 27, 31–34, 48–52; *Richmond Daily Dispatch*, May 30, Jun. 2, 1862.

16. John B. Jones, *A Rebel War Clerk's Diary*, ed. Earl Schenk Miers (Baton Rouge: Louisiana State University Press, 1993), 85.

17. Elizabeth R. Varon, *Southern Lady, Yankee Spy: The True Story of Elizabeth Van Lew, a Union Spy in the Heart of the Confederacy* (New York: Oxford University Press, 2003), 56–57, 68, 73–75.

18. Varon, *Southern Lady, Yankee Spy; Richmond Daily Dispatch*, May 30, 1862.

19. Elizabeth Van Lew as quoted in Varon, *Southern Lady, Yankee Spy,* 77–78.

20. Matt Spruill III and Matt Spruill IV, *Echoes of Thunder: A Guide to the Seven Days Battles* (Knoxville: University of Tennessee Press, 2006), 132; Wheeler, ed., *Voices of the Civil War,* 141–42 (McClellan quote).

21. Campbell, as quoted in Spruill and Spruill, *Echoes of Thunder,* 72.

22. Holmes, as quoted in Spruill and Spruill, *Echoes of Thunder,* 201.

23. *Richmond Daily Dispatch,* Jul. 9, 1862.

24. Spruill and Spruill, *Echoes of Thunder,* 136.

25. Joseph Glatthaar, *General Lee's Army: From Victory to Collapse* (New York: Free Press, 2008), 144.

26. Mrs. Roger A. Pryor, *Reminiscences of Peace and War* (New York: Macmillan, 1904), 188; Burton, *Extraordinary Circumstances,* 386.

27. Rafuse, *McClellan's War,* 207, 219, 224, 227–31. McClellan's actions reflected, too, his demoralization at the way that events seemed to conspire against him, and his extreme physical and mental exhaustion—he had battled malaria and dysentery over the course of the campaign.

28. Porter as quoted in *Fighting with the Eighteenth Massachusetts: The Civil War Memoir of Thomas H. Mann,* ed. John J. Hennessey (Baton Rouge: Louisiana State University Press, 2000), 43–44.

29. George B. McClellan to Abraham Lincoln, Jul. 7, 1862, in Sears, ed., *The Civil War: The Second Year,* 307.

30. Robert Hunt Rhodes, ed., *All for the Union: The Civil War Diary and Letters of Elisha Hunt Rhodes* (New York: Random House, 1985), 61; Katharine Prescott Wormeley, *The Other Side of War with the Army of the Potomac: Letters from the Headquarters of the United States Sanitary Commission During the Peninsula Campaign in Virginia in 1862* (Boston: Ticknor, 1889), 110, 153; *Papers of Frederick Law Olmsted,* 113.

31. Wongsrichanalai, *Northern Character,* 115–19 (Chandler quote on 119); *When This Cruel War Is Over: The Civil War Letters of Charles Harvey Brewster,* ed. David W. Blight (Amherst: University of Massachusetts Press, 1992), 120; Gallagher, *Union War,* 68.

32. James Clarke to Marshall Huey, Apr. 23–24, May 1, 1862, NCWC; Nathaniel Hawthorne, "Chiefly About War-Matters," *Atlantic Monthly,* Jul. 1862, 50, 53, 55; Cynthia Watchell, "Nathaniel Hawthorne's Funny Civil War," Opinionator blog, *New York Times,* May 17, 2013; Masur, ed., *The Real War Will Never Get in the Books,* 161–66.

33. Alfred Lewis Castleman, *The Army of the Potomac: Behind the Scenes* (Milwaukee, WI: Strickland, 1863), 10, 21, 23, 36, 114, 118–19, 142–43, 196.

34. Hugh Frasier to Sister Anne, Apr. 19, 1862, NCWC.

35. William A. Blair, "The Seven Days and the Radical Persuasion: Convincing Moderates in the North of the Need for a Hard War," in Gallagher, ed., *The Richmond Campaign of 1862*, 167–68; Hattaway, *Shades of Blue and Gray*, 82–83; Robert Stiles, *Four Years Under Marse Robert* (New York: Neale, 1903), 76–77.

36. *Gone for a Soldier: The Civil War Memoirs of Private Alfred Bellard*, ed. David Donald (New York: Little, Brown, 1975), 101–2.

37. Glatthaar, *General Lee's Army*, 131; Oakes, *Freedom National,* 213.

38. Kathryn S. Meier, "'No Place for the Sick': Nature's War on Civil War Soldier Mental and Physical Health in the 1862 Peninsula and Shenandoah Valley Campaigns," *Journal of the Civil War Era*, Jun. 2011, 176–97.

39. Meier, "No Place for the Sick," 199.

40. Jonathan Horn, "White House on the Pamunkey," *New York Times,* Opinionator blog, Jun. 29, 2012; Blair, "The Seven Days and the Radical Persuasion," 162–63 (Lee quote).

41. Castleman, *Army of the Potomac*, 143–44; *Lincoln's Journalist: John Hay's Anonymous Writings for the Press, 1860–1864*, ed. Michael Burlingame (Carbondale: Southern Illinois University Press, 1999), 270; Horn, "White House on the Pamunkey," Jun. 29, 2012; Blair, "The Seven Days and the Radical Persuasion," 162–63.

42. Horn, "White House on the Pamunkey" (Stuart quote).

43. Rable, *Damn Yankees!,* 9, 38, 95; Gallagher, *Confederate War,* 59, 65, 146–47; Quigley, *Shifting Grounds*, 79–83 (quote on 79), 146–48 (second quote), 174–77.

44. Jaime Amanda Martinez, *Confederate Slave Impressment in the Upper South* (Chapel Hill: University of North Carolina Press, 2013), 22–25, 32; Brasher, *The Peninsula Campaign*, 86–88.

45. Martinez, *Confederate Slave Impressment*, 22–25, 32; Brasher, *Peninsula Campaign*, 86–88, 108 (quote), 111–15.

46. Brasher, *The Peninsula Campaign*, 143; *OR*, series 1, vol. 11, pt. 3, 605–6.

47. *A Gunner in Lee's Army: The Civil War Letters of Thomas Henry Carter*, ed. Graham T. Dozier (Chapel Hill: University of North Carolina Press, 2014), 112–13, 118–19.

48. Carter, *Gunner in Lee's Army*, 89–90, 105, 142, 145; Quint as quoted in John H. Matsui, *The First Republican Army: The Army of Virginia and the Radicalization of the Civil War* (Charlottesville: University of Virginia Press, 2016), 113.

49. One context for this policy was the Union government's efforts to generate revenue and resources to pay for the war. The Republican Congress passed a series of measures that would give the government far greater control over the economy. The Legal Tender Act of Feb. 25, 1862, passed to finance the war effort in the face of a gold shortage, authorized the creation of paper Treasury notes or "greenbacks," not redeemable in gold, but valid as legal tender for the payment of debts. This represented a major enhancement of Federal power: although they

had no inherent value, greenbacks counted as money simply because the government said so. Congress followed this with the Internal Revenue Act of 1862, which imposed a wide variety of taxes on goods such as liquor and tobacco, and on business transactions, incomes, inheritances, corporate receipts, and services and professions (through licensing fees). To collect these taxes, a new massive Bureau of Internal Revenue sprang into being. The Union was able to generate 21 percent of its wartime funds using taxation; the Confederacy, by contrast, raised only roughly 5 percent of its funds that way. In 1863, the National Banking Act would round out these reforms by giving new banks chartered and supervised by the federal government the power to issue a uniform national currency secured by U.S. bonds. The new system superseded the state banks, as they were pressured into converting to national charters, and increased both the power of the Treasury Department and the clout of New York City, as the nation's financial and commercial hub. Weigley, *A Great Civil War*, 204–10. See Richard Franklin Bensel, *Yankee Leviathan: The Origins of Central State Authority in America, 1859–1877* (New York: Cambridge University Press, 1990), 157–59.

50. Bensel, *Yankee Leviathan*, 157; Stephen C. Neff, *Justice in Blue and Gray: A Legal History of the Civil War* (Cambridge, MA: Harvard University Press, 2010), 124.

51. "The Second Confiscation Act," Freedmen and Southern Society Project, Department of History, University of Maryland, http://www.freedmen.umd.edu/conact2. htm.

52. Masur, *Lincoln's Hundred Days*, 60.

53. Joint Committee on the Conduct of the War, *Barbarities of the Rebels at Manassas* (Washington, DC, 1862), 5–8, University of Virginia Special Collections; Andrew Coopersmith, *Fighting Words: An Illustrated History of Newspaper Accounts of the Civil War* (New York: New Press, 2006), 77.

54. Masur, *Lincoln's Hundred Days*, 63–64; Silvana R. Siddali, *From Property to Person: Slavery and the Confiscation Acts, 1861–1862* (Baton Rouge: Louisiana State University Press, 2005), 198–201; *Chicago Tribune*, Jun. 7, 1862.

55. Oakes, *Freedom National*, 226; *Life and Writings of Anna Ella Carroll* (Washington, DC: Judd & Detweiler, 1895), 2:121–24. For the argument that confiscation threatened to snuff out Southern Unionism, see also *Speech of Hon. L. W. Powell, of Kentucky, on the Bill to Confiscate the Property and Free the Slaves of Rebels* (Washington, DC: L. Towers, 1862), 9; *Speech of the Hon. John Law, of Indiana: on the "Bill Emancipating Slaves of Rebels"* (Washington, DC: Henry Polkinhorn), 1–3.

56. Elijah Babbitt, *Speech of Hon. Elijah Babbitt, of Pennsylvania, on the Confiscation of Rebel Property: Delivered in the House of Representatives, May 22, 1862* (Washington, DC: Scammell, 1862), 5; Ira Harris, *Confiscation of Rebel Property: Speech of Hon. Ira Harris, of New York, in the Senate of the United States, Monday April 14, 1862* (Washington, DC: Scammell, 1862); A. A. Sargent, *Confiscation of Rebel Property: Speech of Hon. A. A. Sargent of California in the House of Representatives, May 23, 1862* (Washington, DC: Scammell, 1862), 2, 4, 6–7; William Kellogg,

Confiscation of Rebel Property: Speech of Hon. William Kellogg, of Illinois, Delivered in the House of Representatives, May 24, 1862 (Washington, DC: Scammell, 1862), 15–16.

57. Edward Henry Rollins, *Confiscation and Emancipation: Speech of Hon. Edward H. Rollins, of New Hampshire, Delivered in the House of Representatives, Thursday, May 22, 1862* (Washington, DC: Scammell, 1862), 6; Jacob Collamer, *Speech of Hon. J. Collamer, of Vermont, in the United States Senate, April 24, 1862, on the Bill to Confiscate the Property and Free the Slaves of Rebels* (Washington, DC: Scammell, 1862), 10–15.

58. Samuel S. Blair, *Speech of Hon. S. S. Blair, of Pennsylvania, Delivered in the House of Representatives, Thursday, May, 22, 1862* (Washington, DC: Scammell, 1862), 48; Charles Sumner, *Indemnity for the Past and Security for the Future: Speech of Hon. Charles Sumner of Massachusetts on His Bill for the Confiscation of Property and Liberation of Slaves Belonging to Rebels. In the Senate of the United States, May 19, 1862* (Washington, DC: Scammell, 1862), 16; *War Powers of Congress: Speech of Hon. Charles Sumner, of Massachusetts, on the House Bills for the Confiscation of Property and the Liberation of Slaves Belonging to the Rebels. In the Senate of the United States, June 27, 1862* (Washington, DC: Scammell, 1862), 6–7.

59. Siddali, *From Property to Person*, 193, 197; *Boston Daily Evening Transcript*, Aug. 20, 1862; *Liberator*, May 16, 1862.

60. Alonzo H. Quint, *The Potomac and the Rapidan: Army Notes from the Failure at Winchester to the Reenforcement of Rosecrans, 1861–63* (Boston: Crosby and Nichols, 1864), 110, 170, 260.

61. Blair, "The Seven Days and the Radical Persuasion," 176; *Chicago Tribune*, Jun. 25, Jul. 13, 1862.

62. Harris, *Lincoln and the Border States*, 175–77; Hay, *Lincoln's Journalist*, 265.

63. Gallagher, ed., *The Richmond Campaign of 1862*, 17.

64. Lincoln, "Appeal to Border-State Representatives for Compensated Emancipation," Jul. 12, 1862, in *Lincoln's Selected Writings*, 267; Harris, *Lincoln and the Border States*, 177.

65. Harris, *Lincoln and the Border States*, 179–80; Richard J. Behn, "Compensated Emancipation," Mr. Lincoln and Freedom Project, Lehrman Institute, www.mrlincolnandfreedom.org/civil-war/congressional-action-inaction/compensated-emancipation.

66. Harris, *Lincoln and the Border States*, 181; Carwardine, *Lincoln*, 206–8; Masur, *Lincoln's Hundred Days*, 80–81.

67. Carwardine, *Lincoln*, 206–8; Masur, *Lincoln's Hundred Days*, 82; Allen C. Guelzo, *Abraham Lincoln: Redeemer President* (Grand Rapids, MI: Wm. B. Eerdmans, 1999), 343.

68. Chase, *Inside Lincoln's Cabinet*, 106; Hay, *Lincoln's Journalist*, 284; Joshua Zeitz, *Lincoln's Boys: John Hay, John Nicolay, and the War for Lincoln's Image* (New York: Viking, 2014), 122.

69. Mason, *Apostle of Union*, 284–91.

70. Edward Everett, *Orations and Speeches on Various Occasions* (Boston: Little, Brown, 1868), 4:466–67, 477, 482, 501–4, 520–21, 537–38; Mason, *Apostle of Union*, 284–91. For press coverage of Everett's speeches, see, for example, *Boston Daily Advertiser,* Oct. 17, 1861; Jul. 14, 1862; *Daily National Intelligencer* (Washington, DC), Jul. 28, 1862; *Daily Evening Bulletin* (San Francisco), Nov. 13, 1861.

71. Abraham Lincoln, "Address on Colonization," Aug. 14, 1862, in Sears, ed., *Civil War: Second Year*, 366–71; Masur, *Lincoln's Hundred Days*, 90.

72. *New York Tribune*, Aug. 20, 1862; Abraham Lincoln to Horace Greeley, Aug. 22, 1862, in *Lincoln's Selected Writings*, 274–75; Masur, *Lincoln's Hundred Days*, 87; Carwardine, *Lincoln*, 209.

73. James Oakes, *The Radical and the Republican: Frederick Douglass, Abraham Lincoln, and the Triumph of Antislavery Politics* (New York: Norton, 2007), 191–95; Carwardine, *Lincoln*, 208–10; Oakes, *Freedom National*, 309–13; Doris Kearns Goodwin, *Team of Rivals: The Political Genius of Abraham Lincoln* (New York: Simon & Schuster, 2005), 470–71.

74. Oakes, *The Radical and the Republican*, 191–98; Carwardine, *Lincoln*, 208–10; Oakes, *Freedom National*, 309–13; Goodwin, *Team of Rivals,* 470–71; Sebastian Page, "Lincoln, Colonization and the Sound of Silence," *New York Times*, Opinionator blog, Dec. 4, 2012.

75. Paul D. Escott, *"What Shall We Do with the Negro?": Lincoln, White Racism, and Civil War America* (Charlottesville: University of Virginia Press, 2009), xvii, 54–55, 110, 248–49. See also George M. Fredrickson, *Big Enough to Be Inconsistent: Abraham Lincoln Confronts Slavery and Race* (Cambridge, MA: Harvard University Press, 2008).

76. *New York Times*, Aug. 26, 1862; *Douglass' Monthly*, Sept. 1862.

77. Oakes, *The Radical and the Republican*, 195–98, and *Freedom National*, 312–13; Carwardine, *Lincoln*, 209; Phillip W. Magness and Sebastian N. Page, *Colonization After Emancipation: Lincoln and the Movement for Black Resettlement* (Columbia: University of Missouri Press, 2011), 4–5; Masur, *Lincoln's Hundred Days*, 87; *Forgotten Valor: The Memoirs, Journals, and Civil War Letters of Orlando B. Willcox,* ed. Robert Garth Scott (Kent, OH: Kent State University Press, 1999), 4.

78. Oakes, *The Radical and the Republican*, 195–95, and *Freedom National*, 312–13; Carwardine, *Lincoln*, 209; Magness and Page, *Colonization After Emancipation*, 4–5; Masur, *Lincoln's Hundred Days*, 87.

79. Magness and Page, *Colonization After Emancipation*; Varon, *Disunion!*; Dorothy Ross, "Lincoln and the Ethics of Emancipation: Universalism, Nationalism, Exceptionalism," in *Abraham Lincoln and Liberal Democracy*, ed. Nicholas Buccola (Lawrence: University Press of Kansas, 2016), 90.

80. Lincoln, "Appeal to Border-State Representatives for Compensated Emancipation," Jul. 12, 1862, in *Lincoln's Selected Writings*, 267; Lincoln, "Address on Colonization," Aug. 14, 1862, in Sears, ed., *Civil War: Second Year*, 366–71.

81. *Pacific Appeal* (San Francisco), Aug. 9, 1862.

82. *Pacific Appeal*, Sep. 6, Oct. 18, 1862; *Liberator*, Aug. 15, 1862; *Christian Recorder*, Aug. 30, 1862; *Montreal Witness*, Sep. 6, 1862; Purvis as quoted in Margaret Hope Bacon, *But One Race: The Life of Robert Purvis* (Albany: State University of New York Press, 2007), 144.

83. *Liberator*, Aug. 15, 1862; Lincoln, "Meditation on the Divine Will," Sep. 2, 1862, in *Lincoln's Selected Writings*, 275. Lincoln biographer Douglas S. Wilson has questioned the 1862 dating of the "Meditation" and argued that it is "chronologically much closer to, and perhaps even belongs to, the year 1864." Douglas S. Wilson, *Lincoln's Sword: The Presidency and the Power of Words* (New York: Vintage Books, 2006), 254–55, 329–30.

CHAPTER 4

1. Gideon Welles, Sep. 22, 1862, in Sears, ed., *Civil War: Second Year*, 530.

2. Hess, *The Civil War in the West*, 51–62; *Wheeling Daily Intelligencer*, May 1, 1862; W. H. Robert to Wife, Apr. 28, 1862, in Nina Silber and Mary Beth Sievens, eds., *Yankee Correspondence: Civil War Letters Between New England Soldiers and the Home Front* (Charlottesville: University Press of Virginia, 1996), 31.

3. Hess, *The Civil War in the West*, 63–69; U.S. Grant to Julia Dent Grant, Jun. 12, 1862, in *Ulysses S. Grant: Memoirs and Selected Letters* (New York: Library of America, 1990), 1009.

4. *Nashville Daily Union*, Aug. 2, 19, 23, 31, Sep. 4, 1862; Benjamin Franklin Cooling, *To the Battles of Franklin and Nashville and Beyond: Stabilization and Reconstruction in Tennessee and Kentucky, 1864–1866* (Knoxville: University of Tennessee Press, 2011), 15–16.

5. Paul H. Bergeron, *Andrew Johnson's Civil War and Reconstruction* (Knoxville: University of Tennessee Press, 2011), 47–53; Robert Tracy McKenzie, *Lincolnites and Rebels: A Divided Town in the American Civil War* (New York: Oxford University Press, 2009), 204–8, 227; Hannah Rosen, *Terror in the Heart of Freedom: Citizenship, Sexual Violence, and the Meaning of Race in the Postemancipation South* (Chapel Hill: University of North Carolina Press, 2009), 24.

6. Jon L. Wakelyn, ed., *Southern Unionist Pamphlets and the Civil War* (Columbia: University of Missouri Press, 1999), 105, 114, 118 (quote); *New York Times*, Feb. 2, 1862; *Christian Recorder*, May 2, Jun. 21, 1862.

7. Phillip Shaw Paludan, *The Presidency of Abraham Lincoln* (Lawrence: University Press of Kansas, 1994), 235–36; Dilbeck, *A More Civil War*, 46; William A. Blair, *With Malice Toward Some: Treason and Loyalty in the Civil War Era* (Chapel

Hill: University of North Carolina Press, 2014), 138 (quote). As Harold Hyman explains, "Loyalty testing by means of oaths continued on an ever increasing scale as Union forces penetrated the South." Harold Melvin Hyman, *Era of the Oath: Northern Loyalty Tests During the Civil War* (Philadelphia: University of Pennsylvania Press, 1954), 35–38. See also Jonathan Truman Dorris, *Pardon and Amnesty Under Lincoln and Johnson: The Restoration of the Confederates to Their Rights and Privileges, 1861–1898* (Chapel Hill: University of North Carolina Press, 1953) and John Martin Davis Jr. and George B. Tremmel, *Parole, Pardon, Pass and Amnesty Documents of the Civil War: An Illustrated History* (Jefferson, NC: McFarland, 2014).

8. Sherman to Father and Mother, May 14, 1862; Sherman to Wife and Children, May 26, Sep. 17, Oct. 20, 1862, in Charles W. Sherman, *Letters to Virtue: A Civil War Journey of Courage, Faith, and Love*, ed. Ann K. Gunnin (Alpharetta, GA: BookLogix, 2014), 32, 37, 89, 106.

9. Deposition of Octave Johnson, in Berlin et al., eds., *Free at Last*, 51–52.

10. Oakes, *Freedom National*, 246–52.

11. Davis and Tremmel, *Parole, Pardon, Pass*, 47; B. M. Palmer, *Oath of Allegiance to the United States, Discussed in Its Moral and Political Bearings* (Richmond, VA: MacFarlane and Fergusson, 1863), 9, 11, 14, 21–22.

12. Hess, *The Civil War in the West*, 84–91; Coopersmith, *Fighting Words*, 97–101; *Charleston Mercury*, May 26, 1862; *The Diary of Miss Emma Holmes, 1861–1866*, ed. John F. Marszalek (Baton Rouge: Louisiana University Press, 1979), 165. Historians have traditionally argued that sexual violence by Union troops against white Southern women was rare, but more recent scholarship stresses that the "threat of sexual violence and the fear of rape were common to southern women and central to how they experienced the Civil War," and that there were more cases of sexual crimes than previously thought. Crystal Feimster, "General Benjamin Butler and the Threat of Sexual Violence During the American Civil War," *Daedalus* 138 (Spring 2009): 126–34.

13. Butler, *Butler's Book*, 322; Nina Silber, *Gender and the Sectional Conflict* (Chapel Hill: University of North Carolina Press, 2008), 60; Chester Hearn, *When the Devil Came Down to Dixie: Ben Butler in New Orleans* (Baton Rouge: Louisiana State University Press, 1997), 99–101; *New York Times*, May 11, 1862.

14. *Sarah Morgan: The Civil War Diary of a Southern Woman*, ed. Charles East (New York: Simon & Schuster, 1991), 68, 73, 76, 109, 111, 123.

15. *Sarah Morgan: The Civil War Diary*, 141–43, 166, 212–15.

16. Kristie Ross, "Arranging a Doll House: Refined Women as Union Nurses," in Catherine Clinton and Nina Silber, eds., *Divided Houses: Gender and the Civil War* (New York: Oxford University Press, 1992), 108, 112–13; Libra R. Hilde, *Worth a Dozen Men: Women and Nursing in the Civil War South* (Charlottesville: University of Virginia Press, 2012), 25–34 (Hunter quote on page 30).

17. E. Susan Barber, "Sally Louisa Tompkins, Confederate Healer," in Cynthia A. Kierner and Sandra Gioia Treadway, eds., *Virginia Women: Their Lives and*

Times (Athens: University of Georgia Press, 2015), 1:352–54; Hilde, *Worth a Dozen Men*, 25–34.

18. John Pope, "Address to the Army of Virginia," Jul. 14, 1862, and John Pope, "General Orders Nos. 5, 7, 11," in Sears, ed., *Civil War: Second Year*, 323–28; Harsh, *Confederate Tide Rising*, 113.

19. Harsh, *Confederate Tide Rising*, 108–18.

20. John G. Selby, "Virginia's Civilians at War in 1862," in Davis and Robertson, eds., *Virginia at War*, 42–43; Harsh, *Confederate Tide Rising*, 113–18.

21. Harsh, *Confederate Tide Rising*, 134–58.

22. *John Dooley, Confederate Soldier: His War Journal*, ed. Joseph T. Durkin (Washington, DC: Georgetown University Press, 1945), 20–21.

23. Harris, *With Charity for All*, 64; *New York Times*, Aug. 16, 1862.

24. *Fayetteville* (NC) *Semi-Weekly Observer*, Sep. 8, 1862; E. F. "Bull" Paxton to Wife, Sep. 7, 1862, Elisha Franklin Paxton Letters, University of Virginia Special Collections; Harsh, *Confederate Tide Rising*, 158–63.

25. Edwin Stanton to John Pope, Sep. 6, 1862, *OR*, ser. 1, vol 13, 617; Weigley, *A Great Civil War*, 143–44.

26. Bradley R. Clampitt, "The Civil War and Reconstruction in Indian Territory," and Clarissa Confer, "Hardship at Home: The Civilian Experience," both in Bradley R. Clampitt, ed., *The Civil War and Reconstruction in Indian Territory* (Lincoln: University of Nebraska Press, 2015), 4–14 (quote on 5), 38–49.

27. Sylvia D. Hoffert, *Jane Grey Swisshelm: An Unconventional Life* (Chapel Hill: University of North Carolina Press, 2004), 154–55; Swisshelm as quoted in Scott W. Berg, *38 Nooses: Lincoln, Little Crow, and the Beginning of the Frontier's End* (New York: Vintage, 2012), 209.

28. Peter Cozzens, *The Earth Is Weeping: The Epic Story of the Indian Wars of the American West* (New York: Vintage, 2016), Thomas W. Cutrer, *Theater of a Separate War: The Civil War West of the Mississippi River, 1861–1865* (Chapel Hill: University of North Carolina Press, 2017), 121 (Chivington quote); Andrew W. Masich, *Civil War in the Southwest Borderlands, 1861–1867* (Norman: University of Oklahoma Press, 2017), 218–19; Ari Kelman, *A Misplaced Massacre: Struggling over the Memory of Sand Creek* (Cambridge: Harvard University Press, 2013), xi.

29. Robert E. Lee to Jefferson Davis, September 3, 8, 1862, in Sears, ed., *Civil War: Second Year*, 435–36, 446–47; Harsh, *Confederate Tide Rising*, 8–9.

30. "Lord Palmerston and Lord Russell: An Exchange," Sep. 14, 17, and 23, 1862, in Sears, ed., *Civil War: Second Year*, 443; Amanda Foreman, *A World on Fire: Britain's Crucial Role in the American Civil War* (New York: Random House, 2010), 291–95; Lonnie A. Burnett, *Henry Hotze, Confederate Propagandist* (Tuscaloosa: University of Alabama Press, 2008), 149; Harsh, *Confederate Tide Rising*, 18–19.

31. Rafuse, *McClellan's War*, 276–77.

32. John Hay, Sep. 1, 1862, and Edward Bates, "Remonstrance and Notes on Cabinet Meeting," Sep. 2, 1862, in Sears, ed., *Civil War: Second Year*, 425, 429; Weigley,

Great Civil War, 144–47; Rafuse, *McClellan's War*, 274–75, 279 (McClellan quote).

33. Lewis H. Steiner, Sep. 5–6, 1862, in Sears, ed., *Civil War: Second Year*, 450–52.

34. *Richmond Dispatch*, Sep. 11, 15, 1862; Freehling, *The South vs. the South*, 51.

35. Slotkin, *Long Road to Antietam*, 183 (McClellan quotes), 188; Weigley, *A Great Civil War*, 148–49.

36. Rafuse, *McClellan's War*, 301; Slotkin, *Long Road to Antietam*, 206.

37. Weigley, *Great Civil War*, 151–52.

38. Wheeler, ed., *Voices of the Civil War*, 186 (Gordon quotes); Ezra Carmen, *The Maryland Campaign of September 1982*, vol. 2, *Antietam*, ed. Thomas G. Clemens (El Dorado, CA: Savas Beatie, 2012), 87 (Hooker quote).

39. Stanley Harrold, ed., *The Civil War and Reconstruction: A Documentary Reader* (Malden, MA: Blackwell, 2008), 91 (Strother quotes).

40. Rafuse, *McClellan's War*, 325–26.

41. Edward Porter Alexander, *Fighting for the Confederacy*, ed. Gary W. Gallagher (Chapel Hill: University of North Carolina Press, 1989), 153–54; John O. Casler, *Four Years in the Stonewall Brigade* (1983; reprint, Columbia: University of South Carolina Press, 2005), 116.

42. Weigley, *A Great Civil War*, 153; Rafuse, *McClellan's War*, 328–29; George B. McClellan to Mary Ellen McClellan, Sep. 20, 1862, in Sears, ed., *Civil War: Second Year*, 524.

43. Bob Zeller, *The Blue and the Gray in Black and White: A History of Civil War Photography* (Westport, CT: Praeger, 2005), 65–81; J. Matthew Gallman, "Three Roads to Antietam: George McClellan, Abraham Lincoln, and Alexander Gardner," in J. Matthew Gallman and Gary W. Gallagher, eds., *Lens of War: Exploring Iconic Photographs of the Civil War* (Athens: University of Georgia Press, 2015), 43–45; *New York Herald*, Oct. 5, 1862; *New York Times*, Oct. 20, 1862.

44. David L. Thompson, "With Burnside at Antietam," in Sears, ed., *Civil War: Second Year*, 501; James M. McPherson, *For Cause and Comrades: Why Men Fought in the Civil War* (New York: Oxford University Press, 1997), 12–13.

45. Stephen W. Sears, *Landscape Turned Red: The Battle of Antietam* (Boston: Houghton Mifflin, 1983), 178 (first two quotations); Royall W. Figg, *Where Men Only Dare to Go, or The Story of a Boy Company C.S.A.* (1885; reprint, Baton Rouge: Louisiana State University Press, 2008), 53; *Richmond Dispatch*, Sep. 30, 1862.

46. McPherson, *For Cause and Comrades,* 165.

47. "David L. Thompson: With Burnside at Antietam," 500; Edgar Warfield, *Manassas to Appomattox: The Civil War Memoirs of Pvt. Edgar Warfield* (McLean, VA: EPM Publications, 1996), 98; Figg, *Where Men Only Dare to Go*, 44; Wilson J. Barnett to family, Sep. 21, 1862, NCWC.

48. Wilson J. Barnett to family, Sep. 21, 1862, Ephraim E. Brown to family, Sep. 18, 1862, Charles M. Wyvell to "Dear Friend," Sep. 28, 1862, all in NCWC; Castleman, *Army of the Potomac,* 227.

49. George H. Gordon, *A War Diary of Events in the War of the Great Rebellion, 1863–1865* (Boston: James R. Osgood, 1882), 4; Lesley J. Gordon, *A Broken Regiment: The 16th Connecticut's Civil War* (Baton Rouge: Louisiana State University Press, 2014), 39; McPherson, *For Cause and Comrades*, 165.

50. Josiah Marshall Favill, *Diary of a Young Officer Serving with the Armies of the United States During the War of the Rebellion* (Chicago: R. R. Donnelly & Sons, 1909), 191; Castleman, *Army of the Potomac*, 232.

51. Aaron Sheehan-Dean, *Why Confederates Fought: Family and Nation in Civil War Virginia* (Chapel Hill: University of North Carolina Press, 2007), 90–91; Glatthaar, *General Lee's Army,* 173; Lee as quoted in Walter H. Taylor, *General Lee: His Campaigns in Virginia, 1861–1865* (1906; reprint, Lincoln: University of Nebraska Press, 1994), 135.

52. Oliver Wilcox Norton, *Army Letters, 1861–1865* (Chicago: O. L. Deming, 1903), 120; Thomas T. Ellis, *Leaves from the Diary of an Army Surgeon* (New York: John Bradburn, 1863), 312; Rhodes, *All for the Union*, 76.

53. *Daily National Intelligencer*, Sep. 29, 1862; *Wheeling Intelligencer,* Oct. 23, 1862.

54. Jeffery D. Marshall, ed., *A War of the People: Vermont Civil War Letters* (Hanover, NH: University Press of New England, 1999), 114; Samuel W. Fiske to the *Springfield Republican*, Sep. 20, 1862, in Sears, ed., *Civil War: Second Year*, 504.

55. *Christian Recorder,* Oct. 25, 1862.

56. *Pittsburgh Gazette*, Sep. 17, 1862.

CHAPTER 5

1. Abraham Lincoln, Preliminary Emancipation Proclamation, Sep. 22, 1862, in Sears, ed., *Civil War: Second Year*, 534–35; Guelzo, *Abraham Lincoln: Redeemer President*, 343.

2. "Memorial of the Public Meeting of the Christian Men of Chicago," in Richard B. Harwell, ed., *The Union Reader: As the North Saw the War* (1958; reprint, New York: Dover, 1996), 151–54.

3. Lincoln, "Reply to Chicago Emancipation Memorial, Washington, D.C.," in *Lincoln's Selected Writings*, 276–79.

4. Lincoln, "Reply to Chicago Emancipation Memorial, Washington, D.C.," 276–79.

5. Coopersmith, *Fighting Words*, 105 (first quote); Masur, *Lincoln's Hundred Days* (second quote), 103, 146; *Christian Recorder*, Sep. 27 (Harper quote), Nov. 22, 1862 (Turner quote); Frederick Douglass, "Emancipation Proclaimed," Oct. 1862, in Sears, ed., *Civil War: Second Year*, 562–63; *Daily National Intelligencer*, Oct. 11, 1862.

6. Anonymous soldier to "Dear Sister," Oct. 18, 1862, NCWC; Masur, *Lincoln's Hundred Days*, 131 (Campbell quote); Gordon, *War Diary*, 7.

7. Norton, *Army Letters, 1861–1865*, 124–26. See also McPherson, *For Cause and Comrades*, 121–22.

8. *New York Herald*, Sep. 23, 25, Oct. 2, 5, 6, 8, 10, 11, 23, Nov. 22, 1862. See also the *Daily National Intelligencer* (Washington, DC), Oct. 11, 1862.

9. Masur, *Lincoln's Hundred Days*, 106 (first quotation); Coopersmith, *Fighting Words*, 106 (second and fourth quotations); L. A. Whitely to James Gordon Bennett, Sep. 24, 1862, in Sears, ed., *Civil War: Second Year*, 538 (third quotation).

10. Mark E. Neely Jr., *The Fate of Liberty: Abraham Lincoln and Civil Liberties* (New York: Oxford University Press, 1991), 12–19, 35–44, 52–60; George B. McClellan to William H. Aspinwall, Sep. 26, 1862, in Sears, ed., *Civil War: Second Year*, 540.

11. Masur, *Lincoln's Hundred Days*, 134, 145–47, 152, 165.

12. Foreman, *World on Fire*, 268–72.

13. Foreman, *World on Fire*, 272, 281–84, 293, 317–20 (quote on 319), 328–29; Doyle, *Cause of All Nations*, 8–10.

14. Horatio Seymour, *Public Record: Including Speeches, Messages, Proclamations and Other Public Utterances of Horatio Seymour* (New York: I. W. England, 1868), 87; Jack Furniss, "To Save the Union 'In Behalf of Conservative Men': Horatio Seymour and the Democratic Vision for War," in Elizabeth R. Varon and Gary W. Gallagher, eds., *New Perspectives on the Union War* (New York: Fordham University Press, 2019).

15. Masur, *Lincoln's Hundred Days*, 134, 145–47, 152, 165; Orville H. Browning, Nov. 29, 1862, in Sears, ed., *Civil War: Second Year*, 614.

16. *Bangor* (ME) *Daily Whig and Courier*, Sep. 25, 1862; Hay, *Lincoln's Journalist*, 31; Masur, *Lincoln's Hundred Days*, 102.

17. Horace Greeley, "Southern Hate of the North," *Continental Monthly*, Oct. 1862, 449–50; *New York Post*, Oct. 28, 1862.

18. Ralph Waldo Emerson, "The President's Proclamation," Sep. 1862, and Frederick Douglass, "Emancipation Proclaimed," Oct. 1862, in Sears, ed. *Civil War: Second Year*, 556–57, 561; *Pacific Appeal*, Nov. 15, 1862; William Furness, *A Word of Consolation for the Kindred of Those Who Have Fallen in Battle* (Philadelphia: Crissy and Markley, 1862), 10.

19. Masur, *Lincoln's Hundred Days*, 109; Edward McPherson, *The Political History of the United States During the Great Rebellion* (Washington, DC: Philp & Solomons, 1865), 232–22.

20. Oakes, *Freedom National*, 324–27.

21. Holmes, *Diary of Miss Emma Holmes*, 202; "Debate in the Confederate Senate on Retaliation for the Emancipation Proclamation," Sep. 29 and Oct. 1, 1862, in Sears, ed., *Civil War: Second Year*, 569–70; *Staunton Spectator*, Oct. 7, 1862.

22. Jones, *Rebel War Clerk's Diary*, 1:125, 142, 150, 154, 161 (quotes on 150, 154, and 161).

23. Buckner as quoted in Hess, *The Civil War in the West*, 100.

24. Hess, *The Civil War in the West*, 102–4; Sam R. Watkins, "From 'Co. Aytch,' Maury Grays, First Tennessee Regiment," in Sears, ed., *Civil War: Second Year*, 597; McPherson, *Embattled Rebel*, 103–4.

25. Herman Hattaway and Archer Jones, *How the North Won: A Military History of the Civil War* (Urbana: University of Illinois Press, 1983), 231–55; Earl J. Hess, *Braxton Bragg: The Most Hated Man of the Confederacy* (Chapel Hill: University of North Carolina Press, 2016), 58–70 (quote on 70); Braxton Bragg, "To the People of the Northwest."

26. Hess, *The Civil War in the West*, 100–104; *Philadelphia Inquirer*, Oct. 18, 1862.

27. Hess, *The Civil War in the West*, 106–7; Weigley, *A Great Civil War*, 156–59.

28. Michael B. Ballard, *Vicksburg: The Campaign That Opened the Mississippi* (Chapel Hill: University of North Carolina Press, 2004), 24–30.

29. Ballard, *Vicksburg*, 50, 68–69, 107.

30. Christopher Waldrep, *Vicksburg's Long Shadow: The Civil War Legacy of Race and Remembrance* (Lanham, MD: Rowman and Littlefield, 2005), 13–22.

31. Waldrep, *Vicksburg's Long Shadow*, 13–22.

32. John W. Haley, *The Rebel Yell and the Yankee Hurrah*, ed. Ruth L. Silliker (Camden, ME: Down East Books, 1985), 50; George G. Meade to Margaret Meade, Nov. 8, 1862, in Sears, ed., *Civil War: Second Year*, 612; George C. Rable, *Fredericksburg! Fredericksburg!* (Chapel Hill: University of North Carolina Press, 2002), 45–52 (quote on 45).

33. Rable, *Fredericksburg!*, 80–89; Haley, *Rebel Yell and Yankee Hurrah*, 53.

34. William Thompson Lusk, *War Letters of William Thompson Lusk, Captain, Assistant Adjutant-General, United States Volunteers, 1861–1863* (New York: privately printed, 1911), 231–32.

35. Rable, *Fredericksburg!*, 83–87.

36. Stiles, *Four Years Under Marse Robert*, 128; Edward Porter Alexander, "From *Fighting for the Confederacy*," in Sears, ed., *Civil War: Second Year*, 647.

37. Rable, *Fredericksburg!*, 177–81 (quote); *Inside Lincoln's Army: The Diary of Marsena Rudolph Patrick*, ed. David S. Sparks (New York: Thomas Yoseloff, 1964), 189; Haley, *Rebel Yell and Yankee Hurrah*, 57.

38. "Edward Porter Alexander: From *Fighting for the Confederacy*," 653; Rable, *Fredericksburg!*, 226–33 (quote 226).

39. Harwell, ed., *The Union Reader*, 183; Warfield, *Manassas to Appomattox*, 117; Rable, *Fredericksburg!*, 278.

40. *New York Herald*, Dec. 19, 1862; Samuel W. Fiske to the *Springfield Republican*, Dec. 15 and 17, 1862, in Sears, ed., *Civil War: Second Year*, 659; Rable, *Fredericksburg!*, 343–53; Wheeler, ed., *Voices of the Civil War*, 221–22.

41. *Richmond Daily Dispatch*, Dec. 19, 1862; *Charleston Mercury*, Dec. 27, 1862; Rable, *Fredericksburg!*, 343–53; John Esten Cooke, *A Life of Gen. Robert E. Lee* (New York: D. Appleton, 1871), 184.

42. Rable, *Fredericksburg!*, 341.

43. Masur, ed., *The Real War Will Never Get in the Books*, 26 (Alcott quote).

44. Masur, ed., *The Real War Will Never Get in the Books*, 255–56 (Whitman quote). For an analysis of how Alcott and Whitman developed new literary conventions

for writing about common soldiers, see Stephen Cushman, *Belligerent Muse: Five Northern Writers and How They Shaped Our Understanding of the Civil War* (Chapel Hill: University of North Carolina Press, 2014), 52–63.

45. Lawson, as quoted by Clifton Johnson in *Battleground Adventures*, in Sears, ed., *Civil War: Second Year*, 664; *New York Herald*, Dec. 2, 1862; Rable, *Fredericksburg!*, 373; Lusk, *War Letters*, 239; James C. Mohr, ed., *The Cormany Diaries: A Northern Family in the Civil War* (Pittsburgh: University of Pittsburgh Press, 1982), 264.

46. Masur, *Lincoln's Hundred Days*, 181 (*Boston Journal* quote); Abraham Lincoln, Annual Message to Congress, December 1, 1862, in *Civil War: Second Year*, ed. Sears, 630–37.

47. Lincoln, Annual Message to Congress, 630–37.

48. Masur, *Lincoln's Hundred Days*, 185–87.

49. Masur, *Lincoln's Hundred Days*, 193; *Letters and Recollections of John Murray Forbes*, ed. Sarah Forbes Hughes (Boston: Houghton, Mifflin, 1899), 1:349–53.

50. *Pacific Appeal*, Dec. 20, 1862; *Douglass' Monthly*, Jan. 1863, in C. Peter Ripley, ed., *Witness for Freedom: African American Voices on Race, Slavery, and Emancipation* (Chapel Hill: University of North Carolina Press, 1993), 223.

CHAPTER 6

1. Guelzo, *Abraham Lincoln: Redeemer President*, 345.

2. Lincoln, "Final Emancipation Proclamation," in *Lincoln's Selected Writings*, 297–98.

3. Lincoln, "Final Emancipation Proclamation."

4. Oakes, *Freedom National*, 370–73; Testimony of Captain Charles B. Monroe, May 9, 1863, in Berlin et al., eds., *Free at Last*, 107–9.

5. Allen Guelzo, "Emancipation: The Un-Holiday," *National Review*, Jul. 20, 2012.

6. Oakes, *Freedom National*, 357–59; Michael Vorenburg, "Emancipation—Then What?" *New York Times*, Opinionator blog, Jan. 15, 2013.

7. Freehling, *The South vs. the South*, 130–31; Oakes, *Freedom National*, 366.

8. Rosen, *Terror in the Heart of Freedom*, 24–29; William Sooy Smith letter, Mar. 27, 1863, in Berlin et al., eds., *Free at Last*, 99; Bergeron, *Andrew Johnson's Civil War*, 35–44 (quote on 44).

9. Isaac W. K. Handy letter, Jan. 1, 1863, William M. Clements Library, University of Michigan, http://clements.umich.edu/exhibits/online/proclaiming_emancipation/emancipation-january.php.

10. William C. Harris, "After the Emancipation Proclamation: Lincoln's Role in the Ending of Slavery," *North and South*, Dec. 2001, 45–49.

11. Bruce Levine, *The Fall of the House of Dixie: The Civil War and the Social Revolution that Transformed the South* (New York: Random House, 2013), 98–99, 116, 134; Oakes, *Freedom National*, 197–208; Willie Lee Rose, *Rehearsal for Reconstruction: The Port Royal Experiment* (Indianapolis: Bobbs-Merrill, 1964).

12. Levine, *Fall of the House of Dixie*, 98–99, 116, 134; Oakes, *Freedom National*, 197–208; *The New South* (Port Royal, SC), Mar. 15, Aug. 23, 1862; Charlotte

Forten, "Life on the Sea Islands," *Atlantic Monthly*, May 1864, 587, 591; Ben Parten, "The Port Royal Experiment," Essential Civil War Curriculum, www .essentialcivilwarcurriculum.com/the-port-royal-experiment.html, 13.

13. Oakes, *Freedom National*, 201; Thomas Wentworth Higginson, *Army Life in a Black Regiment* (Boston: Fields, Osgood, 1869), 39–40; Susie King Taylor, *Reminiscences of My Life in Camp* (Boston: Susie King Taylor, 1902), 18.

14. Higginson, *Army Life in a Black Regiment*, 39–40.

15. Charlotte Forten, Jan. 1, 1863, in Masur, ed., *The Real War Will Never Get in the Books*, 151.

16. Higginson as quoted in Blaine Roberts and Ethan J. Kyle, "This Grove of Gladness," Opinionator blog, *New York Times*, Dec. 31, 2012.

17. *Douglass' Monthly*, Feb. 1863.

18. *Emilie Davis's Civil War: The Diaries of a Free Black Woman in Philadelphia, 1863–1865*, ed. Judy Giesberg (University Park: Pennsylvania State University Press, 2014), 17; David Williams, *I Freed Myself: African American Self-Emancipation in the Civil War Era* (Cambridge: Cambridge University Press, 2014), 106; *Weekly Anglo-African*, Jan. 17, 1863 (Hamilton quote); *Christian Recorder*, Jan. 31, Feb. 7, 14, Mar. 21, 1863; *Liberator*, Jan. 16, 1863 (Nell quote). On Robert Smalls, see Andrew Billingsley, *Yearning to Breathe Free: Robert Smalls of South Carolina and His Families* (Columbia: University of South Carolina Press, 2007).

19. *Christian Recorder*, Jan. 31, Feb. 7, 14, Mar. 14, 21, 1863; *National Anti-Slavery Standard*, Jan. 24, 1863 (Purvis quote); *Pacific Appeal*, Jan. 17, 1863; Douglass, "The Proclamation and the Negro Army," Feb. 6, 1863, in Masur, ed., *The Real War Will Never Get in the Books*, 115–16; *Pacific Appeal*, Jan. 1, 1863.

20. Masur, *Lincoln's Hundred Days*, 212 (Phillips quote); Henry Adams to Charles Francis Adams Jr., Jan. 23, 1863, and Harriet Beecher Stowe, "A Reply," *Atlantic Monthly*, Jan. 1863, in Masur, ed., *The Real War Will Never Get in the Books*, 12, 145.

21. *Liberator*, Jan. 16, 1863.

22. Weber, *Copperheads*.

23. James M. McPherson, "Foreword," in Weber, *Copperheads*, ix; *Chicago Times* and *Cincinnati Enquirer*, as quoted in *Detroit Free Press*, Jan. 6, 1863. For Democratic accusations of Lincoln administration "terrorism," see *Syracuse Daily Courier and Union*, Jul. 19, Oct. 8, 1862; *Chicago Times* in *Daily Empire* (Dayton, OH), Nov. 22, 1862; *Cincinnati Enquirer*, Jan. 10, Mar. 6, 1863.

24. *North American and United States Gazette* (Philadelphia), Jan. 2, 1863; *Bangor Daily Whig and Courier*, Jan. 3, 5, 1863; *Daily Evening Bulletin* (San Francisco), Jan. 5, 1863; *Boston Daily Advertiser*, Jan. 2, 1863; *Daily National Intelligencer*, Jan. 3, 1863; *Vermont Chronicle* (Bellows Falls), Jan. 6, 1863.

25. *New York Herald*, Jan. 3, 1863; Coopersmith, *Fighting Words*, 120 (*New York Times* quote); Weber, *Copperheads*, 76–77; *Waynesboro* (PA) *Village Record*, Jan. 9, Mar. 6, 1863.

26. Eric Foner, *Reconstruction: America's Unfinished Revolution, 1863–1877* (New York: HarperCollins, 1988), 36–38; Kevin T. Barksdale, "Creation of West

Virginia," Encyclopedia Virginia, www.encyclopediavirginia.org/West_Virginia_Creation_of.

27. Harris, *Lincoln and the Border States*, 204–6; *North American and United States Gazette*, Jan. 7, 1863; Phillips, *Rivers Ran Backward*, 226; *Bangor Daily Whig and Courier*, Jan. 5, 1863.

28. F. P. Stanton, "The Consequences of the Rebellion," *Continental Monthly*, Jan.–Feb. 1863, 37–38, 231–32; *New Haven* (CT) *Daily Palladium*, Feb. 2, 1863.

29. Coopersmith, *Fighting Words*, 114–15; *Highland Weekly News* (Hillsboro, OH), Jan. 29, 1863; Rable, *Fredericksburg!*, 372; Gallagher, *Union War*, 103; Henry C. Baldwin to Charley, Feb. 1, 1863, NCWC.

30. Sherman to Wife and Children, Mar. 15, 1863, Sherman to Wife and Parents, Mar. 26, 1863, in Sherman, *Letters to Virtue*, 186–87, 192.

31. Charles W. Hill to Martha, Jan. 6, Apr. 3, May 19, 1863, NCWC.

32. George Snell to Dear Brother, Mar. 18, 1863, NCWC.

33. Halleck to Grant, Mar. 31, 1863, in Berlin et al., eds., *Free at Last*, 101–2.

34. Joseph P. Reidy, " 'Coming from the Shadow of the Past': The Transition from Slavery to Freedom at Freedmen's Village, 1863–1900," *Virginia Magazine of History and Biography*, Oct. 1987, 405–7, 411; Chandra Manning, *Troubled Refuge: Struggling for Freedom in the Civil War* (New York: Vintage, 2016), 51.

35. Jim Downs, *Sick from Freedom: African-American Illness During the Civil War and Reconstruction* (New York: Oxford University Press, 2012), 50–51, 55–56.

36. Halleck to Grant, Mar. 31, 1863; Officers' Report, Helena, Arkansas, Dec. 29, 1862; Eaton Questionnaire, Apr. 29, 1863, in Berlin et al., eds., *Free at Last*, 101–2, 180–81, 190–93.

37. *Thank God My Regiment Is an African One: The Civil War Diary of Colonel Nathan W. Daniels*, ed. C. P. Weaver (Baton Rouge: Louisiana State University Press, 1998), 64.

38. Eaton Questionnaire, Apr. 29, 1863, in Berlin et al., eds., *Free at Last*, 105; Thavolia Glymph, "Refugee Camp at Helena, Arkansas, 1863," in Gallman and Gallagher, eds., *Lens of War*, 139; Harriet Jacobs to William Lloyd Garrison, Sept. 5, 1862, in Sears., ed., *Civil War: Second Year*, 385–89; Harriet Jacobs to Lydia Maria Child, Mar. 18, 1863, in Brooks D. Simpson, ed., *The Civil War: The Third Year Told by Those Who Lived It* (New York: Library of America, 2013), 99.

39. Jacobs to Child, Mar. 18, 1863, in Simpson, ed., *Civil War: Third Year*, 99; Yellin, *Harriet Jacobs: A Life* (New York: Civitas, 2003), 167.

40. Levine, *Fall of the House of Dixie*, 142; Colin Edward Woodward, *Marching Masters: Slavery, Race, and the Confederate Army during the Civil War* (Charlottesville: University of Virginia Press, 2014), 119; *Staunton Spectator*, Jan. 6, 1863; *Richmond Daily Dispatch*, Jan. 10, 1863.

41. Jefferson Davis, Annual Message, Jan. 12, 1863, in *Journal of the Confederate Congress* (Washington, DC: Government Printing Office, 1904), 3:7, 18; Lee to James

A. Seddon, Jan. 10, 1863, in *Wartime Papers of Robert E. Lee*, 390; Coopersmith, *Fighting Words*, 123, 128; Rable, *Damn Yankees!*, 124; Holmes, *Diary of Miss Emma Holmes*, 231–32.

42. "North Carolina Slaveholder to the Confederate President," Nov. 25, 1863, in Berlin et al., eds., *Free at Last*, 142–43.

43. McCurry, *Confederate Reckoning*, 225, 296–97; C. R. Barteau letter, Jan. 8, 1863, in Berlin et al., eds., *Free at Last*, 96–97; Scot Nesbit, "Introduction," Visualizing Emancipation website, http://dsl.richmond.edu/emancipation/introduction.

44. Thavolia Glymph, *Out of the House of Bondage: The Transformation of the Plantation Household* (Cambridge: Cambridge University Press, 2008), 110–16; Penrose, as quoted in Adam Rothman, *Beyond Freedom's Reach: A Kidnapping in the Twilight of Slavery* (Cambridge, MA: Harvard University Press, 2015), 87.

45. Oakes, *Freedom National*, 410.

CHAPTER 7

1. *Milwaukee Daily Sentinel*, Mar. 6, 1863; Wakelyn, ed., *Southern Unionist Pamphlets*, 146; John W. Wood, *Union and Secession in Mississippi* (Memphis, TN: Saunders, Parrish & Whitmore, 1863).

2. Hess, *The Civil War in the West*, 126–33; *A Southern Boy in Blue: The Memoir of Marcus Woodcock, 9th Kentucky Infantry (U.S.A.)*, ed. Kenneth W. Noe (Knoxville: University of Tennessee Press, 1996), 118–19.

3. Woodcock, *Southern Boy in Blue*, 121; Stewart, as quoted in Wheeler, ed., *Voices of the Civil War*, 229.

4. Woodcock, *Southern Boy in Blue*, 123–26; "Lot D. Young: From *Reminiscences of a Soldier of the Orphan Brigade*," in Sears, ed., *Civil War: Second Year*, 735; on Fortress Rosecrans, see the National Park Service website for the Stones River battlefield, www.nps.gov/stri/learn/historyculture/foro.htm.

5. Drew Gilpin Faust, *This Republic of Suffering: Death and the American Civil War* (New York: Vintage, 2004), 69, 267; Woodcock, *Southern Boy in Blue*, 136–37.

6. Woodcock, *Southern Boy in Blue*, 136–37.

7. "Ira S. Owens: From *Greene County in the War*," in Sears, ed., *Civil War: Second Year*, 732.

8. Watkins, *Co. Aytch*, 79.

9. Ballard, *Vicksburg*, 156–64.

10. Ballard, *Vicksburg*, 156–64; McPherson, *Battle Cry of Freedom*, 579.

11. Ballard, *Vicksburg*, 190.

12. Ballard, *Vicksburg*, 199; Grant, *Personal Memoirs*, 155.

13. Ballard, *Vicksburg*, 248–49; Waldrep, *Vicksburg's Long Shadow*, 40; Weigley, *Great Civil War*, 265 (Grant quote).

14. Ballard, *Vicksburg*, 249.

15. Ballard, *Vicksburg,* 321 (Pemberton quote).

16. Terry L. Jones, *The American Civil War* (New York: McGraw-Hill, 2010), 372 (quote); Douglas Lee Braudaway, "A Texan Records the Civil War Siege of Vicksburg, Mississippi: The Journal of Maj. Maurice Kavanaugh Simons, 1863," *Southwestern Historical Quarterly,* Jul. 2001, 101.

17. Osborn H. Oldroyd, *A Soldier's Story of the Siege of Vicksburg* (Springfield, IL: for the author, 1885), May 17.

18. Haley, *Rebel Yell and Yankee Hurrah,* 65; Theodore A. Dodge, Jan. 21–24, 1863, in Simpson, ed., *The Civil War: Third Year,* 6.

19. Stephen W. Sears, *Chancellorsville* (New York: Houghton Mifflin, 1996), 55–58, 67–81.

20. Robert E. Lee to Mary Lee, Feb. 8, 1863, in Simpson, *Civil War: Third Year,* 33; Sears, *Chancellorsville,* 42–44.

21. Sears, *Chancellorsville,* 108; Ernest B. Furgurson, *Ashes of Glory: Richmond at War* (New York: Vintage, 1997), 189–94; Varon, *Southern Lady, Yankee Spy,* 102–4; McCurry, *Confederate Reckoning,* 180.

22. Michael Chesson, "Harlots or Heroines? A New Look at the Richmond Bread Riot," *Virginia Magazine of History and Biography* 92 (1984): 131–75; Craig, as quoted in Varon, *Southern Lady, Yankee Spy,* 104.

23. George Rable, *Civil Wars: Women and the Crisis of Southern Nationalism* (Urbana: University of Illinois Press, 1989), 110; *The Journals of Josiah Gorgas, 1857–78,* ed. Sarah Woolfolk Wiggins (Tuscaloosa: University of Alabama Press, 1995), 59; *New York Herald,* Apr. 17, 1863.

24. McCurry, *Confederate Reckoning,* 191–200.

25. Barrett as quoted in Jeff Toalson, ed., *Mama, I Am Yet Still Alive: A Composite Diary of 1863 in the Confederacy* (Bloomington, IN: iUniverse, 2012), 114–15.

26. *New York Times,* Apr. 8, 20, 1863; *Washington Evening Star,* Apr. 8, 9, 14, 1863; *Wheeling Daily Intelligencer,* Apr. 13, 1863; *Cleveland Daily Leader,* Apr. 13, 1863.

27. Sears, *Chancellorsville,* 181–224.

28. Symonds, *A Battlefield Atlas of the Civil War,* 59; Goss in Wheeler, ed., *Voices of the Civil War,* 259.

29. Haley, *Rebel Yell and Yankee Hurrah,* 87; Sears, *Chancellorsville,* 431–34.

30. Casler, *Four Years in the Stonewall Brigade,* 155; Royster, *The Destructive War,* 198, 224, 228; Rable, *God's Almost Chosen People,* 264; Catherine Edmondston, May 5–7, 9, and 11–12, 1863, in Simpson, ed., *Civil War: Third Year,* 194.

31. Cudworth letter, May 9, 1863, in Silber and Sievens, eds., *Yankee Correspondence,* 78–79.

32. Gordon, *War Diary,* 69, 71.

33. *New York Herald,* May 8, 1863; *Valley Spirit,* May 13, 1863.

34. Neff, *Justice in Blue and Gray,* 53, 153–59; Clement L. Vallandingham, "Speech in Congress," Feb. 23, 1863, in Simpson, ed., *Civil War: Third Year,* 63.

35. Weber, *Copperheads*, 94–99.

36. Abraham Lincoln to Erastus Corning and Others, Jun. 12, 1863, in Simpson, ed., *Civil War: Third Year*, 255–60.

37. Greeley as quoted in "Erastus Corning," Mr. Lincoln and New York, Lehrman Institute, www.mrlincolnandnewyork.org/inside.asp?ID=72&subjectID=3.

38. William Henry Harrison Clayton to Nide and Rachel Pugh, Mar. 26, 1863, in Simpson, ed., *Civil War: Third Year*, 103; Weber, *Copperheads*, 101; Benjamin W. Wilber to "Old Chank," Mar. 28, 1863, NCWC; Walter Rundell Jr., " 'Despotism of Traitors': The Rebellious South Through New York Eyes," *New York History*, Oct. 1964, 347–48, 351, 355; *Christian Recorder*, Mar. 7, 1863.

39. On Union Leagues, see Lawson, *Patriot Fires*, 88–120, and Adam I. P. Smith, *No Party Now: Politics in the Civil War North* (New York: Oxford University Press, 2006), 68–80.

40. Lawson, *Patriot Fires*, 119; Smith, *No Party Now*, 73.

41. Lawson, *Patriot Fires*, 121 (first quote); Daniel S. Dickinson, *Speeches, Correspondence, Etc., of the Late Daniel S. Dickinson* (New York: G. P. Putnam and Sons, 1867), 2:64, 135, 183, 239–54, 259–60 (quotes on 242 and 254), 281–85; *New York Times*, Mar. 21, 1863; James MacKaye, *The Emancipated Slave Face to Face with His Old Master,* in Loyal Publication Society, *Pamphlets Issued by the Loyal Publication Society from Feb. 1, 1864, to Feb. 1, 1865, Nos. 45 to 78* (New York: Loyal Publication Society, 1865).

42. Silber, *Daughters of the Union*, 154; *Proceedings of the Meeting of the Loyal Women of the Republic, Held in New York, May 14, 1863* (New York: Phair, 1863), 7 (Stanton quotes), 13 (Weld quote).

43. *Proceedings of the Meeting of the Loyal Women of the Republic*, 41, 43 (Blackwell quotes), 53 (Weld quote).

44. J. Matthew Gallman, *America's Joan of Arc: The Life of Anna Elizabeth Dickinson* (New York: Oxford University Press, 2006), 24–30 (quotes on 29, 30); *Goodhue Volunteer* (Red Wing, MN), Apr. 29, 1863; *Liberator*, May 8, 1863 (*New York World* quotes); *New York Times*, May 3, 1863.

45. D. H. Dilbeck, " 'The Genesis of This Little Tablet with My Name': Francis Lieber and the Wartime Origins of General Orders No. 100," *Journal of the Civil War Era*, Jun. 2015, 234–36; Neff, *Justice in Blue and Gray*, 77–82.

46. Neff, *Justice in Blue and Gray*, 15–18; Dilbeck, " 'The Genesis of This Little Tablet,' " 237.

47. Dilbeck, " 'The Genesis of This Little Tablet,' " 239–40; Neff, *Justice in Blue and Gray*, 77–82.

48. Dilbeck, " 'The Genesis of This Little Tablet,' " 243–44; Neff, *Justice in Blue and Gray*, 136 (quotation); John Fabian Witt, *Lincoln's Code: The Laws of War in American History* (New York: Free Press, 2012), 254–56.

49. Jefferson Davis, General Orders, No. 111, Dec. 24, 1862, at Freedmen and Southern Society Project, Department of History, University of Maryland, www.freedmen .umd.edu/pow.htm; Retaliatory Act, May 1, 1863, at House Divided: The Civil War Research Engine at Dickinson College, http://hd.housedivided.dickinson.edu/ node/39620.

CHAPTER 8

1. Haley, *Rebel Yell and Yankee Hurrah*, 90; Philip Hamlin to Dear Friends, Jun. 23, 1863, Gettysburg National Park (courtesy of Peter Carmichael); D. Scott Hartwig, "In the Footsteps of Sergeant Hamlin, 1st Minnesota Infantry," Jan. 18, 2013, Gettysburg National Military Park blog, https://npsgnmp.wordpress.com/2013/ 01/18/in-the-footsteps-of-sergeant-hamlin-1st-minnesota-infantry.

2. Stephen W. Sears, *Gettysburg* (Boston: Houghton Mifflin, 2003), 13–14.

3. Edmund DeWitt Patterson, Jun. 24–30, 1863, and Arthur James Lyon Fremantle, Jul. 1–4, 1863, in Simpson, ed., *Civil War: Third Year*, 279, 295; *Richmond Enquirer*, May 8, 1863.

4. Lee to Mary Custis, Apr. 23, 1863, Lee to Davis, Jun. 10, 25, 1863, in Lee, *Wartime Papers*, 440, 507–9, 530; *Richmond Daily Dispatch*, Apr. 27, 1863; *Charleston Mercury*, Jun. 17, 1863; *Staunton Vindicator*, Jun. 19, 1863; *Richmond Enquirer*, Jun. 30, 1863.

5. Lee to Davis, Jun. 10, 25, 1863, in Lee, *Wartime Papers*, 507–9, 530; *The Papers of Jefferson Davis*, vol. 9, *January–September 1863*, ed. Lynda Lasswell Crist (Baton Rouge: Louisiana State University Press, 1997), 244.

6. Tally Simpson to his Aunt, Jun. 28, 1863, in Toalson, ed., *Mama, I Am Still Yet Alive*, 96–97, 198–99; Sears, *Gettysburg*, 107–8.

7. Sears, *Gettysburg*, 111–12; Wheeler, ed., *Voices of the Civil War*, 282.

8. Wheeler, ed., *Voices of the Civil War*, 280 (Coffin); Harwell, ed., *The Union Reader*, 227 (Broadhead).

9. Sears, *Gettysburg*, 84; Henry Livermore Abbott to Josiah Gardner Abott, Jul. 6, 1863, in Simpson, ed., *Civil War: Third Year*, 336.

10. Sears, *Gettysburg*, 115, 150–52.

11. Sears, *Gettysburg*, 104, 143; William T. Livermore Diary, May 24, Jun. 15, 17, 29, 30, NCWC; Samuel W. Fiske to the *Springfield Republican*, Jun. 30, 1863, in Simpson, ed., *Civil War: Third Year*, 289.

12. Doubleday, in Wheeler, ed., *Voices of the Civil War*, 291; Broadhead in Harwell, ed., *Union Reader*, 231.

13. Allen C. Guelzo, *Gettysburg: The Last Invasion* (New York: Alfred A. Knopf, 2013), 219–20.

14. Doubleday, in Wheeler, ed., *Voices of the Civil War*, 300; Broadhead, in Harwell, ed., *Union Reader*, 232.

15. Arthur James Lyon Fremantle, Jul. 1–4, 1863, in Simpson, ed., *Civil War: Third Year*, 296.

16. Sears, *Gettysburg*, 239.

17. Gordon, Oates, and Alexander in Wheeler, ed., *Voices of the Civil War*, 309–11, 314; Haley, *Rebel Yell and Yankee Hurrah*, 103.

18. Wilkeson, in Wheeler, ed., *Voices of the Civil War*, 316; Haley, *Rebel Yell and Yankee Hurrah*, 103.

19. Sears, *Gettysburg*, 441; Francis Adams Donaldson, "Narrative of Gettysburg," Jul. 2–3, 1863, in Simpson, ed., *Civil War: Third Year*, 324; Haley, *Rebel Yell and Yankee Hurrah*, 106; Glatthaar, *General Lee's Army*, 281.

20. Guelzo, *Gettysburg*, 443–44.

21. Haley, *Rebel Yell and Yankee Hurrah*, 106; Weigley, *A Great Civil War*, 254.

22. Weigley, *A Great Civil War*, 255–56.

23. Waldrep, *Vicksburg's Long Shadow*, 36 (quote).

24. Oldroyd, *A Soldier's Story*, May 22.

25. Waldrep, *Vicksburg's Long Shadow*, 37 (quote).

26. Ballard, *Vicksburg*, 367–69; Weigley, *A Great Civil War*, 269; Oldroyd, *A Soldier's Story*, 58.

27. Dora Miller, "A Woman's Diary of the Siege of Vicksburg," *Century Magazine*, May 1885, 775; William H. Tunnard, *A Southern Record: The History of the Third Regiment, Louisiana Infantry* (Baton Rouge: published for the author, 1866), 254.

28. Donald S. Frazier, *Blood on the Bayou: Vicksburg, Port Hudson, and the Trans-Mississippi* (Buffalo Gap, TX: State House Press, 2015), 54–57; Stephen J. Ochs, "The Rock of New Orleans," *New York Times*, Opinionator blog, Jul. 31, 2013.

29. Joseph T. Wilson, *The Black Phalanx: African American Soldiers in the War of Independence, the War of 1812 and the Civil War* (1887; reprint, New York: Da Capo Press, 1994), 213–18; Laurence Lee Hewitt, "An Ironic Route to Glory: Louisiana's Native Guards at Port Hudson," in John David Smith, ed., *Black Soldiers in Blue: African American Troops in the Civil War Era* (Chapel Hill: University of North Carolina Press, 2002), 95.

30. Elias D. Strunke letter, May 29, 1863, in Berlin et al., eds., *Free at Last*, 439–41; James M. McPherson, *The Negro's Civil War: How American Blacks Felt and Acted during the War for the Union* (New York: Pantheon, 1965), 189 (Banks quote); Stephen J. Ochs, *A Black Patriot and a White Priest: André Cailloux and Claude Paschal Maistre in Civil War New Orleans* (Baton Rouge: Louisiana State University Press, 2006), 161; Hewitt, "An Ironic Route," 97 (Garrison quote); Wilson, *Black Phalanx*, 216–17 (last quotation).

31. Richard Lowe, "Battle on the Levee: The Fight at Milliken's Bend," in Smith, ed., *Black Soldiers in Blue*, 114–24; Frazier, *Blood on the Bayou*, 94–101.

32. Miller, in McPherson, *The Negro's Civil War*, 190; Frazier, *Blood on the Bayou*, 104–8; Lowe, "Battle on the Levee," 124–28 (Stone quotation on 128).

33. *Richmond Daily Dispatch*, May 22, 1863; Douglas Lee Braudaway, "A Texan Records the Civil War Siege of Vicksburg, Mississippi: The Journal of Maj.

Maurice Kavanaugh Simons, 1863," *Southwestern Historical Quarterly* 105 (Jul. 2001): 110–18.

34. Braudaway, "A Texan Records the Civil War," 119.

35. Miller, "A Woman's Diary"; Joan Waugh, *U. S. Grant: American Hero, American Myth* (Chapel Hill: University of North Carolina Press, 2009), 65; Joan Waugh, "'I Only Knew What Was in My Mind': Ulysses S. Grant and the Meaning of Appomattox," *Journal of the Civil War Era*, Sep. 2012, 307–18.

36. Braudaway, "A Texan Records the Civil War," 123; Oldroyd, *A Soldier's Story*, 75; Ballard, *Vicksburg*, 399.

37. Ballard, *Vicksburg*, 407–13 (Lincoln quote on 411).

38. *New York Herald*, Jul. 6, 12, 1863; *New Haven Daily Palladium*, Jul. 8, 1863, *North American and United States Gazette*, Jul. 8, 14, 1863, *Perrysburg* (OH) *Journal*, Jul. 15, 1863; Bradley R. Clampitt, *Occupied Vicksburg* (Baton Rouge: Louisiana State University Press, 2016), 45.

39. Clampitt, *Occupied Vicksburg*, 42–45; *New York Herald*, Jul. 12, 1863.

40. Ballard, *Vicksburg*, 399 (first quotation); Coopersmith, 180, 183.

41. *A Politician Goes to War: The Civil War Letters of John White Geary*, ed. William Blair (University Park: Pennsylvania State University Press, 1995), 100; *Christian Recorder*, Aug. 8, 1863.

42. Margaret S. Creighton, *The Colors of Courage: Gettysburg's Forgotten History: Immigrants, Women, and African Americans in the Civil War's Defining Battles* (New York: Perseus, 2005), 148–50. On Letterman and medical progress, see Alfred J. Bollet, *Civil War Medicine: Challenges and Triumphs* (Tucson, AZ: Galen Press, 2002); Ira M. Rutkow, *Bleeding in Blue and Gray: Civil War Surgery and the Evolution of American Medicine* (New York: Random House, 2005); Humphreys, *Marrow of Tragedy*, 5–12; Scott McGaugh, *Surgeon in Blue: Jonathan Letterman, the Civil War Doctor Who Pioneered Battlefield Care* (New York: Arcade, 2013).

43. McGaugh, *Surgeon in Blue*, 184–95; Humphreys, *Marrow of Tragedy*, 40–41; Cornelia Hancock to Her Cousin and to Ellen Hancock Child, Jul. 7–8, 1863, in Simpson, ed., *Civil War: Third Year*, 341.

44. John M. Rudy, "Gettysburg College and the Battle of Gettysburg: A Civil War Walking Tour," 2013, http://cupola.gettysburg.edu/cwfac, 8; James L. Bowen, *History of the Thirty-Seventh Regiment, Mass. Volunteers, in the Civil War of 1861–1865* (Holyoke, MA: Clark W. Bryan, 1884), 192; Frank Aretas Haskell, *The Battle of Gettysburg* (Boston: Mollus, 1908), 89; Carol Reardon, *Pickett's Charge in History and Memory* (Chapel Hill: University of North Carolina Press, 1997), 44, 49, 52.

45. Haley, *Rebel Yell and Yankee Hurrah*, 107; Rod Gragg, *Eyewitness Gettysburg: The Civil War's Greatest Battle* (Washington, DC: Regnery History, 2013), 245, 402–3 (Wheeler and Browning quotes); Edward P. Smith, *Incidents Among Shot and Shell* (Philadelphia: Edgewood, 1868), 176, 185; Sophronia E. Bucklin, *In Hospital and Camp: A Woman's Record of Thrilling Incidents Among the Wounded in the Late War* (Philadelphia: J. E. Potter, 1869), 149; *Franklin Repository* (Chambersburg, PA),

Jul. 29, 1863; Edward L. Ayers, *The Thin Light of Freedom: The Civil War and Emancipation in the Heart of America* (New York: W. W. Norton, 2017), 96.

46. Coopersmith, *Fighting Words*, 183 (*News* quote); "A Nurse at Gettysburg," 344–45.

47. Ballard, Vicksburg, 402; George S. Bernard, "The Gettysburg Campaign: The Narrative of a Private Soldier in the Confederate Army," in Hampton Newsome, John Horn, and John G. Selby, eds., *Civil War Talks: Further Reminiscences of George S. Bernard and His Fellow Veterans* (Charlottesville: University of Virginia Press, 2012), 137–38; Gary W. Gallagher, "Lee's Army Has Not Lost Any of Its Prestige: The Impact of Gettysburg on the Army of Northern Virginia and the Confederate Home Front," in Gary W. Gallagher, ed., *The Third Day at Gettysburg and Beyond* (Chapel Hill: University of North Carolina Press, 1994), 4–6.

48. Coopersmith, *Fighting Words*, 207–8.

49. George Winston Smith and Charles Judah, *Life in the North During the Civil War: A Source History* (Albuquerque: University of New Mexico Press, 1966), 58–61; *New York Times*, Jul. 14, 1863.

50. Smith and Judah, eds., *Life in the North*, 59; *News* as quoted in Coopersmith, *Fighting Words*, 195; Barnet Schecter, *The Devil's Own Work: The Civil War Draft Riots and the Fight to Reconstruct America* (New York: Walker Books, 2005), 110.

51. Judith Giesberg, *Army at Home: Women and the Civil War Northern Home Front* (Chapel Hill: University of North Carolina Press, 2009), 50, 78–79, 128–29; Coopersmith, *Fighting Words*, 203 (*New York Times* quote).

52. Christian G. Samito, *Becoming American Under Fire: Irish Americans, African Americans, and the Politics of Citizenship During the Civil War Era* (Ithaca, NY: Cornell University Press, 2009), 126; William B. Kurtz, *Excommunicated from the Union: How the Civil War Created a Separate Catholic America* (New York: Fordham University Press, 2016), 113–15; William L. Burton, *Melting Pot Soldiers: The Union's Ethnic Regiments* (New York: Fordham University Press, 1998), x, 154; Doyle, *Cause of All Nations*, 159.

53. Joseph H. Prime to Hannah, Jul. 21, 1863, and James Clarke to "Dear Friend," Jul. 17, 1863, NCWC; William Wheeler, *In Memoriam: Letters of William Wheeler of the Class of 1855, Y.C.* (Cambridge, MA: G. Houghton, 1875), 417.

54. Iver Bernstein, *The New York City Draft Riots: Their Significance for American Society and Politics in the Age of the Civil War* (New York: Oxford University Press, 1990), 34, 53, 183; Coopersmith, *Fighting Words*, 201.

55. Gooding, *On the Altar of Freedom*, 9, 13, 15; Kantrowitz, *More than Freedom*, 21–23; "Corporal James H. Gooding," National Park Service website for Andersonville National Historic Site, www.nps.gov/ande/learn/historyculture/j-h-gooding .htm.

56. Gooding, *On the Altar of Freedom*, 24.

57. Gooding, *On the Altar of Freedom*, 24, 26–27, 34–35.

58. Catherine Clinton, *Harriet Tubman: The Road to Freedom* (New York: Little, Brown, 2004), 163–74; *North American and United States Gazette*, Jun. 9, 1863;

Ripley et al., eds., *Witness to Freedom*, 244–45; *Daily National Intelligencer*, Jun. 11, 1863.

59. Gooding, *On the Altar of Freedom*, 38–39.

60. Douglass, in McPherson, ed., *The Negro's Civil War*, 194; "Robert Gould Shaw," Civil War Trust website, www.civilwar.org/education/history/biographies/robert-gould-shaw.html.

61. *Pacific Appeal*, Aug. 22, 1863; Glenn David Brasher, "Striking the Blow at Fort Wagner," *New York Times*, Opinionator blog, Jul. 18, 2013.

62. *Christian Recorder*, Jul. 25, Aug. 22, 1863; *Liberator*, Aug. 14, 1863; *Philadelphia Inquirer*, Jun. 26, 1863.

63. *New York Evening Post* as quoted in *Christian Recorder*, Aug. 1, 1863, and *Cleveland Daily Leader*, Aug. 3, 1863; *Mattoon* (IL) *Gazette*, Aug. 19, 1863.

64. *Christian Recorder*, Sep. 5, 1863; Grant in McPherson, ed., *Negro's Civil War*, 195; Lincoln to James C. Conkling, Aug. 26, 1863, in *Lincoln's Selected Writings*, 318–21.

65. Lincoln to James C. Conkling, in *Lincoln's Selected Writings*, 318–21.

66. Tera W. Hunter, *Bound in Wedlock: Slave and Free Black Marriage in the Nineteenth Century* (Cambridge, MA: Harvard University Press, 2017), 179 (first quote); Gooding, *On the Altar of Freedom*, 7, 119; McPherson, ed., *The Negro's Civil War*, 203, 206–7.

CHAPTER 9

1. Arthur Van Lisle, "At Chickamauga Thirty Years Ago," *Blue and Gray*, Sep. 1893, 195–201.

2. Christopher J. Einolf, *George Thomas: Virginian for the Union* (Norman: University of Oklahoma Press, 2007), 186.

3. *Charleston Mercury*, Oct. 3, 1863; Scribner as quoted in Steven E. Woodworth, *Chickamauga: A Battlefield Guide with a Section on Chattanooga* (Lincoln: University of Nebraska Press, 1999), 19; *Daily Cleveland Herald*, Sep. 24, Oct. 23, 1863, *New Hampshire Statesman*, Oct. 23, 1863, *Milwaukee Daily Sentinel*, Nov. 6, 1863.

4. *Charleston Mercury*, Sep. 30, 1863.

5. James A. Connolly to Mary Dunn Connolly, Nov. 26, Dec. 7, 1863, in Simpson, ed., *Civil War: Third Year*, 597–98.

6. Bragg in Wheeler, ed., *Voices of the Civil War*, 374.

7. M. David Detwiler, *The Civil War: The Story of the War with Maps* (Mechanicsburg, PA: Stackpole, 2014), 111.

8. McKenzie, *Lincolnites and Rebels*, 123, 131–33.

9. Lane, *A Soldier's Diary*, 270; McKenzie, *Lincolnites and Rebels*, 149–51.

10. *New York Times*, Sep. 18, 1863; *Wheeling Daily Intelligencer*, Sep. 21, 1863; *New York Herald*, Oct. 9, 1863; McKenzie, *Lincolnites and Rebels*, 174–75.

11. McKenzie, *Lincolnites and Rebels*, 172; Abraham Lincoln, Executive Order, December 7, 1863, American Presidency Project, www.presidency.ucsb.edu/ws/?pid=70002.

12. Tyler Dennett, ed., *Lincoln and the Civil War: In the Diaries and Letters of John Hay* (1939; reprint, Cambridge, MA: Da Capo, 1988), 104 (Hay quote).

13. *New York Herald*, Nov. 28, 1863.

14. Eric Foner, *Reconstruction: America's Unfinished Revolution, 1863–1877* (New York: Harper & Row, 1988), 39–41; Dennett, ed., *Lincoln and the Civil War*, 126 (Hay quote); *New York Times*, Nov. 6, 1863; Daniel W. Crofts, "Holding the Line in Maryland," *New York Times*, Opinionator blog, October 22, 2013; *Anglo-African*, Oct. 10, 17, 24, 31, 1864; Debra Jackson, "A Black Journalist in Civil War Virginia: Robert Hamilton and the 'Anglo-African,'" *Virginia Magazine of History and Biography* 116 (2008): 42–72.

15. Sutherland, *A Savage Conflict*, 129–30.

16. Sutherland, *A Savage Conflict*, 125–30.

17. Harris, *Lincoln and the Border States*, 324–25; Charles D. Drake, "The Wrongs to Missouri's Loyal People," in Wakelyn, ed., *Southern Unionist Pamphlets*, 152.

18. Harris, *Lincoln and the Border States*, 314–28.

19. Harris, *Lincoln and the Border States*, 309, 314–28, 345–46; Foner, *Reconstruction*, 42; Thomas C. Fletcher, *Missouri's Jubilee* (Jefferson City, MO: W. A. Curry, 1865), 4–5.

20. Sutherland, *A Savage Conflict*, 135–38, 206–13; Robert F. Smith, "The Confederate Attempt to Counteract Reunion Propaganda in Arkansas, 1863–1865," *Arkansas Historical Quarterly*, Spring 1957, 54–62; *Cleveland Daily Leader*, Oct. 7, 1863; Brian Craig Miller, ed., *A Punishment on the Nation: An Iowa Soldier Endures the Civil War* (Kent, OH: Kent State University Press, 2012), 100.

21. *New York Times*, Dec. 4, 1863, Edward W. Gantt, "An Address in Favor of Reunion in 1863," in Wakelyn, ed., *Southern Unionist Pamphlets*, 212, 220–21.

22. Quint, *The Potomac and the Rapidan*, 371; Wheeler, *In Memoriam*, 422, 432–33, 445.

23. *Intimate Letters of Carl Schurz, 1841–1869*, ed. Joseph Schafer (Madison: State Historical Society of Wisconsin, 1928), 291–92.

24. Bergeron, *Andrew Johnson's Civil War*, 35–44 (quote on 44).

25. Foner, *Reconstruction*, 45–50; John Hope Franklin, *Reconstruction After the Civil War* (Chicago: University of Chicago Press, 1961), 14–15; Carwardine, *Lincoln*, 237.

26. Foner, *Reconstruction*, 55–58.

27. Gooding, *On the Altar of Freedom*, 31, 54, 61, 103.

28. Charles Sumner, "Our Domestic Relations; Or, How to Treat the Rebel States," *Atlantic Monthly*, Sep. 1863, 507–28.

29. Montgomery Blair, *Speech of the Hon. Montgomery Blair (Postmaster General), on the Revolutionary Schemes of the Ultra Abolitionists, and in Defence of the Policy of the President* (New York: D. W. Lee, 1863).

30. *New York Herald*, Sep. 3, 1863; Lincoln to Rosecrans, Oct. 4, 1863, in *Collected Works of Abraham Lincoln*, ed. Roy P. Basler (New Brunswick, NJ: Rutgers University Press, 1953), 6:498.

31. *New York Herald*, Oct. 8, 1863.

32. This view is captured best in Garry Wills, *Lincoln at Gettysburg: The Words That Remade America* (New York: Simon & Schuster, 1992). See also Martin P. Johnson, *Writing the Gettysburg Address* (Lawrence: University Press of Kansas, 2013), 57–59, 166–67.

33. Johnson, *Writing the Gettysburg Address*, 19, 28–31; Neely, *Lincoln and the Democrats*, 62–65.

34. Edward Everett, "Gettysburg Address," November 19, 1863, Voices of Democracy: The U.S. Oratory Project, http://voicesofdemocracy.umd.edu/everett-gettysburg-address-speech-text.

35. Johnson, *Writing the Gettysburg Address*, 16; Jared Peatman, *The Long Shadow of Lincoln's Gettysburg Address* (Carbondale: Southern Illinois University Press, 2013), 37–51; *Richmond Enquirer*, Nov. 25, 27, 1863.

36. Lincoln, "Third Annual Message to Congress," Dec. 8, 1863, in *Lincoln's Selected Writings*, 331.

37. Lincoln, "Third Annual Message to Congress," Dec. 8, 1863, and "Proclamation of Amnesty and Reconstruction," Dec. 8, 1863, in *Lincoln's Selected Writings*, 331–34.

38. McPherson, *Tried by War*, 207; Lincoln, "Proclamation of Amnesty," 333.

39. *Chicago Tribune*, Jan. 20, 1864; *New York Times*, Jan. 10, 11, 1864; *Alexandria Gazette*, Jan. 13, Feb. 19, 1864; S. Millett Thompson letter, Dec. 6, 1863, NCWC.

40. Mark A. Weitz, "Preparing for the Prodigal Sons: The Development of the Union Desertion Policy During the Civil War," *Civil War History* 45 (Jun. 1999): 99–125; Lincoln to John G. Foster, Jan. 27, 1864, Lincoln to Edwin M. Stanton, Feb. 10, 1864, and Lincoln to Daniel E. Sickles, Feb. 15, 1864, all in *Collected Works of Abraham Lincoln*, 7:153–54, 176–77, 185; "Domestic Intelligence," *Harper's Weekly*, Feb. 6, 1864; Dorris, *Pardon and Amnesty*, 57 (last quotation).

41. Dennett, ed., *Lincoln and the Civil War*, 131 (Hay quote); *New York Tribune*, Dec. 10, 1863; *Chicago Tribune*, Jan. 27, 1864; "The President's Message," *Harper's Weekly*, Dec. 26, 1863.

42. *Franklin Repository*, Dec. 16, 1863; *Constitution* (Middletown, CT), Dec. 16, 1863.

43. Hamilton, "Address to the People of Texas," in Wakelyn, ed., *Southern Unionist Pamphlets*, 247–50. The Union tried to set the stage for the liberation of Texas, and the installation of a pro-Union government there, in the ill-fated Red River campaign in the spring of 1864; moving into east Texas, the Union high command reckoned, would make it possible to seize large quantities of Confederate cotton, and also deter the French in Mexico from allying with the Confederacy. Nathaniel Banks led expeditionary force against Shreveport, Louisiana, only to be turned back by Confederate forces under Lieutenant General Richard Taylor (in Major General Edmund Kirby Smith's Trans-Mississippi Department). See Gary Joiner, *Through the Howling Wilderness: The 1864 Red River Campaign and Union Failure in the West* (Knoxville: University of Tennessee Press, 2006).

44. Stoddard, *Dispatches*, 201, 203; "Domestic Intelligence," *Harper's Weekly*, Jan. 9, Feb. 6, 1864; *Chicago Tribune*, Dec. 22, 1863, Jan. 16, Feb. 2, 1864; *New York Times*, Jan. 5, 1864; *Evening Star* (Washington, DC), Jan. 25, 1864; *New York Herald*, Jan. 8, 27,

1864. While conceding the difficulty of generating definitive numbers, Jonathan Truman Dorris finds that record books of wartime reports sent to Washington, D.C., provide the names and addresses of 22,659 people who took the amnesty oath between Dec. 1863 and May 1865, with Tennessee, North Carolina, and Arkansas leading in the tally. Dorris, *Pardon and Amnesty*, 71.

45. *Metropolitan Record* as quoted in *Richmond Daily Dispatch*, Jan. 27, 1864; *Harper's Weekly*, Mar. 19, 1864; *New York Daily News*, Jan. 10, 1864.

46. Rick Beard, "Lincoln's Ten Percent Plan," *New York Times*, Opinionator blog, December 9, 2013.

47. Larry E. Nelson, "Black Leaders and the Presidential Election of 1864," *Journal of Negro History*, Jan. 1978, 50; Frederick Douglass, "The Mission of the War," in *Frederick Douglass: Selected Speeches and Writings*, ed. Philip S. Foner (Chicago: Chicago Review Press, 2000), 565.

48. *Christian Recorder*, Feb. 20, 1864; *Pacific Appeal*, Jan. 9, 1864.

49. Dennett, ed., *Lincoln and the Civil War*, 77 (Hay quoting Lincoln).

50. *Harper's Weekly*, Sep. 19, 1863, 600–603. See also, for example, *Harper's Weekly*, Jun. 14, 1862, 380, Sep. 27, 1862, 616–17, Jun. 6, 1863, 357, May 7, 1864, 289, Nov. 5, 1864, 708, 717, Dec. 24, 1864, 822–25, 829; Paul F. Mottelay and T. Campbell-Copeland, eds., *The Soldier in Our Civil War: A Pictorial History of the Conflict, 1861–1865* (New York: S. Bradley, 1890), 2:170; *Frank Leslie's Illustrated Newspaper*, Oct. 1, 1864, 21; George N. Barnard's 1862 photograph "Refugees Leaving the Old Homestead," Library of Congress, www.loc.gov/pictures/resource/stereo.1802739; and the Joseph E. Baker lithograph "Union Refugees," Library of Congress, www.loc.gov/pictures/item/90714047.

51. Freehling, *The South vs. the South*, xiii. Historians have estimated that 6,000 rebel soldiers were "galvanized": they were prisoners of war who agreed to switch sides to the Union in order to gain freedom from prison camps. The Union military opted to send most of these men west to fight against Native Americans. Phil Leigh, "The Galvanized Yankee," *New York Times*, Opinionator blog, Jun. 5, 2012. The number of white Southern refugees is also difficult to ascertain. George Rable has estimated that number at 250,000, but it remains unclear how many considered themselves to be Unionists and were fleeing from the Confederate to Federal lines. Silkenat, *Driven from Home*, 8.

52. Rable, *Confederate Republic*, 161–65; Barton A. Myers, *Rebels Against the Confederacy: North Carolina's Unionists* (Cambridge: Cambridge University Press, 2014), 117; Victoria E. Bynum, *The Long Shadow of the Civil War: Southern Dissent and Its Legacies* (Chapel Hill: University of North Carolina Press, 2010); Victoria E. Bynum, *The Free State of Jones: Mississippi's Longest Civil War* (Chapel Hill: University of North Carolina Press, 2001).

53. Myers, *Rebels Against the Confederacy*, 102.

54. Freehling, *The South vs. the South*; Thomas G. Dyer, *Secret Yankees: The Union Circle in Confederate Atlanta* (Baltimore: Johns Hopkins University Press, 1999); Varon, *Southern Lady, Yankee Spy*, 199.

55. Myers, *Rebels Against the Confederacy*, 11–14, 119; Steven E. Nash, "'The Other War Was but the Beginning': The Politics of Loyalty in Western North Carolina, 1865–1867," in Andrew L. Slap, ed., *Reconstructing Appalachia: The Civil War's Aftermath* (Lexington: University Press of Kentucky, 2010), 107–9.

56. Myers, *Rebels Against the Confederacy*, 12.

57. James M. McPherson, *Embattled Rebel: Jefferson Davis as Commander in Chief* (New York: Penguin Press, 2014), 172–73; *Richmond Daily Dispatch*, Oct. 28, 1863; Davis to Zebulon Vance, Jan. 8, 1864, *OR*, ser. 1, vol. 51, pt. 2, 808–10; Rable, *Confederate Republic*, 243.

58. "Address of Congress to the People of the Confederate States: Joint Resolution in Relation to the War," Jan. 22, 1864, *OR*, ser. 4, vol. 3, 126–37.

59. Emory M. Thomas, *The Confederate Nation: 1861–1865* (New York: Harper & Row, 1979), 264–65; Catherine Edmonston, December 11, 1863, in Simpson, ed., *Civil War: Third Year*, 661–63.

60. *Charleston Mercury*, Dec. 17, 1863, Jan. 12, 16, 1864; Jones, *Rebel War Clerk's Diary*, 317; Smith, "Confederate Attempt to Counteract Reunion Propaganda," 59, 61.

61. Fahs, *The Imagined Civil War*, 36; Sarah E. Gardner, *Blood and Irony: Southern White Women's Narratives of the Civil War, 1861–1937* (Chapel Hill: University of North Carolina Press, 2004), 33; Bradley R. Clampitt, *The Confederate Heartland: Military and Civilian Morale in the Western Confederacy* (Baton Rouge: Louisiana State University Press, 2011), 17 (Evans quote); Augusta Jane Evans, *Macaria; or Altars of Sacrifice* (Richmond: West & Johnson, 1864), 161–62.

62. Gallagher, *Confederate War*, 8, 10, 37, 75, 85, 93.

63. Gallagher, *Confederate War*, 38 (Pierson quote); Clampitt, *The Confederate Heartland*, 24 (Barber quote).

CHAPTER 10

1. Varon, *Southern Lady, Yankee Spy*, 136–49.

2. *Hartford* (CT) *Courant*, Mar. 11, 1864; *National Republican*, Mar. 11, 1864; *Evening Star* (Washington, DC), Mar. 10, 1864.

3. John Cimprich, *Fort Pillow, a Civil War Massacre, and Public Memory* (Baton Rouge: Louisiana State University Press, 2005), 72–74; Achilles V. Clark to Judith Porter and Henrietta Ray, Apr. 14, 1864, in Aaron Sheehan-Dean, ed., *The Civil War: The Final Year Told by Those Who Lived It* (New York: Library of America, 2014), 44; Will Hickox, "Remember Fort Pillow!," *New York Times*, Opinionator blog, April 11, 2014.

4. *Daily Cleveland Herald*, Apr. 18, 1864; *Liberator*, Apr. 22, 1864; *Scioto Gazette* (Chillicothe, OH), Apr. 18, 1864; *North American and United States Gazette*, Apr. 16, 1864; *Milwaukee Daily Sentinel*, Apr. 16, 1864.

5. *Christian Recorder*, Apr. 23, 30, Jul. 9, 1864.

6. Cimprich, *Fort Pillow*, 95–97, 99 (quote), 103.

7. Lonnie R. Speer, *Portals to Hell: Military Prisons of the Civil War* (Mechanicsburg, PA: Stackpole Books, 1997), 102; William B. Hesseltine, *Civil War Prisons* (Kent, OH: Kent State University Press, 1972), 172–78; *New York Times*, Aug. 9, 11, 15, 17, 1862.

8. "Myth: Grant Stopped the Prisoner Exchange," National Park Service website for Andersonville National Historic Site, November 27, 2017, www.nps.gov/ande/ learn/historyculture/grant-and-the-prisoner-exchange.htm; Varon, *Southern Lady, Yankee Spy*, 100; Roger Pickenpaugh, *Captives in Blue: The Civil War Prisons of the Confederacy* (Tuscaloosa: University of Alabama Press, 2013), 92–94 (Tippett quote on 92).

9. Gideon Welles, "Debating Retaliation: Washington, DC," May 3–4, 1864, in Sheehan-Dean, ed., *Civil War: Final Year*, 57–59; Charles W. Sanders Jr., *While in the Hands of the Enemy: Military Prisons of the Civil War* (Baton Rouge: Louisiana State University Press, 2005), 219–21; Cimprich, *Fort Pillow*, 102–3; Harwell, ed., *Union Reader*, 284–85 (Tracy quote); Benjamin G. Cloyd, *Haunted by Atrocity: Civil War Prisons in American Memory* (Baton Rouge: Louisiana State University Press, 2010), 11.

10. Cloyd, *Haunted by Atrocity*, 19, 24–27; United States Sanitary Commission, *Narrative of the Privations and Sufferings of United States Officers and Soldiers While Prisoners of War in the Hands of the Rebel Authorities* (Boston: Littell's Living Age Office, 1864), 22–24, 55, 70–71.

11. J. J. Geer, *Beyond the Lines: Or a Yankee Prisoner Loose in Dixie* (Philadelphia: J. W. Daughaday, 1863), 49–54; Safford in Marshall, ed., *A War of the People*, 252.

12. *Unspoiled Heart: The Journal of Charles Mattocks of the 17th Maine*, ed. Philip N. Racine (Knoxville: University of Tennessee Press, 1994), 159–60.

13. Sanders, *While in the Hands of the Enemy*, 217–18.

14. Robert M. Dunkerly, Donald C. Pfanz, and David R. Ruth, *No Turning Back: A Guide to the 1864 Overland Campaign, from the Wilderness to Cold Harbor, May 4–June 13, 1864* (El Dorado Hills, CA: Savas Beatie, 2014), 10–12.

15. Brooks D. Simpson, "Great Expectations: Ulysses S. Grant, the Northern Press, and the Opening of the Wilderness Campaign," in Gary W. Gallagher, ed., *The Wilderness Campaign* (Chapel Hill: University of North Carolina Press, 1997), 14; Robert E. L. Krick, "An Insurmountable Barrier Between the Army and Ruin: The Confederate Experience at Spotsylvania's Bloody Angle," in Gary W. Gallagher, ed., *The Spotsylvania Campaign* (Chapel Hill: University of North Carolina Press, 1998), 103–4, 112; Porter, in Wheeler, ed., *Voices of the Civil War*, 393.

16. Gordon C. Rhea, *To the North Anna River: Grant and Lee, May 13–25, 1864* (Baton Rouge: Louisiana State University Press, 2000), 41–61.

17. Robertson, *Civil War Virginia*, 152–53; Waugh, *U.S. Grant*, 87.

18. Jean Edward Smith, *Grant* (New York: Touchstone, 2001), 367.

19. Carol Reardon, "A Hard Road to Travel: The Impact of Continuous Operations on the Army of the Potomac and the Army of Northern Virginia in May 1864," in Gallagher, ed., *Spotsylvania Campaign*, 195–96; J. Tracy Power, *Lee's Miserables: Life in the Army of Northern Virginia from the Wilderness to Appomattox* (Chapel Hill: University of North Carolina Press, 1998), 75; Gallagher, "The Two Generals Who Resist Each Other: Perceptions of Lee and Grant in the Summer of 1864," in Gary W. Gallagher and Caroline E. Janney, eds., *Cold Harbor to the Crater: The End of the Overland Campaign* (Chapel Hill: University of North Carolina Press, 2015), 5, 11–12; *Richmond Daily Dispatch*, May 28, Jun. 1, 1864.

20. Haley, *Rebel Yell and Yankee Hurrah*, 165; Rhodes, *All for the Union*, 150; Stephen Minot Weld to Stephen Minot Weld Sr., Jun. 21, 1864, in Sheehan-Dean, ed., *Civil War: Final Year*, 217; *Christian Recorder*, Jul. 9, 1864.

21. Gallagher, "Two Generals," 11, 17; *Chicago Tribune*, May 14, 1864.

22. *New York Herald*, Jun. 6, 1864; Andrew Evans to Sam Evans, Jun. 5, 1864, in Robert F. Engs and Corey M. Brooks, ed., *Their Patriotic Duty: The Civil War Letters of the Evans Family of Brown County, Ohio* (New York: Fordham University Press, 2007), 259.

23. Earl J. Hess, *The Battle of Ezra Church and the Struggle for Atlanta* (Chapel Hill: University of North Carolina Press, 2015), 1; James A. Connolly to Mary Dunn Connolly, May 15, 1864, in Sheehan-Dean, ed., *Civil War: Final Year*, 134; Stephen Davis, "Atlanta Campaign," *New Georgia Encyclopedia*, www.georgiaencyclopedia .org/articles/history-archaeology/atlanta-campaign; Albert Castel with Brooks D. Simpson, *Victors in Blue: How Union Generals Fought the Confederates, Battled Each Other, and Won the Civil War* (Lawrence: University Press of Kansas, 2011), 260–65.

24. Hess, *Battle of Ezra Church*, 4; Watkins, *Co. Aytch*, 149; Clampitt, *Confederate Heartland*, 25, 75.

25. William T. Sherman to Ellen Ewing Sherman, Jun. 30, 1864, in Sheehan-Dean, ed., *Civil War: Final Year*, 233.

26. Paludan, *Presidency of Abraham Lincoln*, 276–79; "Louisiana and Black Suffrage," Mr. Lincoln and Freedom Project, Lehrman Institute, www.mrlincolnandfreedom .org/civil-war/reconstruction/louisiana-black-suffrage.

27. Paludan, *Presidency of Abraham Lincoln*, 281.

28. Larry T. Balsamo, "'We Cannot Have Free Government Without Elections': Abraham Lincoln and the Election of 1864," *Journal of the Illinois State Historical Society*, Summer 2001, 183–86; "Pomeroy Circular" [Letter by S. C. Pomeroy in opposition to renomination of President Lincoln], Union Lincoln Association, Feb. 20, 1864, Lincoln Financial Foundation Collection, https://ar-chive.org/stream/letterinoppositoopome#page/no/mode/2up; Smith, *No Party Now*, 104.

29. Paludan, *Presidency of Abraham Lincoln*, 270–71.

30. *Presidential Election, 1864: Proceedings of the National Union Convention Held in Baltimore, Maryland, June 7 and 8, 1864* (Baltimore: Republican National Convention, 1864), 5–8, 29, 53, 69–70.

31. "Transcript of Wade-Davis Bill," www.ourdocuments.gov/doc.php?flash=true&doc=37&page=transcript; Paludan, *Presidency of Abraham Lincoln*, 280–81.

32. Boutwell, *Congressional Globe*, May 4, 1864, 38th Cong., 1st Sess., 2104; Abraham Lincoln, "Proclamation Concerning Reconstruction," Jul. 8, 1864, in Sheehan-Dean, ed., *Civil War: Final Year*, 241–42.

33. Benjamin F. Wade and Henry Winter Davis, "To the Supporters of the Government," Aug. 5, 1864, in Sheehan-Dean, ed., *Civil War: Final Year*, 307–18.

34. Samuel Cox, *Congressional Globe*, 38th Cong., 1st Sess., May 5, 1864, 2096–99.

35. A. Wilson Greene, *Civil War Petersburg: Confederate City in the Crucible of War* (Charlottesville: University of Virginia Press, 2006), 190–95.

36. Greene, *Civil War Petersburg*, 203–8.

37. Joseph T. Wilson, *The Black Phalanx: A History of the Negro Soldiers of the United States in the Wars of 1775–1812, 1861–'65* (Hartford, CT: American Publishing, 1887), 316, 349, 418, 420–21; on Mahone and Confederate commemoration of the battle of the Crater, see Kevin M. Levin, *Remembering the Battle of the Crater: War as Murder* (Lexington: University Press of Kentucky, 2012), 42–51.

38. M. Keith Harris, "We Will Finish the War Here: Confederate Morale in the Petersburg Trenches June and July 1864," and Caroline E. Janney, "A War Thoroughfare: Confederate Civilians and the Siege of Petersburg," in Gallagher and Janney, eds., *Cold Harbor to the Crater*, 221–24 (Pegram quote 223), and 250 (Alexander quote).

39. Harris, "We Will Finish the War Here," 223.

40. Harris, "We Will Finish the War Here," 215–17; Kevin Levin, "The Devil Himself Could Not Have Checked Them: Fighting with Black Soldiers at the Crater," in Gallagher and Janney, eds., *Cold Harbor to the Crater*, 271; C. Chauncey Burr, "From The Old Guard," Aug. 1864, in Sheehan-Dean, ed., *Civil War: Final Year*, 295.

41. *Sam Richards's Civil War Diary: A Chronicle of the Atlanta Home Front*, ed. Wendy Hamand Venet (Athens: University of Georgia Press, 2009), 230; William G. Thomas, *The Iron Way: Railroads, the Civil War and the Making of Modern America* (New York: Cambridge University Press, 2011), 149–57 (quotes on 151 and 157).

42. Hess, *Battle of Ezra Church*, 1–6; Clampitt, *Confederate Heartland*, 81.

43. Wendy Hamand Venet, *A Changing Wind: Commerce and Conflict in Civil War Atlanta* (New Haven, CT: Yale University Press, 2014), 156–66; *Sam Richards's Civil War Diary*, 232.

44. "Uncivilization of the Lincoln War," *Old Guard*, Aug. 1864, 171.

45. Weber, *Copperheads*, 160.

46. Larry E. Nelson, *Bullets, Ballots, and Rhetoric: Confederate Policy for the United States Presidential Contest of 1864* (Tuscaloosa: University of Alabama Press, 1980), 36.

47. William C. Davis, "The Turning Point That Wasn't: The Confederates and the Election of 1864," in *The Cause Lost: Myths and Realities of the Confederacy* (Lawrence: University Press of Kansas, 1996), 132–37.

48. Weber, *Copperheads*, 159–64 (Greeley quote 155); James R. Gilmore, "Our Visit to Richmond," Sep. 1864, in Sheehan-Dean, ed., *Civil War: Final Year,* 355.

49. Weber, *Copperheads,* 159–64 (Lincoln quote 164); "Abraham Lincoln and New Jersey," Abraham Lincoln's Classroom, Lehrman Institute, www .abrahamlincolnsclassroom.org/abraham-lincoln-state-by-state/abraham-lin-coln-and-new-jersey; Balsamo, " 'We Cannot Have Free Government Without Elections,' " 191–92; Lincoln, "Memorandum on Probable Failure of Reelection," Aug. 23, 1864, in Sheehan-Dean, ed., *Civil War: Final Year,* 324 (Raymond quote in introductory text for memorandum).

50. Lincoln, "Memorandum," 324.

51. Jonathan W. White, *Emancipation, the Union Army, and the Re-election of Abraham Lincoln* (Baton Rouge: Louisiana State University Press, 2014), 98–101; "Platform of the Democratic National Convention," in Sheehan-Dean, ed., *Civil War: Final Year,* 336–37.

CHAPTER 11

1. William H. Seward, "The Allies of Treason. The Fall of Atlanta, Sept. 3, 1864," in *Works of William H. Seward,* ed. George E. Baker (Boston: Houghton Mifflin, 1884), 5:491–507.

2. *New York Times,* Sep. 5, 1864; *Sam Richards's Civil War Diary,* 253.

3. Venet, *A Changing Wind,* 172; "James A. Connolly to Mary Dunn Connolly, September 11, 1864," in Sheehan-Dean, ed., *Civil War: Final Year,* 381–82.

4. William T. Sherman to James M. Calhoun and Others, Sep. 12, 1864, in Sheehan-Dean, ed., *Civil War: Final Year,* 384–86.

5. William T. Sherman to John Sherman, Dec. 29, 1863, in *Sherman's Civil War: Selected Correspondence of William T. Sherman, 1860–1865,* ed. Brooks D. Simpson and Jean V. Berlin (Chapel Hill: University of North Carolina Press, 199), 578.

6. William T. Sherman (WTS) to Henry W. Halleck, Sep. 17, 1863; WTS to John Sherman, May 26, 1864; WTS to Ellen Ewing Sherman, Jun. 9, 1864; WTS to John A. Spooner, Jul. 30, 1864; WTS to Emily Hoffman, Aug. 5, 1864; WTS to Schuyler Colfax, Aug. 12, 1864; WTS to James Guthrie, Aug. 14, 1863; WTS to Edwin Stanton, Oct. 25, 1864, all in *Sherman's Civil War,* 548, 640, 643, 677, 683, 691, 694, 741.

7. *Sam Richards's Diary,* 246; Jefferson Davis, "Speech at Macon," Sep. 23, 1864, in Sheehan-Dean ed., *Civil War: Final Year,* 399–402.

8. *Soldiers' Journal* (Alexandria, VA), Oct. 5, 1864; Castel, *Victors in Blue,* 284; Gary W. Gallagher, "Two Generals and a Valley: Philip H. Sheridan and Jubal A. Early in the Shenandoah," in Gary W. Gallagher, ed., *The Shenandoah Valley Campaign of*

1864 (Chapel Hill: University of North Carolina Press, 2006), 15; Grimsley, *Hard Hand of War*, 168.

9. *Christian Recorder*, Oct. 1, 1864; Gallagher, "Two Generals," 19; Castel, *Victors in Blue*, 288; William G. Thomas, "Nothing Ought to Astonish Us: Confederate Civilians in the 1864 Shenandoah Valley Campaign," in Gallagher, ed., *The Shenandoah Valley Campaign of 1864*, 240.

10. Keith S. Bohannon, "'The Fatal Halt' Versus 'Bad Conduct': John B. Gordon, Jubal A. Early, and the Battle of Cedar Creek," in Gallagher, ed., *The Shenandoah Valley Campaign of 1864*, 67 (Waldrop quote).

11. Thomas, "Nothing Ought to Astonish Us," 241 (first quote), 250 (second quote); Grimsley, *Hard Hand of War*, 185.

12. McClellan, "Letter in Acceptance of the Nomination of the Chicago Convention," Sep. 8, 1864, in *New York Times*, Sep. 9, 1864; William C. Harris, "Conservative Unionists and the Presidential Election of 1864," *Civil War History*, Dec. 1992, 314 (Winthrop quote).

13. William C. Harris, *Lincoln and the Border States: Preserving the Union* (Lawrence: University Press of Kansas, 2011), 245–49, 255.

14. *Philadelphia Press*, Sep. 19, 1864.

15. Middletown (CT) *Constitution*, Oct. 12, 1864; *Philadelphia Evening Bulletin*, Sep. 12, 1864; *Philadelphia Press*, Nov. 8, 1864; *Harper's Weekly*, Oct. 15, 1864; *Boston Daily Advertiser*, Oct. 4, 1864.

16. "Who Shall Be Vice-President?," political broadside, 1864, Library Company of Philadelphia.

17. *Campaign Dial* (Philadelphia), Sep. 14, 15, 1864; *Christian Recorder*, Sep. 17, 1864.

18. *Chicago Tribune*, Feb. 17, 1864; *New York Times*, Mar. 31, 1864; *Franklin Repository*, Nov. 30, 1864.

19. *Sacramento Daily Union*, Nov. 1, 1864; *New York Times*, Jun. 11, 1864.

20. Samuel T. Spear, *Our Country and Its Cause: A Discourse Preached October 2, 1864, in the South Presbyterian Church, of Brooklyn* (Brooklyn: Union Steam Presses, 1864); *Soldiers' Journal*, Mar. 9, 16, 1864; *Constitution* (Middletown, CT), Oct. 26, 1864; *Campaign Dial*, Sep. 14, 1864; Smith, *Stormy Present*, 211.

21. *Liberator*, May 20, Jul. 8, Sep. 16, Nov. 18, 1864; "Address of the Colored National Convention," Oct. 6, 1864, in Sheehan-Dean, ed., *Civil War: Final Year*, 419–20; Paludan, *Presidency of Abraham Lincoln*, 273; *New York Times*, Aug. 8, 1864.

22. *New York Times*, Apr. 20, 1864; *Liberator*, Oct. 28, 1864; Lois Leveen, "The Civil War's Oratorical Wunderkind," *New York Times*, Opinionator blog, May 21, 2013.

23. Jason Phillips, "The Grape Vine Telegraph: Rumors and Confederate Persistence," *Journal of Southern History* 72 (Nov. 2006): 769; *Inside the Confederate Government: The Diary of Robert Garlick Kean Hill*, ed. Edward Younger (Baton Rouge: Louisiana State University Press, 1993), 83.

24. *Charleston Mercury*, Apr. 2, 1864.

25. Jefferson Davis, speeches at Macon, GA, Sep. 23, 1864, Augusta, GA, Oct. 3, 1864, and Columbia, SC, Oct. 4, 1864, *Papers of Jefferson Davis*, vol. 11, *September 1864– May 1865*, ed. Lynda Laswell Crist (Baton Rouge: Louisiana State University Press, 2003), 59–60, 63, 86–87.

26. Phillips, "The Grape Vine Telegraph," 770; *Richmond Enquirer*, Nov. 11, 1864; Clampitt, *Confederate Heartland*, 101; *Richmond Dispatch*, Nov. 12, 1864.

27. Stephen Elliot, *"Vain Is the Help of Man," a Sermon Preached in Christ Church Savannah on Thursday September 15, 1864* (Macon, GA: Burke, Boykin, 1864).

28. Neely, *Lincoln and the Democrats*, 125; Horatio Stebbins, *The President, the People, and the War: A Thanksgiving Discourse* (San Francisco: Charles F. Robbins, 1864), 19, 21; *Christian Recorder*, Dec. 31, 1864; Abraham Lincoln, Annual Message to Congress, Dec. 6, 1864, in Sheehan-Dean, ed., *Civil War: Final Year*, 504–5, 507–8.

29. Balsamo, "We Cannot Have a Free Government," 196–97; Jonathan W. White, *Emancipation, the Union Army, and the Reelection of Abraham Lincoln* (Baton Rouge: Louisiana State University Press, 2014), 115–21. For an excellent account of the National Union party's coalition building, see Smith, *No Party Now*, esp. 102–12.

30. Richtmyer Hubbell, *Potomac Diary: A Soldier's Account of the Capital in Crisis, 1864–1865*, ed. Marc Newman (Charleston, SC: Arcadia, 2000), 34; John C. Myers, *A Daily Journal of the 192d Reg't Penn'a Volunteers Commanded by Col. William B. Thomas in the Service of the United States for One Hundred Days* (Philadelphia: Crissy and Markley, 1864), 97, 100, 146–47 (quote); J. A. Mowris, *A History of the One Hundred and Seventeenth Regiment, N.Y. Volunteers (Fourth Oneida), from the Date of Its Organization, August, 1862, Till That of Its Muster Out, June, 1865* (Hartford, CT: Case, Lockwood, 1866), 307–8 (McLean quotes).

31. White, *Emancipation, the Union Army, and the Reelection of Abraham Lincoln*, 115; Sam Evans to Andrew Evans, Jun. 11, 1864, in Engs and Brooks, eds., *Their Patriotic Duty*, 263.

32. Jane Evans to Samuel Evans, Sep. 11, 1864, in Engs and Brooks, eds., *Their Patriotic Duty*, 287–89.

33. Sam Evans to Andrew Evans, Sep. 24, 1864, and Sam Evans to Jane Evans, Oct. 15, 1864, in Engs and Brooks, eds., *Their Patriotic Duty*, 294, 299–300.

34. Andrew Evans to Sam Evans, Nov. 14, 1864, in Engs and Brooks, eds., *Their Patriotic Duty*, 309.

35. Holmes, *Diary of Miss Emma Holmes*, 382; *Charleston Mercury*, Oct. 15, 21, 1864; *Richmond Daily Dispatch*, Nov. 8, 9, 10, 1864; *Confederate Union* (Milledgeville, GA), Nov. 8, 1864.

36. Cooling, *To the Battles of Franklin and Nashville*, 294, 328.

37. Lisa Tendrich Frank, *The Civilian War: Confederate Women and Union Soldiers During Sherman's March* (Baton Rouge: Louisiana State University Press, 2015), 61, 73.

38. Frank, *The Civilian War,* 6–8, 60–62 (Sherman quote on 62), 105–6; Holmes, *Diary of Miss Emma Holmes,* 402.

39. Sherman to Abraham Lincoln, Sep. 17, 1864, and Sherman to Caroline Carson, Jan. 20, 1865, in *Sherman's Civil War,* 716; *Chicago Tribune,* Dec. 3, 1864; Christian McWhirter, "The Song That Drove Sherman Crazy," *New York Times,* Opinionator blog, Mar. 8, 2015.

40. Jacqueline Glass Campbell, *When Sherman Marched North from the Sea: Resistance on the Confederate Home Front* (Chapel Hill: University of North Carolina Press, 2003), 22–29 (quote on 25); *New York Times,* Jan. 5, 1865.

41. Campbell, *When Sherman Marched North,* 27; *Richmond Dispatch,* Jan. 9, 1865.

42. Marion B. Lucas, *Sherman and the Burning of Columbia* (Columbia: University of South Carolina Press, 1976); J. Cutler Andrews, *The South Reports the Civil War* (Princeton, NJ: Princeton University Press, 1970), 492; Coopersmith, *Fighting Words,* 224–25.

43. Levine, *Fall of the House of Dixie,* 234; Frank, *Civilian War,* 111–12; Anne Sarah Rubin, *Through the Heart of Dixie: Sherman's March and American Memory* (Chapel Hill: University of North Carolina Press, 2014), 22–23.

44. "Meeting of Colored Ministers with Edwin M. Stanton and William T. Sherman," Jan. 12, 1865, in Sheehan-Dean, ed., *Civil War: Final Year,* 558–65.

45. William T. Sherman, "Special Field Orders No. 15," in Sheehan-Dean, ed., *Civil War: Final Year,* 566–68; Levine, *Fall of the House of Dixie,* 238.

46. *Christian Recorder,* Feb. 4, 1865; *The Elevator* (San Francisco), Apr. 7, 1865; Eric Foner, *Forever Free: The Story of Emancipation & Reconstruction* (New York: Vintage, 2006), 64.

47. *Christian Recorder,* Jan. 7, 1865.

CHAPTER 12

1. Lee to William P. Miles, Jan. 19, 1865, in *Wartime Papers of Robert E. Lee,* 885–86; *New York Times,* Feb. 22, 1865; *New York Herald,* Mar. 10, 1865.

2. *Richmond Daily Dispatch,* Feb. 21, 22, 1865.

3. Power, *Lee's Miserables,* 181–87.

4. Power, *Lee's Miserables,* 192, 210–11; Glatthaar, *General Lee's Army,* 423; Lee to Seddon, Jan. 11, 1865, in *Wartime Papers of Robert E. Lee,* 881.

5. William A. Frassanito, *Grant and Lee: The Virginia Campaigns, 1864–1865* (Gettysburg: Thomas, 1983), 268–71; David W. Miller, *Second Only to Grant: Quartermaster General Montgomery C. Meigs* (Shippensburg, PA: White Mane Books, 2000), 233; Elizabeth R. Varon, "City Point, Virginia: The Nerve Center of the Union War Effort," in *Lens of War: Exploring Iconic Photographs of the Civil War,* eds. Gary W. Gallagher and J. Matthew Gallman (Athens: University of Georgia Press, 2015), 205–12.

6. Cornelia Hancock, *Letters of a Civil War Nurse* (Lincoln: University of Nebraska Press, 1998), 116; *Meade's Army: The Private Notebooks of Lt. Col. Theodore Lyman*, ed. David W. Lowe (Kent, OH: Kent State University Press, 2007), 229.

7. Miller, *Second Only to Grant*, 233; A. Wilson Greene, *The Final Battles of the Petersburg Campaign: Breaking the Backbone of the Rebellion* (Knoxville: University of Tennessee Press, 2008), 54, 57; A. Wilson Greene, *Civil War Petersburg: Confederate City in the Crucible of War* (Charlottesville: University of Virginia Press, 2006), 224; Varon, "City Point," 205–12; *Christian Recorder*, Jun. 18, Nov. 26, 1864.

8. *New York Times*, Mar. 27, 1865; *Christian Recorder*, Sep. 24, 1864; *Charleston Mercury*, Mar. 11, 1864.

9. *Thomas Morris Chester, Black Civil War Correspondent: His Dispatches from the Virginia Front*, ed. R. J. M. Blackett (Baton Rouge: Louisiana State University Press, 1989), 123–24, 229–31, 246, 253, 274–75, 279–80.

10. Haley, *Rebel Yell and Yankee Hurrah*, 210, 217, 221.

11. Varon, *Southern Lady, Yankee Spy*, 168–75.

12. Horace Porter, *Campaigning with Grant* (1897; reprint, New York: Konecky and Konecky, 1991), 392; Adam Badeau, *Military History of General Ulysses S. Grant, from April, 1861 to April, 1865* (New York: D. Appleton, 1881), 2:243; George Henry Sharpe to Cyrus Comstock, Jan. 1867, Elizabeth Van Lew Papers, New York Public Library.

13. Varon, *Southern Lady, Yankee Spy*, 178–82; Testimony of Mary C. Van Lew, Letters Received by the Confederate Adjutant and Inspector General, 1861–1865, Oct. 15, 1864, RG 109, National Archives, Washington, DC.

14. Bruce Levine, *Confederate Emancipation: Southern Plans to Free and Arm Slaves During the Civil War* (New York: Oxford University Press, 2006), 27–30 (Cleburne quote on 27).

15. Levine, *Confederate Emancipation*, 51, 95 (first quote), 101 (second quote); Robert E. Lee to Andrew Hunter, Jan. 11, 1865, in Sheehan-Dean, ed., *Civil War: Final Year*, 555–56.

16. Bruce Levine, "The Riddles of Confederate Emancipation," History Now, Gilder Lehrman Institute, http://new.gilderlehrman.org/history-by-era/american-civil-war/essays/riddles-%E2%80%9Cconfederate-emancipation%E2%80%9D; Levine, *Confederate Emancipation*, 119.

17. Christian G. Samito, *Lincoln and the Thirteenth Amendment* (Carbondale: Southern Illinois University Press, 2015), 53–59; Michael Vorenberg, *Final Freedom: The Civil War, the Abolition of Slavery, and the Thirteenth Amendment* (Cambridge: Cambridge University Press, 2001), 174.

18. Samito, *Lincoln and the Thirteenth Amendment*, 114; Vorenberg, *Final Freedom*, 177.

19. Daniel W. Crofts, *Lincoln and the Politics of Slavery: The Other Thirteenth Amendment and the Struggle to Save the Union* (Chapel Hill: University of North Carolina Press, 2016), 261; Bliss speech, *Congressional Globe*, Jan. 7, 1865, 38th Cong., 2nd Sess., 150; Vorenberg, *Final Freedom*, 187.

20. Ashley speech, Jan. 6, 1865, *Congressional Globe*, 38th Cong., 2nd Sess., 138–41.

21. Scofield speech, Jan. 6, 1865, and Davis speech, Jan. 7, 1865, *Congressional Globe*, 38th Cong., 2nd Sess., 144–46, 154–55.

22. Coffroth speech, Jan. 31, 1865, and Yeaman speech, Jan. 9, 1865, *Congressional Globe*, 38th Cong., 2nd Sess., 170–72, 523–24.

23. *New York Daily Tribune*, Feb. 1, 1865.

24. Samito, *Lincoln and the Thirteenth Amendment*, 41 (quote), 92, 114.

25. Guelzo, *Abraham Lincoln*, 417–20; Abraham Lincoln, Second Inaugural Address, March 4, 1865, http://avalon.law.yale.edu/19th_century/lincoln2.asp.

26. Douglas L. Wilson, *Lincoln's Sword: The Presidency and the Power of Words* (New York: Knopf, 2006), 269; Ronald C. White Jr., *Lincoln's Greatest Speech: The Second Inaugural* (New York: Simon & Schuster, 2006); Guelzo, *Abraham Lincoln*, 418–19.

27. *Cleveland Daily Leader*, Mar. 6, 1865; *Burlington* (IA) *Weekly Hawk-Eye*, Mar. 18, 1865; *Pittsburgh Gazette*, Mar. 7, 1865.

28. *Liberator*, Mar. 17, 1865; *Brooklyn Daily Eagle*, Mar. 6, 1865; *Daily Milwaukee News*, Mar. 5, 1865.

29. Nelson Lankford, *Richmond Burning: The Last Days of the Confederate Capital* (New York: Viking Press, 2002); Robertson, *Civil War Virginia*, 167.

30. Lankford, *Richmond Burning*.

31. *Richmond Whig*, Apr. 4, 1865; Putnam, *Richmond During the War*, 366–67, 375.

32. Varon, *Southern Lady, Yankee Spy*, 193–94.

33. *Evening Star* (Washington, DC), Apr. 3, 5, 1865; *Wilmington Herald*, Apr. 8, 1865; *Harper's Weekly*, Apr. 13, 1865; *New York Herald*, Apr. 13, 1865.

34. Sheridan to Grant, Apr. 5, 1865, *OR*, ser. 1, vol. 46, pt. 3, 582; Henry Edwin Tremain, *Last Hours of Sheridan's Cavalry* (New York: Silver & Bowers, 1904), 141. For a detailed account of the Appomattox campaign and surrender, see Elizabeth R. Varon, *Appomattox: Victory, Defeat, and Freedom at the End of the Civil War* (New York: Oxford University Press, 2013). For a detailed account of Sailor's Creek, see Chris M. Calkins, *Thirty-Six Hours Before Appomattox: The Battles of Sailor's Creek, High Bridge, Farmville and Cumberland Church* (Farmville, VA: Farmville Herald, 2006), 5–17, 29–32.

35. Varon, *Appomattox*, 18–22.

36. Varon, *Appomattox*, 33–39.

37. Varon, *Appomattox*, 31–33; James M. McPherson, "No Peace Without Victory, 1861–1865," *American Historical Review* 109 (Feb. 2004): 1–18.

38. Steven E. Woodworth, "The Last Function of Government: Confederate Collapse and Negotiated Peace," in Mark Grimsley and Brooks D. Simpson, eds., *The Collapse of the Confederacy* (Lincoln: University of Nebraska Press, 2001), 13–39; William C. Davis, *An Honorable Defeat: The Last Days of the Confederate Government* (New York: Harcourt, 2001), 28–30, 40–46.

39. Grant, *Personal Memoirs*, 604–8; Haley, *Rebel Yell and Yankee Hurrah*, 265.

40. William Chase to sister, Apr. 14, 1865, NCWC; Grant, *Personal Memoirs*, 101, 114–19, 601; Grant interview, *New York Herald*, Jul. 24, 1878; Hubbell, *Potomac*

Diary, 84; Hallock Armstrong, *Letters from a Pennsylvania Chaplain at the Siege of Petersburg, 1865*, ed. Hallock F. Raup (London: Eden Press, 1961), 22.

41. *Pittsburgh Gazette*, Apr. 8, 1865; *National Republican* (Washington, DC), Apr. 8, 1865.

42. *New York Times*, Apr. 11, 1865.

43. *Cleveland Daily Leader*, Apr. 15, 1865.

44. Henry Ward Beecher, *Patriotic Addresses in America and England, 1850–1885, on Slavery, the Civil War, and the Development of Civil Liberty in the United States* (New York: Fords, Howard & Hulbert, 1888), 676–700.

45. Beecher, *Patriotic Addresses*, 676–700.

46. *New York Tribune*, Apr. 10, 11, 12, 13, 1865; *New York Evening Post*, as quoted in the *Liberator*, May 5, 1865; McCoslin quoted in Noah Andre Trudeau, *Like Men of War* (New York: Little, Brown, 1998), 423; *Christian Recorder*, April 22, 1865; Chester, *Thomas Morris Chester, Black Civil War Correspondent*, 302, 313, 332.

47. *New York Times*, Apr. 12, 14, 1865; *Pittsburgh Daily Gazette*, Apr. 13, 1865.

48. Coopersmith, *Fighting Words*, 253–54; *Lancaster Intelligencer* in *Valley Spirit* (Franklin, PA), Apr. 12, 1865.

49. Robert E. Lee, "Farewell Address," *OR*, ser. 1, vol. 46, pt. 1, 1267; Varon, *Appomattox*, 70; Walter H. Taylor, *Four Years with General Lee* (New York: Appleton, 1877), 191; Susan P. Lee, *Memoirs of William Nelson Pendleton* (Philadelphia: Lippincott, 1893), 414.

50. Varon, *Appomattox*, 72–73; Gary W. Gallagher, "An End and a New Beginning," in *Appomattox Court House* (Washington, DC: Government Printing Office), 77.

51. Memoir of Dr. [Hodijah Baylies] Meade, Small Special Collections, University of Virginia, 102; *Diary of Captain Henry A. Chambers*, ed. T. H. Pearce (Wendell, NC: Broadfoot's Bookmark, 1983), 262; Edward A. Moore, *The Story of a Cannoneer Under Stonewall Jackson* (New York: Neale, 1907), 302; Edward M. Boykin, *The Falling Flag* (New York: E. J. Hale & Son, 1874), 64–65.

52. Varon, *Appomattox*, 161–62; *Anderson Intelligencer* (Anderson Court House, SC), Apr. 27, 1865; *Southern Watchman* (Athens, GA), Apr. 26, 1865; *Edgefield (SC) Advertiser*, Apr. 26, 1865; *Columbia* (SC) *Phoenix*, Apr. 21, 1865.

53. *When the World Ended: The Diary of Emma LeConte*, ed. Earl Schenck Miers (Lincoln: University of Nebraska Press, 1987), 90–91; *Sarah Morgan: The Civil War Diary*, 606; Diary of Mary Washington (Cabell) Early, Apr. 11, 17, 1865, Virginia Historical Society, Richmond.

54. Geary, *A Politician Goes to War*, 238.

55. William E. Gienapp, *Abraham Lincoln and Civil War America: A Biography* (New York: Oxford University Press, 2002), 201 (quotations); Varon, *Appomattox*, 135.

56. Lincoln, "Last Public Address," in *Collected Works of Abraham Lincoln*, 8:399–405; Michael W. Kauffman, *American Brutus: John Wilkes Booth and the Lincoln Conspiracies* (New York: Random House, 2004), 209–11; Gienapp,

Abraham Lincoln, 199–200; Michael Burlingame, *Lincoln and the Civil War* (Carbondale: Southern Illinois University Press, 2011), 128.

57. *Green-Mountain Freeman* (Montpelier, VT), Apr. 18, 1865; Davis, *Emilie Davis's Civil War*, 157–58, 193; Edward Steers Jr., *Blood on the Moon: The Assassination of Abraham Lincoln* (Lexington: University Press of Kentucky, 2001), 14, 293; *Christian Recorder*, Apr. 29, 1865.

58. Marshall, ed., *A War of the People*, 301, 307 (Smith and Rutherford quotes); Coopersmith, *Fighting Words*, 274; *Dayton Empire* as quoted in *Nashville Daily Union*, Apr. 21, 1865.

59. Hodes, *Mourning Lincoln*, 130–35; *Chicago Tri-Weekly Journal*, May 6, 1865; M. P. Gaddis, *Sermon on the Assassination of Abraham Lincoln Delivered in Pike's Opera House, April 16, 1865* (Cincinnati: Times Steam Book and Job Office, 1865), 6, 14.

60. *Zachariah Chandler: An Outline Sketch of His Life and Public Services* (Detroit: Post and Tribune, 1880), 281; George S. Boutwell, *Speeches and Papers Relating to the Rebellion and the Overthrow of Slavery* (Boston: Little, Brown, 1867), 368–70; George Henry Gordon, *A War Diary of Events in the War of the Great Rebellion, 1863–1865* (Boston: James R. Osgood, 1882), 405.

61. Hodes, *Mourning Lincoln*, 135; *Liberator*, May 26, 1865.

62. *Washington Evening Star*, Apr. 22, 1865; *Daily National Intelligencer*, May 2, 1865; *New York Herald*, Apr. 16, 1865; *Milwaukee Daily Sentinel*, May 10, 1865; *Freedom's Champion* (Atchison, KS), May 4, 1865.

63. Levine, *Fall of the House of Dixie*, 283–87.

64. Varon, *Appomattox*, 152; *Highland Weekly News* (Hillsborough, OH), Apr. 27, 1865; *National Anti-Slavery Standard* (New York), Apr. 29, 1865, 14–19; *Brooklyn Eagle*, Apr. 29, 1865; *Franklin Repository*, May 10, 1865.

65. *Sacramento Daily Union*, May 15, 1865; *New York Times*, May 5, 1865. For the history of Juneteenth, see, for example, Elizabeth Hayes Turner, "Juneteenth: Emancipation and Memory," in Gregg Cantrall and Elizabeth Hayes Turner, eds., *Lone Star Pasts: Memory and History in Texas* (College Station: Texas A&M University Press, 2007), 143–75.

66. *North American and United States Gazette*, May 29, 1865.

CONCLUSION

1. Robert J. Breckinridge, "The Great Deliverance and the New Career," *Littell's Living Age*, Sep. 30, 1865, 577–92; Nicholas Guyatt, *Providence and the Invention of the United States, 1607–1876* (Cambridge: Cambridge University Press, 2007), 297.

2. Charles R. Bliss, *Deliverance from the Furnace: A Thanksgiving Sermon, Delivered at South Reading. December 7, 1865* (Boston: T. R. Marvin & Son, 1865), 8–10, 21–23.

3. On rebelism, see Ayers, *Thin Light of Freedom*, 387, 398.

4. Paul H. Bergeron, "Introduction," in *The Papers of Andrew Johnson*, ed. LeRoy P. Graf, Ralph W. Haskins, and Paul H. Bergeron (Knoxville: University of

Tennessee Press, 1967–2000), 8:xxviii–xxix (hereafter *PAJ*); Paul H. Bergeron, *Andrew Johnson's Civil War and Reconstruction* (Knoxville: University of Tennessee Press, 2011), 74–76; Brooks D. Simpson, Leroy P. Graf, and John Muldowny, eds., *Advice After Appomattox: Letters to Andrew Johnson, 1865–1866* (Knoxville: University of Tennessee Press, 1987), 39–41.

5. Thaddeus Stevens, "Reconstruction," Sep. 6, 1865, in John David Smith, ed., *A Just and Lasting Peace: A Documentary History of Reconstruction* (New York: Penguin, 2013), 77–78.

6. Mark Wahlgren Summers, *A Dangerous Stir: Fear, Paranoia, and the Making of Reconstruction* (Chapel Hill: University of North Carolina Press, 2009), 74–78; Gregory P. Downs, *After Appomattox: Military Occupation and the Ends of War* (Cambridge, MA: Harvard University Press, 2015).

7. Eric Foner, *A Short History of Reconstruction* (New York: Harper Perennial, 1990), 94–95; Simpson, Graf, and Muldowny, eds., *Advice After Appomattox,* 121–22.

8. *Bangor Daily Whig and Courier,* Aug. 7, 1865; *New Hampshire Statesman,* Sep. 8, 1865; *Boston Daily Advertiser,* Mar. 10, 1866; *Daily Cleveland Herald,* May 17, 1865; Lewis Hayden, *Caste Among Masons: Address Before the Price Hall Grand Lodge of Free and Accepted Masons of the State of Massachusetts* (Boston: Edward S. Coombs, 1860), 8–10.

9. North Carolina Blacks to Andrew Johnson (AJ), May 10, 1865; Joseph Noxon to AJ, May 27, 1865; Delegation Representing the Black People of Kentucky to AJ, Jun. 9, 1865; Committee of Richmond Blacks to AJ, Jun. 10, 1865; South Carolina Black Citizens to AJ, Jun. 29, 1865, all in *PAJ*, 8:57–58, 119, 203–4, 211–13, 317–19.

10. John Hope Franklin, *Reconstruction After the Civil War* (Chicago: University of Chicago Press, 1961), 43; *Appendix to the Congressional Globe,* 39th Cong., 1st Sess., Mar. 2, 1866, 140–41.

11. Downs, *After Appomattox,* 67–72, 104–6; *Andrew Johnson, President of the United States: His Life and Speeches,* ed. Lillian Foster (New York: Richardson, 1866), 216–22. On Johnson's motivations, see, for example, Hans Trefousse, *Andrew Johnson: A Biography* (New York: W. W. Norton, 1989), 228.

12. Alfred R. Wynne to Andrew Johnson, Sep. 8, 1865, and R. Weakley Brown to Andrew Johnson, Sep. 30, 1865, in *PAJ*, 9:49–50, 153–54; *Staunton Vindicator,* Sep. 22, 1865; *Buffalo Commercial Advertiser,* Aug. 17, 1865; *Daily National Intelligencer,* Apr. 9, 1866.

13. John David Smith, " 'The Work It Did Not Do Because It Could Not': Georgia and the 'New' Freedmen's Bureau Historiography," *Georgia Historical Quarterly* 82 (Summer 1998): 334; Joseph S. Fullerton to Andrew Johnson, Feb. 9, 1866, in Smith, ed., *A Just and Lasting Peace,* 167–70; Hans L. Trefousse, "Andrew Johnson and the Freedmen's Bureau," in Paul A. Cimbala and Randall M. Miller, eds., *The Freedmen's Bureau and Reconstruction: Reconsiderations* (New York: Fordham University Press, 1999), 28–39 (quote on 37); Isenberg, *White Trash,* 178.

14. Foner, *Forever Free*, 114–15; Andrew Johnson, "Veto of the Civil Rights Bill," Mar. 27, 1866, http://teachingamericanhistory.org/library/document/veto-of-the-civil-rights-bill/.

15. *The Independent* (New York), Apr. 5, 1866; "The Political Situation," *New Englander and Yale Review*, Apr. 1866, 359; Foner, *Short History of Reconstruction*, 113; Rosen, *Terror in the Heart of Freedom*, 61–69.

16. Summers, *A Dangerous Stir*, 100; Mark Wahlgren Summers, *The Ordeal of the Reunion: A New History of Reconstruction* (Chapel Hill: University of North Carolina Press, 2014), 97–98; *Speeches of Andrew Johnson*, 264; *The Great Impeachment and Trial of Andrew Johnson, President of the United States* (Philadelphia: T. B. Peterson & Brothers, 1868), 21; Bergeron, *Andrew Johnson's Civil War*, 126–29.

17. Thomas Nast, "Andy's Trip," *Harper's Weekly*, Oct. 27, 1866, accessed at http://www.andrewjohnson.com/ListOfCartoons/AndysTrip.htm.

18. Franklin, *Reconstruction*, 101–3, 106; Summers, *Ordeal of the Reunion*, 44.

19. Bergeron, *Andrew Johnson's Civil War and Reconstruction*, 205–11; Randolph Harrison McKim, *A Soldier's Recollections* (New York: Longmans, Green, 1910), 5–6.

20. Peter C. Luebke, "Union Regimental Historians and the Meaning of the Great Rebellion in Immediate Retrospect," in Varon and Gallagher, eds., *New Perspectives on the Union War*; Barbara A. Gannon, *The Won Cause: Black and White Comradeship in the Grand Army of the Republic* (Chapel Hill: University of North Carolina Press, 2011), 169.

21. Summers, *Ordeal of the Reunion*, 395; Joseph T. Wilson, *Emancipation: Its Course and Progress, from 1491 B.C. to A.D. 1875* (Hampton, VA: Normal School Steam Power Press Print, 1882), 49; Wilson, *Black Phalanx*, 316, 349, 418, 420–21.

22. Frederick Douglass, "There Was a Right Side in the Late War," May 30, 1878, in *Frederick Douglass: Selected Speeches and Writings*, 627–33. On Douglass's efforts to counter Lost Cause propaganda and promote the emancipationist memory tradition, see David W. Blight, *Frederick Douglass' Civil War: Keeping Faith in Jubilee* (Baton Rouge: Louisiana State University Press, 1989), 234–35, and David W. Blight, *Race and Reunion: The Civil War in American Memory* (Cambridge: Harvard University Press, 2001), 91–92.

23. Douglass, "There Was a Right Side in the Late War," 627–33.

24. Coffey, *Exodus and Liberation*, 183–97 (quote on 183).

Index

Note: Photographs, illustrations, and maps are indicated by an italic page number.